RETURN OF A KING

RETURN OF A KING

The Battle for Afghanistan

William Dalrymple

BLOOMSBURY

LONDON · NEW DELHI · NEW YORK · SYDNEY

First published in Great Britain 2013

Copyright © 2013 by William Dalrymple
Maps and chapter illustrations by Olivia Fraser
Tribal trees by ML Design
Endpaper images, 'Sketches in Afghanistan', 1838–1842, by Louis and
Charles Haghe after James Atkinson © National Army Museum

Bloomsbury Publishing Plc
50 Bedford Square
London
WC1B 3DP

www.bloomsbury.com

Bloomsbury Publishing, London, New Delhi, New York and Sydney
A CIP catalogue record for this book is available from the British Library

ISBN 978 1 4088 1830 5 (hardback edition)
ISBN 978 1 4088 2287 6 (trade paperback edition)

10 9 8 7 6 5 4 3 2 1

Typeset by Hewer Text UK Ltd, Edinburgh

Printed and bound by CPI Group (UK) Ltd, Croydon, CR0 4YY

To my beloved
Adam

And also to the four people who did most
to encourage in me a love of history:

Veronica Telfer
Fr Edward Corbould OSB
Lucy Warrack
and
Elsie Gibbs
(North Berwick, 10 June 1922 – Bristol, 4 February 2012)

Great kings have always recorded the events of their reigns, some writing themselves, with their natural gifts, but most entrusting the writing to historians and writers, so that these compositions would remain as a memorial on the pages of passing time.

Thus it occurred to this humble petitioner at the court of the Merciful God, Sultan Shuja al-Mulk Shah Durrani, to record the battles and events of his reign, so that the historians of Khurasan should know the true account of these events, and thoughtful readers take heed from these examples.

Shah Shuja, *Waqi'at-i-Shah Shuja*

Contents

THE INVASION OF AFGHANISTAN 1839~42

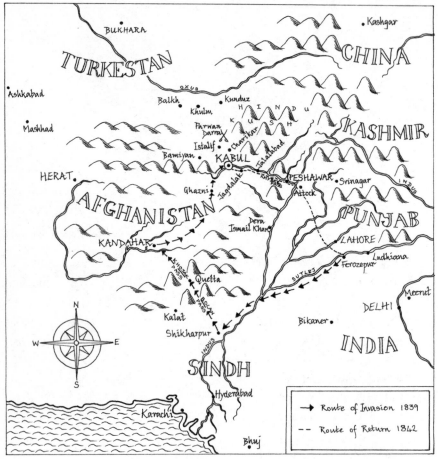

Legend:

→ Route of Invasion 1839

-- Route of Return 1842

KABUL 1839~42

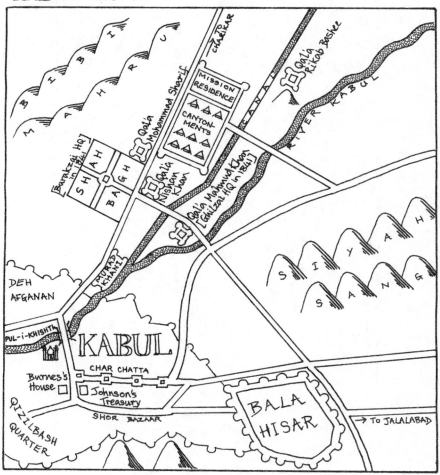

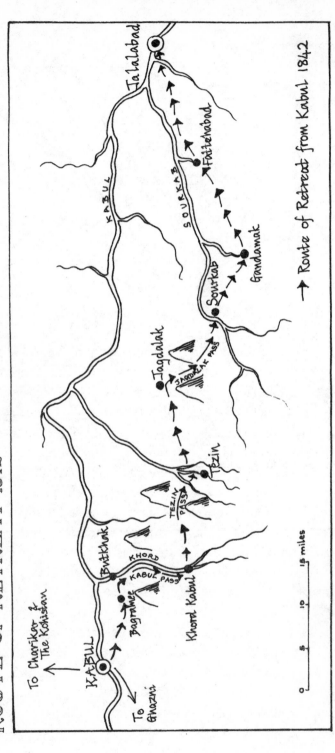

ROUTE OF RETREAT 1842

→ Route of Retreat from Kabul 1842

Dramatis Personae

THE AFGHANS

The Sadozais

Ahmad Shah Abdali (1722–72): Born in Multan, Ahmad Shah rose to power in the service of the Persian warlord Nadir Shah. On the latter's death, Ahmad Shah seized control of the Shah's chest of Mughal jewels, including the Koh-i-Nur diamond, and used it to fund the conquest of Kandahar, Kabul and Lahore, then later launched a series of lucrative raids into India. Taking the title Durrani ('Pearl of Pearls') he created an empire that was built out of the collapse of three other Asian empires – the Uzbeks to the north, the Mughals to the south and to the west the Safavids of Persia. At its height it extended from Nishapur in modern Iran through Afghanistan, the Punjab and Sindh to Kashmir and the threshold of Mughal Delhi. Ahmad Shah Abdali died after contracting a tumour which ate away his nose and finally attacked his brain.

Timur Shah (r. 1772–93): Son of Ahmad Shah Abdali and father of Shah Mahmoud, Shah Zaman and Shah Shuja. Timur successfully maintained the Afghan heartlands of the Durrani Empire his father had bequeathed to him, but he lost the Persian and Indian extremities. It was he who moved the capital from Kandahar to Kabul, to keep it out of the turbulent Pashtun heartlands. At his death, his legacy was violently disputed by his twenty-four sons, throwing the Durrani Empire into civil war.

Shah Zaman (r. 1793–1800, d. 1844): Shah Zaman succeeded his father Timur Shah in 1793, attempting with limited success to save his grandfather's Durrani Empire from collapse. Having been thwarted in an attempt to invade Hindustan in 1796, he lost control of his dominions and was captured and blinded by his twin enemies, the Barakzai clan and his half-brother Shah Mahmoud, in the winter of 1800. Released by Shah Shuja at his accession in 1803, he lived in Kabul until he was forced to flee to India after the defeat at Nimla in 1809. He came back to Afghanistan in 1841 and briefly joined Shuja for the uprising in Kabul. The following year, after his brother's assassination, he left Afghanistan for the last time, returning to exile in Ludhiana where he died in 1844. He was buried at the Sufi Shrine in Sirhind.

Shah Shuja (1786–1842): Shuja first rose to prominence after his elder brother Shah Zaman was captured and blinded by his enemies in 1800. Escaping arrest, he wandered the mountains until returning to seize power in Kabul during sectarian riots in 1803. His rule lasted until his defeat by the Barakzais and his half-brother Shah Mahmoud at the Battle of Nimla in 1809. For several years he then wandered north India as a fugitive, stripped of his wealth and, in 1813, of his most precious possession, the Koh-i-Nur. In 1816 he accepted the offer of asylum in Ludhiana extended by the British East India Company. Three failed attempts to retrieve his throne were finally followed by a successful fourth attempt in 1839, but this time he was installed as a puppet ruler by the Company, who decided to place him back in Kabul to further their own strategic ends; when he tried to exercise independent sovereignty, the British quickly marginalised and humiliated him. In November 1841, at the outbreak of the Kabul uprising, Shuja refused offers to take over the leadership of the rebellion and unlike the British in the cantonment, successfully held his own in the Bala Hisar. By

February 1842, after the British army in Kabul had abandoned him and marched off to its own destruction, it looked as if Shuja might manage to keep his throne through manipulation of the different rebel factions; but he was assassinated by his own godson on 5 April, and with his death the rule of the Sadozais ended and the Barakzais took power.

Shah Mahmoud (r. 1800–3, 1809–18; d. 1829): Shah Mahmoud succeeded in seizing control of Kabul in 1800 after the blinding and capture of his half-brother Shah Zaman. He ruled until he was overthrown by his other half-brother Shah Shuja in 1803. Shuja chose not to blind Mahmoud, only to imprison him. When Mahmoud escaped from the Bala Hisar in 1808, he joined forces with his brothers' Barakzai rivals and led a successful rebellion, defeating Shuja at the Battle of Nimla in 1809. He ruled what was left of the Durrani dominions until 1818 when he blinded, tortured and killed his over-mighty Barakzai wazir, Fatteh Khan, and was in turn ousted from Kabul by Fatteh Khan's outraged brothers. Shah Mahmoud clung on in Herat until his death in 1829, when he was succeeded by his son **Prince Kamran Shah Sadozai of Herat (r. 1829–42)**, who ruled until deposed and strangled by his powerful wazir, **Yar Mohammad Alikozai (r. 1842–51)** in 1842.

Prince Timur, Prince Fatteh Jang, Prince Shahpur and Prince Safdarjang: These were all sons of Shah Shuja, the first three by Wa'fa Begum. None of them inherited their father's ambition or their mother's ingenuity, and Prince Timur was renowned as an especially uncharismatic figure. Prince Fatteh Jang was remembered mainly for the homosexual rapes he inflicted on members of his own garrison in Kandahar. He ruled in Kabul for five months after the death of Shah Shuja, and abdicated in October 1842 after learning that the British would not stay to keep him in power. He handed over to his younger brother Prince Shahpur, who ruled for less than a month before being expelled by his own nobles at the request of Wazir Akbar Khan. The darkly beautiful Prince

Safdarjang, Shuja's son by a Ludhiana dancing girl, was little more effective. All four princes died in exile in Ludhiana, having failed to retain the throne after the departure of the British.

The Barakzais

Haji Jamal Khan (d. 1771): Topchibashi, or commander of artillery, to Ahmad Shah Abdali. A rival of Ahmad Shah Abdali after the death of Nadir Shah, he accepted Abdali's elevation after the latter received the blessing of the 'ulema, and he gave his support to Abdali in return for a commanding role in the army.

Payindah Khan (r. 1774–99): Son of Haji Jamal Khan, Payindah Khan was the most powerful noble in Timur Khan's durbar and it was his support that enabled Shah Zaman to rise to power. The two fell out over Shah Zaman's attempts to limit the power of the hereditary nobility, and when Payindah Khan attempted to engineer a coup to replace Shah Zaman, the Shah had him executed in 1799. Far from bringing down the power of the Barakzais, however, the execution ultimately led instead to the fall of Shah Zaman and the rise of Payindah Khan's twenty-one sons, especially the eldest, Wazir Fatteh Khan and his younger brother and ally, Dost Mohammad Khan. The killing of Payindah Khan began the blood feud between the Barakzais and the Sadozais which would cast a shadow over the region for half a century.

Wazir Fatteh Khan (1778–1818): Fatteh was the eldest of Payindah Khan's children. After the execution of his father he managed to flee to Iran. In the following years he revenged himself on the Sadozais, first by engineering the blinding and overthrow of Shah Zaman by his half-brother Shah Mahmoud, then by defeating Shah Shuja at the Battle of Nimla in 1809. He ruled as the powerful Wazir to Shah Mahmoud until he assisted in the rape of the Sadozai harem in Herat in 1817, after which he was blinded, scalped, tortured and executed by Shah Mahmoud in 1818. The brutal killing reopened the feud between the Barakzais and the Sadozais which was to divide the region until the expulsion of the last Sadozai from Afghanistan in 1842.

Dost Mohammad Khan (1792–1863): Dost Mohammad was the eighteenth son of Payindah Khan by a low-status Qizilbash wife. His rise to power was initially brought about by his eldest brother Wazir Fatteh Khan and then, after the latter's death, by his own ruthlessness, efficiency and cunning. Between 1818 and his accession in 1826, Dost Mohammad slowly increased his hold on power, and in 1835 he declared a jihad against the Sikhs and had himself formally declared as Amir. He was greatly admired by Alexander Burnes, who wrote despatches praising his justice and popularity, but despite Burnes's efforts, Calcutta continued to see him as an enemy of British interests. After he received the Russian envoy, Ivan Vitkevitch, in 1838, Lord Auckland decided to replace him with his Sadozai arch-rival, Shah Shuja. After the British took Kabul, he spent eighteen months on the run, before surrendering to Sir William Macnaghten on 4 November 1840. He was sent off to exile in India. He was released following the assassination of Shah Shuja and the subsequent British withdrawal from Afghanistan in 1842, and was allowed to return to Kabul. Over the next twenty-one years of his reign he succeeded in enlarging his dominions to the current borders of the country. He died in 1863 shortly after conquering Herat.

Nawab Jabar Khan (1782–1854): The notably Anglophile seventh son of Payindah Khan and close ally of his younger brother, Dost Mohammad Khan. Despite his interest in western ways and personal fondness for many of the British officials, he remained loyal to Dost Mohammad and was prominent in the resistance against the British following their invasion in 1839.

Wa'fa Begum (d. 1838): Daughter of Payindah Khan and half-sister of Fatteh Khan and Dost Mohammad. Wa'fa married Shah Shuja early in his first reign, soon after 1803, when Shuja was attempting to soothe the blood feud between the Barakzais and the Sadozais. Praised by the British for her 'coolness and intrepidity' she managed to get her husband released from imprisonment in Kashmir in 1813 by offering Ranjit Singh the Koh-i-Nur, and according to some sources helped Shuja escape a second time, from Lahore in 1815. On her arrival in Ludhiana she managed to persuade the British to give her asylum, thus providing the Sadozais with the base from which they would eventually return to their throne. She died in 1838 and some attributed the failure of Shuja's policies after that to the absence of her wise advice.

Wazir Mohammad Akbar Khan (1816–47): Dost Mohammad's fourth and most capable son, born of a Popalzai wife. Akbar was a sophisticated and complex character, who was regarded in Kabul as the most dashing of the resistance leaders. The *Akbarnama* even includes a detailed description of the pleasures of his wedding bed. He first came to notice when he helped defeat the Sikh general Hari Singh at the Battle of Jamrud in 1837 and according to some sources personally killed and decapitated the Sikh leader. After his father surrendered to the British in 1840, and on his own release from the pit of Bukhara, he stayed at large in the Hindu Kush aiming to lead the resistance against the British. His arrival in Kabul on 25 November 1841 transformed the uprising and it was he who led the negotiations for a British withdrawal. On 23 December 1841, during a parley by the banks of the Kabul river, he personally killed the British envoy, Sir William Macnaghten. He subsequently led the siege of Jalalabad, and commanded the Afghan forces which tried to stop Pollock retaking Kabul on 13 September 1842. After the British withdrew he retook the capital and remained the most powerful figure until the return of his father, Dost Mohammad, in April 1843. He died four years later, some said poisoned by Dost Mohammad who had come to regard him as a potential threat to his rule.

Nawab Mohammad Zaman Khan Barakzai: Zaman Khan was a nephew and close adviser of Dost Mohammad Khan, for whom he had served as Governor of Jalalabad between 1809 and 1834. He fled Kabul with Dost Mohammad in 1839, but Mohan Lal Kashmiri facilitated his return from exile and had him received into the court of Shah Shuja in 1840. At the outbreak of hostilities he initially showed signs of siding with the British, but was soon persuaded to take on the leadership of the uprising. Despite being known as the 'rich nomad' and regarded as a country bumpkin, he was crowned Amir in early November. He was sidelined by his cousin Akbar Khan after the latter's arrival at the end of November 1841, and by February 1842 had entered an alliance with Shah Shuja, for whom he agreed to act as wazir. The alliance broke down owing to his rivalry with Naib Aminullah Khan Logari, and it was owing to Shuja's perceived favouritism of Logari's son Nasrullah over Zaman Khan's son, **Shuja ud-Daula Barakzai**, that the latter assassinated the Shah, his own godfather.

Other Leaders of the Resistance

Naib Aminullah Khan Logari: Aminullah Khan was a Yusufzai Pathan of relatively humble origins – his father had been assistant to the Governor of Kashmir at the time of Timur Shah – and he had risen through his intelligence and loyalty to the Sadozais. By 1839 he was a very old man, but still powerful, commanding substantial funds and large tracts of strategically important land in addition to his own private militia. Despite being a committed pro-Sadozai loyalist, he strongly objected to the presence of the infidel British in his lands and when he was insulted by a junior British officer, Captain Trevor, and lost his lands for refusing to pay increased taxes to the Crown, he became the leading centre of the resistance along with Abdullah Khan Achakzai. After the slaughter of the British in the Khord Kabul he rejoined the service of Shah Shuja, and only went across to the Barakzais after Shuja's death. On the return of Dost Mohammad in 1843 he was imprisoned 'for inciting peaceful people to engage in mischief' and died in the dungeons of the Bala Hisar.

Abdullah Khan Achakzai (d. 1841): Abdullah Khan was a young warrior-aristocrat from one of the most powerful and distinguished families in the region. His grandfather had been a rival of Dost Mohammad's grandfather in the early days of the Durrani Empire, and the Achakzais had never shown much enthusiasm for the Barakzais. But like his friend Naib Aminullah Khan Logari, Abdullah Khan strongly objected to the presence of British troops in Afghanistan and after he had his mistress seduced by Alexander Burnes, and was mocked when he tried to retrieve her, he became one of the two principal leaders of the resistance. He was appointed the Commander-in-Chief of rebel forces at the outbreak of hostilities in November 1841, and was the main military mind behind the British defeat until his death in battle on the Bibi Mahru heights on 23 November. An assassin subsequently claimed he had shot him in the back to win the bounty offered by Mohan Lal Kashmiri for the death of the rebel leaders.

Mohammad Shah Khan Ghilzai: Mohammad Shah was the powerful chief of the Babrak Khel Ghilzai of Laghmanat, and the father-in-law of Wazir Akbar Khan. On the return of Shah Shuja in 1839 he was persuaded to join the court and appointed to the honorary position of the King's Chief Executioner. He joined the resistance after Sir William Macnaghten cut the Ghilzais' subsidies in October 1841: every king had paid the Ghilzais *rahdari* (road-keeping) to maintain the road and protect the armies and traders en route to India, but Macnaghten informed the Ghilzai chiefs that he was abrogating this agreement. After the return of Akbar Khan in 1841 it was Mohammad Shah Ghilzai who supervised the slaughter of the British during the retreat. Like the other leaders of the rebellion he found himself sidelined after the return of Dost Mohammad Khan in 1843, and he died in exile among the Kafirs of Nuristan.

Mir Masjidi (d. 1841) and Mir Haji: These brothers were two powerful and respected hereditary Naqsbandi sheikhs from Kohistan. Mir Haji was also the hereditary Imam of the Pul-i-Khishti Friday Mosque, the leader of the Kabul 'ulema and the chief pirzada of the great Kabul Sufi shrine of Ashiqan wa Arifan. Having been promised large bribes by Wade in 1839, both brothers led their Tajik tribesmen against Dost Mohammad and so played a crucial role in the accession of Shah Shuja; but a year later, when none of the promised money had been paid, they rose in turn against Shuja and his British backers. Having made his protest, Mir Masjidi was about to give himself up when, contrary to all understandings, the British attacked his fort and massacred his family; his lands were then shared among his enemies. Following this both brothers became implacable enemies of the British and led the Tajik Kohistanis against the Anglo-Sadozai regime, first from the Nijrow Valley and then in Charikar and Kabul. Mir Masjidi was killed on the heights of Bibi Mahru on 23 November, but Mir Haji lived on to incite the people of Kabul against Shah Shuja, and it was his call for jihad against the British in Jalalabad that finally lured Shah Shuja out of the Bala Hisar to his death on 5 April 1842.

THE BRITISH

Mountstuart Elphinstone (1779–1859): Elphinstone was a scholarly Lowland Scot who was chosen by Lord Minto to lead the first British Embassy to Afghanistan in 1809. Despite never venturing further than Shah Shuja's fortress in Peshawar, he subsequently published an extraordinary and highly influential book about Afghanistan, *An Account of the Kingdom of Caubul*, which became the main source of English-language knowledge about the region for several generations.

Major-General William Elphinstone (1782–1842): William Elphinstone was an elderly cousin of Mountstuart who, before being appointed as Commander-in-Chief at Kabul at the age of fifty-eight, had last seen action when he commanded the 33rd Foot at Waterloo. After years on half-pay he had returned to active service only in 1837, at the age of fifty-five, in order to pay off his growing debts. To his friends such as Lord Auckland, Elphinstone was a man of great personal charm, but he had no liking or feeling for India or the Indian troops he had to lead, and he described his sepoys as 'negroes'. He arrived in Afghanistan suffering from severe gout and his condition got rapidly worse. General Nott described him as 'incompetent', an assessment that was rapidly proved all too accurate by his failure to act at the start of the uprising and his subsequent retreat into depressive indecision. He was wounded in the retreat from Kabul and after lingering for three months died of a combination of wounds, depression and dysentery at Tezin on 23 April 1842.

Sir William Hay Macnaghten (1793–1841): Macnaghten was a bookish scholar, linguist and former judge from Ulster who had been promoted from his court room to run the Company's bureaucracy: '*our* Lord Palmerston', Emily Eden called him, 'a dry sensible man, who wears an enormous pair of blue spectacles'. He was widely respected for his intelligence, but many disliked his pomposity while others questioned whether this 'man of the desk' was at all suited to his new job as chief adviser to the Governor General. It was Macnaghten who taught Lord Auckland to look upon Dost Mohammad as an enemy of British interests, and in collaboration with Claude Wade pushed for regime change in Kabul by aiding Shah Shuja to regain his throne. Having designed the policy of the invasion, Macnaghten asked to be sent out to Kabul to implement it, but his administration was not a success and he soon found himself sending delusionally optimistic despatches to Lord Auckland about the 'perfect tranquillity' of Afghanistan in the face of the anxious reports his officials were sending in from across the country. He failed to spur his generals into effective action during the rebellion of November 1841 and was killed by Akbar Khan during negotiations outside the cantonment on 23 December 1841.

Major Claude Wade (1794–1861): Wade was a Bengal-born Persian scholar who, during his period as British agent in Ludhiana, transformed the position from just running relations with Ranjit Singh's Sikh court to controlling a network of 'intelligencers' across the Himalayas and Central Asia. In this way Wade effectively turned himself into the first spymaster of the Great Game. It was Wade who first suggested using Shah Shuja to bring about regime change in Afghanistan, and partly out of a sense of competition with Alexander Burnes, who favoured an alliance with Dost Mohammad, pushed forward the policy of restoring the Sadozais to the throne. During the invasion of 1839 he was meant to lead a mixed force of Company troops and Ranjit Singh's Punjabi Muslims up the Khyber, but he failed to gather more than a handful of Punjabis. He nevertheless forced the Khyber on 23 July. On the death of Ranjit Singh, he fell out with the Khalsa, and the Sikhs asked Auckland to have him replaced. He finished his career in the less sensitive posting of Resident in Indore, before retiring to the Isle of Wight in 1844.

Sir Alexander Burnes (1805–41): Burnes was an energetic, high-spirited and resourceful young Highland Scot whose skill in languages won him swift promotion. He led two expeditions of exploration into Afghanistan and Central Asia in 1830–2 and 1836–8, both nominally commercial, but in reality political, gathering detailed intelligence for the Company. On the second expedition, the discovery of a rival Russian delegation also wooing Dost Mohammad of Kabul led Burnes to urge Calcutta to sign a treaty of friendship, but his advice was ignored and Lord Auckland decided instead to replace Dost Mohammad with the more pliable Shah Shuja. Burnes strongly opposed this course, but agreed to support it after he was offered a baronetcy and the position of deputy to the Envoy, Sir William Macnaghten. In Kabul, his talents were wasted as Macnaghten took sole control of the administration and he threw himself instead into the pursuit of the women of Afghanistan. In this way he made himself the hate figure he remains to this day in Afghanistan; and it was this, according to the Afghan accounts, that helped sparked the final fatal explosion in Kabul and his own gruesome death on 2 November.

Charles Masson (1800–53): After faking his own death and deserting his regiment during the siege of Bharatpur in 1826, Masson crossed the Indus and explored Afghanistan on foot. He became

the first westerner to explore Afghanistan's archaeology, locating
the remains of the great Bactrian city of Bagram and excavating
Buddhist stupas. Somehow Claude Wade learned the secret of
Masson's real identity as a deserter, and before long had blackmailed him into becoming an 'intelligencer', so ensuring a stream
of regular and accurate reports from Afghanistan. Masson assisted
Burnes during his 1837–8 negotiations with Dost Mohammad, but
unlike Burnes failed to find a position in the subsequent invasion
and occupation, despite knowing Afghanistan better than any
other Englishman. He eventually made his way back to England
where he died in poverty near Potters Bar in 1853 'of an uncertain
disease of the brain'.

Brigadier General John Shelton of the 44th Foot (d. 1844):
Shelton was a cantankerous, rude and boorish man who had lost
his right arm in the Peninsular War. He was a rigid disciplinarian
and known to be 'a tyrant to his regiment'. On arrival in Kabul he
soon made himself disliked in the cantonment, quickly falling out
with the gentle and gentlemanly Major-General Elphinstone. 'His
manner was most contumacious from the day of his arrival,' the
General wrote later. 'He never gave me information or advice, but
invariably found fault with all that was done.' This dysfunctional
pair of commanders could not agree on a strategy at the outbreak
of the uprising in November 1841, but eventually Shelton got his
way and at his suggestion the Kabul army marched out of the
cantonments on 6 January 1842, only to be annihilated in the snows
of the high passes. Shelton was taken hostage, and later tried by
court martial, but honourably acquitted. When he was thrown
from his horse and died in Dublin in 1844, his men turned out on
the parade and gave three cheers to celebrate his demise.

Colin Mackenzie (1806–81): Originally from Perthshire,
Mackenzie was renowned as the most handsome young officer in
the Indian army. In 1841, as Assistant Political Agent in Peshawar,
he went to Kabul where he was caught at the outbreak of the uprising. One of the few British officers to distinguish himself with

intelligence and bravery during the fighting, he was eventually taken hostage by Akbar Khan but survived the war to raise and command a Sikh regiment on the Frontier.

George Lawrence (1804–84): George was the elder brother of the more famous Henry and John Lawrence, both of whom later found fame as heroes of the Raj. A bright young Ulsterman, he was fast-promoted by Sir William Macnaghten to be his military secretary. As such, he fought both in the 1839 invasion and in the pursuit of Dost Mohammad, and was present at the latter's surrender on 4 November 1840. He narrowly escaped death three times: at the outbreak of the uprising in November 1841, at the time of the murder of Macnaghten on 23 December and again during the retreat from Kabul, when he was taken hostage. He survived the war, only to be made prisoner again during the subsequent Sikh war in 1846.

Eldred Pottinger (1811–43): Pottinger was the nephew of the spymaster of Bhuj, and Burnes's former boss, Sir Henry Pottinger. His presence in disguise in Herat during the Persian siege of 1837–8 was probably more than fortuitous, and provided a stream of much-needed information for the British. In British accounts he is usually credited with steeling the resolve of the Heratis to defend their city, though this is not a version of events which is supported by any of the many Persian or Afghan chronicles of the siege, where Pottinger is notable for his absence. At the outbreak of the uprising in November 1841, Pottinger was besieged a second time at Charikar to the north of Kabul, and almost alone of the garrison there made it through alive to the Kabul cantonments. When the capitulation to the rebels was made, against his advice, he was one of the hostages left with Akbar Khan and was in captivity for nine months, until General Pollock took Kabul in Sept 1842. He was subsequently court-martialled and although completely exonerated, received no reward for his work in Afghanistan and resigned from the Company service. He went off to stay with his uncle, Sir Henry Pottinger, in Hong Kong and there Eldred died in 1843.

General William Nott (1782–1845): Nott was a plainspoken yeoman farmer's son from the Welsh borders who arrived in India in 1800, and slowly worked his way up to become one of the most senior Company generals. A brilliant strategist and ever-loyal to his sepoys – 'the fine manly soldiers' to whom he was fiercely attached – he showed less talent in dealing with his superiors. Lord Auckland regarded him as chippy and difficult and far from a gentleman, and for this reason he was to be passed over again and again for the position of Commander-in-Chief in Kabul. He was eventually given the command of Kandahar, which he managed to keep quiet while the rest of Afghanistan was in violent revolt. He was to prove much the most effective of the British military commanders, and in August 1842 he marched across Afghanistan, defeating all the forces sent against him, and arrived in Kabul on 17 September, two days after Pollock had retaken the city. He returned to India via Jalalabad and was appointed Resident at Lucknow as a reward for his services in Afghanistan.

Lieutenant Henry Rawlinson (1810–95): Rawlinson was a talented Orientalist who helped decipher the ancient Persian cuneiform script. It was he who, in October 1837, as part of the British military mission to Persia, first alerted the British to the Russian mission of Ivan Vitkevitch when he accidentally came across Vitkevitch and his Cossack escort in the disputed borderlands between Persia and Afghanistan. He was subsequently posted to Kandahar, where he was Political Agent with General Nott, and together with Nott formed the most capable administration in the country. He accompanied Nott on his march across Afghanistan in August 1842, only to be horrified by the war crimes committed by British troops in Kabul and Istalif. He returned via the Khyber to India, but spent the rest of his career in Persia and the Arab world.

Sir Robert Sale (1782–1845): Sale was a veteran of the Company army known to his men as 'Fighting Bob' as he refused to stay at the back and always threw himself into the fiercest hand-to-hand fighting. Sale fought at the capture of Ghazni, and it was his violent punitive expeditions in Kohistan in 1840 that did much to unite the Tajiks in their opposition to the Anglo-Sadozai regime. At the end of October 1841 he was ordered back to India, punishing the Ghilzai for their resistance on the way out. As his force progressed down the Khord Kabul and Tezin passes they were caught in a series of well-executed ambushes and the expedition, which was supposed to chastise the tribesmen, ended by having a very different victim: in the narrow web of the mountain passes, the hunters found that they had now become the prey. With what remained of his force, Sale reached Jalalabad on 12 November. There his brigade remained under siege until finally breaking out and defeating Akbar Khan on 7 April 1842. They were relieved by Pollock's Army of Retribution nine days later, and accompanied it to Kabul. On 18 September, Sale was reunited with his formidable wife, **Florentia, Lady Sale (1790–1853)**, who had survived the Retreat from Kabul and subsequently spent nine months as a hostage of Akbar Khan. 'Fighting Bob' was killed three years later during the Anglo-Sikh War of 1845. Lady Sale emigrated as a widow to South Africa and died in Cape Town in 1853.

Sir George Pollock (1786–1872): Pollock was a precise, ruthless and doggedly efficient Company general who had been in India more than thirty years when he received his orders to relieve the besieged British garrison in Jalalabad. His reputation had been built on careful planning and meticulous logistics, and he was determined not to be bullied into acting prematurely. After carefully collecting supplies in Peshawar, he forced the Khyber with his Army of Retribution, finally relieving Jalalabad on 16 April. After another pause to collect more transport and ammunition, he advanced, defeating Akbar Khan in the Tezin Pass and retaking Kabul on 16 September. After destroying Istalif, and burning much of Kabul, he withdrew from Afghanistan and was received by Lord Ellenborough at Ferozepur on 19 December 1842.

Lord Auckland (1784–1899): George Eden, Lord Auckland, was a clever but complacent Whig nobleman. A confirmed bachelor of fifty-one, on arrival in Calcutta he knew little about Indian history or civilisation, and did little to illuminate himself about either. He knew still less about Afghanistan, and in 1838 allowed himself to be manoeuvred by his hawkish advisers into launching an entirely unnecessary invasion to replace Amir Dost Mohammad with Shah Shuja. Unwilling to commit the necessary resources to the unpopular occupation, he was wholly unprepared for the British defeats which followed. The complete destruction of the Kabul army, as Emily Eden noted, aged 'poor George' ten years in as many hours, and he seems to have suffered some kind of stroke. After his replacement by Lord Ellenborough, Auckland lived on in semi-disgrace in Kensington, and died aged only sixty-five in 1849.

Lord Ellenborough (1790–1871): The son of Warren Hastings's defence lawyer, he was a brilliant but difficult and unappealing man, whose physical appearance was so distasteful that George IV was alleged to have claimed that the very sight of Ellenborough made him sick. Ellenborough made his career out of Russophobia and was in many ways the father of the Great Game, that contest of Anglo-Russian imperial competition, espionage and conquest that engaged Britain and Russia until the collapse of their respective Asian empires. In October 1841, he was appointed Governor General to succeed Lord Auckland and arrived in India in time to take credit for the success of the Army of Retribution which allowed the British to withdraw from Afghanistan with some of their military reputation intact. He was 'flighty and unmanageable in all matters of business', wrote one observer, but 'violently enthusiastic on all military matters, and they alone seem to occupy his interests or his attention'.

OTHERS

Count Vasily Alekseevich Perovsky (1794–1857): Governor of the Russian steppe frontier garrison at Orenburg and the Russian counterpart of Claude Wade, Perovsky determined to match British intelligence operations in Central Asia with intelligence work of his own. In Ivan Vitkevitch, he found a man who he hoped would 'play the part of Alexander Burnes'. As soon as it became clear that the British were about to invade Afghanistan, Perovsky began lobbying to revive Russian prestige in the region by conquering the Turkman Khanate of Khiva. The Russian attack on Khiva ended as disastrously as the British retreat from Kabul would do, with Perovsky losing half his camels and nearly half his men. It put back Russian ambitions on the steppe for a generation: Khiva would not fall to Russian arms until 1872.

Ivan Vitkevitch (1806–39): He was a Roman Catholic Polish nobleman, born Jan Prosper Witkiewicz in Vilnius, today the capital of Lithuania. Jan had helped found a secret society called the Black Brothers, an underground 'revolutionary-national' resistance movement begun by a group of Polish students intent on fighting the Russian occupation of their country. Witkiewicz and the five other ringleaders were arrested and interrogated, stripped of their titles and rank in the nobility and sent to different fortresses on the Kazakh steppe. At the time, Witkiewicz had just celebrated his fourteenth birthday. Witkiewicz resigned himself to his fate and decided to make the best of his situation. He learned Kazakh and Chagatai Turkish, allowed his name to be changed to the more Russian-sounding Ivan Viktorovitch Vitkevitch, and rose to become the first Russian player of the Great Game. He made two expeditions to Bukhara before being sent to Kabul to make an alliance with Dost Mohammad. Here he outmanoeuvred his British rival, Alexander Burnes, but when his alliances were countermanded by his superiors, and the British invaded Afghanistan, he returned to St Petersburg where he was found dead in a hotel room on 8 May 1839, having apparently committed suicide.

Mohammad Shah II Qajar (1808–48) was the Qajar ruler of Persia who, by embracing a pro-Russian alliance and trying to recapture the disputed Afghan border town of Herat, helped alarm and provoke the British into their 1839 invasion of Afghanistan.

Maharajah Ranjit Singh (1780–1839): The brilliant and wily Sikh ruler, who created a powerful, well-organised and well-ruled Sikh kingdom in the Punjab. In 1797 he had helped Shah Zaman save some cannon lost in the mud of the River Jhelum during the chaos of the Afghan retreat, and he was given charge of much of the Punjab, although he was only nineteen years old. In the years that followed, Ranjit Singh slowly prised the lucrative eastern provinces of the Durrani Empire from his former overlord and took his place as the dominant power in the Punjab. In 1813 he seized the Koh-i-Nur from Shah Shuja and put the Shah under house arrest, but the latter succeeded in escaping the following year. During negotiations with Sir William Macnaghten in 1838, he outmanoeuvred the British and managed to turn what was planned as a Sikh expedition into Afghanistan in British interests into a British invasion in Sikh interests. He died in 1839, with the British midway through their invasion of the lands of his great enemy, Dost Mohammad.

Mohan Lal Kashmiri (1812–77): Mohan Lal was Burnes's invaluable munshi (secretary) and closest adviser. His father had been a munshi on the Elphinstone mission twenty years earlier, and on his return had chosen to make Mohan Lal one of the first boys in north India to be educated according to the English curriculum in the new Delhi College. Clever, ambitious and fluent in English, Urdu, Kashmiri and Persian, Mohan Lal had accompanied Burnes on his trip to Bukhara, after which he worked for some time as an 'intelligencer' for Wade in Kandahar. Burnes relied on and trusted Mohan Lal completely, and took him with him during the 1839 invasion as his intelligence chief. His failure to listen to Mohan Lal's warnings about an imminent uprising led directly to Burnes's death. During the uprising, Mohan Lal took out large loans in his own name for the benefit of Macnaghten during the siege, and again in 1842 borrowed more money to secure the release of hostages. He was never repaid the 79,496 rupees he calculated he was owed; as a result he was dogged by debt for the rest of his life. In pursuit of justice, he travelled to Britain where between attempts to lobby the Company directors he also visited Scotland, where he delivered Burnes's journals to his family in Montrose. While in Britain he published in English a memoir of his Central Asian travels with Burnes and an enormous 900-page, two-volume biography of Dost Mohammad. He even had an audience with Queen Victoria. But the Afghan War haunted his life and effectively ended his career.

The Sadozais

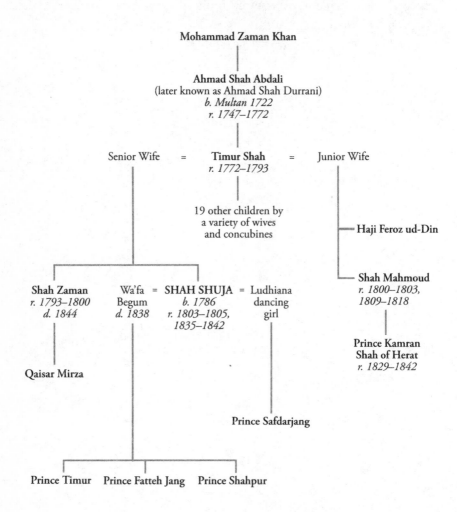

Mohammad Zaman Khan

Ahmad Shah Abdali
(later known as Ahmad Shah Durrani)
b. Multan 1722
r. 1747–1772

Senior Wife = **Timur Shah** = Junior Wife
r. 1772–1793

19 other children by
a variety of wives
and concubines

Haji Feroz ud-Din

Shah Mahmoud
r. 1800–1803,
1809–1818

Shah Zaman   Wa'fa = **SHAH SHUJA** = Ludhiana
r. 1793–1800   Begum   *b. 1786*   dancing
d. 1844   *d. 1838*   *r. 1803–1805,*   girl
                               1835–1842

Prince Kamran
Shah of Herat
r. 1829–1842

Qaisar Mirza

Prince Safdarjang

Prince Timur   Prince Fatteh Jang   Prince Shahpur

The Barakzais

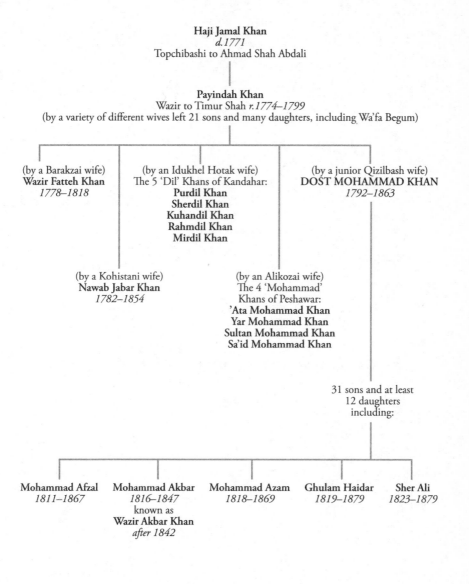

Haji Jamal Khan
d.1771
Topchibashi to Ahmad Shah Abdali

Payindah Khan
Wazir to Timur Shah *r.1774–1799*
(by a variety of different wives left 21 sons and many daughters, including Wa'fa Begum)

(by a Barakzai wife)
Wazir Fatteh Khan
1778–1818

(by an Idukhel Hotak wife)
The 5 'Dil' Khans of Kandahar:
Purdil Khan
Sherdil Khan
Kuhandil Khan
Rahmdil Khan
Mirdil Khan

(by a junior Qizilbash wife)
DOST MOHAMMAD KHAN
1792–1863

(by a Kohistani wife)
Nawab Jabar Khan
1782–1854

(by an Alikozai wife)
The 4 'Mohammad'
Khans of Peshawar:
'Ata Mohammad Khan
Yar Mohammad Khan
Sultan Mohammad Khan
Sa'id Mohammad Khan

31 sons and at least
12 daughters
including:

Mohammad Afzal
1811–1867

Mohammad Akbar
1816–1847
known as
Wazir Akbar Khan
after 1842

Mohammad Azam
1818–1869

Ghulam Haidar
1819–1879

Sher Ali
1823–1879

Acknowledgements

There may be easier places to research a history book than Afghanistan and Pakistan, but few which provide more unexpected diversion in the course of hunting down texts, letters and manuscripts. On the way, I have amassed a huge debt to a number of friends who kept me safe and sane while gathering the raw material for this book.

In Afghanistan: Rory Stewart put me up in his Kabul fort where I was beautifully looked after by everyone at Turquoise Mountain – Shoshana Coburn Clark, Thalia Kennedy and Will and Lucy Beharel. Siri Trang Khalsa took me on a weekend trip to explore Istalif and Charikar; she also linked me up with Watan in Kandahar. Mitch Crites provided reassuring company and sage advice about what was and wasn't possible, as did Paul Smith at the British Council.

It is not every day you find a Chief of Secret Police who has closely read your work, and I am grateful to Amrullah Saleh of the NSD, President Karzai's then security chief, both for his fearsome critique of *The Last Mughal* (in his view Zafar, a despicable weakling, lacked patriotic zeal and deserved no sympathy) and more particularly for connecting me with Anwar Khan Jagdalak, under whose protection I was able to trace the route of the retreat. Anwar Khan put his own life at risk to show me his home village – I remain forever in his debt.

I also remain hugely indebted to Najibulla Razaq who came with me to Jagdalak, Jalalabad and Herat. He was a fund of calm guidance when confronted with unexpected Afghan situations. I'll never forget how on my first trip, when we touched down together at Herat, we found that the old 1950s airport terminal was locked, as the man who had the key to the building had gone off for noon prayers. This followed a check-in at which I had been given a boarding pass marked 'Kabul – Riyadh' and when I pointed out that I was going to Herat, the airline official had replied that it didn't matter, 'they'll let you on the plane anyway'. When an old tractor arrived and dumped our bags at the edge of the apron, in the absence of trolleys, Najibulla quickly found two little boys with wheelbarrows who carried our bags to the line of shrapnel-marked cars which acted as the Herat taxi fleet. Najibulla was also an excellent guide to the Herat Museum of the Jihad: a collection of objects left behind by the various foreigners who have foolishly tried to conquer Afghanistan, ranging from British cannon from the First Afghan War through to Russian tanks, jets and helicopter gunships. It won't be long, one can be certain, before a few shot-up American Humvees and British Land-Rovers are added to the collection.

Sir Sherard Cowper-Coles, the British Special Representative, took me on his farewell picnic to the Panjshir, where under the willows by the side of a river, we had an oddly English lunch in the drizzle, with rugs and cucumber sandwiches and plastic cups of Chardonnay. If you ignored his ever-alert phalanx of bodyguards, their walkie-talkies crackling and assault rifles primed, as well as the litter of wrecked Soviet APCs and downed helicopter gunships, it could almost have been the Cotswolds. There Sherard briefed me on the political situation and its parallels with the First Afghan War. He also passed on detailed security advice and provided me with a tiny high-tech satellite tracking gizmo in case I got kidnapped on my way to Gandamak: if I pressed a panic button it would reveal my location and record a few seconds of audio in which I was supposed to identify my would-be captors. I took it with me, and was glad to be able to return it unused.

Brigadier General Simon Levey gave me a very helpful satellite map of the route of the retreat. Jayant Prasad and Gautam Mukho-padhaya were both wonderfully hospitable at the Indian Embassy. Saad Mohseni and Thomas Ruttig both provided useful advice and contacts across Afghanistan. I owe a lot to other friends made in Kabul including Jon Lee Anderson, Jon Boone, Hayat Ullah Habibi, Eckart Schiewek and Summer Coish.

Dr Ashraf Ghani, an erudite historian as well as former Finance Minister, gave me invaluable help with Persian and Afghan sources, while Jawan Shir Rasikh took me to the Kabul book bazaar at Jowy Sheer where we found many of them. Andy Miller of UNESCO helped get me access to the Bala Hisar and helped steer us both clear of Soviet era minefields as we explored it. Sayed Makdoum Rahin and Dr Omar Sultan got me into the Kabul archives and Ghulam Sakhi Munir helped me once inside. The fabulous Philip Marquis of the French Archaeo-logical Mission DAFA provided access to his brilliant library as well as Gallic good cheer, Camembert and the best claret in Afghanistan.

Jolyon Leslie was generous with his learning and experience and helped me get into Timur's tomb and the citadel in Herat, both of which he has beautifully restored for the Aga Khan, marshalling for the purpose more workmen than usually toil in biblical epics into moving quantities of soil and so revealing the fabulous Timu-rid tile decoration which had lain hidden for centuries. During this restoration Jolyon had to remove dead Soviet cannon and anti-aircraft emplacements, as well as a massive Soviet booby trap left as a farewell present to Herat: a network of live shells connected to an old tank battery at the top of a thirteenth-century hexagonal tower: bastions first built to defend Herat from the Mongol hordes were still being used to defend the Russians from the Mujehedin little more than two decades ago.

The warm and fearless Nancy Hatch Dupree walked me around the site of the Kabul cantonments and the hill of Bibi Mahru and helped in a thousand other ways. At the age of eighty-four she continues to commute between her homes in Kabul and Peshawar, sometimes driving herself down the Khyber Pass, sometimes by Red Cross flights: 'I am their only frequent flyer,' she told me when I bumped into her in Kabul airport recently. One of my fondest memories of my first research trip to Kabul was taking Nancy out to dinner at the Gandamak Lodge. In the middle of the entrée bursts of automatic gunfire were let off immediately outside whereupon all the hardened hacks abandoned their meals and dived under the tables. Only Nancy continued unfazed, announcing from her seat, 'I think I'll just finish my chips.'

I was looked after in Kandahar by Hazrat Nur Karzai, guided (over the telephone) by Alex Strick von Linschoten and (in the flesh) by Habib Zahori, and generously given shelter and guarded by Mark Acton, William Jeaves and Dave Brown of Watan Risk Management at their Watan Villa: who would guess that a house full of ex-Scots Guardsmen living in such tense conditions could remain teetotal for weeks at time? But I am very grateful: Kandahar is no place to visit without a little assistance.

In Pakistan: Mohsin and Zahra Hamid had me to stay while I researched in Lahore and provided diverting entertainment and delicious Punjabi khana in the evenings. I should especially thank Mohsin's father for giving over his study for my camp bed. While in Lahore Fakir Aijazuddin, Ali Sethi, Sohaib Husayn Sherzai and Mr Abbas of the Punjab Archives were generous with advice and getting me access to documents and new Persian and Urdu sources. Farrukh Hussein helped me find Mubarak Haveli and told me about the taikhana through which his ancestor had helped Shah Shuja escape from his house arrest.

In India: my neighbour Jean-Marie Lafont instructed me on Sikh history and the role of the French generals of the Fauj-i-Khas; Michael Axworthy tutored me on the Qajars; and James Astill shared invaluable Afghan contacts. The great Professor B. N. Goswamy in Chandigarh found some remarkable images and went out of his way to send me .jpgs and help get permissions. Reza Hosseini with huge generosity told me about his important find in the National Archives, a Persian manuscript copy of the *Muharaba Kabul wa Qandahar*, and even more sweetly brought me a copy of the Kanpur published edition of 1851. Lucy Davison of Banyan ably organised logistics for a research trip following the route of Shah Shuja's disastrous 1816 attempt to invade Kashmir over the high passes of the Pir Panjal range.

In the UK: David Loyn, James Ferguson, Phil Goodwin and my cousin Anthony Fitzherbert all gave advice on how to find my way around modern Afghanistan. Charles Allen, John Keay,

Ben Macintyre, Bill Woodburn and Saul David were invaluable in sharing their knowledge of Afghanistan's past history and enabled me to track down new sources. Farrukh Husain of Silk Road Books sent me parcel after parcel of Victorian accounts of the war. Peter and Kath Hopkirk, whose epic work on the Great Game first introduced me – and many of my generation – to the First Afghan War, helped with Alexander Burnes, as did his engaging new biographer, Craig Murray, whose forthcoming work looks set to be an important re-evaluation of this most intriguing figure. Sarah Wallington and Maryam Philpott tracked down invaluable sources in the British Library while Pip Dodd in the National Army Museum, Sue Stronge at the V&A and John Falconer in the British Library went out of their way to give me access to their artworks. I have the happiest memories of an afternoon with Elizabeth Errington going over the pick of Charles Masson's lovingly boxed and minutely catalogued Afghan finds in the store rooms of the British Museum.

In Moscow Dr Alexander Morrison and Olga Berard successfully hunted down the lost intelligence reports of Ivan Vitkevitch for me. A number of scholars helped me tackle the Persian and Urdu sources: Bruce Wannell came to stay in a tent in my Delhi garden for several weeks to work with me on the *Waqi'at-i-Shah Shuja*, the *Muharaba-i Kabul y Qandahar*, and the *Naway Ma'arek*. Aliyah Naqvi took a break from her dissertation on the court of Akbar to help me with a different Akbar and helped tackle Maulana Hamid Kashmiri's *Akbarnama*. Tommy Wide worked on the *Jangnama* and the *'Ayn al-Waqayi*, as well as helping double-check the identities of the different Sadozai graves in and around Timur's Tomb. Danish Husain and his mother, Professor Syeda Bilqis Fatema Husaini, worked together on the *Tarikh-i-Sultani* and the *Letters* of Aminullah Khan Logari. I am especially grateful to Robert McChesney for generously sending me his translation of the *Siraj ul-Tawarikh*.

Several friends were good enough to read through portions of the book and offer useful critiques, among them Chris Bayly, Ayesha Jalal, Ben Hopkins, Robert Nichols, Alexander Morrison, Ashraf Ghani, Anthony Fitzherbert, Chiki Sarkar and Nandini Mehta – the brilliant dream team at Penguin India – Akash Kapur,

Fleur Xavier, David Garner, Monisha Rajesh, James Caro, Jawan Shir Rasikh, Maya Jasanoff, Jolyon Leslie, Gianni Dubbini, Sylvie Dominique, Pip Dodd, Tommy Wide, Nile Green, Christine Noelle, Michael Semple and Shah Mahmoud Hanifi. Jonathan Lee put in weeks of work minutely annotating an early draft of this manuscript and helped me understand much about the complicated dynamics of the uprising that I had managed to miss. One of the most interesting and useful few days I had in the preparation of this book was spent visiting him in New Zealand and walking along stormy winter beaches north of Auckland as he explained the complexities of Afghan tribal history.

I have been lucky as ever to have as my agent the incomparable David Godwin, and my brilliant primary publishers at Bloomsbury: Michael Fishwick, Alexandra Pringle, Nigel Newton, Richard Charkin, Phillip Beresford, Katie Bond, Laura Brooke, Trâm-Anh Doan, David Mann, Paul Nash, Amanda Shipp, Anna Simpson, Alexa von Hirschberg, Xa Shaw Stewart and Diya Hazra, who have all thrown themselves into this project with huge energy and enthusiasm; thanks too to Peter James, Catherine Best, Martin Bryant and Christopher Phipps; at Knopf, Sonny Mehta, Diana Coglianese and Erinn B. Hartman; Vera Michalski at Buchet Chastel and in Italy the incomparable Roberto Calasso at Adelphi. I am also very grateful for all that Richard Foreman has done for my books since *The Last Mughal*.

A writer relies more than anything else on the love and tolerance of his family. Olive, Ibby, Sam and Adam have all been complete sweethearts as their increasingly obsessed husband and father roved the Hindu Kush then returned only to sit banging away on his laptop at the end of the garden, mentally removed from family life and dwelling instead amid the troubles and traumas of 1840s Afghanistan: apologies, and thank you.

This book is dedicated to the last of our children still based full-time in Delhi, my beloved youngest, Adam.

William Dalrymple
Delhi – Kabul – Chiswick,
December 2009 – September 2012

I

No Easy Place to Rule

The year 1809 opened auspiciously for Shah Shuja ul-Mulk. It was now March, the very beginning of that brief Afghan spring, and the pulse was slowly returning to the veins of the icy landscape long clotted with drifts of waist-high snow. Now the small, sweet-smelling Istalif irises were pushing their way through the frozen ground, the frosted rime on the trunks of the deodars was running to snowmelt, and the Ghilzai nomads were unlatching their fat-tailed sheep from the winter pens, breaking down their goat-hair tents and readying the flocks for the first of the spring migrations to the new grass of the high pastures. It was just then, at that moment of thaw and sap, that Shah Shuja received two pieces of good news – something of a rarity in his troubled reign.[1]

The first concerned the recovery of some lost family property. The largest diamond in the world, the Koh-i-Nur, or Mountain of Light, had been missing for more than a decade, but such was the turbulence of the times that no attempt had been made to find it. Shah Zaman, Shuja's elder brother and predecessor on the throne of Afghanistan, was said to have hidden the gem shortly before being captured and blinded by his enemies. A huge Indian ruby known as the Fakhraj, the family's other most precious gem, had also disappeared at the same time.

So Shah Shuja summoned his blind brother and questioned him on the whereabouts of their father's most famous jewels: was it really true that he knew where they were hidden? Shah Zaman revealed that nine years earlier he had hidden the Fakhraj under a rock in a stream near the Khyber Pass, shortly before being taken prisoner. Later, he had slipped the Koh-i-Nur into a crack in the wall of the fortress cell where he was first seized and bound. A court historian later recorded, 'Shah Shuja immediately dispatched a few of his most trustworthy men to find these two gems and advised them that they should leave no stone unturned in their efforts. They found the Koh-i-Nur with a Shinwari sheikh who in his ignorance was using it as a paperweight for his official papers. As for the Fakhraj, they found it with a Talib, a student, who had uncovered it when he went to a stream to wash his clothes. They impounded both gems and brought them back in the king's service.'[2]

The second piece of news, about the arrival of an embassy from a previously hostile neighbour, was potentially of more practical use to the Shah. At the age of only twenty-four, Shuja was now in the seventh year of his reign. By temperament a reader and a thinker, more interested in poetry and scholarship than in warfare or campaigning, it was his fate to have inherited, while still an adolescent, the far-flung Durrani Empire. That Empire, founded by his grandfather Ahmad Shah Abdali, had been built out of the collapse of three other Asian empires: the Uzbeks to the north, the Mughals to the south and to the west the Safavids of Persia. It had originally extended from Nishapur in modern Iran through Afghanistan, Baluchistan, the Punjab and Sindh to Kashmir and the threshold of Mughal Delhi. But now, only thirty years after his grandfather's death, the Durrani Empire was itself already well on its way to disintegration.

There was, in fact, nothing very surprising about this. Considering its very ancient history, Afghanistan – or Khurasan, as the

Afghans have called the lands of this region for the two last millennia – had had but a few hours of political or administrative unity.[3] Far more often it had been 'the places in between' – the fractured and disputed stretch of mountains, floodplains and deserts separating its more orderly neighbours. At other times its provinces formed the warring extremities of rival, clashing empires. Only very rarely did its parts happen to come together to attain any sort of coherent state in its own right.

Everything had always conspired against its rise: the geography and topography and especially the great stony skeleton of the Hindu Kush, the black rubble of its scalloped and riven slopes standing out against the ice-etched, snow-topped ranges which divided up the country like the bones of a massive rocky ribcage.

Then there were the different tribal, ethnic and linguistic fissures fragmenting Afghan society: the rivalry between the Tajiks, Uzbeks, Hazaras and the Durrani and Ghilzai Pashtuns; the schism between Sunni and Shia; the endemic factionalism within clans and tribes, and especially the blood feuds within closely related lineages. These blood feuds rolled malevolently down from generation to generation, symbols of the impotence of state-run systems of justice. In many places blood feuds became almost a national pastime – the Afghan equivalent of county cricket in the English shires – and the killings they engendered were often on a spectacular scale. Under the guise of reconciliation, one of Shah Shuja's chiefs invited some sixty of his feuding cousins 'to dine with him', wrote one observer, 'having previously laid bags of gunpowder under the apartment. During the meal, having gone out on some pretext, he blew them all up.' A country like this could be governed only with skill, strategy and a full treasure chest.

So when at the beginning of 1809 messengers arrived from the Punjab bearing news of an East India Company embassy heading north from Delhi seeking an urgent alliance with him, Shah Shuja had good reason to be pleased. In the past the Company had been a major problem for the Durranis, for its well-disciplined sepoy armies had made impossible the lucrative raids down on to the plains of Hindustan which for centuries had been a principal source of Afghan income. Now it seemed that the Company wished to woo the Afghans; the Shah's newswriters wrote to him that the Embassy had already crossed the Indus, en route to his winter capital of Peshawar. This not only offered some respite from the usual round of sieges, arrests and punitive expeditions, it potentially provided Shuja with a powerful ally – something he badly needed. There had never been a British embassy to Afghanistan before, and the two peoples were almost unknown to each other, so the Embassy had the additional benefit of novelty. 'We appointed servants of the royal court known for their refinement and good manners to go to meet them,' wrote Shah Shuja in his memoirs, 'and ordered them to take charge of hospitality, and to treat them judiciously, with caution and politeness.'[4]

Reports reaching Shah Shuja indicated that the British were coming laden with gifts: 'elephants with golden howdahs, a palanquin with a high parasol, gold-inlaid guns and ingenious pistols with six chambers, never seen before; expensive clocks, binoculars, fine mirrors capable of reflecting the world as it is; diamond studded lamps, porcelain vases and utensils with gold embedded work from Rome and China; tree-shaped candelabra, and other such beautiful and expensive gifts whose brilliance the imagination falls short in describing'.[5] Years later Shuja remembered one present that particularly delighted him: 'a large box producing noises like voices, strange sounds in a range of timbres, harmonies and melodies, most pleasing to the ear'.[6] The Embassy had brought Afghanistan its first organ.

Shah Shuja's autobiography is silent as to whether he suspected these British bearing gifts. But by the time he came to write it in late middle age, he was well aware that the alliance he was about to negotiate would change the course of his own life, and that of Afghanistan, for ever.

The real reason behind the despatch of this first British Embassy to Afghanistan lay far from both India and the passes of the Hindu

Kush. Its origins had nothing to do with Shah Shuja, the Durrani Empire or even the intricate princely politics of Hindustan. Instead its causes could be traced to north-eastern Prussia, and a raft floating in the middle of the River Nieman.

Here, eighteen months earlier, Napoleon, at the very peak of his power, had met the Russian Emperor, Alexander II, to negotiate a peace treaty. The meeting followed the Russian defeat at the Battle of Friedland on 14 June 1807, when Napoleon's artillery had left 25,000 Russians dead on the battlefield. It was a severe loss, but the Russians had been able to withdraw to their frontier in good order. Now the two armies faced each other across the meandering oxbows of the Nieman, with the Russian forces reinforced by two new divisions, and a further 200,000 militiamen waiting nearby on the shores of the Baltic.

The stalemate was broken when the Russians were informed that Napoleon wished not only for peace, but for an alliance. On 7 July, on a raft surmounted by a white classical pavilion emblazoned with a large monogrammed N, the two emperors met in person to negotiate a treaty later known as the Peace of Tilsit.[7]

Most of the clauses in the treaty concerned the question of war and peace – not for nothing was the first volume of Tolstoy's great novel named *Before Tilsit*. Much of the discussion concerned the fate of French-occupied Europe, especially the future of Prussia whose king, excluded from the meeting, paced anxiously up and down the river bank waiting to discover if he would still have a kingdom after the conclave concluded. But amid all the public articles of the treaty, Napoleon included several secret clauses that were not disclosed at the time. These laid the foundations for a joint Franco-Russian attack on what Napoleon saw as the source of Britain's wealth. This, of course, was his enemy's richest possession, India.

The seizure of India as a means of impoverishing Britain and breaking its growing economic power had been a long-standing obsession of Napoleon's, as of several previous French strategists. Almost exactly nine years earlier, on 1 July 1798, Napoleon had landed his troops at Alexandria and struck inland for Cairo. 'Through Egypt we shall invade India,' he wrote. 'We shall re-establish the old route through Suez.' From Cairo he sent a letter to Tipu Sultan of Mysore, answering the latter's pleas for help against the English: 'You have already been informed of my arrival on the borders of the Red Sea, with an invincible army, full of the desire of releasing you from the iron yoke of England. May the Almighty increase your power, and destroy your enemies!'[8]

At the Battle of the Nile on 1 August, however, Admiral Nelson sank almost the entire French fleet, wrecking Napoleon's initial plan to use Egypt as a secure base from which to attack India. This forced him to change his strategy; but he never veered from his aim of weakening Britain by seizing what he believed to be the source of its economic power, much as Latin America with its Inca and Aztec gold had once been that of Spain.

So Napoleon now hatched plans to attack India through Persia and Afghanistan. A treaty with the Persian Ambassador had already been concluded: 'Should it be the intention of HM the Emperor of the French to send an army by land to attack the English possessions in India,' it stated, 'HM the Emperor of Persia, as his good and faithful ally, will grant him passage.'

At Tilsit, the secret clauses spelled out the plan in full: Napoleon would emulate Alexander the Great and march 50,000 French troops of the Grande Armée across Persia to invade India, while Russia would head south through Afghanistan. General Gardane was despatched to Persia to liaise with the Shah and find out which ports could provide anchorage, water and supplies for 20,000 men, and to draw up maps of possible invasion routes.* Meanwhile, General Caulaincourt, Napoleon's Ambassador to St Petersburg, was instructed to take the idea forward with the Russians. 'The more fanciful it sounds,' wrote the Emperor, 'the more the attempt to do it (and what can France and Russia not do?) would frighten the English; striking terror into English India, spreading confusion in London; and, to be sure, forty thousand Frenchmen to whom

---

* In Napoleon's luggage, captured on the retreat from Moscow, was found a portfolio full of 'the reports, maps, and routes, drawn up by General Gardane at the request of the Emperor', for the invasion of India which he was still planning to pull off after the subjection of Russia. NAI, Foreign, Secret Consultations, 19 August 1825, nos 3–4.

Persia will have granted passage by way of Constantinople, joining forty thousand Russians who arrive by way of the Caucasus, would be enough to terrify Asia, and make its conquest.'[9]

But the British were not caught unawares. The secret service had hidden one of their informers, a disillusioned Russian aristocrat, beneath the barge, his ankles dangling in the river. Braving the cold, he was able to hear every word and sent an immediate express, containing the outlines of the plan, to London. It took British intelligence only a further six weeks to obtain the exact wording of the secret clauses, and these were promptly forwarded to India. With them went instructions for the Governor General, Lord Minto, to warn all the countries lying between India and Persia of the dangers in which they stood, and to negotiate alliances with them to oppose any French or Franco-Russian expedition against India. The different embassies were also instructed to collect strategic information and intelligence, so filling in the blank spaces on British maps of these regions. Meanwhile, reinforcements would be held in readiness in England for despatch to India should there be signs of an expedition being ready to sail from the French ports.[10]

Lord Minto did not regard Napoleon's plan as fanciful. A French invasion of India through Persia was not 'beyond the scope of that energy and perseverance which distinguish the present ruler of France', he wrote as he finalised plans to counter the 'very active French diplomacy in Persia, which is seeking with great diligence the means of extending its intrigues to the Durbars of Hindustan'.[11]

In the end Minto opted for four separate embassies, each of which would be sent with lavish presents in order to warn and win over the powers that stood in the way of Napoleon's armies. One was sent to Teheran in an effort to impress upon Fatteh Ali Shah Qajar of Persia the perfidiousness of his new French ally. Another was despatched to Lahore to make an alliance with Ranjit Singh and the Sikhs. A third was despatched to the Amirs of Sindh. The job of wooing Shah Shuja and his Afghans fell to a rising young star in the Company's service, Mountstuart Elphinstone.

Elphinstone was a Lowland Scot, who in his youth had been a notable Francophile. He had grown up alongside French prisoners of war in Edinburgh Castle, of which his father was governor, and there he had learned their revolutionary songs and had grown his curly golden hair down his back in the Jacobin style to show his sympathy with their ideals.[12] Sent off to India at the unusually young age of fourteen to keep him out of trouble, he had learned good Persian, Sanskrit and Hindustani, and soon turned into an ambitious diplomat and a voracious historian and scholar.

As Elphinstone made his way to his first posting in Pune, one elephant was reserved entirely for his books, including volumes of the Persian poets, Homer, Horace, Herodotus, Theocritus, Sappho, Plato, *Beowulf*, Machiavelli, Voltaire, Horace Walpole, Dryden, Bacon, Boswell and Thomas Jefferson.[13] Since then Elphinstone had fought alongside Arthur Wellesley, the future Duke of Wellington, in his central Indian Maratha wars and had long since given up his more egalitarian ideals. 'As the court of Kabul was known to be haughty, and supposed to entertain a mean opinion of European nations,' he wrote, 'it was determined that the mission should be in a style of great magnificence.'

The first Embassy to Afghanistan by a western power left the Company's Delhi Residency on 13 October 1808, with the Ambassador accompanied by 200 cavalry, 4,000 infantry, a dozen elephants and no fewer than 600 camels. It was dazzling, but it was also clear from this attempt to reach out to the Afghans that the British were not interested in cultivating Shah Shuja's friendship for its own sake, but were concerned only to outflank their imperial rivals: the Afghans were perceived as mere pawns on the chessboard of western diplomacy, to be engaged or sacrificed at will. It was a precedent that was to be followed many other times, by several different powers, over the years and decades to come; and each time the Afghans would show themselves capable of defending their inhospitable terrain far more effectively than any of their would-be manipulators could possibly have suspected.

It was Shah Shuja's grandfather, Ahmad Shah Abdali, who is usually considered to have founded the modern state of Afghanistan in 1747. His family came from Multan in the Punjab and had a long tradition of service to the Mughals. It was appropriate therefore that his power derived in part from the enormous treasure chest of Mughal gems plundered by the Persian marauder Nadir Shah from the Red Fort in Delhi sixty years earlier; these Ahmad Shah had seized within an hour of Nadir Shah's assassination.*

Putting this wealth at the service of his cavalry, Ahmad Shah hardly ever lost a battle, but he was ultimately defeated by a foe more intractable than any army. He had had his face eaten away by what the Afghan sources call a 'gangrenous ulcer', possibly leprosy or some form of cancer. At the height of his power, when after eight successive raids on the plains of north India he finally crushed the massed cavalry of the Marathas at the Battle of Panipat in 1761, Ahmad Shah's disease had already consumed his nose, and a diamond-studded substitute was attached in its place. As his army grew to a horde of 120,000 and his Empire expanded, so did the tumour, ravaging his brain, spreading to his chest and throat, and incapacitating his limbs.[14] He sought healing in Sufi shrines, but none of this brought him the cure he craved. In 1772, having despaired of recovery, he took to his bed and, as one Afghan writer put it, 'the leaves and fruit of his date palm fell to the ground, and he returned whence he had come'.[15] The great tragedy of his new Durrani Empire was that its founder died before he could fix the boundaries of his country, build a working administration or properly consolidate his new conquests.

Ahmad Shah's diminutive son, Timur Shah, successfully maintained the heartlands of the Empire his father had bequeathed to him. He moved the capital from Kandahar to Kabul, to keep it out of the turbulent Pashtun heartlands, and looked to the Qizilbash – Shia colonists who first came to Afghanistan from Persia with the armies of Nadir Shah – for his royal guard. Like the Qizilbash, his

---

* What is left of Nadir Shah's Mughal loot is still kept locked up in the vaults of Bank Meli in Teheran. This includes the 'sister' of the Koh-i-Nur, the Dariya Nur, or Ocean of Light.

own Sadozai dynasty were Persian-speaking and culturally Persian-ised and Timur Shah looked to his Timurid predecessors – 'the Oriental Medici' as Robert Byron dubbed them – for his cultural models. He prided himself on being a man of taste, and revived the formal gardens of the Bala Hisar fort in Kabul first constructed by Shah Jahan's Governor of Kabul, Ali Mardan Khan. In this endeavour, he was inspired by the stories of his senior wife, a Mughal princess who had grown up in the Delhi Red Fort with its court-yards of fountains and shade-giving fruit trees.

Like his Mughal in-laws, he had a talent for dazzling display. 'He modelled his government on that of the great rulers,' records a later court history, the *Siraj ul-Tawarikh*. 'He wore a diamond-studded brooch on his turban and a bejewelled sash over his shoulder. His overcoat was ornamented with precious stones, and he wore the Koh-i-Nur on his right forearm, and the Fakhraj ruby on his left. His Highness Timur Shah also mounted another encrusted brooch on his horse's forehead. Because he was a man of short stature, a bejewelled stepstool was also made for him to mount his horse.'[16] Though Timur Shah lost the Persian territories of his father's empire, he fought hard to preserve the Afghan core: in 1778–9, he recovered the rebellious Punjabi city of Multan, his father's birthplace, return-ing with the heads of several thousand Sikh rebels laden on camels. The heads were then put on display as trophies.[17]

Timur left twenty-four sons, and the succession struggle that followed his death – with all the competing claimants energeti-cally capturing, murdering and maiming each other – began the process of undermining the authority of the Durrani monarchy; under Timur Shah's eventual successor, Shah Zaman, the Empire disintegrated. In 1797, Shah Zaman, like his father and grandfa-ther before him, decided to revive his fortunes and fill his treasuries by ordering a full-scale invasion of Hindustan – the time-honoured Afghan solution to cash crises. Encouraged by an invitation from Tipu Sultan, he descended the switchbacks of the Khyber Pass and moved into the old monsoon-weathered walls of the Mughal fort of Lahore to plan his raid on the rich plains of north India. By 1797, however, India was increasingly coming under the sway of a frighteningly alien intrusion into the region: the East India Company. Under its most aggressive Governor General, Lord Wellesley, the elder brother of the future Duke of Wellington, the Company was expanding rapidly out from its coastal factories to conquer much of the interior; Wellesley's Indian campaigns would ultimately annex more territory than all of Napoleon's conquests in Europe. India was no longer the source of easy plunder for the Afghans that it once was, and Wellesley was an especially cunning adversary.

He decided to thwart Shah Zaman, not through direct force of arms, but through diplomatic stratagem. In 1798, he sent a diplomatic mission to Persia, offering arms and training, and encouraged the Persians to attack Shah Zaman's undefended rear. Shah Zaman was forced to retreat in 1799, and in the process left Lahore under the governorship of a capable and ambitious young Sikh. Rajah Ranjit Singh had helped Shah Zaman save some cannon lost in the mud of the River Jhelum during the chaos of the Afghan retreat, and by charming the Shah, and impressing him with his efficiency, he was given charge of much of the Punjab, although he was only nineteen years old.[18] In the years that followed, as Shah Zaman marched and counter-marched trying to maintain his fracturing empire, it was Ranjit Singh who would slowly prise the lucrative eastern provinces of the Durrani Empire from his former overlord and take his place as the dominant power in the Punjab.

'The Afghans of Khurasan have an age-old reputation,' wrote Mirza 'Ata Mohammad, one of the most perceptive writers of Shah Shuja's age, 'that wherever the lamp of power burns brightly, there like moths they swarm; and wherever the tablecloth of plenty is spread, there like flies they gather.'[19] The reverse was also true. As Zaman retreated, thwarted from plundering India and hemmed in by the Sikhs, British and Persians, his authority waned and one by one his nobles, his extended family and finally even his half-brothers rebelled against him.

The end of Shah Zaman's rule came during the icy winter of 1800, when the Kabulis finally refused to open the city gates to their luckless king. Instead, one cold winter's night, with the falling snow soft on his lashes, he took shelter from the gathering blizzard in a fortress between Jalalabad and the Khyber. That night, he was imprisoned by his Shinwari hosts, who locked the gates, murdered his bodyguard and later blinded him with a hot needle: 'The point', wrote Mirza 'Ata, 'quickly spilled the wine of his sight from the cup of his eyes.'[20]

The proud and bookish Prince Shuja was only fourteen years old when his elder brother was blinded and deposed. Shuja was Shah Zaman's 'constant companion at all times' and, in the coup d'état that followed, troops were sent out to arrest him. But he eluded the search parties and with a few companions wandered on unmarked tracks from the poplars and holly oaks of the valleys to the crystalline snows of the high passes, cresting the kerfs and shelves of the mountains, sleeping rough and biding his time. He was an intelligent, gentle and literate teenager, who abhorred the violence spiralling around him, and in adversity sought solace in poetry. 'Lose no hope when faced with hardships,' he wrote at this time, while moving from mountain village to mountain village, protected by loyal tribesmen. 'Black clouds soon give way to clear rain.'[21]

Like Babur, the first Mughal Emperor, Shah Shuja crafted a beautifully written autobiography where he talks of his days as a homeless wanderer on the snow-slopes of the Safed Koh, padding around the silent shores of high-altitude lakes of turquoise and jade, waiting and planning for the right moment to recover his birthright. 'At this time,' he wrote, 'fate afflicted us with much suffering. But we prayed for strength, as the gift of victory and of kingship lies only with God. By His grace, our intention was that from the moment of mounting the throne, we would so rule our subjects with justice and mercy, that they should live in happiness within the shade of our protecting wings. For the purpose of kingship is to watch over the people, and to free the weak from oppression.'[22]

His moment came three years later, in 1803, when sectarian rioting broke out: 'The people of Kabul', wrote the Shah, 'remembered the gentleness and generosity of my brother Zaman's governance; and they compared it to the insolence of the usurper and his ruffianly troops. They had had enough, and had recourse to the pretext of religious differences in order to obtain some change. The quarrel between Sunni and Shia blazed again, and soon there were riots in the streets of Kabul.'[23]

The fighting was between the Shia Qizilbash and their Sunni Afghan neighbours. According to a Sunni source,

> a Qizilbash rogue seduced a young Sunni boy who lived in Kabul into going home with him. He invited some other pederasts to take part in this loathsome business and they performed a number of obscene acts on the helpless lad. At the end of several days, during which they plied him with drugs and alcohol, they threw him out into the street. The boy went home and told his father what had happened. His father, in turn, demanded justice . . . The boy's family assembled at the Pul-i-Khishti Mosque on Friday, with their heads and feet bared, and their pockets turned inside out. They stood the boy beneath the pulpit and called on the chief preacher to redress the wrong. The preacher then declared a war against the Qizilbash.[24]

Most serious Afghan feuds tend to involve close blood-relations, and the 'usurper' in this case was Shah Shuja's estranged half-brother, Shah Mahmoud. When he refused to punish the overmighty Qizilbash who made up both his bodyguard and administrative elite, outraged Sunni tribesmen poured into Kabul from the surrounding hills and besieged the walled Qizilbash compound. In the chaos, Shah Shuja arrived from Peshawar as a champion of Sunni ortho-doxy, freed one brother – Shah Zaman – from imprisonment, then locked up the other – Shah Mahmoud – in his stead. He forgave all who had rebelled against Shah Zaman, with the single exception of the clan of the Shinwari chieftain responsible for blinding his brother: 'The officers arrested the culprit, and his supporters, and razed his fort to the ground. They looted everything and dragged the man to Shuja's court. Then for his sins, they filled his mouth with gunpow-der, and blew him up. They threw his men in prison, and brutally tortured them until they became an example for any who claimed they were so fearless they were capable of resisting the exquisite pain of the torturer.'[25] Finally, according to Mohammad Khan Durrani, they strapped the offender's wife and children to Shuja's artillery and blew them from the mouths of the cannon.[26]

Amid all this civil and fratricidal war, Durrani Afghanistan quickly fractured into anarchy. It was during this period that the country accelerated its transformation from the sophisticated centre of learning and the arts, which led some of the Great Mughals to regard it as a far more elegantly cultured place than India, into the broken, war-torn backwater it was to become for so much of its modern history. Already Shah Shuja's kingdom was only a shadow of that once ruled by his father. The great colleges, like that of Gauhar Shad in Herat, had long shrunk in size and reputation for learning; the poets and artists, the calligraphers and miniaturists, the architects and tile makers for which Khurasan was famous under the Timurids, continued their migration south-eastwards to Lahore, Multan and the cities of Hindustan, and westwards to Persia. Afghans still regarded themselves as sophisticates, and Mirza 'Ata, the most articulate Afghan writer of the period, sounds like Babur when he talks proudly of Afghanistan as 'so much more refined than wretched Sindh where white bread and educated talk are unknown'. Elsewhere he talks of his country as 'a land where forty-four different types of grapes grow, and other fruits as well – apples, pomegranates, pears, rhubarb, mulberries, sweet watermelon and musk-melon, apricots, peaches, etc – and ice-water, that cannot be found in all the plains of India. The Indians know neither how to dress nor how to eat – God save me from the fire of their dal and their miserable chapattis!'[27]

Yet the reality was that the great days of high Timurid culture and elegant Persianate refinement were fast disappearing. Virtually no miniature painting survives from Afghanistan during this period, in striking contrast to the Punjab where Pahari artists were then producing some of the greatest masterpieces of all Indian art. A once great city like Herat was now sunk in squalor and filth. Ravaged by repeated outbreaks of cholera, Herat had shrunk within living memory from a population of 100,000 to less than 40,000.[28] The Durrani state, with its severe institutional weakness, was on the verge of collapse and Shuja's authority rarely extended further than a day's march beyond wherever his small army of supporters happened to be camped. This chaos and instability created increasing difficulties for the kafilas – the great caravans heading to and from the cities of Central Asia – which in the absence of central authority could be taxed, tolled or looted by any tribal leader at will. This in turn severely threatened the political economy of Afghanistan by clogging the arteries through which passed the financial lifeblood of the Afghan state.

Afghanistan was still capable of supplying the whole region with three lucrative products – fruit, furs and horses. The looms of Kashmir still produced the finest shawls in Asia, and its crocuses the best saffron. Multan was famed for its gaudy chintzes. In good years there were also taxes to be collected from the kafila merchants travelling the Afghan trade routes bringing silk, camels and spices from Central Asia to India, and carrying back cotton, indigo, tea, tobacco, hashish and opium. But during the political unrest of Zaman's and Shuja's reigns, fewer and fewer kafilabashis were willing to take the risk of travelling through the dangerous Afghan passes.[29] In contrast to the confidence of previous generations, more and more Afghans were beginning to see their own country as an impoverished dead-end, 'a land that produced little but men and stones', as one of Shah Shuja's successors later put it.[30]

With little money coming in through taxes or customs, Shuja's only real assets were the loyalty of his blind brother, Shah Zaman, and the advice of his capable wife, Wa'fa Begum, who some believed to be the real power behind the throne. There was also the additional asset of the family's fast-diminishing treasure chest of Mughal jewels.

An alliance with the East India Company was therefore of the greatest importance for Shah Shuja, who hoped to use it to gain the resources with which he could unite his fracturing empire. In the long term, the British would indeed succeed in uniting the Afghans under a single ruler, but in a rather different way to that planned by Shuja.

By the end of October 1808, Elphinstone and his ambassadorial caravan were heading through the Shekhawati towards Bikaner, out of the Company's dominions and into the wind-blown wastes of the Thar Desert – virgin territory for the British.

Soon the Embassy's two-mile-long procession of horses, camels and elephants found itself in 'sand-hills, rising one after another, like waves of the sea, and marked on the surface by the wind, like drifted snow . . . Off the road our horses sunk into the sand above the knees.'[31] Two weeks' hard trudge brought them through 'a tract of more than ordinary desolation, until we discovered the walls and towers of Bikaner, a great and magnificent city in the midst of a wilderness'.[32]

Beyond Bikaner lay the borders of Shuja's remaining Durrani dominions, and before long Elphinstone's party encountered their first Afghans – 'A party of one hundred and fifty soldiers on camels', lolloping through the empty desert towards them. 'There were two men on each camel, and each had a long and glittering matchlock.'[33] Soon after passing the Durrani strong-hold of Dera Ismail Khan, Elphinstone received a welcoming letter and a dress of honour from Shuja, who sent a hundred cavalrymen, all 'dressed like Persians, with coloured clothes, boots, and low sheepskin caps'. By late February 1809 the Embassy had passed Kohat. In the distance rose the white snow peaks of Spin Garh; on the lower hills were the fortresses around which Elphinstone could see 'many marauders . . . but our baggage was too well guarded to allow of their attacking it', forc-ing the predatory tribesmen to sit watching, 'looking wistfully at the camels passing'.

Here the valleys were as benign and inviting as the hills were wild. The Embassy passed along straight avenues of poplar and mulberry, criss-crossed by streams and bridged with arches of thin Mughal brickwork shaded with tamarisks. Occasionally they saw a hunting party, where the men had hawks on their fists and pointers at their heels, or groups of fowlers out to catch quails or partridges. Soon the British emissaries found themselves passing walled gardens full of familiar plants: 'wild raspberry and blackberry bushes . . . plum and peach trees, weeping willows and plane trees in leaf'. Even the birds brought back memories of home: 'some of the gentlemen thought they saw and heard thrushes and blackbirds'.[34]

Peshawar was at that time 'large, very populous and opulent'. It was the winter capital of Durrani Afghanistan as well as being a major centre of Pashtun culture.[35] Within the last century it had been the base of the two greatest Pashtun poets, both of whom Elphinstone had read. Rehman Baba was the great Sufi poet of the Pashtun language, the Rumi of the Frontier. 'Sow flowers, so your surroundings become a garden,' he wrote. 'Don't sow thorns; for they will prick your feet. We are all one body, Whoever tortures another, wounds himself.' But it was the more worldly Khushal Khan Khattak who appealed to Elphinstone's Enlightenment heart. Khushal was a tribal leader who had revolted against the Mughal Emperor Aurangzeb and eluded his armies as they chased him through the passes of the Hindu Kush. In his diary, Elphinstone compared him to William Wallace, the medieval Scottish freedom fighter: 'Sometimes succeeding in destroying royal armies, sometimes wandering almost alone through the mountains'. But, unlike Wallace, Khushal Khan was also a fine poet:

> Fair and rosy are the girls of Adam Khel . . .
> Slender of belly, their breasts full and firm,
>
> Like the hawk has been my flight upon the mountains,
> And many a pretty partridge has been my prey.
>
> Love's affairs are like fire, O Khushal,
> Though the flame be hidden, the smoke is seen.[36]

Or, more succinctly:

> There is a boy across the river with a bottom like a peach
> But alas! I cannot swim.[37]

The Embassy marched into Peshawar six months after leaving Delhi, and was lodged in a large courtyard house off the main bazaar. Just as Elphinstone's Scottish Enlightenment education determined the way he responded to Afghan poetry, so when the time finally came for his first audience with Shah Shuja, the Ambassador's reading guided the way he perceived the Durrani monarch. On his way towards Peshawar, Elphinstone had been immersed in Tacitus' account of the German tribes confronting the Roman Empire, and in his diary he transposed the action to his current situation: he imagined the Afghans to be like the wild Germanic tribes, while the 'decadent Persians' were the soft and dissolute Romans. Yet when he was finally led in to see the Shah, Elphinstone was astonished by how different the cultured Shuja was from his expectations of a rough barbarian chief from the mountains: 'The King of Kabul was a handsome man,' wrote Elphinstone,

> of an olive complexion, with a thick black beard. The expression of his countenance was dignified and pleasing, his voice clear, his address princely. We thought at first that he had on an armour of jewels; but, on close inspection, we found this to be a mistake, and his real dress to consist of a green tunic, with large flowers in gold and precious stones, over which were a large breastplate of diamonds, shaped like two flattened *fleur de lis*, an ornament of the same kind on each thigh, large emerald bracelets on the arms and many other jewels in different places. In one of the bracelets was the Koh-i-Nur . . . It will scarcely be believed of an Eastern monarch, how much he had the manners of a gentleman, or how well he preserved his dignity, while he seemed only anxious to please.[38]

Yet the best, and certainly the fullest, record of this first meeting of the Afghans and the British was written not by Elphinstone, but by a junior member of his staff. William Fraser was a young Persian scholar from Inverness and the letter he wrote back to his parents in the Highlands, wide-eyed with wonder at the reception given by the Shah, provides the sharpest-focused and most palpable image that survives of Shuja at the peak of his power. Fraser described the magnificent procession that escorted the British officers in their frogged and braided pigeon-tailcoats through the streets of Peshawar. They passed crowds of Afghan men in flowing mantles and caps of black sheepskin, while some of their women, unlike the unveiled peasants of the country, wore full-length white burkhas, a novel sight for the British.

The British were summoned through the outer courts of Peshawar's great fortress named, like that in Kabul, the Bala Hisar. They were marched past the King's elephants and pet tiger, 'which was by far the finest object of what might be called the palace yard', and found themselves in the main courtyard in front of the hall of audience. In the middle, three fountains on different levels were playing, 'throwing up the liquid in a thin mist to a considerable height'. At the furthest end was a building two storeys high painted with figures of cypresses, the upper being open and supported on pillars, and having a domed pavilion in the centre. Under the gilt dome, on an elevated polygonal throne, sat the Shah: 'Two attendants holding in their hands the universal ensign of royalty in Asiatic monarchies, chowries [horse-hair fly-whisks], immediately determined the situation to be the same as that which the imagination pictures in reading fairy tales, or the Arabian Nights,' wrote Fraser. 'When we first entered, we made the obeisance required by taking off our hats three times and uniting the hands together, as you would to hold water, held them opposite the bottom of the face and muttered something supposed to be a prayer. We concluded by making the motion of stroking our beards.'

One-half of the armed troops who were lined either side of the avenue were then ordered to withdraw, and they went out at a trot, their breastplates and dented pauldrons clanking against each other, 'making as much rattle with their armour and clatter on the pavement as they could'. When they had retired a court official stood before Elphinstone, 'and called out in a loud voice looking up to the King, this is Mr Alfinistan Bahadur Furingee, the Ambassador, God bless him; then Astarji Bahadur [Mr Strachey] and so successively down the line, but had increasing difficulty managing our uncouth names, such as Cunninghame, McCartney, Fitzgerald, and by the time he had passed nearly through, blundered out any sound that struck him.'

When their names had been gone through, the diplomats stood for a minute in perfect silence and stillness, until Shah Shuja 'in a very loud and audible voice' uttered from aloft 'Khush Amuded' – you are welcome. Shuja then left his high gilt throne in the front of the building and, helped down by two eunuchs, walked to a low *takht* [throne dais] in the corner of the hall. When he was seated, the diplomats advanced up the cypress avenue, and into the arcaded hall of audience. 'On entering we ranged ourselves along the side of the apartment, where the floor was covered with the richest carpets. The silence was first broken, by the King's asking if His British Majesty, the Padshah o Ungraiseestan, and his Nation were all well and that the British and his nation had always been on the best terms, and trusted would always remain so. To which Elphinstone replied, "If it pleases God".

'The Governor General's letter was then delivered to Shuja . . . Elphinstone explained the causes and objects of his mission, to which the Shah was pleased to give the most gracious replies and flattering assurances.' The British visitors were invested in robes of honour, after which they rose and rode home in them.

Late that night, Fraser sat up and wrote to his parents about the impression Shuja had made on him: 'I was particularly struck with the dignity of his appearance,' he scribbled, 'and the romantic Oriental awe which his situation, person and Majesty impressed on me.' He went on:

> The king sat with his legs doubled under, but in an erect posture, not reclining, each hand resting on the upper part of the thigh, the elbows sticking out. This is the posture which fierce independent fellows assume generally when sitting in a chair leaning forward dogmatically and brow-beating the rest of the company, such as I have seen [Charles James] Fox assume in the House of Commons when preparing to rise and thunder his invective against corrupt

ministers. The spot we stood upon is the same which his subjects first humble themselves in the presence; where his public demands are executed and where justice receives his sanction; but where perhaps tyranny obtains more speedy obedience . . . My eyes rested at the ground by my feet: it was stained with blood.

When the Shah came down from the throne to move to the hall of audience, Fraser judged him to be about five feet six inches tall, and described his colour as 'very fair, but dead, without any ruddiness. His beard was thick jet black and shortened a little by the scissors. His eyebrows were high but unarched, and had a slope obliquely upwards, but turned again a little at the corners . . . The eyelashes and the edges of his eyelids were blackened with antimony, and his eyebrows and beard were also blackened by art.' His voice, he added, was 'loud and sonorous'.

His dress was superb, the crown very peculiar and ornamented with jewels. I believe it was hexagonal, and at each corner rose a rich plume of black heron's feather . . . a badge of sovereignty and a mark of God's chosen upon earth. The frame of the crown must have been of black velvet, but the feathers and gold so completely covered the ground that I could not accurately discover every precious stone that had a place, but emeralds, rubies and pearls were the most prevalent, and of extraordinary size and beauty.[39]

Negotiations between Shuja and the British about their alliance continued for several weeks.

Shuja was keen for an alliance with the Company, and was especially anxious for British assistance in protecting his lands which had been promised by Napoleon to the Persians. But he was distracted by the bad news arriving in Peshawar from all sides. For all the magnificence of his court, the Shah's hold on the throne was far more tenuous than the British had realised. As Elphinstone and

Fraser both soon came to suspect, Shah Shuja's obsession with the theatre of his court was to some extent a front to disguise the extreme weakness of his position.

Shuja's problems stemmed partly from his own declared intention to bring a new dignity to Afghan politics. In 1803, when he had first come to power and released Shah Zaman from imprisonment, he had disdained to exercise the customary punishment of blinding his defeated half-brother, Shah Mahmoud. 'We find greater sweetness in forgiveness than in revenge,' he wrote in his memoirs. 'So following the Holy Quran's recommendation of mercy, and the dictates of our own mild and forgiving nature, and recognising that humankind is a compound of mistakes and carelessness, we listened favourably to his excuses and granted him our royal pardon, trusting that such disloyal behaviour would not occur again.'[40]

So it was that Mahmoud was put under house arrest in the palace at the top of the Bala Hisar. This policy backfired badly when in 1808 Shah Mahmoud managed to escape and join forces with Shuja's greatest enemies, the rival Barakzai clan. The feud between the two clans, the Barakzais and the Sadozais, was already bitter and bloody, and was soon to cause a conflict that would ravage the whole country, dividing the tribes and providing a range of opportunities for the neighbouring powers to intervene. Before long it would become the central conflict of early nineteenth-century Afghanistan.

Payindah Khan, the patriarch of the Barakzais, had been wazir – prime minister – to Shuja's father Timur Shah. He was the king-maker responsible for bringing Shah Zaman to power on Timur's death in 1793. He had initially been a loyal wazir, but after six years the two had had an angry disagreement.[41] A few months later, the Shah discovered that his Wazir had been plotting a palace coup to protect the interests of the old nobility. Shah Zaman then made the mistake of murdering not just the Wazir to whom he owed his throne but all the ringleaders, most of whom were senior tribal elders. Shah Zaman compounded this by failing to secure any of the Wazir's twenty-one sons. Far from neutralising the Barakzai threat, Shah Zaman had effectively kicked a hornet's nest. By starting this blood feud between Afghanistan's two leading families, he opened a fracture in the Afghan political class that would soon widen into the chasm of a civil war.

The eldest of the Wazir's sons was Fatteh Khan, who took his father's place as the head of the Barakzais. But it gradually became clear that the most determined and threatening of the Barakzai boys was a much younger brother by a Qizilbash wife, named Dost Mohammad Khan. Dost Mohammad was only seven years old and working as the Wazir's cupbearer when he saw his father executed in court, and the horror of the event seems to have marked him for life.[42] He grew up to be the most dangerous of all the enemies of Shah Shuja and by 1809, at the age of seventeen, was already a ruthless fighter as well as a canny and calculating strategist.

When Shah Shuja first came to power in 1803, he had gone out of his way to try and end the blood feud with the Barakzais and bring them back into the fold. The Barakzai brothers were forgiven and welcomed to court, while to seal the new alliance Shuja married their sister, Wa'fa Begum. At first all seemed well; but the Barakzais were merely waiting for their opportunity to avenge their father, and as soon as Shah Mahmoud escaped from the Bala Hisar, Fatteh Khan and Dost Mohammad immediately rallied to his standard and joined the rebellion.

Shortly after Elphinstone's Embassy arrived in Peshawar, Shah Mahmoud and the Barakzai rebels seized the southern Afghan capital of Kandahar. A month later, on 17 April 1809, just as Elphinstone and Shuja were finalising the wording of their treaty, the rebels captured Kabul itself. They then made preparations to attack Shah Shuja in Peshawar. The situation was made more critical by the fact that the bulk of Shuja's army was away fighting another rebellion in Kashmir, and around the same time as the news came of the loss of Kabul, reports began to arrive that all was not well with the Kashmir campaign either: the two nobles put in charge of the attack had quarrelled, and one had gone over to the rebels.

With the King distracted, Elphinstone and his party were left to their own devices and began their intelligence gathering, questioning traders and scholars from different parts of Afghanistan, and asking about the geography and trade and tribal customs. Emissaries were sent out: one Mullah Najib, for example, was paid fifty rupees and despatched to gather information about the Siyah Posh of Kafirstan, said to be the descendants of Alexander the Great's Greek legions. Elphinstone found Shah Shuja's munshi, or secretary, an especially rich source of information: 'a man of retired and studious habits, but really a man of genius, and of insatiable thirst for knowledge. Though well versed in metaphysics, and the moral sciences known in his country, his passion was for mathematics, and he was studying Sanskrit with a view to discovering the treasures of Hindoo learning.' There were other thinkers and intellectuals in the court too, who between them were 'in possession of the greatest part of the learning of the country . . . Moollas, some learned, some worldly, some Deists, some rigid Mahommedans and some overflowing with the mystical doctrines of the Soofees'.[43]

The Shah allowed Elphinstone and his party to use the royal pleasure gardens, and having risen early to pursue their researches, they would break for the afternoon in the Shah Zeman Bagh, where the fruit trees were so thickly planted 'that the sun could not penetrate them at noon, which afforded a cool retreat . . . after luncheon we retired to one of the pavilions which was spread with carpets. Here we spent our time reading the numerous Persian verses written on the walls: most of them alluded to the instability of fortune, some very applicable to the King's condition.'[44]

Here Elphinstone sat scribbling in his diary, trying to make sense of the Afghan character in all its rich contradictions. 'Their vices', he wrote, 'are revenge, envy, avarice, rapacity, and obstinacy; on the other hand, they are fond of liberty, faithful to their friends, kind to their dependents, hospitable, brave, hardy, frugal, laborious, and prudent.'[45] He was astute enough to note that success in battle in Afghanistan was rarely decided by straightforward military victory so much as by successfully negotiating a path through the shifting patterns of tribal allegiances. 'The victory is usually decided by some chief going over to the enemy,' wrote Elphinstone, 'on which the greater part of the army either follows his example or else takes flight.'[46]*

Shuja was now negotiating for the survival of his regime. William Fraser's letters home written from Peshawar show how quickly the initial optimism of the Embassy began to give way to anxiety. 'The reports afloat today are very bad for our poor friend Shuja ul-Mulk,' wrote Fraser on 22 April. 'Kabul and Ghazni are both said to be taken by the rebels, and the Kashmerian army is supposed to be defeated. These are the rumours of the town, but generally credited and I fear, too true. So this man is no longer really King, and must fly, at least for a time, or stake the whole on one battle.'[47]

The British were beginning to understand that Afghanistan was no easy place to rule. In the last two millennia there had been only very brief moments of strong central control when the different tribes had acknowledged the authority of a single ruler, and still briefer moments of anything approaching a unified political system. It was in many ways less a state than a kaleidoscope of competing tribal principalities governed through maliks or vakils, in each of which allegiance was entirely personal, to be negotiated and won over rather than taken for granted. The tribes' traditions were egalitarian and independent, and they had only ever submitted to authority on their own terms. Financial rewards might bring about co-operation, but rarely ensured loyalty: the individual Afghan soldier owed his allegiance first to the local chieftain who raised and paid him, not to the Durrani shahs in faraway Kabul or Peshawar.

Yet even the tribal leaders had frequently been unable to guarantee obedience, for tribal authority was itself so elusive and diffuse. As the saying went: Behind every hillock there sits an

---

* The same was often true in India: Clive's 'victories' at Plassey and Buxar were actually more like successful negotiations between British bankers and Indian power brokers than the triumphs of arms and valour that imperial propaganda later made them out to be.

emperor – *pusht-e har teppe, yek padishah neshast* (or alterna-
tively: Every man is a khan – *har saray khan deh*).⁴⁸ In such a
world, the state never had a monopoly on power, but was just one
among a number of competing claimants on allegiance. 'An
Afghan Amir sleeps upon an ant heap,' went the proverb.⁴⁹
Elphinstone grasped this as he watched Shah Shuja's rule disinte-
grate around him. 'The internal government of the tribes answers
its ends so well', he wrote, 'that the utmost disorders of the royal
government never derange its operations, nor disturb the lives of
its people.'⁵⁰ No wonder that Afghans proudly thought of their
mountains as Yaghistan – the Land of Rebellion.⁵¹

Many of the tribes had lived for centuries by offering neighbouring empires their services in return for the political equivalent of
protection money: even at the height of the Mughal Empire, for
example, the emperors far away in Delhi and Agra had realised that
it was hopeless even to think of attempting to tax the Afghan tribes.
Instead the only way to keep open communication with the Mughals'
Central Asian homelands was for them to pay the tribes massive
annual subsidies: during Aurangzeb's rule 600,000 rupees a year was
paid by the Mughal exchequer to Afghan tribal leaders to secure
their loyalty, Rs 125,000 going to the Afridi tribe alone. Yet, even so,
Mughal control of Afghanistan was intermittent at best, and even the
victorious Nadir Shah, fresh from looting Delhi in 1739, paid the
chiefs huge sums for providing him with safe passage through the
Khyber, in both directions.⁵²* There were other options: the Afghans
could be lured into accepting the authority of a leader if he tempted
them with a four-fifths share of the plunder and spoils of conquest,
as Ahmad Shah Abdali and Timur Shah had both done.⁵³ But without a ruler with a full treasure chest, or the lure of plunder to cement
the country's different interest groups, Afghanistan almost always
tended to fragment: its few moments of coherence were built on the
successes of its armies, never of its administration.

This was certainly how it was beginning to look for Shah Shuja

---

* The British later learned to follow the Mughal model. According to a piece of
imperial doggerel it became British policy to 'Thrash the Sindhis, make friends with
the Baluch, but pay the Pathans.'

and what was left of his grandfather's empire. By May 1809, two months after the arrival of Elphinstone's Embassy, the full scale of the disaster facing him was becoming clear: 'The roads are unsettled, and all the clans and chiefs relieved from the slight control which did exist, plunder, quarrel and fight with one another,' wrote Fraser.

> The King's army in Kashmir has been wholly destroyed . . . Out of 15,000 men, only 3,000 have returned. The rest have either perished, or gone over to the enemy . . . Meanwhile Shah Shooja exerts all his energies and endeavours to raise money in every possible manner, cheers some, coaxes others, and secures the rest by promises. He intrigues too with the sardars [commanders] of the other party, and makes every sacrifice and does everything that a brave man, and an anxious king can do, with an empty treasury, a defeated, dispersed army, and proud independent nobles.[54]

In desperation, the Shah recruited a new army from the tribes of the Khyber, and spent May drilling whatever recruits he could afford to raise; a few more troops continued to straggle in from Kashmir 'dismounted, disarmed and almost naked'.[55] Such was the tension in Peshawar that an angry mob gathered outside the Embassy's quarters after a rumour spread that the British had been in communication with the rebels and that Shuja had ordered the house to be plundered.[56] On 12 June, with the safety of the Embassy now in jeopardy, and the roads becoming daily more dangerous, Elphinstone and his assistants said farewell to the Shah, and headed off south-east towards Delhi and Calcutta.

Shuja meanwhile prepared to make his stand. 'Though the Shah was engulfed with catastrophic news from everywhere and helplessly watched malevolence and ill-fate taking over his administration, he stood steadfast and didn't let fear overcome him,' recorded Sultan Mahmoud Durrani in the *Tarikh-i-Sultani*. 'Instead he marched off to resist Shah Mahmoud's attack.'[57]

Less than a week later, the British were camped on the left bank of the Indus, under the sheltering walls of Akbar's great fort at

Attock, when they saw a bedraggled royal caravan arrive on the north bank and hastily prepare to make the crossing. It was the blind Shah Zaman and Wa'fa Begum, leading the Sadozai harem to safety. 'To describe to you the effect of such a meeting upon the minds of all our party would be as difficult as melancholy,' wrote Fraser. 'Many with difficulty restrained their tears. The blinded monarch was seated on a low cot . . . His eyes at a moderate distance would not be perceived to be defective, merely as if there was a speck on each, with a little irregularity of the surface. After we were seated, he welcomed us in the usual manner and said only that he regretted Shuja's present misfortunes, and trusted it would please God to favour him again.'[58]

The news Shah Zaman brought with him could not have been worse. Shuja's defeat had been absolute. His army had been advancing from Jalalabad towards Kabul and its vanguard had just reached the cypresses of the Mughal garden at Nimla when his forces had been ambushed while still strung out along the road. The rebels had ridden them down with their lances and their sharp Khyber knives, screaming and spearing and clubbing with the buttstocks of their muskets. The lanced and punctured bodies fell as if suddenly deflated. Then the riders dismounted to gut and desecrate the torsos of the fallen, and slice off their genitals to place in the corpses' mouths. Within minutes, Shuja's general was dead, and the new recruits had bolted. Many of his noblemen, won over by the bribes offered by Fatteh Khan Barakzai, now changed sides.[59] Shah Shuja had been towards the rear of the procession. By the time he came to hear of the ambush, it was already over. His new army had disintegrated, and in the chaos of the headlong flight he became detached even from his own bodyguard.

Later, in the thunderous twilight, a storm crashed over the broken army, the noise drowning out the dull clop of the exhausted horses. 'The scourge of heaven was such that it rained enough that day to flood the river, and it became almost impossible to cross it,' recorded the *Tarikh-i-Sultani*. 'But Shah Shuja trusting to the Almighty entered the stream with his horse.' At first, the keel of the horse's breastbone cut through the waters, and the stallion kept its footing on the shingled strands of the Kabul River. But Shuja 'had forded only till midway when a torrent came, and he slipped from his mount. Eventually he and the horse, with much difficulty, swam across to the other side; but the rest of the soldiers refused to make the crossing. So it was that the Shah ended up spending the night alone, deserted by every one of his courtiers and servants.'[60] Shuja himself put it more succinctly. 'We were left alone and unprotected,' he wrote, 'like a precious stone in its setting.'[61]

The king whose year had begun so auspiciously, and who had put on such a dazzling and theatrical display of absolute power only a few weeks earlier, was once again, as in his youth, a lone fugitive, cantering blindly through the darker provinces of the Afghan night.

2

An Unsettled Mind

After the defeat at Nimla, Shah Shuja experienced a prolonged period of humiliation and exile. His wanderings were made all the more perilous by the fact that he was carrying on his person the single most valuable jewel in the world.

For several months Shuja visited the durbars of his allies, asking for their help in mounting a campaign to regain his kingdom and depose Shah Mahmoud and the Barakzais. One night, a former courtier named Atta Mohammad invited him to stay at the great fortress of Attock which guards the principal crossing over the Indus. There, according to Mirza 'Ata,

> they invited Shah Shuja to a private party where they served sweet water melons and started playfully throwing the melon skins at each other. But the jest bit by bit turned to scorn and effrontery, and Shah Shuja soon found himself arrested, held first in Attock then sent under close surveillance to Kashmir where he was kept prisoner in a fort . . . The lancet was frequently held over his eyes; and

his keeper once took him into the Indus, with his arms bound, threatening him with instant death if he didn't hand over the celebrated diamond.[1]

Wa'fa Begum, meanwhile, was loyally working to get him out. After her husband's defeat she had made her way to Lahore, where according to Sikh sources she independently took it upon herself to negotiate a deal with the Sikh Maharajah, Ranjit Singh, offering him the Koh-i-Nur if he helped release her husband from prison.[2] Ranjit Singh agreed to her terms. In the spring of 1813, the Sikh leader sent an expedition to Kashmir, which defeated the Governor who was holding Shuja and released him from his dungeon. Ranjit Singh then took the deposed Shah to Lahore. There he was separated from his harem, put under house arrest and told to fulfil his part in his wife's bargain by handing over the diamond. 'The ladies of our harem were accommodated in another mansion, to which we had, most vexatiously, no access,' wrote Shuja in his memoirs. 'Food and water rations were reduced or arbitrarily cut off, our servants sometimes allowed to go and sometimes forbidden from going about their business in the city.' He regarded this as a breach of the laws of hospitality. 'It was a display of oafish bad manners,' he wrote, dismissing Ranjit Singh, his one-eyed captor, as 'both vulgar and tyrannical, as well as ugly and low-natured'.[3]

Slowly, Ranjit increased the pressure. At the lowest ebb of his fortunes, Shuja was put in a cage, and, according to his own account, his eldest son, Prince Timur, was tortured in front of him until he agreed to part with his most valuable possession.[4] On 1 June 1813, Ranjit Singh arrived in person at Mubarak Haveli in the heart of the walled city and waited upon the Shah with a few attendants.[*]

---

[*] Mubarak Haveli still survives in Lahore's old city, a five-minute walk from the Punjab Archives in Anarkali where much of the research for this book was done. The haveli [courtyard house] is still as it was in Shah Shuja's day, with a succession of courtyards giving on to living quarters reached through wooden fretwork lattices and carved balconies. After the First Afghan War it was given by the British to exiled Qizilbash leaders from Kabul and it remains a centre of Shia activity today, with its own ashurkhana in the furthest courtyard. When I was last there a bomb went off outside the haveli as a Shia Muharram procession left the building, and the area now has a strong police presence.

He was received by Shuja:

> with much dignity, and both being seated, a pause and solemn
> silence ensued, which continued for nearly an hour. Ranjit then,
> getting impatient, whispered to one of his attendants to remind the
> Shah of the object of his coming. No answer was returned, but the
> Shah with his eyes made a signal to a eunuch, who retired, and
> brought in a small roll, which he set down on the carpet at an equal
> distance between the chiefs. Ranjit Singh desired his eunuch to
> unfold the roll, and when the diamond was exhibited and recog-
> nized, the Sikh immediately retired with his prize in his hand.[5]

The Shah had honoured the agreement made by Wa'fa Begum, but
at this point, having got what he wanted, Ranjit Singh reneged on
his promise to release Shuja. Shah Shuja's jewels were not all that
was of value; the deposed Shah too was potentially a lucrative asset.
So the Maharajah kept him under house arrest, allowing him only
the occasional carefully guarded outing for a picnic in the Shalimar
Gardens. 'In flat contradiction to the treaty we had made,' wrote
Shuja, 'it now transpired that, whenever we desired to take the air
and visit gardens or shrines, spies would secretly follow us all
around. We did not deign to take notice of them.'[6]

Shuja was at least allowed to summon the poets of Lahore to amuse
him. One celebrated poet of the period, Rukn-ul Din Lahori 'Mukam-
mal' ('Accomplished'), describes in his memoirs being summoned by
Shuja to Mubarak Haveli, only to have the Shah choke with tears at
the memories his verses stirred. 'O breeze what have you done to the
long hair of my beloved?' replied Shuja with lines in the same metre.

> You have disturbed the peace of my heart.

> The bird of my heart is lamenting the memory of my homeland
> This bulbul is lamenting its separation from the garden.[7]

A few months later, Ranjit Singh decided to seize what was left of
Shah Shuja's treasures. Shuja was invited to take part in a Sikh

attack on Peshawar where his estranged brother-in-law Fatteh Khan Barakzai was trying to consolidate his rule. 'Even though we were then suffering from an extremely sore throat,' wrote Shuja, 'we left our ladies encamped in the Shalimar Gardens and set out to join the Sikh by forced marches.' After Shuja had been lured out of Lahore into the countryside, the campaign was mysteriously called off, ostensibly because Fatteh Khan had withdrawn to Kabul. It was on the return journey that Shuja had his camp plundered by a group of armed robbers who descended on the royal tents in the middle of the night. When one of the dacoits was captured by Shuja's Afghan bodyguard, he revealed that he was working for Ranjit Singh himself. 'We were astonished and horrified at this evidence of the heartless treachery of these crass, ignorant Sikh dogs,' commented Shuja. He then wrote to Ranjit: 'What sort of behaviour is this? Whatever it is that you are plotting to do, do so openly – but stop this sly and underhand harassment! It is shameful!'

The following evening, the stolen trunks were brought back into the camp. 'Making a complete uproar, our Sikh escort brought the trunks, carpet bags and treasure chests into Our Royal Presence – all of them empty!' Shuja lamented:

> Everything was gone, apart from a few old clothes of no particular use. The boxes full of lustrous pearls, the Ottoman and Sindhi guns with gold bands, the fine Persian swords, jewel-encrusted gilt pistols, chests of coins in red and white gold, fine cashmere and silk shawls, all of it gone! And the black-hearted hypocrites had the gall to say to us: 'Here we bring your possessions, which we've fearlessly saved from the robbers! Let His Majesty inspect now to see if anything might by any chance be missing!' Such shameless robbery, and then the effrontery to protest loyalty: it is quite repulsive! God save us from all such!

Knowing that Ranjit Singh himself was behind the robbery, Shuja added, we mentally dismissed all the stolen property as an illusion or a bad dream . . . After these repeated betrayals, we entertained no further hopes of any help coming from these monsters. But given that our womenfolk and our honour were held hostage in Lahore, we had to submit, though sick at heart. We spent the next five months under the strictest surveillance, which was vexatious in the extreme: like clothes too tight in the heat. The feet of resilience stubbed toes on the rocks of oppression, but we could only beat our breasts to relieve the painful heart.[8]

Shah Shuja was not, however, the sort of man who would tolerate being detained at someone else's pleasure, and before long he had come up with an escape plan. His first action, as after his defeat, was to ensure the safety of his womenfolk, and before escaping himself he decided to smuggle his harem out of Lahore. This he did with the help of a Pashtun horse dealer and the Lahori traders who came to sell his women their groceries. According to traditions collected in the later *Siraj ul-Tawarikh*,

> He secretly purchased a number of horse-drawn wagons through some Indian women whom he had met because it was the custom in the homes of the great for them to come and go with goods for sale. In four trips, transporting ten persons at a time, the women left the city dressed in the clothes of Hindu women as if they were either going to swim in the river, as is the custom of the Hindus, or else to have an outing in the countryside. His retainers delivered his wives to Ludhiana, just over the border of the Company's territories, as he had ordered.[9]

When Ranjit Singh heard that Wa'fa Begum and the other women had made their escape, 'he bit the finger of astonishment with the teeth of regret' and increased the number of guards to 4,000, 'infesting every alley in the city, guarding all gates, all the mansions, even kitchens and lavatories, and especially our sleeping quarters . . . The soldiers would heat up oil and threaten torture, saying: "Give us your jewels, or else you'll feel the heat of this boiling oil!"' On a whim they would place Shuja in an iron cage installed in the courtyard. 'Wherever I went, even to do my ablutions, they would watch me. The world was becoming narrower for me and my household, and we soon became tired of observing the activities of these ill-educated and low-born Sikh people.' The Shah and his household took to reciting the verse from the Quran 'Deliver us from the tribe of the oppressors'.

> In answer to our midnight cries of despair, the following idea came as guidance: immediately below the chamber where we slept at night was the royal wardrobe, the quarters of faithful royal servants. We instructed them to make a hole in the ceiling of the lower chamber right under the bed, otherwise the guards would have noticed, and to dig a tunnel from the lower chamber under the neighbouring seven houses, all of which we had rented, breaching walls and digging through the earth. Over the course of three months, they dug through seven walls, one after another, until they reached a side-gulli near the bazaar.*

Leaving a faithful follower to take his place in his bed and disguised as a wandering dervish – 'I polished my body and face with ashes, and made my hair messy with dreadlocks, covering it with a black turban' – Shuja fled through the tunnel with two aides. They then made their way through the city past 'infidel guards and other malevolent individuals who were made deaf and blind by God'.

> At last we reached the main drain of the Fort, which at this season was dry. It was dark and narrow and difficult to pass through, but we were determined to get out, and commending ourselves to God and His Prophet, pushed through, getting scratched and bloodied on the way. Eventually we emerged on to the riverbank. There, servants were waiting with suitable clothes; they had also pre-paid for the boatmen and his skiff. We quickly embarked and crossed to the far side of the river. Not for a moment did we feel the discomforts and dangers of the road, as we rode and occasionally went on foot, thinking neither of

---

* Mubarak Haveli has a large underground cool room, or tykhana, which apparently dates from this period. Its existence must have made the breakout much more feasible than it at first appears.

food nor sleep . . . So it was that we escaped naked, with our bare
existence from Lahore. But we had no material, no funds, no supplies,
so were soon reduced again to a state of near-despair.[10*]

Within a few months of his escape from Lahore, Shah Shuja made
his first attempt to recover his kingdom.

Aligning himself with Ranjit Singh's enemies among the disaffected rajahs of the Punjab Hills, Shuja planned to gather a small
army, make a surprise raid on Kashmir and seize the valley. It was
a smart move, and could have provided a rich base from which to
begin the reconquest of his lost throne – for, as William Fraser
observed, Shuja was still 'beloved as a sovereign for his mellow-
ness, leniency and liberality'.[11] Moreover the political timing was
impeccable: in the aftermath of Ranjit Singh's raid to free Shuja, the
Kashmir Valley was without a clear ruler and was disputed by
several powers. But one thing Shah Shuja consistently lacked in his
campaigning life was that quality which Napoleon famously
remarked was most important for a general: luck.

The first disaster occurred when Shuja tried to get his finances in
order and despatched a man to Lahore to bring the 150,000 rupees
that he had deposited with the money-changers of the city. Ranjit
Singh found out about the plan through his spies, intercepted the
money and deposited it in his own treasury.[12] Raising more money
led to delays, giving Kashmir's Governor time to garrison and refortify all Shuja's likely invasion routes. By the time the Shah had
succeeding in raising sufficient money to finance an army against the

---

* The Afghan war artist James Rattray claims in the notes to his celebrated Afghan
lithographs that it was Wa'fa Begum, not Shuja, who organised his escape (as well as her
own), and he calls her conduct 'an example of coolness and intrepidity'. It seems
unlikely that even Wa'fa Begum could have organised the tunnelling and boatmen from
across the Company border in Ludhiana, but it is a measure of the extent to which the
legend of Wa'fa's abilities had flourished that Rattray was told this thirty years later,
long after her death. See James Rattray, *The costumes of the Various Tribes, Portraits of
Ladies of Rank, Celebrated Princes and Chiefs, Views of the Principal Fortresses and
Cities, and Interior of the Cities and Temples of Afghaunistaun*, London, 1848, p. 29.

jewels Wa'fa Begum had smuggled out to Ludhiana, then to recruit and train the mercenary force, the secret was out and the campaigning season was over.

But Shuja disdained advice to wait until the arrival of spring. He set off with his new troops over the Jot Pass, up the Chamba Valley, just as the first of the winter snow was beginning to dust the peaks of the Himalayas. In an attempt to reach the Kashmir Valley by an unexpected and unfortified route, he decided to take his troops across the heights of the Pir Panjal. Here, on a bleak ridge high above the dark spires of the deodar forests, only a few days' march from Srinagar, the force was caught in a blizzard. Shuja's men found themselves trapped just below the top of the pass, blocked in by snow and exposed to the elements. 'There was no way to advance or retreat,' Shuja wrote later, 'and soon no food and no water. Not knowing how to survive in the snow, the Hindustani troops began to die of the cold.' Before long the small army was almost wiped out. Only Shah Shuja and a small group of survivors made it over the top of the pass, and hence back to the plains.[13] As one British writer put it when he heard the news, 'Misfortune seemed to follow in the footsteps of this Prince . . . It seemed as if he was but warring against his Fate, which was, over and again, to experience hardships such as fall to the lot of few men.'[14]

Shuja's condition was now desperate. In disguise once again, he took an arduous and circuitous route over the mountains with his last few attendants and finally reached the British frontier post of Subbathu in the monsoon of 1816. Met at the border by a small escort, he was taken to Ludhiana. Here his harem had found shelter in a modest haveli near the principal bazaar. 'Our cares were now forgotten,' he wrote. 'Giving thanks to Almighty God who, having freed us from our enemies and led us through the trackless snows, now conducted us to our friends, we passed a night for the first time with comfort, and without dread.'[15]

In 1816, Ludhiana was the British garrison town on the Company's North West Frontier. From the flagpole of its Residency flew the last Union Jack between the Company's Indian possessions and the British Embassy in St Petersburg.

Before Shah Shuja's arrival, Ludhiana was known mainly as a centre of the flesh trade, through which girls from the Punjab Hill States and Kashmir – considered the fairest and most beautiful in the region – passed into slavery in the Sikh-controlled Punjab and Hindustan.[16] Shah Shuja's arrival with his court-in-exile began its transformation from a centre of slave dealing into a major hub of political intrigue and espionage. Over the decades to come it was to transform into the principal British listening post for the Punjab, the Himalayas and Central Asia: a place full of chancers and hoaxers, deserters, mercenaries and spies, the meeting place of the plotters and malcontents of Afghanistan, Ranjit Singh's dominions, the disputed valley of Kashmir and the dominions of the Company.[17]

The Boston-born, hookah-smoking, pyjama-wearing Sir David Ochterlony was the first British Agent in Ludhiana. From there he had established the Company's exact frontiers with Ranjit Singh. These were guarded by a regiment of Irregular Horse belonging to Ochterlony's friend James Skinner, the dashing Rajput-Scottish warlord. From their twin bases in Hansi and Ludhiana, Skinner's 'Yellow Boys' became the Company's first North West Frontier Force, and the first line of defence against whatever might come down the Khyber or over the Sutlej.[18] With their scarlet turbans, silver-edged girdles, black shields and bright yellow tunics, Skinner's men were, according to one contemporary observer, 'the most showy and picturesque cavaliers I have ever seen'.

When Wa'fa Begum first sent her eunuchs ahead to request asylum from the British in 1812 there had been a disagreement between Ochterlony and his colleagues about taking in the family of the fallen Shah. The Delhi Resident Charles Metcalfe, who had negotiated the Company's original treaty with Ranjit Singh at the time of Napoleon's planned invasion of India, argued strongly against the move, saying it would strain relations with an important ally with little benefit to the Company. It was, he wrote, 'an event so pregnant with inconvenience, embarrassment and probable expense, as to render it extremely desirous that it should not take place, and should be discouraged by every means consistent with the observance of respect due to her rank and misfortunes'.[19]

Ochterlony was having none of it. He knew from personal experience what it was like to be a defeated refugee: his father was a Highland Scot who had settled in Massachusetts and fought as a Loyalist during the American Revolution. When Washington's Patriots saw off the British, the Ochterlonys had been forced to flee to Canada; from thence, via Britain, David had entered the Company's army in 1777. Ochterlony also knew better than most of his contemporaries the etiquette concerning the protection of Muslim women: according to Delhi gossip, he had no fewer than thirteen Indian wives and every evening during his years in Delhi was said to have taken all thirteen on a promenade between the walls of the Red Fort and the river bank, each wife on her own elephant.[20]

Now, with characteristic gallantry, he took up the cause of Wa'fa Begum, accusing Metcalfe of heartlessness in abandoning the fallen Queen: the Begum, he wrote, 'was in a forlorn and helpless state . . . A foreigner, a stranger, and a woman of high birth is in misery, and has thrown herself on the protection of a government famed for its humanity and generosity. As the agent of that government I am most anxious to do every justice to its high character.' He then added, presciently, 'England has long afforded an asylum and support to exiled princes, and the most unexpected revolutions have restored them to their thrones under circumstances much more improbable than the restoration of Shah Shuja. In which case, though the gratitude of princes is not proverbial, the hospitality of the British government might give us a friend in a quarter where one may someday be required.'[21] Ochterlony's argument persuaded the Governor General, and the Begum was given asylum.

Wa'fa Begum and her women had limped into Ludhiana from

Lahore on 2 December 1814. The one British official in the town that day reported their bedraggled arrival, and their nervousness about crossing the British frontier without passports or permissions. 'I thought it would allay their apprehensions to send them word that they might rest assured of their personal security,' he wrote. 'I was sorry that I had no better accommodation to offer them than the tent I had prepared for them. They expressed their gratitude for the kind reception, but begged to decline troubling me for anything – saying that the protection of the British government was all they would ever ask or receive from us.'[22]

Within a few months, however, once news of her reception had spread, the number of the Begum's dependants had increased to ninety-six, and she moved to a semi-ruinous haveli that Ochterlony found for her. As she had no means of support, Ochterlony initially paid the Begum's bills from his own pocket. Later, he managed to secure her a small annuity from the government.

Two years later, when Shuja announced his intention of joining Wa'fa Begum, 'from affection for our August Consort and a desire to see our friends, the illustrious English', Ochterlony's mix of generosity and strategic foresight again trumped Metcalfe's caution, and he was allowed to send his assistant, William Fraser, to welcome him at the border.[23]

Fraser was quick to note the great changes that had taken place in the Shah since their last meeting in Peshawar. Seven years of defeat, betrayal, humiliation, torture and imprisonment had taken their toll, and it was clear that Shuja had become damaged, difficult and depressive. He was also almost pathologically determined to ensure that the façade of his royal status should be maintained despite the reality that he was now no more than what Ochterlony called 'an illustrious fugitive' – a refugee dependent on the charity of his former allies. But if Fraser had expected a broken man, he was to be surprised. 'The Shah arrived at the frontier yesterday,' he wrote to Ochterlony. 'I am sorry to learn that he is very Ultra-Royal in his wishes and expectations. He summoned your Munshi and told him he expected that the people of the country should keep at the distance of half a coss from his person, which was a customary observance towards Majesty.' Like the last Mughals, having lost an empire, his court became the focus of his ambitions, and the more powerless he became the more he insisted on public acknowledgement of his royal status. Yet for all the pretension, the reality of his situation was desperate:

> He has not fifty armed attendants and is greatly changed since I saw him last, having greatly increased in bulk and acquired a heavy, almost inanimate look. He has already been abandoned by most of those who arrived with him, and of the few attendants left, I did not recognise one who was of any note during the Kabul mission, nor one indeed whom I had seen before. The scene to me was a painful one. The reverse of fortune is nothing, but the ingratitude and abandonment which seem its consequence are indeed a sorry sight. The former is what all may expect and all should have, but the desolating nature of the latter might shake to its foundation the finest philosophy.[24]

Shuja arrived in Ludhiana at the end of September 1816, nearly two years after his wives. From the beginning he made it clear that the accommodation arranged for him was inadequate for his needs. He demanded as a king and an ally bound by treaty that the British provide him with more than just asylum and a pension: he should have a decent house with walls sufficiently high that his women could be secluded without being ogled by men sitting on the backs of elephants in the street. He also made it clear he didn't intend spending very long in the town: as he put it in one letter to Ochterlony, 'What advantage have I in remaining here?'[25]

The Shah had many faults, but lack of energy or an excess of self-doubt were never among them. Undeterred by his defeats, from the first months of his enforced exile he began to make plans to raise another army to retake his throne, 'dreaming sweet dreams of re-conquering the Kingdom of Khurasan'. In his memoirs, he recounted how he took comfort in the example of previous monarchs who had lost their kingdoms only to regain larger dominions later in life: 'Amir Timur [Timurlane], among modern rulers, was twelve times driven from Samarkand,' he wrote, 'while among the ancients, Afrasyab fought Kai Khusro in seventy battles, was defeated over and again, but never gave up. In the same way [the Mughal Emperor] Humayun inherited the provinces of India, but was defeated by Sher Shah and was forced to flee and beg help from Shah 'Abbas Safavi in Iran. In truth, unless God wills it, nothing will succeed. But when God wills it, we shall surely be successful.'[26]

At this time, Shah Shuja tended to swing wildly between excitement, self-delusion and depression. One day he would dream up what Ochterlony described as 'altogether visionary' plans to surprise his adversaries by returning to Afghanistan via 'the snowy mountains and Thibet'.[27] The next, he would sink into gloom as the impracticality of his schemes became obvious. 'The mind of the Shah remains in an unsettled and restless state,' wrote one Ludhiana officer, 'and he often observes that inactivity and want of employment ill-accord with the tenor of his disposition.' The officer added:

> It has been and will be a part of my duty to soothe, as much as possible, the troubled breast of the Shah . . . I use every persuasive argument that suggests itself to me to dissuade him from entertaining notions that cannot be gratified, such as that of getting British assistance for the recovery of his Throne, the wish of proceeding to Calcutta, or a strong desire to reside at some other post within the British territories. I have even delicately told the Shah's advisers, that these proceed from an unsettled mind and that no place but Kabul would ever be found fully to answer the Shah's expectations.[28]

Nonetheless, only a year after his arrival, concrete plans were in place, and anxious reports began to reach Calcutta about the number of cavalrymen descending on Ludhiana to seek service with the Shah. The government sent back pleas to Ochterlony that 'His Majesty should be induced to continue to reside calmly at Ludhiana with his family on the provision assigned to him.'[29] But it was clear to everyone that this was never going to happen.

After the fiasco of the winter raid on Kashmir, Shuja chose his moment with great care. In 1817, the feud between Afghanistan's two great families, the Barakzais and the Sadozais, had suddenly erupted again, this time following an insult by the Barakzais to a Sadozai princess. The two leading Barakzai brothers, Wazir Fatteh Khan and his younger brother Dost Mohammad, had been sent by Shah Mahmoud and his son Prince Kamran Sadozai on a mission to Herat, the most magnificent city of western Afghanistan. The brothers were to mount a surprise attack and take the great Timurid citadel from a rebellious governor who was plotting to hand it over to the Persians. This they did; but during the plundering which followed, Dost Mohammad and his followers looted the harem and there 'seized the jewelled band which fastened the trousers of the wife' of the Governor.[30] What they didn't take into account was that the Princess in question was Shah Mahmoud's niece.

A week later, when Prince Kamran arrived in Herat, he received a delegation from the harem, demanding that their honour be avenged. Like Shah Zaman before him, Kamran had begun to be worried about the growing power of the Barakzais, and seized the opportunity that the violation of the Sadozai harem presented.

A few days after his arrival in Herat, the Prince announced that he was to throw a party in the royal garden outside the fortress, and he invited Fatteh Khan and his brothers to celebrate their capture of Herat. 'Dancers and musicians gathered amidst the fruit trees, platters of kababs and decanters of red wine were prepared, and the nautch party was warming up,' wrote Mirza 'Ata.

When the Wazir and his brothers entered the garden they drank cup after cup of wine, ate kababs and lost themselves in amazement at the dancing of the lovely women musicians of Herat. Soon they were hopelessly drunk, and the bird of sense had flown out of the

Wazir's brain, and he lay befuddled. Prince Kamran had already arranged everything in advance, so at a sign all the others present at the party got up and seized the Wazir, tied his hands and feet and proceeded to blind him, drawing the tip of their daggers across his eyes to spill the clear liquid on to the dark ground of blindness.[31]

Fatteh Khan was then scalped, and brutally tortured. Sometime later he was led, blind and bleeding, into a tent where had assembled a group of his enemies. He was told to write to his brother Dost Mohammad and order him to surrender. When he refused, saying he was a poor blind captive and without influence, his tormentors closed in. One – Atta Mohammad, the nobleman who had imprisoned Shuja and threatened to drown him in the Indus, and whose father Fatteh Khan had accused of plotting rebellion and had executed – hacked off his ear, naming his grievance as he did so. A second hacked off the other, voicing another complaint; a third the nose. One hand was cut off, then the other. As the blood haemorrhaged out, each of the nobles named the slight done to him for which he was now claiming vengeance, 'thus depriving Fatteh Khan of the highest consolation the mind of a man can possess under torment – a conscience void of offence'. The Wazir bore the torture without complaint, until, when his beard was cut off, he burst into tears. When both feet had been hacked off, Atta Mohammad finally cut Fatteh Khan's throat.[32]

As before, with Shah Zaman's murder of Fatteh's father Payindah Khan, it was one thing to kill the chief of the Barakzais, but quite another to round up the clan. Several of the brothers managed to escape from the garden party and fought their way out of Herat. Two others who were still luxuriating in a hamam 'heard what had happened, quickly ran from the steam room, and fled. They laid hands on two horses belonging to merchants in the covered bazaar, and rode off towards Kandahar. At the fortress of Nad Ali, they joined the Wazir's mother and resolved to avenge their brother's execution.'[33] Fatteh Khan may have been killed, but the rest of the clan now declared war on Shah Mahmoud and Prince Kamran and began to encourage rebellion across their dominions.

As the revolt spread, invitations from tribal elders began to arrive in Ludhiana for Shah Shuja, encouraging him to reclaim his throne and restore order. This was the moment Shuja had been waiting for. With Wa'fa Begum's assistance, he managed to procure weapons and recruit a ragtag assortment of soldiers of fortune, including the American mercenary 'General' Josiah Harlan. Though shadowed all the way by a British intelligence officer, Captain Ross, and his two assistants, all of them disguised as Gurkhas, he made his way to the Sindhi banking centre of Shikarpur.[34] There he secured a loan from the Hindu money-lenders.* He quickly raised a body of troops, then marched northwards and within weeks had managed to recapture his old base of Peshawar.

His triumph was, however, short-lived. Shuja's haughty manner and insistence on the old forms of court etiquette alienated the tribal leaders of the area, so that before long 'the premature exhibition of his exalted notions of regal dignity led to a battle between him and his inviters'.[35] At this critical moment, a shell landed in the Shah's gunpowder store, setting off an enormous explosion which killed large numbers of his troops; 'a huge plume of smoke rose into the sky', remembered Shah Shuja, 'and legs, hands, arms and bodies were scattered in all directions. The enemy pressed their attack, and we were forced to take shelter in the mountains of the Khyber.'[36]

Yet again, Shuja had to retreat. Driven back by the now increasingly powerful Barakzai brothers, he had no option but to return to the territories of the Company, losing more of his troops during a sandstorm on a reckless summer crossing of the desert shales between Shikarpur and Jaisalmer. He also failed to repay the bankers of Sindh, who vowed never to lend to him again. As Mirza 'Ata put it, quoting a Persian proverb, 'those once bitten by a snake fear even a twisted rope'.[37]

---

* The Shikarpuri Sindhi money-lending community had long specialised in financing wars and dealing in arms, and the tradition continues to this day: the most notable Shikarpuris in this business today are the Hinduja brothers, who, among many other such deals, were allegedly involved in the controversial sale of the Bofors guns to Rajiv Gandhi's government in the 1980s.

By October 1818, after a pilgrimage to the great Sufi shrine in Ajmer, and a visit to the Mughal Emperor Akbar Shah II in Delhi, Shuja returned to Ludhiana to plot his next move.

The Shah now had no option but to accept that a long period of exile lay ahead, and, with more resignation than pleasure, he embraced the inevitability of setting up his court-in-exile in Ludhiana.

There was, however, to be no compromise on the Shah's ceremonial, and his durbar was to be maintained in its full theatrical entirety. Remarkably, thanks to the intervention of Ochterlony, the Company was prepared not just to tolerate this pantomime, but to finance it annually to the tune of 50,000 rupees. Shuja and his entourage moved to more substantial quarters, and visitors to the dusty bazaars of Ludhiana were treated to a lavish piece of political theatre: 'His Majesty might be seen almost daily in the vicinity of Loodhiana in regal state,' wrote the American soldier of fortune Josiah Harlan. 'The throng of a long procession proclaimed the approach of the King, shouting to the listless winds and un-peopled highways, as though he was in the midst of obedient subjects, with the deep and sonorous intonation of self-important command, where there was none to obey.'[38]

A bizarre durbar assembled around the deposed Shah. The head of Shuja's household was Mullah Shakur Ishaqzai – 'a short, fat person', wrote Harlan, '[whose] rotundity . . . was adequately finished by the huge turban characteristic of his class, encased in voluminous outline by a profusion of long thick hair which fell upon his shoulders in heavy sable silvered curls'. The curls were there for a purpose: to hide the absence of his ears, which had been removed at Shuja's orders as a punishment for an earlier failure of courage on the field of battle. But the mullah was in good company, at least according to Harlan, who claimed that Shuja had developed the habit of removing pieces of his household's anatomy whenever they failed to perform: many of the ears, tongues, noses and genitals of Shuja's servants had been forfeited at different points, resulting in 'an earless assemblage of mutes and eunuchs in the ex-king's service'.

The unfortunate Chief Eunuch, an African Muslim named Khwajah Mika, had allegedly lost his manhood when a harem screen protecting Wa'fa Begum and the King's other wives had been blown down by a gust of wind, though 'the executioner was of a tender conscience', reported Harlan, and 'merely deprived Khwajah Mika of the lower part of the organ'. After this, the subsequent loss of his ears had been but a minor blow, and, unlike Mullah Shakur, the Chief Eunuch had 'shaved his head and now fearlessly displayed the mark of royal favour'.[39]

Visitors who spent time with Shuja continued to be impressed by his charm, manners and dignity. The pioneering Central Asian traveller Godfrey Vigne, for example, reported that Shuja was 'good natured . . . looking more like a gentleman who has lost an estate than a monarch who had lost his kingdom'.[40] Moreover, Shuja was also ahead of his time in establishing a school for his dependants: by 1836 there were approximately 3,000 school-age males enrolled.[41] The records of the Ludhiana Agency, which survive in their entirety in the Lahore Archives, do however seem to confirm Harlan's hints that he was in other ways not one of the more enlightened employers in the Punjab: his slave girls, for example, were frequently reported as running off, possibly to escape Shuja's punishments, but in some cases 'to seek the protection' of the handsome young officers of the British garrison in the town. This inevitably led to several diplomatic stand-offs between the Ludhiana barracks and the Afghan court-in-exile.[42]

After the death of Ochterlony in 1825, the man who had to deal with such disputes was the new Ludhiana Agent, Captain Claude Martin Wade.

Wade was a Bengal-born Persian scholar, and godson of the

French adventurer Claude Martin, who had lent money to Wade's impecunious father and after whom he was named. It was Wade's French connections that helped secure him the job of dealing with the Sikh court, as Ranjit Singh's power rested on his remarkable army, the Sikh Khalsa, 85,000 strong, which in turn was trained and officered by a small group of French and Italian Napoleonic veterans. All of these had married locally and produced large half-Punjabi families. Thanks to Wade, these ex-Napoleonic officers became an important source of information about Central Asia for the British.* Wade made a point of being friendly to them and was described by one appreciative French traveller as 'the King of the Frontier and an excellent fellow . . . a clever, well-informed man whose society is equally profitable and agreeable'.[43] His own despatches, however, paint a more complex picture: Wade was affable, certainly, but also shrewd, dry, penetrating and cynical. When crossed he could also be prickly and territorial, strongly resisting any attempts to break his monopoly on controlling British relations with both the Sikhs and Afghans.

From the day of his arrival in the town in 1823, Wade worked to revive the extensive news-writing and intelligence networks left in place by Elphinstone when he retreated from Peshawar and which had been neglected as unnecessary expenses since the passing of the Napoleonic threat. Wade also established a web of his own correspondents stretching through the Punjab and Afghanistan to Khiva, Bukhara and beyond, collecting information mainly through 'intelligent natives specially despatched'.[44] This information was collated, sifted and analysed, then sent on to his masters in Calcutta. Though the boundaries between news-writers, 'intelligencers' and outright spies were very porous at this period, Wade was effectively one of the first two spymasters of what later generations would call the Great Game, that grand contest of imperial competition, espionage and conquest that engaged Britain and Russia until the collapse of their respective

---

* In the 1820s the East India Company spent a massive Rs 5,000 in buying the journal of one of these officers, General Claude August Court, in which he described his overland journey through Afghanistan.

Asian empires, and whose opening moves were being played at this period.[45]

Wade's great rival in this work was an Anglo-Irish bulldog named Sir Henry Pottinger, who from the Gujarati town of Bhuj in Kutch ran a competing operation on behalf of the Bombay Presidency, with a particular focus on the Indus Delta, Sindh, Baluchistan and Sistan. As a young man, Pottinger had himself travelled through Persia and Sindh disguised as a Muslim merchant and, knowing the territory as well as any other Company servant, grew to be every bit as territorial as Wade.

In between dutifully playing his part at Shah Shuja's phantom court, Wade spent his days piecing together a jigsaw of news and gossip through his growing list of informants: Indian clerks, traders, passing mercenaries and sympathetic noblemen were all recruited to provide news and bazaar *gup-shup* [gossip]. Perhaps his most useful correspondent was a remarkable British deserter, originally known as James Lewis, who had fled the Company's service and set himself up in Kabul under the assumed name of Charles Masson.

Masson was a keenly inquisitive Londoner who, after deserting his regiment and faking his own death during the siege of Bharatpur in 1826, had walked through north India, crossed the Indus and explored Afghanistan on foot, living like a wandering dervish. Armed with a copy of Arrian's *Life of Alexander the Great*, he became the first westerner to explore Afghanistan's archaeology. Following in Alexander's footsteps, he located the remains of the great Bactrian Greek city of Bagram in the Shomali Plain, while elsewhere he methodically excavated Buddhist stupas and Kushan palaces, dutifully sending the pick of his finds down to the new Asiatic Society in Calcutta. Somehow Wade learned the secret of Masson's real identity as a deserter, and before long had blackmailed him into becoming an 'intelligencer', dangling both the threat of capital punishment and the lure of a royal pardon in front of him, and so ensuring a stream of regular and accurate reports from Afghanistan for the first time.

This growing intelligence network was developed at a time of rapidly changing geopolitics. The Napoleonic threat was now over. Instead by the 1820s it was Russia that kept the Company's hawks fretting over their glasses of madeira.

Since seeing off Napoleon in 1812, the Russians had moved their frontier south and eastwards almost as fast as Wellesley had moved that of the Company north and westwards, and it was becoming increasingly evident – at least to the armchair strategists in London – that the two empires would at some point come into collision in central Asia. Lord Ellenborough, the hawkish new President of the Company's Board of Control, and minister with responsibility for India in the Duke of Wellington's Cabinet, was the first to turn this growing anxiety into public policy. 'Our policy in Asia must follow one course only,' he wrote in his diary, 'to limit the power of Russia.' Later he added: 'Four months from leaving Khiva the enemy might be at Kabul. The Directors are much afraid . . . [but] I feel confident we shall have to fight the Russians on the Indus and I have long had a presentiment that I should meet them there, and gain a great battle.'[46]

Ellenborough, the son of Warren Hastings's defence lawyer, was a brilliant but difficult and unappealing man, whose physical appearance, dominated by what one observer called 'his horrid grey locks', was so distasteful that George IV was alleged to have claimed that the very sight of Ellenborough made him sick. He suffered a crushing humiliation when his first wife, the beautiful but wayward Jane Digby, left him and took a succession of lovers, first the Austrian Prince Schwarzenberg, with whom Ellenborough fought a duel, then in quick succession the kings of both Bavaria and Greece, and an Albanian general, before ending up happily married to a Bedouin sheikh in Palmyra. The ridicule Ellenborough suffered as a result permanently marked his character and led to him retreating into a cocoon of pride and ambition. But, for all his arrogance, he was energetic and clever, and became the first British politician to build a career on opposition to Russian imperialism.[47]

Though Ellenborough exaggerated the threat to the British dominions in India – St Petersburg had in reality no plans to attack the British there – it was certainly true that Russia had recently shown itself extremely aggressive in its dealings with Ottoman Turkey and Qajar Persia. Only a year after Napoleon's 1812 retreat from Moscow, the Russian artillery had massacred Fatteh Ali Shah Qajar's Persian army, and proclaimed the 'liberation' of the Eastern Christians of Armenia and Georgia. Russia then annexed great swathes of modern Armenia and Azerbaijan – what had been until then the Persian Empire in the Caucasus. 'Persia was delivered, bound hand and foot, to the Court of St Petersburg,' wrote the British Ambassador to Teheran.[48]

This turned out to be only the first of a long series of Ottoman and Persian defeats which marked the Russian army's relentless advance southwards.[49] To make matters worse, the British had failed to come to the aid of their Persian allies, so leaving the Persians to face the Russians alone. Following a further series of catastrophic Persian defeats in the Russo-Persian War of 1826–7, the Persians lost all that was left of their Caucasian empire, including all the passes controlling the road to Azerbaijan.[50]

If Russia had not also been fighting the Ottomans, the surrender terms might have been harsher still. But Russia was simultaneously inflicting defeats on the Turks so damaging that the Duke of Wellington believed they marked a 'death blow to the independence of the Ottoman Porte and the forerunner of the extinction of its power'.[51] By the end of the 1820s it seemed only a matter of time before the Russians seized both Teheran and Constantinople, turning Persia and Turkey into vast Tsarist protectorates. In Chechnya and Daghestan, the Russians were conducting a series of genocidal punitive expeditions during which they sacked villages, killed the women and children, cut down the forests and destroyed the crops.[52] Further south still, in Jerusalem, the British Consul was reporting a build-up of 'Russian agents' preparing for a 'Russian conquest of the Holy Lands'.

Russia's stated intention to recreate the old Byzantine Empire on the ruins of that of the Ottomans made such schemes appear perfectly plausible, at least to the foreign-policy hawks.[53]

This rapid succession of Russian victories, combined with reports of Russian brutality in the lands they controlled, came as a severe shock to the politicians in London, who since the demise of Napoleon had come to see the security of British India as vital to Britain's status as a world power. When in 1823 the Himalayan explorer William Moorcroft managed to intercept a letter from the Russian Foreign Minister, Count Nesselrode, to Ranjit Singh, it seemed to confirm all the hawks' worst fears. These fears, and the political paranoia they generated, triggered a wave of Russophobia in the British and British Indian press where Russia increasingly came to be depicted as a barbaric and despotic menace to liberty and civilisation.

This was given momentum by the publication of Colonel De Lacy Evans's overwrought polemic *On the Practicability of an Invasion of British India*. The book sketched out a scenario whereby 60,000 Russian troops could march across the Hindu Kush, take Herat, then appear at the base of the Khyber Pass and sweep all before them. In reality, at this period this was almost as fantastical a scheme as Shah Shuja's plan to invade Kabul via 'Thibet', and the Russian threat it presented was hugely over-played: there were still only a handful of Russians in Central Asia and none within a thousand miles of Bukhara, let alone Kabul. Yet the book was widely read in political circles in London and, although the Colonel had never been to India or even to the region, this did not stop his alarmist text going on 'to become the virtual Bible' of a generation of Russophobes.[54] It was particularly admired by Lord Ellenborough, who liked it as it confirmed all his existing prejudices.

The evening he finished reading the book, Ellenborough went to his study and wrote to the Duke of Wellington that 'Russia will attempt, by conquest, or influence to secure Persia as the road to the Indus.' The following day, 29 October 1828, having mailed off copies of De Lacy Evans's book to colleagues in Teheran and

Bombay, he took note of the book's recommendation that 'some sort of agent' should be stationed at Bukhara to give advance warning of a Russian attack, and wrote in his diary that 'We ought to have full information as to Kabul, Bokhara and Khiva.'[55]

In the weeks that followed, Ellenborough laid down his plans for how Britain should take measures to pre-empt further Russian advances. 'We dread not so much an actual invasion of India', he wrote to the Governor General of India, so much as:

> the moral effect which would be produced amongst our own subjects and amongst the Princes with whom we are allied . . . [by] any approximation of the Russians to the north of India. It is in our interests to take measures for the prevention of any movement on their part beyond their present limits. But the efficiency of such measures must depend upon their being taken promptly, and you being kept constantly informed of everything which passes on the Russian frontier.[56]

Ellenborough's despatch was to have far-reaching consequences. However much the threat it sought to counter was at this stage only a spectre of overheated British imaginations, by authorising a major new programme of intelligence gathering in Central Asia it gave a huge new momentum to the Great Game – what the Russians would later call 'the Tournament of Shadows' – and created an Anglo-Russian rivalry in the Himalayas where none had existed before. It also put immense resources at the disposal of Wade and Pottinger and those watching the Indian frontiers. From this point on a succession of young army officers and political agents began to be despatched to the Himalayas, the Hindu Kush and the Pamirs, sometimes in disguise, sometimes on 'shooting leave', to learn the languages and tribal customs, to map the rivers and passes, and to assess the difficulty of crossing the mountains and deserts.[57]

In years to come, this process of imperial competition would turn into something far more serious than any game and lead to deaths, wars, invasions and colonisation on a massive scale, profoundly changing the lives of hundreds of thousands of inhabitants of

Afghanistan and Central Asia. More immediately, it radically changed the importance of Shah Shuja to the British: no longer was he an ex-monarch with over-grand ideas being maintained out of a sense of duty to a fallen ally; suddenly he was a major strategic asset against Russian encroachment and a key to British hopes of having an ally as ruler of Afghanistan. Ellenborough's despatch also led to the immediate deployment of two covert intelligence operations.

One, led by Lieutenant Arthur Conolly, was designed to test out, on foot, the feasibility of reaching British India from Moscow. Conolly travelled to the Russian frontier at Orenburg, then changed into disguise and made his way through Bukhara and Afghanistan to Herat and the Indus. The journey turned out to be entirely feasible – at least for a determined individual – and much easier than Conolly had imagined, taking little over a year to complete at a leisurely pace.

The second expedition was a much more cunning and elaborate operation. This was to head in the opposite direction and gather information about the Indus, which Ellenborough believed could be made into the principal British transport route into Central Asia, just as the Ganges had earlier opened up the heart of Hindustan to British commerce.

Ellenborough, like many utilitarians of his generation, believed profoundly in the civilising nature of trade and commerce: 'not a bale of merchandise leaves our shores but it bears the seeds of intelligence and fruitful thought to the members of some less enlightened community'.[58] British manufactures he imagined as the first line of defence against Russian advances – Scottish tweed and bundles of Manchester cottons would assist in transmitting enlightenment from Albion, and somehow stiffen Afghan resolve to resist the Tsarist tyranny of St Petersburg. He therefore proposed to send a boat up the Indus manned by a team of disguised draughtsmen, cartographers and naval and military surveyors. They would accurately map the river's banks, plumb its depth and test the practicality of sending British steamers upstream. In this way he hoped to bring about the beginning of the British conquest of Central Asian trade. In order to disguise its true purpose, however, the raft would be given a cover, and officially said to be carrying diplomatic presents for Ranjit Singh deemed too delicate to send by road.

Given the Maharajah's almost obsessive love of fine horses, Ellenborough agreed to the ruse of sending out from Suffolk a team of huge English dray horses, a breed never before seen in India. A heavy gilt English carriage was later added to the gifts, just in case Ranjit Singh ordered the carthorses to be sent by road. Later it was agreed to extend the expedition so that a British intelligence officer disguised 'in the character of a merchant' would pass on through Afghanistan to Bukhara, to assess the possibilities of 'introducing English manufactures into Central Asia'. This officer was of course to take covert notes and make maps as he went, to test the degree of Russian influence in the Central Asian oasis towns, and to report on the ease with which a troop of Cossacks might sweep past the Oxus into Afghanistan, and hence down into India.[59]

Ellenborough's first choice for an 'able and discreet officer' to lead the expedition had been William Fraser's brother, the artist, writer and spy James Baillie Fraser, who had travelled extensively in Persia a decade earlier, had made friends with the Shah and spoke perfect Persian.[60] But Fraser was busy at that moment trying to save his family estates in Inverness – he had got into debt building a massive extension of his house in order to have the Persian princes to stay. So Ellenborough settled instead on an unknown but ambitious twenty-five-year-old linguist and Pottinger protégé who had just won a prize for producing the first new map of the mouth of the Indus since Alexander Dalrymple's celebrated chart of 1783.

The name of this young officer was Alexander Burnes.

In the summer of 1830, five dapple-grey Suffolk carthorses arrived at the docks of Bombay after a voyage of six months; one of the original six, a mare, had died at sea. A fortnight later, after recovering their strength grazing on the green meadows of Malabar Hill, they were packed off again, this time towards the Indus estuary, accompanied by the large gilt carriage.

Waiting for permission to land, the ships were tossed about by gales, dismasting two of the boats and splitting the sails of a third, the one in which Burnes was sailing. The horses, now used to life on the waves, seem to have taken it in their ample stride; but the carriage was badly damaged by seawater and was never quite the same again.[61] Twice the expedition set off, only to be obliged to return after the Amirs of Sindh refused permission for the boats to travel any further.

The necessary permissions were finally received on 4 March 1831, after Ranjit Singh was induced to make various unpleasant threats to the Amirs. From this point the expedition made slow progress upstream for the 700 miles to Lahore. Burnes ducked potshots from the banks, while making detailed jottings on the landscape, peoples and politics of the country they were drifting past. Meanwhile his companions discreetly took soundings and bearings, measuring the flow of the river and preparing detailed maps and flow charts. The Indus proved unexpectedly shallow and Ellenborough's ideas of introducing steamers on the Ganges model was quickly shown to be implausible. But the expedition proved that the River Indus was navigable as far as Lahore in flat-bottomed boats. Barges would be able to take British manufactures as far as the Sikh capital, where they could be unloaded on the banks of the Ravi, and hence carried over the passes to Afghanistan and Central Asia on foot. The only obstacles were political.

Alexander Burnes, the man chosen to lead this mission, was a tough, high-spirited and resourceful young Highland Scot, the fourth son of the Provost of Montrose. He had a broad face, high forehead, deeply inset eyes and a quizzical set to his mouth which hinted at both his curious and enquiring nature and his sense of humour, something he shared with his cousin, the Scottish national poet Robbie Burns.[62]

At the Montrose Academy where he and his brothers had been educated, Burnes was remembered as the 'foremost in bold adventures' rather than for any scholarly achievements, though his classical education there kindled his obsession with Alexander the Great which first drew him to Afghanistan and the Indus.[63]

Shipped off to India with his elder brother James at the age of sixteen, he had now, at the age of only twenty-six, spent a decade in India and grown to be a confident speaker of Persian and Hindustani; he had also perfected a clear and lively prose style, and developed his earlier historical interests: his first publication – 'On the Indus', in the *Transactions of the Bombay Geographical Society* – was more concerned with Hellenistic precedents than with present-day politics.

Like many others who would play the Great Game after him, it was Burnes's quick intelligence and skill in languages that got him his swift promotion, and despite coming from a relatively modest background in a relatively remote part of Scotland, he rose faster in the ranks than any of his richer and better-connected contemporaries. He was also assisted by the recommendations of his talented brother James and the connections both brothers made through their prominence in the Freemasons.*

An angular, wiry and witty man of five foot nine, 'spare and thin', Burnes was ambitious and determined, and had a cool head in an emergency. His friends admired his imagination and his intellectual agility: one wrote that he was 'sharp, quick and rapidly decisive, expressive and penetrating'. On this journey, he had ample opportunity to deploy both his intelligence and his wit, not least when he crossed the frontier to the Punjab and his lumbering cart-horses caused a sensation among Ranjit Singh's officials. 'For the first time,' wrote Burnes, 'a dray horse was expected to gallop, canter and perform all the evolutions of the most agile animal.'

Burnes and his presents were received in great state in Lahore on 18 July 1831. A guard of cavalry and a regiment of infantry were

---

* It is a book written by James Burnes, *A Sketch of the History of the Knight's Templars* (1840), that first links the Freemasons to the Templars and Roslyn Chapel near Edinburgh. It is the ultimate progenitor of a wash of popular nonsense like *The Holy Blood and the Holy Grail* and *The Da Vinci Code*.

sent to meet them. 'The coach, which was a handsome vehicle, headed the procession,' he recorded, 'and in the rear of the dray horses we ourselves followed on elephants, with the officers of the maharajah. We passed close under the city walls and entered Lahore by the palace gate. The streets were lined with cavalry, artillery and infantry, all of which saluted as we passed. The concourse of people was immense; they had seated themselves on the balconies of houses, and preserved a most respectful silence.' The British party was led across the outer courtyard of the old Mughal fort, and into the entrance of the arcaded marble reception room, the Diwan-i-Khas. 'Whilst stooping to remove my shoes,' Burnes wrote, 'I suddenly found myself in the arms and tight embrace of a diminutive, old-looking man.'[64]

This was Ranjit Singh, the Lion of the Punjab himself. Leading Burnes by the hand, he brought him into the court where 'all of us were seated on silver chairs, in front of his Highness'. It was now more than thirty years since Ranjit Singh had come to power, assisting Shah Zaman to save his cannon from the mud of the Jhelum, and thirteen years since Shah Shuja had fled Ranjit's enforced hospitality through the city sewers. Since then, the Sikh leader had taken the opportunity presented by the Afghan civil war to absorb most of the lands of the Durrani Empire east of the Indus and build a remarkably rich, strong, centralised and well-governed Sikh state in its place. As well as training his remarkable army, Ranjit had also modernised his bureaucracy and ran a formidable intelligence network, whose reports were sometimes shared with Wade in Ludhiana.

The British generally got on well with Ranjit Singh, but they never forgot that his army was the last military force in India which could take on the Company on the field of battle: by the 1830s, the Company had stationed nearly half the Bengal army, totalling more than 39,000 troops, along the Punjab frontier.[65] It was therefore extremely important that Burnes establish a good rapport with Ranjit.

The French traveller Victor Jacquemont penned a revealing portrait of the Maharajah just a couple of months before Burnes arrived in Lahore. He depicted Ranjit Singh as a clever and charming rogue – as disreputable in his private habits as he was admirable in his public ones. 'Ranjit Singh is an old fox,' he wrote, 'compared with whom the wiliest of our diplomats is a mere innocent . . .' Jacquemont reported a number of encounters with the Maharajah: 'His conversation is a nightmare. He is almost the first inquisitive Indian I have seen, but his curiosity makes up for the apathy of the whole nation. He asked me a hundred thousand questions about India, the English, Europe, Bonaparte, the world in general and the other one, hell and paradise, the soul, God, the devil, and a thousand things beside . . .' Ranjit Singh regretted that women 'no longer give him any more pleasure than the flowers in his garden'.

> To show me what good reason he had for his distress, yesterday in the midst of his whole court – that is to say in the open country, on a beautiful Persian carpet where we were squatting surrounded by a few thousand soldiers – lo and behold, the old roué sent for five young girls from his seraglio, ordered them to sit down in front of me, and smilingly asked what I thought of them. I said in all sincerity that I thought them very pretty, which was not a tenth what I really thought . . .

Jacquemont also noted that the Maharajah 'has a passion for horses which is almost a mania; he has waged the most costly and bloody wars for the purpose of seizing a horse in some neighbouring state which they had refused to sell or give to him . . . He is also a shameless rogue who flaunts his vices as Henri III did in our country . . . Ranjit has frequently exhibited himself to his good people of Lahore with a Moslem public woman, indulging in the least innocent of sports with her on the back of an elephant . . .'[66]

Burnes was just as taken with Ranjit Singh as Jacquemont had been, and the two quickly became firm friends: 'Nothing could exceed the affability of the Maharajah,' he wrote. 'He kept up an uninterrupted flow of conversation for the hour and a half which the interview lasted: he enquired particularly about the depth of water in the Indus and the possibility of navigating it.' The dray horses and the carriage were then inspected: 'The sight of the horses excited his utmost wonder; their size and colour pleased him: he said they were little elephants, and as they passed singly before him, he called out to the different sardars and officers, who joined in his admiration.'[67] Indeed such was Ranjit's pleasure in his gifts, and Lord Ellenborough's letter which accompanied them, that he ordered an unprecedented artillery salute of sixty guns, each firing twenty-one times, so that the people of Lahore would be in no doubt as to his enthusiasm for his new English alliance.

For two months, Ranjit laid on a round of entertainments for Burnes. Dancing girls performed, troops were manoeuvred, deer were hunted, monuments were visited and banquets were thrown. Burnes even tried some of Ranjit's home-made hell-brew, a fiery distillation of raw spirit, crushed pearls, musk, opium, gravy and spices, two glasses of which was normally enough to knock out the most hardened British drinker, but which Ranjit recommended to Burnes as a cure for his dysentery. Burnes and Ranjit, the Scot and the Sikh, found themselves bonding over a shared taste for fire-water. 'Runjeet Singh is, in every respect, an extraordinary character,' wrote Burnes. 'I have heard his French officers observe that he has no equal from Constantinople to India.'[68]

At their final dinner, Ranjit agreed to show Burnes the Koh-i-Nur. 'Nothing', wrote Burnes, 'can be imagined more superb than this stone; it is of the finest water, about half the size of an egg. Its weight amounts to 3½ rupees, and if such a jewel is to be valued, I am informed it is worth 3½ millions of money.'[69]

Ranjit then presented Burnes with two richly caparisoned horses, dressed in costly Kashmiri shawls, their necks adorned with necklaces of agate and with heron plumes rising from between their ears. While Burnes thanked Ranjit for the present, one of the dray horses was paraded for a final inspection, now decked in cloth of gold and saddled with an elephant's howdah.[70]

Like Ranjit Singh, Burnes clearly had immense charm. It was this which, time after time, managed to disarm the most hostile situations.

The normally suspicious Ranjit wrote to the Governor General on the day of Burnes's departure to say how much he had enjoyed meeting this 'nightingale of the garden of eloquence, this bird of the winged words of sweet discourse'. After the Governor General had authorised Burnes to continue his journey into Afghanistan, the Afghans were no less delighted by him: the first chieftain he came across as he set foot on the Afghan bank of the Indus told him that he and his friends could 'feel as secure as eggs under a hen'. Burnes duly repaid the affection. 'I thought Peshawar a delightful place,' he wrote to his mother in Montrose a month later, 'until I came to Kabul: truly this is paradise . . . I tell them about steam ships, armies, ships, medicine, and all the wonders of Europe; and, in return, they enlighten me regarding the customs of their country, its history, state factions, trade &c . . .'[71] He felt a genuine fondness for the people, who 'are kind-hearted and hospitable; they have no prejudices against a Christian, and none against our nation. When they ask me if I like pork, I of course shudder and say it is only outcastes that commit such outrages. God forgive me! For I am very fond of bacon, and my mouth waters as I write the word.'

Burnes liked Kabul, liked its people, enjoyed its poetry and landscapes, and he admired its rulers. He went on to describe his warm reception by his Barakzai host, Dost Mohammad Khan, 'the most rising man in the Kabul dominions', and faithfully recounted the sparkling intelligence of his conversation, as well as the beauties of the gardens and fruit trees of his palace, the Bala Hisar.[72] If Burnes had charmed Dost Mohammad and his Afghans, they, in turn, had charmed him.

One man who remained stolidly immune to Burnes's attractions was Shah Shuja's keeper, the Ludhiana spymaster Claude Wade. Wade was never happy with anyone who stepped on his territory, which he tended to guard as jealously as any Afghan mastiff protecting its patch. He was certainly not going to put up with some social-climbing twenty-something overtaking him as the

Governor General's preferred adviser on Afghanistan. While Ellenborough's Memorandum potentially gave Wade increased power, supplementing the resources the Company would be prepared to pour into Himalayan intelligence gathering, and increasing the number of operatives Wade could employ, it had also authorised an operation directly into Wade's territory over which he had no control, and which had emerged from Pottinger's competing Bhuj Agency and was run out of the rival Bombay Presidency. Wade quickly came to see Burnes as a major threat to his position, and as the number and quality of Burnes's reports from Kabul began to increase, Wade began annotating them with sarcastic and patronising comments as they passed through Ludhiana, gleefully pointing out any errors he spotted.[73]

Aware that he was now suddenly the desk-bound Afghan expert who had never actually been to Afghanistan, Wade grew still more irritated with his dashing younger rival when Burnes began to come to very different conclusions about British interests in the region to those canvassed by Wade's Agency. Wade had always seen the relationship with Ranjit Singh as the Company's primary alliance in north India, and strongly believed that the Sikhs were by far the most powerful military force in the region. Indeed having spent much time in the Sikh court throughout the 1820s, Wade was close to becoming a partisan to their cause, something his superiors were aware – and indeed wary – of. He was much less interested in Afghanistan, disliked what he had heard of Dost Mohammad and mentally had his Ludhiana friend and neighbour, Shah Shuja, lined up as Britain's potential puppet in Kabul, if the need should arise.

Wade's views had, however, not kept up with the changing reality. Since Shuja's last failed attempt to recapture his throne, Shah Mahmoud had died and Afghanistan had fallen almost completely under the sway of the Barakzai brothers; only in Herat did Shah Mahmoud's son, Prince Kamran, hold out as a last bastion of Sadozai rule. Despite this, Wade continued to look on the Barakzais as Shuja saw them: as ambitious and unprincipled usurpers.

Burnes, coming to it with fresh eyes, saw things differently. On his way through Ludhiana to see the Governor General, in between saying goodbye to Ranjit Singh and setting off for Afghanistan, he had come to pay court to Shah Shuja and had been unimpressed. Despite Shuja telling Burnes that 'had I but my kingdom, how glad I should be to see an Englishman at Kabul, and open the road between Europe and India', Burnes remained unconvinced. 'I do not believe that the Shah possesses sufficient energy to seat himself on the throne of Kabul,' he wrote in a despatch, 'and that if he did regain it, he has not the tact to discharge the duties of so difficult a situation.' Later he expanded on the same theme: 'The fitness of Shuja ul Mulk for the station of sovereign seems ever to have been doubtful,' he argued in his bestselling *Travels into Bokhara*, which collated his reports into a travel narrative.

> His manners and address are certainly highly polished; but his judgement does not rise above mediocrity. Had the case been otherwise, we should not now see him an exile from his country and his throne, without a hope of regaining them, after an absence of twenty years; and before he had attained the fiftieth year of age ... The total overthrow of the dynasty is attributed to misplaced pride and arrogance of the last kings, who now receive no sympathy from the Afghans for their overthow. Shuja, indeed, might have regained his power, but for his rash attempts to exercise the authority of king before he was firmly fixed in it. The Afghans cannot control their feelings of jealousy towards men in power: for the last thirty years, who has died a natural death? To be happy under government they must either be ruled by a vigorous despot, or formed into many small republics.[74]

A vigorous despot was, however, exactly what Burnes had found in Kabul. Burnes had met all the Barakzai brothers on his travels, but there was no question in his mind who was the most impressive. Dost Mohammad Khan was now the sole ruler of Kabul and Ghazni, and well on his way to being acknowledged as the head of the clan despite his youth and his elder brothers' jealousy of his rise. Burnes was unequivocal in his admiration: 'The reputation

of Dost Mohammad Khan is made known to a traveller long before
he enters his country,' he wrote in his *Travels*,

> and no one better merits the high character which he has obtained.
> He is unremitting in his attention to business, and attends daily at
> the court house . . . This sort of decision is exceedingly popular
> with the people. Trade has received the greatest encouragement
> from him . . . and the justice of this chief affords a constant theme of
> praise to all classes: the peasant rejoices at the absence of tyranny;
> the citizen at the safety of his home; the merchant at the equity of
> the decisions and the protection of his property, and the soldiers at
> the regular manner in which their arrears are discharged. A man in
> power can have no higher praise. Dost Mohammad Khan has not
> attained his fortieth year; his mother was a Persian [Qizilbash], and
> he has been trained up with people of that nation, which has sharp-
> ened his understanding, and given him advantages over all his
> brothers. One is struck with the intelligence, knowledge and curios-
> ity which he displays, as well as his accomplished manners and his
> address. He is doubtless the most powerful chief in Afghanistan,
> and may yet raise himself by his abilities to a much greater rank in
> his native country.[75]

Burnes wrote that he had heard that in his youth Dost Mohammad
had been wild and dissolute, but had become a reformed man now
he had gained power. He had given up wine, taught himself to read
and write, and affected piety and a simplicity of manner and dress.
He was available to all, and anyone could come and ask for justice.
Nor was it just that Burnes thought Dost Mohammad was personally impressive. He also saw him clearly as Britain's best bet for
attaining influence in Afghanistan. As far as he was concerned the
Sadozais had had their day, and as Dost Mohammad was so well
disposed towards the British it would be possible to form an alliance with 'no great expenditure of public funds'.[76]

This was a radically different strategy to the one Wade had been
suggesting to Calcutta, and it left Wade with two options: either to
accept the opinion of the younger man who had spent little time in

the region, but unlike him had now seen Kabul for himself; or to
stand on his authority as the regional expert of twenty years and to
continue to back Shah Shuja as Britain's best asset. He chose the
latter course. 'The people are tired of wars and factions,' he wrote
in May 1832, while Burnes was still in Kabul. 'They look for the
reestablishment of their former [Sadozai] government as the only
chance which presents itself of ensuring tranquillity.'[77] This was at
variance with everything Burnes was reporting from the ground;
but Wade made his case in exactly the way he knew would win the
argument in Calcutta. He waited for Burnes to head on north from
Kabul, where he was to reconnoitre the unmapped routes over the
Hindu Kush, and then he made his move.

Wade was assisted by events in western Afghanistan, where the
last bastion of Sadozai rule in Herat was about to be besieged by
the Persians. Since the British had failed to come to the assistance
of the Persians in the 1826–7 Russo-Persian War, the Persians had
concluded that it was wiser to hug their Russian enemy close than
entertain any further flirtations with the British who had proved
unwilling to risk outright war with Russia in their support. Now
the Persians were planning a campaign to retake Herat, and the
hawks in Calcutta strongly suspected that this was really a Russian
initiative in Persian disguise, part of an old Tsarist plan to set up a
forward base in Afghanistan: an article inserted into a treaty signed
five years earlier had given St Petersburg the right to set up a consu-
late in Herat if the Persians were ever to capture it. These fears
were in reality erroneous – in 1832 the Russians were actually
trying to dissuade the Persian Crown Prince Abbas Mirza from
going ahead with the attack. Nevertheless, Wade now played on
these fears, writing to the Governor General that 'the opinion that
Russia is connected with these events has gained an ascendency in
the minds of men . . .'[78] He was emphatic: if something was not
done and Shuja not replaced on his old throne as shah, Russia
would gain control of Herat and use it as the ideal forward base for
an invasion of India.

Along with his letter, Wade sent the Governor General an illuminated Persian manuscript from Shah Shuja, in which he formally

asked for British assistance in what he described as a bid to outflank the Russian interference in Afghanistan. He had buried his former differences with his old enemy Ranjit Singh, he wrote, and he now wanted to return to Afghanistan and lead the resistance to the new joint Russo-Persian threat. While Ranjit Singh would create a diversion by attacking Peshawar, he would take his force by a southern route and lay siege to Kandahar. 'The conquest of my country is an affair of easy attainment,' he wrote. 'With six lakh rupees, I am confident that I shall be able to establish my authority in Afghanistan . . . The people of Afghanistan are anxious for my arrival, and would flock to my standard, and acknowledge no other Chief . . . The Barakzais are not the people around whom the Afghans will rally . . . If I can raise a loan even of two or three lakh rupees, I entertain every expectation that with the favour of God, my object will be accomplished.'[79]

On 1 December 1832, William Fraser, who had recently been appointed the Resident in Delhi, began to receive reports from his informers in the city that there were Afghans in the bazaars buying up very large quantities of arms and ammunition. It was unclear whether these sales were legitimate, or what they were for, so Fraser had the dealers arrested and their purchases impounded. He then wrote to Calcutta to ask what should be done with the men.[80]

An answer arrived at Fraser's Residency direct from the office of the Governor General Lord Bentinck. The dealers, it explained, were as they had claimed agents of Shah Shuja. They had been sent to Delhi to buy muskets, uniforms, ammunition, flints, buttons and cartridge pouches for his long-planned reconquest of his kingdom – all with the Governor General's covert assent and assistance. Shah Shuja was preparing for a military expedition to Afghanistan with the direct, if secret, sanction of Bentinck himself.

As late as 1828, the Governor General had refused pleas from Shah Shuja even to be granted an interview. Now the Persian threat to Herat, and Ellenborough's determination to resist the Russians, had changed political calculations. Bentinck now ruled that, while the British official position would remain one of studied neutrality, Shah Shuja would be allowed discreet help to mount his expedition, including a four-month advance on his pension – a total of 16,000 rupees.[81]

The very same month, while Dost Mohammad Khan was receiving friendly messages from Bentinck thanking him for his hospitality to Burnes and expressing his 'deep desire that friendship and union should be established between this Government and yourself', Bentinck's new Private Secretary, William Macnaghten, was secretly instructing Fraser not only to release Shuja's arms dealers from jail, but also to waive all duty for their purchases at the Delhi Customs, so facilitating a Sadozai counter-revolution against the Barakzai government.[82]

Macnaghten, the man behind this new covert operation, was a bookish orientalist and former judge from Ulster who had been promoted from his court room to run the Company's bureaucracy. Originally a protégé of Henry Russell, the smooth and ambitious Resident at Hyderabad, he was widely respected for his intelligence, but many disliked his pompous, preening vanity while others questioned whether this 'man of the desk' was at all suited to his new job as private secretary and chief adviser to the Governor General.[*] Macnaghten, by contrast, had absolutely no doubts about his own abilities, and instead rather fancied his facility for political intrigue. He also believed he knew Afghanistan far better than he actually did, although he had never been anywhere near the region and all he knew came from his reading of Wade's despatches. Like Wade, Macnaghten may also have been slightly jealous of Burnes's rapid rise: as a born bureaucrat who always wished to maintain the existing protocol, he disapproved of the way Burnes had managed to reach the ear of the Governor General and the Cabinet in London without going through the usual channels. He had also known Wade for many years, liked him, trusted his judgement and

---

[*] For more on Henry Russell, see my *White Mughals* (London, 2002).

approved of the more conventional way he worked and thought.

So was born a dangerously contradictory and two-faced British policy towards Afghanistan, with Burnes making friendly over-tures to Dost Mohammad and the Barakzais, even as another arm of the government was secretly backing an uprising against them. As time would show, this approach was not just duplicitous: it was a recipe for diplomatic disaster that would soon blow up in the faces of everyone involved.

On 28 January 1833, ten years after his previous attempt, having armed his men with the new weapons from Delhi, Shah Shuja rode out from Ludhiana at the head of a small force of Rohilla cavalry. He was confident of the success of what would be his third attempt at recovering the throne of Khurasan. 'I never hesitated to take upon myself difficulties and hardships to regain my kingdom,' he wrote in his memoirs.

> A treasury of pain has been the reward;
> but the key to that treasury lies with the Almighty:
>
> As long as there is life and a horse, ride it, O Shuja,
> Never lose hope to give a horse the reins.
>
> If a hundred times your heart breaks,
> Still carry on, O Shuja!
>
> Ride with God's grace and greatness,
> For nothing is impossible to God.[83]

To lead and train his troops, Shuja hired the services of a dogged old Anglo-Indian mercenary named William Campbell. Their first destination was again the financial centre of Shikarpur on the borders of the Punjab and Sindh. The British had advanced Shuja only a fraction of the money he needed to wage war and this time he was determined to be as ruthless as necessary to make sure he would not fail. He showed his intentions as soon as he left British territory by ambushing a caravan of merchants heading to Sindh and seized the goods and baggage camels.[84] With money to hand out, his followers quickly began to increase.

Wade, following at a distance, sent back optimistic reports of the Shah's progress. Shuja had now gathered 3,000 men 'of respectable appearance', he wrote, as well as 'four pieces of horse artillery, and a treasury with Rs 2 Lakh in it'. There was little doubt, he believed, that this time the Shah would succeed, and, without naming names, went on to ridicule Burnes's ideas about the popularity of the Barakzais. 'The Europeans who have lately travelled in Afghanistan have generally formed an idea that the Afghans are indifferent if not opposed to the restoration of their ancient King,' he observed. 'It ought to be borne in mind that these travellers have in every case been the guests and intimates of that very reigning family [the Barakzais] who would have an interest in impressing them with an opinion favourable to their own reputation.'[85]

By mid-May, Shuja had crossed the Indus and entered Shikarpur without opposition. He then taxed the town's bankers, filled his coffers with their coin and began drilling his troops. Six months later, on 9 January 1834, Campbell's troops saw off an attack by a force of Baluchi tribesmen sent by the Amirs of Sindh to arrest Shuja. 'A party of Baluch danced with their swords as they came into the fight,' recorded Mirza 'Ata, who was an eyewitness.

They harvested with their blades many heads of the royal army, shouting their war-cries till they too were killed. Bravo for their bravery – but alas for their total ignorance of tactics! They dismounted from their horses in the midst of battle and charged on foot uphill, brandishing their swords and yelling like demons, only to be mown down by enemy gunfire before reaching the top. Thus died many Baluch great and small; and the harvest of their lives was scattered to the winds of non-existence . . .

On hearing of their defeat, Shuja gave the order that no one should

be allowed to cross the river, and that all boats were to be seized. Thus
trapped between fire and water the Baluch panicked – and those not
daring to return to face their commander preferred to throw themselves in to the river: many were the sights of drowning Baluch
begging the ferrymen and sailors to save them, and others holding
onto horses' tails until both horse and man were swept away.[86]

For Shuja, success now bred success. A month later, when he
finally set off northwards, his army had grown to 30,000 men and
the Shah was in good spirits. 'Thinking about the huge numbers
of my army,' he explained in his memoirs, 'it occurred to me to
ask what ruler has ever had such a sea of men under his banners,
and if so how will anyone be able to stand up to him?'[87] To the
Amirs of Sindh who were still trying to raise a new army to
oppose him, he sent a challenge which reflected his bullish confidence. 'Execrable dogs!' he wrote. 'God willing, I will give you
such a lesson that you shall be an example to the whole world.
The only way to treat a rabid dog is to put a rope around his neck.
If you are coming to attack us, by all means come. I do not fear
you. God is the disposer of events. The country shall belong to
the conqueror.'[88]

In April Shuja marched his troops through the Bolan Pass, and
as agreed Ranjit Singh moved north-west from Lahore, the armies
of the Sikh Khalsa providing a diversion by crossing the Indus at
Attock and taking Peshawar. The troops of the Barakzais, divided
between the two fronts, could offer effective opposition to neither
invading army. Everything for once was going to plan. Shuja now
wrote to Wade in triumph, barely able to conceal his excitement.
He ridiculed the Amirs of Sindh, 'these short-sighted people who
forget that I am under special protection of God', and expressed
optimism that victory over the Barakzais was near: 'By the divine
favor, victory will continue to open her gate for me.'[89]

Only in May 1834, when Shuja's troops finally marched into the
Kandahar oasis, did his run of luck begin to fail. The Barakzais had
had time to prepare for his arrival and, by the time Shuja marched
up to the city walls, supplies had been laid in and the city's defences

were ready to withstand a lengthy siege. Moreover, Shuja's troops had little experience in siege warfare, and insufficient training, artillery and equipment to carry out an escalade on the city walls. 'The besieging forces had attacked the city unsuccessfully with heavy losses,' wrote Mirza 'Ata.

> Now they tried to scale the Fort walls at night with scaling ladders. These they carried in furtive silence in the dark to below the walls, and waited for sleep to disarm the watchers within. Then they planned to erect the ladders and storm the unsuspecting citadel. Sleep however attacked the royal besiegers first . . . At sunrise the King, impatient of news of the attack, and hearing no uproar from within the fort, had the reveille cannon fired. The besiegers suddenly awoke from their sleep, saw that the sun was rising and that the guards on the Fort walls were already awake and raising the alarm – but from fear of His Majesty, the besiegers went ahead and raised their ladders and swarmed up them, only to be met by a barrage of fire, to be thrown off the ladder of life into the ditch of death.[90]

After two months, the siege had become a stalemate, with both sides holding firm in their positions. It was at this point that news arrived that Dost Mohammad was approaching with 20,000 Barakzai troops from Kabul to aid his besieged half-brothers within the walls. Although Shuja had great numerical advantage – some estimates talk of his army having now swelled to 80,000 – he was anxious that Dost Mohammad might cut off the water supply to his troops, so he fell back from his safely entrenched position in front of the city walls to a well-watered belt of gardens along the Arghandab River to the north-east. Hearing this, Dost Mohammad rode ahead on his own to investigate. 'When the Dost got wind of this retreat, he thanked his good fortune and disguised himself to go and check on the truth of the rumour,' recorded Mirza 'Ata.

> He rode out to see the royal soldiers all resting flat out in the shade, thinking the Kabul army to be still many miles distant. The Dost then took just 3,000 of the best of his troops, rushed them forward,

and quickly attacked the royal troops scattered amid the gardens
before they had realised what was happening. In the heat of battle,
Shaikh Shah Aghasi who at Dost Mohammad's bidding had come
over to the King's side a few days earlier, threw off the mask of
deceit, shouting 'The King has run away, the King has run away.'
He then used the ensuing confusion to attack the royal army from
within. Shuja's troops were amazed to hear the cry of defeat and to
see the Shaikh busy plundering. Smoke from the guns and cannon
was rolling up into the sky, as Campbell and his platoon staunchly
defended their position. But the young men of Kabul were fearless . . . and rushed the gun-emplacement, wounding and capturing
Campbell and taking all the artillery. Shuja's army now panicked.
Soon everyone had fled and the royal army was dispersed, wandering lost in the hills and plains. The Shah, contemplating this total
defeat, had no choice but to flee too.[91]

Yet again, Shuja was forced to retreat. Among the captured baggage
lying strewn in the gardens of Kandahar were letters of support
from Wade, proving British complicity in the failed coup. Wade
tried to put a good face on it all, saying that it was a result no one
could have anticipated; but it now looked more and more as if
Burnes had been right about the popularity and efficiency of the
Barakzais, and that Wade had all along been backing a serial loser
in Shah Shuja.

The secret report drawn up at the Governor General's request to
analyse the policy failure in Afghanistan summed up the position
with devastating brevity. 'Shah Shuja has been engaged in a series
of unfortunate attempts to regain his throne,' it stated, listing
Shuja's four great defeats: the first army ambushed at the Mughal
gardens of Nimla, the second frozen in the snows of Kashmir, the
third blown up in Peshawar by its own exploding ammunition and
now the fourth taken by surprise in the gardens of Kandahar. 'He
has shown great activity and enterprise in preparing and conducting his expeditions, and great fortitude in defeat, but his personal
courage has always failed at the crisis of his affairs and to this defect
his misfortunes are attributed.'[92]

Even Wade was now prepared to admit that his protégé looked like a spent force. But in a private conversation with the American mercenary Josiah Harlan he nevertheless foresaw there was one thing that could yet bring his friend back into play. 'There is now no possible chance for Shuja's restoration,' he said, 'unless an ostensible demonstration of Russian diplomacy should transpire at Kabul.'[93]

If the Russians were to make a direct move on Afghanistan with Barakzai assistance, then Shuja might yet find himself indispensable to British ambitions.

3

The Great Game Begins

The low, barren desert hills on the disputed borderlands between Persia and Afghanistan are no place to get lost at night. Even today it is wild, arid, remote country, haunted only by soaring hawks, packs of winter-wolves and opium smugglers working the old caravan routes. Figures move small and slow through the immensity of the sun-blasted landscape. Two hundred years ago it was an area travellers tried to avoid even during the day, its valleys and passes the refuge of brigands who took full advantage of the debatable lands between the region's warring principalities to pursue their trade.

It was the dog days of October 1837, and the end to a long week for Lieutenant Henry Rawlinson. For three years, he had been drilling a new regiment of the Persian army in a remote barracks near Kirmanshah in western Persia. During this time he had become fascinated by the trilingual inscriptions carved on the orders of the Achaemenid King Darius at nearby Behistan, the Rosetta Stone of ancient Persia. Every evening he would clamber his way up the

near-vertical rock face, or even have himself lowered in a laundry
basket, to take rubbings, then return to his tent to labour away into
the night in an ultimately successful attempt to decode the Persian
cuneiform script on the cliff wall.[1] But his studies had been interrupted when he had been sent on an urgent mission to north-east
Persia, and since receiving his orders at the British Legation in
Teheran he had ridden over 700 miles in six days. Normally the
caravanserais lining the military road from Teheran to the shrine
city of Mashhad on the Afghan border contained ample post-
horses for travellers on official business. But the Shah of Persia was
on his way to besiege Herat, and such was the volume of couriers
passing between the camp and court that Rawlinson had been
unable to change his mount for the entire journey.

Now, both his party and their horses were, as Rawlinson put it,
'pretty knocked up, and in the dark, between sleeping and waking,
we had managed to lose the road'. It was at this point, just as
dawn was breaking over the jagged rim of the Kuh-e-Shah Jahan
mountains, that Rawlinson saw another party of horsemen riding
down on them through the half-light. 'I was not anxious to accost
these strangers,' Rawlinson later reported, 'but on cantering past
them, I saw, to my astonishment, men in Cossack dresses, and
one of my attendants recognised among the party, a servant of the
Russian mission.'[2]

Rawlinson knew immediately he had stumbled on to something.
There was no good reason for a party of armed Cossacks to be on
these remote desert tracks heading for the Afghan frontier, and at
this particular moment there was every reason for a British intelligence officer to be suspicious of any Russian activity in these
crucial border marches. Rawlinson had been recruited from his
regiment in India to the new intelligence corps and sent to Persia
specifically to try to counteract growing Russian influence there.
He had been in the country three years, training the Persian army
and providing them with large quantities of British arms, as part of
a calculated strategy to win back Persia into the British fold.

Within a few months of their arrival, Rawlinson and his party
had realised they were being closely watched by the Russians. 'A

Russian officer, an aide de camp of Baron Von Rosen [the Russian
Viceroy of the Caucasus], arrived in camp today,' Rawlinson had
reported in October 1834. 'He was despatched by his General to
pay his respects to the Ameer. His real object of course is to ascer-
tain our position with the army, the state of the Persian troops, and
such other objects as may fall under his observation affecting the
interests of his country.'³

The cold war between Russia and Britain in 1830s Persia had
turned particularly chilly in March 1833 with the arrival in Teheran
of the suave Count Ivan Simonitch. Like the French officers who
had come to the court of Ranjit Singh, Simonitch was a Napoleonic
veteran who was looking for wider horizons after Waterloo and
the exile of Napoleon. Originally a native of Zara, south of Trieste
on the Dalmatian coast of modern Croatia, Simonitch had joined
up with the Grand Armée just in time for the invasion of Russia,
and like so many others was taken captive by Tsarist forces on the
disastrous midwinter retreat from Moscow. By the time he was
released, his homeland had been absorbed into the Austro-Hungar-
ian Empire and he decided to switch sides and join the Russian
army. He was given the rank of major, sent to the Georgian grena-
dier regiment and fought with bravery in the Russo-Persian Wars.
Badly wounded in a bayonet charge against the Persian Royal
Guard, he was promoted to major-general for his bravery in holding his ground despite his injuries. Soon afterwards, he married an
eighteen-year-old widow, Princess Orbeliani, 'the most beautiful
woman in Georgia', and in a short time became one of the leading
figures in the Russian administration of Tiflis.⁴ Transferred as
ambassador to Teheran, he soon made it his mission to outmanoeu-
vre his British counterpart, Sir John MacNeill, who was as
resolutely Russophobic as Simonitch was doggedly anti-British.

Since the arrival of Rawlinson and his military mission, Simonitch
had managed to gain the Shah's confidence, and achieve far more
access and influence than the stolid MacNeill, the former Legation
doctor, originally from the Outer Hebrides, who proved no match
for Simonitch in terms either of sophistication or of strategy. By
1837 Simonitch had helped nudge the newly crowned Shah to use

his British-armed troops to make yet another attack on the disputed city of Herat, offering him a lure of 50,000 gold tomans and the remittance of debt, in return for the Shah's promise to allow the establishment of a Russian legation in Herat once the conquest was completed. It was a brilliant stroke – encouraging the Shah's ambitions in such a way that they threatened British interests in India – and turned the British-trained regiments directly against the interests of their trainers and suppliers. In this way, Simonitch hoped to use the Shah as a cat's paw for the Tsar, though in fact the new Shah, Mohammad II, had anyway been long obsessed with the recapture of Herat – he even mentioned it in his Coronation speech – and needed little Russian encouragement to attempt to retake it.[5]

Simonitch also gave a Russian guarantee to a proposed treaty of mutual defence between the Shah and Dost Mohammad's Barakzai half-brothers in Kandahar. Simonitch was well aware of the effect this would have on British paranoia. Looking back at this moment of triumph four years later, in 1841, he boasted in his memoirs that Persia had at this period become a 'spectre' which robbed the London Cabinet of sleep, knowing as they did the ease with which Russia could swoop down from Herat and ignite Hindustan. 'In order to set India on fire, Russia had but to wish it,' he wrote.[6]

MacNeill was left with no alternative but to sit in his Teheran study and scribble an alarmist polemic which he published anonymously as *The Progress and Present Position of Russia in the East*. 'The only nation in Europe which attempts to aggrandize itself at the expense of its neighbours is Russia,' he fumed. 'Russia alone threatens to overturn thrones, subvert Empires, and subdue nations hitherto independent . . . The integrity and Independence of Persia is necessary to the security of India and of Europe; and any attempt to subvert the one is a blow struck at the other – an unequivocal act of hostility to England.' This spirited diatribe ignored the obvious fact that the expansion of British possessions in India had continued without interruption throughout the first half of the nineteenth century, gobbling up far more land and overturning many more thrones than anything achieved by Russia; but the book was nevertheless well received and widely read in London, and added to the growing certainty in Westminster that a major clash with Russia was looming in Persia and Afghanistan.[7]

MacNeill was right however that, whatever the more cautious views of Tsar Nicholas and his ministers in St Petersburg, his rival Count Simonitch certainly did have strategic ambitions, at the heart of which lay his hopes of establishing a Russian base at Herat, a six-week march from the British frontier at Ludhiana. Recently, MacNeill's spies at the Russian Legation in Teheran had passed on confusing intelligence – 'absurd stories about a Muscovite prince' who was said to be expected on the Iranian frontier at the head of a body of 10,000 men who would assist the Persians in their siege of Herat. The details of the intelligence sounded suspect; but they seemed to hint at the existence of some Russian move on Afghanistan via Persia. Rawlinson realised that the blond officer leading the Cossack party he had just cantered past 'could be the man alluded to . . . My curiosity was of course excited. In such a state of affairs as preceded the siege of Herat, the mere fact of a Russian gentleman travelling in Khorasan was suspicious. In the present case, however, there was evidently a desire for concealment . . . and I thought it my duty to try and unravel the mystery.'[8]

So Rawlinson wheeled his escort around: 'Following the party, I tracked them for some distance along the high road, and then found that they had turned off at a gorge in the hills. There at length I came across the group seated at breakfast by the side of a clear, sparking rivulet. The officer, for such he evidently was, was a young man of light make, very fair complexion, with bright eyes and a look of great animation.' The Russian, Rawlinson continued,

rose and bowed to me as I rode up, but said nothing. I addressed him in French – the general language of communication among Europeans in the East – but he shook his head. I then spoke in English, and he answered in Russian. When I tried Persian, he seemed not to understand a word; at last he expressed himself hesitatingly in Turcoman or Usbeg Turkish. I knew just sufficient of this language to carry on a very simple conversation, but not to be inquisitive. This was evidently what my friend wanted; for when he found that I was not strong enough in Jaghetai [Chagatai] to proceed very rapidly, he rattled on with his rough Turkish as rapidly as possible. All I could find out was that he was a *bona fide* Russian officer carrying presents from the [Russian] Emperor to [the Persian ruler] Mohammad Shah. More he would not admit; so after smoking another pipe with him, I remounted.[9]

Rudyard Kipling's novel of the Great Game, *Kim*, contains a celebrated scene in which the Raj spymaster, Colonel Creighton, trains Kim to remember detail by making him play the game subsequently known as Kim's Game: being given a short period of time to memorise a tray of random objects, then to turn off the light, remove the tray, and make the student attempt to write a complete list of every detail. It will never be known if Rawlinson was ever trained in such a technique, but the remarkably detailed description of the mysterious officer which he later sent to Calcutta 'lest he should attempt to penetrate in disguise into India' suggests that he might have been. The officer, he wrote,

is a young man of middle stature, with a short neck, high square shoulders, and thin waist. He is extremely fair, and without any colour in his cheeks. He has a broad open forehead, very bright eyes and rather wide apart, a well formed nose, short upper lip, and smiling mouth. He wears a beard and moustachios of a light brown color. The moustachios are not long, but the beard which covers the lower part of his cheeks and his entire chin is particularly full, short and bushy ... He wore a round white Cossack cap, a dark green Georgian coat, narrow cross belts ornamented with silver across his breast wearing *furshungs* or cartridges on his left side after the Georgian fashion, and a sword with steel scabbard attached to a black waist-belt which was fastened with a plain silver plate. He had full dark grey cloth *shulwars* and well-made Russian boots. He had two good looking large grey horses, one of which he rode and the other was led ... He rode on a plain Persian saddle covered with dark cloth and had a short black cloth *shabrac*. He had Persian holsters and the stock of his pistols which appeared of Turkish

workmanship were of ebony inlaid with silver. He spoke Persian
fluently, but with a short, sharp foreign accent, never pronouncing
the 'a' broad and full as the Persians do. He was a perfect master of
Jagatai Turkish, but he did not speak the Constantinople or Persian
dialects of that language.[10]

Rawlinson reached the Persian camp beyond Nishapur after dark,
and asked for an immediate interview with the Shah. Admitted to
Mohammad Shah's tent, he told him about the Russians he had
encountered on the road, and repeated their explanation of what
they were doing. 'Bringing presents to me!' said the Shah in astonishment. 'Why I have nothing to do with him; he is sent direct
from the [Russian] Emperor to Dost Mohammad in Kabul, and I
am merely asked to help him on his journey.'[11]

Rawlinson understood immediately the importance of what the
Shah had just told him: it was the first proof of what British intelligence had long feared: that the Russians were trying to establish
themselves in Afghanistan by forging an alliance with Dost
Mohammad and the Barakzais, and to assist them and the Persians
in extinguishing the last bastion of Shah Shuja's Sadozai dynasty in
Herat. Rawlinson also realised he needed to get back to Teheran as
quickly as possible with this information.

Shortly afterwards, the Russians themselves arrived in the
Persian camp. To the ordinary Persians of the army, the Russian
officer 'gave himself out to be a Musselman of the Soonee persuasion and declared his Musselman name to be Omar Beg. No one
doubted in camp that he was actually a Musselman.' Unaware that
Rawlinson had discovered the truth about their mission, the officer,
introduced now as 'Captain Vitkevitch . . . addressed me at once in
good French, and in allusion to our former meeting, merely
observed with a smile that "it would not do to be too familiar with
strangers in the desert"'.[12]

Later in life, Rawlinson would be famous for two things, firstly
for deciphering cuneiform, and secondly, along with Arthur Conolly,
for coining the phrase 'the Great Game'. But now it was his skill as
a rider which proved most useful. He was, after all, the son of a

racehorse breeder in Newmarket and had grown up in the saddle; he was also a man of enormous physical strength: 'six feet tall, with broad shoulders, strong limbs and excellent muscles and sinews'.[13]

That same night, Rawlinson headed straight back to Teheran, making the 800 miles across Persia in record time, and brought the news of the existence of the Russian delegation to Afghanistan to MacNeill on 1 November 1837. MacNeill in turn immediately sent an express messenger to Lord Palmerston in London and another to the new Governor General of India, Lord Auckland, in Calcutta. 'The Russians have formally opened their diplomatic intercourse with Kabul,' he wrote. 'Captain Vicovich or Beekavitch, alias Omar Beg, a soonee Mahommedan subject of Russia, has been accredited, I am informed, as chargé d'affairs to Ameer Dost Mohammed Khan.' In the despatch, MacNeill included Rawlinson's detailed description of the officer, and added a few more details that his envoy had picked up in the Persian camp: 'He called himself an aide de camp of the Emperor's, but I understood that he was in reality an ADC of the Governor commanding at Orenburg . . . The year before last he was at Bokhara for some time, employed officially by the Russian Government. He learned his Persian and Jagatai Turkish at Orenburg and Bokhara.'[14]

Rawlinson's sighting of Vitkevitch seemed to validate all the over-heated fears of his boss, MacNeill, Lord Ellenborough and other British policymakers who had long feared that the Russians wanted to take over Afghanistan and use it as a base for attacking British India. Rawlinson's description of Vitkevitch was immediately sent to intelligence officials at Peshawar, the Khyber Pass and the other crossing points to India in case the Russian was planning to continue on to British India, or enter into negotiations with Ranjit Singh.

But the mysterious officer was not heading to India. His mission was to undermine British interests in Afghanistan and forge an alliance between the Tsar and Dost Mohammad.

One or two of Rawlinson's suppositions about the officer were correct, but most were mistaken. He was not a Muslim, nor was he a Russian, nor was he ADC to the Governor of the Russian frontier post of Orenburg, nor was his name at birth either Beekavitch or Vitkevitch. Instead the officer was in fact a Roman Catholic Polish nobleman born Jan Prosper Witkiewicz in Vilnius, today the capital of Lithuania.

While still at the Krozach Gymnasium Jan had helped found a secret society called the Black Brothers, an underground 'revolutionary-national' resistance movement begun by a group of Polish and Lithuanian students intent on fighting the Russian occupation of their country. In 1823, the Brothers were exposed after they wrote anti-Russian letters to the principal and teachers of the Gymnasium, and began posting revolutionary slogans and verses on prominent public buildings in the town. Witkiewicz and the five other ringleaders were arrested and interrogated. On 6 February 1824, in an attempt to stamp out any further democratic aspirations among Polish students, three were sentenced to death and three to flogging followed by life exile to the steppe. At the time, Witkiewicz had just celebrated his fourteenth birthday.

At the last minute, thanks to the intervention of the Grand Duke Pavlovitch, the Regent of Poland, the death sentences were commuted to life imprisonment with hard labour in the Bobruisk Fortress, where one of the boys eventually went mad and died in jail. Witkiewicz and two others were stripped of their titles and rank in the nobility and sent to different fortresses on the Kazakh steppe as common soldiers, without the right to promotion. They were forbidden all further contact with their families for ten years, and sent off on the long march south on foot and in chains.[15]

Immediately after his arrival on the steppe, Jan made a plan to escape. With one of his Black Brother colleagues, Aloizy Peslyak, he plotted a route south to India over the Hindu Kush; but the escape plan was exposed and the plotters severely punished.[16] In the years that followed, Peslyak nearly shot himself, while another of their fellow Polish exiles actually did so. But Witkiewicz resigned himself to his fate and decided to make the best of his situation. He learned Kazakh and Chagatai Turkish, and allowed his name to be changed to the more Russian-sounding Ivan Viktorovitch Vitkevitch.

One of his later patrons subsequently wrote:

Exiled to a remote garrison on the Orenburg line, Vitkevitch served as a private soldier for over 10 years and, placed under the command of drunken and debauched officers, he managed to preserve a pure and noble soul and, moreover, to develop and educate his intelligence; he learned oriental languages and so familiarized himself with the steppe that one can positively claim that ever since the Orenburg District came into being, no one around here knew the Kazakhs better than he does ... all the Kazakhs respect him for his upright behaviour and for the hardiness he has shown more than once on his outings into the steppe.[17]

Soon Vitkevitch had memorised the entire Koran by heart, and began inviting the nomadic Kazakh elders back to his lodgings, giving them tea, pilaf and lamb, and learning from them their customs and manners as well as the rich idiom of their language. He also collected books, especially about the steppe and exploration, and it was this that finally began his rise through the ranks of the Russian military.

Vitkevitch's love of literature had attracted the attention of the Commandant of the fortress of Orsk, on the Ural River, who invited him to become a tutor to his children. In 1830, the Commandant hosted the celebrated German explorer Alexander von Humboldt, who was amazed to see his most recent book, *Tableaux de la Nature*, about his travels in Latin America, lying on a table in the house. When he asked how it had got to be there, he was told about the young Pole who had a complete collection of the great traveller's works, and Humboldt asked to meet him. Vitkevitch was brought in:

The young man's pleasant appearance despite the rough private soldier's overcoat, his good looks, modest manner and learnedness all impressed the great scientist. Upon his return from his Siberian journey to Orenburg, he immediately informed the Governor, Count Pavel Suhktelen, of the deplorable position of Vitkevich and asked the Count to lighten the young man's lot. The Count summoned Vitkevich to Orenburg, promoted him to an NCO, appointed him his orderly, transferred him to the Orenburg Cossacks and later found him work at the Kirghiz Department office.[18]

Before long, Vitkevitch was being used as an interpreter, then later was sent out alone on missions through the Kazakh steppe. He had found his career, but only at the cost of joining the Russian imperial machine he had grown up hating, and faithfully serving the state that had destroyed his life, and about which he presumably still harboured the most bitter feelings.

If Humboldt had begun Vitkevitch's rise, the person who did more than anyone else to continue it was, quite unknowingly, Alexander Burnes. On his return from his expedition to Bukhara, Burnes had published his *Travels into Bokhara*, and found himself an overnight celebrity. He was invited to London to meet both Lord Ellenborough and the King, was lionised by society hostesses and gave standing-room-only lectures to the Royal Geographical Society, which presented him with its Gold Medal. On the publication of the French translation of his book soon afterwards, *Voyages dans le Bokhara* was again a bestseller and Burnes went to Paris to receive further awards and more medals.

It was this French translation that brought Burnes's journey to the notice of the Russian authorities. His expedition had been intended to spy out Russian activity in Afghanistan and Bukhara at a period – the early 1830s – when both areas were in reality not part of St Petersburg's ambitions, which were closely focused on Persia and the Caucasus. Ironically, it seems to have been Burnes's writings that first provoked Russian interest in Afghanistan and Bukhara, not least to head off British intrigues so close to the Russian frontier. As so often in international affairs, hawkish paranoia about distant threats can create the very monster that is most feared. According to General Ivanin, Chief of Staff to V. A. Perovsky, Governor of the Russian steppe frontier garrison at Orenburg, St Petersburg was becoming as frustrated as London had been with its poor intelligence from Central Asia. 'All the information that Russia procured was meagre and obscure and was supplied by Asiatics, who either through ignorance or timidity were not able to furnish really useful accounts,' he wrote, reflecting the same prejudices as his British rivals.

> We had reliable information that the agents of the East India Company were continually appearing either at Khiva or Bokhara; we were also aware that this enterprising company had enormous means at its disposal and was endeavouring not only to establish its commercial influence throughout the whole of Asia, but was also desirous of extending the limits of its Asiatic possessions . . . It was accordingly decided in 1835, in order to watch the English agents and counteract their efforts, to send Russian agents into Central Asia. In order to watch the march of events in Central Asia, sub-Lieutenant Vitkevitch was despatched thither in the capacity as an agent . . .[19]

Twice, Vitkevitch was sent off to Bukhara. The first time he travelled in disguise with two Kirghiz traders and made the journey in only seventeen days through deep snow and over the frozen Oxus. He stayed a month, but found it much less romantic than the Oriental Wonder House described by Burnes. 'I must note that the tales told by Burnes, in his published account of his journey to Bukhara, presented a curious contrast to all that I chanced to see here,' he wrote back to Orenburg. 'He sees everything in some glamorous light, while all I saw was merely disgusting, ugly, pathetic or ridiculous. Either Mr Burnes deliberately exaggerated and embellished the attractions of Bokhara or he was strongly prejudiced in its favour.'[20] Despite his distaste, Vitkevitch managed to make a rough set of plans of the city while maintaining his disguise. 'No one, least of all the fanatical Bokharans, could recognize a European and a Christian in this Kazakh-dressed, Kazakh-speaking man, who had assimilated the Kazakh manners and customs,' wrote one of his admirers. 'Moreover, his handsome dark eyes, beard and cropped hair made him look like an Asian and a Muslim.'[21]

On his second visit, in January 1836, Vitkevitch went openly as a Russian officer, to request the release of several Russian merchants who had been detained by the Amir of Bukhara. On arrival in the caravan city he recorded that he was immediately asked: 'Do you know Iskander? I thought they meant Alexander the Great but they were, in fact, talking of Alexander Burnes.' This early indication of British influence did not stop Vitkevitch almost immediately trying to reverse it, and it took him only a couple of weeks to uncover the intelligence network that Burnes had established in order to send news back to India: 'The British have their man in Bukhara,' Vitkevitch soon reported to St Petersburg.

> He is a Kashmiri called Nizamuddin and has been living in Bukhara for four years now under the pretext of trade . . . He is a very clever man, rubs shoulders with everyone and entertains the Bukharan noblemen; at least once a week he sends letters with secret messengers to Kabul, to the Englishman Masson who passes them on. The most curious thing is that Dost Mohammed is aware of Masson's activities; the Khan has even intercepted his letters but leaves the spy alone, saying: one man cannot harm me. Apparently, Dost Mohammed does not want to incur their displeasure out of respect to Europeans in general, and he tolerates Masson too. This man lives in Kabul under the pretext of looking for ancient coins.

Nizamuddin had a kinsman in Bukhara, added Vitkevitch,

> who does all the paperwork for him. They have taken lodgings, rather luxurious by local standards, in Koosh Begee's [chamberlain] caravansarai, where they entertain the nobility; Nizamuddin dresses in fine clothes and is a man of rare physical beauty; his companion is very clever if unseemly and behaves as a subordinate although it

is obvious that he is the one who runs the affairs. They receive their money from Indian bankers. Nizamuddin sought my acquaintance as soon as I arrived and asked me many questions: about Novo-Alexandrovsk, the New Line, our relations with Khiva, etc. Having been forewarned, I did not give him any definite answers. All the same, he sent a letter to Kabul the very next day.[22]

It was on this second visit to Bukhara that Vitkevitch had an extraordinary break. By chance, his visit coincided with that of an Afghan emissary, Mirza Hussein Ali, who had been sent by Dost Mohammad Khan on a mission to Tsar Nicholas. After defeating Shah Shuja outside Kandahar in 1834, Dost Mohammad had discovered letters from Wade encouraging the Afghan chiefs to support the restoration of the Sadozai monarchy with Shuja at the helm. Britain's secret aid for the Shah had come as a great shock to Dost Mohammad, who had believed that he and the Governor General were on excellent terms. In response he decided to appeal to Russia as diplomatic insurance in case the British made any further attempts to interfere in Afghanistan. 'Afghanistan's independence is threatened by British expansion,' he wrote to the Tsar. 'This expansion is also a threat to Russian trade in Central Asia and the surrounding countries to the south of it. Should Afghanistan be defeated in its lone struggle against Britain, it would also mean the end of Russia's trade with Bokhara.'[23]

Vitkevitch stumbled across Mirza Hussein Ali when he took lodgings in the same Bukhara caravanserai and, realising the opportunity, offered personally to escort the Ambassador first to Orenburg, then on to St Petersburg. 'Dost Mohammed Khan, the ruler of Kabulistan, is seeking the patronage of Russia,' he reported excitedly, 'and is prepared to do anything we ask for.'

First, however, he had to fight his away out of Bukhara, as the Amir had abruptly placed sentries around his lodgings, confiscated his camels and refused him permission to leave. 'I grabbed my pistols,' he wrote later,

and thrust them beneath my belt, threw a coat over my shoulders, donned my travelling fur cap and ran to the Koosh Begee. As I entered, I realized they were talking about me and my departure, although I did not listen carefully. I ran straight into the room . . . [and said:] 'I am telling you once again, and this is final, that for the life of me I shall not remain here and anyone who dares detain me on my way or even enquire of my destination, as I have already told you and a hundred of others who never stopped bothering me about it, anyone who stands in my way shall have the following reply' – here I threw off the flap on my coat and pointed at the pistols. The Koosh Begee was so astonished he did not know what to say. I requested that he should give me a laissez-passer bearing his own seal, so that nobody would dare stop me, but he would not give me one, just said: go. I bid him farewell and left, repeating once again that a bullet would be my answer to anyone who provoked me on my way, be it with one word only. The Koosh Begee could not entirely keep up his pretence and said 'We shall see' – but he appeared pleased to see me leave.[24]

Over the months that followed, Vitkevitch and Hussein Ali made their way slowly through the steppe to Orenburg, and then on across the length of Russia to St Petersburg. Hussein Ali was struck down with dysentery on the road, but Vitkevitch nursed and encouraged him, using the enforced periods of rest to learn fluent Dari from his companion. The two finally arrived in the capital in March 1837. Vitkevitch had left Europe fourteen years earlier as a chained convict. This time, Tsar Nicholas personally sent him congratulations on his arrival in the city, promoting him to the rank of lieutenant, and he was ushered straight into the office of Count Nesselrode, the Russian Vice Chancellor and Foreign Minister.

News of Mirza Hussein Ali's mission had been greeted with enormous excitement by all the officials concerned with the incipient Great Game. Count Simonitch had written from the Teheran Legation urging that this opportunity should not be lost.

British influence in Persia was already on the wane, he wrote. Now the chance had come to include Afghanistan in a tripartite alliance of Russia, Persia and 'Kabulistan'. In this way, an arc of Russian influence could be established from Kabul to Tabriz. With the Russians supreme in Afghanistan, the British would be on the back foot, struggling to maintain their position on the Indus, and would have no chance of creating more trouble in Russia's natural zone of influence in Central Asia. Moreover, Russian political influence in Kabul would open up the markets of Afghanistan to Russian produce.[25]

The Governor of Orenburg agreed. It was, he wrote,

absolutely necessary to support the Kabul leader [Dost Moham-mad Khan]. For if the British puppet Shuja becomes ruler of Afghanistan then the country will come under British influence, and the British will only have to take one step to be in Bukhara. Central Asia will then be altogether under British influence, our trade with Asia will cease, and the British will be able to arm the neighbouring Asian countries as well as provide them with power, arms and money against Russia. If the patronage of Russia can support Dost Mohammad on the throne, he will undoubtedly, in gratitude, remain a good friend of ours and an enemy to the English; he will cut them off from Central Asia, will place a barrier to their beloved trading power.[26]

The Governor also urged that Vitkevitch should be given the job of escorting the Afghan Ambassador back home as he was 'an effi-cient, clever man who knows his job, is of a practical nature, more prone to act than to write or talk, and knows the steppe and its inhabitants better than any person living or dead'.[27]

On arrival in St Petersburg, the letter from Dost Mohammad was closely examined and proved to be all that was hoped. Dost Mohammad wrote that the British were on the verge of conquering all of India, and that he alone was capable of stopping their advance, if only he were to be supplied with arms and money in the way that the Russians were doing with the Persians: 'We hope that the magnanimity and unparalleled bounties showered on the Persian court will also stream on the Afghan government and on our dynasty which, with the beneficent gaze of your imperial greatness, without doubt will return to its former favourable state.'[28]

So it was that Nesselrode recommended the Tsar to send what he described as a trade and diplomatic mission to Afghanistan: 'No matter how far removed the above countries [Afghanistan and India] are from us,' he wrote, 'and how limited our knowledge of them, it is undeniable that any broadening of trade relations is profitable.'[29] The only problem was that Mirza Hussein Ali showed no signs of recovering from his illness. So, after many meetings, it was finally decided that Vitkevitch should set off ahead of the Ambassador, who was too unwell to attempt the journey south without at least one month of rest.

On 14 May 1837, Vitkevitch was given a set of written instructions, which talked of opening trade relations with Dost Mohammad. According to one Russian source, he was also given a set of secret oral instructions about buying Dost Mohammad's full support by offering him financial aid of two million roubles to be used against Ranjit Singh's Sikhs, and the promise of military supplies with which the Afghans could reconquer their winter capital of Peshawar, lost since Shah Shuja's failed expedition of 1834.[30] In addition, he was to try to bring Dost Mohammad's Barakzai half-brothers in Kandahar into the new alliance too and urge them to unify and act as one with their brother in Kabul. It was, he was told, of the utmost importance 'to achieve peace between the Afghan rulers ... and to make them understand the immense advantages of a close and amicable relationship between them, advantages for them personally and for their domains, which could thus be much better defended against external enemies as well as against internal disturbances'. Throughout, Vitkevitch was to take detailed notes and on his return write a full report on 'the current state of Afghanistan, its trade, finances and army, and the attitude of the Afghan rulers towards the British'.[31]

Vitkevitch was to travel through the Caucasus, accompanied by Captain Ivan Blaramberg who had just been appointed to the

Russian delegation in Teheran as Simonitch's adjutant.[32] After resting at Tiflis, they were to disguise themselves and, with the greatest secrecy and discretion, make their way to Teheran. 'Once in Teheran,' Vitkevitch was told, 'you shall report to Count Simonitch, and place yourself under his orders. It will be up to him to decide whether to send you on to Afghanistan or to cancel your mission if he considers it incompatible with the political situation in Persia or impossible for any other reason. He will also decide on the further travel arrangements for the Afghan Ambassador Hussein Ali.'[33] 'We need not remind you', wrote Count Nesselrode, at the end of his instructions, 'that all the aforesaid must be kept strictly confidential and nobody but our envoy to Persia, Count Simonitch, and Baron von Rosen should know of these instructions. Caution also requires that you leave all instructions with Count Simonitch when you set off to Afghanistan so that, should some misfortune befall you, nothing could reveal the secret of your mission.' It was of particular importance, warned Nesselrode, that the British discover nothing of these plans, and there was an implicit warning that he could be disowned by St Petersburg if the British did so.

Vitkevitch's notes for his journey south were burned just before his mysterious death, but Captain Blaramberg's memoirs survive. 'Having spent two months in St Petersburg and received my instructions,' he wrote, 'I was preparing to leave the city, but first I met my travelling companion Lieutenant Vitkevich. He turned out to be a pleasant young Pole, 28 years old, with an expressive face, well-educated and energetic . . . all the necessary qualities to play in Asia the role of Alexander Burnes.'[34]

The two travelled south in a carriage laden with presents and bribes for Persian and Afghan officials, and on arrival in Tiflis they met Baron von Rosen, the Commander-in-Chief, and visited Countess Simonitch, who 'became a frequent guest; her charming daughters bore a great resemblance to their astonishing mother'.

The further south they went from Tiflis, the more idyllic the countryside became. The two travellers slept out under the stars, and spent nights in the camps of nomads. 'On 11 July we crossed the border of the Yerivan province and the oppressive heat forced us to halt at a ruined mosque,' wrote Blaramberg.

> It was here that we saw the magnificent Mount Ararat for the first time: its double peak covered in glittering snow rose in the south over the plain. On the 13th we went over the last mountain ridge and descended into the Araxes valley. It was a beautiful day, not a cloud in the sky. We settled in the shade of a small grove by a babbling stream and admired the magnificent Ararat towering before us. Our Armenian manservant made a delicious pilaf and we, being in high spirits, emptied a bottle of Madeira.[35]

It was once they had crossed the Persian border that Vitkevitch's volatile temperament darkened. 'During our journey through Persia, Vitkevitch was often in a melancholy mood,' remembered Blaramberg, 'and he would say that he had had enough of life.' Only when the party reached Teheran did Vitkevitch's spirits revive.

For here Simonitch informed Vitkevitch of two pieces of intelligence which greatly excited the Pole. The first – which later turned out to be false – was that Mirza Hussein Ali's mission had already aroused the suspicion of British intelligence, which, said Simonitch, had tailed the two travellers all the way from Kabul. Simonitch further warned him that as a result he might now be a target for 'intrigues and provocations by British agents'. None of this was true – the British were at this stage entirely ignorant of the Afghan mission to the Tsar – but in order to safeguard the mission Vitkevitch was provided by the Embassy with a Cossack escort to look after him as he headed on to Nishapur and hence to the Shah's camp at Herat. It was this escort that did finally alert British intelligence – in the person of Rawlinson – to the existence of Vitkevitch's mission.

The second piece of news was even more to Vitkevitch's taste. For Simonitch's spies in Afghanistan had just informed him that Vitkevitch would not be alone in Kabul. His British counterpart Alexander Burnes was heading in the same direction, on his second mission to Central Asia. Like Vitkevitch he had specific instructions to win over Dost Mohammad Khan. The man whom Vitkevitch had shadowed and to some extent modelled himself on was heading to the same destination, charged with exactly the same task.

The two men had in fact much in common. They were of nearly the same age; both came from the distant provinces of their respective empires, with few connections to the ruling elite, and having arrived in Asia within a few months of each other had both worked their way up through their own merit and daring, and especially their skill in languages. Now the two would come face to face, in the court of Kabul, and the outcome of the contest would do much to determine the immediate future not only of Afghanistan, but of Central Asia. The Great Game had begun.

On his arrival in Peshawar in October 1837, Alexander Burnes was not impressed with the changes in the city since his last visit.

In the three years since his conquest of Peshawar at the time of Shah Shuja's attack on Kandahar in 1834, Ranjit Singh had moved half his army into the city, turning the former Durrani winter capital into a massive Punjabi barracks. In the process the Sikh Khalsa had destroyed many of Peshawar's most beautiful sights. An enormous new brick fort had been built over the delicate pleasure gardens and pavilions of the Bala Hisar where Shah Shuja had in 1809 received the Elphinstone mission. Another new fort bristling with artillery had just been erected at Jamrud at the mouth of the Khyber. Burnes recorded that one of Ranjit Singh's former Napoleonic officers, Paolo Avitabile, now governed Peshawar, 'and the Sikhs had changed everything: many of the fine gardens around the town had been converted into cantonments; trees had been cut down; and the whole neighbourhood was one vast camp. Mahommedan usages have disappeared – the sounds of dancing and music were heard at all hours and all places.'[36]

Burnes also noted that, despite the massive army of occupation

garrisoning the Peshawar valley, the Sikhs had found it very difficult
to rule the rebellious Pashtuns who inhabited the area and that there
had been so many tribal uprisings, assassinations and acts of insurrection in and around the city that the occupation of Peshawar had
become a major drain on Sikh resources. This, he realised, was actually good news for his mission, as it could only make Ranjit Singh
more willing to come to an accommodation with Dost Mohammad
about the future of the city, and with luck allow Burnes to reconcile
the two rivals, bringing both into alliance with the British.

The decision to send Burnes back to Kabul had been taken by
the new Governor General, Lord Auckland, who had been alarmed
by MacNeill's reports of the Russians' growing activity in Persia
and their purported ambitions towards Herat and the rest of
Afghanistan. Auckland had only just arrived in Calcutta and knew
very little about the region, but he had met Burnes at a houseparty
at Bowood during the latter's triumphant book tour two years
earlier and assumed he was a safe pair of hands. So Burnes was sent
off up the Indus for the second time, this time with instructions to
make a more comprehensive study of the river, laying down buoys
and erecting navigational landmarks. He was then to head on to
Kabul, instructed to gather intelligence on 'the recently created ties
between the rulers of the Afghan principalities and Persia', on the
attitude of the Afghan population towards Russia and on Russian
activity in the region and 'the measures taken by Russia for the
increase of her trade in Central Asia' – a very similar remit to that
Nesselrode had given Vitkevitch.[37]

Auckland's protocol-obsessed Political Secretary, William
Macnaghten, meanwhile, had ordered that given the dubious nature
of Kabul's Barakzai rulers, who in the official view of Calcutta had
usurped the throne of Afghanistan's true monarch, Shah Shuja, a
'strict economy' was to be observed, and Burnes's mission was to
travel with far less pomp and many fewer presents than that of
Elphinstone: Burnes in fact had only a single pistol and one telescope to give to Dost Mohammad. In the light of lingering Afghan
memories of the lavishness of the gifts given by the last Embassy to
Shah Shuja, these instructions did not bode well for the success of

Burnes's mission. Nor did the news of a pitched battle between the Sikhs and the Afghans which had erupted even as Burnes was heading towards the new Khyber frontier separating the two.

The Battle of Jamrud on 30 April 1837 was the climax of three years' growing hostility between the Afghans and the Sikhs over Ranjit Singh's occupation of Peshawar. As soon as he had dealt with Shah Shuja's invasion of 1834, Dost Mohammad had turned his attention to trying to liberate the Afghan winter capital from Sikh control. Whether out of piety or strategy, or a mixture of the two, in February 1835 he had himself awarded the Islamic title of Amir al-Muminin, the Commander of the Faithful, by the 'ulema [clergy] of Kabul: the most senior Sunni cleric in Kabul, the Mir Waiz, had led him to the Id Gah on the edge of the town and placed barley shoots in his turban, an echo of the ceremony by which a sufi saint had consecrated Shah Shuja's grandfather, Ahmad Shah Abdali, in June 1747.* As the *Siraj ul-Tawarikh* noted,

Calling the men of the surrounding region into Kabul, Dost Mohammad declared a jihad [holy war] and announced that the Punjab, Peshawar, and the other regions would be regained.

The religious scholars who called for jihad as an obligation to God, and who considered killing and being killed on the path of religion the catalyst of a better age, and the way to obtain life itself, gathered in joy and declared that: 'The command to jihad is dependent on the existence of an amir and the establishment of an Amirate. Whoever should turn away from his command or prohibition, it would be like disobedience to the order of God and the Prophet. For others, it is absolutely essential that they render him obedience and punish those who disobey.' Thanks to this declaration . . . Dost Mohammad began laying the foundations of his Amirate. In a short time, he had put everything in order, ascended the throne, and had the coinage and the *khutbah* [the Friday sermon] issued in his name. The following verse was inscribed on the coinage:

---

* The same title was later taken by Mullah Omar of the Taliban who in 1996 looked explicitly to the example of Dost Mohammad for inspiration for the founding of the Taliban Islamic Amirate of Afghanistan.

> Amir Dost Mohammad resolved to wage jihad,
> And to mint coins – May God grant him victory.

After his enthronement, Amir Dost Mohammad decided to fulfil the jihad. He left Kabul for Peshawar with an army made up of 60,000 men – royal horse and foot as well as irregular tribal forces.[38]

The declaration of jihad against the Sikhs brought with it a useful legitimisation of Dost Mohammad's seizure of power. He had never dared to claim the Sadozai title of shah, and up to this point his only legitimacy lay in the reality of his power and his reputation for justice. But he could now justify his rule by appeal to a higher Qur'anic authority, and the fulfilment of his duty as a good Muslim to wage holy war against the infidel and so – in theory – usher in a millennial Islamic Golden Age of purity and godliness. At the same time Dost Mohammad used the leadership of the jihad as a way to claim leadership of all the Afghan peoples, writing to the Governor General, 'these people are tribes of my nation, and their protection & support is an obligation as well as a duty . . . Reflect & consider if the Afghans can quietly submit to be injured and oppressed without resisting? As long as I retain life in my body, I can neither separate myself from my nation nor the nation from me.'[39]

Dost Mohammad made a first abortive attempt on Peshawar later that month, gathering a motley horde of jihadis – 'savages from the remotest mountains', according to Josiah Harlan, 'many of them giants in form and strength, promiscuously armed with sword and shield, bows and arrows, matchlocks, rifles, spears and blunderbusses, prepared to slay, plunder and destroy, for the sake of God and the Prophet, the unenlightened infidels of the Punjab'. In the event, the rabble were no match for the beautifully drilled and disciplined troops of the Khalsa and succeeded in doing little except provoking a massacre of the Muslim citizens of Peshawar by an angry Sikh soldiery. But the raid also allowed Dost Mohammad quietly to annex the Afghan provinces of Wardak and Ghazni which separated Kabul from the Khyber and the Sikh border; he had now increased his revenues five times over since first seizing control over the country immediately around Kabul eleven years earlier, and had become unquestionably the most powerful ruler in the country.

At the end of February 1837, the Amir opened hostilities against the Sikhs for the second time. 'Your occupation of Jamrud on the frontier of the valley of Khyber, which is in the possession of the Khyberis, my subjects, has greatly angered these people who will of course do what they can to prevent it,' he wrote to Ranjit Singh's General, Hari Singh, the leader of the Sikh forces in Peshawar. 'My son Mohammad Akbar Khan will also do everything in his power to assist them . . . If you will exert yourself with the Maharaja to restore Peshawar to me, I will not fail to send him horses & other presents from the produce of this country. In the event of you effecting this object, I will agree to whatever you propose. If not, you know my response.'[40]

The Sikhs ignored the warning. Two months later, soon after Ranjit Singh had withdrawn his elite European-trained force, the Fauj-i-Khas, so that they could be guards of honour at a royal wedding in Lahore, 20,000 Afghan cavalry descended the Khyber, and on 30 April succeeded in surrounding Hari Singh near the walls of the new fort at Jamrud. According to the *Siraj ul-Tawarikh*, 'In the heat of the furious combat, Akbar Khan encountered Hari Singh. Without recognising each other, they exchanged blows and after much thrusting and parrying, Akbar Khan won out, knocking Hari Singh to the ground, and killing him. With their commander dead and the army of Islam rolling towards them like a tide in flood, the Sikhs abandoned the field. They were pursued by the sardars as far as Jamrud Fort where they barricaded themselves inside.'[41] The Fauj-i-Khas quickly turned around and a fortnight later drove off the besieging Afghans; but it was a huge boost to the prestige of Dost Mohammad and the first great victory of Akbar Khan, demonstrating how far he had inherited his father's military talents. From this point he would increasingly become the most formidable Afghan commander.

Burnes was halfway up the Indus when he heard of the battle.

For a time, it was unclear whether the hostilities would block his route into Afghanistan and bring about the cancellation of his mission. Either way, he realised the fighting would put the British in the awkward position of trying to remain allies of both sides in a war. But by the time Burnes had reached Peshawar and saw the difficulties the Sikhs were having holding the province and that they had found it 'impossible to keep the country in order', he became convinced that the occupation was proving so troublesome and expensive for the Sikhs that it left him ample room to negotiate a solution. In a letter to John MacNeill in Teheran, he mulled over the idea of an agreement whereby Peshawar could remain under Ranjit Singh's nominal control until his death, when it would revert to the Afghans.[42]

Certainly it was with the confident hope that his mission could bring about some sort of compromise between the Sikhs and the Afghans that Burnes headed up the Khyber Pass on 30 August, passing through the no man's land separating the two warring parties. 'We took our departure from Peshawar,' he wrote later,

> and were driven by M Avitabile in his carriage to Jamrud, scene of the late battle between the Sikhs and the Afghans . . . We found the situation by no means agreeable. The deputation sent to escort us through the Khyber Pass had not yet arrived; and although some months had now elapsed since the battle, the effluvia from the dead bodies, both of men and horses was quite revolting. Some camel-keepers who had left the place the day of our arrival, escorted by a few soldiers, were attacked by the Afridi mountaineers, who came down upon them, drove off the camels, and beheaded two of the people, whose mangled trunks were brought into camp . . . [Half-way up the Khyber] by the road they showed us many small mounds, built to mark the spots where they had planted the heads of the Sikhs whom they had decapitated after the late victory: on some of these mounds locks of hair were yet to be seen.

As they passed from the territory of one tribe to another, 'stopped at every by-road and defile as we came among the different subdivisions of the tribe', the Embassy crossed slowly into Dost Mohammad's area of control. A few days later, after passing the chinars and cypresses of Shah Jahan's great Mughal garden at Nimla, site of Shah Shuja's first defeat by Dost Mohammad in 1809, Burnes was met by two men who would both play important roles in his life.

The first to ride into his camp was the British deserter turned spy and archaeologist Charles Masson. Burnes recorded in his account his pleasure at meeting Masson, who had now earned some celebrity in India thanks to his pioneering work digging the Bactrian Greek and Kushan Buddhist sites around Kabul and Jalalabad; Burnes described Masson in his diary as 'the well-known illustrator of Bactrian reliques', and praised him for his 'high literary attainments, long residence in this country, and accurate knowledge of people and events'.[43] But Masson, who had for many years known Afghanistan intimately and who was a confidant of Dost Mohammad, was much less enamoured by his ambitious and self-promoting celebrity visitor. Like many others, he strongly resented Burnes's fame as a traveller on the basis of his single journey to Bukhara, and was extremely dubious about both Burnes's geographical knowledge and his diplomatic skills. 'I must confess I augured very faintly on the success of his mission,' he wrote later, 'either from his manner or from his opinion "that the Afghans were to be treated as children".'[44] On one matter, however, the two agreed: the occupation of Peshawar was proving a financial disaster for the Sikhs, 'unprofitable, and a constant source of alarm and inquietude to Ranjit Singh', and the opportunity was now there to resolve the conflict by bringing the Sikhs, the Afghans and the Company together in an alliance that would keep Russian and Persian machinations at bay. 'Afghan affairs were capable of settlement,' Masson concluded, 'and the settlement was in our power at that time.'[45]

The second man to enter Burnes's camp was a much grander figure, and arrived that evening on elephant-back preceded by a 'fine body of Afghan cavalry'. This was Dost Mohammad's increasingly powerful fourth son, Mohammad Akbar Khan, whose path to fame had just begun when he had killed Hari Singh two months earlier. Akbar Khan was a strong, hard-bodied, hawk-faced young man. He resembled his father in his bravery, his charm, his ruthlessness and his sense of strategy, all qualities for which he was later celebrated as a heroic figure in Afghan song and epic poetry, where he appears as the Achilles, Roland and King Arthur of the Dari epic all rolled into one:[46]

> When Akbar the Brave, Master of the Sword
> Conquered and defeated the enemy forces
>
> When he fought the fierce armies of the Punjab
> He was but a youth, yet he had the mettle of a Sohrab
>
> He became a legend potent and brave
> As famed through the land as the mighty Rustam
>
> When he reached the season of his manhood
> He was tall and graceful as a young cypress
>
> He mastered every science
> And excelled in every art
>
> His luminous countenance shone with a light divine
> Worthy of crown and throne
>
> All the world was drawn to his face
> Every eye turned towards him[47]

Indeed, such was his beauty that Akbar Khan seems to have become something of a sex symbol in 1830s Kabul. Maulana Hamid Kashmiri, the author of the *Akbarnama*, the first epic poem written in his honour, gives over several pages to his wedding-night athletics with his lovely bride, the daughter of Mohammad Shah Ghilzai, 'this houri of paradise, as bright as the sun, who put the moon and stars to shame'.

Desire moved on both sides
Passion was inflamed as they sought each other

They laid bare their faces from the curtain of modesty
The veil of clothing they threw off

They clasped one another so close
As perfume to the rose and colour to the tulip

They lay with each other in pleasure and delight
Body to body, face to face, lip to lip

Sometimes the fingers would hit upon the moon and the Pleiades
Sometimes the hand would hasten towards the musk of conquest

His desire swelled from the sweetness of her kiss
They both redoubled their labours for the prize

Shining, jewel upon jewel, he planted seed
By a single pearl, the rubies of Badakhshan were scattered[48]

Yet for all his glamour, Akbar was clearly a complex and intelligent man, more emotionally volatile than Dost Mohammad, and also more aesthetically sensitive. He and Masson knew each other well; in fact Akbar Khan had taken Masson under his protection and showed more interest than any other Afghan in the Hellenised Gandharan Buddhist sculptures that Masson had been excavating from the Kushan monasteries around Jalalabad. 'He was enraptured with two female heads,' wrote Masson in his memoirs,

and lamented that the ideal beauties of the sculpture could not be realized in nature. From this time on a kind of acquaintance subsisted between us, and the young sirdar would frequently send for me. I became a pretty constant visitor at his tea-table, and procured from him an order, addressed to several of the maleks [tribal leaders] and chiefs, to assist me in any researches I might undertake ... I was as much gratified as surprised to witness the good sense displayed by the young sirdar as to the nature of my researches, and their object. He remarked to those about him, who suggested that I might be seeking treasure, that my only purpose was to advance science, which would lead to my credit on my return to my native country; and he observed, that whilst among Durranis the soldier was held in honour, amongst Europeans respect was paid to men of 'illam' or science.[49]

Another European traveller, Godfrey Vigne, also described Akbar as the most progressive, enquiring and intelligent of all the Afghan nobles. He closely questioned Vigne on the taste of pork, forbidden to all good Muslims, and was 'so far from being a bigot that he several times ordered his servant to hand me water from his own cup', at a time when most Afghans refused to eat or drink with Christians.[50]

The following day, Akbar Khan led Burnes into Kabul on elephant-back. 'We were received with great pomp and splendour,' wrote Burnes. 'He did me the honour to place me on the same elephant upon which he himself rode, and conducted us to his father's court, whose reception of me was most cordial. A spacious garden, close by the palace and inside the Bala Hisar of Kabul, was allotted to the mission as their place of residence.'[51]

Burnes was received in full durbar by his old friend Amir Dost Mohammad the following morning. As before, Burnes's charm soon won over the Amir. Even though Dost Mohammad charged the British with duplicity in aiding Shah Shuja, and with knowing in advance of Ranjit Singh's plan to seize Peshawar, he had clearly decided not to let this interfere with his friendship with Burnes. Moreover, he calculated that opening diplomatic relations with Britain was his best hope of outflanking the Sikhs. Before long the two men were on the same warm terms as before, and Burnes as admiring of his host as he had been in 1831. 'Power frequently spoils men,' he wrote, 'but with Dost Muhammad neither the increase of it, nor his new title of Amir, seems to have done him any harm. Instead he seems even more alert and full of intelligence than when I last saw him.' When Burnes was led into the audience hall and formally presented his credentials and his slightly disappointing presents, Dost Mohammad received them politely. 'I informed him that I had brought with me, as presents to his Highness, some of the rarities of Europe: he promptly replied that we ourselves were the rarities, the sight of which best pleased him.'[52]

Later, Burnes reflected perceptively on this meeting:

Dost Mohammad's comprehension is very quick; his knowledge of character very great; and he cannot be long deceived. He listens to every individual who complains, and with a forbearance and temper which are more highly praised than his equity and justice . . . Whether his religious wars and government have resulted from a strong spirit of orthodoxy or from ambition is a question yet to be solved . . . The republican genius [of the Afghans] is unchanged; and whatever power a Sadozai or a Barakzai may acquire, its preservation can only be ensured by not infringing the rights of the tribes, and the laws by which they are allowed to govern themselves.[53]

Dost Mohammad may have been impressed by Burnes and vice versa, but there is evidence from a variety of Afghan sources even at this early stage that not all of his courtiers, nobles and chiefs were pleased by the growing friendship of their Amir with the Firangi [foreign] infidel. The more orthodox were especially anxious about such an alliance, and wondered how it sat with the Amir's stated intention of declaring war on the enemies of Islam.

In the Afghan sources, Burnes is always depicted as a devilishly charming but cunning deceiver, a master of *zarang*, of flattery and treachery – an interesting inversion of British stereotypes of the devious Oriental. Mirza 'Ata in the *Naway Ma'arek* talks of Burnes's progress up the Indus:

to spy out conditions in Sindh and Khurasan, which he succeeded in doing thanks to his Plato-like intelligence. Burnes realised that the states of the region were built on very insecure foundations and would need only a gust of wind to blow them down. When the people crowded to stare at the foreigners, Burnes emerged from his tent and jokingly remarked to the crowd 'Come and see my tail and horns!' Everyone laughed, and someone called out: 'Your tail stretches all the way back to England, and your horns will soon be appearing in Khurasan!'[54]

This image is developed by Maulana Kashmiri in his 1844 *Akbarnama*. In this poem, Burnes, the arch-enemy of Akbar Khan, is the demonically charismatic incarnation of all the two-faced treachery and deceit of Crusading Christendom:

One of the Firangi lords of high stature
By name Burnes, and called Sikandar

Gathered all the necessaries for commerce
And set out with every appearance of a trader

When he arrived, with all haste, in the city of Kabul
He sought intimacy with its illustrious men

With many gifts and open display of favours
He made a place for himself in every heart, he held everyone spellbound

The Amir, with his kindness and natural grace
Treated him as a most honoured guest

He elevated him above all others
And bestowed every mark of distinction upon him

But Burnes had mixed poison into the honey
From London, he had requested much gold and silver

With dark magic and deceit he dug a pit
Many a man was seized by the throat and thrown in

When Burnes had bound them 'in chains of gold', the khans 'swore allegiance to him one and all'. Eventually someone warned the Amir:

'O Lion-slaying Commander of great fame!

This sedition-sowing Burnes – he is your enemy
On the outside he seems a man, but inside he is the very devil

Beware this evil-spreading foe
Do you not remember the advice of [the poet] Sadi?

It is better to hold back from strangers
For an enemy is strong when in the guise of a friend

You have been nurturing this enemy day and night
Turn away from him before you find yourself betrayed.'[55]

According to several Afghan sources, the Qajar Shah of Iran, Mohammad Shah, also wrote to warn Dost Mohammad about Burnes's devilish schemes. This letter is mentioned in the *Siraj ul-Tawarikh*, where is it said, 'talks on friendship and cordial relations had not yet begun when an emissary with a note from Mohammad Shah arrived and was admitted to an audience. The Shah of Iran had written an account of Alexander Burnes's double-dealing and had candidly stated that because of his duplicity there would be no peace until his impostures were exposed.'[56] But it is Maulana Hamid Kashmiri who gives the fullest account of the Shah's alleged intervention:

One day, the evil-wisher, arrogant and intoxicated, was sitting
As had become his custom, in a privileged place at court

The blessed Amir of good fortune
Gave into his hand an illuminated letter

And said to him: 'Read it out loud and without pause'
Burnes opened that letter and began to read

After declarations of the Shah's great love
The letter gave a warning: 'I have heard, O Great Ruler

That the evil-sowing devil Burnes
Has arrived and sits in your court day and night

With a hundred marks of love you have called him son
And have placed him as high as any honoured guest

Know there is none second to him amongst the Firangis
Whether it be in malevolence and knavery or in deceit and perfidy

Many have been killed by his hidden hand
Many hearts wounded by an arrow loosed from his bow

Why are you showering gold upon him when you should be spilling blood?
Know and fear his spreading of strife

He can incite corpses to rebellion
The Firangi can attack even the peace of the grave

There is no honour and loyalty among the men of Firang
They have no idol but fraud and deceit

Listen to my words and take them to heart
Hear my counsel and be alert, be alert'

Maulana Kashmiri also hints that Burnes had already developed a
fondness for leading astray not just the men but also the women of
Kabul. In one set of couplets he has Burnes tell the King of Firang:

'In beauty, the people of Kabul
Are the very *houris* and *ghilmans** of paradise

---

* The hunky male eighteen-year-old Chippendales of Islamic heaven, counterparts to
the supermodel houris.

The women of that land
Are of such delectable beauty
One could slay a hundred Firangis
With the power of her buttocks'[57]

This was apparently not just the fertile imagination of the Maulana at work – Masson also notes with some anxiety that Burnes had shown far more interest in the women of Kabul than was wise, especially for an accredited diplomat. Masson wrote that the Amir was kept updated on Burnes's 'revels' with what Maulana Kashmiri calls 'the delectable houris of Kabul' and 'rejoiced perhaps that the envoy's intrigues were of any other than of a political nature'. Masson records that, because of Burnes's appetites, before long he received a visit from Mirza Sami Khan, Dost Mohammad's Minister, who 'proposed I should imitate the example of my illustrious superior, and fill my house with black-eyed damsels. I observed that my house was hardly large enough, and anyway where were the damsels to come from? He replied that I might select any I pleased, and he would take care I should have them. I told him his charity exceeded all praise, but I thought it better to go on quietly in my old ways.'[58]

This was not Masson's only anxiety. It was not just that Burnes's behaviour lacked the 'decorum . . . [with which] it was supposed that a British mission would be conducted', he was worried by Burnes's diplomatic instincts and feared that his manner with the Amir was too 'compliant and obsequious', that he was overdoing the flattery, 'prefacing his remarks with Garib Nawaz, your humble petitioner'.[59] Masson was also concerned that Burnes was encouraging the Amir to hope for the full restoration of Peshawar through British mediation, when it was still far from certain that Ranjit Singh would be at all amenable to this, or that Calcutta would be prepared to press him on that matter, or even that the young Ambassador had the authority to conduct such negotiations in the first place.

Nevertheless, only ten days after his arrival in Kabul, Burnes set out for a quick break in the Afghan countryside, full of optimism about his mission and in the highest spirits. 'A vast vista of gardens extended for some thirty or forty miles in length terminated by the

Hindoo Koosh, white with snow,' he wrote happily from the Shomali Plain the following day, exhilarated to be travelling again in the landscape he loved. 'Every hill with a southern aspect had a vineyard on it.'

More satisfying even than the landscape, or the prospects of a week's rest in the Mughal Emperor Babur's favourite pleasure resort at Istalif, was Burnes's firm conviction that an anti-Russian alliance was all but in the bag. 'Dost Mohammad Khan has fallen into all our views,' he wrote to his brother-in-law from Istalif the following day.

> Things now stand so that I think we are at the threshold of negotiations with King Ranjit, the basis of which will be his withdrawal from Peshawar and a Barakzai receiving it as a tributary of Lahore, the Chief of Kabul sending his son to ask pardon. Oh! What say you to this after all that has been urged [by Wade and Macnaghten] of Dost Mohammad Khan putting forth extravagant pretensions! Ranjit will accede to the plan, I am certain. I have, on behalf of the Government, agreed to stand as mediator between the parties, and Dost Mohammad has cut asunder all his connections with Persia and Russia and refused to receive the ambassadors from the Shah now at Kandahar.[60]

Burnes was not to know that, even as he wrote, several hundred miles to the south his mission was being sabotaged so as to make it almost impossible for him to reconcile the two warring partners. Still less was he to suspect as yet that the man who would effectively kill off his Embassy was the very same man who had despatched it, the new Governor General, Lord Auckland.

Around the same time as Burnes was writing in triumph from Istalif, and Vitkevitch and his Cossacks were cantering across the Afghan frontier south of Herat, a red cordon of ceremonial cavalry was lining up between the gates of Government House in Calcutta and the lapping waters of the riverfront ghats on the Hoogly.

Lord Auckland was about to leave Calcutta for his first trip outside Bengal. His imperial progress was planned to allow him to inspect the famine-struck plains of Hindustan, from the Kingdom of Avadh to the British-controlled North West Provinces. He was to travel first by a 'flat', a special viceregal barge pulled by a steamer, then at Benares to continue by road, in carriage and palanquin, and on elephant-back, up through the Punjab to the newly established hill station of Simla.

George Eden, Lord Auckland, was a clever and capable but somewhat complacent and detached Whig nobleman. He was of a delicate build, with a thin, boyish face, narrow lips and long, elegant fingers. A confirmed bachelor of fifty-one, but looking a decade younger, he made little secret of how bored he was with the bourgeois civil servants and obsequious Indian rajahs he was forced to mix with. Too diffident for politics in England, and a bad public speaker, he took the job of governor general as it was the best administrative job available for him, though he knew or cared little for Indian history or civilisation, and on arrival did remarkably little to illuminate himself about either.

Reliance on his staff had made him popular at the Admiralty, his previous job, but it proved disastrous when he moved to India. Here, sent to rule a world of which he was completely ignorant, he quickly fell into the hands of a group of bright but inexperienced and hawkishly Russophobic advisers led by William Macnaghten – the man who had covertly supported Shah Shuja's 1834 expedition – and his two private secretaries Henry Torrens and John Colvin. As one of the members of his council, Thoby Prinsep, put it, 'Auckland was a good man of business, an assiduous reader of all papers, and very correct and careful in any of the drafts he approved and passed; but he was much wanting in promptness of decision, and had an overweening dread of responsibility which caused the instructions he gave to be so unsatisfactory that his agents had generally to decide for themselves what to do in any difficulty.' Prinsep added, 'He was considered to have yielded too much to his Private Secretary, John Colvin, who on occasions when the Governor General called his Members of Council into private consultation with himself, would take the whole initiative of discussion while his Lordship sat listening with his hands at the back of his head; and having thus so much thrown upon him he got the nickname of Lord Colvin among the younger Civil Servants.'[61]

On his leisurely journey 'Up the Country', Auckland was to be accompanied by his two waspish but adoring unmarried sisters, Emily and Fanny Eden, his pompous and pernickety Political Secretary, Macnaghten, and various other viceregal officials, attachés, wives and babies as well as Macnaghten's notoriously bossy and demanding wife, Frances, and her entourage of a Persian cat, a rosy parakeet and five attending ayahs.

The morning of departure dawned clear and fresh, and the Macnaghtens' friend Thomas Babington Macaulay got up early to come to see them off. Emily Eden noted in her diary – later to become one of the most celebrated travel accounts of the period – that the staff had laid on a 'very pretty procession . . . two lines of troops led from the door of Government House to the River'.[62] Only later that evening did she note the startling extent of the Governor General's entourage: 'We went down on our elephants to see the advance guard of the camp pass over,' she wrote in a letter to her other sister in England. 'It was a red Eastern sky, the beach of the river was deep sand, and the river was covered with low flat boats. Along the bank were tents, camel-trunks, the fires by which the natives were cooking, and in the boats and waiting for them were 850 camels, 140 elephants, several hundred horses, the Body Guard, the regiment that escorts us, and the camp follow-ers. They are about 12,000 in all.'[63]

The scale of the Governor General's establishment underlined the oddness of Auckland's position. As his nephew and Military Secretary, Captain William Osborne, remarked, 'Of all human conditions, perhaps the most brilliant and at the same time the most anomalous, is that of the Governor General of British India. A private English gentleman, and the servant of a joint stock company [that is, the East India Company], during the brief period of his government is the deputed sovereign of the greatest empire in the world; the ruler of a hundred million men. There is nothing in history analogous to this position . . .'[64]

Yet, for all the attendants, the spectacle, the beauty of the Ganges and the greenly tropical monsoon-washed Bengali countryside, it was not a very happy party. Emily had not wanted to come to India in the first place, feeling 'a savage despair' when she first set sail. She disliked her new home from the day her ship turned into the Hoogly from the Bay of Bengal and found itself becalmed. 'I thought we should be coming home with our fortunes made by this time,' she wrote in irritation even before sighting Calcutta, 'but . . . at last, by dint of very great patience and very little wind, we have arrived . . . We are surrounded by boats manned by black people, who, by some strange inadvertence, have utterly forgotten to put on any clothes whatsoever.'[65] Later she was horrified by the elaborate ceremonial and stiff formality of Government House, as well as by the number of attendants who followed her around, writing home about 'the utter bewilderment in which I live . . . [it feels like] a constant theatrical representation going on around me . . .'[66]

Fanny, meanwhile, was already irritated by the Macnaghtens. In her diaries she depicts her brother's bespectacled Political Secretary as a grating pedant, even by the standards of the British government in India. When Auckland asked the boat to stop at Buxar so he could jump ashore and take a look at the site of the battleground where the British had first defeated the Mughals, Macnaghten was reported by Emily to be 'half mad . . . actually dancing about the deck with rage' at the breach of protocol.[67] 'Mr Torrens and Mr Macnaghten nearly fainted away on their deck because George ventured ashore after a bit of impromptu amusement,' agreed Fanny. The following day in Ghazipur the Edens 'gave another shock to Mr Macnaghten's constitution by going ashore without a single aide-de-camp or any other badge of a Governor General about George. When we get to camp we mean to reform and behave better, though as it is, it seems to me that we are always going to be sailing about in a cloud of peacock's feathers, silver sticks and golden umbrellas.'[68] Emily conceded that Macnaghten, for all his pomposity, had a reputation as a clever aide, and refers to him as '*our* Lord Palmerston, a dry sensible man, who wears an enormous pair of blue spectacles . . . he speaks Persian rather more fluently than English; Arabic better than Persian; but for familiar conversation rather prefers Sanscrit'.[69]

Mrs Macnaghten meanwhile was busy trying to stop her Persian cat eating her parakeet – one ayah was employed solely to guard and feed the bird – while worrying about being robbed by foot-pads creeping aboard the boat during the night: 'the previous year they broke into Mrs Macnaghten's tent and stole all her clothes so that Macnaghten had to sew her up in a blanket and drive her to Benares for fresh things'.[70]

Fanny found the Macnaghtens especially insufferable during the formal durbars that were held intermittently along the banks of the Ganges:

> The only amusing part of this business is the extreme gravity and emphasis with which Macnaghten translates every word that passes, never moving a muscle of his very unmovable countenance. 'He says, my Lord, that your Lordship is his father and mother, his uncle and aunt, that you make his night and day, that he has no pillar to lean upon but you.' All the attar of rose ceremonies he conducts with the same solemnity. I never saw a man more born for this business.

Later, during a visit to an elderly rani, 'Macnaghten, in the most solemn manner, returned this answer: "The Rani, my Lord, says it is utterly impossible for her to express how inconceivably well she feels that your Lordship has entered her dwelling . . . she was feeling as a locust in the presence of an elephant . . ." Mrs Macnaghten, who does not in fact understand the language much, acts as interpreter [for Fanny and me]. O my dear, such a woman, she will be the death of me.'[71]

From the very beginning, Lord Auckland, his sisters and their guests suffered from an enervating imperial ennui born of a

patronising – if mildly amused – disdain for the distant colony
through which they were forced to pass. On the second day of
the trip, Emily remarked that their guests 'were all, like our noble
selves, so much bored that they went to bed at eight'. As for her
brother, 'G is already bored to death,' she wrote a week into the
trip. 'Disgust is turning him yellow.'[72] 'We get on much slower
than we expected,' agreed Fanny, 'and George, cut off from his
papers and office-boxes and his "members in council" has a sort-
of deposed Governor General feel which makes him
impatient . . . He is growing rabid with his tent life, and scolds
me every morning because the view is not prettier.'[73] Only the
prospect of some parties upstream cheered the sisters: 'invitations
to a ball have reached us from Brigadier Richards . . . I fancy this
is the beginning of a constant course of dancing we are going
through till we reach the Himalayas . . . I think it would be fitting
if George would learn to walk through the minuet de la cour.
Emily or I could take it in turns to follow with the reigning brigadier of the station . . .' Meanwhile, there was trouble to deal with
in the provision department: 'General Casement and Mr
Macnaghten came on board this evening. We think there is something wrong with the apple jelly they have had at breakfast. A
mysterious allusion was made to it by Mr Macnaghten, which
was hastily nipped in the bud by General Casement.'[74]

It was in the midst of such cares that Lord Auckland was forced to
turn his attention to matters Afghan.

Afghanistan was a country Auckland knew or cared about even
less than he knew or cared about India, and from the beginning he
showed a marked antipathy to its most powerful ruler, Dost
Mohammad Khan. Dost Mohammad, by contrast, had gone out of
his way to court the new Governor General. As soon as he heard
of Auckland's arrival he had sent a letter telling him that 'the field
of my hopes which before had been chilled by the cold blast of

wintry times, has by the happy timing of your Lordship's arrival become the envy of the garden of paradise . . . I hope that your lordship will consider me and my country as your own.'[75] He then came to the point, asking Auckland to intervene on his behalf with Ranjit Singh and to use his influence to retrieve Peshawar for Afghanistan, so bringing peace to the region.

Lord Auckland was however quickly persuaded by Macnaghten to oppose any sort of pact with the Amir. 'Nothing but the offence and jealousy of other powers would be the result of an ostensible alliance with Dost Mohammad,' Auckland wrote in a memorandum soon after receiving the Amir's letter.[76] He did not write back for several months, and then his reply was friendly but hardly encouraging. He said he was pleased that Dost Mohammad wanted good relations with the Company, but regretted he could not intervene in the dispute between him and Ranjit Singh, and hoped that the two would sort out their differences. He also said he wished for 'Afghanistan to be a flourishing and united nation' benefiting from 'a more extended commerce'. He then concluded, in words that his actions would soon disprove, 'My friend, you are aware that it is not the practice of the British government to interfere in the affairs of other independent nations, and indeed it does not immediately occur to me how the interference of my government could be exercised for your benefit.'[77]

The root of the impasse lay in departmental politics and jealousies. All Auckland's information on Afghanistan came through Macnaghten and Wade, neither of whom had ever visited the country. The advice of Burnes, whose despatches from Kabul gave a more accurate assessment of the real balance of power in the country, could only reach the Governor General heavily filtered through the double distorting lens of Macnaghten's summaries and Wade's patronising commentaries, both of which tended to undermine all that Burnes was suggesting. Dost Mohammad's 'tenure of power has actually been very insecure', wrote Wade witheringly in a covering letter appended to one of Burnes's first despatches from Kabul in which he had praised the strength and stability of the Amir's rule. 'Popular commotions have occasionally broken out which he has found it difficult to suppress . . . My own sources of information lead me to believe that the authority of the Ameer is by no means popular with his subjects . . . The greater part of his Troops are disaffected & insubordinate and, though well equipped with arms, are generally very deficient in the qualities which constitute good soldiers.'[78]

In this way, Wade and Macnaghten kept assuring Lord Auckland that Burnes was simply wrong in his assessment of Dost Mohammad: the Amir, they insisted, was an unpopular and illegitimate usurper, with only the most tenuous hold on power. Contrary to what was said in Burnes's despatches, they maintained that Dost Mohammad was actually the least powerful of the various rulers of Afghanistan, with less influence than his half-brothers in Kandahar or 'the most respectable ruler' Kamran Shah Sadozai, Shah Shuja's ineffectual cousin in Herat. In reality, none of this had ever been the case and was now less true than ever – Dost Mohammad had established his suzerainty from the Hindu Kush to the Khyber, had got his half-brothers in Kandahar to accept his leadership after saving them from Shah Shuja's siege and, to crown it all, had now been declared the Amir and the leader of the Afghan jihad. Burnes was right: Dost Mohammad was the dominant power in Afghanistan and potentially a powerful pro-British ally to the Company's north, if only Calcutta could change its course and embrace him.

Burnes was on the spot, and clearly in a better position to weigh up the relative strengths of the different powers than any other British official, but Macnaghten had never liked the ambitious young Scot whom he believed to be naive, inexperienced and over-promoted. He therefore encouraged Auckland to trust instead the veteran spymaster of Ludhiana. 'Where there is a difference of opinion between them,' wrote Macnaghten to Auckland, 'I should be disposed to concur with Capt Wade, whose arguments and conclusions rest on recorded facts, whereas those of Capt Burnes seem for the most part to be formed from the opinion of others, or from the impression made on his mind by circumstances which have come within his observation but which may in reality not be so unusual as to justify inferences which he has derived from them.'[79]

Meanwhile, Wade, as before, was encouraging Auckland to bring Shah Shuja back into play. 'Less violence would be done to the prejudices of the people, and to the safety and well being of our relations with other powers, by facilitating the restoration of Shah Shuja than by forcing the Afghans to submit to the sovereignty of the Ameer,' he advised. 'After the late encounter with the Sikhs, the disputes of parties at Kabul ran so high that had the Shah appeared in the country, he might, I am informed, have become master of Kabul and Kandahar in two months.'[80]

In addition to these distortions, neither Wade nor Macnaghten seemed to have briefed Lord Auckland on how recently Ranjit Singh had occupied Peshawar, or how central its importance was to the Afghans, who still regarded it as their second capital. As a result, Auckland took the factually inaccurate position that the town was unequivocally a Sikh possession, and that Dost Mohammad was being unreasonable and aggressive in wanting it back. For this reason he continued to discourage Burnes from altering in any way the status quo.

Auckland also began to take on Wade's view that it was in the interests of the Sikhs, and therefore of the British, for Afghanistan to remain fragmented, rather than to help Dost Mohammad consolidate his rule and accept him as an ally. 'A very powerful Mahomedan State on our Frontier might prove to be a source of constant excitement or even serious danger,' he told London. 'Chiefships, balancing each other, and disposed by their position and circumstances to court our friendship, are surely far more safe and preferable neighbours.' Nor did Lord Auckland believe, contrary to all the evidence, that Herat was in danger from the Persians or that the Barakzais were likely to make an alliance with the Shah of Persia. 'These Afghans have no natural sympathy with the Persian Government and will retain no close connection with it if left secure in their remaining possessions,' he wrote.[81] It was a comprehensive misreading of the situation: by underrating Dost Mohammad's power, Auckland and his hawkish advisers misunderstood both the reality of his steadily growing hold on Afghanistan south of the Hindu Kush and the balance of power between the Sikhs and the Afghans. They also underestimated how cleverly Count Simonitch, exceeding his instructions from Moscow, was manoeuvring to bring the entire region within the Russian-led, anti-British coalition that the Russian envoy hoped would soon encompass not just Persia and Afghanistan but also Bukhara and Khiva.[82] These errors would lead in turn to more serious misjudgements.

To add to Burnes's problems, Lord Auckland felt no sense of urgency. He was much more concerned with the trials of his vice-regal camping trip and the famine in Hindustan, whose victims were now floating down the Ganges past his boat every morning. Only Burnes in Kabul was beginning to see that Auckland was in danger of sleep-walking into a major diplomatic disaster. He was acutely aware that if the British did not act quickly to secure the friendship of the Barakzais, then the Persians and the Russians would do so instead. In that case Afghanistan would be lost to British influence and handed over on a plate to its rivals. He therefore received with growing incredulity the Governor General's successive letters ordering him not to promise anything to Dost Mohammad and refusing to act as intermediary on Peshawar.

In an effort to change Auckland's mind, Burnes sent a long report on 'the Political State of Kabul' to Calcutta towards the end of November. In this he argued persuasively for the consolidation and extension of Dost Mohammad's power as the surest means of shutting out the Russians from Afghanistan. Again he emphasised that it was not necessary to choose between the Company's long-standing alliance with Ranjit Singh and the one he proposed with Dost Mohammad: with a little imagination and quick action on Peshawar it would be possible for the British to befriend both parties. He could not have known that in Calcutta around the same time Macnaghten was writing to Wade and strongly backing the latter's opposing policy: one that advocated an exclusively pro-Sikh position, leaving Ranjit Singh in possession of Peshawar, and planning north of it a divided Afghanistan, with a weak Shah Shuja reinstalled in Kabul in the Amir's place.[83]

Moreover, Auckland was now becoming increasingly entrenched in his oddly rabid hostility towards Dost Mohammad who, he wrote to London, 'ought to be satisfied that he is allowed to remain at peace and is saved from actual invasion. But he is reckless and intriguing, and will be difficult to keep quiet . . . It is a fine imbroglio of diplomacy and intrigue . . .'[84]

As the Afghan winter brought in the first snows in early December, some bad news arrived in Kabul, which made Burnes more anxious still.

The Persian army was now reported to be moving in its full strength to invest the mighty Timurid walls of Herat. This had been expected: the Persians had long-standing claims to western Afghanistan, had occupied Herat in 1805 and had plotted another attack in 1832. This latest Persian attack had been several years in the planning, and did not in fact need any Russian pressure or encouragement. But the size of the army sent to take the capital of western Afghanistan – over 30,000 strong – and the presence in the Persian camp of a large number of Russian military advisers, mercenaries and deserters working for the Persians still came as a shock to Burnes.

One reason why Burnes knew so much about what was happening in Herat was that a young British officer and player of the Great Game happened to be in the city at that moment, disguised first as a Muslim horse trader then as a sayyid [divine]. Lieutenant Eldred Pottinger was the nephew of the spymaster of Bhuj, and Burnes's former boss, Sir Henry Pottinger. His presence in Herat was probably more than fortuitous, and provided a stream of much-needed information for the British during the siege. In British accounts, 'the Hero of Herat' (as Pottinger was dubbed in Maud Diver's jingoistic Victorian novel) is usually credited with steeling the resolve of the Heratis to defend their city and more or less keeping the Persians at bay single-handedly. This is not, however, a version of events which is supported by any of the many Persian or Afghan chronicles. Here the siege is seen as a titanic struggle between the two peoples, one Sunni, one Shia; and the fortitude of the Herati defenders, subject to the most horrific privations, was depicted as an epic of Afghan bravery and resistance. Indeed two of the most important Afghan historians living at the time devote almost as many pages to the siege of Herat as they do to the British invasion which followed it. Both were seen as equally formidable threats to the independence of Khurasan.

According to these Afghan sources, as soon as news arrived that the Persian army was heading towards Herat, Shah Kamran ordered grain and forage to be brought in, and the fruit trees in the gardens outside the walls to be cut down. Levies were summoned from the Sadozais' Uzbek and Hazara tribal allies, and the city's massive earthen walls were repaired and reinforced. So were those of the Ikhtiyar al-Din, the vast citadel of Herat that occupied an area that was equivalent to two-thirds of the city itself.[85] By 13 November, the advance guard of the Persian army had arrived outside the border fortress of Ghorian. The Herati chronicler Riyazi in the 'Ayn al-Waqayi recorded how the Persians captured the mighty castle in less than twelve hours with the aid of their British-trained artillery: 'so many cannon were fired at the Qala'-i Ghorian that three of its sides completely collapsed'. In this way, wrote Fayz Mohammad, 'the touch-paper of war was lit and preparations were made in the army of Iran for a major assault on Herat'.

A few days later, the first divisions of the enormous 30,000-strong Persian army marched along the valley of the Hari Rud towards the walls of Herat, easily driving off the squadrons of cavalry sent out against them. 'A skirmish was fought and many men died,' wrote Fayz Mohammad, 'but when the vast numbers of the main Iranian army hove into view, the Heratis were unable to continue the fight and retired into the city . . . Seeing no hope of resisting the Iranians in the open field, Kamran devoted all his efforts to defence works. The Shah's forces, like the waves of the sea, lapped against and enveloped the four sides of the city.'[86]

On the morning of Tuesday 19 December, two days after this

unwelcome news had reached Kabul, Burnes and his assistants were looking out of their Bala Hisar residence, waiting for a messenger to bring in the latest despatches from India. Burnes had been hoping that Auckland would change his position on Afghanistan after he had read his long report, and he desperately wanted to be able to give Dost Mohammad some good news. The influence of his enemy, the newly arrived Persian envoy, was growing daily stronger since the news of the encirclement of Herat, and he knew he badly needed to boost British popularity and prestige. Only an undertaking by the British to mediate the return of Peshawar was likely to do that.

Instead, a message came from Dost Mohammad asking to see him. In formal durbar, the Amir gave him the worst news imaginable: a Russian agent, sent by the Tsar to open diplomatic relations with Afghanistan, had just arrived in Ghazni and was expected in Kabul within the week. The agent's name, Burnes learned, was Lieutenant Ivan Vitkevitch.[87]

'We are in a mess here,' wrote Burnes to his brother-in-law, Major Holland, shortly afterwards. 'Herat is besieged and may fall, and the Emperor of Russia has sent an Envoy to Kabul to offer Dost Mohammad Khan money to fight Ranjit Singh!! I could not believe my eyes or ears, but Captain Vitkevitch, for that is the agent's name, arrived here with a blazing letter, three feet long, and sent immediately to pay his respects to myself. I of course received him and asked him to dinner.'[88]

The dinner between the two great rivals – the first such meeting in the history of the Great Game – took place on Christmas Day 1837. The two agents turned ambassadors got on well and found much in common, though we know frustratingly little of the detail of what they wore or ate or spoke about, or how much Vitkevitch revealed of his troubled background. Burnes merely records that the Pole was:

a gentlemanly, agreeable man, about thirty years of age, and spoke French, Persian and Turkish fluently, and wore a uniform of an officer of Cossacks which was a novelty in Kabul. He had been to Bokhara, and we had therefore a common subject to converse upon, without touching on politics. I found him intelligent and well informed on the subject of Northern Asia. He very frankly said it was not the custom of Russia to publish to the world the result of its researches in foreign countries, as was the case in France or England.

Burnes then added: 'I never again saw Mr Vitkevitch, although we exchanged sundry messages of "high consideration", for I regret to say I found it impossible to follow the dictates of my personal feelings of friendship towards him, as the public service required the strictest watch.'[89] This was no understatement: Burnes had already begun to intercept his dining companion's letters back to Teheran and St Petersburg, and vice versa.

In the weeks that followed, Burnes put a brave face on his increasingly uncomfortable situation. He was well aware how close he was to having his mission unravel, especially as there was still no sign that Lord Auckland had grasped the seriousness of what was happening in Kabul, or that he had taken in how close he was to losing both Persia and Afghanistan to the Russians. As it was, Burnes was having difficulty in keeping up with the presents that Vitkevitch was showering on the Amir: 'Captain Vitkevitch informs the Ameer that the value of the rarities sent to him by the Emperor amounts to 60,000 Rs,' he wrote on 18 February 1838. 'The opposing faction have not failed to contrast this with the few trifles which I have presented to him, and to adduce it as a proof of the indifference of a nation famed, and above all in Afghanistan, for its liberality . . . Under all these circumstances it may be naturally expected how anxiously I look for the commands of Government to guide me.'[90]

But with letters taking three to four weeks to reach India, and Calcutta failing to reply to his missives, and with the news from Herat becoming ever grimmer, Burnes decided to seize the initiative. That same month he promised Rs 300,000 to the Kandahar

Barakzais to help them defend themselves against the Persians if Herat fell and the Shah's army marched into Afghanistan.

He also decided to breach protocol and, bypassing Wade and Macnaghten, wrote an impassioned letter directly to Lord Auckland pleading with him to understand what was at stake and telling him clearly that a deal was still easily within his grasp, one which without effort or expense could achieve all British aims, and which at one stroke would head off the designs of Russia and Persia. He blamed the Sikhs for their aggression in taking Peshawar and building the fort at Jamrud, and reiterated how much Dost Mohammad still longed for a British alliance, despite suffering multiple rebuffs. He also pointed to the Sikh seizure of Peshawar as the reason why Dost Mohammad had been forced to look elsewhere for allies. Most of all, he emphasised the immediate danger represented by Vitkevitch, and stressed that the unresolved state of Peshawar 'while it hangs over, brings intrigues to our door, and if not checked may shortly bring enemies instead of messengers'. He concluded that 'much more vigorous proceedings than the Government might wish or contemplate are necessary to counteract Russian and Persian intrigue in this quarter, than have been hitherto exhibited. It is indubitably true that we have an old and faithful ally in Maharaja Ranjit Singh but such an alliance will not keep these powers at a distance, or secure to us what is the end of all alliances, peace and prosperity in our country and on our frontiers.'[91]

Burnes did still have one trump card: Dost Mohammad had made it very clear that he would have preferred an alliance with Britain to one with Russia, and had gone out of his way to demonstrate this. Vitkevitch was being kept virtually under house arrest in the haveli of Dost Mohammad's Minister, Mirza Sami Khan, a much less grand lodging than that given to Burnes, and had still not yet been received by Dost Mohammad; all communication between the two still took place through the Minister. Vitkevitch was also kept under constant surveillance, and wrote to Simonitch that Dost Mohammad was behaving 'very coldly to me'. As Burnes wrote to a confidant,

The Amir came over to me sharp, and offered to do as I liked – kick him [Vitkevitch] out or anything. I said not to do any such thing, but to give me the letters the agent has brought, all of which he surrendered sharp. I sent an express at once to my Lord Auckland with a confidential letter to the Governor General himself bidding him to look at what his predecessors had brought upon him, and telling him that after this, I know not what might happen, and it was now a neck and neck course between the Russian and us.[92]

The astonishingly undiplomatic orders that Burnes eventually received from Lord Auckland in answer to his repeated pleas were written on 21 January and arrived in Kabul exactly a month later. At one stroke Auckland undid all of Burnes's work and hopes. In the covering letter, Macnaghten dismissed his anxieties, explaining that he did not believe that Herat was in any real danger from either Persia or Russia, and that, bafflingly, 'His Lordship attaches little immediate importance to the mission of the Russian agent.' He was also told that he had no authority to offer any money or an alliance to the Kandahar Barakzais, and his initiative to try and buy their support was disowned and countermanded.

In particular Auckland continued to show a complete lack of interest in the idea of an alliance with Kabul, as he made very clear in the letter he addressed to Dost Mohammad. Auckland told the Amir he must forget Peshawar and 'relinquish the idea of govern-ing that territory'. He must also 'desist from all intercourse with Persia, Russia and Turkistan'. All the British would do in return, 'which is all I think that can in justice be granted', would be to persuade the Sikhs not to invade Kabul and so save the Amir 'from a ruinous war'. Ranjit Singh for his part 'through the generosity of his nature has acceded to my wish for the cessation of strife, if you should behave in a less mistaken manner to him. It becomes you earnestly to think on the mode in which you may effect reconcili-ation with that powerful prince, to whom my nation is united by the direct bonds of friendship, and to abandon hopes which cannot be realised.'

Finally there was a warning: if Dost Mohammad should continue to consort with Persia and Russia, the Indian government would support Sikh expansion into Afghanistan and 'Captain Burnes . . . will retire from Kabul where his further stay cannot be advantageous'.[93] There was not the slightest hint of compromise to meet Dost Mohammad's entirely legitimate anxieties and aspirations. Instead Auckland had actually hardened his position against the Amir, who was now being told he could not correspond with Persia and Russia except with British permission, that he must surrender all claims to Peshawar and Kashmir and, most unpalatable of all, beg Ranjit Singh for forgiveness.

It was difficult to see how Burnes could salvage anything from this suicidal set of instructions, especially when Russia was prepared to offer so much: not only friendship and protection, but two million roubles in hard cash to raise an army against the Sikhs – everything Dost Mohammad wished for. In an apparent fit of absent-mindedness, Auckland had in a single stroke handed over to the Russians a great swathe of territory from Persia through Central Asia to Afghanistan – something Vitkevitch realised as soon as he came to hear of the letters' contents. 'The British', he wrote, 'are losing for a long time any hope of re-establishing their influence in this area.'[94]

Burnes was devastated. All his views had been ignored, and all his work destroyed. As Masson later reported, for a while Burnes 'abandoned himself to despair. He bound his head with wet towels and handkerchiefs, and took to the smelling bottle. It was humiliating to witness such an exhibition, and the ridicule to which it gave rise.'[95] But over the weeks which followed Burnes recovered and fought a brave rearguard action, pushing at the boundaries of his instructions to see if there was a loophole with which he could keep Vitkevitch at bay.

He worked with the more pro-British nobles to see if Dost Mohammad could be persuaded to accept merely a promise of British protection. He also seems to have thrown money around, in an attempt to gather support, something that is mentioned in all the Afghan sources. 'Burnes started meeting secretly with the great nobles and chiefs of Kabul,' remembered Mirza 'Ata, 'all of whom had one great love, a love of money and the clink-clink of gold coins – so he soon perverted them and bought their support with bribes.'[96] But the conclusion was still inevitable. Intermediaries, including Nawab Jabar Khan, Dost Mohammad's Anglophile brother who had sent his son to be educated by Wade in Ludhiana, attempted to bring the two sides together, but the insulting and patronising tone of Auckland's letter, as much as its actual contents, had made a compromise impossible. As the Amir observed, the one thing he could never abandon was his *izzat* – his honour. 'It was Auckland who had abandoned the Afghans,' he told Burnes, 'and not he who had deserted the British.'[97]

Events at Herat strengthened Russia's hand, even as the British were undermining their own position. The siege of the town was tightening its grip. Eldred Pottinger wrote to Burnes reporting that:

> The country is utterly and totally ruined for the next year, there is neither seed to sow or cattle to sow it if there were. I really fear that the unfortunate Shiahs [within the town] will be sold into slavery in a mass . . . In the city there is great distress as few calculated the siege lasting more than a few weeks . . . Sheep have become almost unknown in the city and the supply of water being stopped, the public reservoirs and cisterns have become nearly too foul to use.[98]

Moreover, Count Simonitch had now arrived in the Shah's camp and was playing an increasingly active role in directing the siege operations. As MacNeill reported, 'The evidence of concert between Persia and Russia, for purposes injurious to British interests, is unequivocal and the magnitude of the evil with which we are threatened is, in my estimation, immense.'[99]

In a sign of the way the winds were blowing, on 20 March Dost Mohammad's Minister, Mirza Sami Khan, invited Vitkevitch as his guest of honour to celebrate Nauroz, the Persian New Year. Burnes was pointedly not invited until the party had already begun and then refused to go; but he asked his Indian assistant, Mohan Lal Kashmiri, to go in his stead.

Mohan Lal had now been Burnes's invaluable munshi (or secretary) and adviser for seven years, since the two had first met in
Delhi in 1831, when Mohan Lal was only twenty. His father had
been a munshi on the Elphinstone mission twenty years earlier,
and on his return had chosen to make Mohan Lal one of the first
boys in north India to be educated according to the English
curriculum in the new Delhi College. Clever, ambitious and
fluent in English, Urdu, Kashmiri and Persian, Mohan Lal had
accompanied Burnes on his trip to Bukhara, after which he
worked for some time as an 'intelligencer' for Wade in Kandahar,
corresponding frequently with Masson, his counterpart in Kabul.
Burnes relied on and trusted Mohan Lal completely, not least as
he had shown himself willing to pay the ultimate price for his
loyalty and friendship to Burnes: in December 1834 his own
Kashmiri Pundit community had formally outcaste him as a result
of his open expressions of religious scepticism and frequent caste
violations. He was now forbidden 'to drink out of the same cup
with them . . . They discarded me from their society . . . so I am
now left without friends and without a place to reside in my
native city of Delhi.'[100]

Mohan Lal later wrote in English a remarkable book of his travels and a scholarly two-volume biography of Dost Mohammad. In
the latter he gives his own account of his meeting with Vitkevitch
at Mirza Sami Khan's Nauroz party. On arrival he found that the
Minister and Vitkevitch:

> sat a little higher than the others, on the 'nihali' [dais], and the
> former, to show his civility . . . placed me by the side of the
> Russian envoy. While the music was going on, the minister was
> conversing on politics, sometimes with M Vitkevitch and some-
> times with me, inquiring about the number of English troops
> stationed at Ludhiana, the distance between the divisions at
> Kurnal, Meerut and Kanpur; and whether the Mahomedans were
> the major part of the army or the Rajputs; and what were the
> feelings of the natives of India towards the decayed household of
> the great Timur [the Mughals]. Understanding the manner in

which the inquiries were made, I came to the conclusion that every question was put to me according to arrangements made previous to my joining the party ...

The conversation then moved on to the flourishing trade between Russia and Kashmir, which Vitkevitch said he hoped to help the Afghans reclaim from the Sikhs. Vitkevitch claimed he was 'authorized to say to Maharajah Ranjit Singh that if that chieftain did not act in a friendly manner to the Afghans, Russia will send money easily ... to Kabul to raise troops to fight the Sikhs for the recovery of his country ...' He added that 'fifty thousand men of Russian regiments were in readiness to land at Astarabad ... who would then march towards the Punjab; that such movements would rouse all the discontented chiefs of India to rebel; and that the English, who are not soldiers, but merely mercantile adventurers, would not dare to assist Ranjit Singh, knowing that the Afghans are succoured by the warlike nation of Russia'.[101]

Vitkevitch was on the verge of winning the contest for Kabul. On 23 March, Dost Mohammad went to see Burnes for the last time. He had lost hope, he told his friend. 'I wish no countenance but that of the English,' said the Amir, 'but you refuse all pledges and promises, and mean to do nothing for me.'[102] Meanwhile, certainty was growing that the Persians and their Russian allies would soon take Herat and march on into Afghanistan; in response the ethnically Persian Qizilbash Shias of Kabul processed triumphantly through the Kabul streets with a new confidence. 'An event', wrote Burnes, 'unknown to the eldest inhabitants, and which a short time since would have caused a religious tumult.'[103]

Finally, a month later, on 21 April, Dost Mohammad summoned Vitkevitch and had him escorted with a troop of his own cavalry through the streets of Kabul. He received him in the Bala Hisar with full honours. In formal durbar, while Burnes sat alone in his rooms on the other side of the palace complex, Vitkevitch told the Amir that Russia did not recognise the Sikh conquests in Afghan territory and that in the eyes of Russia Peshawar, Multan and Kashmir all still belonged de jure to Afghanistan. He said Russia wished to see a strong and united Afghanistan which Russia would protect diplomatically as an unbreakable barrier against British expansion into Central Asia. He admitted that Russia was too far away to despatch troops at short notice, but promised to give Dost Mohammad money to fight Ranjit Singh, and told him, according to Mohan Lal, much that was 'anything but complimentary about the British'. He also promised that Russia would protect Afghan traders in Russia. In response, Dost Mohammad offered to send his son, Mohammad Azam Khan, to meet Count Simonitch at the Persian camp outside Herat and to confirm in person the Amir's intentions of opening permanent friendly relations with Russia.

For Burnes it was all over: Vitkevitch had won. There was now no longer any point in the Scotsman prolonging his stay in Kabul. On 25 April he and Dost Mohammad exchanged sad notes of farewell to each other. The following morning Burnes, Mohan Lal and Masson rode out of Kabul. Masson wrote that the sudden departure of the British 'partook a little of the nature of flight', and Maulana Hamid Kashmiri in his *Akbarnama* actually has Burnes fleeing for his life:

> His cheeks became yellow like saffron
> Inwardly he gave up his life
>
> The Amir said: 'Up and out with you! Fly from this place!
> Set out on your journey with all haste
>
> Lest in your greed for money and treasure
> You get from me suffering and punishment
>
> I fear that contrary to what one may think
> Great affliction will fall upon you
>
> I see it as very far from my principles
> To kill someone after showing favour
>
> I do not wish to lose my honour for gold
> By handing a guest of mine over to another'

Sikandar [Burnes,] who had no hope of life
Could not have imagined such a deliverance

He set out from Kabul upon the road to Hind
Like a sheep running away from a roaring lion

Every step of the way he would look back
Lest the falcon should seize him again[104]

In reality, it was not quite as bad as Afghan hindsight remembered it. The British were escorted out of town by the Amir's youngest son, Ghulam Haidar Khan, and as a last gesture of personal friendship Dost Mohammad sent Mirza Sami Khan with three stallions which reached the party at the village of Butkhak, twelve miles from Kabul. Burnes and Dost Mohammad would not meet again for another three years, and when they did so it would be under very different circumstances.

Before Jalalabad, Burnes boarded a raft which would take him down the Kabul River to Peshawar. By this stage Vitkevitch was already well on his way to Kandahar. This was the next stage in his mission where he was to negotiate a treaty with Dost Mohammad's Barakzai half-brothers who, having been rejected by Auckland, had now also agreed to join Dost Mohammad, the Persians and the Russians in the siege of Herat.

Herat was Vitkevitch's final Afghan destination. He was accompanied there by Barakzai princes from both Kabul and Kandahar, and was received in triumph in the Persian camp by Count Simonitch on 9 June. Vitkevitch had achieved more for Russia than any of his superiors had even dared hope. His triumph over Burnes and the British was total.[105] Shortly afterwards the Shah of Persia invested him with Order of the Lion and the Sun.[106]

Burnes by then was back in Peshawar, awaiting further instructions. Meanwhile he vented his frustration to Major Holland. 'The game is up,' he wrote. 'The Russians gave me the coup de grâce and I could hold no longer at Kabul so I have fallen back on Peshawar. Our government would do nothing and the Russian legation came down with the most direct offers of assistance and money, and as I had no power to counter act him by a similar offer I was obliged of course to give in.'[107]

His public letters to Simla were, however, more diplomatic. Burnes realised that ironically the failure of his mission meant that the need for an Afghan expert was now greater than ever. He knew that war with Kabul was now possible, perhaps even probable, and despite all his misgivings about the direction British policy was taking, he was sufficiently ambitious still to want to be at the helm of whatever it was that Lord Auckland now had planned.

Even before Burnes reached Peshawar, the wheels of the Company machine were cranking into action to demonise Dost Mohammad and punish him for what Auckland interpreted as his defiance. 'Dost Mahomed Khan has shewn himself to be so disaffected and ambitious that with him we could form no satisfactory connection,' Auckland reported, most inaccurately, to London.[108] If the Amir would not co-operate with Auckland's wishes, then he clearly needed to be replaced by Shah Shuja, who Auckland believed would be more reasonable and do as he was told. But exactly how this was to happen, and in what form, Auckland had yet to decide.

Auckland and his sisters had now arrived in Simla at the end of their Indian tour, and found it to be the first place in India that they really liked. 'The climate is English and exhilarating,' wrote Emily. 'It really is worth all the trouble. Such a beautiful place . . . deep valleys on the drawing room side to the west, and the snowy range on the dining room side, where my room also is.'[109]

The existence of Simla was itself a comment on the astonishing complacency of the British in India at this period: for seven months of the year, the Company ruled one-fifth of mankind from a Himalayan village overlooking the borders of Tibet and connected to the outside world by a road little better than a goat path. Here, over the two decades since the area had been 'discovered' by Captain Charles Kennedy in 1822, the Company had begun building on a long, narrow, high-altitude Himalayan saddle a small fantasy England, a sort of early Victorian theme park of their own imagination, complete with Gothic churches, half-timbered cottages and Scots baronial mansions. Simla was all about homesickness and the nostalgia of the exile for home: it was an escape from the heat, but it was also, tacitly, an escape from India. As one disapproving official later put it, 'Sedition, unrest and even murderous riots may have been going on elsewhere in India, but in Simla the burning questions are polo finals, racing and the all-absorbing cricket tournaments.'

Here, finally, Lord Auckland brought himself to focus on events in Afghanistan in a way he had not previously. For the past two months he had seriously underestimated the threat posed by Vitkevitch and the Russians; now, reading the latest intelligence from Peshawar and Herat, he was belatedly plunged into a state of high anxiety and began to swing instead towards a major overreaction. One reason for this was the arrival of a series of apocalyptic despatches from MacNeill outside Herat, who was just about to withdraw from the Persian camp in protest at the way the Shah was ignoring and humiliating him and his staff, much to the delight of Count Simonitch. Before breaking diplomatic relations with Persia, and retreating to Ottoman Turkey, he fired off a call to arms. 'Lord Auckland should now take a decided course,' he advised, 'and declare that he who is not with us is against us, and shall be treated accordingly. If the Shah should take Herat we shall not have a moment to lose, and the stake will in my opinion be the highest we have yet played for ... We must secure Afghanistan.'[110]

As a preliminary measure, Auckland ordered a naval flotilla to sail from Bombay to the Persian Gulf and occupy the island of Kharg off the coast southwest of Shiraz as a warning to the Shah. Then, while Emily organised amateur theatricals on one side of the drawing room – 'six plays for the benefit of the starving people at Agra' – on the other George turned his attentions to changing the ruler of Afghanistan.

His first hope was that Shah Shuja or Ranjit Singh would dispose of the troublesome Amir, so saving him the trouble of doing so. As Emily noted in a letter to her sister in England, 'Whenever we want to frighten our neighbours into good conduct, we have one sure resource. We always have a large assortment of Pretenders in store. They have had their eyes put out, or their children are in hostage, or the usurper is their own brother, or they labour under sundry disadvantages of that sort. But still there they are, to the good. We have a Shah Shuja all ready to *lacher* himself at Dost Mohammed if he does not behave himself, and Ranjit is ready to join us in any enterprise of that sort . . .'[111] In a letter to his masters in London Auckland put it more formally, writing that he was exploring the idea of 'granting our aid, in concert with Ranjit Singh, to enable Shah Shuja ul-Mulk to re-establish his sovereignty in the Eastern division of Afghanistan, under engagements which shall conciliate the feelings of the Sikh ruler and bind the restored monarch to the support of our interests'.[112]

So it was, on 10 May, that Macnaghten was despatched down to Lahore along with Lord Auckland's nephew and Military Secretary, Captain William Osborne, to sound out the Lion of the Punjab. Having learned the lesson not to economise on gifts, they carried a generous set of presents – 'A sword, the workmanship of which is reported to have been of high merit, two horses agreeable to ride and of a much esteemed English breed and to these I have added two Pistols specially selected by the Commander-In-Chief and understood by him to be admired by Your Highness.' For good measure, Auckland also sent several camel loads of alcohol for the bibulous Maharajah, who according to Emily 'had requested George to send him samples of all the wines he had, which he did, but took the precaution of adding some whisky and cherry brandy, knowing what Ranjit Singh's drinking habits are. The whisky he highly approved of, and he told Macnaghten that he could not understand why the Governor General gives himself the trouble of drinking seven or eight glasses of wine when one glass of whisky would do the same work.'[113] Some of the crates were robbed en route by Punjabi footpads, along with an assortment of items from the bag of the assistant doctor accompanying the party: 'The stomach pump was cut to pieces by the thieves – such a blessing for Ranjit's courtiers,' wrote Emily when she heard of the robbery. 'He tries all medical experiments on the people about him. How they would have been pumped!'[114]

On 20 May, Macnaghten crossed into Sikh territory. Ranjit Singh, as was his custom, received the Embassy at his favourite summer palace at Adinagar. Osborne described how Ranjit received them:

> cross-legged in a golden chair, dressed in simple white, wearing no ornaments but a single string of enormous pearls round the waist, and the celebrated Koh-i-Noor, on his arm – the jewel rivalled, if not surpassed, in brilliancy by the glance of fire which every now and then shot from his single eye as it wandered restlessly round the circle. On Ranjit sitting, his chiefs all squatted around his chair, with the exception of Dheean Singh [his eldest son] who remained standing behind his master. Though far removed from being handsome himself, Ranjit appears to take pride in being surrounded by good-looking people, and I believe few, if any other courts either in Europe or the East, could shew such a fine looking set of men as the principal Sikh sardars.

As was also Ranjit Singh's custom, he then proceeded to interrogate his visitors: 'Our time was principally occupied in answering Ranjit's innumerable questions,' wrote Osborne,

> but without the slightest chance of satisfying his curiosity. It is hardly possible to give an idea of the ceaseless rapidity with which his questions flow, or the infinite variety they embrace: 'Do you drink wine?' 'How much?' 'Did you taste the wine which I sent you yesterday?' 'How much of it did you drink?' 'What artillery have you brought with you?' 'Have they got any shells?' 'How many?' 'Do you like riding on horseback?' 'What country horses do you prefer?' 'Are you in the army?' 'What do you like best, cavalry or infantry?' 'Does Lord Auckland drink wine?' 'How many glasses?' 'Does he drink it in the morning?' 'What is the strength of the

Company's army?' 'Are they well disciplined?' After passing upwards of an hour in conversation, Ranjit Singh rose, and, according to custom, having half smothered us with sandal-wood oil, embraced and allowed us to depart . . .[115]

One subject that fascinated the Maharajah in particular was the private life of the British, and as the negotiations got under way the handsome Captain Osborne had to go through intermittent grillings on his sexual preferences:

'Did you see my Cachmerian girls?' 'How did you like them?' 'Are they handsomer than the women of Hindostan?' 'Are they as handsome as English women?' 'Which of them did you admire most?' I replied that I admired them all very much, and named the two I thought handsomest. He said, 'Yes, they are pretty; but I have got some more that are handsomer, and I will send them this evening, and you had better keep the ones you like best.' I expressed my gratitude for such unbounded liberality; his answer was: 'I have plenty more.' He then led the subject to horses.[116]

Nor did Lord Auckland's proclivities escape Ranjit's scrutiny:
'Is Lord Auckland married?'
'No.'
'What! Has he no wives at all?'
'None.'
'Why doesn't he marry?'
'I don't know.'
'Why don't you marry?'
'I can't afford it.'
'Why not? Are English wives very expensive?'
'Yes; very.'
'I wanted one myself some time ago and wrote to the government about it, but they did not send me one.'[117]

Such banter was partly a smokescreen to disarm the British and disguise from them the acute political intelligence Ranjit Singh always displayed in negotiation. This was something Osborne was perceptive enough to recognise: 'Ill-looking as he undoubtedly is, the countenance of Runjeet Singh cannot fail to strike everyone as that of a very extraordinary man . . . so much intelligence, and the restless wandering of his single fiery eye excites so much interest, that you are forced to confess that there is no common degree of intellect and acuteness developed in his countenance, however odd his first appearance may be.'

Ranjit Singh's negotiating skills soon made themselves apparent and before long the wily Sikh leader was running rings around the uptight Macnaghten. One colleague wrote that 'poor Macnaghten should never have left the secretary's office. He is ignorant of men, even to simplicity, and utterly incapable of forming and guiding administrative measures. The judicial line would probably have best suited him, and even then only in the court of appeal, judging only written evidence.'[118]

Auckland had not initially thought of committing British troops to the project of unseating Dost Mohammad: the fighting he hoped was all to be done by Ranjit Singh and Shah Shuja, and, as on Shuja's last expedition, the British would provide only money, equipment and moral and diplomatic support. But given the trouble he was already having holding his new conquests in Peshawar, Ranjit had little enthusiasm for Lord Auckland's invitation to invade Kabul. Keen to get rid of Dost Mohammad, and seeing opportunities to increase his wealth in the process, but unwilling to get entangled in Afghanistan, he played his hand with consummate skill.

In early June, Macnaghten reported discouragingly that Ranjit 'would not dream of marching a force to Kabul'.[119] Slowly, however, the Maharajah made it clear that he might be open to persuasion, hinting that if he were given the financial centre of Shikarpur, the Khyber and Jalalabad he might be prepared to join a punitive expedition to chastise and unseat his old Afghan enemy. Macnaghten refused, and for a fortnight the talks were deadlocked. In reality, Ranjit was probably only using these demands as a bargaining counter. For when he gave in and said that he now only wanted to be confirmed for perpetuity in possession of Peshawar and Kashmir, to receive £20,000 from the British as well as a large cash payment from the Amirs of Sindh, and for Shah Shuja in addition to pay him an annual tribute including '55 high bred horses of approved colour and pleasant paces', camel loads of 'musk melons of sweet and delicate flavour' and '101 Persian carpets', Macnaghten accepted the offer immediately, and promised to press Shuja and the amirs to deliver. As the negotiations inched forward, what had originally been planned as a Sikh expedition in British interests slowly began to transform itself over the course of several weeks into a British expedition to further Sikh interests.

Only at the end of June, after the negotiations had moved to Lahore, and Burnes and Masson had joined the British delegation from Peshawar, was it confirmed that Ranjit would be prepared to join a largely British force, which together would place Shuja on the throne.

'Your Highness some time ago [in 1834] formed a treaty with Shah Shuja ul-Mulk,' said Macnaghten. 'Do you think it would still be for your benefit that the treaty should stand good, and would it be agreeable to your wishes that the British government become party to that treaty?'

'This', replied Ranjit, 'would be adding sugar to milk.'[120]

Up to this point, no one had thought of informing Shah Shuja that he was imminently to be placed back on his old throne. Nor had Macnaghten, who had done so much to drag Shuja back out of retirement, ever actually met the man he had been championing for so long.

Shuja had now spent thirty years in exile in Ludhiana – half his life – but had never for a minute given up hope of returning home and ruling the country he regarded as given to him to rule by God. Recently, he had lost his remarkable wife, the formidable Wa'fa Begum, and, to add to the pain, fanatical Sikh *akalis* almost immediately desecrated the tomb he built for her at the dargah [shrine] of Sirhind.[121]

On 14 July 1838 Macnaghten arrived in Ludhiana, relieved finally to have reached an agreement with Ranjit Singh. Shuja had been kept briefed by his own network of spies and informers, and he was all too aware that he was being treated as a puppet – or a *mooli*, a radish, as the Afghans call it. He was especially humiliated that the action for which he had been waiting three decades had finally been arranged behind his back without even the most cursory reference to him as to how it would be executed. Nor was he at all happy about paying any tribute to Ranjit Singh, the man who had tortured his son and stolen his most valuable possession, even if in the treaty the tribute was disguised as a 'subsidy'.

In the *Jangnama*, the first Afghan epic poem to be written about the British invasion, this meeting between the British and Shah Shuja is imagined as one where Macnaghten ('His heart had no transparency – only smoke') and Burnes ('that seditious man') used their devilish charms and flattery to overcome the reservations of the Shah ('Shuja the Vile') about returning to Afghanistan as a British puppet:

They said: 'O Shah, we are your servants!
We bow down humbly before your command.'

When the Shah listened to their stories
The key to the lock of speech did appear.

He said to them: 'O my companions!
Let us start trouble within the Amir's kingdom.

I will take his country and crown
I will place a noose around his neck.

Where can he escape the flash of my sword?
He will certainly give up his throne to me.

Then the kingdom of Kabul will immediately
become the possession of you foreign *sahibs*.'

This *Lat* [Lord – that is, Macnaghten] – that wise and wily man –
When he heard these words

Became excited and said:
'O Shah! May your fortune be blessed!

If it suits you thus
Get your things in order for heading to Kabul

My only fear is this: that the people there
Might find the taste of my sherbet bitter.

But now is the time to set to the chase
When will you ever have such a hunt again?'[122]

The reality seems to have been slightly different. Macnaghten was impressed by the sexagenarian's dignity and 'much struck with the majestic appearance of the old pretender, especially with the flowing honours of a black beard descending to his waist . . . patiently awaiting the *kismet*, or fate, which was to restore him to his throne'.[123] But he was in no mood to be further delayed in implementing his plans by the sensitivities of Sadozais, who were hardly in a position to strike a bargain in the way the Sikhs had. Shuja was curtly informed of the plans, and of the boundaries of the somewhat diminished and truncated Afghanistan he was going to be allowed to rule. He received some assurances about the British not interfering with his family or in his internal affairs without his royal approval, and about being given financial assistance for reconstructing Afghanistan and consolidating his rule after the conquest. Given his long-standing problems with runaway slave girls in Ludhiana, according to his own account of the negotiations Shuja asked for a clause in the treaty guaranteeing that 'The maid-servants who run away from one land to another shall be exchanged and given back. It is impossible that a King can have honour and pride without maid-servants.'[124] He was also assured he would be allowed to enter Afghanistan at the head of his own troops, using the same route as he had done in 1833–4, and not merely be placed on the throne trailing behind British regiments. Finally, he was also promised additional funds which he could use to train up his own forces as he had done on the previous campaign.

On 16 July, only forty-eight hours after his first meeting with Macnaghten, Shuja signed what later became known as the Tripartite Alliance.

The Simla season, thought Emily Eden, had got off to a most satisfactory start. 'We give sundry dinners and occasional balls,' she wrote happily to her sister in England, 'and have hit on one popular device. Our band plays once a week on one of the hills here, and we send ices and refreshments to the listeners, and it makes a nice little reunion with very little trouble.'[125] Her only complaint was that the steamer *Semiramis* which was meant to take her letters to London had sailed off to deliver the naval squadron to Kharg in the Gulf, and her post was still stuck in Bombay: 'We try all sorts of plans; but, first, the monsoon cripples one steamer, and the next comes back with all the letters still on board that we fondly thought were in England. Then we try an Arab sailing vessel; but I always feel convinced that an Arab ship sails wildly about drinking coffee and robbing other ships . . .'[126]

Meanwhile, high on his Himalayan ledge, her brother was finalising his plans for a full-scale British invasion of Afghanistan. He was still, however, racked with indecision and rattled by the critical letters he began to receive from old India hands. Charles Metcalfe, who had been acting Governor General in the period up to Auckland's arrival, and who many believed should have had the job in preference to him, had expressed his deep forebodings about Auckland's Afghan policies. 'We have needlessly and heedlessly plunged into difficulties and embarrassments,' he wrote, 'from which we can never extricate ourselves without a disgraceful retreat. Our sole course is to resist the influence of Russia, yet our measures are almost sure to establish it . . . The only certain results, even in the event of brilliant success in the first instance, are permanent embarrassments and difficulties, political and financial . . .'

Britain's foremost Afghan expert, Mountstuart Elphinstone, was equally sceptical. 'If you send 27,000 men up the Bolan Pass to Candahar (as we hear is intended) and can feed them, I have no doubt you will take Candahar and Cabul and set up Shuja,' he observed. 'But for maintaining him in a poor, cold, strong and remote country, among a turbulent people like the Afghans, I own it seems to me hopeless. If you succeed I fear you will weaken your position against Russia. The Afghans were neutral and would have received your aid against invaders with gratitude – they will now be disaffected and glad to join any invader that will drive you out.'[127]

Nor did the Company's local allies believe that the invasion would be at all easy. The Nawab of Bahawalpur, through whose territory the British troops would have to pass, expressed his deep anxieties, which were echoed by all his courtiers. As the British official sent to negotiate with him reported,

> They dwelt on the difficulties of the country, our ignorance of the road and the passes and what appeared to the British Government an easy enterprise, but which to their profound apprehension they said was beset with no ordinary difficulties. With respect to the Shah's fortune, their opinion was most unfavourable. With regard to Dost Muhammad Khan, the general opinion here seems to be that he will never be brought to sue for terms until everyone has deserted him and every door has been closed for him.[128]

When Burnes was summoned to give advice at the Governor General's Residence in Simla on 20 July, he was warned not to muddle Auckland or attempt to change his mind. According to Masson, 'when he arrived, Torrens and Colvin came running to him and prayed him to say nothing to unsettle his Lordship; that they had all the trouble in the world to get him into the business and that even now he would be glad of any pretext to retire from it'.[129] As late as August, Auckland was still oscillating between plans and examining all possible options.

Nonetheless, the pieces were now slowly falling into place, with the invasion plans driven forward relentlessly by Macnaghten and the hawks in the administration despite Auckland's anxieties and reservations.[130] Every day, the scale of the invasion and the degree of British participation gradually increased until a full 20,000 British troops were committed: the largest military operation undertaken by Company forces for two decades, and the first really major conflict since the defeat of Tipu Sultan forty years earlier.

On 10 September, the order for mobilisation was given: Lord Auckland formally asked his Commander-in-Chief to assemble an army for the march into Afghanistan. Across India, sleepy cantonments slowly began to stir into action. In Landour, Captain William Dennie scribbled in his diary: 'We are on the verge of something momentous. They say we are going to fight the Russians or Persians.'[131] The same day, Burnes was sent off to prepare a way for the army through Sindh. 'Twenty thousand men are now under orders to do what a word might have done earlier,' he wrote to Holland, 'and two millions of money must be sunk in to do what I offered to do for two lakhs!'[132] But he was not unhappy: his orders had come in an envelope inscribed 'Sir Alexander Burnes'. At first he thought it was an error; only on opening it did he discover he had been given a knighthood. His mission may have failed, and Macnaghten may have been given the political command of the expedition he had hoped for; but his willingness publicly to support a policy he had always opposed, against a ruler he had liked and whose hospitality he had enjoyed, had been noted by his superiors. So had the fact that he had kept quiet when his despatches from Kabul were edited in such a way that made it appear he had always supported the restoration of Shuja before being published as a Parliamentary Blue Book.* For all the frustrations of the last few

---

* The selective editing of Burnes's despatches for the Blue Book in order to win Parliamentary approval for the war later became a major scandal, the 'dodgy dossier' of its day. See G. R. Alder, 'The Garbled Blue Books of 1839', *Historical Journal*, vol. XV, no. 2 (1972), pp. 229–59.

months, he had kept his mouth shut and been rewarded for his silence. His star was still in the ascendant.

On 1 October, Auckland issued what came to be known as the Simla Manifesto, formally declaring war and announcing Britain's intention to restore Shah Shuja to the Afghan throne by force. 'Poor, dear peaceful George has gone to war,' wrote Emily to her uncle, the former Governor General Lord Minto, who had first despatched Elphinstone to Afghanistan. 'Rather an inconsistency in his character.'[133]

Auckland's manifesto was more or less pure propaganda – a deliberate and blatant inversion of the available intelligence – and was recognised at once by the Indian press as 'a most disingenuous distortion of the truth'.[134] One Indian civil servant pointed out that the manifesto used 'the words "justice" and "necessity", and the terms "frontier", "security of the possessions of the British Crown" and "national defence" in a manner for which fortunately no precedent existed in the English language'.[135]

In the manifesto Auckland accused Dost Mohammad of 'urging the most unreasonable pretensions, avowing schemes of aggrandizement and ambition injurious to the security and peace of the frontiers of India' in pursuit of which 'he openly threatened . . . to call in every foreign aid which he could command', and of having 'made a sudden and unprovoked attack on our ancient ally, Maharajah Ranjit Singh'. He was also accused of giving 'undisguised support to Persian designs . . . of extending Persian influence and authority to the banks of, and even beyond, the Indus'. The war, he claimed, was intended 'to set up a permanent barrier against schemes of aggression on our North West Frontier'. This was of course a complete travesty of the facts, but it was too late now for Auckland to change his position even if he wanted to; thanks to the hawks he had surrounded himself with, events had now acquired their own momentum.

The popularity of Shah Shuja, the document went on, was 'proved to his Lordship by the strong and unanimous testimony of the best authorities'. For this reason the British were to assist the legitimate ruler of Kabul 'to enter Afghanistan, surrounded by his own troops'. This was also far from truth. After thirty years in comfortable retirement, the Shah, now in his late fifties, was about to lead his fourth expedition to reclaim his throne. This time, however, it would be at the head of a British Indian army, for British interests, and closely supervised by British officials.

It was not by any means the homecoming he had spent decades dreaming of. But for Shuja, at this advanced stage in his life, it hardly mattered. As far as he and his courtiers were concerned this was not an unjustified, unprovoked and unnecessary British invasion of an independent country. This was the return of a king.

4

The Mouth of Hell

Shah Shuja's fourth attempt at recapturing his throne – what would be remembered by British historians as the opening of the First Afghan War – got off to as chaotic a start as any of its predecessors.

The plan was, in principle, a good one. First there would be a ceremonial send-off at Ferozepur in the Punjab, attended by all three of the signatories of the Tripartite Alliance. Then, as with Shah Shuja's previous expedition five years earlier, Afghanistan would be invaded by two routes. One army, led by the Shah's eldest son, the Crown Prince Timur, assisted by Colonel Wade and a regiment of Punjabi Muslims supplied by Ranjit Singh, would move north through Peshawar up the Khyber Pass and hence towards Jalalabad. The other – much the larger of the two – would nominally be led by Shah Shuja under the watch of Macnaghten, assisted by troops from the Company's Bengal and Bombay armies. This force would loop south around the Punjab, as Ranjit had now banned British soldiers from marching through his lands. It would then head through the Bolan Pass to attack southern Afghanistan below Kandahar before heading on to Ghazni. Both forces would converge on Kabul to restore Shuja to his throne in the Bala Hisar. At the same time, Shah Shuja's many eager allies in Afghanistan would rise up in his favour, expelling the 'usurper', Dost Mohammad. 'Almost every chief of note should begin to tender his homage to Shah Shooja before he has entered the country,' Wade assured Auckland.[1] But, from the beginning, almost nothing went as planned.

The Simla Manifesto had been explicit that the Shah would return home 'surrounded by his own troops'. The problem was that Shuja at this point had no troops; indeed his only followers were his usual handful of mutilated household servants. So the first thing was to recruit a new army, the Shah Shuja Contingent. Would-be recruits began arriving in Ludhiana throughout the summer of 1838. A few of them were Indian Afghans of Rohilla descent whose ancestors had migrated to the Ganges basin in the eighteenth century, but most of them were local 'Hindoos . . . camp followers from the Company's military stations'. The recruits were so wild and raw, however, and so undisciplined, that it was soon decided that this 'rabble' of 'ragamuffins' were not fit to be put on public parade at the grand ceremonial launch of the expedition at Ferozepur.[2] There was also the issue, as one British officer put it in a letter, that it was clearly a 'fiction [that] the "Shah [was] entering his dominions surrounded by his own troops" when the fact is too notorious to escape detection and exposure, that he has not a single subject or Affghan amongst them'.[3]

So in late August, ahead of the rest of the army, Shuja and his Contingent were quietly marched off out of sight through Ferozepur to Shikarpur, there to begin intensive drilling. Before long, the Contingent had deviated from its intended route, run amok and looted Larkana.[4*] This revived memories across Sindh of the violence and 'great excesses' committed by Shuja's troops on their last promenade up the Indus, rendering the Amirs of Sindh even less willing to help than they had been. To make

---

* Home of the future Bhutto dynasty.

matters worse, the first Bombay troops arriving by sea at Karachi mistook an artillery salute from the lighthouse for an attack, and reduced to rubble the principal coastal fort of their supposed Sindhi allies.

This was not the only problem. Ominously, the revival of Shuja's fortunes seemed already to have gone to his head. Before long the Shah – whose good nature had clearly been corroded and hardened by his long run of ill-fortune – had fallen out with all his British officers, alienating them with his haughtiness and his insistence on making them remain standing in his presence.[5] He also alarmed his British minders by referring to the Afghans, his future subjects, as 'a pack of dogs, one and all'.[6] 'We must try', noted an exasperated Macnaghten, 'and bring him gradually round to entertain a more favourable view of his subjects.' Meanwhile, Prince Timur had failed to set off from Ludhiana at all – 'The Prince is such a fool that he has not budged an inch,' wrote his father in one of a series of apoplectic notes sent to Wade from Shikarpur.[7]

So it was that the ceremonial send-off for Lord Auckland's war took place without the presence of the man in whose name the expedition was being sent, or indeed of any of his dynasty. In lieu of the Sadozais, the Edens set off from Simla in the middle of a monsoon downpour. Emily was not at all happy to leave her beloved Himalayan retreat. 'It is impossible to describe the squalid misery of a really wet day in camp,' she complained soon after hitting the plains.

> The servants looked soaked and wretched, their cooking pots not come from the last camp, and the tents were leaking in all directions: wherever there is a seam there is a stream . . . The camels are slipping down and dying, the hackeries sticking in the rivers. And one's personal comfort! Little ditches running around each tent, with a *slosh* of mud that one invariably slips into . . . I go under an umbrella from my tent to George's, and we are carried in palanquins to the dining tent on one side, where the dinner arrives in a palanquin on the other . . .[8]

On the way they stopped in Ludhiana to meet Prince Timur, who had still failed to leave for Peshawar. 'We had an enormous dinner at Major Wade's yesterday,' wrote Fanny, 'and the city was illuminated after the native way in long lines of little lamps . . . Shuja's son came to it, and having no elephant as well as no kingdom, they sent my own particular one to fetch him.'[9] Meanwhile, Macnaghten had lost his plates and cutlery in the chaos of the move, a cause of much anxiety for one so obsessed with the finer points of etiquette. 'Great terror reigns in the camp on account of that,' reported Fanny. 'What will Shah Soojah who eats with his fingers think of Macnaghten if he does the same?'[10]

The Governor General's damp encampment was only one part of a much larger monsoon mobilisation of troops across the entire north and west of India.

In the Bombay rain, regiments were streaming from their barracks down to the beaches to be loaded on board troop transports and ferried across the stormy sea to Karachi, Thatta and other landing points around the mouth of the Indus. In the cantonments below the Delhi Ridge, the riders of the new experimental camel batteries – mobile camel-borne mortar and Congreve rocket systems – were struggling to harness their obstinate camels. In Hansi, Colonel James Skinner was attempting to call up his reserves from the flooded pasturelands of Haryana while orderlies polished the rusting helmets and chain mail of the troopers. In Meerut and Roorkee the cantonments were awash with mud as the Company sepoys packed up their kit and began the march up the Grand Trunk Road towards Karnal and Ferozepur, their bedraggled wives and mistresses streaming through the quagmire behind them.

Leading one regiment through the monsoon mud was William Nott, a plainspoken yeoman farmer's son from the Welsh borders who had arrived in India forty years earlier, fresh from Caernarvon, and had slowly worked his way up to become one of the most senior Company generals in India. He and his sepoys – 'the fine manly soldiers' to whom he was fiercely attached – struggled up the road to Karnal from their base in Delhi where he had just buried his 'beloved and lamented Letitia', his wife of twenty years. 'The road was covered with troops, guns, gun-carriages, ammunition and treasure,' he wrote. 'It required patience in man and horse to wend their way between these hackeries and implements of war.'

If younger soldiers were hoping the war might bring them glory, plunder and promotion, Nott merely hoped it would help him forget. 'Passed a miserable day in thinking of times gone by, and those I dearly love,' he wrote to his daughters the night of his arrival in Karnal. He added: 'strange to say, my mind was in some degree relieved' by the distraction of a war to be fought; only for him to be horrified by this thought and scribble in the margin: 'When will man cease to destroy his fellow man?'[11]

It came as little comfort that he had finally been promoted to major-general, a distinction that might have come much earlier had he not been so quick to speak truth to power. For Nott was not a man to keep quiet in the face of a perceived slight, and he was already gearing up to take offence at the precedence that was being given to newly arrived commanders of the British army. These men, though usually richer and better connected than their counterparts in the army of the Company, did not speak Hindustani or have any experience of fighting in India or with sepoys. He had heard rumours that the Commander-in-Chief, Sir John Keane, was to take several sepoy regiments away from the control of the Company's generals, and he was already squaring up for a fight about the issue. 'The truth is he is a Queen's officer, and I am a Company's,' he explained to his daughters. 'I am decidedly of the opinion that a Queen's officer, be he ever so talented, is totally unfit to command the Company's Army.'

To everyone's relief, the rains had stopped by the time the now grandly named Army of the Indus began to assemble on the plains of Ferozepur in early November. To try and cheer up the camp, Ranjit Singh sent 600 of his gardeners to arrange impromptu gardens of potted roses around the officer's tents. But a more serious obstacle to the war now confronted the gathering armies. To Auckland's embarrassment, in the midst of all the preparations for the invasion, news came that the Persians, alarmed by the British naval occupation of the island of Kharg, had unexpectedly abandoned the siege of Herat and withdrawn to Mashhad. Soon afterwards came confirmation that Count Nesselrode in St Petersburg had also given way, this time to diplomatic pressure from the Foreign Secretary, Lord Palmerston, in London. Count Simonitch, the author of the entire Russian diplomatic campaign to outflank the British in Persia and Afghanistan, was to be sacrificed – removed from his job as ambassador to the Persian court on the grounds that he had exceeded his instructions.* Vitkevitch was also to be recalled to St Petersburg from Kandahar, where he had been busy reinforcing the Russian–Barakzai alliance by promising Dost Mohammad's half-brothers Russian military support in the event of a British invasion.

Both of Auckland's original *casus belli* were now removed: Russia and Persia were publicly backing down. If there had ever been any real threat to British India it was now over. This would have been an ideal moment to reopen negotiations with Dost Mohammad and achieve all the aims of the war without a shot being fired. There was, after all, still a major famine in north India which had left tens and quite possibly hundreds of thousands starving to death – there are no official statistics – and whose horrors had been greatly exacerbated by the British encourage-ment of poppy growing over food crops. There was also the increasing likelihood that Auckland would choose to fight a second illegal war of aggression on a different front – this time with China – in order to protect the Company's profitable trade in the opium grown from those very poppy fields which had once produced such rich harvests of grain. Then there were all the

---

* This at least is what Nesselrode told Palmerston. In reality it is clear that Simonitch was ready to rejoin the beautiful Princess Orbeliani and their ten children in Tiflis. Since the murder of Griboyedov, a previous Russian envoy to Iran, the Teheran Legation had been considered unsafe for spouses or children, much like the British and American embassies in modern Pakistan. After Simonitch's return to Georgia, his successor Duhamel initially took a similar diplomatic line to Simonitch.

uncertainties of Shuja's reception in Afghanistan, and the unanswered question as to whether it would be possible to maintain him on his throne once re-established. But, astonishingly, no one at Ferozepur seemed to have given a moment's thought to the option of reopening negotiations.

Instead, now that there was no danger of encountering the Cossacks or the Imperial Persian army in Afghanistan, an announcement was made that several regiments would be withdrawn from the Army of the Indus and a significantly smaller force would be sent into action. Auckland nonetheless made a strong public declaration that he intended to 'prosecute with vigour' the existing plan. 'Of the justice of the course about to be pursued, there cannot exist a reasonable doubt,' he asserted. 'We owe it to our own safety to assist the lawful sovereign of Afghanistan in the recovery of his throne.' The Tripartite Treaty would be honoured, and Shah Shuja would still be 'replaced on the throne of his ancestors'.

On 27 November, the Sikh and Company armies finally converged on the plains of Ferozepur. Lord Auckland's normally cynical ADC, William Osborne, was astonished at the sheer scale of the gathering. 'In the *Champs de Drap d'Or* of Ferozepore, Lord Auckland appeared with the imposing magnificence of an Indian potentate,' he recorded, 'and though the uniforms of the vice-regal staff were eclipsed by the jewels and chain armour of the Sikh sardars, the Governor General with his immense retinue and escort of 15,000 men was quite a match for the monarch of the Punjab.'[12] Emily, unusually, was also completely won over by the spectacle. 'Behind us there was a large amphitheatre of elephants belonging to our own camp,' she wrote. Facing them were 'thousands of Runjeet's followers, all dressed in yellow or red satin, with quantities of their led horses trapped in gold and silver tissues, and all of them sparkling with jewels. I really never saw so dazzling a sight. Three or four Sikhs would look like Astley's [Circus] broke loose, but this immense body of them saves their splendour from being melodramatic.'[13]

Others, however, were less impressed. Sir John Kaye, the

future historian of the Afghan War, was a young officer in the artillery at the time, and remembered the first meeting of Lord Auckland and Ranjit Singh as being 'amidst a scene of indescribable uproar and confusion'. Indeed such was the chaos amid the collision of two lines of trumpeting elephants and the subsequent rush to follow the two leaders into the Durbar Tent that many of the Sikh troopers suspected there might be a British plot to do away with their beloved leader 'and began to blow their matches [that is, prime their matchlocks] and grasp their weapons with an air of mingled distrust and ferocity'.[14] Lord Auckland, excited by the hubbub, then 'made a most splashy answer' to Ranjit's speech of welcome 'about their united armies conquering the world. You will be much taken aback, I guess,' wrote Fanny to her sister in England, 'when they march hand in hand and take Motcombe.'[15]

That night Fanny sat next to Ranjit Singh at the banquet and was intrigued and charmed by her dining companion. He had turned up in a pair of plain white kurta pyjamas, with one single jewel, the Koh-i-Nur, glinting on his arm – not perhaps the most tactful ornament for the occasion, given how he had come to own it. The Sikh monarch spent much of the evening trying to get Fanny to drink his home brew. 'The composition he calls wine is like burning fire, and much stronger than brandy,' she noted afterwards.

At first he was content to let George and Sir W Cotton swallow it. Then he began plying me with gold cupfuls. I got on very well for some time, pretending to drink it and pass it to his cupbearer. But he grew suspicious, put it up to his one eye, looked well into the cup, shook his head and gave it back to me again. The next time he put his finger into the cup to see how much had gone. I made Major Wade explain that ladies do not drink so much in England, upon which he waited until George's head was turned away and passed a cup to me under his arm, thinking George was a horrid tyrant who prevented me.[16]

George meanwhile was fending off persistent questions from his new colleague about why he did not possess even one wife. 'George said that only one was allowed in England,' reported Emily, 'and if she turned out a bad one, he could not easily get rid of her. Runjeet said that was a bad custom; that the Sikhs were allowed twenty-five wives, and they did not dare to be bad, because he could beat them if they were. G replied that was an excellent custom, and he would try to introduce it when he got home.'

The next morning the Sikhs showed off their drill and impressed their allies with their discipline and particularly with the accuracy of their artillery. Then it was the turn of the British. 'The consummate skill with which the British chief attacked an imaginary enemy', wrote Kaye, 'was equalled by the gallantry with which he defeated it. He fought indeed a great battle on the plain, and only wanted another army in his front to render his victory a complete one.'[17]

Two days later, after further displays of military and equestrian prowess, many more speeches and several more banquets, the troops finally set off to war. Led forward by lancers with scarlet cloaks and plumed shakos, the columns of cavalry and infantry regiments headed downstream towards Shikarpur, where they were supposed to liaise with the Bombay army and Shah Shuja's Contingent. The Sikhs meanwhile headed north towards Lahore.

The Army of the Indus now consisted of around a thousand Europeans and 14,000 East India Company sepoys – excluding the 6,000 irregulars hired by Shuja – accompanied by no fewer than 38,000 Indian camp followers. The baggage for these men was to be carried to war on over 30,000 camels, which had been collected for the purpose from as far away as Bikaner, Jaisalmer and the Company's camel stud at Hisar in Haryana.

No one was planning to travel light. One brigadier claimed that he needed fifty camels to carry his kit, while General Cotton took

260 for his. Three hundred camels were earmarked to carry the military wine cellar. Even junior officers travelled with as many as forty servants – ranging from cooks and sweepers to bearers and water carriers.[18] According to Major-General Nott, who had had to work his way up throughout his career without the benefit of connections, patronage or money and who looked with a jaundiced eye on the rich young officers of the Queen's Regiments, it was already clear that the army was not enforcing proper military austerity. Many of the junior officers were treating the war as if it were as light-hearted as a hunting trip – indeed one regiment had actually brought its own foxhounds along with it to the front. 'Many young officers would as soon have thought of leaving behind their swords and double-barrelled pistols as march without their dressing cases, their perfumes, Windsor soap and eau de Cologne,' he wrote. 'One regiment has two camels carrying the best Manila cigars, while other camels carry jams, pickles, cheroots, potted fish, hermetically sealed meats, plate, glass, crockery, wax-candles, table linen, &c.'[19]

It did not bode well for the effectiveness of the fighting force. Nor did the lack of communication between the different wings of the Army of the Indus. By now Alexander Burnes was supposed to have completed the negotiations with the Amirs of Sindh and to have received the necessary permissions for the army to pass up the river and through their lands. But the attack on Karachi coupled with the looting of Larkana instead nearly sparked a second war between the British and the Sindhis even before the planned war against Dost Mohammad had got under way. The Sindhis, quite understandably, did not want a British army tramping across their territory, so dragged their feet over permissions and refused to find camels or transport animals for the Bombay troops who were still stranded where they had landed on the shores of the malarial Indus Delta.

Things got worse before they got better. The following week Macnaghten was hurrying to catch up with the army after accompanying the Sikh leader to Lahore, where Fanny and Emily had visited 'a select number of Mrs Runjeets'. On his way he heard to his horror that General Sir Willoughby Cotton, without any

orders, had left the agreed place of rendezvous and was fast heading south, away from Afghanistan, and about to launch an illegal
attack on the Sindhi capital of Hyderabad. 'Cotton is clearly going
on a wild goose chase,' wrote Macnaghten to Simla in desperation.
'He seems to be travelling by a route which has no road. He will
soon, I fear, be in the jungle. If this goes on as it is now doing, what
is to become of our Afghan expedition?' Mirza 'Ata, who appears
to have been attached to Shah Shuja's Contingent, reported the
rumour current in the Sadozai camp that Cotton had wandered so
badly astray that it took the miraculous intervention of a saint to
get him back on track. 'The army lost its way in the scrub jungle,'
he wrote, 'and wandered confused and alarmed for one whole
watch, until a white-bearded old man like the prophet Khizr
appeared and guided them to their camping grounds by the river.'[20]

Macnaghten sent a series of increasingly desperate notes by
camel express, urging Cotton to stop. The General reluctantly
agreed to call off the attack, just hours before the assault was due to
begin, but only after the amirs had fully submitted to him. As
Mirza 'Ata put it, 'when these Mirs – an uncouth and subversive
lot, always eager to pick a fight – saw waves and waves of British
soldiers like a tidal wave, or black clouds of a gathering storm
converging both through land and water towards their land, they
were intimidated and gave in'.[21] Nevertheless the incident caused a
loss of face for the General in front of his troops, who were much
looking forward to looting the city that was supposed to contain
great riches.

The reunion of Macnaghten and one of his principal commanders was far from a happy one: 'Sir Willoughby is evidently disposed
to look upon His Majesty and myself as mere ciphers,' Macnaghten
complained to Colvin. 'Any hint from me, however quietly and
modestly given, was received with hauteur; and I was distinctly
told that I wanted to assume command of the army; that he, Sir
Willoughby, knew no superior but Sir John Keane [the Commander-
in-Chief], and that he would not be interfered with &c, &c. All this
arose out of my requesting 1000 camels for the use of the Shah and
his force.'[22] This request was an allusion to a growing crisis with

the baggage animals, which had just got much more serious after half of the Shah's camels had died from eating a poisonous Sindhi plant, a cousin of the foxglove, so leaving the Shah and his troops, like those still broiling in the humidity of the Indus Delta, 'in the lurch without the means of moving'.

Relations between Shuja and Macnaghten did not get off to a much better start. 'The Shah, I am sorry to say, talks foolishly every time I see him on the subject of how confined his territories are to be,' wrote the Envoy, 'and frequently says it would have been much better for him to have remained in Ludhiana. The next time he touches on the subject, I intend to remind him of the verse of Sa'adi, "If a King conquers seven regions he would still be hankering after another territory."' He then added, ominously for the future, 'I hardly think the 50,000 rupees per mensem will suffice for the Shah's expenses.'[23]

There were also, as ever, tensions between Macnaghten and Burnes, exacerbated by the fact that Macnaghten had been given the job Burnes wanted, while Burnes had been awarded the knighthood the profoundly snobbish Macnaghten would have loved. As a result Macnaghten routinely patronised Burnes, whom he tended to treat as an over-promoted teenager, while Burnes regarded Macnaghten as 'a man of no experience and quite unskilled with natives. He is also very hasty in taking up and throwing off plans.'[24]

It was therefore a disgruntled and disunited army that finally began to converge in one place at Shikarpur at the end of February 1839, a full three months after the scheduled start of the invasion. The only people impressed by the Army of the Indus were the Afghans who, unaware of the lack of co-ordination, discipline and foreplanning, or the squabbles between the commanders, heard only exaggerated stories about the size of the enormous force heading towards them. Dost Mohammad's Barakzai half-brothers in Kandahar felt particularly vulnerable: as in 1834, they would be the first target of any advance into Afghanistan through the Bolan, and now that Vitkevitch had been withdrawn and his promises of Russian military support disowned, they knew all too well how ill prepared they were to meet a modern, well-drilled and

well-equipped colonial army. Years later, the epic poets of the
country recalled the rumours that spread of the huge British invasion force marching towards their mountains and valleys:

On the appointed day, at the appointed hour
Replete and multitudinous, the army set out for Kabul

When the horde was set in motion from that land
The earth shook to its very foundations

Accompanying the Shah, by way of Sindh
Were one hundred and fifty thousand hand-picked soldiers

By another route, Timur, Wade and *Daktar* [Doctor] Lord
Were on their way with five thousand other soldiers

Two raging rivers from two different directions
Made their way to Kabul from Ludhiana

The ruler of every region and province
Was as obedient as wax to the Shah's seal ring

The stamping horses reached the mountains of Sindh
And entered the deserts of Hind

Sweating and over-loaded camels
Flooded through the mountainous road

The cannon and the elephants marched together
Like a mountain moving from its place with the force of the River Nile.[25]

Once a British camp and bridgehead had been established at
Shikarpur, in the absence of further camels to move the supplies

of war, ammunition and food stores began to be sent down the Indus by fleets of hastily requisitioned barges – 'flat bottomed, very shallow and broader at the stern than at the bow, which rise to a peak some fourteen feet out of the water', remembered a young infantryman, Thomas Seaton, who was given charge of one supply convoy. 'In this queer conveyance a straw hut of two rooms had been built, and as all the boats in the fleet – about fifty – were exactly like mine, they looked like a floating village.'[26] By the end of February the entire arsenal had arrived at Shikarpur; and by the end of the month the last of the Bombay troops had marched in too.

All that was now needed was a bridge. The river was more than a thousand yards wide 'with a torrent like a mill stream', and initially the engineers had only eight boats 'and nothing near us but a small village . . . First we seized, by great exertion, about 120 boats,' reported the Orcadian James Broadfoot, who was put in charge of the operation,

> then cut down lots of trees; these we made into strong beams. There was no rope, but we made 500 cables out of a peculiar kind of grass which grows 100 miles from here; the anchors were made of small trees joined and loaded with half a ton of stone. Our nails were all made on the spot. We then anchored the boats in the middle of the stream in a line across leaving twelve feet between each; strong beams were laid across the boats; and planks nailed on these for a roadway. This is the largest military bridge which has ever been made, and you may conceive what labour we had in finishing it in eleven days.[27]

On the very last day of February, the invasion force finally crossed the Indus. Mirza 'Ata was profoundly impressed: 'the astonishing technical skills of the British army would have humbled Plato and Aristotle themselves', he wrote. 'Indeed anyone who saw the structure was astonished.'[28] But the limits of British skills were made very evident in the days that followed.

It was only at this point, after crossing the Indus and entering the 150 miles of sterile salt marshes separating Shikarpur from the Bolan Pass, that it seemed to have dawned on Macnaghten and his generals exactly what they had taken on: a campaign far from their own territory, through a hostile, parched and largely unmapped landscape, with only the most tenuous communications and guarded on all sides by unwilling and unreliable allies.

Because of the delays, summer was now approaching and the desert was rapidly beginning to warm up. So the marches through the empty wilderness now had to be conducted at night. Insufficient surveying of water and supplies ahead of the intended route meant that no one knew how much food and water would be needed. Nor was anyone prepared for the heat. Seaton found it almost unbearable from the very beginning. 'We commenced our march at sunset,' he wrote two days after leaving Shikarpur. 'As soon as we entered into the Desert, a wind sprang up, gentle at first, then hot and fierce, bringing with it particles of dust, fine as the finest powder, which penetrated everything, and, with the heat still radiating from the soil, created an intolerable thirst.' He went on:

> The sepoys, each with his heavy musket, sixty rounds of ammunition, clothing, haversack with necessaries, accoutrements, and his brass pot filled with water, were heavily laden for such a march, the burden doubling the already unbearable oppression of their tight-fitting woollen uniforms. The condition of the men in such circumstances was pitiable, and every minute their sufferings increased. The water in the men's pots was soon exhausted. At midnight they began to flag, then to murmur, and shortly there was a universal cry of 'water – water!' Many were half-raving . . . One sepoy was in such a state that, when I spoke to him, he could scarcely reply; his tongue rattled in his mouth, and his whole countenance was distorted in agony.

It was not just the sepoys who were suffering:

The poor, heavily laden camp-followers, some carrying infants, were in a more pitiable state still, and the children's cries were heartrending. Strong men, exhausted from carrying loads, were scattered on the ground moaning and beating their breasts . . . One of the native officers in camp had with him a little girl, his only child, whose mother was dead. She was a pretty, lively, prattling thing of about six years of age, the delight of everybody. I used to see her every day chattering to her father, helping him light the fire, and cook their food; and her pretty little ways were a delight to witness. I saw her at ten o'clock all well, and at 3pm she was dead and laid out for burial . . . [When they reached the camp at dawn] out of thirty-two wells dug in the bottom of a ravine, only six contained water. One of them was poisoned by an animal which had fallen into it, and of the others the water was so bitter and brackish that the men said it turned their lotas [brass pots] black.[29]

Then there was the gathering crescendo of attacks by Baluchi brigands. Inadequate diplomacy, high-handedness and a lack of co-ordination with local chieftains meant that the tribes of the area looked on the vulnerable British columns as fair game. The troops were generally left well alone, but the unprotected camp followers began to be robbed and murdered on a daily basis.

Neville Chamberlain was a young cavalry officer on his first campaign, and it was a week after leaving Shikarpur, near a water-hole, that he saw his first casualty: 'One woman lay – poor creature! – on the edge of the water, with her long black hair floating in the ripples of the clear stream.' Her throat had been cut from ear to ear. Many other casualties followed. 'The unburied dead were left rotting on the road. Not a tree or a shrub or a blade of grass could be seen through the light the moon afforded us. It was all sand, not a bird exists on this plane, not even a jackal – for we frequently passed camels in a putrid state and if there had been jackals they would be sure to have found them out. Our camels had nothing to eat for several days and forty-five died in one night from hunger and the length of the marches.'[30]

It was on these hot moonlit night marches that the troops caught what was for many of them their first glimpse of the man for whom they were risking their lives. 'Shah Shuja is an old man, about sixty years of age,' wrote Chamberlain. 'His beard reaches down to his waist, and it is naturally white, but to make himself look younger he dyes it black. He goes about in a sort of tonjon [litter] carried by twelve men, and attended by horsemen, running footmen, elephants, horses and a hundred sepoys.'

Shuja put a good face on the privations of the march, but was as anxious as everyone else about the lack of planning and the growing problems with Baluchi marauders and dying baggage camels. He was also worried by the slow response from his future subjects to his letters entreating them to rally to his standard. Ever since Macnaghten had informed him of the plan to reinstate him, Shuja had been engaged in an energetic correspondence with the different tribal leaders of his old dominions, inviting them 'in accordance with their family traditions to come forward and offer allegiance, and have their ancient rights and lands confirmed in perpetuity'. But the response had been a deafening silence, except from some of the Ghilzai and the Khyber chiefs, who had replied asking him to send money.[31]

There was also an ominous silence from the leader whose territory the army was now heading into – Mehrab Khan of Qalat. In the past the Khan of Qalat had been a fairly loyal follower of Shuja and had given him shelter after he fled from his defeat in Kandahar five years earlier. But he strongly disapproved of Shuja returning to power as the puppet of the British. When Burnes was sent to try and win him over – and to try and procure 10,000 sheep for the troops who had now been put on half-rations – Mehrab Khan was frank in declaring that he regarded the policy as tactless, ill planned and strategically wrong-headed. 'The Khan, with a good deal of earnestness, enlarged upon the undertaking the British had embarked in, and declared it to be one of vast magnitude and difficult accomplishment,' reported Burnes.

He said that instead of relying on the Afghan nation, our Government had cast them aside, and inundated the country with foreign

troops; and that if it was our end to establish ourselves in
Afghanistan, and give Shah Shuja the nominal sovereignty of Kabul
and Kandahar, we were pursuing an erroneous course; that all the
Afghans were discontented with the Shah, and all Mahometans
alarmed and excited at what was passing; that we might find
ourselves awkwardly situated if we did not point out to Shah Shuja
his errors; and that the Chief of Kabul (Dost Mohammad) was a
man of ability and resource, and though we could easily replace him
by Shah Shuja even in our present mode of procedure, we could
never win over the Afghan nation.[32]

It was wise advice. As Burnes prepared to return to his army,
having failed to procure any of the supplies he needed, or even the
most tenuous support of Mehrab Khan, his host was no less presci-
ent in his final warning. 'You have brought an army into the
country,' he said. 'But how do you propose to take it out again?'[33]*

From the blinding white salt marshes of Dadur, the shimmering
heat haze of the desert flatlands slowly gave way to rolling foot-
hills. These in turn scrolled up to the silvery outlines of
dragons'-backs rising in the distance from a summer dust storm:
the great mountains of southern Afghanistan. The country
remained burned out and ash-coloured, and as arid as before, but

---

* This has become a famous line and is widely remembered even today. In 2003 it was
repeated to me by Javed Paracha, a wily Pashtun lawyer who has successfully
defended al-Qaeda suspects in the Peshawar High Court. In his fortress-like
stronghouse in Kohat, deep in the lawless tribal belt that acts as a buffer between
Pakistan and Afghanistan, Paracha had sheltered wounded Taliban fighters – and their
frost-bitten women and children – fleeing across the mountains from the American
daisy-cutters at Tora Bora, and was twice imprisoned in the notorious prison at Dera
Ismail Khan. There he was kept in solitary while being questioned – and he alleges
tortured – by CIA interrogators. Despite seeing at close quarters what modern
western weaponry was capable of, he knew his history, and never believed NATO
would succeed in its occupation of Afghanistan. When I went to interview him in
Kohat soon after the installation of President Karzai he quoted Mehrab Khan's line to
me as evidence of the futility of the attempt to install another Popalzai in power.

the gradient became increasingly steep and tortuous until the gaping funnel of the Bolan Pass suddenly opened blackly in front of the troops.

For the first four of the pass's seventy miles, the enfilade was so narrow that only a single camel could advance at a time. Now, as the feet of the cavalry clattered uneasily over the rockfalls blocking the dry riverbed, the errors of the commanders began to multiply the casualties: the stifling winter uniforms of the infantry were far too hot for a steep ascent in baking summer temperatures, and even if the vertical cliff walls initially shielded the sepoys from the direct rays of the sun, the rocks reflected the heat into their faces like an open tandoor. By day, the thermometers in the airless tents registered 119 degrees.

The roads, which had not been properly surveyed or improved by the military engineers, were almost impossible to move artillery along. At first eight horses had to be attached to each gun, as well as lines of sepoys with drag ropes. Then as it grew steeper and stonier, the guns had to be dismantled and carried through by hand: 'each gun, each tumbril, wagon &c was to be separately *handed* down by manual labour,' recorded Major William Hough. 'The ascent was so steep that some did not like to ride up it. A few camels fell and stopped the rest behind . . . The baggage was attacked with considerable spirit [by the Baluchis] at the head of the Pass; 49 camel loads of grain were carried off . . . [The rearguard] found on the road the mutilated bodies of many camp followers.'[34]

At night, the air was filled with the bedlam moans of dying camels and camp followers. Many sepoys also collapsed, sucking at the thin, dry, hot air, calling for water, only to be told that there was none. In addition to everything else, 'the stench of the dead camels rendered our lives intolerable', wrote Seaton. 'I cannot describe our sufferings from the heat, the dust, the desert wind, the myriad of flies. The whole camp smelled like a charnel house. No person could take three steps in camp, anywhere, without seeing a dead or dying man or animal.'[35]

Lack of provisions meant that the soldiers' food had now to be cut from half- to quarter-rations. The camp followers were reduced to eating 'the fried skins of sheep, the congealed blood of animals, and such roots as they could pick up in the neighbourhood'.[36] Random incidents of savage violence continued to unnerve everyone. On 3 April William Hough recorded in his diary: 'Two Serjts. Of Arty. trepanned while out shooting, and mutilated while in the act of giving a pinch of snuff.'[37] Horses too weak to continue had to be shot in large numbers, while much baggage had to be abandoned and burned to prevent it falling into the hands of the Baluch.[38]

'It was the mouth of hell,' remembered the sepoy Sita Ram.

The water in the few wells was bitter and everything, even the firewood, had to be transported by camels. The Baluchis now began to harass us by night attacks and drove off long strings of our camels. The heat was such that many died from the effects – one day thirty-five fell victim to it. At this stage the sepoys of the Company army had almost determined to return to India and there were signs of mutiny in several of the regiments. However, partly on account of the lavish promises of Shah Shuja, and partly for fear of the Baluchis who grew in number every day, the armies marched on. Many people were killed by the tribesmen. They murdered everyone whenever they had the opportunity and rolled large boulders down the mountain sides.[39]

Mirza 'Ata wrote that the entourage of Shah Shuja also felt lucky to make it through alive, as they dodged the bullets raining down on the column from Baluch snipers sheltering in the faults and crevices of the rocks above. 'The army entered the defiles of the Bolan Pass,' he wrote.

The pass was rugged and stony, ringed with mountain peaks scraping the sky: the army gazed in dismay, and the Baluch mountain tribesmen did not delay to snipe and plunder. Thousands of pack-animals, camels, horses, elephants and their loads were lost.

Crossing the pass was extremely difficult: already two months earlier the English had sent two cannons and thousands of donkey-loads of gun-powder to the pass in order to clear the route, and had had to drag them up one by one with ropes; other supplies were transported with similar difficulty, at the cost of losing a great number of camels, horses, bullocks, as well as soldiers who died from lack of water and food – not to mention the military equipment that was plundered. In that waterless hellish defile they spent three days and nights, and supplies were so scarce that half a seer of flour could not be had even for a gold rupee.[40]

For his part, Shuja wrote to Wade from the pass that he intended to punish the tribesmen of the area 'for their criminal attitude, at a proper time'. He also wrote that he was anxious that 'the usurpers' were using scholars and the 'ulema to turn the people against him 'and raise disturbances'.[41] He was right to be worried: his association with the hated Firangi infidels would remain his most vulnerable point. Religious xenophobia was always the most powerful weapon in the armoury of his Barakzai rivals.

Beyond the Bolan lay Quetta, then 'only a miserable village of some 500 houses'. After that lay a second difficult pass, the Khojak, which was shorter and less steep than the Bolan, but even more arid. 'They passed the night without water,' remembered Mirza 'Ata. 'What water they could find was filthy and putrid with the bodies of dead animals that had fallen in, and any who drank of it immediately had stomach cramps and diarrhoea. They were suffering so much from lack of water that for two days humans and animals all were shaking like willows.'[42] Food had by this stage almost completely run out among the camp followers: some 'were to be seen gouging carrion and picking grains of corn from the excrements of animals', reported one officer. 'I saw one day the body of a man who had died by the way side in the act of gnawing gristle from the carcass of a dead bullock.'[43] Before the army had fought a single Afghan it was already a wreck.

But there was relief ahead. On the far side of the Khojak, the invading army found itself in rolling pastureland where the scrub grass was dotted with clumps of dwarf oak and ilex. Occasional herds of fat-tailed sheep and shaggy brown goats belonging to

Kuchi nomads were watched over by tall men in white turbans and purple robes, huge mastiffs at their heels. It was still arid and there was still a hot wind blowing, but wherever there was water a cool shade could be found behind the screens of poplar, some of which had vines entwined up their trunks.*

The army had now crossed an invisible border out of Baluch territory and into the lands of the Pashtuns. After the furtive Baluch brigands, Nott was impressed by the fearlessness of the Achakzai tribesmen, who strode proudly and proprietorially into the British camp and began interrogating their would-be colonisers. 'They are very fine looking fellows indeed,' wrote Nott to his daughters. 'Quite the gentlemen.' When one Afghan asked him why the British had come, Nott replied that Shah Shuja had returned to claim his rightful inheritance and that Dost Mohammad had no right to the throne. The Afghan retorted: 'What right have you to Benares and Delhi? Why, the same right that our Dost Mahomed has to Kabul, and he will keep it.' After this encounter, Nott grew increasingly sceptical about the reception Shah Shuja would receive. 'I differ from the government and the others, and I really believe that the people of Afghanistan will not give up their country without fighting for it,' he observed. 'I know I would not, were I in their situation.'[44]

Other officers had similar conversations. Lieutenant Thomas Gaisford's Indian orderly was asked by one Pashtun visitor to the camp, '"Do they really call these Feringhees, 'Sahibs' [Sir]?" The inquirer asked in such a way as if he thought "Dog of an Infidel" might have been a more appropriate appellation.'[45] 'We fell in with a well-dressed Afghan horseman,' wrote George Lawrence, a bright young Ulsterman whom Macnaghten had just promoted to be his military secretary. 'He told me he had visited our camp, and seen our troopers, saying with much contempt, "You are an

---

* The land appears to be much drier today – the 'Dasht which stretches from Spin Boldak at the foot of the mountains south of Kandahar is now a virtual desert with only a little spring grazing and the dwarf oaks confined to the mountain slopes. But the descriptions left by members of the Army of the Indus reveal a greener landscape, as do the place names: Chaman, the present-day border post between Pakistan and Afghanistan in these parts, means 'meadow' in Persian.

army of tents and camels: our army is one of horses and men."
"What can induce you", he added, "to squander crores of rupees
in coming to a poor rocky country like ours, without wood or
water, and all in order to force upon us a *kumbukht* [an unlucky
rascal] as a king, who the moment you turn your backs, will be
upset by Dost Mohammad, our *own* king?"'[46] In time the horseman's predictions would prove quite correct and when the
rebellion did break out, it would be Achakzais from this region
who would be in the vanguard.

Nott may have been impressed with the Afghans, but he was less
taken with his own colleagues. It was around this time that the
Commander-in-Chief Sir John Keane arrived in the camp and
decided to promote General Willshire, a Queen's officer, over the
much more senior and experienced Nott, so giving Willshire
command of the whole of the Company's Bombay sepoy infantry.
Though he had long suspected something of the sort would happen,
and was inured by now to being passed over on account of his
humble origins and the lack of prestige of the Company regiments
relative to those of the regular army, Nott was still furious. He
immediately confronted the Commander-in-Chief in his tent. The
interview was very short, and went very badly:

'I see I am to be sacrificed because I happen to be senior to the
Queen's officers,' said Nott.

'Ill impression Sir!' replied Keane. 'You insult my authority. I
will never forgive your conduct as long as I live!'

'Your Excellency, since that is the case, I have only to wish you
a very good evening.'[47]

The fight would cost Nott dear. Although he was by far the most
popular, able and experienced general in the Army of the Indus,
from this point on he came to have a reputation for being cantankerous with his superiors, and Auckland as well as Keane now
believed him to be too difficult and undiplomatic ever to take full
command. It was an impression that would lead to a further series
of disastrous appointments, with Nott being passed over time and
time again in favour of much less able men – something which
would before long have fatal consequences for the occupation.

The Army of the Indus was now closing in on its first serious challenge: Kandahar. There were rumours that Barakzai cavalry units were in the vicinity, circling the army, ready to strike, and one night there was a false report of an imminent attack which caused the sleeping soldiers to rise in alarm from their tents and form up into defensive squares. They stayed there, muskets to the ready, until the break of dawn. Only the night-time diversion of a stream that was watering the camp, and the mysterious disappearance of Macnaghten's two elephants, indicated that there were still unseen hostile forces round about, waiting for their opportunity.

It was just as well for the invaders that the Afghans did not attack with full force for the army was more or less broken by the journey they had just undergone through the passes. 'We were at this time utterly unfit for active warfare,' noted Thomas Gaisford in his journal. 'Every man was greatly in need of repose and the horses could scarcely have crawled another march. As for the followers they were nearly starved. Our Commissariat supplies were quite exhausted. Indeed we were in a sorry plight for an advancing army.'[48]

Then around 10 a.m. on 20 April, the Army of the Indus had its first real break. A messenger arrived at the tent of Burnes's intelligence chief, Mohan Lal Kashmiri, announcing that one of Dost Mohammad's most prominent nobles was waiting beyond the camp with 200 followers, ready to offer his allegiance to Shah Shuja.[49] At last one of the letters sent by the Shah had borne fruit.[50] Mohan Lal was sent out to escort the nobleman in and to conduct him to the tent of the Shah.

Haji Khan Kakar was a slippery, ambitious and unscrupulous figure even by the standards of nineteenth-century Afghan power politics. His ancestors had long played the role of regional power-brokers and king-makers. Having risen in the service of Dost Mohammad, who had appointed him first governor of Bamiyan and then commander of his elite cavalry, he had already twice deserted the Amir, most recently at the Battle of Jamrud in 1837. But he always played his hand with skill. He managed to choose his moment of side-changing with perfect timing, rising in power and importance with each successive act of treachery. Maulana Hamid Kashmiri, in the *Akbarnama*, describes him as 'the outsider, the traitor, the master of betrayal' who would use charm and flattery to achieve his duplicitous ends, 'mixing poison in sugar'. Now, at this crucial juncture, on the excuse of leading a raid on the British camp, he took the opportunity to cross sides with all his followers, hoping to make his fortune from the rich and naive foreigners, and to take up Shuja's written offer of a senior place in his government. In the process, he began a haemorrhage of defections and broke the already wavering morale of Kandahar's defenders.

Unaware of the wrecked and starved state of the invading army, in the four days that followed an ever-growing number of Kandahari noblemen crossed the lines into Shuja's camp and offered their fealty to the returning King. For Shuja it was the miracle he had almost despaired of ever seeing take place. For Dost Mohammad's two Barakzai half-brothers in Kandahar, there was nothing to be done but watch the defections with growing despair:

> In disarray, like maddened elephants
> They were tormented by boundless rage
>
> Those two fierce lions, all they wanted
> Was to unsheathe the sword of revenge and enmity
>
> But they lacked friends and their army was too small
> After the treachery of Haji Kakar
>
> They sat locked up behind the gates of the fort
> Their hearts broken from this turn of fortune
>
> When they saw the division in their own ranks
> Particularly in the Shah's tribe of Popalzai

They did not see any other way
But to remove themselves to another country

By night they took their near and dear
And set off on the road to Iran . . .

Meanwhile the heart of Shah Shuja rejoiced to see the devilish Haji
And became free from any fear of the enemy

He showered upon Haji the Sinistrous so many riches
It seemed as if he was stoning him with gold.[51]

Five days later, on 25 April 1839, Haji Khan was on the left side of
Shah Shuja as he rode in triumph through fields of ripe wheat and
barley, and the rich belt of walled gardens and orchards that still
surround the outskirts of Kandahar. On the way, he received delegation after delegation of townspeople coming out to welcome
him. 'The poor crowded around him,' wrote Burnes, 'making
offerings of flowers and strewing the road he was to pass with
roses. Every person, high and low, strove to see how they could
most show their devotion and their delight at the return of a Sadozai
to power.'[52] Followed by Burnes and Macnaghten and only a small
escort of close supporters, Shah Shuja rode unprotected through
the open gates and streets of Kandahar, the city that had successfully defied him only five years earlier.

Kandahar's ancient fortunes had been revived by the Shah's
grandfather, Ahmad Shah Abdali. He laid out the new town
after the old one had been burned and destroyed by Nadir Shah
in 1738, and Abdali had chosen to be buried in a delicate
Mughal-inspired tomb in its heart. Shuja's first action was to
make his way to the tomb garden, take off his riding boots and
enter the dome chamber alone. Having prayed at the grave, and
asked for his grandfather's *barakat* [blessing] he then went to
the building next door. This was the shrine built by Abdali for
Afghanistan's most sacred relic, the woollen *khirqa* or mantle
said to have belonged to the Prophet Mohammad. This Shuja

took in his hands and hugged to his chest, tears streaming down his face.

Three years earlier Dost Mohammad had come here when he wished to declare a jihad against the Sikhs and receive the title Amir al-Muminin, the Commander of the Faithful. One hundred and fifty years later in 1996, Mullah Omar would come too when he was awarded the same title by the Pashtun 'ulema and here he too would swathe himself in the Prophet's cloak to give him the religious authority to bring all the people of Afghanistan under Taliban control. Now Shuja wrapped himself in the same cloth as a symbol of the legitimacy of his return as the king to the dynastic throne of his brother, father and grandfather. He had lost that throne over thirty years earlier when he was defeated at the Battle of Nimla. But he had never lost faith and, though it had taken four attempts, he was now back in his country and on the verge of defeating his lifelong Barakzai enemies.

'This is a very delightful place,' wrote Thomas Gaisford in a letter the following week.

> The scenery is most romantic, the climate fine and the fruit such as you cannot conceive in abundance, quality and price. The finest peaches – some measuring 9½ and 10½ inches round – are to be had at 6 a penny! Rosy cheeked apples for half a penny. The dried peaches, apricots, raisins, plums and mulberries are in profusion – sherbet iced, kabobs, bread, sweetmeats and other dainties are sold at every corner dirt cheap. Never was such a place for a half-starved army to refresh in. But what have we gone through to get here! Our advance into Kandahar over the last two or three hundred miles can be compared to nothing but the retreat of the French from Moscow.[53]

The Army of the Indus had made it against the odds as far as Kandahar, and through good luck and exaggerated reports of their might and numbers had sufficiently unnerved their enemies to capture the ancient capital of southern Afghanistan without firing a shot. Macnaghten in particular was elated. He had faced down his critics, and the reception of Shah Shuja was to him proof of the popularity of the man he had been championing ever since he joined the Governor General's staff five years earlier. Macnaghten believed it showed that he was right and that Burnes had always been wrong: Shuja was legitimate and popular, and the Barakzai were hated usurpers. From the palace of Kandahar he wrote to Auckland in triumph, declaring that it was as if the army had suddenly 'dropped into paradise . . . I am happy to be able to report that the town and territory of Kandahar are in a state of profound tranquillity. It is really wonderful that, with such a dense and motley population in the town, some serious disturbance should not have occurred. The Shah's authority is being gradually established over all the country.'

He added that Shuja had begun to thaw a little, and was behaving in a more relaxed and less imperious manner. 'I am now happy at being able to state that an experience of the conduct of the Shah for a period of between four and five months has led me to form a most favourable opinion of His Majesty's character,' he wrote.

> The repeated reverses which His Majesty had sustained in his efforts to recover his Kingdom have had the effect of inducing many to suppose either that his cause was unpopular, or that he was deficient in spirit or ability; but such persons make no allowances for the arduous circumstances under which those efforts were made. Few men would have attempted the enterprises in which His Majesty failed . . . The Shah is at least not deficient in energy or resolution. From my observation of his character, I should pronounce him to be a mild, humane, intelligent, just and firm man. His faults are those of pride and parsimony. The former defect appears to the Chiefs in a more glaring light from its contrast with the behaviour of the Barakzai usurpers, who in order to preserve their power were compelled to place themselves more on a level with their adherents.

Macnaghten said he had reason to hope that 'His Majesty will gradually assume a less condescending demeanour, or at all events that his subjects will become more reconciled to the distant formalities of their Sovereign'. As for his parsimony, 'it is certainly misplaced at the present crisis, though there is much to be urged in defence of it. His means are very limited, and the claims upon his liberality are very numerous.'[54]

Ten days later, on 8 May, just after the last troops of the rearguard of the Bombay column had finally limped into the camp outside the city, Macnaghten organised a grand durbar for Shuja. This was intended as a public declaration of the resumption of his rule and as an opportunity for the people of Kandahar to pledge their formal allegiance. A magnificently canopied throne was raised on a small platform of mud at the Id Gah outside the city walls. It looked on to the Camel's Back where the mud ruins of the old city of Kandahar lay scattered beneath the Forty Steps and the Cave of Babur – the exact site of the Shah's defeat five years earlier. Shuja was led from the Timurid arcades of the great palace in the citadel by Macnaghten, who had taken the opportunity to dress up for the first time in his new viceregal regalia: 'full court dress such as is usually worn by officials at her Majesty's levees in England', noted one officer.

> Sir Alexander Burnes followed in a plain suit, surrounded by the Afghan chiefs, with whom he appeared to be in close and friendly converse. The winning smile, and frank and courteous manner of the latter gentleman appeared to have gained for him a degree of consideration which no other European could boast of . . . Nothing could exceed the splendour of the costumes in which the chiefs were clad, their turbans and weapons being studded with diamonds and other precious stones, whilst the horses on which they were mounted were perfect specimens of beauty.[55]

Haji Khan Kakar and the other chiefs who had declared for Shuja were followed by Keane, Cotton, Nott and the various British army commanders. They passed out of the Herat Gate and through an avenue formed by the tattered troopers of Shah Shuja's Contingent. To the sound of an Indian regimental brass band playing an English anthem – God Save the King – Shuja was ceremonially enthroned as King of Afghanistan, while the Army of the Indus marched past in all its ragged glory. Cannon fired a 101-gun salute and bags of Indian rupees were thrown into the disappointingly small crowd of Afghans who had assembled to watch the spectacle. 'Everyone became rich!' wrote Mohammad Husain, a merchant of Herat who was one of Shuja's more enthusiastic followers, and his first posthumous biographer.

> His Majesty ordered two lakhs of rupees to be given out for relief of the poor. Those who, in the time of the Barakzais, were too poor to be able even to tie a donkey in their own backyards, now were able to afford luxury saddles for horses and camels; their purses were full of silver coins, their hearts free of care. Indeed, money was so common that little children played with gold and silver coins in the alleys. Such was the benevolence of His Majesty and the English towards the soldiery and peasantry![56]

Yet, for all this optimism among the Shah's supporters, an event took place immediately after this durbar that is not referred to in a single British source, but which according to all the Afghan accounts was crucial in beginning the process of discrediting Shah Shuja in the eyes of his new subjects. Mohammad Husain Herati gives the earliest as well as the fullest account of what happened. 'At this time, an unfortunate incident occurred,' he wrote.

> A girl from a good family was going about her business when an inebriated foreign soldier crossed her path, grabbed her and dragged her into a near-by water-channel where he took her virginity. The girl's shrieks alerted passers-by to her unhappy fate, and they ran to inform her family: a large crowd gathered, including sayyids and clerics, and went to demand justice from His Majesty. Even though apologies were offered and regrets expressed, the Afghans, who are most sensitive on these points of honour,

were bitter in their hearts, saying: 'If, at the beginning of this foreign occupation, such an outrage to a girl of noble lineage can be countenanced, and if the current state of affairs continues, then no one's honour will be safe! It is becoming clear that His Majesty is a mere puppet and a king in name only!'

Herati went on to explain that:

The people of Kandahar have always taken pride in their valour and self-respect, and regarded this incident as too serious to be dismissed with just an apology. Though the girl's family and supporters were bullied into silence by the display of British power, the Durrani clan was seething with anger because their pride and honour had been compromised, and their blood was boiling in their veins. Shame and embarrassment was visible on their faces. Even loyal allies among the Durrani khans, such as Haji Khan Kakar, showed that the insult to the tribe rankled with them, and although they contained their anger, their disaffection showed in their behaviour.[57]

The *Siraj ul-Tawarikh* put it more succinctly: 'The seeds of revenge had been planted in the fertile breasts of honour-conscious Afghans, and they eventually bore terrible fruit. The tribal leaders started thinking that the Padishah only wanted wine from the cup of authority, with no regard for his own good name. The Durrani khans were alienated from the Shah by this incident and secretly nursed their grievances until an opportune moment should arrive.'[58]

One who did exactly this was a leading landowner named Aminullah Khan Logari. Aminullah was an elderly Yusufzai Pathan of relatively humble origins – his father had been assistant to the Governor of Kashmir at the time of Timur Shah – and he had risen in the service of the Sadozais. Like many then present in Kandahar he had no objection to the return of the King, but he was horrified that he had done so on the back of an army of foreign infidels. After the incident of the rape, he made his way to Kabul, where he based himself in the Nawab Bagh and 'sought opportunities to foster a coalition with like-minded Mujehedin to oust the British from the country'.[59]

The first acts of resistance to the British soon began to take place. Two officers of the 16th Lancers who had gone off fishing along the banks of the Arghandab were set upon by a crowd of Durranis as they made their way home; one was stabbed and later died. Attacks on British pickets along the road to the Khojak Pass increased, as did attacks on mail runners and messengers. Two hundred camp followers who attempted to make their way back to India 'were betrayed, disarmed and butchered to a man. Every convoy of treasure, ammunition and stores was compelled to fight its way through the passes, and suffered much loss, both in life and baggage.'[60]

The sepoy Sita Ram felt the atmosphere change radically during the two months that the army stayed resting at Kandahar. 'At first people seemed pleased at the Shah's return,' he recalled.

> But it was said that they despised him in their hearts and were offended that he had returned with a foreign army. They said he had shown the English the way into their country, and that shortly they would take possession of it. They would use it as they had done all Hindustan and introduce their detested rules and laws. It was this that enraged them. They said that if the Shah had come with his own army alone, all would have been well, but their anger grew when they saw the English army was not returning to Hindustan... Although they were repeatedly told that the British had not come to take their country away from them, they could not forget the history of Hindustan.[61]

Before long orders had gone out that no sepoys or British troops could stray out of the camp 'unless going in a body and well armed'.[62] It was a ruling that would never be lifted for the rest of the occupation. For all their claims to be restoring peace to Afghanistan, and to be there at the invitation of the lawful sovereign of the country, the British were under no illusions as to how unpopular they were, and knew that the minute they stepped

outside their heavily guarded cantonments they were likely to have
their throats cut.

It was in response to this crescendo of attacks that Lord
Auckland now took the fatal step of deciding to keep British troops
in Afghanistan after Shah Shuja had been re-established on his
throne, writing to London that 'we must for a time be prepared to
support the Shah where we have placed him'.[63]

While Shah Shuja was being installed in Kandahar, Wade and Prince
Timur were making rather less progress in Peshawar. Despite
Wade's disbursement of over 50,000 rupees in bribes, there was no
sign that the Khyber tribes were ready to let Shuja's forces through.
Still less were they willing to perform any of the acts of subterfuge
suggested by Wade such as seizing the fort of Ali Masjid just below
the top of the pass or 'invading and taking possession of Jalalabad
and destroying and plundering the property' of the Barakzais
there.[64] One chief replied bluntly that now that the Shah had
become the friend of the infidels, 'he would fight for the sake of his
religion even if all the Barakzais were exterminated'.[65]

Like Mehrab Khan of Qalat, the Afridis and the other frontier
tribes had been loyal followers of Shuja and repeatedly protected
him at the lowest ebb of his fortunes; at least one – Khan Bahadur
Khan of the Malikdin Khel tribe – was closely related to Shuja by
marriage. But all were suspicious of his new alliance with the infidel Sikhs and British. This was something Dost Mohammad
successfully played on, sending messages to each that 'if you want
more money say so, but remember that you are an Afghan and a
Muslim and that the Shah is now a servant of the Kafir infidels'.[66]
In case the call to blood and faith was not enough, Dost Mohammad
had been careful to ensure the chiefs' loyalty by taking hostages
from all the leading maliks, and these he carefully kept at his side in
Kabul.

It did not help that Prince Timur was far from a charismatic figure. The nervous and ineffectual Crown Prince was meant to act as a lure for the Khyber chiefs. But Timur was not a natural leader – his portrait shows him to be a slight and anxious-looking man – and his stumbling performance at the durbar Wade had laid on to introduce him to Peshawar did not bode well. 'On entering the Durbar tent,' wrote one observer, 'we found the poor Shahzada, unaccustomed to the royal part he was henceforth to play, standing to do the honours . . . On a motion from the Colonel [Wade] he instantly rectified it by popping with much alacrity on his gadi or throne.' But he soon lost interest, sitting 'with a listless indifference to his situation and an unyielding apathy to everything around him . . . Only recently drawn from comparative obscurity, and unaccustomed to the gaze of strangers, he seemed ill at ease with this public exhibition of his greatness, and was clearly glad when the ceremony was concluded.'[67]

Nor was there any sign as yet of the Sikh forces Ranjit Singh had promised for the invasion. For the previous two months it had been clear that once Lord Auckland had disappeared back to Simla, the wily Maharajah was doing all he could to drag his feet rather than provide the troops or supplies he had pledged. On 19 March 1839, Wade wrote to the Maharajah regretting 'that the appointment of the Muslim army and a Muslim Commander has not yet been made', and asking him 'to give immediate attention to the matter'.[68] Two days later he wrote again to point out that it was now four months since the Army of the Indus had left Ferozepur and only the household troops of two of Ranjit Singh's nobles had so far reported for duty.[69]

A stream of other complaints followed as spring turned to high summer: Sikh officials on the Indus at Attock were not co-operating in getting Prince Timur's forces ferried across; other officials were failing to provide soldiers, shelter, fodder or food supplies; troops had still not arrived – 'the services of Muslim soldiers are urgently required', wrote Wade, again and again. A month later he complained that 'the army appointed at Peshawar was in great trouble as the salaries of the soldiers have not been paid . . . the recruitment of the army, according to the agreement, has not been completed as yet'.[70]

Only at the end of April were orders finally despatched to General Avitabile, Ranjit's Governor in Peshawar, to organise a regiment of local Muslims to assist with the invasion.[71] By mid-May, when Shah Shuja and the main army were already gorging on the peaches, apricots and apples of Kandahar, only one battalion of irregular cavalry – around 650 sowars [cavalrymen] – had yet turned up in Peshawar.[72] Throughout May, as the Khyber chiefs sent down further requests for advance presents and payments – 'I have been successful winning over the people of my hills,' wrote one chief, 'and Rs 20,000 will now be required' – Ranjit sent a message to the now frantic Wade, telling him that there was no hurry and could he come back to Lahore for further consultations about the planned attack?[73]

A month later, Wade received worse news still: Ranjit Singh had taken to his bed 'after a fainting fit'; he died on 27 June, at the age of fifty-eight. His last act was to make a series of huge charitable disbursements. 'Two hours before he died he sent for all his jewels,' reported William Osborne, 'and gave the famous diamond called the Mountain of Light to a temple, his celebrated string of pearls to another, and his favourite horses, with all their jewelled trappings, to a third. His four wives, all very handsome, burnt themselves with his body, as did five of his Cashmerian slave girls . . . Everything was done to prevent it, but in vain . . .'[74]

In Simla, Emily Eden, who had been celebrating the taking of Kandahar – 'Our ball tomorrow will be very gay, and I have just arranged to stick up a large "Kandahar" opposite the other illuminations' – was now horrified by the fate of the 'Mrs Runjeets' she had visited only a few months earlier. 'We thought them so beautiful and so merry,' she wrote. 'The deaths of those poor women is so melancholy, they were such gay young creatures, and they died with the most obstinate courage.' She added: 'I begin to think that the "hundred wife system" is better than the mere one wife rule; they are more attached and faithful.'[75]

It was Wade who immediately realised the much more serious implication for the invasion of Afghanistan. If it had been difficult to gather the promised army when Ranjit Singh was alive, it was going to be next to impossible now he was gone: few of Ranjit's noblemen had shared his enthusiasm for an alliance with the British, and with the succession disputed and a civil war potentially looming, it was likely to be some time before British diplomacy could be brought to bear on whoever finally succeeded the dead Maharajah.

More serious still were the implications for feeding and supplying the Army of the Indus: what chance would there be of sending food, arms, money and reinforcements into Afghanistan when disorders looked almost certain to engulf the Punjab plains separating the invading army from its supply base in British India? Already isolated, the Army of the Indus was now looking increasingly cut off, with the Punjab closing up behind it. Meanwhile, the army was marching ever deeper into the mountains of Central Asia, with ever longer and more vulnerable supply routes, and beyond any easy assistance should anything go wrong.

A difficult expedition, whose success was far from assured, had just become much more difficult.

The same day that Ranjit Singh was dying in Lahore – 27 June 1839 – the Army of the Indus resumed its march from Kandahar towards Kabul.

The force was now split into three units and moved steadily forward at around ten miles a day. This was a little faster than before due to Keane's decision to leave the vast siege guns that had caused such trouble in the passes. He took this decision having been advised that the fortifications of Ghazni and Kabul were not especially formidable and having been assured by Shuja that his Popalzai clansmen would seize control and open the gates of Ghazni when the army arrived there. In Kandahar a garrison of 3,000 men was left behind under the nominal sovereignty of one of Shuja's younger sons, Prince Fatteh Jang, and under the actual military control of Major-General Nott. Most of the Durrani nobles who had just sworn their allegiance to Shuja also chose to stay; only Haji Khan, ambitious for promotion, chose to accompany the army.

The two-month break in Kandahar had been brought to a close after worrying intelligence had arrived from both Herat in the west and Ghazni to the east. In Herat, the Wazir Yar Mohammad Alikozai was not showing the gratitude that the British had expected him to demonstrate for their part in ending the terrible Persian assault on his city. Instead, within weeks of the Persian retreat, he had quarrelled with the British envoy, Eldred Pottinger, who had just spent £30,000 in charitable disbursements in the city, cut the hand off one of Pottinger's servants and attempted to have the envoy himself assassinated. The Wazir had then opened secret negotiations with Mohammad Shah of Persia whose armies had until recently been encamped before his city, declaring, 'I swear to God that I prefer the fury of the King of Kings [the Shah] to the kindliness of a million of the English.'[76]

Macnaghten was uncertain if the fault for the breakdown in relations lay with Yar Mohammad or with the inexperienced Pottinger, so he decided to despatch an embassy to try to win back Herat. Macnaghten asked Burnes to lead this mission, but the latter shrewdly declined, wanting to be around in Kabul ready to step in and replace Macnaghten when the latter returned and suspecting – rightly as it turned out – that the mission to Herat was unlikely to succeed. So Macnaghten sent in his place the Persian-speaking D'Arcy Todd, a former colleague of Henry Rawlinson in the British military mission to Teheran. 'Young Pottinger allowed himself to be apologised to for their threatening to murder him,' wrote Burnes to a friend. 'Major Todd starts tomorrow for Herat, and I predict can do nothing, for nothing is to be done with them.'[77]

Todd's orders were simple: to befriend Yar Mohammad and turn Herat into a pro-British ally on the Persian border, and to settle the frontier with Shah Shuja's dominions. But instead, before long, Todd was writing back in horror at the 'arbitrary and oppressive exactions' being committed by Yar Mohammad, Britain's nominal ally, in his efforts to restore the Herat treasury:

> The person selected was generally a Khan who had enjoyed favour and was therefore supposed to possess wealth, or an executioner convicted of amassing wealth in the non-performance of his duties. The culprit was then put to the torture, the commonest method being by boiling or roasting or baking over a slow fire. The horrible ingenuities practised on these occasions are too disgusting to be more than alluded to. The wretch, writhing in agony, gradually disgorged his wealth and learned before he died that his wives and daughters had been sold to the Turkomans, or divided amongst the sweepers and servants of his murderers. Of two recent victims one was half-roasted and then cut into very small pieces, the other parboiled and afterwards baked.[78]

Herat presented the British with a dilemma they would become increasingly familiar with during the occupation – and one that later colonisers of the region would also have to face: should you try to 'promote the interests of humanity', as Todd put it in one letter to Macnaghten, and champion social reform, banning traditions such as the stoning to death of adulterous women? Wade at the Intelligence Department was, for one, clear where he stood on the issue. The British were there for reasons of strategic self-interest. They were not there to nation-build or encourage gender reform. 'There is nothing more to be dreaded or guarded against', he wrote, 'than the overweening confidence with which we are too often accustomed to regard the excellence of our own institutions, and the anxiety that we display to introduce them in new and untried soils. Such interference will always lead to acrimonious disputes, if not to a violent reaction.'[79]

Meanwhile, Wade's spies in Kabul were reporting that Dost Mohammad was living up to his reputation for efficiency and had been energetically preparing for the British advance by building up his army and repairing the fortifications of Ghazni. He sent a mass of stores down the Kabul River to Jalalabad, and procured a fatwa of jihad against Shah Shuja from the 'ulema of Kabul. He also wrote to Teheran to try to persuade Mohammad Shah to return to the field of battle, 'urging his Majesty to assist him without delay' and declaring that this was now the last opportunity he had before the British established themselves in Afghanistan. 'The mouth of a fountain may in the beginning be stopped by a needle,' he wrote, 'but when it overflows even the elephant has not the power to arrest its course.'[80] Intelligence of all this activity reached the British camp around 20 June and it was decided that the quicker Dost Mohammad was attacked the better.

The 200-mile march from Kandahar to Ghazni initially took the troops through the rich and fertile Arghandab Valley, with its brown waters and silvery willows, its mud-walled orchards of pomegranates and vines and deep red mulberries lining the irrigation ditches. But beyond that, the further the troops marched from the banks of the Arghandab and the network of bubbling irrigation runnels which extended the cultivation to the melon beds at the edge of the valley, the drier the land became. White grasslands blowing in the wind around Qalat e-Ghilzai slowly gave way to a rockier, hillier, more marginal landscape of quartz and shale-scrub, dotted with white opium poppies and purple thistles. The army was now passing into the territories of the Ghilzais: it was barren, 'wild and mountainous country', wrote William Taylor,

over roads extremely difficult and at times almost impassable. The Ghilzies fled at our approach to the numerous mud forts with which these hills abound, and seldom ventured on our track. In the dwellings they had abandoned we found only a few old crones and hungry dogs, both of whom received us with a sort of howling welcome . . . We were lucky enough to discover the stores of corn and *bussorah* [fodder] which the natives had buried at the first news of our approach. We were also well supplied with water, the country being traversed in all directions by rivers and streams. To counterbalance these advantages we were annoyed with shoals of locusts, which literally darkened the skies and kept up a perpetual buzzing

and humming in our ears. The locust appears to be a favourite article of food with the Afghans, who roast it on a slow fire and devour
it with eagerness. We could not bring ourselves to relish this equivo-
cal dainty, even though our rations were not of the best or most
varied description.[81]

On 18 July, Keane received two pieces of intelligence. Firstly, the
Popalzai plot to open the city gates had been discovered, and
Shuja's loyalists had been replaced with Ghilzai tribesmen loyal
to the Barakzais. Secondly, it was learned that the Barakzais were
preparing to make a strong resistance around Ghazni. The
cautious Keane decided to pause to let the centre column led by
Shah Shuja and Willshire's rearguard catch him up.[82] Having
collected his forces, he then marched forward in close formation.
By sunrise on the 20th, the minarets of Ghazni were seen rising
over the scrub, and beyond them the massive fortress, one of the
largest and most impregnable in Central Asia. 'Instead of finding
it, as the accounts had suggested, very weak and incapable of
resistance,' wrote Keane, 'a second Gibraltar appeared before us:
a high rampart in good repair built on a scarped mound, flanked
by numerous towers and surrounded by a well constructed [esca-
lade] and a wide wet ditch. In short, we were astounded.'[83] The
existence of such impregnable fortifications represented a major
intelligence failure on the part of the British, and it was unclear
what could now be done as the siege guns had been left 200 miles
away with Nott in Kandahar. It was not possible for the invaders
to move on, leaving the Ghazni garrison behind them to threaten
their communications. Nor did they have the supplies for either a
retreat or a long siege.

As had been feared, the garrison put up stiff resistance as soon as
the British closed in. They harassed the advancing lines of sepoys
with their cavalry and outgunned them with heavy fire from the
ramparts as the invaders attempted to take up positions around the
fortress. 'The enemy came out in great force,' remembered Sita
Ram, 'and sharp firing took place. The Afghans felt confident in
the strength of this place. The walls were too high to scale and our

light horse artillery guns were of no use against them. This was the first time we had any fighting since we entered Afghanistan.'[84]

This was also the first time the Afghans showed the accuracy of their long-barrelled jezails, the sniper-rifle of the nineteenth century, as their marksmen found their range and began to bring down large numbers of exposed sepoys. 'Every bullet fired from the Ghazni Fort struck the English troops like a Divine punishment,' wrote Mirza 'Ata. 'The soldiers remained hungry and the animals stood exhausted from the long march, still carrying their loads till evening, when the camp was finally prepared behind temporary fortifications and entrenchments. A massive cannon called Zuber Zun, the Hard Hitter, was fired from the fort and camels, soldiers and horses were blown into the air like paper-kites.'[85]

That night the British could see signalling with blue lights from the ramparts. The signals were answered by other lights on the mountains to the east. The purpose of these signals did not become apparent until early the following morning when the army was attacked from the rear by a party of 2,000 wild-eyed ghazis [holy warriors] on horseback. Soon after dawn they appeared on the heights behind the camp carrying the green flags of jihad. As bugles sounded the alarm, the foremost of the jihadis managed to ride over the defensive ditches straight into the middle of Shah Shuja's part of the camp screaming 'Allah hu-Akbar!' and fighting with suicidal bravery until they were surrounded.

Only fifty eventually agreed to surrender, and even they, when hauled before Shuja, insulted him as 'an infidel at heart and a friend of infidels'.[86] As the Shah stood there fuming, one of the ghazis produced a hidden dagger and tried to lunge at him. As soon as the man was overpowered and killed, Shuja's bodyguards beheaded the entire group of prisoners, much to the horror of Macnaghten. It was reported that Shuja's executioners were laughing and joking

Shah Shuja, grandson of Ahmad Shah Abdali and the head of the Sadozai clan, ruled the remains of his grandfather's empire from 1803: 'Our intention,' he wrote, 'was that from the moment of mounting the throne, we would so rule our subjects with justice and mercy, that they should live in happiness within the shade of our protecting wings.' Within six years he had been defeated by his Barakzai enemies and had had to flee into exile in India.

The Barakzais

Dost Mohammad was his father's eighteenth son by a low-status wife. His rise to power was brought about by his own ruthlessness, efficiency and cunning. Dost Mohammad slowly increased his hold on power, until in 1835 he declared a jihad against the Sikhs and had himself formally anointed as Amir.

Akbar Khan (*above* and *right*), the most
intelligent and effective of the sons of
Dost Mohammad, pictured below.

The Peoples of Afghanistan

A family from Kafirstan (*above left*), a Kharoti Ghilzai (*above right*) and (*below*) Pashtun horse traders. Afghanistan was a country sharply divided along tribal, ethnic and linguistic lines.

Three courtly Afghan horsemen, as drawn by the artists of the Elphinstone Mission in 1809.

'The Chaous Baushee in his dress of office'

'The Umla Baushi in his dress of office'

'A Dooraunee Gentleman'

Ranjit Singh, the Sikh ruler and great enemy of Dost Mohammad who created a powerful kingdom in the Punjab.

Ranjit Singh, the 'Lion of the Punjab', and his nobles.

Sikh horsemen.

Two infantrymen from Ranjit Singh's state of the art Fauj-i-Khas regiment, trained for him by ex-Napoleonic veterans.

Playing the Great Game

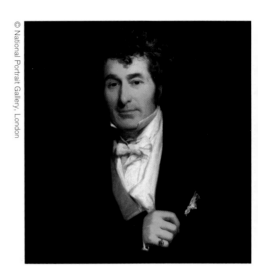

Sir Claude Wade, a Bengal-born Persian scholar, was one of the original spymasters in the Great Game – that grand contest of imperial competition, espionage and conquest that engaged Britain and Russia until the collapse of their respective Asian empires, and whose opening moves were being played out at this period.

Edward Law, 1st Earl of Ellenborough, was the first to turn anxiety about Russia into public policy. 'Our policy in Asia must follow one course only,' he wrote in his diary, 'to limit the power of Russia.'

MacNeill, the Russophobe British ambassador in Teheran whose cable, 'The Russians have formally opened their diplomatic intercourse with Kabul' convinced the British that Dost Mohammad needed to be replaced. 'Lord Auckland should now take a decided course,' he advised, 'and declare that he who is not with us is against us... We must secure Afghanistan.'

Major Eldred Pottinger, nephew of Wade's great rival Sir Henry Pottinger, was in Herat disguised as a Muslim horse trader when the Qajar Persian army attacked it.

Mohan Lal Kashmiri, Alexander Burnes's brilliant Indian assistant and intelligence chief, understood Afghanistan better than any of the British. As long as they followed his advice, all went well.

The Scottish agent of the Great Game, Alexander Burnes, in the field in Afghan dress. He always complained that this famous image did not look in the least like him.

Henry Rawlinson ran into Vitkevitch's Cossacks by chance in the half-light of dawn while lost on the Persian-Afghan frontier. His record-breaking ride from Mashhad to Teheran brought news of the secret Russian mission to Afghanistan. He later become political agent in Kandahar during the British occupation.

Ivan Vitkevitch was a young Polish nobleman who, while in exile on the Cossack steppe, became fascinated with the Turkic culture of what is now Uzbekistan, Kazakhstan and Tajikistan. He was the perfect intelligence agent to take on Burnes, and after much shadowing of each other's footsteps, the pair finally met for Christmas dinner in Kabul in 1838.

Alexander Burnes, the dashing Scottish intelligence officer sent out to gather information on the non-existent Russian threat to British interests in the east. When the book he wrote about his travels became a huge success, the Russians, who read it in French translation, were prompted to embark on intelligence gathering of their own, sending Vitkevitch first to Bukhara then Kabul. Hawkish paranoia in London thus ended up bringing into being the very threat it had most feared – and so was born the Great Game.

Sir William Hay Macnaghten, seen here with his famous blue-tinted spectacles. A bookish former judge from Ulster who had been promoted from his court room to run the Company's bureaucracy, he became Lord Auckland's Russophobe, protocol-obsessed Political Secretary. His jealousy of the fast-promoted Burnes led him to support the idea of replacing Dost Mohammad Khan with Shah Shuja, an idea Burnes strongly opposed. The two men, who never got on, became the dysfunctional centre of the British administration in Afghanistan.

The Edens

George Eden, Lord Auckland, the British Governor General, a clever but complacent man with little knowledge of the region.

Emily Eden, one of Lord Auckland's unmarried sisters and the writer of some of the Raj's most witty and waspish letters.

Reliant on the Russophobic filtering of intelligence by Wade and Macnaghten, Lord Auckland failed to heed the more accurate message from Burnes on the ground, and became convinced of Dost Mohammad's anti-British position. 'Poor, dear peaceful George has gone to war,' wrote his sister Emily. 'Rather an inconsistency in his character.'

In July 1838, Macnaghten visited Shah Shuja and his court in Ludhiana and curtly informed him that after thirty years in exile he was to be replaced on his throne in Kabul with the help of the British.

Shah Shuja's court in exile. From left to right: Prince Timur, Shah Shuja, Prince Safdarjang and Mullah Shakur Ishaqzai.

Two sepoys of the Bengal Native Infantry.

A Bajaur jezailchi.

Kabul infantry.

Skinner's Horse riding out to war.

The British-Indian Army of the Indus make their way east...

as they set about their work, 'hacking and maiming the poor wretches indiscriminately with their long swords and knives', as the prisoners lay pinioned with their hands tied behind their backs. 'The execution of numerous persons in the vicinity of the British camp threw a very unpleasant light on our proceedings,' wrote Mohan Lal. 'Surely no country will admit and approve of the butchery of fifty men in the most cruel and barbarous way for the offence of one individual?'[87]

In the hours that followed, it was Mohan Lal who played the most crucial role in saving the British from the mess they had created for themselves. The previous day, as the invading army had been approaching the fortress, a senior Barakzai prince and rival of Dost Mohammad, Abdul Rashid Khan, had crossed the lines and surrendered himself to Mohan Lal, whom he knew from the munshi's days as an 'intelligencer' in Kandahar working for Wade in the mid-1830s. Debriefing him in his tent, Mohan Lal discovered that according to the Prince the fortress had one major weak point. Most of the fortress gates had been bricked up as the British approached, but the Kabul Gate had been left open so as to allow continued communication with Dost Mohammad. When Burnes passed the information to Keane, the Commander-in-Chief decided he had no option but to attack that very night and hope that surprise would make up for the lack of intelligence and planning.

A plan was quickly put together. An artillery barrage and a diversionary attack to the south would provide cover for a party of engineers to creep up and lay the charges to blow the Kabul Gate. This would be followed by a mass assault with fixed bayonets. 'Such an operation was full of risk,' wrote Henry Durand, who volunteered to lead the explosives party. 'Even success could only be anticipated at the cost of a heavy loss of men.' When Durand raised these risks with Keane, the Commander-in-Chief replied that there was simply no alternative, as there was only two or three days of food left in the commissariat.[88]

The rest of the day was spent in reconnaissance as Keane and the engineers rode around the outer walls of the fort, using the shelter of the belt of walled gardens of apricots and walnuts at its foot to avoid the bullets of the jezail-snipers on the battlements. Just before midnight, orders were sent out that the troops should assemble at 4 a.m., and should remove the white covers of their caps so as to be less visible from the ramparts. At 2 a.m. Shuja was taken to the hill immediately above the Kabul Gate by Macnaghten. According to his biographer, Mohammad Husain Herati, 'William Macnaghten was honoured to enter the royal presence and to invite His Majesty to proceed to the hill of the shrine of the wise Sufi saint Bahlul, from where he would be able to observe the storming of Ghazni fort. As soon as His Majesty had taken up his position, the blazing fire of cannons started.'[89] In his exposed position Shuja came under heavy fire from the ramparts, but remained there with icy courage, impressing his British minders who had been told misleading stories about his previous premature exits from the field of battle.

Sita Ram was part of the diversionary force. 'Orders were given to keep up a hot fire to deceive and distract the attention of the ghazis,' he wrote. 'The wind blew hard on that night and the clouds of dust which were flying about made everything darker than usual. When the guns opened fire we saw the ghazis running with torches, which suddenly made the place look like Diwali puja.'[90]

In contrast to the noise of the barrage on the south, the northern side of the fortress was completely silent as Durand and the other engineers began creeping up towards the walls in the darkness. They were anxious as Macnaghten had divulged the whole plan to Shuja's staff 'and the scheme of attack, success in which depended on secrecy, had become generally known in the Shah's camp'. But the plan had not reached the ears of the defenders. In the pre-dawn glimmer, Durand crept up to within 150 yards of the gate before being challenged by a sentry. 'A shot, and a shout, told that the party had been discovered,' he wrote later. 'Instantly the garrison were on alert; their musketry rang free and quick from the ramparts, and blue lights suddenly glared on the top of the battlements, brilliantly illuminating the approach to the gate. A raking fire from the lower outer works, which swept the bridge at half-pistol shot, would have annihilated the engineers and their men, but strange to say, though the ramparts flashed fire from every loophole, the bridge passed without a shot from the lower works.'

The powder bags were deposited and the fuse lit, 'while the defenders, impatient at the restraint of the loopholes, jumped up onto the tops of their parapets, and poured their fire at the foot of the wall, hurling down stones and bricks'. Running back to cover, the engineers dived into the moat-ditch as a massive explosion rang out, and a bugle sounded the advance.[91] The troops were led into the breach by William Dennie, followed after a pause by a column led by General Robert Sale, known to his men as 'Fighting Bob' as he refused to stay at the back and always threw himself into the fiercest hand-to-hand fighting.

Mohammad Husain Herati was watching from the top of the hill near Shah Shuja. 'The gates of the fortress were blown up,' he recorded, 'and the English rushed in fighting hand to hand till the cries of submission rose to the skies "al-Aman! Spare us!" as the Afghan soldiers threw down their arms. Those whose allotted span had reached the limit were killed; others, men and women, were taken off prisoner while all their wealth and possessions and livestock were given over to plunder.'[92] Mirza 'Ata felt a deep and growing sympathy for the defenders. 'When they set the fuses alight,' he wrote,

the gate was reduced to a lattice of holes and collapsed to the ground, while the explosion filled the air with a storm of dust making everything invisible in all six directions. The Shah's troops rushed to storm the fort, and faced 300 ghazis, fighters for the faith, who drew their swords to defend their religion and three times drove back the British beyond the gates. The troops were forced to fall back and fired from a range of beyond 1,000 feet. But General Sale and the Commander-in-Chief rallied the men who entered the Fort and cut down the ghazis. The Bengal army once again charged and the Commander of the fortress Nawab Ghulam Haidar Khan [Dost Mohammad's son, who had escorted Burnes out of Kabul a year previously] was treacherously abandoned by his companions who hoped to save themselves and earn filthy English gold. They accepted English bribes, their faces blackened by treachery, and fled without fighting. The remaining ghazis fought till they drank the cup of martyrdom from the heavenly streams and were taken to the gardens of Paradise 'beneath which rivers flow', may God have mercy on their souls! Only after the death of the ghazis, did the English gain possession of the Ghazni Fort, and sound victory.[93]

As looting was raging in the lower wards of the fortress, a last doomed resistance was still continuing bravely at the very top. 'The Affghans fought gallantly with their swords, and succeeded in wounding several of our men even when themselves transfixed with a bayonet,' wrote George Lawrence.[94] His friend Neville Chamberlain was less impressed by the behaviour of the British troops. Atrocities were now taking place all around with 'soldiers breaking into the houses to look for plunder, and in this way many were killed . . . I shall not describe the cruelties and actions I saw that day as I am sure it would only disgust you with mankind; but I am happy to say very few women and children were killed, and that was a wonder, as when any person was heard moving in a room ten or twelve muskets were fired into it immediately, and thus many an innocent person was killed.'[95]

By dawn, the flight of the defenders had become a rout. 'Numbers of the enemy were seen dropping down from the ramparts with the aid of ropes,' remarked Thomas Gaisford.

Some were shot while letting themselves down in this way while many that made good their escape were sabred in the field by the cavalry. After all the works were in our possession, bands of the Garrison who had shut themselves up in houses continued to fire upon the troops. Those who surrendered were given quarter but the standard bearer and others who killed many of our men long after the place was ours were shot on their being taken. After all had become quiet, a body breaking from a house endeavoured to cut their way out and wounded many men in the attempt . . .

The slaughter, Gaisford added, was 'dreadful'.

> In a porch leading by a wide staircase to the rampart I found between
> 30 and 40 bodies lying together, many of them on fire and partially
> burnt . . . Some affecting scenes took place in removing the bodies.
> The party who had taken a corpse from a house found it dragged
> back immediately their backs were turned and a woman and child
> crying over it. Every house and shop was ransacked and scarce a
> household remained unstained by blood. Between 500 and 600
> bodies were counted into pits and the probability is that not less
> than 1000 were killed altogether. The wounded were in a sad plight
> and were to be seen for the remainder of our stay in the town . . . some
> burnt, some with gunshot and bayonet wounds, others with shat-
> tered limbs and thirteen even blown up in one explosion at a Gun.
> The Governor of the Fort, Dost Mahomed's son Hyder Khan, was
> discovered in a tower over a gateway and gave up his sword on
> being promised his life.[96]

By nine in the morning, resistance was at an end. It was now time
for the prize agents to begin systematically collecting the loot
which would be shared among the troops. It took five days to cart
everything out, according to Mirza 'Ata. They removed 'to their
own godown 3,000 horses of Turkish, Arabian and Iranian breed;
2,000 camels from Kabul, Balkh, Bukhara and Baghdad; sword
hilts from Isfahan and Tehran in Iran; hundreds of pashmina shawls
from Kashmir; thousands of maunds of raisins, almonds, salted
pistachios, clarified butter, rice, flour; thousands of pistols'. The
scholarly Mirza 'Ata was especially interested in a part of the booty
which no British source seems to have noted: the Kandahar palace
library – 'Several thousand precious and unique books in Persian
and Arabic, covering all the sciences, logic, literary criticism, principles of jurisprudence, syntax and grammar'.[97]

It was a spectacular victory: the impregnable fortress of Ghazni
had been captured within seventy-two hours of the army first
sighting it. As well as a thousand fatalities, around 300 Afghans
were wounded and 1,500 taken prisoner. In contrast, the British

suffered only seventeen killed with around sixty-five wounded.[98] But, as Durand later pointed out, the success of the assault was largely due to luck, as by leaving behind the siege guns and marching without sufficient supplies Keane had 'committed a grievous military error; but as if in mockery of human prudence and foresight, war occasionally affords instances in which a mistake becomes, under the inscrutable will of Providence, the immediate cause of brilliant and startling success: and such this error ultimately proved'.[99]

If the British had won a remarkable victory against the odds, the Afghans had hardly disgraced themselves. They had shown their fighting skills, and the bravery of the defenders, even when all was lost, created legends that began to grow almost immediately. Mirza 'Ata, who like many Afghans began to feel his own loyalties turning at this point, recorded that many believed that miracles attended the bodies of the fallen. 'The dead ghazis, like the martyrs of Kerbela, were left on the battlefield without grave or shroud,' he wrote,

and in spite of entreaties by pious Muslims to give them proper burial the English refused permission. But during the night, thanks to the Almighty, all the corpses of the martyrs disappeared and not a trace of their blood remained on the ground. Another curious story was of a ghazi who remained in a tower of the Fort for 3 days, sniping and killing all who came near – he accounted for 70 Company soldiers, then suddenly disappeared – and no one knew where he went. Inside the Ghazni Fort there are many large underground tunnels of which the English for some months were quite unaware, until, it is said, some 800 virgin girls and infants, 300 horses, 500 Afghan men suddenly appeared and walked away, and not one of the occupying troops making any attempt to stop or challenge them. So it was that English rule descended on Ghazni.[100]

News of the fall of Ghazni reached Dost Mohammad in Kabul in less than forty-eight hours. He had spent three months renovating and strengthening the greatest fortress in the land, and it had fallen to the Kafir [infidel] invaders within three hours. In the next few days there was further bad news that both eroded his own confidence and undermined the resolve of his supporters.

First, and most damagingly for the Amir, his favourite and most effective son Akbar Khan, whom he had deputed to guard the Khyber and block the advance of Wade and Prince Timur, had fallen suddenly sick. There were rumours of poison, and for two days Akbar Khan's life hung in the balance. According to the Afghan sources, this more than anything else affected the spirits of Dost Mohammad: 'When the Amir saw his son, as dear to him as his own liver, the pain of grief tore his heart to shreds and he beat his head with the hands of desperation.'[101]

The illness of Akbar Khan finally provided Wade with the opportunity he had been waiting for. In the confusion he decided to risk an assault on the Khyber although he had managed to gather fewer than 5,000 troops, and these of indifferent quality. The assault was fiercely opposed both by the local Afridis and by the tribesmen of Mohammad Shah Khan of the Babrak Khel Ghilzai, who was the father of Akbar Khan's famously beautiful bride. But on 26 July Wade captured Ali Masjid below the summit of the pass, and before long was marching on towards Jalalabad, from which the prostrate Akbar Khan had to be hurriedly removed on a litter.

The capture of Ali Masjid and Ghazni within forty-eight hours of each other encouraged other disaffected tribesmen. In Istalif, thirty-five miles beyond Kabul, the Tajik Kohistanis rose up against the Barakzais under their religious leader, the Naqsbandi Pir and hereditary Imam of the Pul-i-Khishti mosque, Mir Haji, and expelled their Barakzai Governor, Dost Mohammad's eldest son, Sardar Sher 'Ali Khan. They pursued him into his mud-walled compound in Charikar which they then besieged, 'tightening the noose around his neck'.[102] As a young man, Dost Mohammad had had many of the Kohistani maliks killed when he ruled the area for his elder half-brother Fatteh Khan, and having been offered financial inducements by Wade, Mir Haji now encouraged his people to rise up and claim the revenge for which they had been waiting twenty years.[103]

With one army advancing on him from Ghazni, and another from Jalalabad, and with the Kohistanis rising in revolt to his rear, Dost Mohammad's options were now rapidly diminishing. His first reaction was the traditional Pashtun response to a defeat – negotiations. Nawab Jabar Khan was the most pro-British of all the Kabul nobles: he had hosted Burnes and sponsored Charles Masson's excavations as well as sending his son to be educated in the English fashion at Wade's school in Ludhiana. Morever, during the face-off with Vitkevitch the previous year, the Nawab had worked hard to win over his brother to the British cause.

So Jabar Khan was sent to Ghazni with an offer – Shah Shuja could return to the throne, on the condition that under the Sadozai crown Dost Mohammad could continue as wazir, 'which situation, by hereditary claim, he had a right to secure'. After all, his half-brother Fatteh Khan had been wazir to Shah Zaman, and his father Payindah Khan was wazir to Shuja's father Timur Shah. To Pashtun eyes it was both the customary and the obvious solution to the problem, and Jabar Khan was amazed when the offer was peremptorily turned down by the British. He was also appalled at the rejection of his second request: 'the deliverance of his niece, the wife of Haidar Khan'. As one young British officer, Henry Havelock, noticed, Jabar 'felt or affected, the utmost indignation at the rejection'.[104] Only Mohan Lal, with his long experience of Afghan notions of honour, understood how insulting this rejection was: 'it was quite unnecessary to offend such a valuable friend as the Nawab at this critical time', he wrote. As a result,

[Jabar] really lost confidence and hope in us. In the conversation which he had with us, the topic turned to Shah Shuja ul-Mulk whose name we mentioned with great deference; on which the Nawab smiled, and said to the Envoy, 'If Shah Shuja is really a king, and come to the kingdom of his ancestors, what is the use of your army? You have brought him by your money and arms into Afghanistan, and you have behaved towards him in a friendly and liberal manner in every way. Leave him now with us Afghans, and let him rule us if he can.' Such plain language was not palatable to us ... and the good Nawab, sunk in disappointment and distress of mind by our unfriendly manner towards him, left our camp about noon on the 29th July. I was told to escort the Nawab beyond our piquets; and on the road we heard the shrieks of some woman captured from the fortress of Ghazni. The Nawab turned his face towards me, and nodded his head ... The tone of the language of the Nawab, on his return to Kabul, was not friendly towards us.[105]

As negotiations had now failed, Dost Mohammad had only one remaining option: he gathered his supporters in Kabul and summoned a public meeting in the gardens surrounding the unfinished tomb of Timur Shah. There he made an emotional speech, several accounts of which have survived. 'You have eaten my salt these last thirteen years,' he told his last followers. 'Grant me but one favour in return for that long period of maintenance and kindness – enable me to die with honour. Stand by the brother of Fatteh Khan while he executes one last charge against the cavalry of the Firangi dogs; if in that onset he will fall, then go and make your own terms with Shah Shuja.'[106] The plea was met with silence. The fullest account of what happened next is that given by Maulana Hamid Kashmiri in the *Akbarnama*, who has Dost Mohammad debate his own legitimacy with his followers. The Amir claims to represent the rule of Islamic law and justice, but his followers, seeing which way the wind is blowing, reply that a crowned and legitimate king should always have the first call on their loyalty, not an amir. For this reason they dismiss Dost Mohammad's argument that Shuja has lost the protection of law as he has chosen to ally himself with the Firangi infidels. 'What has the world become in these times?' asked the Amir.

'When of a hundred friends not one remains a friend?

When men become more faithless than women
Why then should the faith of women be given a bad name?

I fear that the state will fall into the hand of the Firangis
Then laws, a creed and religion of their own they would place here

No one's honour would remain intact
No one's suffering would be spared.'

They said to him in reply: 'O leader of this assembly
In this war, aid from us you will not find . . .

For rebelling against Kings is forbidden by God
To be an Amir and a Shah is quite different

We do not dare to draw swords upon him
Let whatever comes to us come.'

The Amir responded: 'Obedience to a King is right
If he is on the rightly guided path of *Shari'a*

Not a king who has become faithless
The world from his oppression would be rendered terrible

Now with the aid of infidels
He has come prepared with a great army

The helpers of infidels, by the law of the *hadith*
Become *kafirs*, wicked and impure

The killing of such an impure Shah is right
Helping him is unrighteous and wrong'

He was answered by the Qizilbash leader, Khan Shirin Khan. Dost Mohammad had a Qizilbash mother and hoped the Qizilbash would stand and fight with him, but they, like everyone else, could see which way the wind was blowing.

'Silence! [replied Khan Shirin Khan.] Do not speak words so
    wicked and infelicitous
For after all we have eaten the salt of the Shah

Stop your idle boasting! The time of your pretensions has gone
The time of your arrogance and vanity has passed.'

When night fell, with a hundred furies and much presumption
The Qizilbash and others worthy of the gibbet and cross . . .

Like fearless thieves plundered the treasury
They carried away much wealth and loot

Then within one night like the wind they flew
To join the Firangi army

The Amir, betrayed by his own forces, was heartbroken.

All his friends he saw become strangers to him
He became sunk in anxiety for his own cause

As the poet Sa'adi said, 'When you see that your friends are no
    longer friendly
Look upon flight from the field as your gain'

So he plucked out of his heart all thoughts of war
From weapons, arms and those things dear to him

He took such that he could carry by himself, the rest he let be
Then he beat the kettledrums of departure and raised the flag

He set out with one thousand and five hundred
Of his own tribe, and went towards Khulm by way of Bamiyan[107]

News of Dost Mohammad's flight arrived in the British camp on 3 August 1839. It took only three more days for the army to march the final few miles to Kabul. On 7 August, eight months after they had left Ferozepur, the Army of the Indus finally marched into the Afghan capital with Shah Shuja at its head, 'dazzling in a coronet, jewelled girdle and bracelet', and Macnaghten not to be outdone in 'a cocked hat fringed with ostrich feathers, a blue frock coat with raised buttons, richly embroidered on the collar and cuffs, epaulettes not yielding in splendour to those of a field marshal, and trousers edged in very broad gold lace'. It was thirty years since the Shah had last seen his magnificent Timurid palace on the great rock of the Bala Hisar, which occupied nearly a quarter of the area of Kabul. Silent crowds filled the street, standing up as the Shah passed, and reseating themselves as the British officials followed; but there were no cheers and no rejoicing. According to George Lawrence, the Kabulis showed 'the most complete indifference [at the return of the Shah], expressing no sign of welcome or satisfaction at his accession to the throne. Evidently their hearts and affections were with their previous sovereign, now a wanderer beyond the Hindu Kush.'[108] Another young officer went further. 'It was more like a funeral procession', he wrote, 'than the entry of a king into the capital of his restored dominions.'[109]

Only the Shah himself showed any pleasure or emotion. 'His Majesty led the way into the palace and gardens,' wrote Major Hough. 'The former were so much dilapidated after the lapse of thirty years that the old man wept, while he explained to his grand-sons and family the state of its former splendour.' As he mounted the familiar staircase to the upper wards of the palace and could see Kabul spread out below him, his spirits rose as he realised that his dream, thwarted for three decades, had finally been fulfilled: 'Ascending the great staircase, the Shah ran with childish eagerness from one small chamber to another of the well-remembered abode of royalty, deploring aloud the neglect and damage which was everywhere visible, and particularly lamented the removal of the panels of mirror from the sheesh mahal.'[110]

But, for all the complaints, Shah Shuja was happy. Finally, he was home.

5

The Flag of Holy War

On the morning of 8 May 1839, just as Shah Shuja was riding in triumph through the gates of Kandahar, the dead body of a man in his early thirties was discovered by a cleaning lady. The discovery took place in a top-floor room of the Paris Boarding House in the shuttered backstreets of St Petersburg. The man had apparently locked his door from within. He had then blown his brains out.

A short and matter-of-fact note lay on the desk beside the body. It read as follows:

> Not knowing anyone who would care about my destiny in any way, I find it sufficient to explain that I am taking my own life voluntarily. As I am currently employed by the Asian Department of the Ministry of Foreign Affairs, I humbly beseech the said Department to dispose of the 2 years' wages due to me from the 1st Orenburg Regiment in the following way: 1. Settle the bill for officer's uniform articles, for the total sum of about 300 roubles; 2. Give 500 roubles to the tailor Markevitch for the dress I ordered from him but haven't

collected; 3. Allow my man Dmitry the use of all my belongings that I have with me at the moment. I have burnt all the papers relating to my last journey and, therefore, all search for them would be entirely useless. I have settled the bill with the landlord of the Paris Inn up until May 7, but should he have any other requests I humbly beseech the Department to satisfy him from the above-mentioned sum. May 8, 1839, 3 a.m. Vitkevitch[1]

Nothing about Ivan Viktorovitch Vitkevitch's notably Dostoyevskian death made much sense, and almost from the moment the body was discovered the mysterious end of Russia's first agent of the Great Game became the subject of speculation. The British believed the suicide was evidence of all that they most disliked and feared about the autocratic callousness of the Tsar's regime. Vitkevitch had, after all, been barbarously exiled from his native Poland to a punishment posting on the distant steppe at the age of only fourteen. Then, having worked his way up against all the odds and excelled as an intelligence agent, at the moment of his triumph, when he had outmanoeuvred his rival Burnes and won over the Barakzais, he had been callously disowned and cast out by his Russian masters.

The British Ambassador in St Petersburg wrote to Palmerston that 'the cause is said to have been the disapprobation & disavowal of his conduct in Afghanistan by the Russ. Govt. instead of the reward & promotion he expected'.[2] According to Russian 'refugees and émigrés' contacted by Sir John Kaye when he was enquiring into the matter in the late 1840s, Vitkevitch had arrived in the capital 'full of hope, for he had discharged the duty entrusted to him with admirable address'. But Count Nesselrode had refused to receive him, and when he presented himself at the Ministry he had been turned away. The Count had sent word that he 'knew no Captain Vitkevitch, except an adventurer of that name, who it is reported, has lately been engaged in some unauthorised intrigues in Kabul and Kandahar'. Vitkevitch 'understood at once the dire portent of the message. He knew the character of his government.' Aware that in the apparently successful British invasion of

Afghanistan he had already been checkmated by Burnes, he now 'saw clearly' that in addition 'he was sacrificed' by the politicians he had served so faithfully and effectively.[3]

The British agent and news-writer in Bukhara, Nazir Khan Ullah, independently confirmed this version of events in a secret despatch sent from Central Asia. Vitkevitch had felt himself compromised when his superiors failed to honour his promises of military support to the Barakzais, leaving them to face the British alone. 'The Russian agent here is my acquaintance,' wrote Nazir Khan to his handler, Burnes. 'He said that when Vitkevitch returned from Kabul to Russia, he told the Russian authorities that he had sent them many letters soliciting Military and Pecuniary assistance and that they never sent him any reply, and delayed the business, and that this neglect had made him out a liar in the country of Kabul and Kandahar. He therefore felt disgraced, and on hearing of the answer of the Cabinet of St. Petersburg, he shot himself.'[4]

For many Russian observers, however, the mysterious death coupled with the suspicious disappearance of Vitkevitch's Afghan papers bore all the hallmarks of British foul play. After all, Vitkevitch's papers contained details of the British intelligence and news-writing networks in Central Asia that he had successfully penetrated. As L. G. Sinyavin, the new director of the Asiatic Department, noted in a letter shortly afterwards:

> He burned our papers without handing them over. Those papers constituted various observations to assist him in drawing up a report on the affairs of Afghanistan and copies of the despatches of British agents to various individuals in Afghanistan. In a word, with him perished all the valuable information about Afghanistan which would now be particularly precious and useful to us and which, from his remarkable talents and gifts of observation, we have every reason to suppose his papers contained. Only what he personally managed to relate to me is known.[5]

All this led to speculation that Vitkevitch's shooting was in fact a covert assassination by British intelligence agents. There was, after

all, no reason why Vitkevitch should commit suicide, given that –
according to the official Russian version of events – he had been
received with honour, promoted, told he was in line for a medal,
and was about to be received by Tsar Nicholas I for a personal
interview on the very morning of his death. Why would such a
man kill himself on the eve of his great moment of glory? Sinyavin
for one was baffled. 'Vitkevitch had only arrived in St Petersburg
eight days previously,' he wrote to Perovsky, Vitkevitch's patron in
Orenburg. 'He was extremely well received by the Ministry and on
the very day of his death the report came through authorising his
transfer to the guards, and on top of that, rewards of promotion,
honours and money.' Sinyavin continued:

> During my meeting with him, I recounted what a favourable inter-
> est you took in him, of your anxiety on hearing [falsely that] he had
> gone to Khiva and been killed, and how before his departure you
> had especially recommended that I organise a decent reward for
> him for such a difficult expedition. He seemed very satisfied and
> merry, and a day before his death I saw him at the theatre, where he
> sat the whole evening and chatted with Prince Saltykov. On the eve
> of his suicide they saw him again in the middle of the day, and again
> he was merry; in the evening he visited Count Simonitch . . . It is all
> very strange . . .'[6]

According to this Russian version, Vitkevitch was in the highest
spirits throughout his trip to St Petersburg. Vitkevitch's Orenburg
friend K. Bukh described how they got together that morning and
'went for a ride in the islands', then saw a play in the
Kamennoostrovsky Theatre. 'He did not show any signs of melancholy,' Bukh wrote later. 'I went to see him on the eve of his tragic
death; he was excited about some article in a German newspaper
referring to him. He showed me the rifles and pistols, his life-long
passion, he had bought in the East. On his return to the hotel he
was in good spirits, and had asked to be woken at nine.'

The oddly terse tone of the suicide note also fuelled speculation:
why was there no mention of his mother, his brother or any of his

colleagues and friends? The first to express his suspicions in print was the Tsarist military historian M. A. Terntyev. 'The investigation did not lead to anything,' he wrote, 'but it is difficult to believe that someone who had worked hard for so many years to further his career would give it up the night before his most ardent dreams were to come true ... Many suspected the British to be involved in this mysterious incident ... Who but the British were interested in Vitkevich's papers? Who but the British were exasperated by Burnes's failure and angry with Vitkevich? ...Vitkevich's death deprived us of important intelligence on Afghanistan; the treaty he had signed with Amir Dost Mohammad also vanished.' This was certainly a version of events that appealed to N. A. Khalfin, the Cold War-era Soviet historian of the Great Game: 'What was it then?' he asked. 'Murder, committed in the centre of St Petersburg, upon the order of a certain foreign power?'[7]

But there is a third version of the events in the Paris Boarding House, which is the one that is generally believed in Vitkevitch's native Poland, and which perhaps rings most true. For, according to one of his Orenburg colleagues, at the theatre the night before he died Vitkevitch – or rather Jan Prosper Witkiewicz as he was still known to his fellow Poles – ran into an old friend from Vilnius. This friend, Tyshkevitch, berated him, angrily asserting that he had at one time been willing to sacrifice himself in the name of his motherland but had now lost all his ideals, abandoning his dearest principles for the sake of naked ambition.

The earliest source for this are some notes of Colonel P. I. Sungurov, who served in Orenburg for thirty years and knew Vitkevitch well. According to Sungurov, after the play Vitkevitch had returned to his hotel to pull together his plans and notes in preparation for the audience with the Tsar the following morning. Late that night, Tyshkevitch came to see Vitkevitch in his rooms, knocking on his door as the traveller sat surrounded by his papers and journals. Vitkevitch's tale of his travels, of the 'great service' he had done to Russia and of his exciting future career provoked Tyshkevitch's indignant response: 'You ought to be ashamed of yourself, Pan Vitkevitch ... You talk of your mission as if it were some sacred feat . . . You, who did not hesitate to sacrifice your life, wealth, and position for the sake of freeing your dear motherland from slavery . . . you now assist with enslaving independent nations. You, who used to despise spies and traitors, have become one yourself . . .' Tyshkevitch lectured his friend for some time. When he had finished, Vitkevitch collapsed, deflated and depressed: 'A traitor, he whispered, yes, a traitor. God damn it all!' As soon as Tyshkevitch left, seized with remorse, Vitkevitch had lit his fire, burned his papers and taken a pistol from the trunk on his hotel-room floor. This he put in his mouth, then pulled the trigger.[8]

The idea of a depression – or melancholia as the Victorians called it – provoked by shame and guilt being the cause of Vitkevitch's suicide was also the explanation favoured by his travelling companion Ivan Blaramberg, who knew him well in his final months. 'In April we received the sad news of our friend Vitkevitch's suicide,' Blaramberg later wrote in his memoirs.

> This was a tragic end for a young man who could yet have been of much use to our government for he had the energy, the enterprise, and all the necessary qualities to play in Asia the role of Alexander Burnes. During our journey to Persia and the sojourn there he was often in a melancholy mood and would say that he had had enough of life. Pointing at a breech-loading Bertran pistol, he once remarked: 'Avec ce pistolet-là, je me brulerai un jour la cervelle.' And he kept his word, as it was with this very pistol that he shot himself in a moment of deep melancholy.[9]

The suicide of Vitkevitch was only one of many far-reaching repercussions of Shah Shuja's return to the throne of Afghanistan.

In Orenburg, Vitkevitch's champion, Count Perovsky, was determined that Russia would not be outmanoeuvred by British machinations in Central Asia. As soon as it became clear that the British were about to invade Afghanistan, Perovsky began lobbying to revive Russian prestige in the region by conquering the Turkman Khanate of Khiva, something he had been pushing for since 1835. For many years the Khivans had been buying the kidnapped and enslaved Russian serfs abducted from the border region by the Kazakhs; the British advance into Central Asia gave Perovsky the excuse he had been waiting for to put his invasion plan into action. A committee assembled in St Petersburg to consider his proposal and decided that the expedition to Khiva should 'consolidate the influence of Russia in Central Asia, weaken the long-standing impunity of the Khivans, and especially that constancy with which the English government, to the detriment of our industry and trade, strives to spread its supremacy in those parts. Looking on this enterprise from this point of view, the committee is entirely convinced of the necessity of it.'[10]

In London, meanwhile, there was great satisfaction that the first military expedition undertaken during the reign of Queen Victoria had been such an effortless success: in London society, a new dance – a gallop named 'The Storming of Ghuznee' – became the fashionable strut of the season.[11] The young Queen wrote in her diary that the invasion was 'a stroke for the Mastery of Central Asia', while her politicians assured her that the war had for the time being settled the question of whether it was Britain or Russia which was to have 'possession of the East'. As the Prime Minister, Lord Melbourne, observed, from the day Shah Shuja returned to the Bala Hisar, it was Macnaghten who was now the real King of Afghanistan.[12] Downing Street authorised baronetcies for Macnaghten, Wade and Keane, and an earldom for Auckland.

In Simla too, there was great relief at the way the campaign had gone: the Governor General's ball to celebrate the victory 'went off with the greatest success', wrote Emily Eden, 'with transparencies of the taking of Ghazni, "Auckland" in all directions, arches and verandahs made up of flowers; and a whist table for his Lordship. Every individual in Simla was there.'[13]

In Kabul itself, there were also celebrations, at least among the Royalist supporters of the Sadozais and among those who were able to gain profit or promotion from the occupation. Shah Shuja settled into the Bala Hisar, and restored his old durbar, making Mullah Shakur, his faithful aide in Ludhiana, his chief of staff, and summoning Colonel Wade, his long-time champion, to receive a special robe of honour. To the assembled nobility he announced a fresh start for Afghanistan: he would forgive his enemies and honour his commitments to the British who had looked after him when he had lost everything. As his faithful biographer Mohammad Husain Herati remarked:

> His Majesty would often repeat that he had spent thirty years as a guest of the English and had never experienced anything except kindness and respect from them, and that this in turn demanded his utter loyalty and that of his heirs, generation after generation. He compared his case to that of the Emperor Humayun who had sought refuge at the Safavid court in Iran and had received help to reconquer his kingdom. He also had it loudly proclaimed in the public audience at court that any of the Barakzai khans who had fled and left their homes would be pardoned on their return to Kabul, and their possessions restored to them: several, such as Nawab Zaman Khan Barakzai with his sons and brothers and with all their dependants and tribesmen, took advantage of the offer of reconciliation, and were restored to their former positions.[14]

Meanwhile, the British troops and sepoys wandered happily around the autumnal palace gardens and the Kabul orchards heavy with fruit, while 'parties rode hither and thither to visit such objects of curiosity as were described to them'.[15] The city that the British had just seized from Dost Mohammad was then at the peak of its prosperity and with a population of around seventy thousand was by 1839 probably the greatest commercial entrepôt in Central Asia and the centre of the region's caravan trade. The security that Dost Mohammad had been able to guarantee in his kingdom and the tolerance he had shown to religious minorities meant that Kabul had become a major centre for Hindu traders from Sindh and especially the Sindhi banking capital of Shikarpur; there were also flourishing communities of Jewish, Georgian and Armenian traders.[16]

The narrow streets gave on to the mud-walled compounds of rich merchants and the townhouses of the landowners and tribal chiefs, though from the streets all that could be seen were grandly carved wooden gateways, the wooden shutters and lattices of the overhanging upper rooms and the tops of the mulberry trees visible above the walls. If the gates opened, however, passers-by could catch glimpses of large courtyards in which trickling fountains were placed in the middle of a raised platform, spread with carpets and bolsters and shaded by fruit trees. Recesses in the arcades would be ornamented with intricate plasterwork. Here, under the trellising, the chiefs would loll during the evenings, smoking pipes and listening to musicians play their rababs or the poets recite the great Persian epics.

Between the great houses stretched miles of bustling brick-built bazaars, arranged by trade, with separate streets for shawl merchants, the sellers of spice and rose water, and the importers of Bukhara silks, Russian tea, Lucknavi indigo, Tartar furs, Chinese porcelain and the celebrated stabbing daggers of Isfahan. 'The shop windows are open to the ground,' noted James Rattray, a young officer who would later go on to draw some of the finest sketches of Kabul,

> and the immense display of merchandise, fruits, game, armour, and cutlery defies description. These articles are arranged in prodigious piles from floor to ceiling; in front of each sits the artificer or from amidst the heaped up profusion peeps out the trader at his visitors. The streets are so narrow, that a string of laden camels takes hours to press through the dense, moving, ever-varying crowds who all day long fill the thoroughfares ... In and out of the crowds the women in their shroud-like veils, thread their passage, or seek an easier plan of forcing it, astride on horse-back ... The multitude is suddenly pushed aside by a long train of foot soldiery, the advance guard of some great chief, who rides proudly on, followed by a troop of cavaliers, glittering in embroidered cloaks and trappings, and brandishing their spears and matchlocks ... After these waddle the elephants of the Shah,

tearing down the outstanding water pipes from the flat roofs, or backing onto an ice or fruit shop.[17]

Through the noise and the press would come the cry of the water seller with his brass cup and leather bag, 'Ab! Ab!', the cry of the lines of blind beggars asking for alms and, at the end of the summer, the rhubarb sellers with their call of 'Shabash rawash!' ['Excellent rhubarb!'].

After all the hardships they had been through, the British troops were enchanted and even a little dazzled: 'They marvelled at the wonderful Chatta covered bazaar,' wrote Mirza 'Ata, referring to the great arcaded market built by Shah Jahan's Governor, Ali Mardan Khan, in the 1640s, around the same time as the Taj was coming up in Agra.

> They admired the fine cut-masonry pools and cisterns, the gardens equal to those of paradise, the fine buildings of a capital city, and the well-stocked shops ... The English troops, numerous as the waves of the sea, had experienced much hardship on the route into Khurasan, and now rested in Kabul, eating meat and rice, almond marzipan, faluda [vermicelli pudding], grilled meats and kababs, with various fruits, grapes of the sahebi and khalili varieties, and the finest of all, khaya-e ghulaman, young men's testicles. They nibbled raisins and grew plump after being semi-starved on vile Indian chillies, dal and chapatis. The proverb 'the women of Kabul all have lovers, just as the wheat flour of Peshawar is all cut with maize flour' was also quickly proved, as the soldiers rode the steed of their lust unbridled day and night.[18]

This latter entertainment was something the jaunty regimental chaplain, the Rev. G. R. Gleig, chose to draw a veil over when he described in his memoirs the various wholesome masculine activities which kept the British troops occupied in Kabul. 'Wherever Englishmen go,' he wrote,

> they sooner or later introduce among the people whom they visit a taste for manly sports. Horse racing and cricket were both got up in

the vicinity of Kabul; and both the chiefs and the people soon learned to take a lively interest. Shah Shuja himself gave a valuable sword to be run for, which Major Daly, of the 4th Light Dragoons had the good fortune to win: and so infectious became the habit that several of the native gentry entered horses. The game of cricket was not, however, so congenial to the taste of the Afghans. Being great gamblers in their own way, they looked on with astonishment at the bowling and batting of the English players. But it does not appear that they were ever tempted to lay aside their flowing robes and huge turbans and enter the field as competitors. On the other hand, our countrymen attended their cocks, quails and other fighting animals, and, betting freely, lost or won their rupees in the best possible humour.[19]

More surprisingly, Gleig claimed that the Afghans also developed a taste for amateur theatricals. 'The British officers got up some plays,' he wrote.

A theatre was constructed, scenery painted, dresses prepared and excellent bands in attendance. The pieces chosen were chiefly comedies, such as the 'Irish Ambassador' and others of the same sort, and great amusement was afforded the audience. For on such occasions they changed the titles of the *dramatis personae*, so as to bring them and the offices of the parties bearing them to the level of Afghan comprehension, while Burnes translated the speeches as they were uttered. The Afghans are a merry people, and have a keen relish of the ludicrous and satirical; and as the interpreter never failed to bring the jokes of the actors home to them, they marked their delight by bursting into peals of laughter.[20]

As late summer turned to autumn, and the nights began to grow longer and colder, the troops were issued with sheepskin clothes, warm gloves and quilts. It was now deemed to be the hunting season and those foxhounds which had made it alive through the Bolan Pass without starving or being eaten by the camp followers were now taken out daily to hunt jackals. Snipe- and duck-shooting also became popular diversions, as did, a little later, skating and snowman building. 'We appeared in skates manufactured by ourselves,' wrote Thomas Seaton, 'and figured away on the ice to the utter amazement of the Kabul people who as they had never seen such a spectacle, came running together to witness the performance. We enjoyed the winter as thoroughly as circumstances would permit – shooting, snow-balling, making snow giants, and picnics to the lake, for the weather was frequently most enjoyable. How clear, how blue and how cloudless it was!'

Shuja meanwhile was busy rebuilding the Bala Hisar and trying to return it to the glories he remembered from his youth, remaking it as a palace which befitted his elevated ideas of kingship. The high walls and bastions ringing the high rock were in good repair; what was not to his liking was the refinements of the palace buildings perching on the terraces within. So, starting with the durbar hall, Shuja refurbished and repainted the plasterwork and repaired the balustrades and the arcades. The Mughal gardens were replanted and a new harem sarai designed from scratch to be ready for his womenfolk when they arrived from Ludhiana. At the same time the court ceremonial was altered to bring back the more formal court style of the Sadozais, which the Barakzais had abandoned. The old offices of state were reinstated and with them the elaborate uniforms which so amazed British observers: 'The court officials should really be viewed in a body of some hundreds,' wrote the artist James Rattray, 'dressed in crimson jackets, and bearing on their heads their high fantastic caps of every conceivable semblance. Some are ornamented with huge ears like asses, or spikes like those of porcupines, while others take the form of goat and buffalo horns, and many are conical, spiral or bell-shaped. These caps are all more or less decorated with figures and devices, some bearing a spear head as an emblem of superior rank.'[21] In formal durbar, Shuja himself was dressed no less remarkably, with a long choga hanging loose over his shoulder, ornamented with jewels at the loops, while the corners of his doge-like hat were edged with velvet pendants. He would remain seated on his octagonal white marble throne while receiving petitioners, and would rise only to receive the most senior British officials. On these occasions he would lean on a long curvilinear antelope horn, 'the expression on his face grave and careworn'.

As winter tightened its grip, the days grew colder and the low, heavy clouds filled with snow that would not fall, Shuja decided to award selected officers with a new medal of his own invention. This was the Order of the Durrani Empire, whose shape and physical form seems to have been modelled on that of the Freemason medal, the Guelphian Order, which Burnes had been awarded after his return from Bukhara.[22] These were given out as the first regiments began the long march back to India, before the first flurries of winter snow thickened into drifts and closed the higher passes. As George Lawrence, Macnaghten's young Military Secretary, noticed: 'The recipients were entirely composed of British officers of the force, as none of his own subjects were regarded as worthy of the honor.'[23]

By late November the first returning regiments had reached Simla, 'and very flourishing they look', wrote Emily Eden. 'They cannot now make out that their sufferings have been all that the papers described. Rather than having undergone privations, they are all looking uncommonly fat. Indeed Captain Dawkins, of Lord Auckland's bodyguard, has come back looking fatter than most Falstaffs.'[24]

While Shah Shuja was being installed in the Bala Hisar, its previous occupant, Dost Mohammad Khan, was fleeing north as fast as he could. Like Shah Shuja after the Battle of Nimla thirty years earlier, the loss of power immediately changed everything for him, and brought with it a series of humiliations which nearly resulted in his ruin and death.

The Barakzais struggled with difficulty over the icy passes, in headlong flight from the British trackers who had been sent out to hunt them down. Yet Dost Mohammad could not move with any real speed as he was 'accompanied by a throng of wives, infants, brothers, sons, and servants'.[25] His heir Akbar Khan, moreover, was still recovering from the poison apparently administered to him at the Khyber, possibly on Wade's orders. Unable to ride, he had to be carried on a litter. The Afghan epic poets remembered the flight of Dost Mohammad with as much sympathy as their Scottish counterparts romanticised that of Bonnie Prince Charlie after Culloden. 'Then forward went the brave sovereign,' wrote Ghulam Kohistani in his *Jangnama*,

> And with him a thousand courageous cavalry.

> And behind them passed the harem
> Remembering the old custom

> After him came the chattels and gold
> And vigilant sentries, ever watchful

> On their trail, with feet like lightning,
> Travelled the vengeance-seekers

> Both night and day they rode
> Like clouds that rush across the sky[26]

The tracking party was led by two tough and resourceful young officers, James Outram and George Lawrence, who were given Haji Khan Kakar and a thousand of Shah Shuja's cavalry as their guides and escort. Travelling at speed, it should not have been difficult to ride down the slow-moving Barakzai caravan. Yet, for all their efforts, Outram's party never succeeded in capturing the Amir, and it soon became clear that Haji Khan was as usual playing a double game, deliberately leading the British off the trail and doing all he could to slow the pursuit.

The search party picked up the scent of the Barakzais when, after two weeks on the hunt, they caught up with some deserters from Dost Mohammad's bodyguard and learned that they were only one day behind the fugitives. 'At five pm we resumed our march,' wrote an exhausted Lawrence,

contrary to the protest of the Hadjee, who expressed himself most
unwilling to proceed, alleging the dangerous and precipitous character of the road for a march at night.* It was quite apparent his
heart was not in the cause. His objections were not listened to, and
we proceeded by a very bad road, over high hills and along the dry
channels of mountain streams, for ten miles, where we halted and
lay down by our horses ... Not fifty of our Affghans reached the
ground with us; but they came in during the day. Here we received
intelligence that the Dost was at a place called Youk, only one march
ahead of us. Hadjee Khan again showed great reluctance to advance,
begging Outram to halt there, as the Dost had 2,000 horsemen with
him. Outram however ordered the party to march at four pm, and
on mustering the Affghans found they numbered only 350, and
they badly mounted.[27]

These delaying tactics continued over the days that followed. The
Haji insisted that they needed to wait for reinforcements, and
when Outram tried nevertheless to set off on a night ride, 'whether
through accident or design, we had not advanced four miles,
before the guides, who were under the charge of Haji Khan's
men, were reported to have deserted. It was then pitch-dark, and
being left in the midst of interminable ravines, where no trace
even of a footpath existed, we had no alternative but to halt until
day break.'[28] The next evening as the British tried to press on,
Haji Khan seized Outram by the arm 'and loudly entreated me
not to think of advancing, threatening rather to detain me by
force, than to permit my rushing on certain destruction'. He also
warned him, no doubt truthfully:

if you do encounter Dost Mohammad, not one of the Afghans will
draw a sword against him, nor will I be responsible if they do not

---

* The Haji in fact had a point. The Hajigak Pass is extremely formidable even in
daytime and during summer. Moreover he had especially good reason to be cautious
as the pass was controlled by Hazaras whom Haji Khan had suppressed some years
earlier and who would no doubt have seized the opportunity to take revenge on their
former persecutor.

turn against yourself in the melee . . . Failing in his object of shaking
our resolution, the Khan at last left and seating himself a few yards
from the door of my tent, conversed in the dark in an undertone of
voice, with three or four of his chiefs for more than an hour. The
latter were heard to upbraid him for assisting the Firangis in their
endeavours to arrest Dost Mohammad, enquiring whether the Amir
had ever injured him . . . and Haji Khan was heard to admit the
truth of all they had advanced.[29]

The following day, as snow began to fall, the Afghans of the party
turned increasingly mutinous. 'We realized', wrote Outram, 'that
our own Afghans were traitors upon whom no reliance could be
placed.' Outram and Lawrence then decided to go on a mission
that seemed almost suicidal, heading on through a blizzard to
apprehend Dost Mohammad with only thirteen British officers.
That night, Outram slept in thick snow, aware he might well die
the following morning, but determined to do what he could to
arrest or else kill the Amir. Afterwards he remembered that he had
never been 'more happy than on this night, under the exciting
expectation of so glorious a struggle in the morning'. But the struggle never took place. Outram and his men galloped down the pass
into the wide Bamiyan valley to find that Dost Mohammad had
just that morning fled north of the Hindu Kush, escaping out of
their reach beyond Saighan to Tash Qurgan, and into the territory
of the independent Uzbek leader, the Mir Wali, 'who is at enmity
with Shah Shuja'. Outram now had no option but to write back to
Macnaghten that 'there being, under such circumstances not the
slightest hope of our now overtaking the fugitive within the Shah's
territories, to which we have been restricted, and the officers of our
cavalry having represented that their horses are incapable, through
want of food or rest, of making further forced marches immediately, we have here been compelled to relinquish the pursuit'.[30]

That night, Dost Mohammad and his followers made it safely to
the shelter of Khamard, the fortress of the slave-trading Mir Wali.
'The Amir spent the next two months as honoured guest of the
Uzbeks,' wrote Mirza 'Ata,

and from there he went on to Balkh where the governor received him in a guest-house in a beautiful garden. While he was in Balkh, letters arrived from Nasrullah Khan, the ruler of Bukhara, by camel-post, requesting the Amir to grace his court with his presence. The Amir left his family and dependents in Balkh and rode together with his heir Akbar Khan to Bukhara, the city of the Islamic sciences, where he was received with royal hospitality and he was given a private palace as his residence and a small allowance to meet his daily expenses.[31]

It is not entirely clear what went wrong in Bukhara, but after a few weeks Dost Mohammad fell out with his hosts: Mirza 'Ata suggests that this was due to some disrespectful remarks made by Akbar Khan, the Amir's hot-tempered son. It may also have been because Nasrullah resented Dost Mohammad's earlier attempts to seize the disputed border city of Balkh, claimed by both amirs, and now objected to his plan to have the 'ulema of Bukhara declare a jihad on his behalf. Either way, harsh words were then exchanged between the two, and the Barakzais left the city having deeply offended Nasrullah Khan. The cunning and ruthless (and possibly even mildly psychotic) ruler of Bukhara then tried to have Dost Mohammad assassinated. 'The Bukharan Amir secretly instructed the escort that when the party crossed the Oxus they were to scuttle the boat in which Dost Mohammad and the princes were riding and so cause them to drown,' wrote Fayz Mohammad in the *Siraj ul-Tawarikh*.

The Afghans were thus taken under guard to the banks of the Oxus and put in boats. A hole was surreptitiously opened in the skiff in which the Amir chose to sit. When the boats moved off, one of the Bukharan Amir's men who was unaware of his master's plot sat as the Amir's escort in the same boat. He planned to cross the river with him and then return. Another man who knew what was going on, spoke to him in Turkish and told him to get out of the boat so that he would not drown with the Amir. But the Amir, whose mother was the daughter of one of the leading Qizilbash of Kabul and was herself a Turk, understood Turkish. When he heard what the man said, he got out of the boat and refused to cross the river. No matter how hard the Bukharan Amir's people tried to persuade him to get back in and cross he refused and said to his companions, 'It is better to roll in my own blood than to die by drowning. For to die by the sword's edge will remain as a reminder of the undeniable injustice of the Amir of Bukhara. But if I were to drown, no one would speak of the ill-treatment which he has shown me, his guest.'[*]

The Amir headed back towards Bukhara with his party, now under guard. 'But a very severe snowstorm blew up which brought everyone to the brink of death. Many of the younger princes were unable even to talk because of the extreme cold. The Amir ordered his personal servants to each take one of the princes and warm them by breathing heavily on them' in order to save their lives.

In short, they limped back to Bukhara, and only reached it after the greatest difficulties. Now even the inadequate stipend which had been allotted the first time was withheld by the Amir of Bukhara. Eventually, some seventy of the group fled ... Nasrullah Khan learned of their escape and ordered seven thousand cavalry to pursue with orders to cut off their escape and, if the sardars chose to fight, then to shed their blood; if not, then to bring them back in chains. At Chiraghchi, they overtook the sardars, surrounded them, and attacked. While bullets and powder lasted, the Afghans held the Bukharans off and spilled much of their blood. But in the end, when they had exhausted their ammunition, the Bukharans fell upon them and took them prisoner. Afzal Khan and Akbar Khan were both wounded in the fight, while several others were killed and many of the rest sustained serious wounds. The Bukharans carried Dost Mohammad and his men back to their city and at the Amir of Bukhara's order, threw them all in a dark dungeon.[32]

---

[*] This was rather rich coming from Dost Mohammad, who had in his time killed several of his enemies after pledging them safe conduct, notably the Mirs of Tagab, Kohistan and Deh Kundi.

On 2 November 1839, with the puddles in Kabul bazaars now iced over and frost glinting on the willows beside the Kabul River, Shah Shuja left the Bala Hisar to winter in Jalalabad, which, in the absence of Peshawar, he now named as his winter capital. Macnaghten went with him. Arriving ahead of Shuja, while the Shah was delayed burying a junior prince amid the poplars of the Nimla Gardens, Macnaghten took for himself the best quarters in town, leaving the Shah to shelter in what one British observer called 'a hovel'.[33]

Mullah Shakur was left in charge in Kabul, with Burnes standing in for Macnaghten. On the last night of the year, as the winter cold grew more intense, Burnes threw a Hogmanay party, and presided over it all in kilt and sporran. Neville Chamberlain, up for the week from Kandahar, was one of the guests. 'We had a very merry party,' he wrote the following morning.

> Though we had nothing to drink but brandy and gin. At about 2 in the morning we took to the mess tables and commenced dancing reels, Captain Sinclair standing on the table, dressed in the Highland costume, playing the bagpipes. Burnes was extremely civil to us. He is liked by everyone, as there is no political humbug in him unlike most persons in that employ ... [He is in fact] a general favourite, and very justly so as he is, I think, the most unaffected, gentlemanlike, pleasant and amusing man that I have had the good fortune to meet.[34]

The celebrations that continued in Kabul throughout the winter were not to everyone's taste. The American adventurer 'General' Josiah Harlan, who had fought successively for the East India Company, Shah Shuja, the Sikhs and finally Dost Mohammad, and who claimed he had briefly had himself crowned the Prince of Ghor, looked on with an increasingly jaundiced eye at the British at play, before finally quitting Afghanistan in disgust. 'Kabul, the city of a thousand gardens, in those days was a paradise,' he wrote later on the steamer back home after Burnes had had him deported from India as an unwanted alien. 'I have seen this country, sacred to the harmony of hallowed solitude, desecrated by the rude intrusion of senseless stranger boors, vile in habits, infamous in vulgar tastes, callous leaders in the sanguinary march of heedless conquests, who crushed the feeble heart and hushed the merry voice of mirth, hilarity and joy . . .' He added prophetically, 'To subdue and crush the masses of a nation by military force, when all are unanimous in the determination to be free, is to attempt the imprisonment of a whole people: all such projects must be temporary and transient, and terminate in a catastrophe . . .'[35]

Yet in that first winter of the occupation there were few signs that Harlan was anything more than an embittered old Afghan hand who had seen his moment of greatness pass. Instead, to the surprise of many, the nobles of Kabul were not unwelcoming. The Rev. G. R. Gleig was not alone in imagining that the Afghans showed 'a good deal of personal liking' for individual British officers, though he quoted one chief who told him: 'We wish that you had come among us as friends, and not as enemies, for you are fine fellows one by one, though as a body we hate you.'[36]

It helped that Dost Mohammad had ruled with an iron rod and imposed unusually heavy taxes on his people, as well as confiscating many estates to help finance his projects of jihad. This made the beginning of Shah Shuja's rule seem relatively mild, and initially many Kabulis and most of the Durrani elite appear to have been willing to give their restored ruler the benefit of the doubt. As Mirza 'Ata put it, 'In the first months of their occupation of Kabul, the English brought most of the chiefs and the city and its environs into submission and obedience: the very few who disobeyed were imprisoned and their forts and property confiscated by the Company government.'[37] Moreover, Macnaghten wisely opted for a generous political settlement. Prominent Durrani nobles in the south were bought off, while the Ghilzai chiefs in the east were heavily subsidised, as were the 'ulema. It was a massive drain on the Indian exchequer, and it quickly became clear that occupying

Afghanistan was not going to be cheap; but the strategy succeeded in keeping the peace for the first autumn and winter of Shah Shuja's reign.[38] As a result Auckland was able with some satisfaction to report to London, 'The country is said to be quiet, the roads to be safe, commerce to be reviving, and the monarchy and change of government are still popular . . . Col. Roberts writes, "I have got acquainted with many of the chiefs. They are in general very desirous to be intimate with the *Sahib Loge*, and when I return to Kabul my house shall be open to them. They are happy to dine with us and to see us at their homes."'[39]

This bright mood was only slightly dimmed by widespread scepticism as to whether the returning Barakzais would really accept Shuja's olive branch and end the feud with the Sadozais that had now been carefully nourished for two generations. 'Many of the Sadozai nobles found Shuja's policy of reconciliation unpalatable,' reported Mohammad Husain Herati. 'They grumbled to each other while travelling or at court, saying: "Now that this clan of Barakzais is so highly respected, restored to all their old privileges and positions, it will not be long before the evil flames of discord rise high. How do these English, with all their claims to science and rationality and political experience, think it will all end, fostering the enemies of their friend? It will end in grief and regrets!"' A traveller who had just arrived from Peshawar related that:

> General Avitabile, the Sikh's governor of that city, on enquiring about the state of affairs in Kabul, and on being told that all groups, including the Barakzais, were equally favoured, turned to his entourage and sighed: 'God help that Shah Shuja and forgive him!' Those present were surprised at the expression, normally used for the dead, and asked: 'Is the King not still alive?' Avitabile answered: 'Anyone who gives room to his deadly enemies, and trustingly embraces them, will not last long. For as Firdawsi put it:
>
> > You killed a father and sowed the seeds of revenge,
> > When will he whose father was killed have peace?

You killed a snake and are raising its young,
What foolishness is this?

Eventually the fruits of all the enmity will ripen. Soon you will hear that Shuja ul-Mulk has been murdered by these very same Barakzais!'[40]

There were other shadows too: one regiment returning to India had its rearguard ambushed and massacred as it descended the Khyber Pass, with the loss of 150 baggage camels; shortly afterwards the garrison of Ali Masjid had to be evacuated down to Peshawar.[41] At the same time, a senior officer, Colonel Herring, was murdered by a party of Afghans while out walking in Wardak. He had disobeyed orders and strayed from the road to chat with some Afghans on a hill. They cut him to pieces. 'It was our melancholy fate to discover his dead body,' wrote Thomas Seaton. It was 'an awful sight, hacked and mangled in the most frightful manner, with every vestige of clothing torn off, except the wristbands of his shirt. The body was nearly severed at the loins, and there was a dreadful gash across his chest and through the ribs. There were altogether sixteen or seventeen wounds, each sufficient to cause death.'[42] Yet by and large the country was at peace. Once the Ghilzai chiefs had received their subsidies from Macnaghten, they fulfilled their part of the bargain. 'The passage from Khyber to Kabul was infested with dacoits and robbers,' recounted the *Tarikh-i-Sultani*. 'They threatened all the wayfarers and travellers on that route. However, once the Ghilzai Khans took over the management of this route, these threats were removed and peace reigned for the rest of the winter.'[43]

More worrying was the arrival of intelligence from Nazir Khan Ullah in Bukhara that the Russians were now finishing their preparations to invade Khiva. 'The Russians have collected a great number of camels, carriages and boats on the bank of the Caspian Sea,' he wrote. 'They have resolved to send their army and provision by way of the Caspian to the vicinity of Kir, a distance of three days' journey from Khiva.'[44] Still ignorant of Dost

Mohammad's detention in Bukhara, Macnaghten feared that the Russians could again be plotting with the Amir, planning to install him in Herat, which was now in 'a comparatively defenceless state'.[45]

Only Burnes seems to have understood that the Russian move was simply a direct response to British aggression in Afghanistan. 'Russia has put forth her force merely to counteract our policy,' he wrote to his friend Captain G. L. Jacob. 'By our advance on Kabul we thus hastened the great crisis.' Even at this stage Burnes instinctively grasped how fleeting could be the hold of either Russia or Britain on such an independent people as the Afghans. 'England and Russia will divide Asia between them,' he wrote prophetically, 'and the two empires will enlarge like the circles in the water until they are lost in nothing, and future generations will search for both in these regions as we now seek the remains of Alexander and his Greeks.'[46*]

Such realism was in increasingly short supply during the winter of 1839–40. Already the idea of permanently annexing Afghanistan was being discreetly discussed; there was even talk of moving the summer capital of the Raj from the inaccessible Himalayan ridge of Simla to the rich gardens of the Kabul valley, just as the Mughals had once migrated each May from Delhi and Agra to Kashmir and the lovely Nimla Gardens near Jalalabad.[47] Such over-confidence soon began to lead to a series of major strategic errors.

Firstly, rather than concentrating on consolidating Shah Shuja's fragile rule in Afghanistan, and providing the resources needed to make the occupation viable and secure, Lord Auckland – like more recent invaders – instead took the premature view that the conquest was already complete and so allowed himself to be distracted by launching another war of aggression in a different theatre. 'China

---

* The Russian attack on Khiva ended as disastrously as the British retreat from Kabul would do, with Perovsky losing half his camels and nearly half his men to the blizzards of the Central Asian winter. It put back Russian ambitions on the steppe for a generation: Khiva would not fall to Russian arms until 1872, just as a British army did not return to Afghanistan for almost forty years. See Alexander Morrison, *Twin Imperial Disasters: The Invasion of Khiva and Afghanistan in the Russian and British Official Mind, 1839–1842* (forthcoming).

promises to be amusing,' wrote his sister Emily in a revealingly flippant letter around this time. 'The Chinese are arming themselves and fitting up little innocent American ships, and collecting war junks; and it is my own belief that they are so conceited that they will contrive some odd way of blowing up all our 74s with blue and red fireworks, take all our sailors and soldiers prisoners, and teach them to cut ivory hollow balls.'[48] By withdrawing a large part of the Bombay army from Afghanistan and diverting much-needed resources away from consolidating the occupation of Afghanistan to his new Opium War, Auckland ensured that Macnaghten would never have the troops or the money he would need to make Shah Shuja's rule a success.

One direct result of the limited funds with which Shuja and Macnaghten were supposed to govern the country showed itself when Auckland turned down requests from the Commander-in-Chief for building both a new citadel in Kabul and a new fort at Kandahar, noting, 'I would see more clearly than I do at present what is to be the ultimate form of Afghanistan before I would incur any very great expense in buildings even for this purpose.'[49] This left the military in a dilemma. With winter now tightening its grip on the Kabul valley, some of the troops were billeted in the Bala Hisar while others were dotted around lodgings within the walled city and many more were shivering in tents in the camp out on the Kohistan Road. Moreover, Shuja was now pressuring Macnaghten to remove the troops that were in the easily defensible Bala Hisar, saying it would disgrace him in the eyes of Afghans if British soldiers were still there when his harem finally arrived from Ludhiana. As Auckland had forbidden the army from constructing a properly defensible new fort, the generals had little option but to build a lightly defended cantonment to shelter their troops as if they were in the peaceful rice paddies of Bengal rather than amid the hostile mountains of Afghanistan.

It is unclear who took the decision to build the cantonment in a fertile plain, bounded on every side by irrigation ditches and walled gardens and overlooked by the fortifications of several Afghan nobles. As one observer put it, 'it must always remain a wonder that any government, any officer, or set of officers, who had either science or experience in the field, should in a half-conquered country fix their forces in so extraordinary and injudicious a position.' Even Gleig – no tactical genius – could see immediately that it was a far from defensible spot. It was, he wrote, a very surprising place to find a fortification:

> There were forts and towers so planted that one or more overlooked each of the circular bastions by which the British lines were protected . . . Moreover, as if to convince the people that by their conquerors they were neither feared nor suspected, the principal magazine or store, both of provisions and ammunition, was not brought within the entrenched camp. On the contrary, an old fort, quite indefensible, and detached from both the cantonment and the Bala Hisar, was filled with stores, on the safety of which the very existence of the army depended; and a hundred sepoys, commanded by a subaltern officer, were considered adequate to protect them. A camp which is itself commanded by heights, and overlooked by towers, cannot command anything, and is wholly worthless for the preservation of order in a city from which it is cut off by a river.[50]

But it was not simply that the worst possible site had been chosen – the cantonment was also built to the worst possible design. It was obvious to Gleig that something was badly wrong with the layout of the hurriedly planned barracks, whose perimeter wall, nearly two miles long, was far too extended to be effectively manned by the garrison, and whose only defences were a low, easily escaladed rampart and a narrow ditch.[51]

Yet remarkably, distracted by their jackal hunting and theatrical debuts, few of the officers made the same simple deduction. Captain James Skinner of Skinner's Horse, the young Anglo-Indian who had been put in charge of the commissariat, did point out that the stores should be brought within the cantonment perimeter wall, but received the unhelpful answer from Sir Willoughby Cotton 'that no such place could be given to him, as they were far too busy in erecting barracks for the men to think of commissariat stores'.

One other man who questioned the design was Colonel Abraham Roberts, the Commander of Shah Shuja's Contingent. As the cantonment began to come up he realised not only that the position would be wholly untenable, but that the design of the barracks' wallwalks, without loopholes or machicolations, made it more or less impossible to defend in the event of an attack. He wrote a letter pointing this out to Lieutenant John Sturt, of the Bengal Engineers, who was designing the cantonment, but received a curt reply that nothing could be done. 'Your recommendation has come too late,' wrote Sturt, 'for I have already laid the foundations of one half. I know little about what is convenient or not – I submitted a plan to Sir W. Macnaghten; whether it went further than his military councils I cannot say, but as I heard no more about it I took silence for consent and worked away. Now the most must be made of it; it is useless questioning its expediency.'[52]

To make matters worse, the Afghans' sense of honour was now beginning to be seriously offended by the growing number of affairs taking place between British officers and Afghan women. The most prominent was probably the marriage between Captain Robert Warburton and the beautiful Shah Jahan Begum, a niece of Dost Mohammad, to which both Burnes and Lieutenant Sturt were witnesses.* Equally sensitive was between Lieutenant Lynch, the Political Agent at Qalat, and the beautiful sister of Walu Khan Shamalzai, the local Ghilzai chieftain. But the most visible activity was certainly in Kabul where a flourishing prostitution racket quickly sprang up to service the needs of all the single soldiers lodged around the town.[53] 'The English drank the wine of shameless immodesty,' wrote Mirza 'Ata, 'forgetting that any act has its consequences and rewards – so that after a while, the spring garden of the King's regime was blighted by the autumn of these ugly events . . . The nobles complained to each other, "Day by day, we

---

* The child born to the Warburtons went on to become Colonel Sir Robert Warburton, who put his mixed heritage and bilingualism to good use when he commanded the Frontier Force in the Khyber between 1879 and 1898, where he founded the Khyber Rifles. See Robert Warburton, *Eighteen Years in the Khyber, 1879–1898*, London, 1909.

are exposed, because of the English, to deceit and lies and shame. Soon the women of Kabul will give birth to half-caste monkeys – it's a disgrace!" But nothing was done.'[54]

Among those taking full advantage of the opportunities offered by Kabul was Alexander Burnes himself, who had now moved into his old lodgings in the centre of town. These he did up in some style, and, by purchasing Russian mirrors in the bazaar and scraping the quicksilver off the back, fitted his house with the first glass windows in Kabul. Given that Macnaghten in Jalalabad was daily taking over more of the duties of government, Burnes found himself with time on his hands. 'I am now a highly paid idler,' he wrote to one friend.

> I give paper opinions, but never work them out . . . These are my watchwords: Be silent. Pocket your pay. Do nothing but what you are ordered, and you will give high satisfaction . . . I lead, however, a very pleasant life; and if rotundity and heartiness be proofs of health, I have them. Breakfast I have long made a public meal. Covers are laid for eight, and half a dozen officers drop in, as they feel disposed, to discuss a rare Scotch breakfast of smoked fish, salmon gills, devils and jellies, and puff away at their cigars until ten . . . Once in every week I give a party of eight, and as the good River Indus is a channel for luxuries as well as of commerce, I can place before my friends at one third in excess of the Bombay price, champagne, hock, Madeira, sherry, port, claret, not forgetting the hermetically sealed salmon and hotch potch, all the way fra Aberdeen. And deuced good it is . . .[55]

If Afghan gossip was anything to go by, 'devils and jellies' were by no means the limit of his pleasures. The ever-loyal Mohan Lal explicitly states that Burnes brought his own troops of Kashmiri women who were 'in his service' and that he did not intrigue with the women of Afghanistan; but Kabul gossip maintained otherwise.[56] 'Burnes was especially shameless,' believed Mirza 'Ata. 'In his private quarters, he would take a bath with his Afghan mistress in the hot water of lust and pleasure, as the two rubbed each other down with flannels of giddy joy and the talc of intimacy. Two memsahibs, also his lovers, would join them.'[57]

Such rumours quickly began to sour the initially good relations between the people of Kabul and the occupying army. Kabul already had a discreet red-light district in the quarter occupied by Indian musicians and dancers close to the walls of the Bala Hisar. But there were not nearly enough Indian *rundis* around to cope with the demand created by the garrison of 4,500 sepoys and 15,500 camp followers, and a growing number of Afghan women seem to have made themselves available for a short but profitable ride into the cantonment. Indeed this became so common that the British began to compose rhymes about the easy availability of Afghan women:

> A Kabul wife under burkha cover,
> Was never known without a lover.[58]

Mohammad Husain Herati wrote:

It was reported to His Majesty by well-wishers that there was a thriving market in female prostitutes who were publicly, day and night, carried on horseback into the English camp. These prostitutes wore fine clothes and jewellery and make-up, fearlessly came in and out unchallenged, so that one could not tell if they were of noble lineage or common sluts – all this undermined public morality and the very basis of the state. It was the hypocrites of the Barakzai faction who first showed the way to this corruption and then blamed His Majesty, hoping thereby to arouse the moral indignation of simple people. His Majesty raised the matter with Macnaghten, who had little experience of the treachery and baseness of these people and only answered: 'If we stop the soldiers having sex, the poor boys will fall quite ill!' His Majesty answered: 'That may well be true; however, in this kingdom at least, it would be better to discipline the soldiers and to respect the outward appearance of morality!'[59]

Fayz Mohammad wrote in the later *Siraj ul-Tawarikh* that this growing slight to Afghan honour was the biggest cause of the alienation of the Afghans from their new government.

> The Shah's well-wishers, who were adherents of the Shar'ia of the Prophet and knew that this disgraceful business ripped the veil of religious honour . . . complained to the Shah who told Macnaghten, 'Better that you should stop the traffic in this market's goods by punishment. Otherwise, this tree of wickedness is going to bear unwholesome fruit.' But Sir William Macnaghten did not heed the Shah's words and soon forgot all about them . . . Until then it was still not generally known that when it came to affairs of state and matters affecting the army the Shah had no influence. Now the Barakzais went about revealing the way things really stood saying, 'The Shah is Shah in name only and has no hand in state matters.' Moreover, for their own purposes, they would play up the role of the English. Dangerously flirting with the fire of sedition they even mocked their neighbours, 'Even your women', they said, 'do not belong to you.'[60]

In March 1840, Shah Shuja returned to Kabul from his winter quarters, and the court reassembled amid the pavilions of the Bala Hisar. With Dost Mohammad now immured within a Bukhara dungeon, Shah Shuja and his backers had a real opportunity to consolidate their joint rule. Instead the spring thaw saw the two rival administrations, British and Sadozai, beginning to compete with each other for control of the country. At the same time a growing realisation began to spread that it was Macnaghten, not Shuja, who was really running the new regime.

The cause of dissension was not a personality clash: Macnaghten remained as enamoured of the Shah as he had ever been. 'My longer experience of His Majesty's character more thoroughly convinces me that there is not an abler or a better man than himself in all his dominions,' he wrote to Auckland on his return from Jalalabad.

His Majesty sits in durbar every morning except Thursday for
about two hours and listens with the greatest patience to the representations of his chiefs. One day is set apart for hearing the
complaints of all those who may allege that they have not received
redress from the authorities to whom their cases had been referred.
Though stern in the execution of justice, as was exemplified only
the other day in the case of the murderer for whose pardon much
influence was exerted, yet His Majesty is merciful and kind hearted
in the extreme, and if the personal qualities of a monarch could
ensure popularity, Shah Shoojah could not fail to obtain it.[61]

There were however several issues of policy, as well as the simple
realities of divided power which were now slowly coming to divide
the Shah from his British backers. As Mohan Lal put it, 'we neither
took the reins of power in our own hands, nor did we give them in
full measure into the hands of Shah Shuja ul-Mulk. Inwardly or
secretly we interfered in all transactions, contrary to the terms of
our engagement with the Shah; yet outwardly we wore the mask of
neutrality.' This annoyed Shuja and disappointed the people. 'The
Shah became jealous of our power, and of the influence which he
thought we were daily gaining for our own benefit, contrary to
treaty, and to suspect that all the people looked upon us as sover-
eigns of the land.'[62]

   The first point of dissension was a growing disagreement over
the army. Already aware of the massive cost of defending
Afghanistan, and of the way it was beginning to turn a small
profit in the East India Company's account into a large loss,
Auckland was under strict instructions from London to train up
in Afghanistan an efficient Afghan national army for Shah Shuja.
This would allow the Company to pull back its troops to India
while leaving Shuja secure and able to defend himself. 'I have
earnestly impressed it upon Macnaghten that every exertion must
be made to consolidate the power of Shah Shooja,' wrote the
Governor General, 'to give efficiency to his army and popularity
to his government [as] our regular troops cannot remain there
beyond the present season . . .'[63] Auckland was equally frank with

the Shah: 'I have been ready, so long as any have seemed to threaten mischief, to allow British troops to remain in Afghanistan, but your Majesty is well aware of my desire to withdraw them as soon as it may be safely done, and your Majesty's army shall be organised as to enable you fully to rely upon them for the maintenance of the legitimate Afghan monarchy.'[64]

This may have seemed a good plan in Simla, but in Kabul Shuja was all too aware that Macnaghten's strategy of diverting resources from the old tribal cavalry levies towards a professional standing infantry army removed his principal means of extending patronage to the chiefs. As far as the nobles were concerned, the Shah was duty-bound to give out money, land and estates to them in return for which they would provide cavalry. The system was certainly corrupt: 'ghost-payrolling' allowed the tribal leaders to claim financial allowances for much larger numbers of men than they actually raised. But it was nevertheless the glue that cemented the local and regional tribal leaders' loyalty to the regime at the centre. By aiming to create a modern, drilled force at the expense of the chieftains, Macnaghten was taking away Shah Shuja's only real opportunity to reward his nobility for their support and undermining the power and wealth of his most important followers.

Nevertheless, Macnaghten insisted on driving the reforms through, maintaining that the benefits and savings would outweigh the risks involved. Payments to the chiefs duly fell by a quarter, from 1.3 million rupees in 1839 to one million two years later, with the bulk of the cuts falling on the eastern Ghilzai tribes who controlled and policed the vital passes between Kabul and the Khyber. To make matters worse, the chiefs had naturally hoped that the wealthy Firangis would actually increase their allowances rather than reduce them. These high expectations increased their feeling of betrayal, especially when they saw that the recruits to the new Uzbek Janbaz and the Hazara Hazirbash regiments were, as Mohan Lal put it, not from the nobility but 'low and petty persons'. When the chiefs complained of this, Captain R. S. Trevor, the young, tactless and unpopular Burnes protégé to whom Macnaghten had delegated the reforms, bluntly wrote that 'in the course of two years all the chiefs of the military class should be dismissed from his [the Shah's] service, and what support they may receive till that time they should consider as charity'. This was a very serious matter. By appearing to threaten the entire traditional order and to take away the income of the Afghan tribal leaders, Macnaghten succeeded in alienating many of the Shah's natural supporters who, until that point, had been quite happy to see the return of the Sadozais. It was certainly not a policy designed to endear Shah Shuja's rule to those who could do most to disrupt it.[65]

Two strongly Royalist nobles were especially furious about the way the British were eroding what they regarded as their traditional rights. The two men were from different backgrounds. Abdullah Khan Achakzai was a young warrior-aristocrat from one of the most powerful and distinguished families in the region. His grandfather had been a rival of Dost Mohammad's grandfather for the post of wazir in the early days of the Durrani Empire under Ahmad Shah Abdali, and Achakzais had never shown much enthusiasm for the Barakzais. But from his impregnable fortress Qila Abdullah, south of Kandahar, Achakzai controlled a great swathe of territory, and Dost Mohammad had always been careful to win his support. In comparison to Achakzai, the elderly Aminullah Khan Logari was almost a self-made man: his father had been a senior administrator under the governor of Kashmir at the time of Timur Shah, and it was through his intelligence and loyalty to the Sadozais under Shah Zaman, Shah Mahmoud and finally Shah Shuja that he had first come to control large areas of the strategically important areas of Logar, to the south of Kabul, and Kohistan to its north, as well as the vital Khord Kabul Pass, which dominated the routes into Kabul from the south. He was now a very old man, but still powerful, commanding substantial funds in addition to his own private militia.

Both men were committed pro-Sadozai loyalists who would naturally have preferred the government of Shah Shuja to that of Dost Mohammad, but they strongly objected to the presence of the infidel British in their land, and were determined that no Kafir innovations would deprive them of their right to serve their monarch or to pay their many followers. When they went to complain about the reductions in their salaries to Captain Trevor, according to Mohan Lal, Trevor insulted them and threw them out.[66] For men of such rank and status to have to subject themselves to such treatment from a junior figure was unacceptable to both nobles' sense of honour. They complained to the Shah, who said he sympathised and sent them on to Macnaghten. Macnaghten refused to help them. Shortly afterwards, Aminullah 'was requested either to give up the chiefship' of his district 'or to increase the sum of revenue paid by him'.[67] Aminullah refused and shortly afterwards control over his district was taken from him.[68] From that moment onwards, Abdullah Khan Achakzai and Aminullah Khan Logari became the two most active centres of opposition to the British in Kabul, waiting and plotting for the moment when they could take their revenge.

Shuja himself had other reasons to be wary of Macnaghten's new Afghan national army. In particular he was unclear if a British-trained, British-officered army would ever actually be obedient to him. As he pointed out to Auckland, already the Shah Shuja Contingent seemed to show little inclination to do as he said. 'I am not personally acquainted with many of the officers in the force,' he wrote. 'Nor do I know the duties they perform. They do not even seem to know that they are my soldiers. I am desirous that the officers as well as the Battalions which you have kindly placed at my service should know that they are in my employ, so that the natives of this country should consider those attached to me to be my servants.' The Shah added: 'It is about 29 years since this country has been deprived of the Royal Authority. This has caused insurrection and every family to be the master of itself . . . I therefore wish that all the officers and Battalions should be entirely under my orders which will create a good feeling between them and the natives of this country, and put off all ill doubts from their minds.'[69]

For the Shah, his inability to control his own corps of the army brought home as nothing else did his own powerlessness. It was at this period that he began to sink into a deep melancholy. 'He often sat at the windows of the palace,' wrote Durand, 'whiling away time, his eye wandering over the different objects which the city and its plain offered. On one of these occasions, after a long silent pause, Shah Shuja made the remark "that everything appeared to him shrunk, small and miserable, and that the Kabul of his old age in no respect corresponded with the recollections of the Kabul of his youth".'[70] Even the perennially insensitive Macnaghten noticed that 'His Majesty has of late been subject to a depression of spirits.'[71]

As much as Shuja wanted to control the new regiments and demonstrate his sovereignty, he was also painfully aware that he simply could not afford to maintain a sizeable army without British financial support. As ever in Afghanistan, it was a struggle to find the money to pay for the enormous army needed to secure so poor, fractured and uncontrollable a country. The army of the old Durrani Empire had been raised on taxes from the rich tributary regions such as Sindh and Kashmir. Since those areas had been lost all Afghan rulers had struggled to pay their troops without imposing unacceptable tax burdens on the relatively barren and unproductive regions that remained to them: 'In the time of the Sadozais there was in every family and tribe one man of dignity, and the expenditure of the cavalry under them was provided from the revenues of the dependant countries of Punjab, Sindh, Cashmere and Moultan and part of Khoorasan,' Shuja explained to Auckland. 'Now from every family and house ten or twenty individuals have sprung up, and each begs the honours of chiefship to be bestowed upon them. I cannot think of any remedy but to apply to Your Lordship for friendly assistance.' He added:

Dost Mohammad Khan notwithstanding his oppressive habits and extortions could not meet the expenses from his income. All his people were displeased with him and deserted him for they did not receive pay for six months in the whole year, and what remuneration they did get was in woollens. If I keep up a force equal in number to that of Dost Mohammad there will be no difference between me and himself. If I maintain a greater number than the revenue of this country, which cannot be equal to their expenses, there will not be sufficient to feed the troops. If I employ an army smaller than that of Dost Mohammad, it will disappoint the natives of this country who are daily swelling in number and petitioning to enter my service. Consequently I am involved in troubles and pass days and nights in vexation. When I look upon the payment of the soldiers I find no other source than to rely on Your Lordship's favour.[72]

If it was the army reforms that first brought Macnaghten and Shuja into conflict, then there was also the problem of Shuja's loyal Chief of Staff, Mullah Shakur, whom Burnes and Macnaghten found increasingly resistant to their ideas. 'Whatever money he gained by public or private means he added to the coffers of the Shah,' wrote Mohan Lal,

and he was therefore in great confidence with the king. Mullah Shakur was however very old, and totally unfit to occupy any high post. He had lost his memory to such an extent that he could not recognise a person whom he had well known before, if he had not seen him even for a day; but he perfectly understood the real meaning of our treaty with the king, and by it he knew that we had no right to take over the administration of the country.[73]

Long before Shah Shuja lost his patience with the interference of Macnaghten and Burnes in his internal affairs, Mullah Shakur was trying to resist British encroachment into the daily running of the country, while maintaining the appearance that Shuja was really running everything. 'As long as Mullah Shakur was in office, the polite fiction was maintained that His Majesty did have some say in the affairs of the kingdom and the army,' wrote Mohammad Husain Herati.

For example, if the price of wheat was fixed at a particular rate, any trader who flouted the rules would be punished by Mullah Shakur in his role as assistant governor of Kabul – but whenever Alexander Burnes sent his chaprasi messenger to protest that the trader in question was under his protection, the offender would be released. By such means, Mullah Shakur attempted to maintain the appearance of the legitimacy of the government. But Burnes and Macnaghten did not like to be contradicted in any way, nor to pay attention to the intricacies of government, and day by day they grew more hostile to the Mullah.[74]

These were not the only things that undermined the popularity and effectiveness of Shah Shuja's government as spring turned to summer in 1840. Many were now complaining of Shuja's distant style, which formed a sharp contrast with the consciously egalitarian approach of Dost Mohammad. It had long been a pattern with Shuja that the more he felt his status diminished, the more he wished to make public demonstrations of his rank. So it was in 1840, just as he began to feel his grip on power slipping, that we begin to read reports of grand perorations of the King and his court around Kabul and its vicinity. 'The wild grandeur' of Shuja's company 'baffles description', wrote the artist James Rattray when he came across them around this time. In front came the royal dromedaries 'with bells suspended from their harness, ringing in time to their dreamy gait, with outstretched necks tasselled and ornamented. There were hundreds of them,' and many bore small cannon decorated with green and scarlet flags which the camel drivers fired at random: 'plumes were carried away and whiskers singed, much to the delight of the unearthly marksmen'. As the deafening camel batteries passed on, next came the royal stud, 'glistening in cloth of gold and jewelled housings'. There followed the officers of the household,

> executioners, stave, sword, kettledrum and standard bearers in their many-horned and pointed scarlet caps, clearing the way by choking it up, restoring order by creating confusion. A clattering array of Afghaun horse followed them, beplumed and armed cap-a-pie, their kettledrums beating, and their bossed and ornamented furniture jingling as they swept past, followed by a host of bare-legged, long-haired groom-boy runners. After them pranced a

squadron of the Envoy's body-guard, in blue and silver, and then – Majesty itself.

The Shah was splendidly mounted, sat well and upright, and looked every inch of him the King. The imperial velvet crown, with drooping leaves of emerald pendants branching from the upper part of it, encircled his high brow, which glistened in a band of costly gems. His dress was a tight-fitting purple satin tunic, embroidered in gold and precious stones, and from shoulder to wrist were bound armlets of massive plates of jewellery. Shagreen leather, pointed-toed and iron-heeled boots, and a flat compact cashmere shawl girdle, from which was suspended a splendid Isfahan scimitar, completed his attire. The Shah was a man of great personal beauty, and so well got up that none could have guessed his age. The character of his countenance was one of excessive hauteur, blended with melancholy; an expression which was increased tenfold by his regularly marked eyebrows, long dark eyes, and beard of jettest black.

Rattray was dazzled, and noted that the people of Kabul were not uninterested: 'As the royal train swept on through the narrow winding streets, every window, doorway and roof was crowded with spectators.' But they were not cheering the man they called 'the Firangi's King'. Instead they showed no sign of 'pleasure or loyalty' but merely looked on 'mute and dogged, counting their beads as they stood motionless, with arms crossed over their breasts. The silence was unbroken save for the voice of a petitioner driven back in an attempt to reach the royal ear, the tramp of cavalry, and the shout of the officer proclaiming the power, excellence and majesty of the Shah of Shahs, the pearl of the Durrani dynasty.' Another officer-turned-artist, Lockyer Willis Hart, went further: 'This form and ceremony, so hateful to the Affghans, was the King's foible, and was sometimes carried to an absurd extent.'[75]

It was not just the people on the street. Many of the chiefs also felt humiliated and belittled by the grandeur and distance of Shuja's ultra-royal style: 'By the late ruler the nobles were treated very attentively, almost on equal terms and enjoyed much influence,' recorded Colonel Wade's munshi, Shahamat Ali, 'while now . . . they found it very difficult to obtain admittance to the royal presence; and those who by flattering the ushers could do so, were made to stand at a respectful distance from his Majesty with their hands folded in a most humble manner, and often compelled to retire from the durbar without being allowed to say a word to the King.'[76] It was also this that made the British officers of Shuja's Contingent so loath to attend on their nominal employer. As Burnes tried to explain to the Shah, 'he might remedy the non-appearance of the British Officers at his Durbar by fixing a day in the week to receive them as they often came and after waiting for a long time departed without an audience'.[77]

But the biggest problem of all, as Macnaghten was frank enough to recognise, was simply the growing taint to Shuja's reputation brought by his continued association with the infidel British and the spreading conviction that he was merely their puppet. 'His Majesty labours under peculiar and complicated difficulties,' Macnaghten wrote to Auckland,

the foremost of which is his connection with us. We have placed him on his throne, but it will be some time before our motives in doing so are understood and there are many who wilfully misunderstand them. The difference of our religion is of course the chief cause of antipathy on the part of the people. The Afghans are a nation of bigots. Besides an intolerance of our creed, there is an intolerance of our customs and it behoves us therefore to be very wary in our attempts at innovation, nor ought it ever to be forgotten that a system, though excellent in itself, may not be good as applied to this country, nor may it be such as to meet appreciation. It requires the most cautious steering to refrain on the one side from alarming popular prejudices, and on the other from leaving the government in the same imbecile state in which we found it.[78]

To Colvin, Macnaghten developed a similar theme: 'You rightly conjecture that the Barakzais have the most inflammable material to work upon. Of all moral qualities, avarice, credulity and bigotry are the most inflammable, and the Afghans have all these three in perfection.' While Macnaghten was correct to point to religious difference as lying at the heart of Afghan objections to the new regime, and to realise that the Muslim 'ulema were fast establishing themselves as the centre of opposition to Shuja, he was wrong to interpret their objection as mere 'bigotry'. The mullahs had initially been co-opted by the Anglo-Sadozai regime, which from the beginning paid salaries to those among the 'ulema who came out in support of the Shah. But the mullahs grew in time to have good reason to dislike a regime which only intermittently patronised their institutions or helped restore their mosques, and which seized for itself many of their *waqf* endowments to help augment the regime's tax revenues: particular horror was caused when the British 'went so far as to usurp control of the endowments of the great Sufi shrine of Ashiqan wa Arifan, which had been registered from the days of bygone rulers'. This was an especially tactless move as the shrine, formerly a Buddhist monastery, was Old Kabul's most important and ancient cult centre, and for several generations had been the burial place of the Barakzais. Moreover, it was controlled by two powerful and respected hereditary Naqsbandi sheikhs from Kohistan, Mir Masjidi and his brother Mir Haji, who was also the hereditary Imam of the Pul-i-Khishti Friday Mosque and the leader of the Kabul 'ulema.[79] They were enormously influential figures and the Anglo-Sadozai regime should have done all it could to keep them within the Shah's inner circle. Instead it seemed to be doing all it could to alienate them.

To aggravate matters further, the British also interfered in the mullahs' administration of justice. The 'ulema understandably didn't like being lectured on the Sharia by the conceited Macnaghten who was now writing, 'I have gained a complete victory over the Moollas who have since freely admitted that my knowledge of the Mahomedan Law is superior to their own.'[80] Most of all they disliked the way the 'licentious infidels' were corrupting their city, and strongly objected to the daily spectacle of carousing British and Indian squaddies openly drinking and whoring in their streets.

These conservative objections to the British presence were shared by the nobility. In the summer of 1840, the

British intercepted a letter from a senior Barakzai leader, Sultan Mohammad Khan, the former Governor of Peshawar, who wrote to his half-brother Dost Mohammad complaining, 'I cannot tell you what oppression is committed by the Firangis. Some of the people have publicly turned Christians and others have turned prostitute. Grain has got very dear. May God turn this accursed set out of the country as their appearance has discarded both religion and modesty.'[81]

All this came to a head in July 1840 when, at the instigation of Mir Haji, the 'ulema began to omit proclaiming the name of Shah Shuja at Friday prayers, on the grounds that the real rulers were the Kafirs. According to Burnes, the Shah immediately summoned him to the Bala Hisar and told him:

> that in the city of Kabul he was assailed night & day by mullahs and others who represented the present state of things as anything but a Mahommedan Kingdom and asked him that if the Shah was of the same opinion a rebellion or insurrection was easily raised against the British. Of course, said His Majesty, I have endeavoured to correct the erroneous opinions of these men by assuring them that the English and I are as two hearts in one body. Yet I cannot hope to get them to think so when in the capital the troops are not my own and their movements take place without my knowledge ... H.M. observed that it was a plain fiction to call the officers and men whom the Gov. Genl. had placed at his disposal as his own, that none of the officers ever came near him, or even acted as his, and it was no wonder therefore that his subjects increasingly considered him a puppet ('a moolee', or radish, was the word he used) & that he had no honour in his own country ...[82]

It was around this time that the more perceptive of the British in Afghanistan began to realise the very delicate nature of their position and the fragility of the regime they had installed. Abraham Roberts began to worry about the extended lines of communication, the much reduced size of the British garrison, and the way that small pockets of troops were left in key urban areas where they were vulnerable to insurrection. He was soon writing to Auckland to express his anxieties about the 'numerous Corps being spread over the Country, free from all Military control, and managed by the Political Department and with so little judgement and without any Military experience'.[83] Meanwhile, General Nott in Kandahar blamed Macnaghten and his political advisers. 'They drink their claret, draw large salaries, go about with a rabble at their heels,' he complained to his daughters.

> All are well paid by John Bull, or rather by the oppressed cultivators of the land in Hindustan. The Calcutta treasury is drained of its rupees, and *good natured* Lord Auckland approves and confirms all. In the meantime all goes wrong here. We are hated by the people . . . Thus it is to employ men selected by patronage. The conduct of one thousand and one Politicals has ruined our cause, and bared the throat of every European in this country to the sword and knife of the revengeful Affghan, and unless several regiments be quickly sent, not a man will be left to note the fall of his comrades. Nothing but force will ever make them submit to the hated Shah.[84]

Even the usually optimistic Burnes began to be anxious. 'There is no two days fixity of purpose,' he complained privately to his friend Jacob, 'no plan of the future policy, external or internal, on which you can depend a week. The bit-by-bit system prevails. Nothing comprehensive is looked to . . . and I, for one, begin to think that Wade [who had retired back in Ludhiana] will be the luckiest of all of us, as he will be away from the breakdown; for unless a new leaf is turned, break down we shall.'[85]

The first signs of concerted armed resistance took place in May 1840 when a column marching from Kandahar towards Ghazni was attacked by 2,000 Ghilzai horsemen. The Ghilzai were quickly driven off, leaving 200 dead behind them, but they learned the lesson that a frontal attack in flat open country was not the way to tackle the British. Then, in mid-August, less than a year after Shah Shuja had entered Kabul in triumph, news arrived in the capital of exactly what the British had most dreaded. Dost Mohammad had been sprung from his Bukhara dungeon. 'The English in Kabul were resting in the arms of pleasure and sloth', wrote Mirza 'Ata, 'when the news arrived that Amir Dost Mohammad Khan had escaped from Bukhara, helped by a private merchant who had bribed the watch appointed to guard the Amir – the sum was said to be some 10,000 Rupees'.

Reports began to arrive that the Amir had returned to northern Afghanistan and raised the flag of holy war. In late August the troops of the small British outpost at Saighan on the frontier of the territory of the Mir Wali of Kunduz, where the valley drops to the northern plains, were forced to fall back twenty miles to a more defensible position in Bamiyan. Worse still, a contingent of Shah Shuja's troops sent to attack the Amir mutinied and joined the rebellion. Around the same time, news came that a quite separate rebellion had broken out in Kohistan only a few hours' journey north of Kabul, where the Tajiks felt that the Shah had failed to reward them properly for their help in taking Kabul in 1839 and had betrayed all the promises that had been made to them.*

It had taken just a year for the Afghans to rise in revolution. But the jihad against the British had now begun.

It is the epic poets who give the fullest account of the Amir's escape from Bukhara. Maulana Hamid Kashmiri tells of how a celebrated Kabul merchant, Khan Kabir, arrived in Bukhara with his caravan and heard that the Amir had been thrown into a pit. Grateful to Dost Mohammad for favours when he was in power,

> He put his heart and soul into achieving the Amir's release
> Night and day he searched for a way out

---

* Wade had encouraged the Kohistanis to rise up and had promised their pirs, Mir Masjidi and his brother Mir Haji, inducements of 500 tomans a year if they did so. The money was never paid. So the Tajik rebellion was led by the same members of the 'ulema who had just removed Shah Shuja's name from Friday Prayers in Kabul.

For the Amir's assistance, he opened the hand of generosity
And scattered gold so that the Amir's jailer became his prisoner

So bound was the warder by the Amir's noose
He endeavoured to serve him like a slave bought with gold

When the Amir knew that the gate was open
He found an opportunity one night, and hastened to escape[86]

Akbar Khan, who escaped at the same time, was quickly recaptured before he had managed to leave the city, but his father succeeded in getting away. With the help of Khan Kabir, Dost Mohammad adopted the disguise of a Sufi fakir, just as Shah Shuja had done when escaping from Ranjit Singh in Lahore thirty years earlier. Initially the Amir took the wrong route, and in his panic killed the horse he had been given, riding it to its death over barren mountains. Just as he was wandering lost and alone in the high-altitude desert and about to give up hope, he was picked up by a camel caravan heading for Balkh. 'The Amir was provided with a camel bearing baskets on both sides,' wrote Mohan Lal, who later became Dost Mohammad's first biographer,

and in one of these baskets, the Amir placed himself under the pretence of indisposition. In Chiraghchi [where he had been surrounded and captured the previous year] the servants of the Bukhara government, being previously informed of the escape of the Amir from the city, suspected his being in the caravan. They examined every camel basket, but could not discover him, since he had cunningly coloured his silver beard with ink, which he found by himself for the occasion, and the informer was punished by the officers for bringing them into ridicule with a false report.[87]

For the next few weeks, the Amir kept with the caravan but, as he had no money, lived only on what he could beg. The Afghan oral tradition is full of stories of the Amir's trials and sufferings on his travels, some of which Fayz Mohammad gathered into his history. 'At Shahr-i Sabz, the Amir dismounted before a ramshackle hostel for dervishes,' he recorded. Here a few men were sitting around drinking tea with milk.

> The Amir was very hungry and with an eye to perhaps getting some tea from them, he sat down near the door of the hostel. But those inconsiderate people, who call themselves qalandars [holy fools] but certainly did not have the character of holy men, said not a word to him, and offered him nothing. With stomach still empty, he then went into the city and asked for a certain merchant named Mullah Kabir who was from Kabul and had a family there in Shahr-i Sabz . . . When he saw the Amir, Mullah Kabir kissed his hand and escorted him to his house. As they entered the house, the mullah was overcome with compassion at seeing the Amir dressed as a dervish and wept. He put himself at the Amir's disposal and did everything it was in his power to do.

After he had rested, the Amir despatched Mullah Kabir to the Governor of Shahr-i Sabz to tell him of his arrival.

> As soon as he heard the news, the governor came to Mullah Kabir's house and showed the Amir the highest regard, moving him into the royal guesthouse. After performing the duties of host, he spoke about the ignominious behaviour of the Amir of Bukhara and offered to send an army there to exact revenge. Dost Mohammad thanked him for the offer, but asked him instead to provide 700 horsemen to accompany him across the Oxus. The governor agreed, prepared the necessary supplies and equipment and assigned 700 troopers as escort.[88]

From this point, the Amir's fortunes began to improve. He crossed the Oxus and made his way safely to Balkh. On the way, as he passed through the villages of northern Afghanistan, he realised that the mood had changed while he had been in prison and that disillusion with the Anglo-Sadozai regime was now widespread. 'Along the road he questioned travellers,' wrote Maulana Kashmiri in the *Akbarnama*, seeking news from Kabul and Bukhara.

> One day he saw amongst the wayfarers
> A young man who had set out from Kabul
>
> He asked him: 'What is the state of affairs in the land of Kabul?
> What do they say of the Shah and the Firangi chiefs?
>
> What plans have they for war and peace?
> And what of the Khans? Are they as before . . . ?'
>
> The young man said: 'O mighty ruler of good fortune!
> Shuja is not that Shuja of yore, his mind is not the same as before
>
> Like Kings he has a seat upon the throne
> But he does not rule the land nor have his hand upon the treasury
>
> Secretly, he is in anguish, his soul exhausted
> Less than a watchman, such a king is he.'[89]

The Amir eventually made his way to his former host, the Mir Wali at Khamard, where he found his son Afzal Khan waiting for him. Here the Uzbek leader again offered to help him – the Mir Wali had owed his power and position entirely to Dost Mohammad's patronage – but also brought him bad news. The Amir's brother, Nawab Jabar Khan, had despaired of the Amir ever freeing himself from his prison and had just surrendered himself to the British authorities, along with the Amir's harem. Undaunted, the Amir decided he had no option but to fight, and again publicly declared a jihad on the Firangis. For the Afghan poets this was a heroic moment:

> He girded his loins to battle the enemy
> And sought out his scattered army
>
> Of men and blade-wielding battalions
> He gathered five hundred horsemen

In Kabul *Laat Jangi* Macnaghten heard the news
That the forces of the brave Amir were drawing near

Loins girded and belt tightened for battle
With Uzbek battalions he was coming to war

Laat Jangi, Macnaghten, Lord of War, commanded *Daaktar*
[Dr Percival Lord]
To take forty thousand, with forty commanders

Like a savage tiger, they gave chase
Intent on hunting the brave lion

Roaring and full of passion, they came forth
Driving towards Bamiyan[90]

Dost Mohammad now had at his disposal a small force of under a thousand Uzbek horsemen. Advancing southwards, he managed to drive away the British sepoys of the first British outpost he came across. Shortly afterwards, the Afghan force at Bamiyan under Saleh Mohammad deserted and joined the Amir's army.

Reports of the growing crisis quickly reached Kabul. 'The news put fear into the hearts of the English soldiers,' wrote Mirza 'Ata, 'and even more so into the heart of the King. He was so alarmed by news of the approach of the Amir that he could not sleep, but rather went out at night into the Royal Garden in the lower part of the Bala Hisar, and had a tunnel opened beneath his throne-platform as an escape route.' Whether this was true or not, many British officers sent their families to take shelter in the Bala Hisar, along with their baggage and possessions, while Macnaghten initially refused to send reinforcements to Bamiyan, saying they could not be spared from Kabul. He then sent a series of jittery and paranoid despatches to Simla. 'The Afghans are gunpowder,' he wrote, 'and the Dost is a lighted match . . . We are surrounded by spies.'[91]

But, for all their fears, the cavalry force the Amir had mustered was still insufficient to meet a disciplined Company army in open battle. When British reinforcements were finally sent up to Bamiyan under William Dennie, the two sides met on Friday 18 September. Dost Mohammad had possession of the chain of forts that commanded the entrance of the valley and drew up his horsemen in the centre. He sent his son Afzal Khan to command one wing crowning the heights to the left, while the Mir Wali took the high ground on the opposite side of the valley.[92] But, as the Afghans were still learning to their cost, it was always an error to concentrate their troops in a plain when the British were armed with modern cannon. The British horse artillery was able to mow down the charging Afghan cavalry long before they were able to reach the guns:

> Frenzied and foaming, the army of Firang
> Did not delay the fight for a moment
>
> All at once the entire horde
> Attacked like a pestilential wind
>
> With their cannonballs and gunfire
> They made the very earth and heavens tremble
>
> The Firangis appeared in those flames
> As would the demons of hellfire.

Seeing the way the battle was going, and with a severe wound on his thigh, Dost Mohammad withdrew, leaving a hundred dead on the battlefield, but saving most of his forces to fight another day. He remained, however, undaunted and instead of retreating he headed on by goatpaths and dry riverbeds over the mountains towards Kabul, intent on meeting up with the Tajik insurgents in Kohistan.

This was both a brave and a risky strategy. Macnaghten had sent Burnes with 'Fighting Bob' Sale and two regiments to occupy the district headquarters at Charikar, and these troops were now blocking the main road between the Amir and the Kohistan rebels. Moreover, Dost Mohammad had many Kohistani enemies. Only a year previously the Kohistanis had risen against him as the British advanced on Kabul. But the Amir gambled that it was his best hope, and that a mutual hatred of the new Kafir govern-ment would for the moment trump earlier enmities. He sent emissaries ahead to the Tajik chiefs, and delegated his ally, the Safi Mir of Tagab, to persuade the sheikhs and mirs of Kohistan and Ghurband to combine under his leadership. He was therefore greatly relieved when his overtures received an immediate reply. Ghulam Kohistani, the author of the *Jangnama*, was himself from the area and recorded local memories of how Dost Mohammad's arrival was greeted in Tagab:

The first to come forward was the triumphant warrior from Parwan
Wise and knowing, Rajab Khan was his name

'You are the Amir and we are your servants,' he said,
'We bow our heads before your command

These unworthy hovels of ours, this land of rock and thistle
You have made worthy by your presence.'

At the Amir's order, those courageous rebels
Rode their horses through the mountainous lands

Nowhere was there a moment's respite or hesitation
Dreading in their hearts a Firangi attack

For fear that *he* would beat them to it –
That wretched Burnes at Charikar[93]

There followed weeks of guerrilla warfare, with Dost Mohammad making surprise attacks on government outposts and inflicting casualties, but lacking the strength to take on the massed forces of the Company. Meanwhile General Sale systematically laid waste to rebel-held villages, destroyed the rebels' trees and crops, and

besieged the rebel-held forts around the Koh Daman, while Burnes
tried to bribe the Kohistan chiefs to betray and hand over the Amir.
By the end of September, Burnes had managed to pry the Mir Wali
and his Uzbeks away from Dost Mohammad, leaving the Amir
with just a few hundred Kohistani supporters; but still he eluded
capture. 'The fighting between the Amir and the English lasted two
months,' wrote Mirza 'Ata. 'There were 13 clashes and skirmishes,
and never in that time did the English even glimpse the lovely face
of victory. Rather it was the Amir who carried off the polo-ball of
victory from the field of battle. Eventually the English abandoned
their search and straggled back into Charikar half-dead, leaving
much of their supplies and equipment behind.'

According to Mohan Lal, much of this fighting and destruction
was anyway ill judged and unnecessary: the Kohistan chiefs had
made it clear that they were willing to call a halt to their insurgency
and only wished for the promises made to them the previous year
to be honoured. One particularly important chief, Mir Masjidi
Khan, the revered Naqsbandi Pir who was the most influential
leader in the area, was actually on the verge of surrendering, and
had given his word he would come into Kabul and 'take refuge in
the mausoleum of Timur Shah, and thence proceed to wait upon
the Shah and the Envoy'. Burnes had agreed to this, when 'contrary
to previous arrangements' Sale and Prince Timur set off to besiege
Mir Masjidi's fort. The fort at first proved too strong to storm, and
the wounded and embittered Mir Masjidi managed to escape to
Nijrow. In his absence his fort was destroyed, his family slaughtered and his lands distributed to his enemies. The brutality of the
destruction of the fort and all its inhabitants horrified the Kohistanis. 'They broke down its walls,' wrote Ghulam Kohistani,

> In every gold-spangled house
> Bedecked like a spring garden
>
> They set fire to the doors and roofs
> Which carried their message up to the skies

> They destroyed the central arch
> They made it like a wasteland
>
> No one saw any sign of life
> No, no one had ever heard a more devastating tale[94]

Thus, concluded Mohan Lal, 'we made the Mir our enemy for ever'.[95] In due course, Mir Masjidi would return and succeed in driving the British out of Kohistan, pursuing the last survivors of the garrison to Kabul. Making an enemy out of him was one of the most serious errors made by the British in the whole campaign.

In mid-October, matters took another turn for the worse when a whole squadron of British-trained Kohistani troops in Charikar crossed over and joined Dost Mohammad.[96] Mohan Lal thought that this was one of the most serious threats the British would ever face in their occupation of Afghanistan, with the Amir on the loose, Kohistan in flames and the rest of the tribes waiting to see who would come out victorious, 'the people and chiefs being equally discontented by our not adhering to the engagements and promises we had made them'.[97]

When the two sides did finally clash, neither was expecting it. On 2 November 1840, Sale and Burnes had cleverly been drawn by the Amir across the Panjshir and away from their base at Charikar. They were moving up the wooded valley Parwan Darra, with its lines of mud-walled forts and rich apricot orchards, heading on to attack a distant rebel fortress, when intelligence came that Dost Mohammad was just ahead and riding fast towards them. Within minutes, the Amir and his 400 cavalry had appeared in view on an elevated piece of ground just ahead of the British. Sale's guns were at the rear, so, without waiting for them to be brought up, those at the head of the column, including Burnes's close friend Dr Percival Lord – known to the Afghan poets as 'Daaktar' – decided to lead the attack. The British officers spurred their horses into a charge, only to realise too late that their own Indian cavalry squadrons had turned and fled. What followed was for the Afghan poets a supreme moment of triumph for Dost Mohammad.

Then the *Daaktar* leapt up like smoke
With all the war-like cavalry that was with him

The Amir eyed up the *Daaktar*
That wretched dog

And he leapt on his horse
With all speed, as fast as fire

Down from the granite hills
Went he, his cavalry following behind

Drawing the sword of rancour from its sheath
They leapt forward without delay

They pounced on the Christians,
The field grew warm with Firangi blood

The clamour of the brave rose up to the heavens
Dust filled the eyes of the Sun and of Jupiter

Soon the earth was 'stained rose-red with heroes' blood'.

The heroes slaughtered the men of Firang
That day of war was like as to the apocalypse

Then from under his saddle Afzal brought out his gun and fired
The shot entered the body of *Daaktar*

It passed through his chest and out his back
His body was rent, and his soul fled out

The British began to retreat, 'The brave ones of Kabul on their tail'.

Then Burnes, of swift decision, ordered them
To bring artillery to the fight

It roared and rumbled like the sky
The sound of it shook the world

At this, the hearts of the believers were astonished
The world had been darkened

They saw that there was nothing they could do
How can one drop of water conquer a river in spate?

So too went Afzal and the Amir
They hurried from the battlefield to the high mountains

There they chose a place to camp
And rested awhile from their trials, and their rage.[98]

Two days later, on the evening of 4 November, a very anxious Macnaghten was taking his evening ride on the outskirts of Kabul in the company of his Military Secretary, George Lawrence, and a small escort of cavalry. The news of the death of Dr Lord and several other officers had arrived the day before, and had been followed that afternoon by an apocalyptic despatch from Burnes, urging that the British abandon all their positions north of Kabul and concentrate their troops in the capital. The day had been spent in nervous discussion – should the troops be pulled in? Should a second force be gathered and sent north? Was it wise to drain Kabul of yet more troops? 'Just as we were approaching the Residency,' remembered Lawrence, 'we were surprised by a horseman suddenly riding up, who, pushing his horse between the Envoy and myself, asked me "if that was the Lord Sahib".'

On my saying yes, he caught hold of Sir William's bridle, exclaiming 'the Ameer, the Ameer!' The Envoy, surprised and agitated, called out, 'Who, who? Where, where?' Looking behind me on the instant,

I saw another horseman close to us, who riding up, threw himself
off his horse, and seized hold of the Envoy's stirrup-leather and
then his hand, which he put to his forehead and lips as a sign of
submission. Sir William instantly dismounted and said to the Ameer,
'You are welcome, you are welcome'; and then led him through the
Residency garden to his own room. Dost Mohammad, on entering,
prostrated himself in Oriental fashion, and taking off his turban,
touched the floor with his forehead. On rising he delivered up his
sword in token of surrender, saying 'he had no more use for it.' The
Envoy immediately returned him the sword, assured the Ameer of
every consideration being shown to him, notwithstanding he had so
long opposed the British Government. To which the Ameer replied
that 'it was his destiny, and he could not oppose it.'

Dost Mohammad was 'a robust, powerful man, with a sharp
acquiline nose, highly arched eyebrows' and an untrimmed beard
and moustache. 'He . . . told us that previous to the action of
Purwan Durrah, he had made up his mind to surrender, and his
temporary success in that affair did not in the least alter his determination . . .' Lawrence added, 'Tents were pitched for the Ameer's
reception, who was put under my immediate care, and a most
anxious duty it was. I scarcely closed my eyes during the two nights
he remained under my charge, every now and then getting up to
look into the tent to see he was still there; it all seemed so much like
a dream that *at last* we should have the Dost safe in our hands, that
I could scarcely credit it except by frequent visits to his tent.'[99]

If there was surprise on the British side at the arrival of the Amir,
where it was presumed that he had not realised how close to victory
he had come, from his own point of view Dost Mohammad was
following normal Turko-Persian protocol by his surrender. It was
not uncommon for defeated rulers of states to surrender to victorious and growing regional powers in the hope of becoming
feudatories. The Durranis and Hotaki Ghilzais had both risen to
power as Safavid governors in the late seventeenth century, and the
Durrani Empire as it was expanding had often reappointed local
rulers as their governors. The system allowed for continuity and

stability, and, for the defeated rulers, preservation of life and the possibility of a return to power if circumstances changed.

As Mohammad Husain Herati put it: 'When the English army advanced, like ocean waves one after the other, they had it proclaimed that whoever captured and delivered to them Dost Muhammad Khan would receive a reward of two lakh rupees. The Amir thought: "In this country where people murder each other for one rupee, or five people for five rupees, what chance do I stand of not being betrayed, with such a price on my head?"' By riding into Kabul and surrendering to Macnaghten on his own terms, the Amir was recognising that for the time being the game was up and a new regional force had emerged. He clearly hoped that the British might sooner or later bring him back as ruler, or that their ultimate defeat would provide opportunities for his return on his own in the future. It was to prove a canny calculation.[100]

Arrangements were swiftly made to convey the Amir to India. He would be given a generous pension and reunited with his harem, who were then being held in the fortress of Ghazni. It was soon agreed that he should be given Shah Shuja's vacated quarters in Ludhiana, as Shuja's harem were shortly due to leave for Kabul. Unexpectedly, in the nine days he stayed in Kabul, Macnaghten and the Amir became friends: 'The candle of intercourse and conversation burned brightly between them,' noted Mirza 'Ata.[101] Macnaghten even intervened on the Amir's behalf with Auckland. 'I trust the Dost will be treated with liberality,' he wrote. 'His case has been compared to that of Shah Shuja; and I have seen it argued that he should not be treated more handsomely than His Majesty was; but surely the cases are not parallel. The Shah has no claim upon us. We had no hand in depriving him of his Kingdom, whereas we ejected the Dost, who never offended us, in support of our policy, of which he was the victim.'[102] It was the closest Macnaghten would ever come to admitting that 'the gallant old Ameer', who had always been friendly to the English, had been quite unnecessarily deprived of his throne and his kingdom.

The Amir was so pleased and relieved by his honourable surrender to the British, and the way in which he had been able to prove his valour on the field of Parwan Darra before he did so, that he was prepared to forgive even Burnes, whom everyone else in the Barakzai camp regarded as a devious and slippery *namak haram* [literally 'impure salt' – a serious insult, meaning one who had played traitor to his host]. As Burnes wrote to a friend,

> My interview with Dost Mohammad was very interesting and very affectionate. He taunted me with nothing, said I was his best friend, and that he had come in on a letter I had written to him. This I disbelieve, for we followed him from house to house [through Kohistan] and he was obliged to surrender. On that letter, however, I hope I have got for him an annual stipend of two lakhs of rupees instead of one. On our parting I gave him an Arab horse; and what do you think he gave me? His own, and only sword, which is stained with blood. He left for India . . . and is to live at Ludhiana. In Kohistan I saw a failure of our artillery to breach, of our European soldiers to storm, and of our cavalry to charge; and yet God gave us the victory . . . If we could turn over a new leaf here, we might yet make Afghanistan a barrier.[103]

Only in one matter did the Amir refuse to co-operate with the British. Macnaghten repeatedly urged him to visit Shah Shuja, but Dost Mohammad flatly refused, and even sent back the trays of food that the Shah had sent to his surrendered rival – a mortal insult in the Afghan honour system. According to Mirza 'Ata, 'the Amir angrily replied to Macnaghten's entreaties, "It is enough that I have come to see you with the result that I am to be taken abroad a prisoner. What would I gain from going to see one who has brought this storm of misfortune on his country? Without the King, you English could never independently have entered Afghanistan."'[104] Fayz Mohammad puts a similar speech into the Amir's mouth: 'I have no business with Shah Shuja,' he is supposed to have said to Macnaghten. 'I have not come to offer an oath of allegiance to him.' Macnaghten insisted, 'In view of the concern for the state that he has, it would be appropriate for you to see him.' The Amir replied, 'It is you who have put him on the throne, not the great mass of those who "loose and bind". If this is true, then you should cease propping him up. When you do, it will be clear to you and to other intelligent people which man deserves to be sovereign and whom the leaders of the country and the subjects will obey. If he has anything to say to me let him come forward and state it in your presence.'[105]

The refusal of the British to hand Dost Mohammad over to the Sadozais for execution caused Shuja huge offence. For weeks he had been urging Macnaghten to send assassins to have the Amir killed, and now at the very least he expected his old enemy to be blinded. But Macnaghten refused even to discuss the matter. 'His Majesty was surprised and could not understand why Dost Mohammad Khan rudely chose not even to pay his respects at court,' wrote Mohammad Husain Herati. 'All the Amir's adherents and followers and Barakzai relatives who remained in Afghanistan went about their business as freely as if they had been infidels just converted to Islam and washed free of sin! The extreme attention and favour paid by the English to the faction and clan of Dost Mohammad Khan led very quickly to a total loss of prestige of His Majesty, as if he had fallen, hard, from heaven to earth.' Meanwhile, continued Herati, 'Macnaghten's efforts to please his guest, and his neglect of the rights of His Majesty, led at length to his own death: again, as the poet said: "If you shower favours on bad men, you harm the good and virtuous."'[106]

On 13 November, Dost Mohammad Khan left Kabul, accompanied by his son Afzal Khan to whom he had written, telling him 'he had been received with much kindness and respect' and urging his son to follow his example and surrender. In Jalalabad the two were reunited with the rest of their harem: Dost Mohammad's nine wives, the twenty-one spouses of his sons, 102 female slaves and another 210 male slaves and attendants, who along with numerous grandchildren and other relations brought the party to a grand total of 381 people in all.[107] As the news of the Amir's honourable treatment spread, the number increased dramatically and, according to Mirza 'Ata, by the time the party arrived at Ludhiana, 'all the family and dependents of the Amir had arrived: 22 of his sons,

13 of his nephews, and another 29 relations as well as 400 male-servants and 300 female-servants, in total 1,115 persons joined the Amir in exile'.[108]

There was great relief in Kabul and Simla when the Barakzais finally reached Ludhiana at the end of December. Sir Willoughby Cotton, who had been given the job of escorting the Amir to his new residence at the end of his stint as British military commander in Afghanistan, even wrote to his successor to say, 'You will have nothing to do here. All is peace.'[109]

But in reality the insurgency was by no means over. Akbar Khan, Dost Mohammad's most warlike son, had just managed to escape from Bukhara. He would soon prove a potent new centre of resistance, and far more violent, ruthless and effective than his father had ever been.

6

We Fail from Our Ignorance

In early February 1840, as the Edens were heading down from Simla on their way back to Calcutta, they bumped into an old acquaintance from Scotland, Major-General William Elphinstone. The two families were friends, and the amiable, ineffective, bumbling old Major-General – an elderly cousin of Mountstuart Elphinstone – had last seen the Edens on his Carstairs estate in the Scottish Borders. Now, as he manoeuvred himself out of his palanquin, Elphinstone was rather put out to have to wait to see his young friend Auckland. 'It seems odd that I have never seen [Lord] A since we were shooting grouse together,' he told Emily, 'and now I have to ask for an audience and for employment.'[1]

The feeling of disappointment was mutual. If Elphinstone was mildly ruffled by their relative change of status, the Edens were worried by the mere sight of Elphinstone. Since their days striding over the border heather, guns under their arms on the Glorious Twelfth, Elphinstone's health had collapsed and he was now 'in a shocking state of gout, poor man! One arm in a sling and very lame', unable to walk unless supported, or aided by sticks. In fact it was so bad that at first Emily didn't recognise him: 'I remember him as "Elphy Bey", and never made out it was the same man till a sudden recollection came over me a week ago.'[2] It was, she wrote, 'almost the worst [case of gout] I ever saw'.[3]

George was more worried still, though in his case the anxiety was professional, for this was the man he had just chosen to take over the command of the army in Afghanistan. His appointment was to be announced after the departure of Sir Willoughby Cotton; General Nott, whom Auckland regarded as chippy and difficult and far from a gentleman, was to be passed over yet again; but, wrote Auckland, he 'had only himself to blame'. Nott, in turn, had all his fears about Lord Auckland's judgement and class prejudices confirmed when he discovered he would be superseded by 'the most incompetent soldier that was to be found among all the officers of requisite rank'.

As Nott was all too aware, Elphinstone's failings were not merely medical. Like many Queen's officers of his generation, he had not seen action since he commanded the 33rd Foot at Waterloo more than twenty-five years previously, and after years on half-pay had returned to active service only in 1837, at the age of fifty-five, in order to pay off his growing debts. His patron, and the man responsible for sending him to India, was Fitzroy Somerset, Lord Raglan, later famous for ordering the suicidal Charge of the Light Brigade.[4] Elphinstone had no knowledge of or interest in the world into which Raglan had just pitched him. 'He hates being here,' noted Emily, 'wretched because nobody understands his London topics, or knows his London people, and he revels in a long letter from Lord W[ellington] . . . He cannot, of course, speak a word of Hindoostanee, and neither can his aide-de-camp: "We can never make the bearers understand us[," he complained.] "I have a negro who speaks English, but I could not bring him [up the country]." He can hardly have picked up a woolly black negro who speaks Hindoostanee. I suppose he means a Native.'[5]

Despite having seen that Elphinstone was more or less an invalid and had no sympathy for India or the Indian sepoys he would have to lead, it did not seem to have occurred to Lord Auckland to question or cancel his friend's command. Instead, he wrote warmly to him throughout the year and when his appointment was finally confirmed in December 1840, shortly after Dost Mohammad's surrender, confided to him his worries about the occupation. 'Though I am impatient gradually to withdraw our regular troops from that country,' he wrote, 'I feel that, before we can do so, the new dynasty must be more strongly confirmed than it yet has been in power, and that there must be better security than is yet established.'[6]

Like Auckland, Elphinstone was not known for his decisiveness and, again like Auckland, had spent much of his career depending on the opinions of his assistants. But while it was Auckland's fate to have fallen into the hands of the hawkish Colvin and the pedantic yet undeniably bright Macnaghten, Elphinstone was more unlucky still in that he was given for his deputy one of the most unhelpful, unpleasant and unpopular officers in the entire army.

Brigadier General John Shelton of the 44th Foot was a cantankerous, rude and boorish man who had lost his right arm in the Peninsular War, and the incessant pain he suffered seemed to have darkened and embittered his character. He was a rigid disciplinarian, known to be 'a tyrant to his regiment'. When Captain Colin Mackenzie first saw him marching his troops into the country, he recorded in his diary that Shelton was 'a wretched brigadier. The monstrous confusion which takes place in crossing the rivers from his want of common arrangement is disgraceful, and would be fatal in an avowed enemy's country.'[7] Later, Mackenzie crossed his path a second time and wrote, 'As I expected, Shelton has marched the brigade off its legs . . . The artillery horses are quite done up, those of the cavalry nearly so, and the beasts of burden, camels etc . . . have died in great numbers, and will continue to die from overwork . . . The unnecessary hardship he has exposed the men to, especially during their passage through the Khyber, has caused much discontent. Part of the horse artillery on one occasion actually mutinied.'[8]

The entire cantonment took an instant dislike to Shelton. The surgeon John Magrath, who had come across him before in India, was soon describing him as 'more detested than ever'.⁹ Nor did Shelton get on with the gentle and gentlemanly Elphinstone. 'His manner was most contumacious from the day of his arrival,' the Major-General wrote later. 'He never gave me information or advice, but invariably found fault with all that was done and canvassed and condemned all orders before officers – frequently perverting and delaying carrying them into effect. He appeared to be actuated by an ill-feeling towards me.'¹⁰

Nor did Elphinstone much take to the political officers or the monarch he was going to have to work with. In April 1841, near the end of his journey from Meerut, he arrived at the winter capital of Jalalabad, to which Shuja had again retreated to escape the blizzards of the Kabul winter. 'My Command I do not think enviable,' he wrote to his cousin shortly after meeting Macnaghten.

> It is one of expense, responsibility, and anxiety . . . There are not many officers to give me much advice, most of them like myself having only lately come into this country. The Political Agents, generally young officers, are frequently proposing schemes for the execution of which they are not responsible. A proposition was lately submitted to Govt. for an advance on Herat, a distance of 600 miles from Kabul through country abounding with difficulties, and where supplies requiring 4000 Camels have to be carried . . .
>
> [Macnaghten] is cold and reserved, but I believe very clever . . . Shah Shuja I saw two days ago, a stout, careworn-looking man. He received me in a wretched garden, his house appeared bad and uncomfortable, as indeed are most here – no one except Sir W. M[acnaghten] possesses much more than a mud hut. The King leaves this on the 10th when I am expected to go too, which is rather annoying as I intended marching by myself and his *ragamuffin* retinue will be a great nuisance on the road.¹¹

A week later Elphinstone finally arrived in Kabul, which depressed him even more than Jalalabad. 'The City is extensive, very dirty & crowded,' he observed. 'The cantonment [meanwhile] is not very defensible without a number of men, as people can come in from without at many points. This, in the event of troops being required elsewhere, would be very inconvenient, & I am a good deal puzzled as to what is now the best thing to be done.'

Elphinstone was not the only one puzzled by what should be done in Afghanistan. Even Macnaghten, the most delusionally optimistic of the British, now recognised that despite the surrender of Dost Mohammad all was not well.

To the south-east, the Punjab was now declining into hostile anarchy: within two years three Sikh rulers had followed each other as leaders of the Khalsa. As a result, a leaderless military regime of evasive and uncertain sympathies now lay between the army of occupation in Afghanistan and its commissariat base in Ferozepur. 'The Punjab remains so unsettled that all the spare troops are obliged to be kept on that frontier,' wrote Emily in April 1841. 'Runjeet's death has been so like the death of Alexander, and of half the great conquerors of ancient history that we used to read about. His army was a very fine thing, and his kingdom a good kingdom while he was there to keep an eye on them, but the instant he died it all fell into confusion, and his soldiers have now murdered their French and English officers, and are marauding all over the country. It is not actually any business of ours, but interrupts our communications with Afghanistan . . .'[12]

This was an understatement. Not only did supply trains heading up the passes into Afghanistan often have to fight their way through ambushes and frequent attempts to hijack the baggage animals, there were a growing number of credible reports that senior Sikh sardars in Lahore and Rawalpindi were actively sheltering rebel Barakzai and Durrani chiefs and other Afghan rebel leaders, giving them a base in the Punjab and the hills around Peshawar from which they could strike back at British troops over the border in Afghanistan. The authorities in India thus found themselves in a difficult situation: the Sikh sardars were still nominal allies, but in reality many were doing all they could to undermine the British in Afghanistan. Before long, Auckland was beginning to flirt with the hawkish plans suggested by Colvin to annex the Punjab in order to close down the insurgents' bases and ease the passage of supplies up to the front: 'I am of the opinion that if Sikh authority should be further dissolved, its restoration is not to be regarded as a thing practicable,' he wrote. 'Things have not yet reached a crisis, but they appear to be fast approaching it.'[13]

Meanwhile, in the west of Afghanistan, there were anxieties that Teheran was busy stirring things up near the Persian border. D'Arcy Todd, the officer who taken on the difficult job of trying to win over the Wazir of Herat, Yar Mohammad Alikozai, had fulfilled Burnes's prediction of the inevitable collapse of his mission by failing to stop the growing rapprochement between the Heratis and the Persians. The final straw was when Yar Mohammad had simply pocketed a large sum of money Todd had given him to finance an attack on the Persian-occupied border fortress of Ghorian. Increasingly convinced that Yar Mohammad was intending to ally himself with Persia and lead an Islamic coalition against Shah Shuja and his British backers, on 10 February 1841 Todd had left his post without official permission and marched back to Kandahar, effectively breaking off diplomatic relations. In due course, Yar Mohammad had Shuja's cousin, Kamran Shah Sadozai, arrested and strangled, so taking over control of the city in name as well as in letter. He then promptly entered into an anti-British alliance with Mohammad Shah of Persia.[14]

Even more threatening was the situation to the south and west of Kandahar, where both the Durranis and the formidable Tokhi and Hotaki Ghilzais had risen up against the British in Helmand and Qalat. Although it was ostensibly the decision to tax the traditionally tax-exempt Tokhi tribe that sparked the rebellion, once again the rhetoric of the resistance concentrated on a specifically Islamic set of grievances with the rebels using the language of the jihad and referring to themselves as 'the soldiers of Islam'.[15] Unlike almost all the other British officers in Afghanistan,

General Nott was proving a notably effective military commander against the rebels, and developed a quick-moving 5,000–strong anti-insurgency column which could be rapidly deployed in any direction; but as soon as he defeated an uprising in one place, another insurgency flared up elsewhere – thanks, he believed, to the 'hatred in which we are held by the Dooranees as Infidels and Conquerers. Akhtar [Khan Durrani, the leading insurgent in Helmand] describes his party as an "assembly of Muslims and 'ulama" and his cause as the "Glory of Islam". He believes the "Feringees are bent on the destruction and expatriation of the whole Mahomedan population".'[16]

Nott now had as his political assistant the able and clever Henry Rawlinson, the man who had first sighted Vitkevitch heading for the Afghan border four years earlier, and whose epic ride back to Teheran had set off the chain of events which had led to the war. Having recently won the Founder's Medal of the Royal Geographical Society for his explorations in Persia and for his work translating the ancient Persian cuneiform script of the trilingual inscriptions at Behistun, Rawlinson now found himself posted to Kandahar where his job increasingly revolved around translating the calls to holy war being issued almost daily by the ghazis of Kandahar and Helmand. 'All holy men & true believers, the blessing of God be upon you,' began one such document that Rawlinson had forwarded to Macnaghten.

I have to inform you that the Mussulmans & 'ulema have assembled 5,000 Matchlock-men, Infantry, and 2000 Horsemen fully armed & equipped, and by the blessing of God we will uphold the Glory of Islam – but we must work together & make our arrangements in concert. On receipt of this letter you must collect your own forces & those of the other Ghazis & come & join us. The illustrious Wazir [Yar Mohammad] has written to us from Herat, and please God by the time our forces can unite & march, the Wazir will have reached Girishk & captured it. In raising your followers, do not be idle and place a perfect reliance on our holy cause & march at once to attack the English.[17]

As more and more of these documents began to accumulate from his informers, Rawlinson started to realise for the first time the full scale of the resistance the occupation was now facing. 'I shall be most thankful when you re-enter this town with the 43rd Regiment,' he wrote anxiously to Nott, 'for it is anything but pleasant to see the spirit of opposition to the government showing itself through all the districts, and to feel that, happen what may, there is no possibility of employing force in support of royal authority [until you return].' A day later he was writing to Nott with even greater urgency: 'I regret to say that affairs to the westward are assuming so alarming an appearance, that I begin to fear that the immediate employment of regular troops will be found necessary in support of the authority of the Govt.'[18] Yet Macnaghten's response when he read Rawlinson's anxious despatches was as patronising as it was wrong-headed. He accused Rawlinson of 'taking an unwarrantably gloomy view of our position, and entertaining and disseminating rumours favourable to that view. We have enough of difficulties without adding to the number needlessly ... I know [such rumours] to be utterly false as regards this part of the country, and have no reason to believe them to be true as regards your portion of the Kingdom.'[19] In a later letter, he again took issue with Rawlinson's assessment that an uprising was imminent. 'I do not concur with you as to the difficulty of our position,' he wrote.

> On the contrary, I think our prospects are most cheering, and with the materials we have there ought to be little or no difficulty ... The people of this country are very credulous. They believe anything invented to our prejudice, but they will soon learn that we are not the cannibals we are painted ... Certainly our troops can be no great favourites in a town where they have turned out half the inhabitants for their own accommodation, but I will venture to say there is not a country town in England where soldiers are quartered in which similar excesses have not happened ...
>
> These people are perfect children and they should be treated as such. If we put one naughty boy in the corner the rest will be

terrified. We have taken their plaything, power, out of the hands of the Dooranee Chiefs and they are panting in consequence. They did not know how to use it. In their hands it was useless and ever hurtful to their master and we are obliged to transfer it to scholars of our own. They instigate the Moollas, and the Moollas preach to the people, but this will be very temporary.[20]

It was the same in Kohistan, to the north of Kabul. In the summer of 1841 Eldred Pottinger, the former 'Hero of Herat', arrived in Charikar with a garrison of Gurkhas to find the British position every bit as indefensible as the Kabul cantonment: the Gurkhas had to camp in tents while their badly located, mud-walled and still gateless barracks was overlooked and dominated by a second much stronger fortress a short distance from it on slightly higher ground. Moreover they had no artillery; yet all around were widespread signs of growing unrest. When one of Pottinger's assistants was taken aside by a fakir to whom he had given alms, and warned that a massacre of their troops was being openly discussed in the bazaar, 'recommending me strongly to spend the winter in Kabul', Pottinger became convinced that another major uprising was about to break out.[21] But Macnaghten refused either to listen to his worries or to send him the reinforcements or the artillery that he believed would be necessary if he were to hold his position. So Pottinger spent weeks collecting more intelligence and then forwarded a second, more detailed assessment to Macnaghten. The Kohistan chiefs, he wrote, had initially supported Shah Shuja, but found that the strictness of the Anglo-Sadozai administration 'was inimical to their interests and power insomuch that it had given them a master who was able to compel obedience instead of one who was obliged to overlook their excesses'. In addition there were other reasons for revolt: 'Hatred of foreign domination, fanaticism, the licentiousness of our troops, and particularly the impunity with which women could be seduced and carried off in a country celebrated for the extreme jealousy of the natives . . .' He went on:

The enemies of the British are increasing in their endeavours to blacken our character, prejudice the populace against us and encourage outlaws. During July and August, while the crops were on the ground, burning of stacks and cutting the banks of the irrigating canals were of frequent occurrence and constant inroads were made by parties of outlaws, without the royal authorities being able to arrest them, even though it was evident that many of the people were cognizant of their comings and goings . . . Nearly every hour brings rumours of the formation of an extensive conspiracy . . . and I feel it my duty to recommend that hostages be demanded from the Kohistan Chiefs.[22]

The reality was that resistance was growing everywhere against the British, and only in Kabul itself was there still some support for the Anglo-Sadozai regime. Even there the popularity of Shuja was crumbling. According to Maulana Kashmiri:

> The people were oppressed by the violence of the Firangi
> They were afflicted by the arrogance of the Firangi
>
> No vestige of honour remained in the city
> Law and order had no standing
>
> The Khans were so disgraced
> Like earth they mixed with water
>
> When in this way Kabul was terror-struck
> With different calamities, stained red and beaten
>
> In every home, they remembered the true justice of the Amir
> Night and day they longed for the Amir[23]

Most British officials now recognised that the Anglo-Sadozai regime was failing – certainly few took so dismissive and over-confident an attitude as Macnaghten – but they differed from each other as to the solution needed to turn the situation around. In

London, John Cam Hobhouse, the President of the Board of Control, who in his youth had been Lord Byron's close friend and travelling companion, argued that what was really needed was radically to increase troop numbers. Either Afghanistan should be relinquished completely, or it should be held in strength. He argued that the number of troops on the ground should be enormously increased from the skeletal garrison to which they had been reduced after the surrender of Dost Mohammad Khan. Expenditure and investment in the country should rise, he wrote, and there should be greater control over the Afghan government. The basic fact that 'the British are masters of the country' should be recognised, and Shuja should be made to obey all the orders given to him. Retreat should be out of the question.[24]

Burnes was also keen on marginalising Shuja and reforming his corrupt government. In August 1840, just before the surrender of Dost Mohammad, he had written Macnaghten a long memo expressing his view that the Shah's government was inefficient, unpopular and expensive, and that greater British interference in the administration was the only way to save the regime. He was not personally in favour of full annexation, and he was clear 'that we shall never settle Afghanistan at the point of a bayonet', but he noted that many of his colleagues were now coming to believe the best solution was to annex both the Punjab and Afghanistan into the Company Raj.[25]

In his private correspondence Burnes was more scathing, and pointed the finger of blame at Auckland and Macnaghten. 'There is nothing here but downright imbecility,' he wrote to his brother-in-law Holland.[26] 'We are in possession of the cities,' he told his elder brother around the same time, 'but have not got the country or the [support of the] people, and have as yet done nothing liberally to consolidate Afghanistan. Lord A has it in his power to take Peshawar and Herat now and restore the Monarchy, enable it to pay itself and relieve India from all expenses, but he will do nothing. *Après moi le déluge* is his motto. He wishes to get home, but is afraid of what he has already done.'[27]

Macnaghten, meanwhile, was pursuing a third approach: he was still toying with the idea of actually bolstering Shuja's power, possibly just to irritate Burnes, but like his deputy wanted to expand the regime's frontiers and to attack Herat, believing, correctly, that Yar Mohammad was encouraging the tribes to rise up against the British. He also wished to annex and 'macadamise' the Punjab, as well as to advance north beyond Bamiyan and annex the Uzbek territories of the Mir Wali, so as to fix Shuja's frontier on the banks of the Oxus, ready to face any Russian advance out of Central Asia.[28]

But against all these ambitious schemes for bringing in more soldiers and hugely extending British control, there stood the unassailable fact of a now almost completely drained treasury in Calcutta. Occupying Afghanistan is always a very expensive business, and by 1841 the combined expenses of the occupation were amounting to a colossal £2 million a year, many times what had initially been expected, and far more than the profits of the East India Company's opium and tea trade could support.

By February 1841, the head of the accounts department working on the figures in Calcutta was forced to write to Auckland and break the news that 'ere six months elapse, the treasures of India will be completely exhausted'.[29] By March, the full scale of the problem was dawning on Auckland. 'Money, money, money is our first, our second and our last want,' he wrote to Macnaghten. 'How long we can continue to feed you at your present rate of expenditure I cannot tell. To add to the weight would break us utterly.'

Once the accounts had been passed to the Commander-in-Chief, Sir John Keane, he was equally depressed. 'We are clearly in a great scrape,' he noted in his diary on 26 March 1841. 'That country drains us of a million a year or more – and we only, in truth, are certain of the allegiance of the people within range of our guns and cavalry . . . The whole thing will break down; we cannot afford the heavy yet increasing drain upon us in troops and money.' A few days later he added, 'it will never do to have India drained of a million and a quarter annually [the real figure was actually much higher] for a rocky frontier, requiring about 25,000 men and expensive establishments to hold it'.[30]

Yet while policy was in confusion, and money was running

out, on the ground the occupation was becoming daily entrenched, with the first and toughest of the memsahibs making the now dangerous journey through the Punjab to the Kabul cantonment. These first arrivals included Macnaghten's socially ambitious wife Frances, along with her cat and parakeet and five attendant ayahs. This at least provided some relief to the Eden sisters, who had been trying to avoid her company ever since her husband had left her with them in Simla. Then there was Florentia Sale, the indomitable Indian-born wife of 'Fighting Bob', who arrived in the summer of 1841 with a grand piano and her winsome youngest daughter, Alexandrina.

Not everyone was delighted by the arrival of the women. John Magrath, the grumpy cantonment surgeon, thought Ladies Sale and Macnaghten were 'both equally vulgar and equally scandalous' (without, sadly, giving more details), and was also dismissive of Lady Macnaghten's abysmal household skills. 'I dined at the Macnaghtens' some days ago,' he wrote in May 1841, 'and got a wretched dinner for my trouble of riding six miles for it.' Alexandrina Sale, he added, was 'ignorant and illiterate', though he conceded that she was at least said to be 'good tempered'.

Despite her alleged illiteracy, Alexandrina was soon being courted by half the officers in the cantonment. This Magrath put down to her 'being the only spinster here and . . . determined to get married . . . One thing in her favour is that she could not lose by comparison.'[31] Lady Sale disapproved of most of her daughter's suitors with their sweet nothings – 'Fair words butter no parsnips,' she was fond of observing – but she liked the handsome Lieutenant John Sturt, the engineer who had designed the indefensible barracks, and before long Sturt was widely judged to be well ahead of the pack, much to the envy of his single colleagues.

Lady Sale had had the foresight to bring enough seeds from her garden in Karnal to fill her Kabul borders with English blooms. 'I have cultivated flowers that are the admiration of the Afghan gentlemen,' she was writing before long. 'My sweet peas and geraniums are much admired and they were all eager to obtain the seed of the edible pea, which flourished well. In the kitchen garden the potatoes especially thrive.'[32]

It was not just the memsahibs who arrived at this time. Seeing Macnaghten reunited with his wife, Shuja now decided to bring his blind brother Shah Zaman and both their harems up from Ludhiana. This was presumably partly because he was missing them, but also because he must have calculated that it was important to move them before the Punjab got any more dangerous, or even closed completely, so cutting him off from his family.

Two young Scottish officers were deputed to the job of escorting the harems from Ludhiana to Kabul, a journey which in calmer times could have been easily accomplished in two to three weeks but which now, with the Khalsa in disarray and with many of its regiments in a state of open mutiny, was a hazardous and uncertain undertaking. To make the commission more difficult still, Shuja decided to send along with his women much of his savings and his celebrated box of Mughal jewels, and word of this soon leaked out.

George Broadfoot, who was put in charge of the caravan, was a practical, red-haired Orcadian giant whose father was the minister of St Magnus Cathedral in Kirkwall. He was assisted by his friend, the dashingly moustachioed Colin Mackenzie, originally from Perthshire, who was renowned as the most handsome young officer in the Indian army. Soon after his arrival in Calcutta, Mackenzie had won the hand of the town's most celebrated beauty, Adeline Pattle, one of six sisters of mixed English, Bengali and French extraction, who had inherited the dazzling dark eyes and skin of their Chandernagore grandmother. The sisters had been brought up between Bengal and Versailles, where their French grandfather, the Chevalier de L'Etang, had been a page to Marie Antoinette, and they spoke Hindustani, Bengali and French among themselves. One of Adeline's younger sisters married Lord Auckland's adviser Henry Thoby Prinsep, which – even though

Emily Eden described Prinsep as 'the greatest bore Providence ever created' – meant that Mackenzie had a direct link over Elphinstone and Macnaghten's head into Lord Auckland's council, something that would later prove extremely useful.

From their barracks at Aligarh, the two men made their way to Shah Shuja's harem via the Taj Mahal and a stop to hunt cheetah in the jungles near Mathura. On arrival in Ludhiana they found that the caravan now consisted of 'the old blind Shah Zaman, a host of shahzadas [princes], and a huge number of ladies of all ranks and ages, [around] 600 from the [two] zenanas [women's quarters], with numerous attendants, together with a large amount of treasure and baggage'. In all, it made up a party of nearly 6,000 people, which together with their baggage needed 15,000 camels to transport. Yet the two young officers expected to protect this temptingly valuable and vulnerable convoy with only 500 men. To make matters worse, at the Sikh border they were met by a further 'escort of picked troops from the Sikh army; but these were affected by the spirit of mutiny then abroad, and were a source of danger rather than protection', wrote Broadfoot. 'The Punjab was verging towards anarchy when we started and daily got into greater confusion as we advanced. The Mutinous troops were moving in all directions towards Lahore, and occasionally crossed our path. They had already murdered or expelled their officers before starting . . .'[33] The caravan made slow progress, but by careful scouting and intelligence work, they managed to pass safely through the first two-thirds of the Sikh dominions.

Matters however took a more serious turn when they got news, just before crossing the Indus at Attock, that there had been a large-scale mutiny in Peshawar. Worse still, the four disaffected battalions – around 5,000 men – who had heard of their coming, were now blocking the road just ahead of them with all their artillery waiting in position, 'and were intending to plunder the kafila'. To avoid having to fight on two fronts, Mackenzie broke the bridge of boats after crossing the Indus, so protecting them from their own Sikh escort. For the several days which followed there was a stand-off, until Broadfoot managed to lure the leaders of the mutineers into an ambush, and by holding them prisoner successfully negotiated a safe-passage. He then crossed around Peshawar, faced down a second stand-off with more mutinous border guards at Jamrud 'who seized a lot of property and made an attempt of a search of the Begum's palkees [litters]', and eventually mounted the Khyber Pass – all without firing a shot.[34]

As they moved on through Jalalabad towards Kabul, both men were appalled by the state of Afghanistan, which they immediately realised was on the verge of breaking out into a major uprising. Broadfoot quickly saw how unpopular the British had become and that the existing garrison was now wholly inadequate to hold the country. 'The army of occupation was reduced in numbers,' he wrote, 'part of it having been sent back to India, while what remained, instead of being concentrated in one or two important places, was scattered in small bodies over a vast country.'[35] Broadfoot was also horrified by the sheer lack of knowledge displayed by the British about the Afghanistan they were trying to rule. 'Our apathy in this respect is disgraceful,' he exclaimed,

> and so is our ignorance of the institutions and manners of the country. When a country is invaded, its resources are always used by the conquering army, the leader of which assumes the government. Lord Wellington administered the civil government of the South of France, collecting the revenues and appointing every functionary. After four years of occupation we are as little prepared to do that effectually here as in 1838; less so, for the desire to learn is diminished, as all think we are soon to quit the country . . . To acquire accurate information of the real resources of the country, the modes of collection, and the rights of the various classes in relation to the State and to each other, never seems to have been thought necessary . . . Consequently, we fail from our ignorance.[36]

Soon after their arrival in Kabul, the two officers were invited to meet Macnaghten and Burnes, and they told them something of their impressions. But 'the Envoy took no notice of any of these warnings', wrote Mackenzie, 'and Burnes did not like to interfere further: his views were, except in the details, those of Macnaghten, and he was nearly as blind as to what was passing around him'.[37] Instead, Macnaghten, ever keen on ceremonial, organised for them to be accorded a grand Bala Hisar reception by Shuja, who he said wished to thank them for safely bringing in his women and treasure, and to present them both with 'a horse, a sword and a dress of honour'.[38]

Mackenzie was appalled by the whole farce, and wrote to his in-laws in Calcutta telling Thoby Prinsep that he believed the occupation in its current form was now untenable and that the whole situation was most 'alarming...our gallant fellows in Afghanistan must be immediately reinforced, or they will perish'.[39]

While waiting for his begums to arrive, Shah Shuja had decided to turn his charm on another young woman. 'Most sacred Queen, whose banner is the Sun,' wrote Shuja to Queen Victoria around this time. 'My Kind and Illustrious Sister, may the Almighty God preserve her! I had the pleasure to receive the congratulatory letter which Your Majesty, out of the excess of your kindness and friendship, wrote me conveying the joyful accounts of your health and prosperity. This caused the garden of affection to bring forth an increase of excellent fruit.'

Never had the Shah felt such fondness for Britain, he wrote, than when he received the Queen's letter: 'At that moment the variegated and perfumed roses of concord, and the odoriferous flowers of love, were blossoming and smiling in the parterre of my affectionate heart.' He went on to tell the Queen what an admirer she now had on the throne of Kabul, and how much he loved her 'mind resplendent as the Sun, the Mighty Majesty exalted as the Heavens, high as the moon, wise as Mercury, joyful as Venus whose standard is the Sun, fortunate as Jupiter of whom Mars is the Hand, Glorious as Saturn, the ornament of the Hall of Justice and Victory, the splendour of the throne of equity and protection, the brilliant full moon of the Heaven of exaltation and fame, and the Shining Star of sovereignty and fortune'.[40]

But, whatever feelings Shah Shuja might have for the young Queen, he was daily feeling less and less affection for her servants in Kabul, despite describing Macnaghten in his letter as 'the high and exalted in rank, the resting place of excellence and valour, the germ of wisdom and discretion, the lofty in worth, the high in place, the distinguished and honourable councillor'. Instead the Shah, 'regarding his position as more secure than hitherto, and feeling himself less dependent on us to maintain him in it, began to evince some impatience at our presence', as Macnaghten's Military Secretary George Lawrence noted. 'He showed how irksome he felt the restraint, necessarily imposed by the Envoy, on the full exercise of his authority . . . and showed how gladly he would be free of the Envoy's controlling supervision.'[41]

At the same time, Burnes was winning the argument within the British administration over the need to increase control over Shuja by replacing the loyal and influential Mullah Shakur with a more pliantly pro-British alternative. Interference in Shuja's administration had been steadily growing for two years, and with the decision now taken to sack Mullah Shakur the real government of Afghanistan was finally taken entirely into British hands.[42] Burnes, wrote Mohammad Husain Herati, favoured Mullah Shakur's rival, 'Uthman Khan, who had previously been known as a Barakzai loyalist. 'This man out of mere self-interest had thrown his lot in with the English and in no way supported His Majesty – so inevitably the flames of discord rose higher. His father before him had been minister to [Shuja's brother] Shah Zaman and, by his hostility to the Durrani khans, had contributed to the downfall of that monarch. But Macnaghten insisted on giving him the position, because it had been his father's, without trying the aptitude or character of the candidate.' He continued:

At the time, Mirza Imamverdi, one of the intimates of Dost Muhammad Khan, notorious for dissimulation and manipulation, who had escaped from Bukhara by pretending to be mad and tearing at his own flesh with his teeth, arrived back in Kabul. He saw no likelihood of success in joining Mullah Shakur's establishment, but contacted 'Uthman Khan who was working at a low level in His Majesty's establishment and within a few days had mounted a propaganda and defamation campaign against Mullah Shakur, so effective that all the Durrani khans and common people repeated the complaints to His Majesty, and Macnaghten and Burnes pronounced: 'The Mullah's not up to the job – he must go!' However much His Majesty countered that Mullah Shakur was a pious, upright and selfless man, and that a better governor could hardly be found, yet it was to no effect. So 'Uthman Khan was appointed and awarded the title and position of Nizam al-Daula, the chief minister, with authority to decide matters throughout the kingdom. Mullah Shakur was dismissed and put under strict house arrest.

Blind to 'the inner rottenness' of Nizam al-Daula, Macnaghten favoured him so excessively that within months 'he became inflated with self-conceit and began to behave towards great men and small with overbearing rudeness'. Added Herati, 'Even in the presence of His Majesty, he failed to observe proper decorum. He undermined the older-established, respectable courtiers, both Durrani and non-Durrani, by bringing unfavourable reports about them to Macnaghten, and then determining to reduce or stop their pensions. However much they protested, and however much His Majesty supported their protests, it was all to no avail.'[43]

As Nizam al-Daula did not get on with Shuja, and was entirely dependent on the British for his position, even the most pro-Sadozai nobles took this as final confirmation of all they suspected: that Shah Shuja was no longer in charge of his own government, and that the British were now holding all the reins of real power. As Fayz Mohammad later put it, 'Without the Nizam al-Daula's consent, the Shah's wishes would go for naught and if a soldier or peasant who had been wronged or oppressed came to the Shah and asked for justice, without Nizam al-Daula's say-so he would receive nothing but words. This became another bit of evidence for the Barakzais who would say to people, "Aside from his title, the Shah has no say in the affairs of state."[44]

For Shah Shuja, it marked a new level of public humiliation. Continually aware of his debt to the British, he wished to show gratitude and be a loyal ally, but was far too proud a man to accept being reduced to an impotent puppet. 'I was again called by the King this afternoon,' wrote Burnes soon after the deposition of Mullah Shakur. It was clear, he noted, that the Shah had 'a deep-rooted jealousy against the [new] Wazir'.

> The King gave me at great length his feelings and his sufferings. He said he had not a trustworthy man in his country; that all were engaged in setting him against us, and us against him – that his enemies were allowed to continue in power – that the portion of his revenue set aside for him was not collected and paid – that his adherents were discontented – that he was kept under by us in all things, yet that they had not gone right; that a pilgrimage to Mecca was his only alternative [in other words, that he should abdicate], and that at Ludhiana he had much power as compared with this part of his reign.[45]

But Burnes had never taken to Shuja, or rated his abilities, and was in no mood to begin feeling sympathy now. Moreover, his boss was belatedly coming to agree. 'An expression from Macnaghten today that Shah Shuja was an old woman, not fit to rule this people, with divers other condemnations,' wrote Burnes in one letter. 'Ay – see my *Travels [into Bokara]*, and as far back as 1831, ten years ago. Still, I look upon his fitness or unfitness as very immaterial; we are here to govern for him, and govern we must.'[46]

Just how badly Nizam al-Daula handled the Afghan nobility became apparent shortly afterwards. At the end of August 1841, Macnaghten received a despatch from Auckland telling him that the financial breaking point had now been reached: the Company had been forced to take out a £5 million loan from Indian merchants at exorbitant rates of interest just to continue paying salaries.[47] Macnaghten was ordered to make extensive and immediate cuts to expenditure. Moreover, in London a Tory government had just come to power by one vote, and the new Prime Minister, Sir Robert Peel, showed no wish to continue financing what he and his colleagues regarded as one of Lord Palmerston's expensive and unnecessary Whig wars.[48] Auckland, a Whig political appointee, was now seriously considering his resignation. Macnaghten was aghast: 'If they – the Tories – deprive the Shah altogether of our support I have no hesitation of saying they will commit an unparalleled political atrocity.' It would not only be a breach of a treaty but a 'cheat of the first magnitude'.[49]

To Auckland, Macnaghten wrote in a rare protest: 'I cannot help feeling some surprise at these repeated communications [asking for more cuts] after the many expositions I have given of the wretched state of the finances of this country and of the numerous and complicated difficulties I have had to contend with ... I cannot do more than I have done.' He went on to outline the trouble he was having managing the increasingly distraught Shuja. 'Of late I have had several most distressing interviews with His Majesty, and I may safely say that the efforts I have been making towards the reduction of the public expenditure have not only been the cause of much mental distress to His Majesty, but have secured for us the hostility of all the men of influence in the country.' In the end, however, Macnaghten as the good civil servant realised he must bow to the inevitable. 'Your Lordship's perpetual exhortations left me no alternative but to counsel unsparing retrenchment. The enormous expenditure already incurred I am aware necessitates the strictest economy. But what can be done with a Kingdom whose net revenues are only fifteen Lakhs [1,500,000] of Rupees per annum?'[50]

Macnaghten decided to leave Shuja's already reduced household budget more or less intact and not to touch the expenditure committed to the new, reformed regiments of the Shah's Afghan national army. Instead he chose to aim the cuts at the extremities rather than the centre. He called the Ghilzai and Khyber chieftains to a durbar in Kabul. There he told them that their subsidies were to be reduced by £8,000, with the worst reductions falling on the eastern Ghilzais and their leader Mohammad Shah Khan, the father-in-law of Akbar Khan, who had been awarded the daunting title of 'Chief Executioner' when he came over and joined the serv- ice of Shah Shuja. To Macnaghten it made perfect sense: he believed that the days of the old nobility, as in India, were numbered. He was merely hastening the inevitable demise of the feudal system and calling the bluff of the more barbaric nomad tribes who had done little to deserve the protection money the Kabul government was in the habit of lavishing upon them.

In the event, however, it proved to be the single biggest misjudge- ment of his entire career and within weeks it had brought the entire edifice of the occupation crashing down. For as far as the Ghilzais were concerned, they had worked hard for their subsidy and believed they were being called to Kabul to be rewarded for their support of the Shah's regime. 'They had prevented even a finger from being raised against our posts, couriers and weak detach- ments,' wrote Henry Havelock. 'Convoys of all descriptions had passed through these terrific defiles, the strongest mountain barri- ers in the world, with little or no interruption from these predatory tribes. The transmission of letters to our own provinces was as regular as between Calcutta and any station in Bengal.' Colin Mackenzie agreed, and emphasised the degree to which the Ghilzai saw it as an outright betrayal: 'Sir William reported that the Chiefs "acquiesced in the justice of the reduction"; but on the contrary they considered it a direct break of faith. The whole deficiency amounted only to Rs 40,000, and this attempt at economy was the main cause of the outbreak and all its subsequent horrors.'[51] Mohan Lal was more succinct: 'For the deductions of a few lakhs of rupees, we raised the whole country against us.'[52]

Part of the problem was that by the autumn of 1841 the chiefs and their dependants simply could not afford the cuts. The military reforms had already eaten into their incomes, the real value of which was fast falling due to hyperinflation: the 4,500 troops and 11,500 camp followers who were resident in Kabul had put a huge burden on the poorly integrated Afghan economy and the effect of the sudden flood of silver rupees and letters of credit into the country was a sharp rise in commodity prices: by June 1841, according to Macnaghten, some basic products had risen by 500 per cent.[53]* This was especially so of grain, driving the Afghan poor to the edge of starvation. Mohan Lal realised this, and tried to warn Burnes of the consequences. 'The purchase made by our Commissariat officers of grain raised the price too high and placed it utterly beyond the reach of the population in general,' he wrote. 'Grass for cattle, meat and vegetables, and in short all the necessities of life, rose to a considerable price. The cry of starvation was universal, and there were very many hardly able to procure a piece of bread even by begging in the streets, while everything would have been in abundance but for our purchases.'[54]

To make matters worse, the exact details of the cuts and how to implement them were left by Macnaghten to the tactless and unpopular Nizam al-Daula to work out. Not only did he reduce the allowances in a manner which insulted many of the most loyal followers of Shah Shuja, on 1 September he forced even the most senior to reapply for their military posts and re-swear their oath of allegiance to the Shah. When the nobles all refused to do so, saying this was unprecedented and beneath their honour, 'that it was not the custom of kings to mistrust their servants, and to demand a paper bond of this nature from them', they were all summarily threatened with exile.[55] It was at the next durbar that the first serious opposition showed itself. Mohammad Husain Herati was in the Bala Hisar at the time. 'One day,' he recalled,

> when all the courtiers were present in the royal audience hall, each according to his rank, Samad Khan, the grandson of Zal Beg Khan Durrani Baduzai, petitioned that 'My pension is not being paid.' His Majesty signalled to the Nizam al-Daula to make an answer, but

---

* The arrival of the US-led coalition in Kabul in 2002 had a similar effect, leading in a few months to a ten-fold hike in house prices.

he merely replied: 'You lie!' Samad Khan answered back: 'It is you
who lie! You have humiliated all those who love and are loyal to the
royal family.' Nizam al-Daula, hearing these truthful words, lost his
temper and shouted: 'I'll have your eyes put out!' Hearing this
boorishness in the royal presence, Samad Khan replied: 'Were it not
that we are in the presence of His Majesty, I would slit your tongue
out of your mouth with my sword! We have both lived in this country long enough before the return of His Majesty, and all well know
that, while my family have enjoyed high and honourable positions
in the state without interruption, you were merely fetching and
carrying Mohammad Zaman Khan Barakzai's pisspot!'

At this point, continued Herati, the Shah rose and left the audience
hall, recognising that Samad Khan was indeed one of the highest-
born of the Durranis. Nizam al-Daula 'slunk off to tell his version
of events to Macnaghten, who promptly wrote to His Majesty that
"Samad Khan is unworthy to remain at court – he must go." His
Majesty considered every order of the English as a command from
heaven, and therefore dismissed Samad Khan from court.
Consternation covered the Durranis, while the Barakzais crowed
in triumph', exulting in this display of the Shah's impotence.

Macnaghten took Nizam al-Daula's advice to reduce particularly the subsidies of the Ghilzai khans on the grounds that 'They
eat up thousands of rupees, all wasted quite unnecessarily: if these
are stopped, no one will dare protest!' However, 'the Ghilzais did
dare protest, and loudly too', recorded Herati. 'No ruler has ever,
at any time, cut back or abolished our subsidy: we work for it, we
guard the roads and the security posts, we restore stolen goods, it
is not given to us for nothing and we will not accept any reduction
at all!' The Ghilzais had a point. Since the time of the Mughals,
both the Ghilzais and the Khyber and Peshawar tribes had been
paid *rahdari* [road keeping] to maintain the road and protect the
armies and traders en route to India. The Khattaks kept the road
open from the Indus to Peshawar and the Afridis from Peshawar to
Jamrud. Every king had paid this subsidy, but now Macnaghten
informed the chiefs that he was arbitrarily abrogating this

agreement in contravention of customary tribal law and his own written undertakings. To make matters worse, as Herati noted, 'Nizam al-Daula foolishly refused to hear the complaints of the chiefs, and spoke roughly to them: so they left him and at night, and fled from Kabul back to their hills to open the doors of sedition, raise rebellion, loot the caravans, and block the roads.'[56]

Maulana Kashmiri in his *Akbarnama* presents the departure of the khans from Kabul less as an angry protest and more as a considered strategy. According to him, the Afghan sardars, fearful that their loss of salaries would be followed by forced exile to India or even London, decided to take action. They met and swore on the Qu'ran to rise up in rebellion so as to lure the bulk of the British troops out of Kabul, then fall on the British leaders when there were few soldiers left in Kabul to defend them:

> When night fell, all the Khans of Kabul came together
> At the house of Abdullah Khan Achakzai to sit and confer
>
> Now the remedy is in our hands, said they
> The bow is ready and the arrow is in our hands
>
> The waters of this storm have not reached our head
> We must get ourselves ready for action
>
> Dying by the sword on the battlefield
> Is better than living in the prisons of Firang
>
> Like the very devil, all evil is the work of Burnes
> Concealed, he goes about whispering to every soul
>
> So this very night Mohammad Shah Khan Ghilzai must go forth
> With his tribesmen, brave and fierce
>
> They will ignite the fire of battle
> And throw brimstone upon the flames

They will sit hidden between the mountain valleys
And seize all the traders and travellers upon the road

So the Shah may send his army forth to make war
Then, when the army leaves, we will deal with Burnes . . .[57]

As fate would have it, the beginning of the Ghilzai rebellion coincided with General Elphinstone going down with a new attack of gout.

A month earlier, Elphinstone's surgeon, Dr Campbell, had inspected his patient and been horrified by what he discovered. According to his confidential report, 'Genl. Elphinstone has been very seriously ill ever since his arrival here. His malady attacked him in all his limbs, making a perfect wreck of him. I saw him a short time since & very much astonished I was at the very great alteration in his appearance. He is reduced to a perfect skeleton, both hands in flour and water, and legs swathed in flannel and in a very low and desponding condition, totally incapable, I feel assured, of giving any attention to any affair howsoever important. I fear in my humble opinion his constitution is shattered beyond redemption.'[58] Elphinstone had sent the report to Auckland and asked to be relieved of his command; now he was finalising his plans for returning to India, and hence to retirement among his beloved Scottish grouse moors.

As part of the cuts, Macnaghten had also decided to further reduce the small British garrison remaining in Afghanistan and to send back to India 'Fighting Bob' Sale and his brigade. Sale was now instructed to make a detour on his return journey to knock down a few Ghilzai forts and quell any signs of the uprising that he encountered on his way out of the country: the tribes, Macnaghten wrote calmly, 'were very kind in breaking out just at the moment most opportune for our purpose. The troops will take them en route to India.'[59]

When Sale's Orcadian Military Engineer, George Broadfoot, went to see Elphinstone to collect intelligence and finalise the plans to 'chastise' the eastern Ghilzais, he found the General 'in a pitiable state of health, absolutely unfit for duty', and so 'lost and perplexed' he ended up asking himself whether the General was still entirely sane.[60]

> He insisted in getting up and was supported to his visitor's room. This exertion so exhausted him that it was half an hour before he could attend to business, indeed several ineffectual attempts to do so had excited him so much that I was sorry I had come at all . . . He said he did not know the number or strength of the [Ghilzai] forts [and] complained bitterly of the way he was deprived of all authority [by Macnaghten] and reduced to a cipher . . . [Later] I went back to the General and found him in bed and quite worn out . . . He told me once more how he had been tormented by Macnaghten from the first; reduced, to use his own words, from a General to a head constable. He asked me to see him before I moved, but he said, 'if anything occurs, for God sake clear the passes quickly, that I may get away. For, if anything were to turn up I am unfit for it, done up body and mind, and I have told Lord Auckland so.' This he repeated two or three times, adding he doubted very much he would ever see home, even if he did get away.[61]

As he left, Broadfoot told the General about his own anxieties: he had tried to get the smiths and armourers in the city to manufacture some mining tools to be used in the siege of the Ghilzai forts, but they had all 'refused to work for the Firangis as they were busy forging arms, for what purpose we have since learned, though Burnes said it was for the wandering tribes about to migrate'.[62]

Macnaghten, meanwhile, had been characteristically unfazed by the departure of his army commander, by the intelligence of intense arms manufacture in the bazaars or even by the angry exit of the Ghilzai chiefs, writing to Auckland that they were simply 'kicking up a row about some deductions which have been made from their pay' and would be 'well trounced for their pains . . . These fellows will require many a hiding yet,' he wrote, 'before they settle down into peaceable citizens.'[63]

The advance guard of Sale's brigade, around one thousand men, left Kabul on the morning of 9 October. They marched to Butkhak, a distance of fifteen miles from the cantonment on the Jalalabad road. That night, just after dark, as the troops were camped near the mouth of the pass, the sentries heard a strange sound echoing from the shadowy slopes and bare crags above them. Among the younger officers was Thomas Seaton, who was looking forward to returning to the pleasures of India.

> Our mess-dinner was just over, when the native officers command-ing the quarter guard sent in a sepoy to tell the colonel that a great number of people were to be seen assembled on the hill above us, and that he had heard them loading their juzzails . . . The ball is put into juzzails naked, and requires to be hammered a great deal with an iron ramrod to get it home. This hammering makes a loud ring-ing noise, that can be heard at a considerable distance and so unmistakable in its character that it can never be forgotten by those whose ears have once been startled by the unfamiliar sound. 'Gentle-men,' said the colonel, 'you had better go and turn out your respective companies instantly, and as quietly as possible. They will be on you immediately.'

The Colonel sent parties round the camp to extinguish all the lights, and Seaton was ordered to take two companies to the foot of the hill where the Afghans were gathered, 'with directions to keep the men as silent as death; to make them kneel or sit down, and not to fire a shot' until the enemy descended from the hill. 'I marched off at the head of my men, and had scarcely reached my post when the whole hilltop seemed to burst into flame from the simultane-ous discharge of hundreds of juzzails. Shouts and yells of "Yelli,

Yelli, Yelli" [short for Ya Allah] at the same time rent the air, accompanied by howlings that would have done credit to a thousand jackals.' This onslaught was maintained for upwards of an hour.

> The long continued darkness and silence in our camp greatly puzzled the Afghans, especially as we did not attempt to return their fire. Imagining we had either run away or that their fierce fire 'had sent all the sons of burned fathers to Jehunnum,' they moved down the hill in two bodies to spoil the camp and slay the wounded, their progress being accompanied by fierce yells and shouts . . .
>
> [Finally] we could just see them looming through the gloom. The men of my two companies had been sitting down on the ground, with their muskets between their knees, but the short word 'Ready!' brought them to the kneeling position; and at the word 'Present!' a volley from 170 men crashed amongst the enemy with awful effect . . . We had some forty men killed and wounded, and but for our colonel's presence of mind and foresight, our loss would have been trebled.[64]

When Macnaghten heard about the ambush he was furious. 'Imagine the impudence of the rascals,' he wrote. 'Taking up a position with four or five hundred men in the Khoord-Kabul Pass, not fifteen miles from the capital.' 'Fighting Bob' Sale was promptly sent off on 12 October with the rest of his brigade – around 1,600 men in all – to relieve the advance guard and reopen the passes.

Their first night at the mouth of the pass was quiet, and the following morning they marched at dawn into the narrow winding heights of the Khord Kabul. 'No opposition met them until they were fairly entangled in the pass,' remembered the chaplain, the Rev. G. R. Gleig, who was planning to return to India with the brigade.

> Then from the rocks and precipices on either side, such a storm of fire opened as told of itself that the heights above were occupied in great force. So skilful too were the Afghans in the art of skirmishing, that, except by the flashes which their matchlocks emitted, it

was impossible to tell where the marksmen lay. Rocks and stones, some of them hardly larger than a thirteen-inch shell, seemed to offer them excellent shelter. They squatted down showing nothing above the crag except the long barrels of their fusils and the tops of their turbans; and with such unerring aim were their shots thrown that, both in the advance guard, and from the body of the column, men began to drop.[65]

It was already becoming clear, as an official report to Calcutta pointed out, that in the high passes 'our regular European and Hindoostanee Troops fight against Afghans in their native hills to a great disadvantage. The superior agility of the latter enables them to evade pursuit and their jezails or long guns carry with deadly precision to a distance where our muskets are harmless.'[66] The ability of the Afghans to melt invisibly into the landscape also alarmed the British; as Sale reported to his wife, 'until they commenced firing, not a man was known to be there'.[67] One of the casualties was 'Fighting Bob' himself, who had his leg shattered with the ball of a jezail within the first minute of the ambush. 'I could not help admiring old Sale's coolness,' said his Brigade Major. 'He turned to me and said, "Wade, I have got it," and then remained on horseback directing the skirmishers until compelled from loss of blood to make over command to Dennie.'[68]

Despite this, Sale's force pushed on down the Khord Kabul Pass, reinforced by more troops from Kabul and taking increasingly heavy casualties as they went, Sale again directing operations, this time from a palanquin. The worst losses took place during another night attack a week later on 17 October. Around 5 p.m., one of the Tezin chiefs sent a note to the British 'saying that they had arrived at the Tung-i-Tareekhi [the Dark Gorge], and that in two hours they would attack us. A polite reply was sent to the effect that we should be happy to receive the chiefs, and would endeavour to give them a suitable welcome.'[69] The note proved a stratagem: by telling the British to expect a frontal attack, and beginning to launch one, the Ghilzai managed to surprise the British when their main force appeared to the rear, where some of Shah Shuja's newly recruited

Hazirbash cavalry had been bribed to let them within the camp: 'They were of the same tribe, and whilst the rest were fighting, these ever-ready gentlemen did a little work of their own, cutting downs surwans [camel drivers] and hamstringing camels.'[70]

That night Sale's brigade lost a further eighty-nine men, as well as much of their baggage and ammunition, which was removed to the Ghilzai fortress in Tezin on ninety of the Company's own camels. The expedition which was supposed to chastise the Ghilzais turned out to have a very different victim to that intended: in the narrow web of the mountain passes, the spider had become the fly; and the hunters found to their surprise and discomfort that they had now become the prey.

On the morning of 23 October, the beleaguered column advanced again, through an especially narrow part of the pass just before Tezin. Turning a corner around two huge rocks, 'the hills which bounded the valley on all sides were suddenly seen to swarm with Afghans'. By a combination of sniping from cover and well-timed rushes on the baggage train and rearguard, 'they again slew this day a great many more of our men, and carried off no inconsiderable portion of booty; of which it would be hard to say whether our people grudged them most the nine new hospital tents, which with all the furniture they appropriated, or certain kegs containing not fewer than thirty thousand rounds of musket ammunition'.[71] That ammunition would later be used on the rest of the Kabul army with deadly effect.

The following day the British again found themselves surrounded; but this time in addition their passage forwards was blocked by an immense force of cavalry obstructing their advance on Tezin. After a brief stand-off, Sale agreed to admit to his camp a delegation which arrived under flag of truce. Negotiations were resumed in the Ghilzai camp, from where George MacGregor, the Political Officer attached to the column, reported 'that the chiefs received him with great politeness, and were pleased at the confidence reposed in them by his going to meet them attended only by one suwar [cavalryman]. They appeared to be unanimous, and many in number, mustering 700 followers, who were daily increasing.'[72]

MacGregor eventually agreed to pay the tribe all they asked. 'They are to get the Rs 40,000 the quarrel began about,' reported Lady Sale, 'and they promise to return any property they can find of ours: so that we can leave off where we set out, barring our killed and wounded, expence, loss of ammunition and baggage, and the annoyance of the detention, if not the loss, of all our daks [post].'⁷³ But it was more serious than Lady Sale realised. Few now believed the negotiations would do more than buy time, while some such as Henry Durand thought it a huge mistake. 'It was a time for action,' he wrote. 'Fighting Bob', he believed, should have been 'striking not talking'.⁷⁴ But the payment did allow Sale to send the wounded back to Kabul with an armed escort in order to warn the authorities there of the scale of the uprising, and for the rest of the column to head on down towards Jalalabad at speed. Moreover, as John Magrath, the morose surgeon of the force, wrote, 'I am glad we are to have no more fighting, for everything Sale and Dennie have a hand in is sure to be bungled.'⁷⁵

Ominously, after a two-day lull, the attacks began again. 'The rear guard has been attacked daily,' reported Sale at the end of the week, 'and the bivouack fired at each night.'⁷⁶ Each morning, 'as soon as the bugle called in the pickets, numbers of Afghans started up as if by magic from behind every rock, boulder, hillock, bush or tuft of grass within half a mile of the camp, forming a vast semicircle of enemies'.⁷⁷ The numbers of Afghans continued to grow. As Lady Sale noted from the cantonment, 'All the forts about Kabul are empty, and the Juwans [young men] have gone (it is said) to aid the fight against us at Tezin.' Only on 2 November did Sale's brigade finally emerge from the pass into the plain and reach the small fertile village of Gandamak, near Shah Jahan's Nimla Gardens, where Shah Shuja's Contingent maintained a small barracks.

Here Sale and his officers paused to rest and recover for ten days – though, as the chaplain was quick to emphasise, it was a sober moment and 'nobody indulged to excess in the use of spirituous liquors'. It was here that what remained of Macnaghten's new Afghan regiment, the Janbaz, 'broke out in open mutiny and tried to kill the English officers . . . It was now evident that the whole country had risen against us, and it was not a mere rising of the Ghilzai chiefs to get their subsidies restored.'[78] The brigade had so far lost over 250 men in only a few days, and their position was clearly worsening fast. Rumours were beginning to arrive of heavy fighting in the passes behind them and around Kabul itself. So a Council of War was convened to decide the best course of action. Rather than keep going on to India, or return to Kabul, Sale and his officers decided to continue the remaining thirty-five miles down-hill to Jalalabad, refortify the town and wait to see what happened next. Though no one was yet aware of it, this decision would change the course of the war.

Sale's brigade arrived in Jalalabad on 12 November and managed to seize the town without serious opposition. The low mud walls were crumbling and the troops found Jalalabad 'a dirty little town', but it was at least fertile and well watered on one side, by the Kabul River, which the hungry troops found to be full of delicious trout and the local *shir maheh* that they barbecued on charcoal. As Gleig commented, 'uninviting to the eyes of the ordinary traveller as this dilapidated city might have appeared, to the eyes of the brave but sorely harassed troops . . . it offered many and great attractions'.[79]

Broadfoot got to work rebuilding the fortifications on the after-noon of their arrival. Breaches in the curtain were filled, parapets and loopholes constructed, and ten artillery pieces were raised on to the bastions and prepared for firing. Foraging parties were sent out to gather food and fodder, and obstacles blocking the line of fire from the walls began to be demolished. The repairs were made just in time. The following morning a large mixed force of Ghilzai and Shinwari tribesmen appeared 'on the low hills to the south of the town and as the day advanced they came swarming up the rocky heights'.[80]

The city gates were closed, but just before that Sale sent a last express messenger out in the hope that he could get safely down the Khyber and reach the British Residency at Peshawar. 'Be pleased to acquaint the Com in Chief', he scribbled on a scrap of paper,

that we are surrounded on every side by the insurgents. Two regts
and a corps of sappers do not more than suffice to man these extensive walls and great efforts are demanded of us. We want treasure
immediately as well as 20,000 rounds of musket ammunition. In
fact we need succour in every way, troops, treasure, provision and
ammunition, and now. Measures must be prompt to be useful to us.
The troops are placed on half rations, and we have only six days rice
and no atta.[81]

The siege of Jalalabad had begun.

Across southern Afghanistan, a mass uprising was now clearly
imminent.

In Kandahar, Rawlinson believed that 'the feeling against us is
daily on the increase and I apprehend a succession of disturbances . . . Their mullahs are preaching against us from one end of
the country to the other.'[82] His military counterpart, General Nott,
was in agreement, writing to his daughters in despair that 'this country is in a sad state . . . Sir Wm Macnaghten's mistakes and weak
system begin to tell most woefully; it must be changed or we must
walk out of this part of the world . . . It may take many years to
undo what that man, Macnaghten, has done. How could Lord
Auckland allow such a man to remain in authority here, bringing
into contempt everything connected with the name of Englishmen?'[83]

In Ghazni, the commander of the garrison there, Colonel
Thomas Palmer, was equally anxious, writing to Nott that 'the
country here is getting more disturbed every day . . . I see not how
General Sale's Brigade is to leave the country. Of course they might
force their way through, but the enemy would close on their rear,
and cut off our communications with India as completely as it has
been done for the past fortnight.'[84] Most alarmed of all was Eldred
Pottinger in Charikar, who was now so certain that his small garrison of Gurkhas was about to be massacred that he rode back to

Kabul to reason with Elphinstone and Macnaghten in person. Elphinstone sat looking panicked, then dithered and fussed, but failed to send him any concrete help, least of all the cavalry and artillery Pottinger had desperately requested, saying that all the troops were needed in Kabul. Macnaghten meanwhile said he did not have time to see Pottinger, and mocked his written report: 'Pottinger writes as if he is about to be invaded by [Mir Masjidi's] Nijrowees, but I can imagine there is little ground for this alarm and the fellows will sneak into their holes again when they hear that the Ghilzais are quiet again.'[85]

Macnaghten seemed by now doggedly determined not to allow any news, however dire, to ruffle his complacency. This was all the more remarkable as the trouble was clearly spreading to Kabul, where the British were now being openly insulted by shopkeepers in the street, 'and the whole demeanour of the people', as Colin Mackenzie noted, 'was that of anticipated triumph in the destruction of the English'. There were several murders: one trooper was pistolled by an Afghan as he slept in his tent; a private soldier was found in a ditch with his throat cut; Captain Waller was wounded by an assassin, and a swordsman slashed at Dr Metcalfe as he rode from the town to the cantonment. Lady Sale was appalled. 'The general impression is that the Envoy is trying to deceive himself into an assurance that the country is in a quiescent state,' she noted in her diary. 'He has a difficult part to play, without sufficient moral courage to stem the current singly.'[86]

Part of the reason for this obstinacy was that he had just received the news that Lord Auckland had rewarded him for his Afghan labours with the most agreeable post the East India Company could offer a civil servant: the governorship of Bombay, complete with its beautiful Palladian Residence on Malabar Hill. It was therefore in his interests to get out as soon as possible, leaving an impression of a job well done; what followed could then be blamed on any successor. 'This is an unlooked for honor,' he wrote ingratiatingly to Lord Auckland, 'and its coming now is the more welcome when I can conscientiously say that I shall leave this country in a state of tranquillity and rapid progress towards improvement.'[87]

The man who was most likely to be appointed to pick up the reins after Macnaghten's departure was Alexander Burnes. For months he had being increasingly sidelined by the Envoy, with little to do but to mug up on his favourite authors. 'This is assuredly one of the idle stages of my life,' he had written home in August. 'I do nothing for the public, except giving advice, but as I have no duties to perform, unless it be to receive my 3500 rupees a month . . . [in the meantime] to study Tacitus is as pleasant as to write despatches.'[88] Hearing of the Envoy's new appointment, he wrote that 'his hopes were up' that he would succeed Macnaghten; and yet, now that the prize he had sought so long was almost within his grasp, he found himself wondering how much he really wanted it. 'I seem hourly to lose my anxiety for power and place,' he told his brother James in his last letter. 'I have been asking myself if I am altogether so well fitted for the supreme control here as I am supposed to believe. I sometimes think not, but I have never found myself fail in power when unshackled . . . I wish this doubt were solved, for anxiety is painful. One trait of my character is thorough seriousness; I am indifferent about nothing I undertake – in fact if I undertake a thing I cannot be indifferent.'[89]

Yet the truth was that Burnes's many talents had largely been wasted during the occupation. He knew Afghanistan better than any other British official or traveller with the single exception of Masson, he loved and understood the country, and his political instincts were as shrewd as his judgement was usually impeccable. His Achilles heel was his ambition, which had led him to get involved with an entirely unnecessary invasion and a mishandled occupation, both run by a foolish martinet who neither listened to nor respected his ideas. Like his rival Vitkevitch, Burnes was a brave and resourceful young man. Like Vitkevitch, he was an outsider who by dint of hard work moved himself centre-stage in the greatest geopolitical struggle of his age; but both had found, in different ways, that in the end they remained pawns in the wider imperial game. When Vitkevitch realised that his life's work had been ignored and wasted, he had shot himself in a fit of depression and disgust. Burnes's response was instead to throw himself into the pursuit of pleasure. In this way he made himself the hate figure he remains to this day in Afghanistan; and it was this, according to the Afghan accounts, that sparked the final fatal explosion in Kabul. It is Mirza 'Ata who gives the best Afghan account of how Burnes provoked that detonation.

The nobles in Kabul, he wrote, had been getting progressively more irritated with the British occupation, and in particular the way they had cut the allowances of the Ghilzai chiefs, sidelined Shah Shuja and sacked his Wazir, Mullah Shakur. It was Shuja's complaints about his own impotence that finally 'roused the Royalist Sardars to a furious pitch of offended honour and religious faith' against the occupying army, according to Mirza 'Ata, 'so each went to his own home, and at dusk when the sun had set in the west and the moon arose in all her splendour, they gathered together to consult and swear unity on the Qur'an'. Maulana Hamid Kashmiri has some of the leaders urge rapid action while Sale's force was still absent in the Khord Kabul:

The King has no army, and *Laat Hay Jangi* [Macnaghten] is drunk
Carousing and singing, flask ever in hand

Burnes is sitting pretty in all his conceit
When will there be a better moment than this?

Time is running out, there is no room for delay
We cannot choose to sit by, we must contrive

Lest the rabbit become aware
And the prey slip through our fingers

Let us make haste towards Burnes, the wicked soul
And take care of this business by daybreak[90]

In the end, however, it was agreed that they would wait for an incident of bad conduct on the part of the occupiers to justify rising up in insurrection. On the evening of 1 November, in the first week of

Ramazan, the leading sardars found the flashpoint they were waiting for. 'It so happened, by God's will, that that night a slave girl of
Abdullah Khan Achakzai ran away from his house to the residence
of Alexander Burnes,' wrote Mirza 'Ata. 'When on enquiry it was
found out that that was where she had gone, the Khan, beside
himself with fury, sent his attendant to fetch the silly girl back; the
Englishman, swollen with pride, cursing and swearing, had the
Khan's attendant severely beaten and thrown out of the house.'
This was a provocation too far. According to Mohan Lal, 'Abdullah
Khan Achakzai, with his relatives, went to Aminullah Khan Logari,
and holding the Qu'ran in his hand, implored him to be his comrade
in exciting sedition in the city. When he had agreed to this, some
other disaffected chiefs were sent for into the house of the Achakzai
chief.'[91] Once the jirga had assembled, the nobles were addressed
by Abdullah Khan:

> 'Now we are justified in throwing off this English yoke: they stretch
> the hand of tyranny to dishonour private citizens great and small:
> fucking a slave girl isn't worth the ritual bath that follows it: but we
> have to put a stop right here and now, otherwise these English will
> ride the donkey of their desires into the field of stupidity, to the
> point of having all of us arrested shortly and deported into foreign
> imprisonment. I put my trust in God and raise the battle standard of
> our Prophet Muhammad, and thus go to fight: if success rewards us,
> then that is as we wished; and if we die in battle, that is still better
> than to live with degradation and dishonour!' The other Sardars, his
> childhood friends, tightened their belts and girt their loins and
> prepared for Jihad – holy war.[92]

When Mohan Lal came to hear about the meeting of the conspirators through his informers, he immediately went over to Burnes's
house to warn him of what was brewing. Burnes had spent the day
fretting about his future: it was the twentieth anniversary of his
first footfall in India and he felt that it must be a life-changing day.
'What will this day bring forth?' reads the last entry in his journal.
'It will make or mar me, I suppose. Before the sun sets I shall

know.'[93] But the Ghilzai uprising had blocked the passes, and no post arrived in Kabul that day.

'On the evening of 1st November 1841,' wrote Mohan Lal,

I visited Sir Alexander Burnes and told him [what was afoot] . . . He replied that he does not like to meddle in the arrangement made by the Envoy, as he goes in a few days to Bombay, and then he [Burnes] will conciliate the chiefs by fixing former allowances. I told him again that it was contrary to the rules of service to allow such unfortunate evils to grow in height and not contrive means to annihilate them before the serious injuries are done to us by the enemies. When he heard this, he stood up from his chair, sighed, then sat back, telling me that the time had already arrived that we should leave this country and lament for the loss of it.[94]

As Mohan Lal was heading back to his house, further down the Pul-i-Khishti Bazaar, the conspirators were preparing for action. 'That very night,' wrote Mirza 'Ata,

before dawn had broken, they went to the house of Burnes, and with their pitiless swords killed the soldiers that were on guard there. The news of the fight spread through the city and the men of Kabul, sturdy fighters, welcomed it as a gift from God long prayed for. They boarded up their shops, took up arms and ran to the scene shouting [the Durrani and Ghilzai battle cry] 'Ya Chahar Yar! O Four Friends, the rightly-guided Caliphs of Islam!' As dawn was breaking, locust-like, they poured into the streets, and assembled around the house of Alexander Burnes.[95]

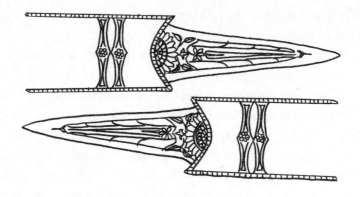

All Order Is at an End

The morning of 2 November 1841 dawned clear and cold. The oblique winter light threw long, sharp shadows from the Afghan pines and cypresses in the gardens outside Kabul's city walls. Beyond the gardens, in the newly completed cantonment, Captain Hugh Johnson, the paymaster of Shah Shuja's troops, had woken early. He had attended a regimental dinner party the night before and, given the worsening security situation, had been persuaded by his brother officers to spend the night in the cantonment, even though his Afghan mistress was waiting for him in his bed in the Shor Bazaar in the centre of the city.

'At about sun rise & before I was up,' he wrote in his diary that night, 'one of my servants came to inform me that the workmen who had for the last few days been employed on a house I had purchased in the Mission Compound refused to leave their houses today as they were afraid of their property being plundered, a rumour having been spread during the night that a disturbance was to take place in the city.'[1] This Johnson thought unlikely. There had been no signs of imminent trouble in the city before he left the previous evening, and as his house was opposite that of Alexander Burnes he felt sure his friend would have warned him if there had been any intelligence of a disturbance. Nevertheless, 'about ½ an hour after my servant left me to return to the city, three chaprasses came to report that a mob had collected in front of my house and Treasury. They were endeavouring to effect an entrance, and Burnes was trying to pacify them.' Johnson's account continues:

> Arose. Ordered my horse to be got ready, but before mounting went to report what I had heard to Captain Lawrence, Military Secretary to the Envoy. The latter had already received a note from Burnes on the subject and was on his way to the General's. Another of my servants then arrived to say the street in which Burnes and I lived was completely taken possession of by the mob. Some of them were trying to break open my gate, and my Treasury guard was keeping up a heavy fire upon them. Seeing my horse was saddled, he told me it would be impossible to reach my house, as the insurgents were increasing every minute, and were murdering any Europeans or Hindoostanees that came in their way. In the supposition that the General would immediately order down a detachment to suppress the tumult, as well as to save my Treasury and the life of the Resident, Sir Alexander Burnes, from whom another letter had been received *imploring immediate assistance*, my horse was kept ready that I might accompany the party. Went on the ramparts to see if anything towards the city indicated a disturbance. Had not been there five minutes before a dense smoke was seen rising and from its direction I was immediately convinced the rebels had set fire to my house. I also heard heavy vollies of musquet firing.

'Terrific reports . . . of murder and plunder' began to reach him.

> Yet to our astonishment no detachment was as yet ordered. Hours slipped away and no steps taken to quell the insurrection. A rumour was current, which afterwards proved but too true, that the insurgents had gained possession of my Treasury by mining the wall and

of my house by setting fire to the gateway, that they had murdered
the whole of the guard consisting of 1 Subadar and 28 Sepoys besides
our [European] commissioned officers, all my servants – male,
female, and children – had plundered the whole of my Treasury to
the amount of about one lakh and seventy thousand rupees, burnt
all my office records for the past 3 years, which comprise unad-
justed accounts to nearly *one million* sterling, and had possessed
themselves of all my private property amounting to upward of ten
thousand rupees.[2]

Johnson could not believe that so little was being done to save
Burnes or the treasury, or his staff, and made repeated enquiries
as to what the plans were. It emerged that the problem lay with
General Elphinstone. When reports came in that a disturbance
had begun in the old city, the ailing General had tried for the
first time since his arrival to mount his horse, but had fallen
heavily, and the horse on him, after which, according to Captain
Vincent Eyre, 'Elphinstone, who I fancy was never a strong or
independent-minded man, was reduced to one remove from
dotage.'[3]

One man in the cantonment who was trying to stir the troops
into action was Macnaghten's energetic young Military Secretary
George Lawrence. Like Johnson, Lawrence had been up early and
had discovered that trouble was afoot. 'A messenger who I had
sent into the town to make some trifling purchases, returned
breathless, in the greatest state of excitement, reporting that the
shops were all closed, and crowds of armed men were filling the
streets . . .' he recorded. 'I instantly rose and sought the Envoy,
whom I found at about eight am in earnest consultation with
General Elphinstone . . .'[4]

Lawrence proposed that the 5,000 British troops in the
cantonment should be marched immediately into the city to
Burnes's residence and that the two known ringleaders of the
uprising, Aminullah Khan Logari and Abdullah Khan Achakzai, should both be arrested: 'Not a moment should be lost!'
But, as he wrote later, 'my proposal was at once put down as one

of pure insanity and, under the circumstances, utterly unfeasible'. A second proposal was, however, accepted: that the recently married garrison engineer, Lieutenant Sturt, should gallop out to Brigadier Shelton, who was encamped on the far side of the city at Siyah Sang guarding the route into the city from the mouth of the disturbed Khord Kabul Pass. Sturt should tell him about the mob marauding around Pul-i-Khishti and encourage him to march to the Bala Hisar fort; from there he could command the walled city and take appropriate action. Lawrence was meanwhile to head on to the Bala Hisar and confirm the plan with Shah Shuja.

With a small escort of four troopers, Lawrence set off from the cantonment at around 9 a.m., directing his escort 'to keep close up to me, to use their spurs if necessary, but on no account to pull up or stop'.

> Near the fort of Mahomed Khan, an Affghan rushed from a ditch on to the road, brandishing a huge double-handed sword, and made a furious lunge at me, which I avoided by throwing my stick at him, drawing my sword and making my horse plunge towards him. One of my escort killed the fellow with a shot from his carbine . . . Just as we emerged from the road we were met by a shout and a rapid fire of musketry from a second party of men concealed in a ditch. Our rapid pace, and the firing being too high, alone saved us from destruction.

When he got to the Bala Hisar, Lawrence was conducted into the presence of the Shah, 'who was walking with great agitation up and down the court'.

> His Majesty exclaimed, 'Is this not just what I always told the Envoy would happen, if he would not follow my advice?' I then informed the King of the object of my visit, and requested His Majesty to authorise me to order up Brigadier Shelton's brigade to occupy the Bala Hisar. 'Wait a little,' the King replied. 'My son Fatteh Jang, and the Prime Minister, Usman Khan [Nizam al-Daula],

have gone down into the city and with some of my troops. I have no doubt they will suppress the tumult.'[5]

As Lawrence was aware, there was no small irony in this. For months, the British had been describing Shuja as lazy and ineffectual, yet when the crisis broke it was Shuja alone who took immediate action to suppress the uprising in the city before it got out of hand. He had sent into action against the mob the loyal and long-standing Anglo-Indian commander of his personal guard, William Campbell, at the head of a thousand troops and two cannon, with Fatteh Jang adding his authority. Indeed, Shuja was the only person to make any effort to try to save Alexander Burnes, despite the fact that he had been the Shah's loudest critic for over a decade. As Lawrence waited with Shuja, reports began arriving of Fatteh Jang's successful progress into the city and his pacification of successive wards.

By mid-morning, however, events began to take a darker turn. First of all, Lieutenant Sturt arrived in the durbar 'sword in hand, bleeding profusely, and crying out that he was being murdered. He explained that just as he was dismounting from his horse at the gate, he had been stabbed three times in the face and throat by a man who rushed out of the crowd.' Reports then arrived that Campbell and Fatteh Jang's levies had been ambushed by insurgents in the narrow streets of the city, and had taken over a hundred casualties from marksmen hidden within the houses of the Shor Bazaar. They had lost their two cannon and were now pinned down a short distance from Burnes's house. Shuja became increasingly worried about his son and, despite Lawrence's pleas, 'influenced by paternal affection, after hesitating, eventually recalled his son and Prime Minister. The latter, a bold, honest, uncompromising man eventually came in panting from the fray, and greatly excited, said in an angry tone to the King, "By recalling us just at the moment of victory, your troops will be defeated, and evil will fall upon us all."'[6]

After a sleep of only three hours, Mohan Lal was woken just before dawn by a maidservant who told him in alarm about the massing crowd outside Burnes's gate, a few houses away at the end of the bazaar: 'Agha,' she said. 'You are asleep and the city is upset.'

Mohan Lal came out into his garden, and saw the people moving their goods to a secure place away from the neighbourhood.

> The merchants were taking off their commodities from the shops, and the whole city appeared in commotion. Mirza Khodad, secretary to Sultan Jan [one of the leading Barakzai rebels who had been with Dost Mohammad in Bukhara], came to my house and being my old acquaintance, warned me of the danger in which I was then standing, by remaining in my house and not sending away my property. Naib Sharif [one of the Qizilbash chiefs and an old carousing companion of Burnes] also sent his father-in-law, to fetch me to the Persian Quarters, with all my valuable things. But I refused to attend to their kind advice, fearing that my stirring from the house might increase the apprehension of the impending danger. So I sent my servant with a note to Sir Alexander Burnes, whose residence was separated by a few buildings from my house, conveying to him the messages I had received . . . His reply was that I must remain in my house, and that he has sent for troops, and that they will soon be in town. Half an hour after this, my servant informed me that the Nizam al-Daula was advising that officer to quit his house and to proceed with him to the Bala Hisar, as there was very great risk to his personal safety.[7]

Burnes had been so confident of his safety and popularity that he had only twelve guards. He had just decided to leave with the Wazir when at the last minute he was persuaded to stay by his old Jamadar (the head of his bodyguard), who reminded him that he had just sent a message to Macnaghten and that he should really wait for the Envoy's reply. So Nizam al-Daula left alone, promising to return with a battalion of Shah Shuja's troops. As he rode away he was fired upon from the rooftops, but managed to fight his way back to the Bala Hisar.

At this point the rebel leaders – a mixed crew of disaffected Royalists, Barakzai sardars, angry aristocrats furious about the military reforms, unemployed former bureaucrats and middle-ranking 'ulema not in the Shah's service – arrived in Ashiqan wa Arifan, at the corner of the Shor Bazaar. Directed by Abdullah Khan Achakzai who had quickly assumed military command of the uprising, they took up positions in the garden next to Burnes's house. As Colin Mackenzie noted in his diary, the rebel leaders 'hated Burnes as the man universally believed to have guided the British into Afghanistan. They alleged he did not behave to them with proper respect. Burnes thought himself popular with the lower classes; but it is doubtful if he was so, while the chiefs regarded him as the chief agent in introducing that system of order which was utterly repugnant to them.'[8] So when Burnes sent two messengers to ask what the complaints of the rebel chiefs were, and inviting them to come to terms, the chiefs merely beheaded the first messenger, leaving the other to report this reply to Burnes. The chiefs' men were then ordered up on to the rooftops, to try and work their way into the back of Burnes's compound. He was to be offered no quarter. 'Now about two hundred people assembled on all sides,' wrote Mohan Lal, 'and Sir Alexander Burnes, from the window of his upper room, demanded the insurgents to pacify themselves, and promised a handsome reward to all.' With him on the balcony was Captain William Broadfoot, the younger brother of General Sale's red-haired engineer, and Burnes's own younger brother, Charles, who had just arrived in Kabul.

> While he was haranguing the mob, Captain Broadfoot received a [musket] ball just below his breast, and was brought down by Sir Alexander and his brother Charles and placed in the room downstairs. The [sepoy] guard, being now under sharp fire from the rebels, opposed the advance. Some of the servants of Sir Alexander desired him to permit himself to be wrapped up in a tent, which

they would carry off on their shoulders, in the way that many others were carrying off plunder, but he said he could neither leave his own brother, nor his wounded friend Captain Broadfoot.

At this point the mob managed to set fire to the gateway of Burnes's house, 'the flames extending to the room where Sir Alexander and his brother were standing, looking at the multitude and begging for quarter. Captain Broadfoot was consumed in it. Lt Charles Burnes then came out into the garden and killed about six persons before he was cut to pieces.'

Mohan Lal was standing on his rooftop, watching on with horror, as musket balls passing on from Burnes's house pitted the walls and shattered the windows around him. Now he was spotted by the rooftop musketeers and had to make a rapid exit. This he made through a hole in the exterior wall of his compound that he had had specially prepared for his escape. His plan was to make a dash for the well-defended walled Qizilbash quarter of Murad Khani and fetch the pro-British Shia leader, Khan Shirin Khan, to the aid of Burnes. As he was rushing through the streets, however, he was seized by a group of insurgents coming from the opposite direction. They had surrounded him and were about to behead him as a Kafir spy when, by good fortune, the group ran into the elderly Barakzai chief and first cousin of Dost Mohammad, Mohammad Zaman Khan, whose surrender and integration in Shuja's court Mohan Lal had facilitated a year earlier:

The Nawab came out of his house and upbraided those who had seized me. Snatching me away from their hands, he took me away and placed me among his ladies, who having received some assistance from me some time before, brought a sumptuous dish of 'pulav' for my breakfast. To enjoy this hospitality from the hands of the Afghan fair on other occasions would have been an unexpected and highly valued nourishment, but at the present disastrous moment, every grain of rice seemed to choak in my throat. I was now locked in a dark room and the good Nawab desired me to take my rings off from my fingers, and to conceal them somewhere, so that the avarice of his son might not tempt him to cut off my fingers with them. My house was in the meantime comprehensively plundered.[9]

Since Mohan Lal, the closest direct observer, was now secreted inside a zenana, there are no eyewitness accounts surviving of the final moments of Burnes, and the different versions that exist are all, to different extents, hearsay. The least likely version – though certainly the most imaginative – is that of Mirza 'Ata. In his narration, when the ghazis burst into the compound,

it is said that Burnes at that moment was in the private quarters of the house, taking a bath with his mistress in the hot water of lust and pleasure . . . At this point, the guerrilla Ghazis burst in and dragged them all from the changing room of life, cut them down with their swords and threw their corpses into the ash-pit of death. Everything in the house was plundered, the fighters breaking open the treasure chests and filling the skirts of their clothes with Company coins which clinked with a loud noise: 'shereng, shereng!' The fighters then attacked the house of the Bakhshi [paymaster] Captain [Hugh] Johnson and plundered the godown of all its stores and treasure; any English who found themselves in the city of Kabul tried to escape as best they could and make their way to the cantonment.[10]

A variant on this story is given by Munshi Abdul Karim in the *Muharaba Kabul wa Kandahar*. Like Mirza 'Ata, Munshi Abdul Karim takes the view that the crisis was largely precipitated by Burnes's allegedly gargantuan sexual appetites. In the view of the munshi, the flashpoint was not a slave girl of Abdullah Khan Achakzai, but 'Burnes' falling in lust with an Afghan woman and imprisoning of her husband'.

It is said that, one day, he was walking to inspect the city and suddenly caught sight of a young Afghan woman, peerless in beauty, standing on the flat roof of her house. Burnes immediately became

obsessed by the sight of her, and, forgetting his duties, or any sense
of piety or shame, as soon as he returned to his office, summoned
the Kotwal, the chief of police, to fetch the householder of that
particular house in that particular quarter. The constable ran to
carry out his orders and arrived back with a young Afghan soldier,
upright and pious, the owner of that house and husband of that
peerless beauty. Burnes said 'I have work for you – if you do my
bidding, I shall make you an officer, I shall make you rich, I shall
make you one of my intimates!'

'And what is that work? That I may strive to fulfil your wishes?'
asked the young soldier.

'You have a wife, beautiful as the full moon, whom I saw standing on the roof of your house: I cannot get her out of my mind;
give her to me, let me assuage my passion, and anything you ask
shall be yours!'

The young soldier trembled with shame, fell into a fury of
outraged honour and hissed: 'You filthy animal! Have you no fear
of God? Am I a pander, to sell my wife to you for gold? Beware!
One more word and I'll answer you with the blade of my sword!'
Burnes, to cover his confusion, had the man clapped into irons and
thrown into a dungeon like a common murderer.

In Munshi Abdul Karim's version, it is this soldier's relatives who
deliver the coup de grâce to Burnes:

Twelve relatives of the young soldier crowded into Burnes's room.
Two grabbed him, forced him down, sat on his chest, shouting:
'You animal! You dare to defile girls of noble birth? If you're
supposed to be head of the courts of justice, just tell us, what
punishment awaits such scum? What do the law books of the Jews,
the Christians, the Zoroastrians have to say?' Burnes pleaded for
his life, begging forgiveness – but the Afghans were not to be
moved. They killed him, hacked his body to pieces, shaved off his
beard and exhibited his head through the streets of the city, after
plundering and setting fire to his house, and killing any who came
to his aid. The rioters ran to the jail, overpowered the guards and

killed them, and set free the young soldier and other prisoners. Another group attacked the Bakshi's treasury, mowing down with their swords all the guards and officials they found there, then plundered the contents of the treasury.[11]

A third version, preferred by the great Victorian chronicler of the Afghan War, Sir John Kaye, has a 'mysterious Kashmiri Mussalman' offer to save Burnes as the flames engulfed his house. This enigmatic figure – who appears in no other account – is alleged to have made his way to the balcony where the two Burnes brothers were defying the crowd and, swearing on the Qur'an, offered to lead them to safety through the back garden. Since it was clear by now that Macnaghten had no intention of saving his young assistant, both the Burnes brothers 'threw on native dresses' and followed their guide down into the garden, hoping that they might yet escape. But they had gone only a few paces before the 'Kashmiri Judas shouted at the top of his voice: "See, friends! This is Sikunder Burnes!" It took the mob less than a minute to finish off the victims.'[12]

Mohan Lal gives a fourth version, probably the most credible, and certainly the most moving. He states that, after spending an hour locked in the zenana closet, he pleaded with Mohammad Zaman Khan, and his host finally consented to allow him up on to his roof. By this time it was all over: Burnes, his travelling companion and intimate friend for ten years, had been killed, and the remains of his house were being gutted by fire. But according to the Nawab's guards, who had watched the final act from their parapet,

after Charles Burnes was killed, and fire had consumed the whole of the room, Sir Alexander Burnes was obliged to come to the door opening to his garden. Here he implored the multitude to save his life, but [instead] receiving a torrent of abuse ... abandoned all hopes of safety. On this he opened up his black neckcloth and tied it on his eyes, that he should not see from what direction the blow of death strikes him. Having done this, he stepped out of the door, and in one minute he was cut to pieces by the furious mob.[13]

'The sharp blades of two hundred brave Afghans worked his body into shreds of bone,' wrote Maulana Kashmiri.

> They strung them up for all to see
> From every corner flowed a river of blood.
>
> In booty they carried off all his wealth and goods
> As the autumn wind strips the leaves off a tree.[14]

Shortly after this, the rebels sent out a proclamation to the chiefs across the country: 'On the third Tuesday of the blessed month Ramadan in the morning time, it occurred that with other heroic champions stirring like lions, we carried by storm the house of Sikander Burnes. By the Grace of the most holy and omnipotent God, the Brave Warriors having rushed right & left from their ambush, slew Sikander Burnes with various other Firangis of Consideration, and nearly 500 Battalion men, putting them utterly to the sword & consigning them to Perdition.'[15]

The trunk of Burnes's headless body was left in the street to be eaten by the dogs of the city. For nearly a week, no one even thought to try and save anything of his mangled remains. Finally Burnes's friend Naib Sharif, with whom he had spent many a lively evening, sent a servant to pick up the rotting remains and bury them in the garden of Burnes's house.[16]

At the time of his death, Sir Alexander Burnes, soldier, spy, traveller, diplomat and thwarted deputy Envoy, was only thirty-six years old.

With Burnes's house and Johnson's treasury in flames, and the occupants of both houses slaughtered, the angry mob rippled out from the Sunni stronghold of Ashiqan wa Arifan and the Shor Bazaar, past Shah Zaman's Pul-i-Khishti Masjid, and over the bridge in search of other targets. At the same time, as the news spread of plunder and profit, armed tribesmen began to pour into town from the rural hinterland. 'The people of the surrounding region heard the news of Burnes's assassination,' wrote Fayz Mohammad. 'Within a short time, while Shah Shuja and the English officers were still trying to devise a plan, many people had gathered in the city . . . The Ghilzais immediately pitched in without hesitating even a moment to unpack – the infantry with their bags of food still on their backs, and the cavalry with theirs in their saddlebags.'[17]

Already, late the previous night, Lady Sale had seen from her rooftop large numbers of armed Kohistani horsemen heading into town; now the stream of armed tribesmen pouring into Kabul from all directions and of all ethnicities swelled to a torrent. 'Abdullah Khan Achakzai and Aminullah Khan Logari welcomed the armed volunteers who came dancing and drumming joyfully from all directions,' wrote Mirza 'Ata. 'They gathered them under the battle standard of Islam outside the walls and ordered them to attack.'[18]

There had been around 300 rebels in the morning when the attack on Burnes's compound took place; but within forty-eight hours some 3,000 fighters had assembled in the city; three weeks later, the numbers had swelled to an almost unprecedented 50,000 as a whole range of groups with quite different motives and grievances were mobilised to take on the British. Having arrived separately the different – and sometimes rival – groups made separate camps: in reality, especially at the beginning, the insurgents were never the united force the British imagined them to be. The supporters of the Barakzais took over the Shah Bagh, the crumbling remains of one of Shah Jahan's old pleasure gardens. The Kohistani Tajiks based themselves in Deh Mazang, the eastern Ghilzais put up in the fort of Mahmud Khan, while the pro-Sadozai Royalists like Aminullah Khan Logari dominated the Old City. Most of the incomers were not from the Durrani elite but were instead drawn from relatively marginal groups: some were restless Pashtuns from the valleys and passes to the south and east of Kabul, from the Koh Daman and Logar, but it was perennially rebellious Tajik Kohistanis, deeply affected by the vicious punitive campaigns of Burnes and Sale the previous year, who initially seem to have made up the majority of the incomers, encouraged by their Naqsbandi pirs and especially by Mir Masjidi's kinsman Mir Aftab, who marched in with a large party on the evening of 3 November. Some, such as the Logaris, arrived with their chiefs; others came as individuals, called to arms by the radical Sunni 'ulema and encouraged by the rumours of rich plunder to be had. Shuja later wrote that he believed that 'these men are not influenced by considerations of religion, they give their lives for the wealth of this world and do not fear death'.[19] But the rebels certainly used the rhetoric of religious war in order to recruit for and justify their revolution – a relative innovation in the internal history of the Afghan peoples as most previous conflict had been between Muslims.[*] 'All the citizens, great and small, rich and poor, civilian and military, were made to swear on the Holy Qur'an to support the struggle,' adds Mohammad Husain Herati.[20]

The first targets of the newly strengthened rebels were the series of small outlying forts and tower houses between the town and cantonment that the British military bureaucrats had commandeered as storehouses. 'All these forts were close to the city,' wrote Herati, 'in a continuous web of orchard walls and irrigation channels, with thick tree-cover, which made it easy for the guerrillas to approach.'[21] There was nothing random about this choice of target: the rebel leaders were well aware that the British had failed to make proper arrangements for guarding their supplies which were stored not within the cantonment but at the forts of Jafar Khan, Nishan Khan and Mohammad Sharif.

They realised that if they could destroy or capture these forts, the British would either die of hunger, or surrender from lack of

---

[*] There were two recent precedents for the use of the language of the jihad in the region: Shuja's grandfather Ahmad Shah Durrani had adopted the jihad as a justification for his invasion of the Punjab, as had Dost Mohammad when he attempted to recapture Peshawar from Ranjit Singh.

ammunition, or both. Thus, as soon as Burnes was dead, they headed out of the city to destroy the forts and loot the godowns there. Within minutes, they pulled down the Fort Jafar Khan and set it on fire. Then they pushed forward to the Fort Mohammad Shareef which was adjacent to the Cantonment, and the Ghazis then turned their attention back to bringing down the walls, and like rats began to dig up the foundations.[22]

That morning, Captain Colin Mackenzie had woken in the third of the walled compounds to be targeted for attack, the Qal'a Nishan Khan, the commissariat fort reserved for the supplies of the Shah's forces. This fort, which contained nine months' supplies of wheat and fodder, as well as all the British medical supplies, lay just over a mile from the British headquarters, flanked by the canal and the Qizilbash quarter of Murad Khani on one side and on the other abutting the Shah Bagh. Mackenzie had already heard rumours of trouble in the town but was absorbed in adding up his regimental accounts, which he wanted to complete before accompanying the Envoy down to Peshawar the following day.

> Suddenly, a naked man stood before me, covered with blood, from two deep sabre cuts in the head and five musket shots in the arm and body. He proved to be a sawar [cavalryman] of Sir W Macnaghten sent with a message to us, but intercepted by the insurgents. This being a rather strong hint of how matters were going, I immediately ordered all the gates to be secured. At the same time I caused loop holes to be bored into the upper walls of Captain Troup's house [a short distance away] in which were stationed a naik [NCO] and ten sepoys. Whilst so employed, the armed population of Deh-i-Afghanan came pouring down through the gardens and began firing at us . . . One of my men was killed, and another badly wounded.

The attackers then occupied the whole of the Shah Bagh and could not be dislodged despite repeated sallies from the fort by Mackenzie's men, who continued to suffer casualties.

The canal was cut off during the day, and so closely watched that one of my followers was shot while trying to fetch some water; but we fortunately found an old well, the water of which was drinkable. Towards the afternoon, having no ammunition but what was contained in the soldiers' pouches, I communicated with Capt Trevor who despatched my requisition for ammunition at least, but did not send assistance. Capt Lawrence's gallant offer to come to our aid, if loaned two companies, was refused [by Elphinstone and Macnaghten]. In the evening I served out provisions from the Government stores. The attacks continued at intervals during the night, and we had the most disagreeable suspicion that the enemy was undermining our northwest tower.[23]

That afternoon, while Mackenzie was fighting for his life, within the city the rebel leaders were reviewing their options. Until early afternoon they had all kept their horses saddled in case the expected British counter-attack broke through to their headquarters.[24] But it was becoming increasingly clear that the British were too shocked to respond in any coherent way, and several chiefs who had initially offered their services to them, seeing the failure of nerve in the cantonment, now began to drift away and to put out feelers instead to the rebels.[25] As Vincent Eyre commented: 'The murder of our countrymen, and the spoliation of public and private property, was perpetrated with impunity within a mile of the cantonment, and under the very walls of the Bala Hisar. Such an exhibition of weakness on our part taught the enemy their strength – confirmed against us those who, however disposed to join in the rebellion had hitherto kept aloof, and ultimately encouraged the nation to unite as one man for our destruction.'[26] As a first step to this, the rebel leaders decided that rather than prepare for a quick exit they had better organise themselves instead into a provisional government, and elect a leader, without which it was not lawful to declare jihad.

As most of the leading nobles at the beginning of the uprising were Royalists, their first thought was to offer Shah Shuja the chance to expel his infidel backers. Shuja had made his frustration with the British widely known, but according to Herati the rebel overtures were nonetheless met with a firm rebuke from the Shah.

> The leaders of the uprising sent a deputation to His Majesty, saying: 'You are our monarch, and we seek your support in our struggle against this foreign occupation: please separate yourself from this tribe of foreigners!' His Majesty replied: 'Our rule is inseparable from the English, whose honoured guest we have been for thirty years; and even though their imposition of the worthless Uthman Khan as the Nizam al-Daula and Wazir has caused us much grief, yet we bear them no grudge: let what is to befall them fall also on us!' Having failed in their attempt to co-opt His Majesty, the rebels declared him an infidel, a kafir.[27]

In the absence of a Sadozai to lead them, the insurgents then turned to the Barakzais. There had been rumours for several weeks that Dost Mohammad's clever and ruthless son, Akbar Khan, had at last escaped from Bukhara. But in his absence the rebels were forced to turn to the most senior of his Barakzai cousins, Mohammad Zaman Khan, the man who had saved Mohan Lal's life earlier in the day. When he had first heard of the outbreak, Zaman Khan had sent his son Shuja, the Shah's godson, to Captain Trevor to offer his services.[28] Now, seeing the way the wind was blowing, he agreed to take on the leadership of the revolt, writing politely to Macnaghten that he had accepted the offer 'not from his own wish, but to prevent greater ills arising'. He said that he was prepared to become Wazir to Shuja and negotiate a British withdrawal by peaceful means. 'They elected Mohammad Zaman Khan Barakzai as their leader,' recorded the disapproving Herati, 'and he who was commonly known as the "rich nomad", a country bumpkin, now became the most powerful man in Kabul.'[29]

The two real leaders of the uprising were not forgotten: Aminullah Khan Logari was elected his Naib, or deputy (a title he proudly retained for the rest of his life), with Abdullah Khan Achakzai acting as the Commander-in-Chief of the rebel armies. A proclamation was issued: 'Nawab Mohammad Zaman Khan

Barakzai, Ghazi, in kindness the flower of the times, and in religious devotion the wonder of the age, has been selected by the Muslims of all tribes, under the title of Amir of the Faithful and Imam of the Holy Warriors, and as such recognised by all.'[30] Soon after this, mullahs and malangs [dervishes] rushed through the streets of the city banging their drums, formally declaring a jihad.

In the Bala Hisar, Shah Shuja, understanding the vital importance of an immediate response before the insurgency gained any more momentum, was increasingly baffled by the failure of Macnaghten to counter-attack: it was not just self-defeating, it was also such a stark contrast to the way he had been so keen to manage every minute detail of Afghanistan's governance in peacetime. Yet, parallel to all the frantic activity in the city, the British leadership within the cantonment remained strangely quiescent, as if frozen with fear. As Herati put it, 'His Majesty eventually sent his Chief Secretary to Macnaghten in the cantonment with the message that: "Now is no time for idleness or delay! Send troops at once to invest the city from all sides and quell this riot before it swells to unmanageable proportions; arrest the leaders before they get fully organised – it can still be done!"' Herati went on:

> Macnaghten – alas – thought His Majesty over-nervous, and merely sent one platoon of Tilingas [sepoys] with artillery to the Bala Hisar fort to calm the royal nerves. His Majesty again sent an urgent message: 'We are currently quite safe in the Bala Hisar fort; but the utmost urgency is security in the city, which must be restored at once, otherwise these turbulent townsmen will never be tamed!' Macnaghten's only answer was: 'Why all this hurry?' If only Macnaghten had followed His Majesty's advice, and had sent immediately some proper English troops to invest the city from all sides, and to make an example of the ring-leaders by burning down their houses, they would have struck the fear of God into the rioters and restored order! As it was, Macnaghten dithered, while His Majesty had only his small personal guard and had to bend to his will.[31]

British eyewitnesses within the cantonment also recorded the degree to which Macnaghten misread the seriousness of what was going on, despite the shocking murder of his deputy. 'Macnaghten at first made light of the insurrection,' recorded Vincent Eyre, 'and by his representations as to the general feelings of the people towards us, not only deluded himself, but misled the General. The unwelcome truth was however soon forced on us.'[32] Indeed, by early afternoon, rather than counter-attacking, Macnaghten had instead decided to retreat, abandoning his outlying Mission Compound and withdrawing his civil head-quarters into the cantonment. Elphinstone meanwhile had ordered the guard along the cantonment walls to be doubled. Beyond that, no action was taken by the British commanders despite having 5,000 armed soldiers, ample horse artillery and a year's store of ammunition at their disposal. 'We must see what the morning brings,' Elphinstone wrote to Macnaghten, 'and then think what can be done.'[33] The formidable Lady Sale was appalled. 'All was confusion and indecision,' she wrote. 'The Envoy mounted his horse and rode to the gateway, and then rode back again . . .'

Soon, however, Lady Sale had other matters to occupy her. Lieutenant Sturt, her new son-in-law, was brought on a stretcher from the Bala Hisar 'covered with blood, and unable to articulate. From the wounds in the face and shoulder, the nerves were affected; the mouth would not open, the tongue was swollen and paralysed, and he was ghastly and faint from loss of blood. He could not lie down from the blood choking him. With some difficulty and great pain he was supported upstairs, and laid on a bed, when Dr Harcourt dressed his wounds, which having been inflicted about ten o'clock, now at one were cold and stiff with clotted blood.'[34]

While this was going on in the cantonment, Brigadier Shelton had belatedly marched his troops around the back of the city and into the Bala Hisar, but had been unsure what to do once he got there. Around 3 p.m. George Lawrence arrived back at Shah Shuja's durbar and reported finding the unimaginative Shelton:

directing a desultory fire on the city from two of his guns. Brig Shelton's conduct at this crisis astonished me beyond expression . . . [He was] almost beside himself, not knowing how to act, and with incapacity stamped on every feature of his face. He immediately asked me what he should do, and on my replying 'Enter the city at once,' he sharply rebuked me, saying, 'My force is inadequate, and you do not appear to know what street fighting is . . .' The King at this time asked me more than once why the troops did not act, and seemed to be, as well he might, deeply annoyed that we did nothing. Shelton well knew the King's anxiety that he should take active measures for quelling the disturbance, but he was in fact quite paralysed . . .[35]

It was this paralysis which allowed a spontaneous protest by some disgruntled chiefs – one they imagined would be a hopeless gesture of anger, not the beginnings of a major revolution – to unite the people under the banner of Islam and grow quickly into one of the most dangerous challenges the British would face anywhere in their Empire in the nineteenth century. 'Vacillation and incapacity ruled in our military counsels and paralysed the hearts of those who should have acted with energy and decision,' concluded Lawrence. 'By their deplorable pusillanimity an accidental emeute, which could have been quelled on the moment by the prompt employment of a small force, became a formidable insurrection, which ultimately involved the ruin of a gallant army.'[36]

By evening, seeing his allies sinking into ever greater despondency, Shah Shuja tried to cheer up the depressed officers by proposing to throw a dinner. The response was glum. How could a dinner be thrown, replied the officers, when they had left their dress uniforms in the cantonment?[37] Even as Kabul burned, and with their position weakening by the minute, the British were determined that proper regimental etiquette should be observed to the end.

On the morning of 3 November, Eldred Pottinger was becoming nervous. With only one hundred troops, he was stationed in a small fortified enclosure – actually a converted caravanserai – at Laghmani, on a hilltop sixty miles north of Kabul and a short distance above the British barracks in Charikar, where the administration for Kohistan was housed. Now ever larger numbers of heavily armed Kohistanis were gathering around his tower house. Ostensibly the tribesmen were there to reconcile Pottinger's administration with some disaffected chiefs from the Nijrao district who had been driven into rebellion in 1840, and who had suffered badly in Sale's punitive expeditions that autumn; but Pottinger had a strong sense that something was amiss. 'I grew greatly alarmed at their increasing numbers,' he wrote later,

> and at their refusal to attack the Castles of the [insurgent] Chiefs who composed [the Kohistan rebel leader] Mir Masjidi's army. This feeling led to my taking sundry precautions for the security of my position against surprise. However as it appeared impolitic to shew any suspicion I was confined to half measures . . . On the 3rd the increase of armed men round my residence was most alarmingly thick and induced me to man the towers [of the fort]. In the morning the Chiefs who brought the Nijraoees were very anxious that I should receive their friends; and those Nijraoees who had come previously demanded presents and were indignant at not getting them. I sent several messages to these latter that if they would perform the services I had pointed out, I would not only give them presents, but procure for them dresses of honour from the King.

Pottinger's assistant, Lieutenant Charles Rattray,* then went to greet the new arrivals who were sitting in the adjoining stubble field, about thirty yards distant. According to the account of the

---

* Charles Rattray was the brother of the artist James Rattray who went on to produce some of the most celebrated lithographs of the war.

Gurkha havildar [NCO] Moti Ram, 'Mr Rattray, who commanded one of the Affghan corps, was lured out to look, he said, at some new recruits which he had brought with him for service. They were mounted men. As Lt Rattray was examining them drawn up in a line, they wheeled up from the left and right, and enclosed Mr Rattray, who was shot with a pistol.'[38] Pottinger meanwhile was talking to some of the Nijrao chiefs when one of his Afghan recruits 'had run up to apprize me of treachery'.

> He had scarcely made me comprehend his meaning, as he spoke by hints, when the sounds of shots alarmed us. The Chiefs with me rose and fled, and I escaped into the Castle through the Postern gate, which having secured I ran onto the top of the rampart. From there I saw Mr. Rattray lying badly wounded about three hundred yards distant, and the late tenderers of service making off in all directions with the plunder of the Camp of the detachment of Hazirbash. A party of the enemy crossing the field observed Mr. Rattray and running up to him one put his gun to his head and dispatched him, while several others fired their pieces into different parts of the body. The Guard having by this time got on the alert and loaded their musquets commenced a fire and speedily cleared the open spaces. But we continued closely pressed by the enemy from under shelter of the numerous water courses and walls.[39]

The following night, running short of ammunition as they had marched up from their main base at Charikar with little 'beyond the supply in the men's pouches', Pottinger and his Gurkha escort broke out of their encircled position under cover of darkness. Leaving behind his armoury and treasury, plus all the Afghan hostages he had taken from the Kohistan chiefs, Pottinger and his force managed to fight their way through to the main British barracks in the valley bottom, where were stationed a full detach-ment of 750 Gurkhas plus around 200 women and children from their families. There were also three guns, but no cavalry. Here Pottinger faced a new problem. The half-finished and still gateless barracks had not yet had a well built, and before long the besieged garrison was running short of water.* Each time a party was sent out at night to fetch it from the nearby canal, the volunteers were shot dead on its banks or else captured alive. What little water was brought in was 'at once seized and drunk by whoever could get hold of it'.

'The men used to steal out at night', remembered Havildar Moti Ram,

> to a nearby spring which the Affghans had diverted to another direction. Those who had canteens filled them; those who had lotas only, took them with them covered in clothes, lest the glitter of the metal should lead to detection. Those who had neither lotas nor canteens resorted to the use of cloths which they dipped in the fountain and brought back saturated with moisture. When any of these adventurous spirits returned to the fort all struggled around them to procure one precious drop. The Affghans, however, found out about this practice, and shot down all those who approached the spring. There was not a drop of water within the walls of the fort, and the men went mad with thirst.[40]

Meanwhile, the Kohistani tribesmen were pouring in; within forty-eight hours, some 20,000 Tajiks had gathered to besiege Pottinger and his Gurkhas in their unfinished barracks. 'It seemed indeed as though the whole male population of the country had assembled against us,' wrote Pottinger's Dublin-born colleague Lieutenant John Haughton.[41] The following day, the besiegers took the neighbouring fort, which overlooked the barracks, 'and shots began to drop into the interior of our square'. Before long Pottinger had been badly wounded with a musket ball in his thigh and his military commander, Captain Christopher Codrington, had been mortally wounded in the chest.

In the days that followed, the defenders grew desperate. '[The last of our] water was served out to the fighting men only,' reported Haughton, 'about half a tea cup full to each man, and

---

* The barracks still stand, a short distance from the US Air Force base of Bagram.

much of this was mere mud . . . Many sucked raw [sheep's] flesh to assuage their thirst. Fighting is at all times dry work, but fighting without water is nearly impossible. The misery was great . . . Soon, our voices were hoarse, our lips were cracked, our faces begrimed with dust and smoke, and our eyes bloodshot.' By the end of the week, the whole garrison was beginning to hallucinate. 'About midday,' wrote Haughton,

> it was announced to me that a body of men were visible coming from the direction of Kabul. I at once went out to look, and saw them sure enough; but were they the relief long expected or enemies? Relief certainly. I could make them out distinctly with a telescope. The foremost were horsemen, our own 5th Cavalry, a fact rendered certain by their white headdresses. We congratulated one another, and tears of joy streamed from my eyes; but alas! It soon appeared we were deceived. The fantastic play of mirage had so acted on a herd of cattle grazing, as entirely to deceive us.[42]

It was a similar story all over eastern Afghanistan. Overnight, every village turned hostile.

In the Khyber Pass, the British picket at Peshbulaq was attacked and the troops forced to fall back to Peshawar.[43] South of Kabul, on 3 November, a small party of sepoys under Captain Crawford was marching a group of captured Afghan rebel chiefs from Kandahar to Ghazni. 'We marched all night, and by daybreak we reached Mooshky,' remembered one of the sepoys, Himat Baniah, when questioned during his subsequent court martial.

> About 8 a.m. the people of Mooshky and the adjacent villages assembled and suddenly came upon us with about 500 men. Armed with matchlocks and swords they came on making much noise and killed many of us. The remainder fled. We were all separated one in one fort and one in another. I heard that Lieutenant Crawford got

on as far as Monee. When the 500 men came upon us I was stripped
of everything, even to my clothes. After this I escaped to a short
distance. About 5 p.m., two horsemen discovered my retreat and
seized me and carried me off captive to a fort called Ghardeh.[44]

Soon after, Ghazni was surrounded and besieged by a large force of
Ghilzais. Only Kandahar, under the watchful eye of General Nott,
continued to remain peaceful. 'I am not to be caught sleeping as my
Kabul friends were,' wrote Nott. 'I have made every preparation
for the safety of this part of the country.'[45]

In Kabul, meanwhile, the siege of the two vital commissariat
forts was intensifying. On 3 November, Captain Trevor's tower
house opposite the Shah's commissariat fort was stormed by the
rebels soon after he and his family had escaped out of the back
gate in the dark. Yet although the forts contained all the British
food supplies that had been gathered for the long Afghan winter,
neither Elphinstone nor Macnaghten sent any troops, or even
further supplies of ammunition, to aid the defenders of either
outpost, although both centres of resistance were less than a mile
and a half from the cantonment where 5,000 armed sepoys were
idly waiting for orders. 'No military steps have yet been taken to
protect our only means of subsistence in the event of a siege,'
wrote an increasingly frustrated Lady Sale in her diary. 'This fort
(an old crazy one, undermined by rats) contains the whole of the
Bengal Commissariat stores. Should the Commissariat fort be
captured, we shall lose not only all our provisions, but our
communication with the city shall be cut off. The envoy and
general still appear perfectly paralysed.'[46]

Brigadier Shelton was no more effective. 'Shelton appeared from
the commencement to despair of success,' wrote Mohan Lal,
'which produced a baneful effect in every fighting man.'[47] 'Although
already supplied with a force superior in numbers to that which
had shortly before carried the strong fort of Qalat by assault in
open day, Shelton had remained totally inactive,' agreed George
Lawrence. 'Even so obvious an action as securing the [old Mughal]
Shah Bagh and Mohammad Sharif's fort [which overlooked the

cantonment] was totally neglected, although these lay between us and that containing the commissariat stores, on which the very existence of the force depended.'[48]

On 4 November, Hugh Johnson, the paymaster of Shah Shuja's force, went to Elphinstone and explained the situation with stark clarity. He told the General that 'there were but two days' provisions left in cantonments . . . that we could not procure supplies from the surrounding country with the enemy out in force in the neighbouring forts, and [that] the consequent destruction of our force [was inevitable] from famine, unless the Commissariat Fort were taken possession of at all hazards'. Elphinstone reluctantly agreed with Johnson's analysis, and sent a message to the defender of the fort, Ensign Warren of the 5th Native Infantry, 'a man of cool determined courage, who said little and always went about with a couple of bulldogs at his heels', telling him that a relief force would be sent to him at two in the morning. He then did nothing to bring the promise to fulfilment. Warren replied with a stream of messages begging for immediate assistance and explaining that unless he were relieved without delay he would have to abandon his position as much of his guard, which initially had been only seventy men strong, had now run away. The following morning at five o'clock, the commissariat fort was finally abandoned, Warren and his handful of men having bravely waited a full three hours beyond the time by which Elphinstone had promised to relieve them. 'The enemy then took immediate possession,' wrote Lady Sale, 'depriving us of [almost] our only means of subsistence.'

This left just one centre of British supplies intact, the Qal'a Nishan Khan, commanded by Colin Mackenzie, which still contained the ample supplies collected for Shah Shuja's force. From their parapets, the defenders watched glumly 'the scene of plunder going on in Trevor's house,' wrote Mackenzie; 'and the enemy, taking possession of the top, which overlooked my defences, pitched their balls from their large jezails with such accuracy as to clear my western face of defenders.' His account continued:

It was only by crawling on my hands and knees up a small flight of steps and whisking suddenly through the door that I could even visit the tower that was being undermined. On one of these visits the sentry told me that there was an Afghan taking aim from an opposite loophole, but I could not see him. As I moved my head, the sentry clapped his eye to the slit, and fell dead at my feet with a ball through his forehead . . . In the afternoon the enemy brought down a large wall piece against us, the balls from which shook the upper part of one of our towers. The disposition to despair was increased by the utter failure of our last ammunition . . . The Afghans also brought quantities of firewood and long poles, with combustibles at the ends, which they deposited under the walls in readiness to burn down my door.

Some of Mackenzie's sawars now embarked on 'a sort of half-mutiny', planning to escape on horseback. 'This I quelled by going down amongst them with a double-barrelled gun. I cocked it, and ordered them to shut the gate, threatening to shoot the first man who should disobey. They saw I was quite determined, for I had made up my mind to die, and they obeyed.' By the evening Mackenzie and his men were exhausted, after 'fighting and working for nearly forty hours without rest'.

Abandoned, as I evidently was, to almost certain destruction by my own countrymen, my Afghan followers remained staunch to the last, in spite of the most tempting offers if they would betray me. When at last we had scarcely a round of ammunition, Hasan Khan [the commander of Mackenzie's Afghan jezailchi troops] came to me and said: 'I think we have done our duty. If you consider it necessary that we should die here, we will die, but I think we have done enough.'[49]

Mackenzie then agreed to make arrangements for a retreat. It was Ramazan, so they planned their escape soon after sunset, to coincide with the time that their besiegers would be busy with their *iftar* dinner. The Afghan marksmen of Hasan Khan's jezailchis were to lead, while the wounded were to be transported on make-shift litters and were to follow with the women and children. Mackenzie was himself to bring up the rear. The plan was to avoid all villages and to follow the canal until the cantonment came in sight, and then to strike out across the fields. All baggage and food supplies were to be abandoned.[50]

This was easier to order than to achieve. 'A night retreat is generally disastrous,' wrote Mackenzie,

and this proved no exception, for notwithstanding my strict order that all the baggage should be left behind, many of the poor women contrived to slip out with loads of their little property on their shoulders, making their children walk, whose cries added to the danger of discovery. Going among the women to see that my order for leaving everything was obeyed, a young Gurkha girl of sixteen or eighteen, who had girded up her loins and stuck a sword in her cumberbund came to me, and throwing all that she possessed at my feet, said: 'Sahib you are right, life is better than property.' She was a beautiful creature, with a fair complexion and large dark eyes, and she stood there with her garments swathed around her, leaving her limbs free, a picture of life, spirit and energy. I never saw her again, and fear she was either killed or taken prisoner on the night march.

The shooting started before the column had moved more than half a mile. Mackenzie's party quickly got separated from the jezailchis who had led the retreat, and he found himself alone and under fire, 'with a chaprasi and two sowars in the midst of the wailing crowd of women and children'. Soon after this he was surrounded. At first he thought it was his own men, but 'they quickly undeceived me by crying out "Feringhee hast" (Here is a European) and attacking me with swords and knives.' Mackenzie spurred his horse and wheeled round,

cutting from right to left. My blows, by God's mercy, parried the greater part of theirs, and I was lucky enough to cut off the hand of my most outrageous assailant. My sword went clean through the man's arm, but just after that, I received such a tremendous blow on the back of the head that, though the sabre turned in my enemy's hand, it knocked me almost off my horse. Hanging on with one foot . . . the next thing I remember was finding myself upright in the saddle in advance of the enemy, with the whole picket firing after me. I passed unhurt through two volleys of musketry. The picket pursued, but I soon distanced them, crossing several fields at speed . . . Proceeding cautiously along, I found to my horror my path again blocked up by a dense body of Afghans. Retreat was impossible, so, putting my trust in God, I charged into the midst of them, hoping that the weight of the horse would clear the way for me, and reserving my sword-cut for the last struggle. It was well that I did so, for by the time I had knocked over a heap of fellows, I found that they were my own Jezailchis.

Eventually they reached the cantonment. 'During the night,' noted Mackenzie, 'many stragglers of my party, principally followers, dropped in. From first to last I had about a dozen killed. Among the errors which led to our downfall, that of omitting to strengthen my post was the worst. Every Afghan of intelligence has confessed that if I had been reinforced by a couple of regiments, we should have remained masters of the city.'[51]

Hugh Johnson, already aghast at the folly of the generals in allowing his treasury to fall into the hands of the rebels, was even more horrified at the loss of all food supplies – and all this within only thirty-six hours of the outbreak of the revolt. 'Four lakh of rupees worth of wheat, barley, wine, beer & every requisite were surrendered without a blow being struck back to our enemy,' he wrote in his diary the following day.

Numbers of people, and especially that large and influential tribe the Qizilbashes, had hitherto kept aloof from the struggle, and much as they might have been astonished at our inactivity for a day or two, and our apparent apathy at the loss of our Treasury and the murder of our Resident, it never entered their most idle dreams that a British force of five thousand men of whose high state of discipline & courage and of the wisdom of their leaders they had always heard such high praise, would sit down tamely and see themselves bearded at the very gates of their Cantonments by a few contemptible ill-assured savages.

The eyes of the whole Afghan nation were now however opened. Every man was our enemy, and in lieu of the high character which we had hitherto borne, we were looked upon with the most utter contempt. The godown fort was this day something similar to a large ants' nest. By noon thousands & thousands had assembled from far & wide to participate in the booty of the English dogs, each man taking away with him as much as he could carry and to this we were all helpless eye witnesses.[52]

Afghan sources state that within twenty-four hours the rebels had taken three years' worth of military and food supplies, removing everything to within the city walls. 'They carried off the booty on their heads, and distributed thousands of maunds of grain among the Afghan villagers and nomads, so that, having eaten their fill, they too joined the revolt,' wrote Munshi Abdul Karim. 'Whatever was judged as too heavy to carry off, they destroyed.'[53]

Lady Sale was quite clear about the seriousness of what had happened: 'It gave both confidence and much plunder to the enemy and created great disgust among Europeans, who lost all their rum. A worse loss was all the medical supplies, sago, arrow root, wine &c, for the sick.'[54] Weeks later, when word of what had happened reached George Broadfoot in the besieged city of Jalalabad, he wrote an angry note in his diary:

Colin Mackenzie was in the outskirts of the city in an old fort. For two days he fought, and then cut his way through to the large force, who did not seem able to cut their way through to him, bringing in all his men and the crowd of women and children safe, himself getting two sabre wounds. A more heroic action was never performed. The unhappy women and children have since perished or gone into slavery, because 5000 men could not do what he did with 50.[55]

Within the besieged cantonment, hunger soon began to set in.

The troops were put on half-rations, but as with the death march through the Bolan two years earlier, it was the camp followers and baggage animals who suffered first. 'Our cattle have been starving for some days past,' wrote Johnson in his diary a week later. 'Not a blade of grass nor a particle of bussorah [fodder] or grain is procurable for them.* The barley in store is served out as rations to camp followers. They only get ¼ of a seer for their daily food. Our cattle are subsisting on the twigs, branches & bark of trees. Scarcely an animal is fit to carry a load.'[56] A week later the situation was even more dire: 'Our camp followers have for the past 2 days had nothing to eat except the carcasses of our camels and horses that have died from want of food. Twigs and the bark of trees was no longer procurable. All the trees in the Cantonments are stript.'[57]

Johnson soon identified the only feasible source of food: the Sufi-shrine village of Bibi Mahru ('Moon-Faced Lady'), known to the British as Bemaroo, which lay on a low ridge half a mile to the north, commanding the rear of the cantonment.† Johnson eventually concluded negotiations with the headman, and a small quantity of wheat now arrived in the cantonment, but it was only enough for the needs of a few days.[58] To add to the misery, the temperature now dropped, and the first snows of winter began to dust the ground. Around the same time the insurgents began to bombard the cantonment with the cannon they had captured within the city and in the commissariat forts. There was little skill or method to the bombardment, and throughout the war the Afghans struggled to find trained gunners, but the random falling of shot within the

---

* One of the tasks of the Ghilzai had been to supply grain and forage to the cantonment. When Macnaghten cut their subsidy they retaliated by refusing to supply provisions.

† The village and its shrine are still there, above the airport road, overlooking the large Kabul ISAF base and the heavily sandbagged American Embassy compound.

cantonment walls still began to wear away at the nerves of the besieged troops.

The cannon fire was soon supplemented by volleys of musketry from the fort of Mohammad Sharif, captured by the rebels the following day. This looked straight on to the main gate of the cantonment, and flanked the road leading to the city. The Afghans, having walked in and captured it unopposed, had quickly loopholed the walls so as to shoot down any British attempt at sorties from their front gate. On 6 November, Elphinstone further stymied British resistance by forbidding returning fire from the walls on the grounds that 'powder is scarce!' wrote an incredulous Lady Sale. 'There being at the time sufficiency for a twelve month siege.'[59]

It was now clear to everyone that Elphinstone was a liability. 'People do not hesitate to say that our chief should be set aside,' noted Lady Sale in her diary. 'The poor general's mind is distracted by the diversity of opinions offered; and the great bodily ailments he sustains are daily enfeebling his powers. There is much reprehensible croaking going on: talk of retreat, and the consequent desertion of our Mussalmen troops. All this makes a bad impression on the men.'[60] This was certainly true: the troops were baffled and unnerved by the lack of leadership and the sudden loss of confidence. 'The spirits of the army were much depressed,' wrote the sepoy Sita Ram. 'There was fighting every day, and because there was no good food for the European soldiers, they lost spirit and did not fight as well as they used to.' To make matters worse,

The cold was so intense that it rendered the sepoy portion of the army next to useless . . . We were annoyed night and day by cannon fire. The enemy seemed to increase by thousands and their long matchlocks outranged our muskets. Although they could never withstand a regular charge, so long as they could find cover behind walls, houses etc, their fire was very distressing . . . The whole army was in a miserable plight . . . The price of food was perfectly absurd and everyone endured great hardship. I saw many sahibs shed tears of vexation, and they blamed their generals and leaders for their humiliation. They said their leaders were too old and virtually useless . . .'[61]

On 9 November, in order to provide an alternative to Elphinstone, who between crippling gout and successive defeats had now sunk into a black hole of depression, Macnaghten decided to bring in Shelton from his post in the Bala Hisar. This was another error. Not only was Shelton every bit as passive as Elphinstone, he was if anything more convinced of the hopelessness of the British position. 'He brought neither help nor comfort,' wrote Colin Mackenzie, 'openly talking of retreat.' On his arrival, when Mackenzie cheerily asked how he was, Shelton replied, 'Pretty well in body.' 'Well,' said Mackenzie, 'that's always something in these hard times.' 'The Brigadier then turned to him with the most lugubrious countenance and uttered the words: "Dust to dust."'[62]

Shelton's arrival also acted to divide the British high command. Macnaghten believed it was the duty of the garrison 'to retain our post at whatever risk', while Shelton 'strenuously advocated an immediate retreat to Jalalabad'. 'This difference of opinion, on a question of such vital importance, was attended with unhappy results,' recorded Vincent Eyre. 'It deprived the General in his hour of need, of the strength which unanimity imparts.'[63]

Calling Shelton down to the cantonment meant abandoning the British position in the one really strong and well-supplied fortress in Kabul. The weakness of the position of the cantonment was obvious to everyone. A much better strategy would have been to abandon it and march the British troops into the Bala Hisar. 'Though we were all starving and eating horse and camel we could have marched into Bala Hisar and held out a year,' thought Mackenzie. 'In a fortnight the tribes would have melted away. There was a strong fortress commanding the town, capable of receiving the whole force, yet nothing would induce the commanders to occupy it.'[64]

No one was more aware of the fundamental indefensibility of the cantonment than Lieutenant Sturt, who had designed it. From his sickbed, propped up in his pyjamas, 'fretting himself half-mad at everything going wrong', he sent repeated messages urging the commanders to move into, not out of, Shuja's ancient fortress. 'Were Sturt's advice taken, we should nightly send ammunition there,' recorded Lady Sale in her diary, 'and, when a sufficiency is conveyed, all make one bold night march in very light marching order, just what we can carry on our horses. In there we can be lodged (not comfortably, I grant) in the houses of the inhabitants. They have laid in their stores for the winter, which would be bought at any price, and then we might defy all Afghanistan for any time.'[65] But the reply to Sturt's plan from the commanders was: 'How can we abandon the cantonments when they have cost us so much money?'

After the departure of Shelton, Shuja was left alone in his fortress with what was left of the Shah's Contingent and the handful of British officers attached to it. According to Lady Sale:

[he] took up his abode at the gate of the harem sarai, where he remained during the rest of the siege; and all day, seated at the window, commanding a fine view of the Cantonments, telescope in hand, watched anxiously the course of passing events in that place, sunk into a state of despondency. He put off for a time all the insignia of royalty, made the officers sit by him on chairs, and seemed for a time quite *gobrowed*, an expressive Eastern term to be rendered something between dumbfounded and at one's wits' end.[66]

By the second week of November, with British positions in the Bala Hisar, the city and all the forts around the cantonment now lost or abandoned, the fighting began to centre instead around Bibi Mahru, which had become the last source of supplies for the increasingly desperate British. Here a series of inconclusive engagements took place around the forts dominating the village and overlooking the cantonment. On 10 November, the insurgents tightened the noose around the British by occupying the heights on either side and, 'more numerous than ants or locusts', seized a tower house on the crest of one hill directly opposite called the Rikab Bashee's fort.[67]

Three days later, the rebels manhandled two captured field guns on to these heights. As before, Shelton declined to take action, citing the risks of defeat. 'Brigadier,' said an exasperated Macnaghten eventually, 'if you will allow yourself to be bearded by the enemy, and will not advance and take these two guns by this evening, you must be prepared for any disgrace that may befall us.'[68] The following morning at dawn Shelton finally made a major infantry sortie, only to be immediately attacked by a strong force of Afghan cavalry who rode straight down through his ranks. 'The Afghans gathered their strength and charged downhill and mowed down hundreds of English soldiers like grass,' recorded Mirza 'Ata. 'Bravery and death were to be seen on both sides.'[69]

Only after leaving eighty of their troops dead on the ground, and with nearly 200 wounded, did the British succeed in spiking one gun and dragging the other back within the cantonment walls.[70] It was not a good precedent for the effectiveness of the terrified garrison against their increasingly confident and emboldened besiegers.

On 15 November, British morale received another blow when two ragged figures broke through the ring of besiegers to bring terrible news. Eldred Pottinger and John Haughton were apparently the only two survivors of the 750-strong garrison of Charikar.

After ten days of siege, driven mad by thirst, made anxious by the growing stream of desertions, and by the growing numbers of Tajiks and Safis massing to join the siege of the barracks, Pottinger had decided that the only hope was to try to make a dash for Kabul. 'The corps was completely disorganised from the privations it had suffered, the utter inefficiency of the native officers who had no sort of control over their soldiers, the exhaustion of the men from constant duty, and the total want of water and provisions,' he wrote later. 'I therefore considered that our only chance of saving any portion of the Regiment was a retreat on Kabul and though that was abundantly perilous, I entertained a hope that the most active men who were not encumbered with wives and children might make it through in safety.'

But, as with Mackenzie's night retreat from the commissariat fort, chaos reigned almost from the minute Pottinger's troops dashed from the building. 'I found it totally impossible to preserve any order after leaving the gate and in vain attempted leading the men,' he confessed in his official report.[71] The fleeing soldiers were shot down as they ran madly to try to find water. All 300 of the wounded who were left behind, as well as any of the sepoys or their wives captured alive, were distributed among the Tajik chiefs and immediately sold as slaves.[72]

While Pottinger and Haughton, who both had horses, eventually made it through to Kabul, riding by night far from the main road, along the western flank of the Koh Daman, and hiding by day, only a handful of their sepoys limped in after them. Among those captured and enslaved was Havildar Moti Ram, who uniquely left an account of his capture. Moti Ram made it further than most, and was captured when within sight of his destination. 'At the time hostilities broke out,' he wrote, 'there were two Gurkha fakirs in the fort who were visiting on a pilgrimage the different Hindoo shrines of Afghanistan.' These fakirs demanded arms and ammunition.

Our officers complied with their requests, and these sturdy and holy personages astonished by all their feats in action: there were none of us who fought the Afghans better than they did. We all marched together during the night without molestation, until we arrived at a village near Kara Bagh. Here opposition commenced, and we advanced skirmishing until about 3 o'clock A.M., by which time our movements became generally known, and our enemies were gathering around us in hopeless numbers every minute. The road ran through the middle of Kara Bagh with walls and vineyards on either side: these the Afghans lined, and from them poured a deadly and frequent fire upon us. Numbers were killed, we were totally vanquished. There was a gateway into a vineyard on one side of the road. I rushed through it; an Afghan laid hold of my clothes to detain me, but I shook him off and continued my flight, taking care to carry my musket with me, for which I had only five rounds remaining in my pouch.

Approaching the British cantonment at dawn, Moti Ram realised that he had wandered into the middle of the besieging Afghan troops. 'I saw at once that all hope of further escape was gone. I had one hundred rupees in my kummerbund, which sum I had amassed in the Shah's service. I took it out and buried it, placing a stone which I thought I could recognise over it, and sat down quietly to await what might happen. Shortly after, a party of horse, about 25 in number approached the spot where I was. Some seized me by the feet, some by the shoulders.'[73] The Afghans tried to shoot Moti Ram with his own musket, but when it three times failed go off, the havildar told them he was a Muslim and that it was God's will that he was not to be killed. He was asked to recite the Kalima, the Muslim profession of faith, and he did so.

> The sabre was then removed from my throat and they carried me to [their chief] Baha-ud-Din, first depriving me of my coat, panta-loons, a silk handkerchief, a pistol, my shoes and some other articles, leaving me only a pair of pyjamas. The people of the village contin-ually threatened to put me to death, but Baha-ud-Din at length released me. I had proceeded a coss when a man ploughing on the roadside seized me, and threatened to kill me unless I worked his plough. Whilst I was with him, I suffered severely during the night time – the weather was bitter cold, and I had nothing to cover me but my chogah. I examined the roof of the house during the day, and it appeared to me that by removing a few of the bricks from the chimney I might get out unobserved. At night I did so, and effected my escape.

But not for long. 'I had got five coss further down the road to Jalalabad when the son of a sirdar who was fighting at Kabul sent some horsemen to take and bring me to him. All the villagers, young and old, male and female, gathered around exclaiming, "a

Kafir or Feringhee: kill him, kill him"; but the young chief protected
me from violence, and told me to groom his horse.' Added Moti
Ram: 'This young man was continually looking in the direction of
Kabul, through a telescope which he said Sir A Burnes had given
his father as a present.'[74]

On 20 November the rebels' guns were suddenly stilled, and for
the next three days there were no attacks on the cantonment. Only
on the morning of the 23rd did it become clear that the days of
quiet had been to allow the rebels to manufacture ammunition and
powder. That morning, before dawn, the Kohistanis under Mir
Masjidi massed in huge numbers on the heights above the cantonment, digging breastworks and trenches, and completely cutting
off the British from their food supplies in Bibi Mahru. They then
began to bombard the cantonment with their artillery. Shelton was
soon sent out to try to clear the heights.

'The sound of artillery fire rolled like thunder,' wrote Mirza 'Ata.
'Abdullah Khan Achakzai Ghazi heard the sound of fierce fighting,
and hastened to reinforce the jihadis at Bibi Mahru: they trampled
the English soldiers under the hooves of their horses, they cut them
down with their sharp swords, then captured the English gun, and
shouting "Allah hu-akbar! God is great!" they charged the English.'

In order to defend himself against the cavalry, Shelton then
formed his infantry into two squares at the summit of the hill, the
standard British defence against mounted attack that had been so
effective against Napoleon's lancers at Waterloo. But it proved a
disastrous tactic in Afghanistan. The Afghans simply pulled back,
allowing the jezail marksmen to come forward and from behind
the cover of stones and rocks fire into the densely packed British
ranks while keeping well out of range of British muskets. The
British were easy targets: a solid mass of scarlet uniforms standing completely still for hours on end silhouetted on a ridge. One
hundred sappers had accompanied the force 'for the express

purpose of raising a *sangar* [shallow trenches and breastworks]
behind which our troops would have been wholly protected from
the fire of the jezails, and infused into our troops a sense of security . . . But no such defence was raised.'[75] Instead, exposed on the
brow of the hill, rank after rank fell where they stood, as Shelton
remained rigid and unmoving under fire, astonishingly brave but
fatally unimaginative, apparently unable to think of any response
to the destruction of his regiment.

To add to their misfortunes, Shelton's one gun had now over-
heated and was unable to reply to the Afghan jezails. Among those
wounded at this point was Vincent Eyre, who received a bullet
through his left hand 'which for the present terminated my active
services', and Colin Mackenzie, who took a bullet in the left shoulder. 'Three times the face of the square had to be made up,'
Mackenzie wrote afterwards.

> The front ranks had been literally mowed away . . . Our ammuni-
> tion was almost expended and by one pm the men were faint from
> fatigue and thirst. But no water was procurable and the number of
> killed and wounded was swelled every instant. I tried to persuade
> Shelton to effect a retreat only to be told: 'Oh no, we will hold the
> hill some time longer.' On Shelton's refusal to retire, Colonel Oliver,
> who was a very stout man, remarked that the inevitable result would
> be a general flight to cantonments, and that, as he was too unwieldy
> to run, the sooner he got shot the better. He then exposed himself to
> the enemy's fire and fell mortally wounded.[76]

To the growing horror of Lady Sale and the other spectators watching from the cantonment rooftops – 'I had a fine view of the field
of action, and by keeping behind the chimneys, escaped the bullets
that continually whizzed past me' – a large party of Afghan ghazis
led personally by Abdullah Khan now began to crawl up a hidden
gully towards the squares, out of sight of the infantry, but clearly
visible to the ladies.[77] Moments later they broke cover and flung
themselves at the redcoats. According to the *Tarikh-i-Sultani*, 'at
that moment, Abdullah Khan Achakzai, who was renowned for

his bravery and had included a wish for martyrdom in his early morning prayers, yelled, "With Allah's grace, Victory indeed is near!" and with his unit launched an assault like a fierce lion or the serpent that inhabits the scented grass. He captured the English cannon and pushed back the British infantry soldiers, dispersing them. The British soldiers couldn't withstand this assault and turned and fled.'[78]

Within minutes the nearest square had collapsed, and the Afghans began to drag away the captured gun. 'It was very like the scenes depicted in the battle of the Crusaders,' wrote Lady Sale. 'The enemy rushed on and drove our men before them like a flock of sheep with a wolf at their heels. As they captured our gun, our artillerymen fought like heroes; two were killed at the gun; Sergeant Mulhall received three wounds; poor Laing was shot while waving his sword over the gun and cheering the men. It was an anxious sight, and made our hearts beat.'[79]

Shelton, however, managed to keep his one remaining square intact and ordered his bugler to sound the halt. Then he counter-attacked with bayonets, retrieving the gun and in hand-to-hand fighting killing both Mir Masjidi and the military commander of the rebellion, Abdullah Khan Achakzai. 'The news of the Ghazi's death bereaved every Muslim, especially the members of Afghani tribes,' wrote Sultan Mohammad Khan Durrani. 'Had he not lost his life, the Ghazis would have captured the British Cantonment on that day itself.'[80]

For a while the British seemed to have the upper hand. But when the Afghans retreated and the remnants of the two squares reformed, the jezail marksmen resumed their fire, and further ranks of sepoys began to fall where they stood. 'The Brigadier was then urged and entreated to seize the decisive moment to charge the enemy,' wrote George Lawrence, who was looking on with horror from the cantonment walls, 'but from some unexplained cause nothing could induce him to stir from the hill.'[81]

Then a second party of rebel swordsmen assembled in the hidden gully, ready for a final assault. This time all the troops broke rank and fled back to the cantonment, pursued by the Afghan cavalry. 'All order was at an end,' noted George Lawrence.

I could see from my post our flying troops hotly pursued and mixed up with the enemy, who were slaughtering them from all sides: the scene was so fearful I can never forget it. On came the fugitives, pouring into the cantonment, which we fully expected the Affghans to enter along with them. Fortunately for us, and most unexpectedly, the Affghan cavalry suddenly swept to the right, directed, as we afterwards heard, by Mahommad Osman Khan Barakzai, who was one of the chiefs then in communication with Sir W Macnaghten. But who can depict the horror of that night, and our consternation, for we felt ourselves doomed men? Nothing of course could justify the conduct of our troops; but the total incapacity of Brigadier Shelton, his reckless exposure of his men for hours at the top of a high ridge to a destructive fire, and his stubborn neglect to avail himself of the several opportunities offered to him throughout the day – by the temporary flight of the enemy, to complete their dispersion – go far to extenuate the soldiers, who had lost all confidence in a leader who had proved himself so incapable of command.[82]

It was the turning point in the war. The day had been a catastrophe. Of the 1,100 men who marched out with Shelton in the morning, well over 300 had been killed, while the wounded who had been left outside were disembowelled as their wives and children looked on helplessly at the bottom of the hill. Many more who had been cut off and failed to make it back within the cantonment walls were hunted down that night. 'Those who had survived the battle and fled back towards the English base but lost their way and tried to hide out in byways and crannies were rounded up one by one and executed,' wrote Fayz Mohammad. 'For the English, the calamities of this day took away whatever control they might have had over events and they were rendered virtually helpless.'[83]

Certainly, after this, the British made no more attempts at taking the initiative. 'Shelton's incapacity neutralised the heroism of the officers,' wrote Mackenzie. 'Their spirit was gone and discipline had almost disappeared.'[84] 'Even such of the officers as had hitherto indulged in the hope of a favourable turn of events began to entertain gloomy forebodings as to our future fate,' agreed Eyre in his diary that evening. 'Our force resembled a ship in danger of wrecking among rocks and shoals, for want of an able pilot to guide it safely through them. Even now, at the eleventh hour, had the helm of affairs been grasped by a competent hand, we might perhaps have steered clear of destruction; but in the absence of any such deliverer, it was but too evident that Heaven alone could save us.'[85]

Instead, that night, worse news still arrived in the cantonment. Welcoming volleys from the city announced the arrival of Akbar Khan, Dost Mohammad's most fiery and militarily effective son. He had just marched in from Bamiyan at the head of 6,000 of the Mir Wali's Uzbek cavalry, and immediately put himself in charge of the resistance.

Akbar Khan spent the first few days after his return receiving the adulation of his people. 'It was as if spring had brought life to a garden,' wrote Maulana Kashmiri.

> All the nobles and chiefs came forward to pay homage
> Men and women, young and old, came out to bless him
>
> They said to him: 'O Protector of us all!
> Our Defender, Refuge and Bedrock!'
>
> Such a resounding chorus of prayer rose from the earth
> That in heaven they asked Jesus what all the clamour was . . .'[86]

Akbar soon proved himself the adversary the British had always feared he would be. Within a few days he had transformed the uprising by blockading the cantonment effectively for the first time. Mullahs were sent into all the villages in the vicinity to stop the farmers selling the British supplies.[87] The villages to the rear were occupied and garrisoned, and the headmen threatened with instant death if they sold a single sack of grain or fodder to the Firangis. The new wooden bridge over the Kabul River which linked the cantonment with the Bala Hisar and the Jalalabad road was burned down. To Macnaghten's anger, the garrison made no attempt to stop the destruction, and merely watched idly from the behind their parapets, even though the Afghans dismantling bridge were easily within range. With two of the leading Royalist leaders killed on the heights of Bibi Mahru, the previously somewhat fractured rebel command now united firmly around Akbar Khan and his Barakzais. 'It is perfectly wonderful how they [the rebels] hang together,' wrote a frustrated Macnaghten.[88]

Akbar Khan's marriage alliance with the daughter of Mohammad Shah Khan, one of the most powerful Ghilzai chieftains, also began to change the ethnicity of the resistance. With Abdullah Khan Achakzai dead and the Kohistani Tajiks increasingly sidelined following the death of Mir Masjidi and the departure of his followers en masse to bury their Pir, it was the unsophisticated but formidable Ghilzai who now came to dominate the uprising. Basing themselves in the fort of Mahmud Khan just outside the city walls, it was their troops who increasingly filled the ranks of men ringing the hilltops around the silent and cowed cantonment, supported by the Barakzai forces who had made their base in the Shah Bagh at the valley bottom.

Within the cantonment walls, the pressure was now intense as icy blizzards and hunger brought morale ever lower. The horses were so hungry they were found gnawing at tent pegs and eating their own dung over and over again; Lady Sale saw one starving horse bite off and devour the tail of its neighbour, while her own mare champed away at a cart wheel. Mirza 'Ata, like many Afghans, relished the discomfiture of the once arrogant British. 'It now happened that so much snow fell that the English troops, who had never seen the snows of Khurasan, became like melting snowmen,' he wrote. 'Many died of hunger; others killed transport camels and oxen for the Muslims to eat the meat and the Hindus to eat the skins! In these extreme circumstances, as in the lowest pit of Hell, all differences of religious practice and taboo were forgotten.'[89] The camp followers who couldn't get access to the dead horses and camels were now seen roasting and spitting pariah dogs in the streets.

Akbar Khan had been released from his prison-pit in Bukhara only a month earlier after a miserable year-long confinement. Shortly before his release, according to Maulana Kashmiri, Akbar had been visited in a dream by a Sufi saint who told him to put on his turban, strap a sword to his belt and go and protect his homeland, which had been given to him by God.[90] Mirza 'Ata, who came greatly to admire the Barakzai heir, learned one version of the story from his followers: 'The 'ulama of the noble city of Bukhara interceded with the ruler Nasir al-Daula to release Sardar Muhammad Akbar Khan and his companions,' he wrote. 'The chiefs of Kabul wrote to Akbar welcoming him, expressing their joy at his liberation and explaining that the English army was much weakened after recent fighting and in no state to resist, so that the Sardar's arrival was most opportune: now was the time for avenging his father, the peerless Amir!' Akbar Khan went straight to Kabul, where all the chiefs and notables told him of the injustices committed by the English, and appealed to him for justice. The Sardar then wrote to Macnaghten asking to see him, and a meeting was arranged.

The next day, Sardar Muhammad Akbar Khan with some trusted companions rode out from Kabul to the appointed place, as did Macnaghten from the cantonment: they met and embraced heartily and retired for private conversation. This much is reported, that the Sardar told the English envoy that it was no longer appropriate for him to remain in Kabul, that he should hand over one of his officers as a hostage and leave for India. Whenever the Sardar's honoured father, the peerless Amir, was released from foreign incarceration and returned to Khurasan, then the English hostage would be honourably dismissed. Macnaghten agreed, and this agreement was put into writing; the English were all of the opinion that after this agreement there would be no further strife.[91]

The reality was a little more complex. Through Mohan Lal, who remained active within the city, Macnaghten had been in contact with several of the rebel commanders from the very beginning of the uprising and had already for several weeks been exploring the possibility of buying military support, dividing the Afghan factions or engineering some sort of honourable exit. Two days after Shelton's crushing defeat, the Envoy received an initial delegation of rebels who came seeking an unconditional British surrender. As Macnaghten put it himself, in a note found on his desk after his death,

> At my initiation, deputies were sent from the Rebels who came into cantonment on the 25th, I having received overtures from them of a pacific nature on the basis of our evacuating the country. I proposed to them the only terms which in my opinion could be accepted with honour. They returned me a letter of defiance the next morning to the effect that unless I consented to surrender our arms and to abandon His Majesty to his fate, we must prepare for imminent hostilities. To this I replied that we preferred death to dishonour and that it would remain with a higher power to decide between us.[92]

Macnaghten having refused to hand over Shuja and his family to Akbar Khan, and having broken off relations, there followed a further fortnight of hungry and anxious inactivity on the part of the British. Macnaghten was now pinning his strategy on the faint hope that a relief force from either Jalalabad, Ghazni or Kandahar might rescue the demoralised troops in the cantonments. To MacGregor, the Political Officer attached to General Sale's brigade in Jalalabad, he appealed repeatedly: 'Dozens of letters have been written, urging your immediate return with Sale's Brigade to Kabul, and if you have not started by the time you receive this, I earnestly beg that you will do so immediately. Our situation is a very precarious one; but with your assistance we shall all do well, and you must render it to us if you have any regard for our lives or the honour of our country.'[93]

The last messenger to make it through the Khord Kabul Pass,

however, carried the news that Sale was himself hopelessly besieged and outnumbered in Jalalabad and in no position to relieve Kabul; he also reported that the Khyber had been lost and was now closed to any potential relief force attempting to make its way up from Peshawar. On 7 December, after thick snow had blocked the route, it became clear that no help was likely to make it through from Kandahar either, at least until the spring thaw. On the morning of the 8th Macnaghten heard from the last remaining garrison, Ghazni, that they too were besieged and unable to come to the aid of their compatriots in Kabul.[94] Now, with only one day's provisions left, there was no hope. Imminent starvation loomed. The military leadership remained paralysed. Elphinstone and Shelton both seemed locked in despair. The defeated and hungry troops were on the verge of mutiny. The numbers of the Afghan resistance were now estimated at over 50,000, outnumbering the British garrison about ten to one.

All these anxieties culminated in a stormy meeting of the British commanders on the evening of 8 December. By this time, Elphinstone, Shelton and Macnaghten were barely on speaking terms, and the childishly obstreperous Shelton was especially disparaging about the Envoy. 'I will sneer at him,' he announced. 'I like to sneer at him.'[95] At Councils of War he was openly insolent to the General, rolling himself up in his quilt on the floor, from which requests for his opinion would be answered with loud snores.

At the meeting, Elphinstone produced the written letter Macnaghten had requested, taking formal responsibility for opening surrender negotiations, explaining that:

> after having held our position here for upwards of three weeks in a state of siege, from the want of provisions and forage, the reduced state of our troops, the large number of wounded and sick, the difficulty of defending the extensive and ill-situated cantonment we occupy, the near approach of winter, our communication cut off, no prospect of relief, and the whole country in arms against us, I am of the opinion that it is not feasible any longer to maintain our position in this country, and that you ought to avail yourself of the offer to negotiate which has been made to you.[96]

The other officers also formally declared the British situation untenable, 'giving it as their decided and unqualified opinion that no more military operations could be undertaken by the troops in their present condition, and that therefore no time should be lost in negotiating for a safe retreat to Hindustan, without any reference to Shah Shuja or his interests, for their first duty was to provide for the honour and welfare of the British troops under their command'.[97] The readiness of the military to abandon Shuja stood in stark contrast to the Shah's remarkable fidelity to the British, despite a stream of tempting proposals from the rebels for him to abandon his unpopular Kafir allies. Macnaghten repeatedly warned that any attempt to abandon Shuja would cover the British with 'everlasting infamy'. But he was overruled and ordered to meet with Akbar Khan to see what terms he could get to guarantee the safety of the British during an immediate withdrawal from Afghanistan.

This first meeting between the two took place on the icy banks of the Kabul River, just beyond the charred remains of the bridge. Macnaghten was accompanied by Lawrence, Trevor and Mackenzie; Akbar brought with him all the leading chiefs of the rebellion.[98] Macnaghten began with a characteristically preening and disingenuous preamble, which he read out in fluent court Persian: 'Whereas it has become apparent from recent events that the continuance of the British army in Afghanistan for the support of Shah Shuja-ool-Moolk is displeasing to the majority of the Afghan nation, and whereas the British government had no other object in sending troops to this country than the integrity, happiness and welfare of the Afghans, therefore it can have no wish to remain when that object is defeated by its presence.' Then came the meat of Macnaghten's draft treaty. '1st, the British troops now at Kabul will repair to Peshawar with all practical expedition, and thence return to India. 2nd, the Sirdars engage that the British troops shall be unmolested in their journey, shall be treated with all honour, and receive all possible assistance in carriage and provisions.'[99] It was at this point, noted Macnaghten in his last memo, that 'Mahommed Akbar interrupted me and observed that we did not require supplies as there was no impediment to our marching the next morning. I mention the above fact to shew the impetuous disposition of this youth. He was reproved by the other Chiefs and he himself, except on this occasion, behaved with courtesy, though evidently elevated by his sudden change of fortune.'[100]

After two hours, an agreement was reached. The British were to withdraw three days later, on 14 December, and their safety was to be guaranteed. Captain Trevor was to be handed over as a hostage. Jalalabad, Ghazni and Kandahar would also be evacuated. In return for a large down-payment, food, grain and transport cattle would be sent to the British to help them on their way. Shah Shuja would be given the choice of leaving with the British or remaining in Kabul as a private citizen. The Bala Hisar would first be evacuated by its few remaining British officers and handed over to Akbar Khan. Meanwhile Dost Mohammad would be released from his house arrest in Ludhiana and allowed to return to the throne. The Afghans would undertake not to ally with any foreign power without the consent of the British, and the British in return promised that 'the English army will not cross into Afghan territory unless the Afghan leaders request it'.

Macnaghten thought the terms as good as he was likely to get and, naive and delusional as ever, wrote to Auckland, 'We shall part with the Afghans as friends, and I feel satisfied that any government which may be established hereafter will always be disposed to cultivate a good understanding with us.'[101]

One person who of course was not consulted about any of this was Shah Shuja – the man in whose name the war had been waged and the occupation administered. His biographer Mohammad Husain Herati gives the only surviving account of the Shah's reaction when he heard of the terms which had been offered by Macnaghten, his one-time champion:

When His Majesty got intelligence of this agreement, he wrote to Macnaghten as follows: 'Did you bring us back to this country only

to hand us over to our enemies? Have you still no idea of the faithlessness of the Barakzais and of the people of this country? By
throwing money at these vengeful people, you are only hastening
your own and our death and destruction! Is that sensible?'
Macnaghten merely countered: 'It is too late to change the agreements that have been made.' His Majesty was distraught, running
hither and thither like liquid mercury, wringing his hands day and
night, saying 'Macnaghten has taken leave of his senses – it will be
the death of both of us!'

Macnaghten ordered the remaining British troops to leave the Bala
Hisar and despatched a message to inform Akbar Khan that the
fort had been evacuated and that he should send his own troops to
garrison it.

> Mohammad Akbar Khan immediately sent 2,000 jezail-bearing
> Ghilzais. The decent citizens of Kabul were horrified, exclaiming 'If
> Akbar Khan takes over the fort, what will happen to Shah Shuja's
> womenfolk and children and dependants? God help them!'
>   At the thought of the imminent rape and pillage, His Majesty was
> sunk in a whirlpool of despondency. However the denizens of the
> Bala Hisar fort were mostly old retainers, born within the
> compound, loyal servants who had grown up under the protection
> and patronage of the royal family: these at least did not weakly give
> in to despair, and as soon as the last of the English forces had
> marched out of the fort, they boldly shut the gates behind them and
> killed any of the rebel soldiers who had already penetrated the fort,
> so that Akbar Khan's troops were forced to retire disappointed.[102]

Akbar Khan's troops tried twice more to assault the main gate of
the Bala Hisar, but Shah Shuja's household troops, whom the
British had long disparaged as 'a useless rabble', successfully drove
them back, inflicting serious casualties. 'We could not but admire
the promptitude and courage he [Shuja] had displayed on this very
critical occasion,' wrote Lawrence, 'and heartily desired that a
similar energy might be shown by our own leaders, who still

appeared quite incapable of adopting any measures to secure our honour and our safety.'[103]

As the British buckled and surrendered, ignoring all Shuja's warnings, the Shah remained strong and successfully held out in the Bala Hisar until he chose to march out from his well-provisioned fortress many months later, at the onset of the spring thaw.

While Macnaghten was quietly sacrificing Shah Shuja, Lord Auckland was, somewhat unexpectedly, entertaining Shuja's old rival, Dost Mohammad, at a ball in Calcutta.

After the 'bracing' air of Simla, the Edens were appalled by the heat and humidity of a Calcutta summer. 'We have subsided from the interests of Afghan politics', wrote Emily to a friend, 'into the daily difficulties of keeping ourselves from being baked alive. I may say we have risen to this higher pursuit, for it is much the more important of the two, and of much more difficult achievement . . .'[104] The heat confirmed her in her opinion that it was time for them all to get out of the horrors of Asia and head quickly back to the safety of Kensington: 'Our George has done very well in India, has he not? You know we always thought very highly of him even in his comical dog days . . . Now I think he has done enough, and might as well go home, but none of the people at home will hear of it, and this month's despatches have made me desperate.'[105]

But duty was duty, and on Queen Victoria's birthday, amid the drenching humidity of a Bengali June, 'the most desperate weather ever felt in India', the sisters decided to throw a ball. 'Our Queen's ball was very magnificent,' Emily wrote soon afterwards, 'and as I fondly hope it is our last, I am glad it went off so well. *I wore my diamonds!*' The star guest, on exhibit to all both as a curiosity and as an advertisement for the great successes of Lord Auckland's foreign policy, was the Amir himself. 'We had Dost Mohammad and his sons and suite at the ball,' continued Emily,

the first time he had ever seen European ladies in their shameless
dress; but he did not see the dancing – George took him to another
room. He is a very kingly sort of person, and carries off his half-
captive, half-lion position with great tact. By way of relieving
George part of the evening, I asked him to play at chess, and we
played game after game, which was rather a triumph considering
native chess is not like ours, and he kept inventing new rules as we
went on. If he were not a Dost it was not quite fair.[106]

Afterwards, Emily asked her chess partner if she could make a
portrait of him and his followers. He agreed to sit for her pencil,
but then, as appalled as she was by the Calcutta humidity, set off
back up country to Ludhiana without telling her and before she
had finished. 'I have been making a sketch of Dost Mohammad and
his family,' Emily reported somewhat tetchily to her sister in
England, 'and he set off this morning for the upper provinces, leaving me with one of their nephews unsketched. So this morning,
with great activity I got up early, and Colvin abstracted the nephew
from the steamer and brought him to sit for his picture before
breakfast. The nephew is very like the picture of Judas Iscariot, but
he is a fine subject. Considering Colvin had no breakfast, he seemed
to talk Persian with wonderful animation.'[107]

The situation in Afghanistan had begun to deteriorate rapidly
soon after Dost Mohammad's departure from Calcutta. News had
arrived a fortnight later that a Tory government had been elected in
London, and after mulling over his options, Lord Auckland
resigned as Governor General. Lord Ellenborough, the man who
had originally written the memo that sent Burnes up the Indus ten
years earlier, was appointed to replace him.

A week later, the news of Burnes's murder and the fast unravelling of Lord Auckland's entire Afghan strategy arrived in Bengal
by courier. The first despatch to make it to Government House
was a short note from General Sale written three weeks earlier in
Jalalabad telling Auckland of the first rumours of disaster in Kabul
and of his own encirclement. 'I need not tell you that these communications very greatly distress me,' Auckland wrote to Sir Jasper

'Scenes from the line of march of a Bengal Regiment.' This Victorian precursor of the strip cartoon probably shows the Army of the Indus heading through Sindh and approaching Afghanistan.

Entrance to the Bolan Pass, from Dadur. In spring 1839 a 12,000-strong British-Indian force, the Army of the Indus under Sir John Keane, forced the Bolan Pass and captured Kandahar. The invasion aimed to replace Dost Mohammad with Shah Shuja, who was considered to be more pro-British.

As they navigated the narrow passes of Baluchistan, the Army of the Indus was vulnerable to ambush by the Baluchis, who hid in the ravines; skirmishes and sniping attacks were common. 'It was the mouth of hell,' remembered the sepoy Sita Ram. 'The Baluchis now began to harass us by night attacks and drove off long strings of our camels. They murdered everyone whenever they had the opportunity and rolled large boulders down the mountain sides.'

In April 1839, the Army of the Indus captured the city of Kandahar without a fight. Here Shah Shuja held a durbar within sight of the dome of the tomb of his grandfather, Ahmad Shah Abdali.

'The Storming of Ghuznee.' After forcing the Bolan Pass and capturing Kandahar, the Army of the Indus advanced on the formidable fortified walls of Ghazni, protected by thick, sixty-foot-high walls, a major problem for the British who had left their heavy artillery in Kandahar. Mohan Lal Kashmiri, Burnes's invaluable intelligence chief, discovered that one of the gates was not bricked up and could be stormed if taken by surprise.

'The Durbar-Khaneh of Shah Shoojah-ool-Moolk at Kabul.' After the seizure of Ghazni, Dost Mohammad fled Kabul and Shuja was re-installed as Shah in August 1839. This Mughal-style reception hall in the Bala Hisar was where he would hold his durbars, and where he irritated his nobles and his British officers by making them stand for hours. As the British officer-turned-artist, Lockyer Willis Hart, noted: 'This form and ceremony, so hateful to the Affghans, was the King's foible, and sometimes carried to an absurd extent.'

The People of Kabul

The Kabul Bazaar during the British occupation.

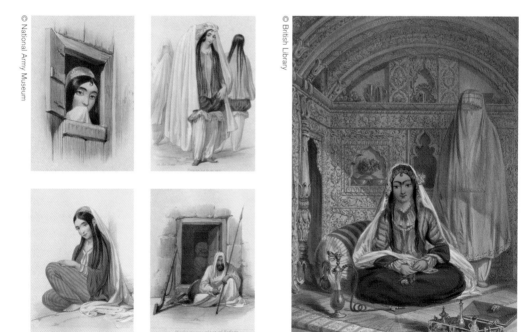

The women of Kabul were to prove irresistible to the occupying British troops – with disastrous results.

'The retinue of Shah Shooja-ool-Moolk'. This image includes Mohammad Shah Ghilzai, Akbar Khan's father-in-law (*on the left*) who was bought over by the Anglo-Sadozai regime and was awarded with the fearsome ceremonial title of Chief Executioner. He would become one of the leading rebels and more than anyone else was responsible for the 1842 massacre of the retreating British garrison in the high Ghilzai passes.

Rattray's sketch of the rows of tents during the early days of the occupation before the building of the cantonments. The rock of the Bala Hisar rises to the rear left of the picture.

Amir Dost Mohammad surrenders to the British envoy Sir William Hay Macnaghten in November 1840. Macnaghten and his aides were out riding in the valley of Qila-Qazi near Kabul when the surrender occurred.

The elderly and ineffective gout-riddled British military commander in Afghanistan, General William Elphinstone, collapsed into nervous indecision at the outbreak of the uprising.

Afghan foot soldiers of the insurrection against the British occupation fire their accurate long-barrelled jezails down onto the indefensible British position in the cantonment.

Afghan insurgents prepare an attack on the British cantonments outside Kabul. This image shows how the elegant colonial cantonments, with the Mission Compound on the left, were surrounded by hills on all sides and almost impossible to defend.

Captain Colin Mackenzie commanded the defence of the commissariat fort against the Afghan insurgents. Both he and Lawrence (*right*) became celebrities on their return and enjoyed posing in Afghan costume.

Lady Sale, turbaned in captivity.

Major-General Sir Robert Henry Sale, known to his men as 'Fighting Bob' for always throwing himself into the fiercest combat.

Alexandrina Sturt (née Sale), taken hostage by Akbar Khan after the massacre in the Khord Kabul Pass.

George Lawrence

Eyre, the artist, in self-portrait.

Captain Skinner, here a hostage prior to the British withdrawal, would be killed in action at the Jagdalak Pass during the Retreat of 1842.

The interior of the fort where the British hostages were kept.

The last survivors of the 44th Foot were exposed and surrounded at dawn as they stood at the top of the hill of Gandamak. Overwhelmingly outnumbered, the troops made their last stand. They formed a square, and defended themselves, 'driving the Affghans several times down the hill' until they had exhausted the last of their rounds, and then fought on with their bayonets. Then, one by one, they were slaughtered.

The British Garrison at Jalalabad, from the top turret of which an eagle-eyed staff officer was able to spot Dr Brydon's approach and send out rescuers.

Lady Butler's famous oil, *The Remnants of an Army*, which depicts Dr Brydon's exhausted arrival at the walls of Jalalabad on his collapsing nag.

The meticulous but merciless Major-General George Pollock, commander of the Army of Retribution which laid waste to south-eastern Afghanistan and burned Kabul to the ground.

General William Nott, one of the most senior Company generals in India, was a brilliant strategist and ever-loyal to his sepoys – 'the fine manly soldiers' to whom he was fiercely attached. He was to prove much the most effective of the British military commanders. In August 1842 he marched across Afghanistan, defeating all the forces sent against him, and arrived in Kabul on 17 September, two days after Pollock had retaken the city.

The Army of Retribution arrived in Kabul in September 1842. After releasing the British hostages, they destroyed the great Char Chatta covered bazaar. A new mosque built in celebration of the British defeat was also razed to the ground, and fires started across the city. 'The cry arose that Cabul was given up to plunder...'

Dost Mohammad (*seated, to the left of the ring of dancers*) is received in Lahore, on his way back to Kabul. He was restored to the throne in 1842 following the final British withdrawal and the treacherous assassination of Shah Shuja by his own godson. He would reign until his death in 1863.

Nicholls, the Commander-in-Chief, that night. 'They leave room for very formidable and serious speculation. I would not however speak of my own feelings. The question is, what is to be done?'

He then laid out various options, but like his generals in Kabul the stream of depressing news seemed to paralyse him and from the beginning he opposed the idea of an immediate military response. 'I propose to have a special Council tomorrow,' he wrote, 'but it seems to me that we are not to think of marching fresh armies for the reconquest of that which we are likely to lose . . . I fear that the Afghan national spirit has been generally roused.'[108]

The truth was that Auckland had already realised months earlier that his whole Afghan policy had been catastrophically mistaken and was in danger of bankrupting the entire Indian government. Now with disaster looming, and with his treasury empty, he had no hesitation in taking the decision that he should simply write off the entire project and not throw any further resources into what was clearly a losing battle.

Shah Shuja, Macnaghten, even his old grouse-shooting companion 'Elphy Bey', were to be left to sort out the mess on their own. No help would be coming from Calcutta.

Snow fell heavily in Kabul during the second week of December, billowing down from the Hindu Kush, instantly turning the dusty grey hills around the city a dazzling white, settling thickly on the parapets of the cantonment and freezing the Kabul River. 'The snow did not trouble the Sardars and ghazis who were in their element,' wrote Mirza 'Ata, 'but the army from India was unused to snow and many died. Many others became incapable of fighting because of the intense cold.'[109]

Yet for Macnaghten the snow was the least of his worries. He had, as agreed, handed over the two remaining fortresses overlooking the cantonment as well as the large down-payments demanded by the sardars, including 20,000 rupees to Akbar Khan,

but still the promised food and fodder had only arrived in dribs
and drabs and the army and their pack animals remained on the
verge of starvation.[110] Nor was there any sign of the promised
carts and baggage animals the English would need to transport
their goods back to India. As a result, the 14 December deadline
for the departure of the army passed without the slightest movement. Meanwhile, any remaining defiance within the cantonment
had ebbed into a cowed anxiety and fear. 'So great was the want
of common sense', wrote Mackenzie,

> that hundreds of the enemy, armed to the teeth, were allowed to
> insinuate themselves into the cantonments and to walk about spying
> everything. A Ghilzai drew his sword on Lt Sturt within a few yards
> of a loaded 6-pounder, because that officer endeavoured to keep
> back the man's insolent comrades. So strictly were the sentries
> forbidden to fire, that our camp followers and friendly Afghans
> were often robbed and even killed a dozen yards from our walls,
> and the mess sheep of the 5th Cavalry were captured within 150
> yards of the ramparts, under the eyes of the whole garrison.[111]

Realising the desperate state the British were in, Akbar Khan now
increased his demands. More cannon were to be surrendered. Yet
more hostages were demanded. Seeing the bottomless pit that they
were falling into, Macnaghten again raised with his commanders
the idea of retreating to the Bala Hisar or even reopening hostilities
with the Afghans now that their guard was down, 'to march out at
once in order of battle [in Lawrence's words], and enter Kabul or
fight the enemy beneath its walls, expressing his own earnest hope
that the General, now that he had been reinforced by the fresh
troops from the Bala Hisar, would adopt this clear and obvious
course'.[112] Again Shelton and Elphinstone opposed all his plans,
seeming more determined than ever to march out of Afghanistan as
quickly as possible. 'The forts were the same evening given up and
immediately occupied by Afghans,' added Lawrence. 'The Envoy
and I stood on a mound near the mosque whilst they were being
evacuated by our men, and I am not ashamed to say that it was

with eyes moistened with tears from grief and indignation, we witnessed these strongholds, the last prop of our tottering power in Kabul, which it had cost us so much blood to seize and defend, made over, one after another, to our treacherous and exulting enemies.'[113]

Then, without warning, a small chink of light and hope appeared. On 20 November, Nizam al-Daula, the Prime Minister Macnaghten had foisted on Shuja, sent news that his old patron, Nawab Zaman Khan, the Barakzai leader who had initially taken on the leadership of the revolt, 'was offended because of the people rallying around Mohammad Akbar, and sent word that he wanted to become an ally of the English. The English, who sought safety from the sharp edge of Afghan swords, considered the Nizam al-Daula's letter tidings from heaven.'[114] At the same time, news came that many of the rebel troops were discontented with Akbar Khan due to the high price of food.[115]

Macnaghten immediately embarked on a renewed attempt to divide and rule. Desperate to avoid the potential catastrophe of a midwinter retreat through hostile mountains, he tried various schemes at once, 'grasping at every new combination that seemed to promise more hope than the last'. Through Mohan Lal, both the Qizilbash and the Ghilzai chieftains were offered the large sum of 20,000 rupees to break with the rebels and rally to the support of the British. 'If any portion of the Afghans wish our troops to remain in the country,' he declared, 'I shall think myself at liberty to break the engagement which I have made to go away, which engagement was made believing it to be in accordance with the wishes of the Afghan nation.'

But Macnaghten was hopelessly out of his depth. 'It is very difficult to know what to do,' he wrote in confusion to Mohan Lal at this time.[116] He didn't understand the strength of the marriage ties which linked the Ghilzais to Akbar Khan, nor did he even begin to comprehend the degree to which most Afghans hated their Kafir occupiers. Moreover, Mohan Lal was being watched and Akbar's spies were passing on detailed information about all the Envoy's amateurish attempts at intrigue. There were also damaging rumours circulating among the rebels that Macnaghten was offering money to anyone who would assassinate Akbar and the other hostile chiefs. According to Mirza 'Ata, 'Macnaghten wrote a secret letter to the chiefs, to the effect that whoever would bring Sardar Muhammad Akbar Khan's severed head would be rewarded with a sum of 10,000 Rupees and would be appointed assistant to the Envoy. As soon as the Khans read this, they immediately passed the original on to Akbar Khan who kept it with him.'[117] The story could well be true. Certainly there is evidence from the correspondence of Mohan Lal that a paid assassin called Abdul Aziz sent in an invoice to Mohan Lal for the killing of Abdullah Khan Achakzai, saying he shot him in the back with a poisoned bullet while he was fighting Shelton on 23 November, implying that Mohan Lal had indeed offered a bounty for the killing of rebel leaders.[118] It is extremely unlikely he would have dared to do so without some sort of authorisation from the Envoy.

Hearing this, Akbar Khan decided to set a trap to expose Macnaghten's duplicity. On the evening of 22 December, he sent out two of his cousins to the cantonment. They were escorted by Captain James Skinner, a young Anglo-Indian cavalry commander and the son of the founder of Skinner's Horse, who had been captured and arrested on the first day of the uprising as he tried to flee from the city in a woman's burkha.

Over dinner, the Barakzai envoys made Macnaghten a startling new offer. The British could stay in Afghanistan until the spring, they said, and Shuja remain as shah, if the British supported Akbar Khan's bid to be wazir and to gain hold of the real reins of power. If Macnaghten would make a written undertaking to help him, make a colossal down-payment of £300,000 and an annuity of £40,000, then Akbar Khan would be happy to bring him the head of Aminullah Khan Logari. Macnaghten was apparently being offered a chance to tear up the recently agreed treaty and cut a secret deal with Akbar Khan. Given the extreme weakness of the British position, the terms were suspiciously generous, but, conceited to the last, Macnaghten seems to have convinced himself that his recent intrigues were so brilliant that Akbar had been forced to compromise in order to safeguard his position. Aminullah's head Macnaghten rejected, saying the arrest of Aminullah Khan and handing him over as a prisoner to the British would be enough; but he swallowed the rest of the bait, and signed a Persian document putting his consent in writing. According to Mohan Lal, 'The offer was not received by the Envoy altogether without suspicion; but as he has no hope of military aid, and considered the idea of a retreat disgraceful to the British name, he was like a drowning man catching at straws.'[119]

For Akbar Khan, this was the final evidence he needed of the duplicity of the Envoy. He showed the document to Aminullah Khan and warned the other chiefs of Macnaghten's willingness to betray his agreements with them and do a secret deal behind their backs. Then he sent a message to Macnaghten to meet him again the following morning to finalise details of the plot. Macnaghten agreed.

George Lawrence, Mackenzie and Trevor were summoned by the Envoy at dawn and told about the offer. According to Lawrence, Macnaghten said:

> that he had every reasonable hope it would bring our present difficulties to an early and happy termination, and that Akbar was to give up Aminoollah Khan as a prisoner to us. Sir William then warned me to be ready to gallop to the King with the intelligence and to acquaint him with Akbar's proposal. On me again remarking that the scheme seemed a dangerous one and asking if he did not apprehend any treachery, he replied, 'Dangerous it is, but if it succeeds it is worth all risks. The Rebels have not fulfilled even one Article of the Treaty and I have no confidence in them, and if by it we can only save our Honour, all will be well. At any rate I would sooner suffer a hundred deaths than live the last six weeks over again.'

At this point, Hasan Khan, the head of Mackenzie's jezailchis who had faithfully led the retreat from the commissariat fort, intervened and 'repeatedly warned Sir William of the likelihood of a fatal termination to his hazardous interviews with the Afghan chiefs. He argued that surely he was the better judge of the intentions of his own countrymen than Sir William could be, and that among them no dishonour was attached to what we call treachery.' Mackenzie also pointed out that the offer sounded very suspicious, but Macnaghten replied: 'A plot! Let me alone for that – trust me for that!' To Elphinstone, who also raised the same objection, Macnaghten replied smugly: 'Leave it to me. I understand these things better than you.'

Shelton was supposed to send a military escort with Macnaghten, but the cavalry, disorganised as ever, were not ready to leave. After a short wait, the impatient Macnaghten decided to head off for his appointment with just his small personal guard, accompanied by his three assistants, Lawrence, Trevor and Mackenzie. Akbar Khan was already waiting at the agreed rendezvous. He had brought with him his relative Sultan Jan Barakzai, his father-in-law, the Ghilzai chief Mohammad Shah Khan, and a third chief whom the British did not recognise but who was in fact Aminullah Khan's younger brother, who had come to bear witness to Macnaghten's act of treachery.

The meeting started courteously enough. The Envoy presented Akbar with a valuable horse that he had previously complimented, and the young rebel leader politely thanked Macnaghten for double-barrelled pistols which the Envoy had sent to him along with his carriage and a pair of horses the day before. The party dismounted, and horse blankets were spread on a small hillock which the Afghans pointed out as being free from snow and whose position partially concealed them from the cantonment. The Envoy then sat down beside Akbar Khan, with Trevor and Mackenzie next to him. Lawrence stood behind Macnaghten until, pressed by Akbar, he knelt on one knee. Lawrence then pointed out the growing number of Afghans converging on the spot, saying that, if the subject of the conference was of a secret nature, the other men had better withdraw. Macnaghten repeated this to Akbar, who replied, 'They are all in the secret.' 'Hardly had he so said,' Lawrence wrote later, 'when I found my Arms locked, my pistols and sword wrenched from my belt and myself forcibly raised from the ground and pulled along. Mahomed Shah Khan Ghilzai who held me called out, "Come along if you value your life!" I turned and saw the Envoy lying, his head where his heels had been and his hands locked in Akbar's, consternation and horror depicted on his countenance.'[120]

As Lawrence was being dragged away, according to Mirza 'Ata:

The Sardar [Akbar] shouted at Macnaghten, 'You are the Minister of a great King, the head of a glorious army, all foreign dignitaries pay tribute to your knowledge and accomplishments. But I must beg to differ, and consider you a fool, one whose word cannot be relied on, who reveals his inner treachery by what he writes! You have not been able to get the better of us in battle and now you seek to destroy us by deceit. You faithless, cheating trickster! So quick to betray our agreement! Do you think I would trust you rather than my fellow citizens of Kabul? Do you think it would be so easy to get us to mutually destroy each other for your conven-ience? Do you realise what a ridiculous figure you cut? Shame on you: you are a laughing stock! My intention was to have you honourably accompanied out of Kabul back to India; but your scheme was to have me assassinated. Your mind is darkened with black smoke and vain imaginings! Now you had better come with me into the city of Kabul!'

Panicking, Macnaghten tried to escape, 'like a pigeon fluttering to fly free from the grip of a hawk'. Akbar 'grabbed him, drew his thirsty sword, then tore open the Envoy's liver and lopped off his head. The headless corpse of the illustrious Saheb Macnaghten, the Chief Minister, like the carcase of a rabid dog, was dismembered and dragged into the city. It was then hung up, with his head and top hat, at the Four-Roofed Bazaar.'[121]

Colin Mackenzie, who was an eyewitness, gives a slightly differ-ent account. He wrote that, as a group of armed Afghans approached the seated party, Akbar Khan asked Macnaghten to move aside as he had something confidential to say to him. As Macnaghten leaned towards him, Akbar Khan suddenly screamed 'Bigir! Bigir!' meaning 'Seize! Seize!' at which he pinioned the Envoy. Akbar's face wore an expression 'of the most diabolical ferocity' while Macnaghten's face was 'full of horror and astonishment'. Macnaghten cried 'Az barae Khooda!' – 'For God's sake' – as Akbar caught him by his waist and tried at gunpoint to force him to mount the horse to go into the city with him. 'The Envoy refused and said, "What do you wish to do with me?"' Sultan Jan then said to Akbar, 'Be quick otherwise we shall all be caught by the troops which are coming out from the cantonment.' On this, Akbar Khan shot the Envoy with the double-barrelled pistol he had just been given. Macnaghten was still alive, but Akbar ordered his servant to finish him off with a jezail, and it was this which put an end to the life of the British Envoy. Akbar then had his head cut off, and ordered his body to be dragged through the streets along with that of Captain Trevor, who had been murdered by Sultan Jan.[122]

As soon as the violence began, Macnaghten's personal escort of sixteen troopers fled, making no effort to rescue the officers.[123] As they were galloping back to the cantonment, they crossed the path of the delayed cavalry escort, which then also turned tail. 'Not a man was despatched [from the cantonment],' wrote Lawrence,

> nor a party sent out to reconnoitre; no sortie made, nor even a gun fired, though bodies of the enemy's horse and foot were seen hurrying from the place of the conference towards Mahomed Khan's fort, and several officers declared they could see distinctly through their field-glasses two bodies lying on the ground where the meeting took place. No attempt was made to recover them. Thus, almost within musket-shot of our entrenched position, and in broad daylight, a British envoy had been barbarously murdered, and his mangled body allowed to remain for hours where he fell, and finally carried off by a savage mob to be insulted in every possible way, and paraded throughout the city, without an attempt being made to save any of the party, or to avenge this unequalled outrage.[124]

Meanwhile, Mackenzie and Lawrence were being abducted. Both men were 'surrounded by a circle of Ghilzai with drawn swords and cocked jezails, and the cries of "Kill the Kafir" became more vehement . . .' But Akbar Khan protected them. He drew his sword 'and laid about himself right manfully', as Mackenzie gratefully noted. 'Pride, however, overcame his sense of courtesy when he thought I was safe; for he then turned around to me, and repeatedly said, in a tone of triumphant derision: *"Shuma mulk-i-ma me-girid!* – You'll seize my country will you?"'[125] At the same time, Lawrence was also being bundled away at gunpoint through crowds of angry Ghilzais all crying for a 'Koorban' [sacrifice] to the Ghilzai headquarters at the fort of Mahmud Khan, where the two captives were shoved into a cell. Just before the door closed, one tribesman took a swipe with his sword at Mackenzie. Mohammad Shah Khan Ghilzai, who was standing close by, put his arm around Mackenzie to protect him, and took the cut on his own shoulder.[126]

Shortly afterwards, Aminullah Khan Logari, the supposed victim of Macnaghten's plot, burst in on the two prisoners and told them that they were soon to be blown from the mouths of cannon. Outside their cell, Ghilzais gathered to taunt the two captive Kafirs. They spat, poked their swords and guns through the bars, and tried to break down the door of the cell. The guards only just managed to stop the crowd murdering the prisoners. A few minutes later there was another commotion and the prisoners looked out to see a human hand impaled on a pole. 'Look well!' screamed the Ghilzais; 'your own will soon suffer a similar plight.'

It was the hand of the Envoy. Macnaghten's and Trevor's heads were then paraded on the tips of spears, while their trunks were dragged through the streets, then skinned, and their hides hung from a meat hook in the bazaar.[127] Even Macnaghten's large blue spectacles were put on display.[128] 'All came to see the remains exposed there,' remarks Mirza 'Ata,

and to spit in disgust. The gold coin of honesty and scrupulous respect for one's engagements is a currency valid everywhere, which will preserve its owner from dishonour even in the most turbulent circumstances. 'If you are faithful and true, people will love you; deceit will only make people shun and loathe you!' As it was, Sardar Muhammad Akbar Khan's fame spread, and everyone repeated how all the English achieved was to drive the famished donkeys of their failed ambition back into India and to force the women of India to wear the weeds of widowhood in mourning for their husbands! It was clear to all that those Englishmen who had boasted of their shrewdness in policy and bravery in battle, were worth nothing compared to the Sardars of Khurasan. They were in fact mere mules stuck in the mud![129]

8

The Wail of Bugles

The retreat from Kabul began soon after 9 a.m. on the morning of 6 January 1842.

The night before, the now almost recovered Lieutenant Sturt had mined a portion of the walls to the left of the rear gate so as to create a wide breach through which the 3,800 remaining sepoys, 700 European cavalry and footsoldiers and 14,000 camp followers could march. At dawn the mine was sprung, and the walls blown outwards so as to create a bridge over the ditch.

Seen through the jagged new gap in the curtain wall, the sun rising over the ring of dazzling white mountains around Kabul revealed a day that was 'beautifully clear and frosty, with the snow nearly a foot deep on the ground'.[1] Yet the troops waiting to march out of the relative safety of the cantonment walls to an uncertain fate in the Afghan mountains were a less inspiring sight. 'A crouching, drooping, dispirited army, so different from the smart light-hearted body of men they appeared some time ago,' thought a depressed George Lawrence, who had been released, along with

Colin Mackenzie, to help supervise the retreat. On marching out into the virgin snow 'the men were [soon] sinking a foot deep each step . . . My heart sunk within me under the conviction that we were a doomed force.'[2]

A fortnight had now passed since the British had heard for sure that their political leader, Sir William Hay Macnaghten, had been murdered by Akbar Khan. After two days of anxious waiting amid contradictory rumours, the army's worst fears were vindicated: the British had indeed lost their leader and Lady Macnaghten had lost her husband.

Among the Afghans, there was jubilation at the astonishing thoroughness of the reversals suffered by the arrogant Firangi invaders, but there was also some chivalrous sympathy for Lady Macnaghten, at least among the poets. In the *Akbarnama*, Maulana Hamid Kashmiri places in her mouth a pained lament that she utters when she is told that her husband will not be returning:

> . . . The wife of *Laat-Hay Jangi*, Lord Hay of War, tore at her collar
> Her grief raged, and out poured her song of bereavement . . .
>
> She cried: 'O Prince in the Land of Firang!
> You were honoured in *Rum* [Rome/Europe] and famed in Ethiopia!
>
> But in this land you were doomed
> Here your death was certain
>
> Come back! With you, I am happy in poverty
> Beggary would be better than such lordship . . .
>
> . . . Today, street urchins and alley rats
> Play with your rolling head as though it were a ball . . .
>
> . . . Come back, O proud conqueror!
> You exalted the very crown and throne that were yours
>
> But in Kabul today, upon the dust of the road
> Lies your body without a head, and your head without a crown'[3]

Yet any sympathy expressed by the Maulana was tempered by a certainty that the extraordinary speed of the fall of the once power-ful British was due above all to divine displeasure: the lying, deceitful Kafirs had got their just deserts. The final proofs of this, as far as Maulana Kashmiri was concerned, were the unprecedented blizzards which then fell on Kabul to further discomfit the accursed disbelievers:

> Despite suffering such grief and sorrow, such pain and misery
> Heaven did not desist from tormenting them yet again
>
> It girded its loins, bent upon desolation
> Gripping Kabul in the coldest of winters
>
> From the sky descended a scourge so great
> That courtyard and roof became one from snow . . .
>
> In the flowing river, there was no more water
> In the shining sun, there was no more heat
>
> The cattle outside, whined and howled
> Torn to shreds by the wind's murderous blade
>
> For the Firangi horde, already battered by misfortune
> The howling of the blizzard and the falling of the snows were a calamity
>
> The soldiers were many and their food was little
> Judgement lay behind and death stood before them
>
> To remain was unwise, to escape impossible
> No hope of peace, no chance of war[4]

By this stage, the British were also beginning to feel as though they were labouring under the curse of heaven. Even indomitable and ever reso-lute Lady Sale accepted that things now looked very bad for the besieged troops, writing in her diary with characteristic understatement,

A dismal Christmas Day, our situation far from cheerful. Lawrence has come in, looking haggard and ten years older from anxiety . . . Naib Sharif paid for the interment of Sir A Burnes's body, but it was never buried; and part of it, cut into many pieces, is still hanging on the trees in his garden. [Now] the Envoy's head is kept in a *bhoosa* bag in the chouk: and Akbar says he will send it to Bokhara to show the King there how he has seized the Firangis here, and what he means to do with them . . . Whether we go by treaty or not, I fear but few of us will live to reach the provinces . . .[5]

She added that while selecting what property she should carry with her on the retreat, she had found a copy of Thomas Campbell's *Poems*,

which opened at *Hohenlinden*; one verse of which haunted me day and night:

> *Few, few shall part where many meet,*
> *The snow shall be their winding sheet;*
> *And every turf beneath their feet*
> *Shall be a soldier's sepulchre.*[6]

To make matters worse, the British troops now learned that Macnaghten had been killed while trying to break the terms of the treaty he had signed with the Afghan chiefs. Not only were the British starving, outmanoeuvred and cut off, they knew now that in addition they had lost any remaining moral high ground. Moreover the Afghans who had outsoldiered and outwitted them turned out not to be the crack troops from the mountains they had imagined them to be, but – in part at least – merely the 'tradesmen and artisans of Kabul, so that we had not even the melancholy satisfaction of knowing that we had been contending with the soldier tribes of the country'.[7]

After the death of Macnaghten, the badly wounded Eldred Pottinger was now the most senior British political officer left alive. Despite his telling Elphinstone and Shelton not to trust Akbar and urging that the only hope lay in heading for the Bala Hisar, Shelton continued to push hard for a withdrawal and Pottinger was put on a litter and sent out to negotiate the surrender and the terms of the retreat. 'I was hauled out of my sick room,' he wrote afterwards, 'and obliged to negotiate for the safety of a parcel of fools who were doing all they could to ensure their own destruction.'[8] In return for supplies and a safe passage, Akbar now demanded the surrender of all their remaining artillery as well as their treasure.

While waiting for food and baggage animals to be delivered, the British continued to be harassed. The worst offenders were the growing number of ghazis who increasingly clustered around the cantonment gates to bait, abuse and rob the now helpless invaders and those Afghans still friendly with them. 'Much annoyance was daily experienced from these people,' wrote Vincent Eyre.

> They were in the habit of plundering the peaceable dealers who flocked in from the city with grain and forage, the moment they issued from the cantonments. They even committed frequent assaults on our Sepoys, and orders to fire on them on such occasions were repeatedly solicited in vain, although it was well known that the chiefs themselves advised us to do so . . . The consequence was that our soldiers were daily constrained to endure the most insulting and contemptuous taunts and treatment from fellows whom a single charge of the bayonet would have scattered like chaff, but who were emboldened by the apparent tameness of our troops, which they doubtless attributed to the want of common pluck.[9]

Most harrowing of all was the knowledge that all the Afghans who still had any contact with the British were completely certain that the garrison were walking into a trap. On 29 December 1841, Hugh Johnson recorded in his diary:

> Several of my native friends in the city come daily to see me, and all agree without one dissenting voice that we have brought the whole of our misfortunes upon ourselves, through the apathy & imbecility displayed at the commencement of the outbreak.

They also tell me that our safety in the retreat depends solely
upon ourselves, that no dependence is to be placed in the promises
of any of the Chiefs, every one of whom knows that they are in a
measure paid beforehand to do their utmost to destroy us.[10]

Mohan Lal, who had unrivalled contacts throughout Kabul, sent a
whole succession of warnings that the British were heading straight
into an ambush, and passed on explicit intelligence from the
Qizilbash chiefs that the British would all be massacred; but he was
ignored.[11] Macabre rumours began to circulate that the Afghans
would seize all the British women and kill all the British men with
the single exception of one who would be taken to the entrance of
the Khyber Pass, where he would be left, legless and armless, with
a note pinned to his chest to warn the British never again to attempt
to enter Afghanistan. Lady Sale, always willing to stare the truth in
the face, wrote bleakly in her diary the night before the retreat that
'the Affghans tell us we are doomed'.[12]

No one did more to warn the British of the fate that awaited
them in the passes than Shah Shuja himself. Mohammad Husain
Herati recorded that 'His Majesty wrote to Pottinger: "To leave
the cantonment in the depths of this harsh winter is an act of
extreme folly, beware, do not think of going to Jalalabad! If you
must leave the cantonment, then come and spend the winter with
us in the Bala Hisar fort, where we will await the end of winter
together, and if supplies run out, we will make sorties to plunder
round about for our survival." But this offer was not accepted . . .'[13]

As Mohan Lal pointed out, the decision of the British to abandon Shuja was of course a major breach of faith. 'No regard was
shown to the articles of the Tripartite Treaty,' he wrote, 'and Shah
Shuja ul-Mulk was left at the mercy of his enemies, to whom we
had given shelter during his government of the last two years. Had
it not been for us, he, acting as an independent sovereign, would
have destroyed the Barakzais, and thus have freed us and himself
from these fatal consequences.'[14]

Shuja himself seemed less upset and resentful of the British
betrayal than simply baffled by the amazing stupidity of his allies.

Over his years in Ludhiana, despite his frequent differences with his British hosts, he had come to admire the smooth efficiency of the Company's administration, but what he had seen over the previous six weeks defied belief: how could the British, and especially the once-masterful Macnaghten, have behaved so idiotically? 'Sir William Macnaghten did not listen to me,' a despairing Shuja wrote to Auckland, saying how over and again he had explained to the Envoy that:

> unless by slaying or enchaining these people nothing is to be done; I know them well; but my speaking was useless ...
>
> Often I said I would leave the country as there would certainly be an insurrection; but the envoy told me to be comforted and that he would settle the country with a few regiments. Again I said, 'beware you are deceived; I will withdraw from the land,' but I was tied down by my family, the winter came and I did not go; and then the affair came to a head. What dogs are these people! I had hoped to have settled all the country between Khorasan and Persia; who were the men to oppose me? But they made it an affair between Kafirs and Islam; on which account all the people turned from me.[15]

Particularly galling for Shuja was the way Macnaghten in his final negotiations had handed over such huge sums to Akbar Khan after so long trimming Shuja's own budget, thus leaving him without any resources to mount a proper defence:

> Mahomed Akbar and others were dying of hunger – you by your money have set them on foot. You gave money to your enemy, you armed him to slay yourself; what he is doing is with your money; but for it he could not have maintained himself for ten days.
>
> I did not even drink water without Sir William Macnaghten's sanction and often I said to him: we will be wrecked. Captain Lawrence is alive, before him I often said this. Captain Burnes is now dead, he followed his own heart, and he was deceived by men's words. I told him men are dissatisfied with you and intend you evil,

do not be deceived; but it was of no use . . . Until now by one device or another I have carried on, but now they send men to me and say that the Shah is sinking Islam, men say that I am with you [British] and on this account they have left me.

He ended, characteristically: 'Whatever may be the will of God, that will happen.'[16]

As George Lawrence was the one officer left alive with whom Shuja still had a close relationship, it was to him that Shuja sent a last urgent message begging him once more to warn the General not to leave the cantonment, and emphasising that no trust whatsoever could be placed in the promises of Akbar Khan. 'As long as we held our position, the king urged, they could not hurt us; but if we once abandoned it we were dead men,' wrote Lawrence. 'Of these warnings I duly informed Pottinger, who took me to General Elphinstone, to whom I repeated them . . . but we were told that it would not now do to remain where we were, and that march we must.'[17]

Having failed to convince the authorities in the cantonment about the impossibility of a safe retreat, Shuja did his best to save his few remaining acquaintances. As Vincent Eyre recorded,

[he] used his utmost endeavours to persuade Lady Macnaghten and as many ladies as would accompany her to withdraw from the army, which he said would all be destroyed, and to take advantage of his protection in the Bala Hisar. He also appealed to Brigadier Anquetil, who commanded the Shah's force, 'if it were well to forsake him in the hour of his need, and to deprive him of the aid of that force, which he had hitherto been taught to consider his own?' All was, however, unavailing. The general and his council of war had determined that go we must, and go we accordingly did.[18]

According to Lady Sale, late on the night of 5 January, Shuja sent one final appeal to his British allies, scribbling 'a message to ask if not even one officer of his force will stand by him?'[19]

But, having deserted him and ignored all his advice, Shuja's officers were now too busy packing for their imminent departure even to bother sending a reply.

At 9 a.m. on the morning of 6 January, to the sound of bugles and drums, the first British troops marched out of the cantonment and trudged off through the knee-high snow towards the Khord Kabul Pass on the Jalalabad road. Despite the bright morning sun, Lady Sale's thermometer registered a temperature 'considerably below zero point'.[20]

There were some optimistic signs: while around one hundred Afghans had gathered to witness the departure of the would-be conquerors, the ghazis who had haunted the gates of the cantonment had mysteriously disappeared, and the advance guard of the column marched out without encountering the slightest resistance. Even the noose of surrounding forts which had peppered the cantonment with shot for the previous six weeks were completely silent, 'with not a man to be seen on the walls', as a relieved Hugh Johnson noted.

For this reason, the advance guard was in high spirits:

After having been cooped up in Cantonments for the last 2 months and 3 days, during which time we had lost in several engagements a great portion of our officers and men, and the latter had also suffered very severely from want of necessary food, cold and over-work, great was the delight of the sepoys at the prospect of being freed from so inclement a climate as is Kabul at this season, and the more especially as the whole of the firewood that had been laid in for the winter's consumption was already expended, and almost the whole of the fruit trees in Cantonments had also been cut and burnt.[21]

Lady Sale's final breakfast was cooked using the wood of her dining-room table. She then donned the turban and Afghan sheepskin *pustin* that her Afghan friends had advised her to wear, and, taking her twenty-year-old pregnant daughter with her, declined Captain Lawrence's offer of protection and chose to travel instead mixed up with the brightly dressed troopers of Skinner's Horse who made up the advance guard.

There was no sign of the escort that the chiefs had promised to send with the British. Nor was the hastily constructed pontoon bridge over the icy Kabul River ready in time to receive the troops, and they had to queue for an hour to make the crossing, despite Lady Sale's wounded son-in-law Lieutenant Sturt having spent the entire night 'up to his hips in water' sinking gun carriages in the river and topping them with planks. But to begin with, for all the delay at the bridge, and the confusion created by the thousands of frightened, starving and benumbed camp followers who for their own safety had deliberately mixed themselves up with the marching sepoys, it still looked as if the snow would be more of a danger to the retreating troops than the swords of the Afghans. 'It was bitterly cold, freezing hard,' noted George Lawrence, 'and I pitied from my soul the poor native soldiers and camp followers, walking up to their knees in snow and slush. It was no easy task to keep all my charges together, some of the bearers hurrying on, others lagging behind with the palanquins and doolies containing the women and children.'[22]

The first problem occurred just after eleven, when word came from Nawab Zaman Khan Barakzai that the British should halt their advance as he had not yet completed the necessary arrangements for their safety. By this time, the advance had at last begun crossing Sturt's makeshift bridge and a long and vulnerable line of troops were standing waiting in the cold snow between the river and the cantonment. Elphinstone, indecisive as ever, ordered a halt, then dithered on what to do next. Around the same time, a swarm of Afghans, including the absent ghazis, began to descend from the village of Bibi Mahru, 'rending the air with their exulting cries' and set about looting and burning the now deserted Mission Compound immediately to the north of the main cantonment. The noise of shooting and the plumes of smoke so close by made everyone nervous, and some of the porters and camp followers now began to break out of line and run out of the gate, leaving the baggage they were meant to be carrying and 'mixing themselves up with the troops to the utter confusion of the whole column'.[23]

An hour later, around noon, the ghazis mounted the walls of the Mission Compound and began to fire down into the waiting troops, while the rearguard returned fire from the wallwalks of the cantonment. By one o'clock, fifty of the European infantry were lying dead or wounded in the snow. Colin Mackenzie could see that a massacre was about to take place, with the troops half in and half out of the cantonment, and, watching Elphinstone still hesitate, he galloped off in defiance of his orders – the General shouting weakly after him, 'Mackenzie don't do it,' and rode to the bridge where he told Shelton to resume his march. Despite Mackenzie's decisive action, thanks to the delay the light was fading and it was nearly five o'clock before the last sepoys of the rearguard finally left the cantonment, having manned the icy walls for eleven hours without food.[24] As they did so, the ghazis rushed straight into the empty cantonment, mounted the wallwalks and immediately began to shoot at the column from the battlements with their long jezails.

At this stage, while most of the troops were now well on their way to Bagramee, the place designated as the camp site for the first night, most of the baggage and all the ammunition of the force was still waiting to cross the bridge. As the ghazis' jezails found their range, the camp followers and the last troops of the rearguard began to fall where they stood, first jostling then fighting in panic for their turn to cross. Amid this scene of fear,

[Colin] Mackenzie always remembered as one of the most heart-rending sights of that humiliating day, fixing his eyes by chance on a little Hindustani child, perfectly naked, sitting on the snow, with no mother or father near it. It was a beautiful little girl about two years old, just strong enough to sit upright with her little legs doubled under her, hair curling in waving locks around the soft little throat, and her great black eyes, dilated to twice their normal size, fixed on the armed men, the passing cavalry, and all the strange

sights that met her gaze . . . Many other children as young and innocent he saw slain on the road, and women with their long dark hair
wet with their own blood . . . [Soon] Afghans were seen [milling in
the snow, finishing off the dying and] stabbing with their knives the
wounded grenadiers.[25]

Although Sturt had pointed out to the General that the river was
perfectly fordable by camels and horses just upstream from the
bridge, this vital piece of intelligence did not seem to have been
shared and, despite the ever increasing strafing from the cantonment walls, the terrified remains of the sepoy column battled with
the women and children of the camp followers to cross by the new
gun-carriage bridge. As a result, by late afternoon, as the sun was
sinking behind the mountains and the shadows fast lengthening,
the bank of the river had turned into 'a swamp encrusted with ice',
and was so slippery as to be impossible for the baggage camels even
to get close. As the fire from the ramparts increased in accuracy
and intensity, tents, barrels of gunpowder, boxes of musket balls,
packs of clothing and food were all abandoned in great piles on the
banks of the Kabul River, the discarded sacks and saddlebags illuminated by the light of the now blazing cantonment. The rearguard
was also forced to spike two of the nine guns the British had been
allowed to take away with them, finding it impossible to drag the
heavy cannon through the snow. In the end, such was the panic
that almost none of the baggage made it over the bridge. So was
repeated for a second time the biggest mistake made by Elphinstone
at the start of the siege: failing to safeguard his commissariat.

'Night had now closed around,' remembered Eyre, 'but the
ghazis, having fired the Residency, and almost every building in the
cantonment, the conflagration illuminated the surrounding countryside for several miles about, presenting a spectacle of fearful
sublimity.'[26] As the temperature dropped ever lower after sunset,
the main body of troops were by now waiting in vain for the arrival
of their food, wood and tents at the camping place of Bagramee,
seven miles further on. As the hours passed, and the night grew
darker and colder, word began to spread that the baggage and food

were lost. Within a few hours of the retreat beginning the force had yet again lost all its supplies.

At Bagramee that night, chaos ruled. The last of the rearguard did not make it in until 2 a.m., having 'had to fight the whole way, and pass through literally a continuous line of poor wretches, men, women and children, dead or dying from the cold and wounds, who, unable to move, entreated their comrades to kill them and put an end to their misery'.[27] Right up until the entrance to the camp the rearguard found 'scores of worn out sepoys and camp followers lining the way, having sat down in despair to perish in the snow'.

Only a lucky few had anything to eat that night. George Lawrence succeeded in finding 'a little cold meat and sherry', which he was given by Lady Macnaghten, who had brought her own supplies. Almost everyone else went hungry, 'obliged to lie down on the bare snow, without either shelter, fire or food . . . The silence of the men betrayed their despair and torpor, not a voice being heard.'[28]

Lady Sale was luckier than most: though she had now lost all her possessions and had nothing to eat, she had given her bedding to her daughter's ayah to ride upon, so unusually she and her household did have some covering that first night. A few others were lucky too: the irritable Dr Magrath for example found an empty dhooly to sleep in. But as now became clear, the Bengali sepoys had no idea how to cope in the snow, a sharp contrast to Mackenzie's loyal Afghan jezailchis who showed how it could be done. 'Their first step on reaching the [camping] ground was to clear a small space from the snow,' recalled an impressed Eyre. 'They then laid themselves down in a circle, closely packed together, with their feet meeting in the centre; all the warm clothing they could muster among them being spread equally over the whole. By these simple means sufficient animal warmth was generated to preserve them from being frost bitten; and Captain Mackenzie, who himself shared their homely bed, declared that he had felt scarcely any inconvenience from the cold.'[29]

Just how necessary such techniques were became clear the

following morning. Many of the troops had simply frozen to death in the night. 'I found lying close to my tent, stiff, cold, and quite dead, an old grey haired conductor named Macgregor, who, utterly exhausted, had lain down there silently to die,' remembered George Lawrence.[30] Many sought out the reticent Scottish assistant surgeon of Shah Shuja's Contingent, the thirty-year-old William Brydon. He had spent the night warmly wrapped in his sheepskin coat and now rushed around the camp at dawn, trying to encourage those still living to jump up and down and warm themselves up. 'I called to the natives who had been lying near to me to get up,' he wrote in his diary, 'which only a few were able to do. Some of them actually laughed at me for urging them, and pointed to their feet, which looked like charred logs of wood. Poor fellows they were frostbitten, and had to be left behind.'[31]

The second day of the retreat proved even more chaotic than the first.

'Less than half of the sepoys were by this stage fit for duty,' wrote Vincent Eyre. 'The cold had so nipped the hands and feet of even the strongest men, as to completely prostrate their powers and incapacitate them for service.' Even the cavalry were 'obliged to be lifted on their horses . . . Large clods of hardened snow adhered so firmly to the hoofs of our horses, that a chisel and hammer would have been requisite to dislodge them. The very air we breathed froze in its passage out of the mouth and nostrils, forming a coating of small icicles on our moustaches and beards . . . Already only a few hundred serviceable fighting-men remained.'[32]

If the bodies of the soldiers were severely weakened, their resolve and self-control was even more badly affected. 'About ½ past 7 a.m. the advance guard moved off without any order given or bugle being sounded,' recorded Hugh Johnson in his diary. 'Discipline is at an end.'[33] The remaining baggage had not even been lifted on to the camels and oxen before large numbers of Afghans began to dart down the mountain slopes, plundering all that they could lay their hands on. Three cannon being dragged by mules were passing a small mudbrick fort close to the camp ground when a party of Afghans sallied straight out and captured them. The sepoys supposed to guard the artillery immediately ran off. As the troops advanced on their road, the number of mounted Afghans around them steadily increased. They travelled parallel to the British, on both flanks of the column, firing randomly into the jostling rabble of refugees they were now driving between them, like shepherds expertly controlling a flock of panicked sheep, the terrified sepoys having already lost all will to fight back.

One entire Hindustani regiment – Shah Shuja's 29th – went over en masse to Akbar Khan that morning. Many other sepoys, already too frostbitten to continue, now threw down their weapons and fled back to Kabul, hoping that their injuries would preserve them from the attention of the town's slavers, and anyway 'preferring to become prisoners there to the certain death which they saw clearly must result from continuing any longer with the main body'. Months later, several hundred maimed former sepoys were still to be seen hobbling on their stumps, begging around the Kabul bazaars.

Although there was now hardly any food or ammunition left to see the main force through to Jalalabad, Elphinstone still called a halt in the middle of the second afternoon at Butkhak, at the mouth of the great Khord Kabul Pass, after the army had made barely five miles' progress, 'thereby losing one more day', as Johnson noted.

We had left Kabul with only 5 days ¼ rations to take us to Jellala-bad, and no forage for cattle, and with no prospect of getting any.

In this way he subjected our unfortunate troops, already nearly paralysed with cold, to another night in the snow with no shelter. No ground being again marked out for the troops, the whole was one mass of confusion. Three fourths of the Sepoys were mixed up with the camp followers and knew not where to find the HQs of their Corps.[34]

Lady Sale was equally scornful of the General's leadership, and became more certain than ever that a wholesale massacre was now imminent. She wrote:

> By these unnecessary halts we diminished our provisions, and having no cover for officers or men, all are perfectly paralysed with cold . . .
>
> The snow still lies more than a foot deep. No food for man or beast; and even water from the river close at hand difficult to obtain, as our people are fired on in fetching it; yet so bigoted are our rulers that we are still told that the sirdars are faithful, that Akbar Khan is our friend &c &c &c; and that the reason they wish us to delay is that they may send their troops to clear the passes for us! They will send them there can be in no doubt; but everything is occurring just as was foretold before we set out.[35]

So it was that for a second night the troops again went to bed hungry in the thick snow.* This time, however, Afghans filled the slopes on all sides, shooting down through the darkness, and rumours spread that Akbar Khan was personally directing their fire. 'A night of starvation, cold, exhaustion, death,' wrote Eyre, 'and of all deaths I can imagine none more agonising than where a nipping frost tortures every sensitive limb, until the tenacious spirit itself sinks under the exquisite extreme of human suffering.'[36]

But the sufferings of the first two days were nothing compared with what would follow the next morning.

---

* It would have been far better for the retreating army to have travelled at night when the snow would have been frozen, and the Ghilzai unable to shoot with any accuracy: the Afghan Mujehedin, travelling in the same terrain in the 1980s always travelled at night for these very reasons. But this was an army untrained and ill-equipped for either mountain or winter warfare.

Butkhak lies a short distance beyond the towering cliffs of the Khord Kabul Pass.* It was in the mouth of the pass, near here, more than two months earlier, that 'Fighting Bob' Sale's brigade had first been attacked as they were retiring for the night. Now the same cliffs were witness to a far more bloody dawn ambush. As before, the killing was preceded by the eerie ringing of unseen jezails loading.[37]

Just before sunrise, large numbers of Afghans had massed in the darkness to the rear of the British camp. As the sepoys were rising to find yet more frozen corpses littering the ground around the few remaining tents, it was there that the fighting began: 'The scene at sunrise was fearful,' wrote Hugh Johnson.

> The Force was perfectly disorganised. Every man appeared to be so paralysed with cold as to be scarcely able to hold his musket or move a step. Some of the enemy having appeared on the rear of the bivouack, the whole of the camp followers rushed to the front in one huge mass: men, women and children . . . The ground was strewn with boxes of ammunition, and property of various kinds. The enemy soon assembled in great numbers. Had they made a dash among us we could have offered no resistance and every one of us would have been slaughtered.[38]

Instead, the frontmost troops and followers were skilfully herded into the mouth of the Khord Kabul Pass, the women led by Lady Sale – 'I felt very grateful for a tumbler of sherry which at any other time would have made me feel most unladylike.' At the same time General Elphinstone's staff spotted a group of Afghan horsemen standing at some distance to the rear under a banner, clearly directing proceedings. It was correctly assumed that this was Akbar Khan, and Mackenzie and Lawrence were sent off to renegotiate the safe passage they had been promised in Kabul. Akbar Khan

---

* The army could have taken the far less dangerous route through the Lautaband Pass. Why they did not do this remains a mystery. In the second Afghan War this was the route used by the British army thus bypassing the terrible Khord Kabul and Tezin Passes where most of the killing took place.

agreed that if his friends Mackenzie and Lawrence were again to be
surrendered as hostages, he would send his most influential men
ahead 'to clear the pass from the Ghilzais who occupied it'.[39] The
terms were accepted.

'We proceeded', wrote Lawrence afterwards, 'escorted by two
of Akbar's dependents, through crowds of the enemy, until we
reached the Sirdar. We found [Akbar] seated on the side of a hill at
breakfast, which he civilly asked us to partake of, ordering at the
same time his men to take away our firearms . . . We then sat down,
not without a shudder at eating from the same dish as the man who
had been so lately the murderer of the Envoy.'[40] Shortly afterwards,
while Akbar gently chided the two young officers for leaving
Kabul before he could arrange for their protection, the two heard
great fusillades of musketry from within the pass. The advance
guard had just been shepherded into a perfectly executed ambush.

For days, so it became clear afterwards, the Ghilzais had been
preparing for this moment. Embankments, shallow trenches and
rubble sangars had been carefully erected out of the range of the
British muskets but sufficiently close to the valley bottom to be
well within the range of the Afghans' jezails. Now, once the front
of the British column had entered far within the towering cliffs of
the pass – making no attempt to send up flankers to crown the
heights as should by now have been automatic drill for the infantry
– the ambush was sprung. 'We had not proceeded half a mile when
we were heavily fired upon,' wrote Lady Sale that night. 'The
Chiefs who rode with the advance desired us to keep close to them.
They certainly desired their followers to shout to the people on the
heights not to fire; but they did so quite ineffectually. These Chiefs
certainly ran the same risks we did; but I verily believe many of
these persons would individually sacrifice themselves to rid their
country of us.'* She continued:

---

* In reality the Jabbar Khel and Kharoti Ghilzai who patrolled these passes would not
have felt any compunction about disobeying the Barakzai chiefs whom the Ghilzais
despised almost as much as they hated the Sadozai. Macnaghten had reneged on their
payments and now they wanted to get their own back.

After passing through some very sharp firing, we came upon Major Thain's horse, which had been shot through the loins. When we were supposed to be in comparative safety, poor Sturt rode back, to see after Major Thain: his horse was shot from under him, and before he could rise from the ground, he received a severe wound in the abdomen. It was with great difficulty that he was held upon a pony by two people, and brought into camp at Khoord Kabul.

The pony Mrs Sturt rode was wounded in the ear and neck. I had fortunately only one ball in my arm; three others passed through my *poshteen* [posting – 'long skin', i.e. sheepskin coat] near the shoulder without doing me injury. The party that fired on us were not fifty yards from us, and we owed our escape to urging our horses on as fast as they could go over the road where, at any other time, we would have walked our horses very carefully . . .

The pass quickly became jammed, and 'for a considerable period we were stationary under heavy fire . . . The 37th [Regiment] continued moving slowly forward without firing a shot, being paralysed with cold to such a degree that no persuasion of their officers could induce them to make any effort to dislodge the enemy, who took from some of them not only their firelocks but even the clothes from their person; several men of the 44th supplied themselves with ammunition from the pouches of their *sipahees* [sepoys] . . . All this time our men were dropping fast from a flanking fire from the heights . . . [At least] 500 of our regular troops, and about 2,500 of our camp followers, are killed . . .'[41]

Yet according to those who followed, the first wave of troops in which Lady Sale was travelling got off comparatively lightly. 'The advance, altho' they suffered considerably, was by comparison with the rear very fortunate,' wrote Hugh Johnson.

There the scene of slaughter was dreadful. We had to run the gauntlet of the whole length of this fearful defile, a distance of about 5 miles. All baggage was abandoned. The enemy not only poured in a murderous fire from every rock and cave in the heights on each side, but descended into the Pass and slew man, woman and child. The whole road for a distance of 5 miles was covered with dead and dying. The 37th Native Infantry lost more than half its men, and other Corps in proportion. Even those who remained could scarcely move from their feet and hands being frost-bitten, and to add to our misery, snow began to fall on our arrival at Khoord Cabul.[42]

All morning, Lawrence and Mackenzie had to sit with Akbar and make small talk, listening as the waves of musketry echoed down the pass. Mackenzie, who was a good linguist, heard Akbar shouting to his men in Dari – a language known to many of the British – to 'spare' the British, while telling them to 'slay them all' in Pashtu, the language of the tribes, which only Mackenzie and very few others on the British side understood. In the late afternoon the two hostages were allowed to follow, captives again as they had been on the day of Macnaghten's murder, but this time protected by Akbar's cousin, Sultan Jan Barakzai. The scene the party passed was one of unparalleled horror. As Lawrence described it:

> sepoys and camp followers were being stripped and plundered on all sides, and such as refused to give up their money and valuables were instantly stabbed or cut down . . . On seeing us, the poor creatures cried out for help, many of them recognising me and calling me by name. But what could we do . . . The Ghilzais had now tasted blood, and clearly showed their tigerish nature, becoming very savage and fierce in their demeanour towards ourselves, demanding that we should be given up to them for a sacrifice, brandishing their long blood-stained knives in our faces, and telling us 'to look on the heaps of the carcasses around us, as we should soon be ourselves among them.' 'You came to Kabul for fruit, did you? How do you like it now?' they cried.

When he saw the body of an Englishman stretched out by the road, Lawrence rode over and found that the soldier was alive:

> the poor fellow raising his head and recognising me, cried out, 'For God sake, Captain Lawrence, don't leave me here!' I jumped

off my horse, and going up to the man raised him up, with the assistance of two of Sultan Jan's men, who had dismounted by his orders. He was a sergeant of the 44th, and at first appeared only to have lost his left hand; but to my grief and horror, on raising him, I saw that from the nape of his neck to his backbone, he had been cut in pieces. 'What use is there lifting him up?' cried the Affghans, 'he cannot live many minutes.' I reluctantly assented, and on telling the poor fellow we could do nothing for him, he said, 'Then for God sake shoot me.' 'Even this I cannot do,' I mournfully replied. 'Then leave me to die,' he said, and this we were forced to do . . .

As we proceeded we met numbers of the enemy's horse and foot returning to Kabul, laden with plunder of all kinds. One miscreant had a little Indian girl seated on his horse behind him . . .[43]

That night, having ascended to the top of the pass, the British found themselves in an even colder camp site than the night before. Snow began to fall towards evening, developing into a full-scale blizzard by nine at night. For the entire army, only four tents remained, one of which was assigned to Lady Sale and her daughter. There was no fuel or food, but at least some of the doctors still had their medicine bags. Dr Brydon's friend and Scottish compatriot Dr Alexander Bryce 'came and examined Sturt's wound', wrote Lady Sale. 'He dressed it; but I saw by the countenance in his expression that there was no hope. He afterwards kindly cut the ball out of my wrist; and dressed both my wounds . . . [That night] the sipahees and camp followers, half frozen, tried to force their way not only into our tent but into our beds . . . Many poor wretches died round the tent in the night . . . Many women and children abducted.'[44]

'The snow was the only bed for all,' wrote Eyre, 'and for many, ere morning, it proved the winding sheet. It was only marvellous that any of us at all should have survived that fearful night!' Maulana Hamid Kashmiri echoed the thought in his *Akbarnama*:

> The winter, with its very heartlessness
> Showered love upon the brave people of Kabul

For if the Kafirs did not die of the snow
Or by the swords of the plundering looters

To hyenas, wolves and jackals, from every side
The fox called out, bidding them to a feast of meat

Kites circled above and cried out far
A generous invitation to all beasts of prey

Upon that road how many escaped alive?
All were thrown down, and laid low in the snow[45]

On the fourth morning of the retreat, 9 January, in the middle of a
high-altitude sub-zero blizzard, desperation finally gave way to
complete despair. 'The flesh from men's feet was peeling off in
flakes,' recorded Captain William Anderson, one of the last survivors of Shah Shuja's Contingent. 'Scores had been frozen to death
in the night.'[46]

As the blizzard continued to rage with greater intensity than
ever, only one mile of progress was made in the entire day. 'The sky
on all sides filled with snow,' recorded Munshi Abdul Karim,

the horizon became invisible, and a fierce wind arose, uprooting
trees. Thick dark clouds blew in with terrifying thunder-claps and
flashes of lightning. As more snow fell, the frost bit hard and all was
covered in white powder like camphor. The English troops froze,
their finger-tips fell off by segments, the soft tissue fell off their
bones, even their feet separated from their ankles; living and dead
were indistinguishable, motionless in the frozen wastes. The Afghan
tribes who were used to such harsh conditions, crowded the hills
and rushed down to plunder the helpless English troops. They
found them half dead, or frozen solid like stones, no longer caring

about their weapons, their gold, their possessions, barely conscious at all, each only just aware of his own dire condition.[47]

That evening, Elphinstone effectively acknowledged that his troops were doomed and gave over all the British women – or at least those of officer class – into the hands of Akbar Khan.* Throughout the day, Akbar had hovered on the tail of the column insisting that he was doing everything he could to restrain the Ghilzai, but claiming that even their chiefs could not restrain them now they had tasted blood. Instead he offered to save the women and children and any wounded officers who wanted to give themselves up. In the end nineteen of them – two men, eight women and nine children – were escorted away. Lady Sale and her daughter Alexandrina had just watched Sturt die, strapped to the back of a shivering pony. 'The rough motion increased his suffering and accelerated his death,' wrote Lady Sale, 'but he was still conscious that his wife and I were with him; and we had the sorrowful satisfaction of giving him a Christian burial . . .' Later, as she recounted,

> overwhelmed by domestic affliction, neither Mrs Sturt nor I were in a fit state to decide for ourselves whether we would accept the Sirdar's protection or not. There was but faint hope of our ever getting safe to Jalalabad; and we followed the stream . . . We were taken by a very circuitous route to the Khoord Kabul forts where we found Mahomed Akbar Khan, and the other hostages. Three rooms were cleared out for us, having no outlets except a small door to each; and, of course, they are dark and dirty . . . At midnight, some mutton bones and greasy rice were brought to us. All that Mrs Sturt and I possess are the clothes on our backs in which we quitted Kabul . . .[48]

For the British, this surrender of their women into the hands of men they had come to regard as brutal savages was the moment of

---

* British women below officer class were left to fend for themselves. According to the tribesmen I talked to in these passes, a great number ended up in local harems, while the less desirable ones were sold as slaves.

their greatest humiliation. For the Afghans, in contrast, the protection offered to the British memsahibs was seen as a mark of their own chivalry. 'Commander Akbar Khan, though taken up with ruthless fighting, saw the dreadful condition of the women and children, and pitied them,' wrote Munshi Abdul Karim.

> Out of love of God and common decency, he ordered the living to be separated from the dead, and for them to be taken to warm places and covered with sheepskins and sable pelisses. He placed them next to braziers to revive them, after the extreme cold had all but stopped the blood circulating in their veins. Such is Afghan hospitality! Even after the fiercest battle, they will succour the weak in extreme distress, as if they were their own family. For if God wills it, even a Kafir can be a cause for good.[49]

For those still on the retreat, however, the horrors continued. By the following morning, 10 January, after a second night on the exposed heights of the Khord Kabul, Hugh Johnson recorded succinctly that 'we had now not a single sepoy remaining of the whole of the Kabul Force. Every particle of our baggage was gone. We all gave ourselves up for lost . . . Every man among us thought that ere many hours should pass he was doomed to die, either by cold or hunger or butchered by our enemies . . . My eyes have become so inflamed from the reflection from the snow that I am nearly blind, and the pain is intense. Several officers are quite sightless.'[50]

Dr Brydon was lucky that morning to find the hoard of food left behind by Lady Macnaghten when she was handed over to Akbar Khan. The meat and sherry she had shared with George Lawrence were now long gone, but there were still 'some eggs and a bottle of wine . . . The eggs were not boiled but frozen quite hard, and the wine also, to the consistency of honey . . .' It was as well for Brydon that he had some sustenance, for there followed the worst day of the retreat yet, as the snow-blinded and frostbitten troops stumbled through the narrows of the Tezin Pass where a second meticulously laid ambush awaited them. 'This was a terrible march,' Brydon recorded in his diary that night, the fire of the enemy incessant, and great numbers of officers and men, not knowing where they were going from snow-blindness, were cut up. I led Mr Banness, the Greek merchant, a great part of the way over the high ground, and often felt so blind myself that from time to time I applied a handful of snow to my eyes, and recommended others to do so, as it gave great relief. Descending towards Tezin, the whiteness was not so intense, and as the sun got low, the blindness went off; but the fire of the enemy increased, and as they were able to get very close to us in the Pass, which we now again entered, it was very destructive.

The enemy all the way pressed hard on our flanks and rear, and, on arriving at the valley of Tezin towards evening, a mere handful remained of the native regiments which had left Cabul . . . Dr Bryce, just on entering the pass, was shot through the chest, and when dying handed his will to Captain Marshall.[51]

'Little or no resistance was made by the sepoys,' noted Elphinstone in his official memorandum to the government, 'most of whom had lost their fingers or toes, and their muskets covered with frozen snow would have been little use even if the men could have handled them. The slaughter was frightful and when we reached Kubber Jubber [actually Khak-i-Jabar] fighting men were with difficulty distinguished from camp followers. Most had thrown away their arms and accoutrements; and fell an easy prey to our barbarous and bloodthirsty foe.'[52] As ever, the orders given by Elphinstone only made things worse. 'Our military authorities, who proved themselves as incapable of conducting a retreat as they had previously shown themselves in the operations preceding it, had with the most strange perversity ordered our men on no account to return the fire,' wrote Lawrence. 'The consequence was that their ranks were forced in, and an indiscriminate slaughter of unresisting men followed all the way to Tezin . . .'[53] 'We were in so thick a mass,' wrote an exhausted and despairing Johnson, 'that every shot told on some part or other of the column.'[54]

By the evening of 11 January, after yet another day-long massacre, as the ever diminishing column stumbled out of the Tezin Pass towards the fertile valley-bottom village of Jagdalak, the number of casualties passed 12,000. There were only 200 troops still left to stumble forward. The small rearguard was under the command of Shelton, who now for the first time showed his steel as he stood at the back of the column holding the Afghans at bay. 'Nothing could exceed the bravery of Shelton,' wrote Johnson. 'He was like a bull-dog assaulted on all sides by a lot of curs trying to snap at his head, tail and sides. Shelton's small band was attacked by horse and foot, and although the latter were fifty to one, not a man dared to come close . . . We cheered him in true English fashion as he descended into the valley, notwithstanding we, at the time, were acting as targets for the marksmen of the enemy on the hills.'

That night, as the remaining troops lay besieged and starving in a small ruined mud-walled enclosure in Jagdalak, Akbar Khan summoned General Elphinstone and Brigadier Shelton for negotia-tions. Hugh Johnson accompanied them. 'We found the Sirdar and his party bivouacked in the open air,' he wrote. 'Nothing could exceed the kind and apparently sympathising manner in which we were received by this Chief who immediately on learning that we were hungry and thirsty ordered a cloth to be spread on the ground where we were sitting.'[55] He welcomed them to his blazing camp fire, offered them dinner, then refused to allow them to return to their troops. Shelton was furious and demanded the right as an officer and soldier to return to lead his men and die fighting. He was refused.

By nine the following night, after a day under continual fire, and when it was clear that all the remaining leaders had either been captured or killed, most of the survivors, 'now almost maddened with hunger and especially with thirst having been marching or rather hunted like wild beasts for 24 hours', decided that their only hope was to press on in the dark. They found however their way blocked by a formidable thorny barrier of 'prickly holly oak, well twisted together, about six feet high', which had just been erected across the narrowest part of the pass.[56] Those who tried to tear it down with their bare hands or claw their way up it were shot down as they did so. Very few made it over. One who failed to do so was the sepoy Sita Ram. He recorded how,

when the General sahib left, all discipline fell away. As a result, the
Afghans were able to annoy us the more . . . A number of sepoys and
followers went across to the enemy in an effort to save their lives. My
regiment had disappeared and I attached myself to the remnants of a
European regiment. I thought that by sticking to them I might have
some chance of getting away from that detestable country. But alas!
Alas! Who can withstand fate? We went on fighting and losing men
every step of the road. We were attacked in front, in the rear, and from
the tops of hills. In truth, it was hell itself. I cannot describe the
horrors. At last we came to a high wall that blocked the road; in trying
to force this, our whole party was destroyed. The men fought like
Gods, not men, but numbers prevailed against them. I was struck
down by a jezail ball on the side of my head.

Sita Ram was knocked unconscious, and when he came to he found
himself:

tied crossways upon a horse which was being led rapidly away from
the fighting towards Kabul. I now learned that I was being taken
there to be sold as a slave. I begged to be shot, or have my throat cut
and abused the Afghans in Pushtu and in my own language . . . but
my captor threatened to make me a Muslim on the spot if I did not
keep quiet. What dreadful carnage I saw on that road – legs and
arms protruding from the snow, Europeans and Hindustanis half
buried . . . It was a sight I shall never forget as long as I live.[57]

One of the very few to make it over the holly barrier was the last
surgeon left alive, Dr Brydon. 'The confusion became terrible,' he
remembered,

and the shouts of 'Halt, Halt, keep back the cavalry,' were incessant.
Just after getting clear of the Pass – I with great difficulty made my
way to the front. We had not gone far in the dark before I found
myself surrounded. At this moment my Khidmutgar [table servant]
rushed up to me, saying he was wounded, had lost his pony, and
begged me to take him up. I had not time to do so before I was

pulled off my horse and knocked down by a blow on the head from an Afghan knife, which must have killed me had I not placed a portion of Blackwood's Magazine in my forage cap. As it was a piece of bone about the size of a wafer was cut from my skull, and I was nearly stunned. I managed to rise upon my knees, and seeing that a second blow was coming I met it with the edge of my sword, and I suppose cut off some of my assailant's fingers, as the knife fell to the ground. He bolted one way, and I the other, minus my cap. The Khidmutgar was dead; those who had been with me I never saw again. I rejoined our troops, scrambled over a barricade of trees made across the Pass, and I got a severe blow on the shoulder from an Afghan who rushed down the hill and across the road.[58]

The badly wounded Brydon was saved by clinging to the stirrup of an officer's horse, and so was dragged clear of the mêlée. Stumbling over more corpses in the moonlight, he then came across a mortally wounded cavalryman. He had been shot through the chest, and was haemorrhaging blood over his scarlet uniform. The man grabbed Brydon by the hand and begged him to take his pony before someone else did. The cavalryman then fell back dead. Grateful to his anonymous benefactor, and desperate to find any other last survivors, Brydon mounted the pony and rode off into the darkness.

There were a few other miraculous escapes. Havildar Moti Ram, one of the last survivors of the Charikar Gurkha garrison, who had been enslaved on arrival in Kabul, heard that the garrison was leaving the Kabul cantonment and managed to effect a further escape from his captors on the night of 6 January.

Pretending to the Afghans who stopped him that he was a camel driver discharged from the service of Shah Shuja, he managed to find the stone under which he had buried his life savings and rejoined his colleagues just in time to be present for the massacre in the Khord Kabul Pass two days later. 'At Jagdalak,' he later recorded,

> the British force was girded round by Akbar Khan's horsemen, who killed all they could. In the darkness I extricated myself from this scene of carnage, and sought safety once more in the hilltops. I remained a day high up in the hills. I had tasted no food for twenty-six hours from the time I made my last insufficient meal. I was benumbed by cold . . . I wished for death to release me from sufferings that had now become intolerable. I descended to the roadside determined to declare myself to the first Afghans who approached and court the blow of some pitying sword. I saw a party approach, and concluded the hour of my death had arrived.

But the party proved to be five Hindu Khatris,[*] or traders:

> These Cutries said, 'As you are a Hindoo, we will save your life, but you must pay us before doing so.' They searched me and took the 100 rupees out of my cummerbund, and returned me ten of them – they conducted me to a dharamasala [pilgrims' resthouse] in which there was a Hindoo Fakir. His protection I also sought, and gave him my remaining ten rupees. He dressed me up in the red dress of a fakir and rubbed wood ashes over my face. I was to pass for his chela [disciple]; and he said I was to accompany him in the character of such on a pilgrimage he proposed making to Hardwar. A party of fruit merchants shortly after arrived. The fakir, the Cutries and myself joined them. We descended the high road considerably to the left of Peshawar. I begged my way until I got to Sir Jasper Nicholls's Camp, one march this side of Ludhiana.[59]

The least lucky were those hundreds of sepoys and camp followers who neither escaped nor were enslaved or killed. In the Tezin Pass alone, 1,500 of these were stripped of their goods and their clothes

---

[*] It was Khatri traders from Multan and Shikarpur who dominated the Central Asian trade between Bukhara and Sindh. See Arup Banerji, *Old Routes: North Indian Nomads and Bankers in Afghan, Uzbek and Russian Lands*, New Delhi, 2011, p. 2.

by the Afghans, then left to starve and freeze to death in the snows, abandoned by their British employers and treated with contempt by their Afghan captors.[60] Lady Sale and the other prisoners of war saw many such in the days that followed, as they headed back towards Kabul. 'The road was covered with awful mangled bodies, all naked,' wrote Lady Sale in her diary.

> We passed some 200 dead bodies, many of them Europeans, the whole naked, and covered with large gaping wounds . . . Numbers of camp followers, we found still alive, frostbitten and starving; some perfectly out of their senses and idiotic . . . The sight was dreadful; the smell of blood sickening; and the corpses lay so thick that it was impossible to look upon them as it required care to guide my horse so as not to tread upon the bodies.

They came upon several camp followers who emerged from caves or from behind rocks 'where they had taken shelter from the murderous knives of the Affghan and the inclemency of the climate'.

> They had been stripped of all they possessed, and few could crawl more than a few yards on hands and knees, being frostbitten in the feet. Here Johnson found two of his servants: the one had his hands and feet frostbitten, and had a fearful swordcut across one hand, and a musket-ball in his stomach: the other had his right arm completely cut through the bone. Both were utterly destitute of covering, and had not tasted food for five days . . . Wounded and starving, they had set fire to the bushes and grass, and huddled all together to impart warmth to each other. Subsequently we heard that scarcely any of these poor wretches escaped from this defile: and that driven to the extreme of hunger they had sustained life by feeding upon their dead comrades.[61]

Only eighty survivors from the column managed to make it alive over the Jagdalak holly-oak barrier on the night of 12 January.

Most of these – some twenty officers and forty-five privates of Shelton's 44th Foot, and a couple of artillerymen and sepoys – were exposed and surrounded at dawn as they stood, uncertain of the correct road, at the top of the hill of Gandamak, ten miles further on. Overwhelmingly outnumbered – 'every hut had poured forth its inhabitants to murder and plunder' – and with only twenty muskets and two rounds of ammunition each between them, the troops decided to make their last stand. They were offered quarter but refused. Many felt their regiment had been disgraced after running away from the hilltop of Bibi Mahru on the evening of 23 November, and now they were determined to die fighting and so redeem the regimental honour. They formed a square, and defended themselves, 'driving the Affghans several times down the hill' until they had exhausted the last of their rounds, and then fought on with their bayonets.[62] Then, one by one, they were slaughtered.* The Afghans took only nine prisoners. One of these was Captain Thomas Souter, who wrapped the regimental colours of the 44th around his waist and was taken captive by the Ghilzai who assumed that someone so colourfully dressed must be worth holding to ransom. 'Thinking I was some great man from looking so flash,' he wrote, 'I was seized by two fellows after my sword dropped from my hand by a severe cut on the shoulder, and my pistol missing fire. They hurried me from this spot to a distance, took my clothes off me, except my trousers and cap, and led me away to a village.'[63]

Fifteen more cavalrymen made it as far as Fattehabad, where ten were killed while sitting down to accept breakfast from some villagers. Four were shot down from the rooftops as they attempted to remount and ride out of the village. One more – Eldred Potting-er's young nephew Thomas – was tracked down, caught and beheaded hiding amid the beautiful cypress trees and water runnels of Shah Jahan's Nimla Gardens, where Shuja had first been defeated and lost his throne in 1809.

Only one man made it beyond this point. Dr Brydon was still

---

* When the writers Nancy and Louis Dupree visited Gandamak in the 1970s they found bones, fragments of Victorian weaponry and military equipment still lying in the scree above the village.

fifteen miles from the safety of Jalalabad. 'I proceeded alone,' he
wrote later.

> Then I saw a party of about twenty men drawn up in my road, who
> when I came near, began picking up large stones . . . so I with diffi-
> culty put my pony into a gallop and, taking the bridle in my mouth,
> cut right and left with my sword as I went through them. They
> could not reach me with their knives and I was only hit by one or
> two stones. A little further on I was met by another similar party
> who I tried to pass as I did the former, but was obliged to prick the
> poor pony with the point of my sword before I could get him into
> a gallop. Of this party, one man on a mound over the road had a
> gun, which he fired close down upon me, and broke my sword,
> leaving only about six inches on the handle.

Brydon managed to get clear of these attackers, only to find that
'the shot had hit the poor pony, wounding him in the loins, and he
could now hardly carry me'.

> Then I saw some five horsemen dressed in red, and supposing they
> were some of our irregular cavalry, I made towards them, but,
> getting near, found they were Afghans, and that they were leading
> Captain Collyer's horse. I tried to get away, but my pony could
> hardly move, and they sent one of their party after me, who made
> a cut at me, guarding against which with the bit of my sword, it fell
> from the hilt. He passed me, but turned and rode at me again. This
> time, just as he was striking, I threw the handle of the sword at his
> head, in swerving to avoid which he only cut me over the back of
> the left hand. Feeling it disabled, I stretched down the right to pick
> up the bridle. I suppose my foe thought it was for a pistol, for he
> turned at once and made off as quick as he could. I then felt for the
> pistol I had put in my pocket, but it was gone, and I was unarmed,
> and on a poor animal I feared could not carry me to Jalalabad.

The surgeon felt suddenly drained of energy: 'I became nervous
and frightened at shadows, and I really think would have fallen

THE WAIL OF BUGLES

from my saddle but for the peak of it . . .' He had been spotted, however, by an eagle-eyed staff officer on the top turret of the Jalalabad fort, and rescuers quickly came to his assistance.

> Among the first of them was Captain Sinclair, whose servant gave me one of his own shoes to cover my foot. I was taken to the Sappers' Mess, my wounds dressed by Dr Forsyth, and after a good dinner, with great thankfulness, enjoyed the luxury of a sound sleep . . . On examination I found that I had a slight sword wound on my left knee, besides my head and left hand, and that a ball had gone through my trousers a little higher up, slightly grazing the skin . . . The poor pony, directly it was put into a stable, lay down and never rose again. Immediately on my telling how things were, General Sale despatched a party to scour the plains . . . but they only found the bodies of Captain Hopkins and Collyer, and Dr Harper . . .[64]

That night, lamps were raised on the gates of Jalalabad and bugles blown to guide in any last stragglers, but none limped in. 'A strong wind was blowing from the south, which sent the sound of the bugles all over the town,' remembered Captain Thomas Seaton. 'The terrible wailing sound of those bugles I will never forget. It was a dirge for our slaughtered soldiers and, heard all through the night, it had an inexpressibly mournful and depressing effect. Dr Brydon's tale struck horror into the hearts of all who heard it . . . The whole army had been destroyed, one man alone escaping to tell the fearful tale.'[65]

In the days that followed, a few other survivors limped in, including Dr Brydon's friend Mr Banness, the Greek merchant, and several hardy Gurkhas. In time the legend grew that the entire British army in Afghanistan had been wiped out. This of course was not the case: large garrisons survived in Kandahar and Jalalabad, and even of the Kabul army there were 2,000 sepoys who ultimately came home along with thirty-five British officers, fifty-one private soldiers, twelve wives and twenty-two children, all of whom were either taken hostage (in the case of the

Europeans) or managed to stumble back to Kabul to beg on the streets (in the case of the Hindustanis). It was nonetheless an extraordinary defeat for the British and an almost miraculous victory for the Afghan resistance. At the very height of the British Empire, at a point when the British controlled more of the world economy than they would ever do again, and at a time when traditional forces were everywhere being massacred by industrialised colonial armies, it was a rare moment of complete colonial humiliation.

The story was immediately retold by Afghan poets and singers, the numbers of casualties and the scale of the victory growing with each retelling. 'It is said that 60,000 English troops – half from Bengal, half from other provinces, without counting servants and camp-followers – went to Afghanistan,' wrote Mirza 'Ata,

> and only a handful came back alive, wounded and destitute. The rest fell with neither grave nor shroud to cover them, and lay scattered in that land like rotting donkeys. The English love gold and money so much that they cannot stop themselves from laying their hands on any area productive of wealth. But what prize did they find in Afghanistan except, on the one hand, the exhausting of their treasury and, on the other, the disgracing of their army? It is said that of the 40,000 English troops who had been in Kabul, many were taken captive en route, many remained as cripples and beggars in Kabul, and the rest perished in the mountains, like a ship sunk without trace; for it is no easy thing to invade or govern the Kingdom of Khurasan.[66]

9

The Death of a King

The news of the massacre of an entire British army spread quickly around the region.

In Bukhara, the Amir celebrated the good tidings by ordering the murder of his two British prisoners, Charles Conolly and Arthur Stoddart. In Herat, the Wazir Yar Mohammad took the opportunity of throttling his monarch, Kamran Shah Sadozai, knowing that neither the British nor Shah Shuja would now be in any position to stop him. The news caused more excitement still in India. In Delhi, the bankers of the Chandni Chowk bazaars heard the news a full two days before the colonial authorities: the letter-writing systems of traditional trade working far faster and more efficiently than the creaking colonial system of harkara runners.[1] By the time the news reached Calcutta, it had already given hope and encouragement to the many opponents of Company rule across the length and breadth of Hindustan: it was no accident that when the Great Rebellion did break out in 1857, it did so in sepoy regiments which had been deserted by their British officers in the snows of the Khord Kabul, and in civilian centres such as Lucknow, Agra and Kanpur where the Persian presses had eagerly reprinted the Afghan epic poems and prose accounts of the British defeat.[2]

Lord Auckland was almost the last to hear about the catastrophe. It took a full two weeks for the express bearing Dr Brydon's tale finally to reach Government House on 30 January 1842. The news, as Emily Eden noted, aged 'poor George' ten years in as many hours: he screamed and raged, then took to his bed. He emerged partially paralysed, and was believed to have suffered some kind of stroke.[3] In the days that followed, his sisters became more and more anxious, watching helplessly as their brother paced pale-faced up and down the veranda by day and lay prostrate on the lawns at night, pressing his face against the cool turf for comfort. Only a few weeks earlier, his trusted adviser Macnaghten had been writing to him from Kabul, telling him not to believe the naysayers and assuring him that all was well. Now his entire Imperial strategy and all his 'plans for public good and public security upon which I had staked so much have all broken under circumstances of horror and disaster of which history has few parallels'.[4] Indeed the entire catastrophe was to Auckland himself 'as inexplicable as it is appalling'. Worse still was the news that followed, that Akbar and the other leaders of the resistance were now moving to finish off the three remaining British garrisons in Jalalabad, Ghazni and Kandahar. Around India, rumours spread that, with much of the Indian army still absent in China fighting Auckland's Opium War, the Afghans would soon be pouring down the Khyber Pass to loot the plains of Hindustan as they had done so often in the past.

It was one week more before London heard what had happened. *The Times* broke the news to the nation: 'We regret to announce that the intelligence which this express has brought us is of the most disastrous and melancholy nature.' In a typically Russophobic leading article published a few days later it hinted heavily – and quite inaccurately – at a Russian hand in the events, pointing out that the first to be targeted for assassination was none other than Sir Alexander Burnes, the great rival of Vitkevitch and 'the keenest antagonist of the Russian agents'.[5]

The new Tory government of Sir Robert Peel had been all set to withdraw from Afghanistan and wash its hands of the mess created by its Whig predecessors. Now, however, it was agreed by the Cabinet that the nation's military reputation had first to be salvaged. Lord Ellenborough, the founding ideologue of the Indus policy and the man the Tories had already sent out to replace Auckland as governor general, heard of the disaster when his ship docked off Madras on 21 February. From the Governor's House he wrote immediately to Peel declaring that he intended to teach the Afghans a lesson they would never forget: 'the honour of our arms must be re-established in Afghanistan . . . Every difficulty should be encountered and overcome for the preservation of India.'6 By the time Ellenborough reached Calcutta on the 28th – addressing barely a word to his disgraced and beleaguered predecessor or his sisters – the news had arrived that Ghazni too had fallen to the Ghilzai, and its garrison, like that of Kabul, had been either captured, slaughtered or enslaved.

By this time, a heavily armed relief force, six regiments strong, with the ominous title of the Army of Retribution had already been despatched from the cantonments of Meerut and Ferozepur with orders to cross the Sutlej and head to Peshawar, ready to wreak revenge. Auckland's first choice of general had been another elderly veteran like Elphinstone, but luckily for the troops the frail and doddering Sir Harry Lumley was ruled out on medical advice. So the command went instead to Major-General George Pollock, who received his orders while smoking his breakfast cheroot on the veranda of his bungalow in Agra. Pollock was a precise, sensible and doggedly efficient Londoner who had been a Company officer in India more than thirty years. A veteran of the Nepal and Burmese Wars, he was, as George Lawrence's younger brother Henry put it, 'as good as any commander that could be sent'. When George Broadfoot heard the news inside the besieged walls of Jalalabad, he also approved. Though no Napoleon, he wrote, Pollock was 'superior to any officer I have yet chanced to meet in these regions'.7

At the same time as Pollock received his appointment, orders were sent to Dost Mohammad's keeper, Captain Nicholson, that their prisoner was to be moved from the Afghan frontier and placed in isolation and under surveillance. 'You will be pleased to lose no time on receipt of this letter in adopting the most strict system for the custody of Dost Mohammad Khan,' Nicholson was instructed by George Clerk, the agent for the North West Frontier, 'making him a close prisoner and preventing all communication with him or his retinue by Afghans or Hindoostanis, except with your permission.'[8]

Within a few days, Dost Mohammad had been moved to an isolated property high in the hills beyond Mussoorie. Nicholson's measures to secure his prisoner reveal the extreme fear and paranoia that overtook the British in India at this time. The small sepoy guard was replaced with no fewer than 110 Englishmen from a newly arrived Queen's Regiment. Even Skinner's Horse, one of whose battalions had just been wiped out – along with Skinner's own son James – on the retreat from Kabul, was sent away from the area as 'the proportion of Mohammadans in the Rissalah was so great that it seemed more prudent not to employ men whose religion (however well inclined to us the men may be) *might* be employed as a means to seduce them from their duty'.

Elaborate measures were taken to make sure that Dost Mohammad did not escape or enter into correspondence with the Afghan rebels. 'The Ameer's premises are guarded day and night by sentries,' wrote Nicholson, 'and the roads leading to it from Landour, as also from Rajpoor, are constantly watched by sentries. None of the Ameer's followers will be allowed to pass out beyond the sentries, no strangers whatsoever admitted within them, except by my pass, which will only be granted when necessary, and the individuals going out will be accompanied by a European guard.' Further precautions were taken to prevent correspondence:

> ... I am establishing a small thannah [police post] at the foot of the hills which will watch the advent of all strangers from the Westward, especially Afghans or Kashmiris, and give me instant notice of the arrival of any suspicious characters ... At the head of this I propose placing an individual of my present establishment who

speaks all the languages of the trans-Indus countries, and with him will be associated a Hindu chupprussie and four hillmen. Their orders are to accompany secretly any suspected individual up the hill, till he reaches the nearest sentry, and then to hand him over to the guard, which is to be posted close to the Ameer's house.

As an additional measure, Nicholson recommended that all Kashmiris be banned from the Mussoorie hills, unless they had a special pass,

> [because] an Afghan messenger would not be likely personally to attempt communicating with the prisoner so closely watched as Dost Mohammad Khan, but would have recourse to one less liable to suspicion; in all probability to a Kashmiri.
>
> Their character as Cossids [messengers] is too well known to need mention and of them I am especially apprehensive. Hence I would suggest that orders be given at Ludhiana and Amballah, that no Kashmiri should be permitted to visit the Dhoon [Valley] or the hills without a pass from yourself. It would probably too aid my efforts if a note of any Kashmiri traveller were to be sent to me by dak by the police officers of the Amballah district, and this would be a check on my own thanna people.

Clerk approved of all Nicholson's measures and in addition gave Nicholson special authority to 'arrest and most closely search any suspicious individual'.[9]

In the meantime, everyone turned their fire on Auckland. In Jalalabad, the night Brydon rode in, Thomas Seaton had written in his diary: 'That Elphinstone's imbecility was the immediate cause of this disgrace and of these terrible disasters is beyond all doubt; but the real author was he who selected for a post of such difficulty and responsibility a man crippled by gout in his hands and feet, whose nerves had succumbed to bodily suffering, and who was in no way remarkable for capacity.'[10] Soon everyone else, including the British press and many Members of Parliament, came to the same conclusion, especially a bright young Tory MP named

Benjamin Disraeli, who began a sustained campaign against Auckland in Parliament.

On arrival in Calcutta, Ellenborough was so rude to his predecessor that George wrote to his friend Hobhouse in London wondering if Ellenborough were entirely sane.[11] Auckland was left with little choice but to take most of the responsibility and return home in disgrace. His letters at this time were, understandably, full of despair. 'I have been greatly depressed,' he wrote to Hobhouse. 'I look upon our affairs in Affghanistan as irretrievable, but we must encounter further risks in the endeavour to save what may be saved from the wreck . . . I fear that we are destined to hear of more horror and disaster.'[12]

What Auckland did not understand was that the regime which he had set up in Kabul was actually by no means finished.

The British had always ignored and underestimated Shah Shuja, and now, with both Burnes and Macnaghten dead and the frozen corpses of their Kabul army feeding the vultures of the snow-clogged Ghilzai passes, Shuja himself remained safe and secure behind the high walls of the Bala Hisar. Indeed, now that his British allies were no more, the Shah's personal popularity was visibly increasing among the people and chiefs of Kabul. Without Macnaghten to give him bad advice, Shuja – as resolute as ever in the face of catastrophe – was able to demonstrate his deftness at handling Afghan tribal politics.

He now played on the jealousy felt by the two remaining original rebel leaders – Aminullah Khan Logari and Nawab Zaman Khan Barakzai – towards the recently arrived Akbar Khan, who had taken the leadership of the rebellion only after they had already defeated the British. He opened negotiations and within a few days – while Akbar was far from Kabul, first escorting his British prisoners of war to a secure fortress in Laghman, then returning to besiege Jalalabad – the Shah had managed to knit together a new

alliance which he hoped would keep him in power and leave Akbar
Khan isolated.

The two men Shuja reached out to brought very different assets
to the table. As Akbar Khan's uncle, Nawab Zaman Khan was a
senior claimant to the Barakzai succession, and controlled the valuable asset of all the British sick and wounded left in Kabul; but he
had few financial or intellectual resources and little military ability.
The elderly but still canny Naib Aminullah Khan Logari, in contrast,
had made a fortune through trade which he had recently augmented
with the large sums he managed to extract from the Hindu bankers
of Kabul on the basis of the bills given to him by the retreating British as part of their surrender. He used this to recruit a force of
sepoys as well as pay his own tribesmen from Logar. He also had
the prestige of being one of the two military leaders responsible for
so comprehensively crushing the British in Kabul. But being neither
a Sadozai nor a Barakzai, and of relatively humble origins, he was
apparently unable to come to power without the support of one or
other of the two leading clans. By allying with Nawab Zaman Khan
and Shah Shuja he was able to gain the support of both.[13] Naib
Aminullah had always been a confirmed Sadozai loyalist, while
Nawab Zaman Khan detested his charismatic cousin Akbar with all
the embittered passion that the ambitiously mediocre sometimes
feel towards those of genuine talent. The alliance looked durable as
it gave something to all three of the parties involved and each
brought something to it that the others needed.

According to his biographer Mohammad Husain Herati, Shuja
had planned the whole strategy with flawless precision. 'The
Barakzai propaganda that His Majesty had become indistinguishable from the English invaders had taken root among great and
small alike,' he wrote.

In order to counter this, and following advice that the only way out
of the present rebellion which threatened to destroy the monarchy
was to conciliate the good graces of Aminullah Khan Logari, His
Majesty decided to send his favourite and most gifted son Prince
Shahpur to the house of Aminullah. He also promised a gift of

200,000 rupees to Nawab Zaman Khan Barakzai. So it was that Aminullah and most of the other Khans now came to support His Majesty, saying that the Nawab had been elected Amir while it seemed that His Majesty was subservient to foreign and infidel interests, but now that he had regained his independence, and was once again a true Muslim monarch, there was no need for an Amir, and Zaman Khan would have to be content with the post of Wazir which was a powerful enough position. Akbar Khan was not party to this new alliance.

To give formal shape to these agreements, on 17 January 1842 Shuja's son Prince Shahpur, Aminullah Khan Logari and Zaman Khan Barakzai attended court at the Bala Hisar fort, 'together with their banners and their horsemen and those of the khans of the Durranis, the Ghilzais, the Farsi-speakers of Kohistan and Kabul, to greet His Majesty and receive his orders'. Herati added, 'From then on, the same ritual was observed every morning and evening, and His Majesty kept these newly co-opted rebels busy with promises of position, stipends and monetary rewards. Meanwhile he wrote to George MacGregor and the British commanders in Jalalabad that the situation was finally coming under control.'[14]

By the end of the first week of February, despite all the disasters of the previous three months, it was becoming increasingly clear that the apparent victory of Akbar Khan was by no means a forgone conclusion, and that Shuja still had everything to play for. Indeed, in one of the strange revivals of fortune which marked Shuja's life, he was now arguably in more direct control of his ancestral lands than he had been at any other point in his reign. Seeing the way the winds were blowing, many of the remaining Durrani and Qizilbash chiefs now cast their lot with the Shah and one by one began coming to his durbar to offer their allegiance and beg his forgiveness. 'As the new alliances grew firm,' wrote Maulana Kashmiri, 'the Shah held court and granted audience to all the Khans.'

He elevated all the high lords even higher
And showered his benevolence upon the soldiery

Kabul became free of violence and sedition
Governance was once again the business of the Shah

But he did not accord Akbar a place
The hatred in his heart had not grown cold . . .[15]

The situation was still delicate. Shuja did not yet dare leave the Bala
Hisar, and he remained dependent on the support of his two new
allies, especially the muscle of Aminullah Khan. According to Mirza
'Ata, the Shah remained a little 'suspicious, as these two Kabul chiefs
had once been partisans of Amir Dost Mohammad Khan: could they
be plotting to take his life? And now the English were said to be
approaching again, and could well attempt to re-conquer Khurasan.
Shuja was between a rock and a hard place. Nevertheless the King
had at that time some 10,000 troops, 12 cannons, uncountable treasures, and plentiful stocks of gun-powder.'[16] These figures were
probably optimistic. But for all his problems, the Shah's prospects
were now brighter than they had been for months.[17]

On 7 February, Shuja wrote in his own hand a heartfelt message
to 'my beloved son' Prince Timur who was with General Nott in
Kandahar. Mohan Lal Kashmiri, who had remained in Kabul and
so escaped the massacre, promised to get the letter through to the
British garrison there using his network of spies and runners. Shuja
opened by writing of his acceptance of the incomprehensible work-
ings of divine will represented by fate, and of the shame and sadness
he felt at what had taken place. 'Here we have had a repetition of
those scenes which the people of this place have so often enacted,'
he wrote. 'I frequently warned the English of what was coming –
but they paid no regard to me. Fate has decreed that those scenes
which I had hoped never to see again should take place. The people
of Kabul sounded a war cry against Unbelievers and even withdrew themselves from me, saying, the Shah is with the English.' He
then explained to his son that he had been forced to dissimulate in

order to survive: 'I told them: "What can the English be to me? They certainly treated me with kindness, and I was a long time a guest of the nation – but what else?" This even was unworthy of me – may God shield me from the shame I feel [for disowning my friends]. If, by the blessing of God, I should ever see you again, I will unfold to you the secrets of my heart. It was my fate to act as I have done.'

He then went on to tell Prince Timur of his hopes. 'Do not grieve,' he wrote, 'a better state of things is now in progress. Be happy and contented – we shall still attain the objects of which we have been disappointed and I shall keep a careful eye upon you. I cannot send you the particulars as I could wish, for the road is full of danger. There is much to communicate – if matters should turn out happily, and according to my heart's desire, you will know all very soon!'[18]

By now, with the rebel Afghan leadership still fractured and disunited, Shuja's letters were showing his increasing confidence. To MacGregor in Jalalabad he wrote urging a rapid British advance on Kabul – 'Not a cat belonging to you shall be injured,' he promised – before returning to his old theme of the faithlessness of the Barakzais. He particularly decried the respect that he imagined the British were still paying to his old enemy, Amir Dost Mohammad. 'I cannot think that you are possessed of a proper sense of honor,' he lectured MacGregor.

> After all that has happened, why do Dost Mahommed and his family remain there in luxury? What has been your treatment of that dog, and what return have you received from this faithless one, Mahommed Akbar? Dost Mahommed and his wives and his children, in revenge for the sahibs who have fallen in this country, should be seen wandering in destitution through the bazaars and streets of Hindustan. May God accomplish this wish of my heart! If Akbar ever falls into my power what treatment shall he receive![19]

One reason the British did not take revenge on Dost Mohammad in the manner suggested by Shuja was the very large number of prisoners of war now held by Akbar Khan.

Some were the wounded who had been left behind in Kabul; some had been given over as hostages by treaty; others had surrendered or been captured and dragged from the caves and villages where they had taken shelter. In all, around 120 Europeans had now been rounded up, of whom Akbar had collected some forty, including Lady Macnaghten and her cat (though the parakeet does not seem to have survived the retreat from Kabul), the widowed Mrs Trevor and the formidable Lady Sale and her pregnant and bereaved daughter Alexandrina.

The first few days had been the worst, as Akbar's prisoners were escorted through the snowbound passes and held in dirty mountain-top forts and remote tower houses. For several days amid 'bitterly cold' winds the hostages had had to ride over the bloody and mutilated corpses of their comrades. Occasionally they recognised close friends, such as when Mackenzie saw the remains of James 'Gentleman Jim' Skinner lying among a pile of corpses near Jagdalak, and had to ask permission to stop and dig him a shallow grave. They also passed small knots of their 'naked, wounded and frostbitten' sepoys 'huddled together . . . Alas! We could do nothing for these poor wretches, none of whom survived the next few days.'[20] It is difficult to assess whether the captive British officers could actually have done much more to save their sepoys, but rumours were soon making their way down the passes to India that the British officer class had saved their own skins while abandoning their men to slavery and death.

One fort refused to admit the prisoners, 'stating that we were Kafirs', and forced them to take shelter in 'a wretched cowshed'.[21] They forded several branches of the freezing Panjshir River 'which was not only deep but exceedingly rapid'. During one of these crossings they were ambushed by 'a body of Afghan plunderers who attacked all those who remained on the bank ... Many in despair threw themselves into the river and were drowned.'²² This was followed by the ascent of a steep pass, 'where I found it requisite to hold tight on by the mane', wrote Lady Sale, 'lest the saddle and I should slip off together'. At the top they then got caught in the middle of an inter-tribal blood feud, but after the volleys they had just experienced in the Khord Kabul this seemed almost trivial in its violence, at least to Lady Sale: 'A few jezails were fired; there was great talking and noise; and then it was over.' Soon even the smallest pleasures seemed to the hostages wild extremes of luxury. 'We enjoyed washing our faces very much,' wrote Lady Sale one morning, and 'had a grand breakfast of dal and radishes'.²³

Once they arrived at the fortress of Akbar Khan's father-in-law, however, conditions improved. In all the Afghan accounts, and in several of the Indian Muslim ones too, Akbar Khan's kindness to his prisoners is regarded as exemplary and in the epic poems he is depicted as a paragon of chivalry, a sort of Afghan Saladin, which is still how he is remembered in Kabul today. Munshi Abdul Karim's account is typical. 'When Commander Akbar's guests had somewhat recovered,' he wrote,

and were able once again to stand and move their frozen limbs, the Commander returned to the Fort to pay them a courtesy visit.

The hostages all stood in line, trembling and fearful, to express their gratitude. Commander Akbar comforted them, and, showing great respect to General Elphinstone and the Minister's widow, offered them sable-lined cloaks of cloth-of-gold, which he himself draped around their shoulders. He gave each of them a warm sheepskin poshteen and with tears in his eyes, said 'No-one can foretell, no-one can alter the decrees of fate and Divine will! The old men of Kabul in my army tell me that such extremes of snow and ice have not been seen in these parts in living memory. Have no fear – I will protect you and send you to the warmer clime of Laghman to rest and recover, until the sun enters the house of Pisces, the snows melt and the road to Hindustan will once again be open.' Commander

Akbar's exemplary behaviour, fine manners, personal modesty, and solicitous care won the universal admiration of his guests, who swore lifelong gratitude. Once the hostage guests had reached Laghman, spacious apartments were set aside for the ladies, with serving girls in attendance. Food too was generously provided: grains and meat, the fat sheeps' tails, chickens, eggs, as well as all kinds of dried and fresh fruits.[24]

What is perhaps more surprising is that while some British accounts do concentrate on the sufferings of the prisoners of war, many also commend Akbar for his care of them. Pottinger formally wrote to General Pollock to assure him 'that in the Afghan fashion, we received every attention which prisoners could expect, and that any incivility we received was from the inferior agents against the wish of Mahomed Akbar Khan who on complaint gave redress as far as lay in his power'.[25] Lawrence went further, noting that 'Akbar gave up his palanquin to Ladies Sale and Macnaghten,' that he was 'invariably most courteous', especially to Lady Macnaghten, and that he assured the ladies 'that they were his "honoured guests, that they should want nothing he could supply them with, and that as soon as the roads were safe enough he would forward them to Jalalabad; in the meantime they could write freely to their friends"'. When Lawrence told Akbar that the prisoners needed a little money he was immediately offered a thousand rupees: 'on my giving him a receipt for it, he tore it up, saying such things were only required among traders, not between gentlemen'. Later, when Lawrence complained that he had been insulted by one of the servants, 'the Sirdar had the man soundly flogged, saying that "if that was not sufficient I might have his ears if I pleased"'.[26]

There was also surprisingly widespread recognition by the hostages of the more positive qualities of the Afghans. 'There is no doubt that Afghans and Europeans get on much better than Europeans and Hindustanis,' wrote Colin Mackenzie during his captivity. 'The Afghans are an extremely hardy, bold, independent race, very intelligent with a ready fund of conversation and pleasantry which renders them very agreeable companions ... The Afghan gentlemen are extremely sensitive to courtesy, having excellent manners themselves.'[27] Vincent Eyre agreed: 'We found the Afghan gentry most agreeable travelling companions.' Lawrence found that on further acquaintance Sultan Jan, who had only a month earlier murdered his friend Captain Trevor, 'was naturally a fine-tempered man, and very fond of children'.[28]*

The prisoners were considerably less positive about some of their own number. Lady Macnaghten, who had somehow managed to save her baggage, but refused to share any of her clothes, or her sherry, remained a figure disliked by all. The Anglo-Indian Mrs Wade was more unpopular still: soon after her arrival at Laghman, she divorced her English husband and eloped with one of her captors, converting to Islam, 'adopting the costume of the Mussalmans and professing to have changed her creed ... She gave information of some plans laid by the men for their escape, which very nearly caused them all to have their throats cut ... Having reported to her Afghan paramour the manner her husband had secreted some gold mohurs in his robes, he was of course plundered of them.'[29] Most hated of all was the crabby Brigadier Shelton, who quarrelled with almost every one of the other prisoners. Even when they were all nearly killed by an earthquake on 19 February, Shelton found a way to use it as a pretext for an argument. When the earthquake struck, he happened to be sitting on a bench with Mackenzie on the flat roof of the fort:

> He looked around fiercely to see who was shaking his bench. Mackenzie cried: 'It's an earthquake Brigadier!' and, calling to

---

* These opinions should not be especially surprising or taken as examples of Stockholm Syndrome. British attitudes towards the Afghans have traditionally been both positive and admiring. Mountstuart Elphinstone thought the Afghans resembled Scottish Highlanders (see the excellent analysis of this in Ben Hopkins, *The Making of Modern Afghanistan*, London, 2008), and in the late nineteenth and early twentieth century British officers identified with the Afghans and saw their frontier fighting in terms of school playing-field athletics – attitudes which seeped into Kipling's writing. This idea of the 'noble Pashtun' is still alive and well among British forces in Afghanistan in the most recent occupation who tend to view the Afghans as 'natural fighters'. For an especially kitsch example of this trope, see the Sylvester Stallone movie *Rambo III* (1988).

Lady Sale, made for the stairs, which were cracking and falling about them, and by God's mercy, they all reached the bottom in safety. In the evening Shelton came up and said: 'Mackenzie, I want to speak to you.' 'Very well, Brigadier.' In a solemn tone, to make him feel the enormity of offence [he said]: 'Mackenzie, you went downstairs first today'; to which the latter coolly replied: 'It's the fashion in an earthquake Brigadier. I learned it among the Spaniards in Manila.'[30]

Lady Sale, meanwhile, took the earthquake with her usual spirit: 'The roof of our room fell in with a dreadful crash. The roof of the stairs fell in as I descended them; but did me no injury. All my anxiety was for Mrs Sturt; but I could only see a heap of rubbish. I was nearly bewildered, when I heard the joyful sound, "Lady Sale come here, all are safe"; and found the whole party uninjured in the courtyard ... Lady M's cat', she added, 'was buried in the ruins, but dug out again.'[31]

On that same morning, 19 February, Thomas Seaton had been sent out of the south gate of Jalalabad with a pickaxe to lead a working party.

He and his men had been ordered to destroy some ruined mud walls just outside the city. The walls had provided cover for groups of Afghan cavalry who had been harassing the foraging parties the British daily sent out to gather fodder, and Seaton was told to knock them down so as to provide a clear line of shot for the cannon on the gate and make the whole sector safer for the grass-cutting syces [grooms] and haymaking camp followers. There was some urgency to this work and Seaton had strict instructions to finish it before sundown as the British had learned from their spies that Akbar Khan and his army were now only a day's ride away from Jalalabad: having deposited his prisoners of war beyond rescue by the British – or abduction by his rivals – Akbar was now returning to finish off the remaining British presence in the country.

A little after eleven o'clock, Seaton had put down his pickaxe and was admiring the view down the valley when he felt a faint shaking beneath his feet accompanied by a low rumbling. There was a pause. Then,

> [in] an instant, the rumbling increased and swelled to the loudest thunder, as if a thousand heavy wagons were driven at speed over a rough pavement. I turned quite sick and an awful fear came over me. The ground heaved and set like the sea, and the whole plain appeared rolling in waves towards us. The motion was so violent that I was nearly thrown down and I expected every moment to see the whole town swallowed up. My eyes being attracted towards the fort, I saw that the houses, the walls and the bastions were rocking and reeling in the most terrific manner, and falling into complete ruin, while all along the south and west faces the parapets which had cost us so much labour, and had been erected with so much toil, were crumbling away like sand. The whole fort was enveloped in one immense impenetrable cloud of dust, out of which came the cries of alarm and terror from the hundreds within.

When 'the dreadful noise and quaking' had stopped, there was a deathly silence. 'The men were absolutely green with fear, and I felt myself that I was deadly pale. Looking around the valley, I saw everywhere indications of the awful visitation. Every village, town and fort was enveloped in dense clouds of dust. From some the dust was streaming away with an appearance as if the place was on fire; from others it rose high up in the air, in thick dense columns, as if a mine had been exploded.' It was evident that not a village, town or fort had escaped.

> When the breeze had cleared away the dust from Jalalabad, the place presented an awful appearance of destruction and desolation. The upper stories of the houses that a few minutes before had reared themselves above the ramparts so trim and picturesque, were all

gone, and beams, posts, doors, planks, windows, bits of walls, ends of roofs, earth and dust, all mingled together in one confused heap, were all that remained. The walls presented an equally awful appearance. The parapet all around had fallen, and was lying at the foot of the wall in heaps of rubbish. The walls were split through in many places; and the outer surfaces of many of the bastions had sheered off. A breach had been made in the eastern wall, large enough for two companies abreast to march through ... A month's cannonading with a hundred pieces of heavy artillery could not have produced the damage that the earthquake had effected in a few seconds.[32]

In the hours that followed, the chief engineer George Broadfoot took General Sale on a tour of the wrecked defences. Sale was appalled by what he saw. He wrote to Calcutta that when he had first arrived at the city two months earlier, 'I found the walls of Jalalabad in a state which might have justified despair as to the possibility of defending them.' Through sheer hard manual labour the fortress had been made secure, and 'the unremitting and almost incredible labours of the troops, aided by the zeal and science of Capt Broadfoot put the town in an efficient state of defence'. Now the defenders had to start all over again as the earthquake had destroyed 'all our parapets, injured a third of the town, made a considerable breach in the ramparts of a curtain in the Peshawar face and reduced the Cabool Gate to a shapeless mass of ruins'.[33]

There was no alternative but to draw up the entire garrison into working squads and immediately begin repairing the breaches. Even as the work was making some initial progress, 'towards sunset, a small body of horsemen from Akbar's camp came to reconnoitre. The artilleryman Augustus Abbott, who was on the look-out, sent a [cannon] shot right into the party, making them scamper off.'[34] Broadfoot muttered, 'Now is the time for Akbar!'[35]

Luckily for the defenders, it seems that the earthquake had affected the besiegers as badly as the besieged, for no more was seen of the Afghans for five crucial days. In that time, the garrison hardly slept. At dawn, wrote Seaton, 'every man in the garrison was on foot, ready to commence work as soon as it was light enough, and officers and men laboured at their appointed task with a will . . . By the evening of the 24th the bastions were repaired, the parapet built all around, and in many places double the strength it was before. The labour was terrible; and in the evenings my hands were so swelled I could scarcely close them on my knife and fork. During those four days not an officer or man took off his clothes. Everyone slept at his post on the ramparts, ready for defence if attacked, or for work at dawn of day.'[36]

Finally, on the morning of 25 February, Akbar Khan crossed the river and the plumes of his Uzbek cavalry were sighted silhouetted as they climbed the Piper's Hill to the south of the town, 'all splendidly mounted and bearing their standards, making a great show'. Minutes afterwards, the cavalry were riding down on the fleeing grass-cutters and foragers. The gates were closed and 'Afghans moved round us in great force, with increased numbers of foot soldiers'. The siege of the city now resumed in earnest, but the garrison's moment of greatest vulnerability had passed.

As in Kabul, Akbar Khan immediately took effective measures to stop supplies getting into the city, threatening all the local villagers with death if they sold food, sulphur, saltpetre or ammunition to the Firangis. Soon Seaton was recording his own growing hunger in his diary: '2nd March. All our comforts are rapidly disappearing. Tea has long been gone; coffee has disappeared today; sugar on its last legs; butter gone; there is no grass for the cows; candles not to be had; wine and spirits are a matter of memory. In a few days we shall be reduced to our rations of half a pound of salt beef and half a pound of coarse sugar, and further reductions are in prospect.' A few days later the entry read, even more ominously: 'No tiffin today; meat becoming scarce.'[37] By 23 March, Sale sent word to General Pollock in Peshawar that he could not hold out much longer: he had already destroyed all his transport camels so that what fodder there was could be given to the cavalry, and he calculated that what remained of the salt meat would run out on 4 April.[38] Ammunition for the muskets was also soon running perilously short.

Akbar again positioned himself as the champion of Islam and used his new-found reputation as a holy warrior to

draw supporters and allies, even among those who were otherwise
sceptical about his leadership. As MacGregor wrote to Pollock in
mid-March: 'He represents himself as one who has now no home,
no family, no ties and no object, but the revival of the true religion
and the extermination of its enemies.'[39] On the evening halts on his
way from Laghman to Jalalabad, Akbar used his time in camp to
send out a stream of diplomatic messages trying to rally the Afghan
nobles to his standard, using the language of the jihad in a more
direct and innovative way than he or any other Afghan had yet
done.[40] Anyone who had allied with Shah Shuja, he hinted, should
be treated as an apostate. No one would be allowed to sit on the
fence. To one noble, Saiyed Ahai-ud-Din, who had been a close
ally of the Shah, he wrote:

> Rest assured of this: if you have any apprehension in consequence
> of having been forced to form connexions with the Firangis, I beg of
> you to dismiss all fears on this account from your heart, for you
> acted as the time required. Everyone great and small has been
> obliged for the sake of his own interests to connect himself more or
> less with the Firangis. But now that the book of that hated race has
> been dispersed into wind-blown leaves, and now that the ranks of
> the Army of Islam are firmly united together, what can be the reason
> for your withdrawing yourself? I write to beseech of you that aban-
> doning all alienation, and considering my house as your home, you
> will return without delay that we may meet each other and the ties
> of friendship between us be drawn even closer. I trust you will start
> in this direction immediately.[41]

To another nobleman, Turabaz Khan, Akbar wrote an even more
explicitly religious – even mystical – appeal: he must forsake the
Kafirs and return to the fold of the true Believers. 'Intelligence was
received that you had left Lalpoora and taken refuge in the hills,' he
wrote.

> From this it would appear that your intention is to separate yourself
> from the race of Islam. My respected friend, this is the word of God

that has now come to pass. The wise and holy men of this land have during the last four happy months had wonderful dreams and seen visions showing that our Holy Prophet and the Four Friends [the first four Caliphs, or Charyar] have girded up their loins and buckled on their swords in the cause of Islam. The whole of Islam is united with one heart, and we have engaged in a war against the Infidel. The race of unbelievers have been overcome and altogether destroyed. This is not a matter of Man's judgement, but for that of God. You should be keeping your eye steadily fixed on the interests of your religion . . . Judge for yourself whether it is better that you and I should live and be respected among Mussulmans, or that we should pass our lives among Kafirs? If you desire the good of Islam consider my own house and wealth as your own, but if you continue to prefer the company of Kafirs we cannot have relations. Let me hear from you quickly.[42]

The appeal struck all the right chords: Akbar Khan's army quickly swelled as news of his growing prestige as a successful wager of the jihad spread through the mountains. Mirza 'Ata was among his many cheerleaders:

Sardar Muhammad Akbar Khan the Ghazi set about besieging the English garrison and had criers go around the countryside calling out 'Whoever is a true Muslim must obey the verse of the Qur'an: "Fight in God's way with your wealth and your own selves, that is best for you, if you but knew."' He encouraged everyone to join the struggle against the Christians. As a result of this proclamation, 2,000 enthusiastic young fighters joined his forces. When this young hero was released from detention in Bukhara and came to Kabul, he had no state or wealth. Now his treasury overflowed with plunder taken from the English, and his armouries with their muskets and powder-stores. Thousands of brave warriors followed his victorious stirrups. His plan was to capture English officers alive and to take over their treasury as he had done already in Kabul, so that he could ensure the release of his father Amir Dost Mohammad Khan from captivity in India. For two months he remained outside Jalalabad besieging the garrison and digging trenches and breastworks.[43]

By the end of March, the besiegers had successfully inched forward and brought their siege engines and stockades to within eighty yards of the city walls. No food at all was now entering the city and supplies were growing daily more depleted. All Akbar Khan lacked was good artillery to effect a breach. But in Sale he had a far more spirited opponent than any he had faced in Kabul. Every camp servant within the walls was now armed, and even the syces and camel men had been issued with home-made pikes so that they could help man the walls, especially when the garrison made sorties. If the defenders were short of ammunition they would hold up a life-size dummy with a cocked hat above the parapet to attract fire, then in the evening, when the besiegers had retired to their camp, they would go outside and collect all the spent bullets, which were then run into moulds for the use of the garrison. 'We all slept at our posts,' wrote Seaton. 'The officers merely unbuckled their swords, and perhaps changed their boots. None of us wore any uniform – these were carefully put away; but we wore clothes made of camel-hair cloth. The digging, felling, moisture, dust and mud could not hurt them and dirt did not show . . . It was not long before Akbar seemed to be awakening to the fact that his only chance of success was to starve us out.'[44]

It was therefore a major blow to the siege when, on 1 April, the defenders augmented their food supplies by successfully stealing those of their besiegers. Towards the end of March, Akbar Khan had decided to try to deprive the garrison of what little fodder remained by driving his flocks of sheep, under cavalry escort, over the meadows of the foraging grounds in an attempt to remove all remaining grass. With the siege daily tightening its grip, the shepherds grew so confident that, on 31 March, they brought their flocks to within 400 yards of the crest of the glacis. At sunset, the hungry defenders were forced 'to watch these perambulating chops and legs of mutton vanish in the distance'. But the following day, Sale was ready for them.

The cavalry had been ordered to mount at dawn, and were silently waiting along with 650 infantry, some volunteer pikemen and a diversionary force of Broadfoot's sappers. As soon as the sheep came within range, the sappers were sent out by the north gate and began firing at the enemy breastworks to draw the attention of the besiegers. Meanwhile, the south gate was quietly thrown open and the cavalry dashed out. The Afghan shepherds and their escort both fled, and the troopers quickly rounded up the sheep and drove them into the city over the drawbridge. The entire manoeuvre took no more than ten minutes. By the time the Afghan cavalry had appeared both sheep and soldiers were safely back within the walls. 'We were all in the highest spirits,' wrote Seaton in his diary that night after a celebratory dinner of roast lamb. 'When the enemy danced with rage, they were saluted with shouts of laughter and "Baa-Baa!" from along the walls. We took four hundred and eighty one sheep and a few goats, which gave sixteen days' meat for the garrison, at three-quarters ration . . . On the 3rd a spy came in and told us that when Akbar learned that we had captured his sheep, he burst into such a transport of fury, that his people were afraid to go near him.'[45]

Shortly after this, Akbar suffered a more serious reverse. He had spent the day leading an attack on the city, and in the evening had retired to the camp to welcome a new group of Khajrani tribal levies who had just appeared to offer their services. After welcoming the new arrivals, according to the reports forwarded to the British by a sympathetic Afghan chieftain,

Sardar Akbar Khan who had not eaten during the day stood up and moved a few paces to one side to eat his dinner which had been brought to him, and to look on while the Khajranis made their approach to attack the defences of Jalalabad. While standing he received a serious wound from a double barrelled gun which struck him on the fleshy part of the arm and passed through his breast. Two men were seized and charged with having done this act. One of them had previously been Shah [Shuja's] Pishkhidmat [table servant]. They pleaded that the gun had gone off by accident. The Sirdar

is confined to his seat and no one but [his father-in-law] Mohammad Shah Khan Ghilzai is allowed to go near him; his troops are
much dispirited.[46]

Afghan sources all assume that the shooting was an attempted assassination. Mirza 'Ata reported rumours that the British were behind it.
'General Sale was using all means to oust the Sardar from his position,
to no effect,' he wrote. 'So at last he managed to have one of the
Sardar's trusted personal attendants offered two lakh (200,000 Rupees)
to murder him. The wretch sold his faith and honour and accepted the
money, and waited for an opportunity to shoot the Sardar. Even
though the shot wounded Akbar Khan in the shoulder, God was
protecting the Ghazi, and he did not die.'[47]

Most observers, however, blamed the Sadozais. According to
Fayz Mohammad,

some of those present immediately grabbed the ingrate responsible
and after dressing Akbar's wound they brought the servant before
the wounded Sardar who reproached him and demanded an explanation. The man expressed repentance, kissed the ground, and
produced a letter from Shah Shuja offering Rs 50,000 for the assassination. He revealed that the Shah and the English had given him
25,000 rupees up front, and the promise of another 25,000 after the
job was done. The Sardar kept Shah Shuja's letter and, since the man
had spoken truthfully, forgave him. But the ghazis summoned him
and another man who was a co-conspirator and killed them both.[48]

This seems to have been the case: according to the report that
reached the hostages from their jailers, the would-be assassin was
'roasted alive for his crime'.[49]

Akbar was not the only one under pressure as March turned to
April. In Kabul, Shuja's new alliance was now under threat as his

two newly co-opted allies, Aminullah Khan Logari and Nawab Zaman Khan, both began jostling for power and control over the city's resources. By mid-March their household troops had fought a pitched battle in the streets over the right to collect revenues from Customs House and the city mint.[50]

More threateningly, Shuja's credentials as a Muslim leader were now being questioned thanks to the success of Akbar Khan's overtly Islamic call to arms. 'Akbar Khan sent letters to the people of the surrounding regions,' wrote Fayz Mohammad,

> and incited them with the message, 'If the Shah is dealing honestly with the people of Islam, has no love for the English, and is discharging the duties of state and religion in your best interests, you should call for him to proclaim jihad so that united we may all attack the English and rid the country of their existence.' The Sardar kept repeating to the people the call for jihad until scholars and their students, at his instructions, placed Qur'ans kept at the tombs of saints on their heads and went among the people, village by village and hamlet by hamlet, and got prayer leaders and muezzins to begin to exhort their people to jihad. In large groups and small, people gathered at the gates of the Shah's palace and clamoured for him to proclaim a holy struggle. They cried out, 'Let us drive the English out of the country!'[51]

This put the Shah in an extremely awkward position. Publicly, he had been forced to disown his British patrons and had declared in durbar that he would work to annihilate the infidel.[52] Privately, he still felt beholden to the British and believed he needed their help to defeat the Barakzais; for this reason he sent a stream of letters to MacGregor begging him to send British troops to Kabul as soon as possible, and asking with increasing desperation when he might expect them. As Mohammad Husain Herati put it,

> His Majesty temporized, promising to send messengers to persuade the English to leave voluntarily but in reality to seek to reassure them of his continuing loyalty: first his private secretary Inayatullah Khan

Bamizai, then his personal servant Din Muhammad Khan were sent. On the third occasion His Majesty wrote secretly: 'How are we to escape the pressure of these scheming dishonest Barakzais and the turbulent folk of Kabul?' MacGregor wrote back that His Majesty should hold out in Kabul for another two weeks, as reinforcements were on their way from Peshawar. His Majesty invented one excuse after another, and so hung on for a whole two months but still no help came.[53]

Given his past, Shuja's lingering pro-British sympathies were still widely suspected in Kabul, and many of the chiefs correctly believed that he was dissimulating. 'Because of his stalling,' recorded the *Siraj ul-Tawarikh*, 'the Barakzai began to say publicly, "Shah Shuja is an English-lover. Don't be misled by his words, which contradict his deeds. If this is not true, why hasn't he started for Jalalabad and why haven't the English left yet, in conformity with the documents he sent them?"'[54] As March progressed, and stories of Akbar's bravery in Jalalabad began to circulate in Kabul, more and more of Shuja's supporters, including his principal ally and Naib, Aminullah Khan Logari, urged him to show his commitment to the cause by marching immediately on Jalalabad, or at the very least to send one of his sons in his place.[55]

Placed in an impossible dilemma, and not wishing to give the British reasons to distrust him, Shuja bribed several of the chiefs to go ahead without him. On 2 March, Prince Timur was ordered off to Jalalabad, but never got any further than Butkhak at the mouth of the Khord Kabul.[56] On the 18th, Aminullah Khan and the Barakzais came to the Bala Hisar and at durbar publicly called upon the Shah to come out of his fortress and lead 8,000 men to join Akbar Khan in his fight against the infidels.[57] Maulana Hamid Kashmiri has the Barakzais compare Shuja's duplicitous diplomacy to Akbar Khan's fearless waging of war:

> One day, a group of chiefs and generals
> Gained access to the Shah's audience chamber

They said to him: 'O Renowned Padshah!
What will you do? Tell us!

You hold your position of royal command
Because we are firm in our pledge of service

We believed you would defend the country
That you would command and protect the rule of law

So tell us what grievous wrong has Akbar committed?
That you have girded your loins for his destruction?

Except that he made you King in this land
And rendered the forces of evil crippled and helpless

Instead of raising him high
You seek to throw him low

You have delegated the task of killing him
To certain men and faithless vermin

Night and day you wear out your pen
Writing letters to our enemies . . .'[58]

On 3 April, the pressure on Shuja was increased still further when the head of the Kabul 'ulema, Mir Haji, the elder brother of the recently killed Mir Masjidi, took up the call for holy war as well, and in his Friday sermons goaded Shuja to lead an Islamic army against the Kafirs. 'The treacherous and hypocrite Mir Haji', as Mohan Lal called him, 'pitched his tent on the way to Jalalabad and sent the criers to proclaim in the city that he was going on a religious war and whoever being Mussalman will not march with him, shall be considered an infidel.'[59] He then set off leading a long procession of 'wild fakirs carrying alam battle standards and Holy Qur'ans and sacred relics from the shrines, chanting prayers in a vast procession, all heading to Jalalabad. It may have been the merest political manipulation,' commented Herati, 'but His Majesty realised that unless he went with them a new revolt would break out in Kabul.'[60]

The situation was now critical. That night Nawab Zaman Khan sent his wife to the palace with a sealed Qur'an to assure Shuja of his fidelity. 'His wife begged the Shah to march fearlessly along with the Barakzais to Jalalabad and said that her husband will promote the cause and stand by His Majesty as a loyal servant. On considering the proclamations made by Mir Haji and having been insisted upon by all the Chiefs to march against Jalalabad, the Shah was obliged finally to send out his tent and consented to proceed with them.'[61]

The royal campaign tent was duly pitched at Siyah Sang on the Jalalabad road. 'I scarcely believe he will ever march,' wrote an anxious Mohan Lal to Jalalabad, 'and if he does he will either be murdered or blinded by the Barakzais.'[62] For one week more the Shah remained within the Bala Hisar, anxiously waiting to hear if General Pollock had yet managed to bring his army up the Khyber. 'It is nearly one month that I have delayed sending troops to Jalalabad,' he wrote in desperation to MacGregor. 'But during this time no letters have been received from you. I know almost nothing of your intentions. If the British troops arrive within the next ten or fifteen days it is well, but the sooner the better. If not what ought to be done? This is not a matter to be trifled with. Whatever you think advisable, write to me plainly that it may be well understood and arrangements made.'

He added: 'I have made myself unpopular with all Mahomedans on your account yet you have not comprehended this. Please understand. They say that I wish to destroy the true faith. This is an affair affecting life and death ... God deliver me.'[63]

Major-General George Pollock was not a man who liked to be rushed. His reputation had been built on careful planning and meticulous logistics, and following the catastrophe of the slaughter of the Kabul army in January he was all the more determined not to be bullied into acting a single moment before he was ready. Sir Jasper Nicholls, the Commander-in-Chief in Calcutta, was entirely behind him in this, writing to London that 'It was as well that a cool, cautious officer of the Company's army' should have the command. 'Any precipitancy on the part of a general officer panting for fame might now have the worst effect.'[64]

Pollock had arrived in Peshawar on 5 February to find morale at rock bottom and many of the sepoys hospitalised: no fewer than 1,800 were on the sick list, and as the trickle of frostbitten survivors of the retreat limped and crawled into Peshawar with their stories of defeat and desertion by their officers, the atmosphere grew increasingly mutinous. Pollock knew he had to turn this around and immediately set about reassuring the sepoys. His first action was to issue worsted gloves and stockings to keep them from the cold. 'I shall visit the hospitals frequently,' he explained to Nicholls, 'and by adding in any way to their comforts, show that I feel an interest in them.' Soon the numbers of sick were decreasing by the day, and the atmosphere in the camp visibly improving.

Over the following two months, as more regiments and supply wagons arrived, he slowly assembled his forces and his provisions, riding out every day with his field glass to study the elaborate defences and stone sangars the Afridis were building across the Khyber to block his advance. He had calculated that he needed around 275,000 rounds of ammunition in order to bring his force up to 200 rounds per man, and these had all arrived by mid-March. Following desertions by his camel drivers he delayed another fortnight until he had the transport capacity he needed. He also wrote to Ferozepur requesting one more regiment of cavalry and several more traps of horse artillery. Meanwhile, to the increasingly desperate Sale in Jalalabad he wrote: 'Your situation is never out of my mind . . . Necessity alone has kept me here. Pray therefore tell me, without the least reserve, the latest day you can hold out.' Sale replied in a message written in rice water, visible only with the application of iodine, that his last supplies of salt meat would run out on 4 April.[65]

The camels, cavalry and artillery finally arrived on 29 March. That evening Pollock gave orders to break camp and move to the fort of Jamrud at the mouth of the Khyber. A week later, at 3.30 a.m. on 5 April, he ordered his troops to advance silently through the darkness, in three columns, up the defiles of the Khyber. By sunrise, the Afridis found that Pollock's sepoys were crowning the heights on either side of their stone sangar. By midmorning, the tribesmen had abandoned all their carefully erected defences and were in headlong retreat. By 2 p.m., Pollock's central column had taken the fortress of Ali Masjid and were already regrouping, ready to head on to relieve Jalalabad.[66]

The same morning that Pollock's sepoys were storming their way up the Khyber, Shah Shuja finally gave up on his British allies. Having heard nothing from MacGregor in reply to his last and most desperate note, the Shah decided he now had no option but to leave the shelter of his fortress and head off to Jalalabad.

He had spent a sleepless night 'restlessly walking up and down, calling on God, and constantly asking the eunuch servants what time of the night it was'. He then performed his ablutions, said goodbye to his wives and packed a small travelling pouch with the pick of his remaining reserves of diamonds, rubies and emeralds. 'At the first glimmer of true dawn, His Majesty prayed the two prostrations of the customary prayer in his private apartments in the fort, intending to pray the remaining obligatory two prostrations at the Siyah Sang camp. He mounted his palanquin and urged the porters to move quickly so as not to be late for the main prayer in camp. His Majesty was accompanied by only a minimal escort of personal servants.'[67]

The previous day, 4 April, Shuja had left the Bala Hisar for the first time since the outbreak of the rebellion on 2 November. He rode out to his tent at the Siyah Sang, and there he held a review of the troops and a public audience for the Kabul nobles. It was at this

audience that he formally announced his departure for Jalalabad
and appointed his favourite son, Prince Shahpur, as governor of
Kabul during his absence. Nasrullah, the eldest son of Aminullah
Khan Logari, was appointed Shahpur's acting chief minister.
According to Mirza 'Ata, the Shah brought with him '200,000
Rupees in cash and several bolts of double shawl cloth with which
to honour the Kabul chiefs, each according to his rank and merit.
He especially favoured Naib Aminullah Khan Logari who had
become his closest confidant. Shuja then mounted his palanquin
with his son and returned to spend a last night with his harem in
the Bala Hisar Fort.'[68]

Unbeknown to Shuja, however, this action of publicly honouring
Aminullah Khan had been interpreted as a deliberate insult to his
other principal ally, Nawab Zaman Khan Barakzai. He and Naib
Aminullah Khan were now barely on speaking terms, and the public
demonstration of the Shah's closeness to Aminullah at the Siyah
Sang durbar had caused huge offence in the camp of the Nawab,
who was from by far the grander lineage. 'Zaman Khan was a great
lord with many fighters in his retinue,' wrote Mirza 'Ata,

> while Aminullah Khan Logari had recently merely been one of his
> attendants. At the durbar Nawab Zaman Khan and others close to
> Amir Dost Mohammad Khan had received no cloaks of honour
> from the King and indeed were quite passed over in the gaze of
> royal favour. This change in fortune did not sit well with the Nawab.
> Had the King seen fit to bestow his favours more equitably, the
> hidden discord might have been healed rather than enflamed. But
> the Nawab and his followers were seething with rage and pique at
> the King's taking no notice of them.

Most upset of all was Shuja' al-Daula, Zaman Khan's eldest son,
'who . . . had received his name from his godfather [Shah Shuja's]
own lips' and at whose birth the Shah had been present.

> Shuja' al-Daula, whose name means bravery or valour, a name
> which influenced his character, complained thus to his father: 'That

THE DEATH OF A KING

Aminullah Khan Logari was a mere servant of ours. He and those other minor chiefs with no solid base in society, they have now received all the King's favours, all the honourable appointments. Meanwhile we have been passed over, all our services to the crown and sacrifices for the cause forgotten: we look on dry-lipped, receiving no sign of gratitude, while the others get all the praise. I'm going to kill him if ever I am able to do so!' In spite of his father remonstrating that now was not the moment and that it was the time to concentrate on fighting the English, the boy took no notice and planned to ambush the King as he came from the fort to the army camping ground in the morning. Before dawn, he hid with 15 gunmen until the royal cavalry escort approached.

As Shah Shuja's party headed down the corkscrewing road from the Bala Hisar, the Nawab's son appeared and hailed his god-father's palanquin. The carriers paused and put down the palanquin. The Shah peered out of the curtains, and at that moment the waiting gunmen opened fire. The bloodied figure of Shuja stumbled out and tried to limp away across the fields. The assassins were already making off from the scene of the crime when one of them spotted the Shah and shouted to his employer to finish the job properly. 'So Shuja' al-Daula gave chase and pounced on the prostrate monarch, stabbing him pitilessly with his sword, shouting "Give me that cloak of honour now!" He stripped the dead King of his jewels and golden arm-band, belt and sword – all worth some one million Rupees. The King's gentle body, bred to rest on soft cushions of fine wool and velvet, was now dragged by the feet on rough stony ground and dumped in a ditch.'[69]

'That blameless monarch', commented Herati,

was martyred between two prayers, all the while repeating the holy names of God in his dawn litany, while the foul murderers earned only eternal damnation! Shahnawaz, one of His Majesty's attendants, tried to resist and wounded two of the assassins, but then seeing that the place was empty and abandoned, and that the travelling case of jewels was unattended, grabbed it and rushed towards the fort. He hid it in a crack in an old wall, intending to retrieve it at a later stage and sell the contents. But his actions were observed and so it was that the jewels fell into the hands of the murderer Shah Shuja and his father Nawab Zaman Khan.

Alas for that monarch, who once walked the avenues of the royal gardens but never picked the flowers of his hopes and ambitions! Instead he remained lying in blood and dust, unburied in the open plain. He died on the 23rd of the month of Safar, fixing his permanent abode in the kingdom of heaven. 'For we belong to God and to Him we return!'[70]

Prince Shahpur hastened at once to the Bala Hisar fort to protect the royal women and children. The body of his father was left to lie where it fell for twenty-four hours, while the Sadozais barred the gates of the fort and gathered together, with the old blind Zaman Shah taking charge, as they tried to work out a strategy to save their position and seek revenge on the murderers. 'Meanwhile the Barakzais shouted out their gleeful congratulations, and Mir Haji promptly returned from his pretended jihad with his battle standards announcing, "We've sent the greater Lord [Shah Shuja] to join the lesser Lord [Macnaghten]." All were congratulating each other, saying "Now we've uprooted these infidel foreigners from our country!"'[71]

Only one man saw it as his duty to attend to the corpse of the murdered Shah. Shuja's faithful water carrier, Mehtar Jan Khan Ishaqzai, who had followed Shuja into exile in Ludhiana, returned to the corpse late that night and remained next to it, guarding it from mutilation. The following morning he and another old retainer of the Shah's, 'Azim Gol Khan, the 'Arz-begi, helped prepare the corpse for burial. Working alone, the two men dug a shallow grave inside a ruined mosque near the place of the murder. This they covered with earth, and placed the King's palanquin on top. They also raised a small cairn of stones to mark the place of the murder.

Later that summer, the stones and the bloodstained palanquin were still lying where the two loyal retainers had left them.[72]

At the beginning of the twentieth century, the historian Fayz Mohammad was told that Shah Shuja Sadozai had eventually been laid to rest in the magnificent Mughal-style mausoleum of his father, Timur Shah. That may well be the case, and it seems probable that his sepulchre is one of three male graves in the basement of that building; but if so the grave remains unmarked, a measure of the Shah's standing in Afghanistan today.

Even in his own time, the victorious Barakzai view of the struggle between the two clans dominated the way the Afghans wrote about the war, not least because they were patronising the poets who did the writing. Maulana Hamid Kashmiri, for example, puts into the mouth of the Shah's assassin a speech which he shouts at the dying Shuja and which represents the Barakzai position on Shuja's legacy: 'O cruel tyrant!' he taunts. 'When were you ever Shah that you call yourself so?' And he adds:

'The country that bestowed upon you this title of Shah
You have destroyed by casting a shadow of doom

Drunk like a maddened elephant
You aided and abetted the Firangi forces

Devastation came to Ghazni and Kabul
Into every home reached the hand of oppression

You turned the land of Islam into the land of infidels
You made the marketplace of infidelity brisk and vigorous

Your outer garb is like that of holy pilgrims in Mecca
But within, you thirsted for the blood of Muslims

You killed many brothers of mine
And now you say that I am murdering you?

I am extracting blood vengeance by law
With the blood of your throat I will wash you clean of blood.'[73]

It is certainly true that the Shah was a deeply flawed man and made many errors of judgement. He was rarely an impressive leader in war and his arrogance and hauteur alienated potential followers throughout his career; as William Fraser noted soon after he crossed the frontier into British India for the first time in 1816, he was indeed 'very Ultra-Royal in his wishes and expectations'.[74] This belief derived from Shuja's essentially Timurid view of his own kingship: as he wrote to Lord Bentinck in 1834, he believed himself to be 'under the special protection of God'.[75]

Yet, for all this, Shuja was a remarkable man: highly educated, intelligent, resolute and above all unbreakable. Throughout his life he was fated to suffer desperate and repeated reverses, often for reasons quite outside his own control, but he never gave up nor ever gave way to despair. 'Lose no hope when faced with hardships,' he wrote in his youth while on the run after the blinding and deposition of his brother. 'Black clouds soon give way to clear rain.'[76] This optimism remained a strength throughout his life. Observers constantly remarked on his 'grace and dignity', even in the most adverse circumstances.[77] The British called him ineffectual, and Burnes in particular mocked him as the man who lost the kingdom of his ancestors; but when the moment of crisis came at the outbreak of rebellion in November 1841, Shuja was the only figure in Kabul to offer an effective military response, and the only person who made any attempt to save Burnes, even though Burnes had always done his best to humiliate him.

Shuja was always unusual for his honourable loyalty to his allies and his faithfulness to his agreements, in a region not known for either. This was one reason he never forgave the Barakzais for breaking the arrangement made between his grandfather, Ahmad Shah Abdali, and Dost Mohammad's grandfather, Haji Jamal Khan, that the Sadozais would rule as King, with the Barakzais as their faithful servants. He saw himself as the true heir to a highly cultured Persian-speaking Safavid and Timurid civilisation, and as well as writing fine verse and prose himself was a generous patron to poets and scholars, as Mountstuart Elphinstone discovered to his surprise when he spent time in Shuja's court in 1809. His vision of his kingdom was one which saw it not as an isolated and mountainous backwater but instead as tied by alliances to a wider world, and which through the common Persianate civilisation was diplomatically, culturally and economically integrated with the other countries of the region. It was sadly not a vision that shows much sign, even today, of being realised, though the idea has never completely died.

Shuja's reign was brought down not by his own faults but by the catastrophic mishandling of the invasion and occupation of Afghanistan as managed by Auckland and Macnaghten, and as lost by General Elphinstone. This left him in the unenviable position of being distrusted and used by the British, while being seen across the country as the Kafir's puppet. Yet the uprising of 1841 was a rebellion not against Shah Shuja but specifically against the British; indeed it is clear from the Afghan sources that many of the participants saw themselves as rescuing the Shah from the gilded cage into which it was believed the British had locked him for their own ends. The rebels even offered Shuja the leadership of their struggle, and only began opposing him when he refused to disown his British patrons. The rebellion only became a Sadozai–Barakzai power struggle much later on with the arrival of Akbar Khan. When Akbar Khan left Kabul for Jalalabad, the allegiance of many nobles reverted to the Shah. Throughout, Shuja remained surprisingly popular, and outlived almost all those who had been involved in the fiasco: not just Burnes and Macnaghten and the rest of the Kabul army, but even the man who took his most precious possession, Ranjit Singh.

Shuja's greatest mistake was to allow himself to become too dependent on the troops of his incompetent British patrons. He should have insisted on the return of all British forces immediately after his installation in 1839, for as the most perceptive of the British observers of Afghanistan, Charles Masson, noted at the time, 'the Afghans had no objection to the match, only the manner of the wooing'.[78] As his renewed popularity after the exit of the British in 1842 showed, there were still great reserves of support for the Sadozai monarchy if he had only had the confidence to rely on it. Instead, he remained for ever hitched to his unpopular allies, and it was his unwillingness to sever his links with the British that was in the end his undoing.

As a result, Shuja's turbulent life ended, as so much of it had been lived, in failure. His premature death left behind him no legacy for his successors: as Maulana Hamid Kashmiri put it, his sons and grandsons were now 'like a flock out to pasture with no shepherd'. Although after the Kabul army was massacred it briefly seemed as if the revival of the Sadozais might be possible, on his death his sons and his blind brother Shah Zaman were left in a hopeless situation, with little chance of consolidating the power of his dynasty. As Herati noted, for the Sadozais 'the day now turned to blackest night . . . His Majesty was 65 years of age when he was murdered: he had tasted the triumphs and misfortunes of a long life, and had learned to distrust his fickle subjects. Shah Shuja' al-Mulk of noble lineage would never have disgraced himself by ingratitude for their years of hospitality, but the repeated wrong choices made by Macnaghten compromised him beyond hope of recovery.'[79]

Shuja's death did not, however, bring the end of the killing, nor the end of the war. For even as Shuja's corpse was lying in the Kabul dust, Pollock's Army of Retribution was marching for Jalalabad and, as Lady Sale had already heard from her anxious jailers, it was taking no prisoners and giving no quarter.[80]

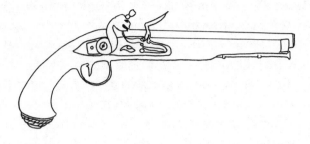

10

A War for No Wise Purpose

On the evening of 6 April 1842, Akbar Khan's artillery around Jalalabad thundered into life and blazed out a series of rolling salutes. All night the guns continued, accompanied – so the garrison could hear from the walls – by the sounds of celebration, music and dancing from beyond the far side of the siege works.

The salutes had been ordered by Akbar Khan to celebrate the death of Shuja and the mortal blow which the Barakzais had just inflicted on their Sadozai rivals and blood-enemies. Within the walls of the besieged city, however, the gun-salutes were assumed to have a quite different meaning. The garrison knew that Pollock was about to attempt the difficult feat of taking the Khyber Pass by force, and supposed the victory salutes were to celebrate his defeat. A false report from a British informer confirmed the error, adding incorrectly that Akbar Khan had just sent reinforcements to the pass to help wipe out what was left of Pollock's force.

Sale had made all his calculations for the defence of Jalalabad around the certainty that Pollock was imminently coming to his rescue. Now, with his ammunition nearly expended and only 500 sheep left to feed the defenders, Sale believed he had few options left. Plunged into deep gloom, he allowed himself to be persuaded by his younger officers to risk everything in a last desperate attempt to break out, even though the garrison was by then outnumbered at least three to one by Akbar's huge army of Ghilzai and Shinwari tribal levies. A Council of War was summoned where 'each gave his opinion that if they must perish, it would be better to die like men, with arms in their hands', as the Rev. G. R. Gleig put it. 'They were about to throw their last die and engage in their final battle; for, let it terminate how it might, there would not remain for them musket ammunition enough to try the fortune of another. It was necessary, therefore, that their victory should not only be sure, but complete; so complete as to open for them a free passage to the head of the Khyber – and perhaps beyond it.'[1]

That evening, a simple strategy was thrashed out. The wounded soldiers and the camp followers with their home-made pikes would man the defences, while every last able-bodied soldier would be divided into one of three columns. The columns would all 'march direct upon Akbar's camp, burn it, drive him into the river, and bring off his guns'.[2] There was no alternative plan in case of failure.

The following day, in the chilly pre-dawn glimmer of 7 April, the city gates were thrown open, and for the first time since they arrived in late December the entire garrison marched out. Sale had expected to surprise the defenders, but word of the General's gamble had somehow leaked out and, as the sun rose over the mountains to the east of Jalalabad, the troops saw that Akbar Khan, far from being taken by surprise, had formed his entire army into battle order 'and they were turning out in their thousands'.[3]

Firing began immediately. The first casualties were inflicted on the westernmost column, which was commanded by the long-bearded Baptist teetotaller Henry Havelock. Akbar launched all his cavalry at Havelock. As 'large masses of horse' closed in, Havelock coolly ordered the column into a square and repulsed the attack, inflicting heavy losses on the circling horsemen. 'I felt throughout that Lord Jesus was at my side,' wrote Havelock later. Havelock's men had become rather bored of his sermons during the siege; they were, however, deeply impressed by their commander's almost mystical sangfroid in battle. 'He was as calm under fire as if he stood in a drawing room full of ladies,' one wrote afterwards.[4]

Throughout the battle, the column was skilfully supported by the artillery from the city walls. This was something the Kabul defenders had never properly achieved but here, as in earlier battles during the campaign, accurate and effective cannonfire made a crucial difference against armies of Afghan tribesmen unused to grapeshot and modern explosive shells. Moreover the flat plains of Jalalabad favoured the British style of disciplined infantry warfare and did not allow the Afghans to bring into play the mountain guerrilla tactics that had proved so devastating in the passes. It was clear almost immediately that, after six months, the tables were now turning in favour of the British.

There was a brief halt in the advance as Sale ordered his second-in-command, William Dennie, to assault one of the small mud forts that lay between the city and Akbar's camp; in the confusion Dennie – the man who had led the assault on Kandahar in 1839 and defeated Dost Mohammad at Bamiyan a year later – was shot dead as he rushed through the fort gate at the head of his men. But the advance continued unchecked. As Akbar's lines drew closer, and the Afghan guns opened up on the columns, the infantry broke into a run, then charged with fixed bayonets. Among those in the lead was Thomas Seaton. 'The columns were soon well up to the camp,' he wrote.

We made a rush at it, and carried it without a check, the enemy flying through the grove of trees beyond. We saw large numbers of them throw themselves into the river which, swollen and rapid, destroyed the greatest portion of them. The enemy's horse hung about for some time, but our cavalry and guns making a demonstration against them they moved off, going along the banks of the stream. The whole of Akbar's camp fell into our hands. His guns,

ammunition, standards, plunder – everything he had with him. The
bugle soon recalled our skirmishers, and I detached with a party to
fire the tents, and the huts made of boughs and reeds. They were
very numerous, and the smoke of the burning proclaimed our
victory to the whole valley. Numbers of camels and mounds of
grain fell into our hands . . . In spite of the woeful mistake made in
attacking the enemy's outpost [where Dennie had been killed] our
loss was surprisingly small, amounting to only eleven men killed.[5]

It was all over by 7 a.m. The beaten and wounded Afghan besiegers
were soon streaming back towards Gandamak, and by midday the
British commissariat staff were already busy moving large quantities of captured grain, powder, shells and shot into the city, as well
as 'a lot of fowls which were flying about loose'. 'Never was a
victory so complete,' wrote a gleeful Gleig. 'Akbar and the wreck
of his army fled towards Kabul, and all the chiefs of the districts in
the other direction sent in their submission.'[6]

When Pollock's relief force finally marched into sight, nine days
later, the garrison was able to ride out to escort them in. The Army
of Retribution, expecting to see 'long beards, haggard faces and
tattered garments' found instead the defenders 'all fat and rosy, in
the highest health, scrupulously clean shaven and dressed as neatly
as if quartered in the best regulated cantonment in India. We on the
contrary, the relieving army, presented the strongest contrast to all
this . . . Our coats and trousers were torn and dirty, our lips and
faces blistered by the sun.'[7]

As Pollock's force streamed into the city, they were pointedly
piped in to the strains of the old Jacobite air, 'Oh, But Ye've Been
Lang a'Coming'.

General Pollock, as ever, was not to be rushed. His progress was as
methodical, and as ruthlessly violent, as ever.

While he was consolidating his hold on the Khyber, Pollock's sepoys had begun the process of taking revenge for earlier Afghan atrocities by decapitating the dead Afridis they had killed and carrying 'the heads into camp in triumph, stuck on the points of their bayonets'. There were also a number of Afridi women among the dead.* When one of Pollock's officers, Lieutenant Greenwood, remonstrated with the sepoys responsible, one of them replied simply, 'Sahib I have lost twelve brethren in this accursed pass, and I would happily bayonet a Kyberee a month old at his mother's breast.'[8]

Pollock showed little sign of wishing to restrain such tendencies and, as his force headed on towards Jalalabad, villages deemed hostile were torched as the Army of Retribution passed by. In one hamlet, where some plundered British property and the uniforms of some murdered soldiers had been discovered, the entire village was methodically reduced to rubble. 'The destruction of Ali Boghan', explained Pollock nonchalantly in his next despatch, 'was caused by one of those sudden bursts of feeling against which, being wholly unexpected, no precautions were considered necessary.'[9]

On arrival at Jalalabad, Pollock paused again. While there were many in the garrison who wished him to pursue the fleeing Akbar Khan to Kabul without delay, Pollock was determined to leave nothing to chance. He felt that since the garrison had already eaten all their camels he did not have enough baggage animals to carry adequate supplies forward; in his view at least 9,000 new camels needed to be found before he could move forward to retake Kabul.[10]

Moreover, it was still unclear how far the new Governor General would authorise him to proceed, and there were increasing signs that the once hawkish Ellenborough was getting cold feet. Anxious about the empty treasury in Calcutta, Ellenborough began sending messages to Pollock and Nott maintaining that, now Jalalabad had been relieved and Akbar Khan defeated, they must begin winding-up operations and prepare to return to India, if necessary leaving the hostages and prisoners of war to their fate. The garrisons of Jalalabad and Kandahar could not believe that they were being

---

* These women may have been water carriers (saqau), a traditional role for Pashtun women during battle.

forbidden to retake Kabul now that they had Akbar on the run. 'There seems to be some falability [sic] attending us in this country,' wrote Broadfoot when he heard the news. 'A vigorous advance on the Capital *now* would be certainly victorious and would almost as certainly lead to the entire submission of the Country . . . [But] the General has not instructions of any kind whatever from the government, and even if he could go on must halt from ignorance of the wishes of the Supreme authorities.'[11]

In Kandahar, Rawlinson – who was still agitating to have the whole of Afghanistan annexed to British India – was aghast when he read that Kandahar was now to be abandoned, along with the rest of the country. 'The peremptory order to retire has come upon us like a thunderclap,' he wrote. General Nott was even more frustrated that his moment of triumph was to be taken from him. 'The people in power are all mad,' he wrote to his daughters.

> Either that, or Providence hath blinded them for some wise purpose. I am very, very tired of working, tired of this country, and quite tired of the folly of my countrymen . . . My soldiers are four months in arrears; there is not one rupee in the Kandahar treasury, and no money can be borrowed. I have no medicine for the sick and wounded, I have no carriage cattle for the troops, nor money to buy or hire, and but little ammunition. I have been calling for all these for six months and not the least aid has been given to me . . . How I do long to be in some nice spot in Australia![12]

Unwilling to retreat, Generals Pollock and Nott both dragged their feet and sent to Ellenborough a long succession of excuses why they could not withdraw – the weather, lack of transport, money and so on – while they got the hawks in India and at home to lobby Ellenborough to change his mind. 'It is impossible to press upon you too strongly', wrote an all-too-willing Duke of Wellington to the Governor General, 'the notion of the importance of the restoration of reputation in the East.'[13] Pollock made the same point in a succession of letters to Calcutta, emphasising that 'with regard to our withdrawal at the present moment, I fear it would have the very worst effect; it would be construed into a defeat, and our character as a powerful nation would be entirely lost in this part of the world'.[14] Realising that he would be accused of throwing away an opportunity of freeing Akbar Khan's hostages and salvaging Britain's military reputation, Ellenborough began looking for a way to reverse his position.

While he waited for Ellenborough to let him off his leash, Pollock kept himself busy revenging himself on those Afghans within his reach. He sent out punitive parties to cow the tribes of the Jalalabad valley, 'unroofing a few villages ... and burning everything combustible'.[15] One brigade was sent south into the Shinwari country, to burn all the forts and villages and fell the trees. One day alone, thirty-five forts were set ablaze. Another brigade under the artilleryman Augustus Abbott was sent towards Gandamak to punish the villagers who had massacred the last survivors of the 44th Foot. 'We destroyed all the vineyards,' he later recorded, 'and cut deep rings around trees of two centuries' growth.* Their forts and houses were destroyed; their walls blown up and their beautiful trees left to perish. The retribution was thorough and enduring in its effects. It is lamentable to see the mischief done, but the example was quite necessary.'[16]

MacGregor, the Political Officer with the force, also wrote approvingly of the brutality and destruction, saying that while demolished walls could soon be repaired, the destruction of trees – 'a measure which might at first seem barbarous to the civilised mind' – was the only way for the Afghans to be made to 'feel the weight of our power, for they delight in the shade of their trees'. In any village believed to have aided Akbar Khan, orders were given 'at once to commence the work of destruction so that neither fort, house, tree, grain nor boosa [fodder] should be spared them'.[17]

Meanwhile, the onset of the summer heat, and with it disease, added to the frustration of the troops left waiting in Jalalabad.

---

* The same tactics were used by the Taliban against the orchards and vineyards of the Shomali Plain when they finally lost patience with the mainly Tajik villages of Parwan in the 1990s.

'Great was the disappointment among the officers,' wrote Lieutenant Greenwood,

> and loud the murmurings among the men, when at first days then
> weeks passed away while we remained inactive . . . The camels and
> baggage animals were dying in numbers daily, and the stench of
> their dead bodies and the filth of the immense camp was insupport-
> able. Millions of flies were bred in the masses of corruption that lay
> on every side. The very air was black with them, and such torments
> they became, that it was almost impossible to get a minute's rest.
> Provisions were bad and scarce. Sickness began to rage among the
> men, who bitterly complained that they were brought there to die
> like cowards in that pest house, instead of being led at once against
> the enemy.[18]

Temperatures soon rose to forty-three degrees Celsius, and many
of the officers disappeared into the underground cool houses, or
tykhanas, that they found in the basements of the old houses.

Within the fort, one man seemed especially miserable. Every
evening when the troops were at dinner, General Sale would slip
off 'ostensibly to have a quiet look around at the progress of our
work', wrote Thomas Seaton, 'but in reality to ponder on the
desperate situation of his wife and daughter, and to debate with
himself the possibility of effecting their rescue'. Seaton realised
that, now that the siege was over and its anxieties passed, Sale's
thoughts were dwelling more and more on the fate of his family,
especially now that Ellenborough seemed to be contemplating
withdrawing from Afghanistan and leaving the prisoners of war
and the hostages in captivity. There were also the rumours which
had been circulating during the siege that Akbar might bring Lady
Sale before the walls of the city and torture her within Sale's sight,
so compelling him to surrender. One evening Seaton found himself
on guard duty as Sale did his lonely rounds, and he plucked up the
courage to ask the General what he would do had such a report
proved true: 'Turning towards me, his face pale and stern, but quiv-
ering with deep emotion, he replied, "I-I will have every gun turned

on her; my old bones shall be buried beneath the ruins of the fort here; but I shall never surrender.'"[19]

Sale's defeat of Akbar Khan turned out to be a very mixed blessing for Lady Sale and her fellow hostages.

Like the Jalalabad garrison before them, they had heard the false rumours of Pollock's defeat, and had been plunged into depression at the thought of their ever-lengthening captivity. But when news came through of Sale's victory and Pollock's successful passage through the Khyber it brought with it a period of renewed uncertainty. After eleven weeks of stability, they were ordered back on to their horses and sent off northwards, away from any attempts that the British might make to rescue them. They later learned that after the Battle of Jalalabad many of the chiefs – especially those of the eastern Ghilzai – had demanded that they be put to death. Only Akbar Khan's personal intervention had saved them.[20]

Before they left on their wanderings, the pick of their goods were plundered by their jailer, Akbar's father-in-law Mohammad Shah Khan, chief of the Babrkhel Ghilzai of Laghmanat. Lady Sale reported that he 'has taken away all of Lady Macnaghten's jewels to the value of above a lakh of rupees; and her shawls, valued at between 30 and 40,000 rupees'. But Lady Sale was not planning to be so easily robbed: 'My chest of drawers they took possession of with great glee – I left some rubbish in them, and some small bottles, that were useless to me. I hope the Afghans will try their contents as medicine, and find them efficacious; one bottle contained nitric acid, another a strong solution of lunar caustic.'[21]

Several days later the caravan containing the prisoners crossed with that taking the wounded Akbar Khan back to Kabul. George Lawrence saw him pass in his palanquin. 'He looked pale and ill,' he wrote,

and he carried his wounded arm in a sling; he returned our saluta-
tions very courteously. He smiled as I passed him, and beckoning
me to join him, spoke in a free and soldierly manner of Sale's victory
and his own defeat, praising the gallant bearing of our men, with
Sale conspicuous on his white charger at their head. He admitted
that his force had fled precipitately, he himself having to get out of
his palanquin and escape on horseback. Had our troops only
followed up a few miles further to the bank of the river, he must
have been captured, as he had to remain some hours until a raft
could be prepared to take him across.[22]

Waving goodbye, Akbar Khan headed on towards Kabul, while
the prisoners were escorted by a different route to a fortress at the
top of the Tezin Pass. On the road they crossed again the route of
the January retreat, passing frequent macabre reminders of its
horrors. 'Many of the bodies, from being imbedded in the snow,
were little altered, but most were reduced to skeletons,' noted
Lawrence.[23] More tragic still were the feral remains of the sepoy
army, some of whom were still hiding out in the caves of the high
passes. Lady Sale saw one cave in front of which lay a huge pile of
human bones, 'and from the blood close to its entrance, there is
reason to believe that the inhabitants were supporting nature by
devouring each other. I saw three spectral figures crawling on
hands and knees just within the cave and heard them calling out for
help as we passed.'[24]

The next few days of the hostages' forced march took place in
pouring rain and through thick mud. It was a particularly violent
downpour near Sarobi that finally finished off the ailing General
Elphinstone; as he had long predicted, he would never make it back
to his beloved Borders grouse moors. Yet it was a measure of his
personal charm that despite being almost single-handedly responsible for the catastrophe that had led to the prisoners' current
situation, he was faithfully tended by the other hostages to the end.
Mackenzie and Lawrence were particularly solicitous and shared
shifts with Moore, his batman, to look after the old General as he
faded away, and, though without any medicine, Mackenzie 'was

able to sooth in some degree his last sufferings by a tonic prepared from pomegranate rinds'.[25] 'He told me repeatedly he wished and even prayed for death,' wrote Lawrence. 'He said, sleeping and waking, the horrors of that dreadful retreat were always before his eyes. We all felt deeply for him and tried to soothe and comfort the old man, but it was of no avail, as he was worn out in body and mind, and evidently heart-broken by what had occurred. His wound remained unhealed, but he heeded it not; his anguish of mind was too intense to be distracted even by bodily suffering . . .'[26]

On his last night, Elphinstone requested Moore to bring him a bowl of water and a clean shirt. Once washed and changed, he had Mackenzie read the prayers for the dying, and asked the weeping Moore to lift his head. 'I lay down on the bare floor near the poor General,' wrote Lawrence.

[He] never appeared to close his eyes all night, so great was the pain he suffered.

I spoke several times to him, but he only thanked me, saying I could do nothing for him, and that all must soon be over . . . His suffering had been intense, but he bore all with fortitude and resignation. He repeatedly expressed to me deep regret that he had not fallen in the retreat. His kind, mild disposition and courteous detachment had made him esteemed by us all, and we could not but regret his removal from amongst us, although his death was to him a most happy release.[27]

When he learned of the General's death, Akbar Khan chivalrously gave orders that the body should be conveyed down to Jalalabad, escorted by Moore. But it was Elphinstone's fate to suffer bad luck even in death. On the way down, a passing party of ghazis discovered what was being carried, opened the casket, then stripped the General's body naked and pelted it with stones. Akbar sent a second party of horsemen to rescue the corpse, and its guardian, and then had both rafted down the Kabul River to the gates of Jalalabad.

There, on 30 April, the ill-fated General was finally laid to rest by Pollock and Sale, with full military honours.*

When news arrived in Kabul of the complete defeat of Akbar Khan, and as his wounded and battered troops began limping in on the evening of 8 April, there was a widespread panic, and many supporters of the Barakzai began to flee for the hills.[28]

Fatteh Jang and the Sadozai princes who had remained nervously holed up within the Bala Hisar since the death of Shah Shuja now found their hopes rising again. They began collecting food, arms and ammunition, and, encouraged by their key ally Aminullah Khan Logari, began negotiating with the Tajiks of Kohistan in a bid to recruit more troops to their cause. As so often in the past, Kabul fractured into rival quarters of Barakzai and Sadozai influence, with Nawab Zaman Khan's Barakzai troops desperately defending their compounds against Aminullah and his Sadozai allies. 'Ameenoollah's power is daily increasing,' reported Mohan Lal Kashmiri in a despatch to Jalalabad on 10 April. 'He has command of the Treasury of the Shah and Futteh Jung, and is collecting the men of his own tribe, the Loghurrees.'[29]

Lady Sale, characteristically, took a more forthright view of events. 'Parties run high at Kabul,' she wrote in her diary. 'Nawab Zaman Khan says he will be king, Akbar ditto, Jubbar Khan the same, and Ameenoollah has a similar fancy, as also Mahommed Shah Khan, and Futteh Jung, the Shahzada.' She added:

> Troops go out daily to fight ... Now is the time to strike the blow, but I much dread dilly-dallying just because a handful of us are in Akbar's power. What are our lives when compared to the honour of our country? Not that I am at all inclined to have my throat cut: on

---

* His body was eventually removed by Pollock and reburied in Park Street cemetery in Calcutta, not far from the tomb erected for whatever remains Lady Macnaghten had managed to retrieve of her husband.

the contrary, I hope that I shall live to see the British flag once more triumphant in Affghanistan; and then I shall have no objection to the Ameer Dost Mahomed Khan being reinstated: only let us first show them that we can conquer them, humble their treacherous chiefs to the dust and revenge the foul murder of our troops; but let us not dishonour the British name by sneaking out of the country like whipped pariah dogs ...

Let our Governors-General and Commanders in Chief look to that; whilst I knit socks for my grandchildren: but I have been a soldier's wife too long to sit down tamely whilst our honour is tarnished ... Were I in power I would make the Chiefs remember it. A woman's vengeance is said to be fearful but nothing can satisfy mine against Akbar, Sultan Jan and Mohammad Shah Khan.[30]

The stalemate and uncertainty was broken on 9 May, when Akbar Khan arrived back in Kabul. With his usual vigour and decisiveness, he immediately laid siege to the Sadozais in their fortress, digging a series of massive mines under the most vulnerable towers. Using the same tactics that had served him so well while gathering supporters in Jalalabad, he again represented himself as the champion of Islam, and depicted the Sadozais as quisling friends of the Kafirs. He wrote to the chiefs that 'it was an object of paramount importance that in the contest with the race of misguided infidels the whole of the members of the true faith should be united together, therefore did the whole of the devoted followers of the true faith consent to choose me as their head, and to place themselves under my counsel'.[31]

In just over a week, he managed to bribe Aminullah Khan to desert the Sadozai camp. A week after that he had won over Mir Haji, and with him the Kabul 'ulema and the Kohistanis.[32] Akbar Khan also recruited and armed an infantry and artillery regiment made up of Indian sepoys who had deserted from the British during the retreat. By the end of May, 12,000 troops had rallied to his standard, outnumbering the Sadozai defenders three to one.[33] After a month of sustained bombardment and the mining, and having exhausted his stock of gunpowder and cannon balls, Fatteh Jang was finally compelled to surrender. Akbar Khan was admitted into the Bala Hisar on 7 June.

By the end of that month, Fatteh Jang had been forced to hand over all powers to Akbar, who formally appointed himself wazir, then promptly seized all the latter's assets. Fatteh Jang was made to write to Pollock and explain, 'I have given to Sirdar Mahomad Akbar Khan the full and entire management of all my property and affairs of every description and have resigned to him in perpetuity full power to judge and settle all questions on all points. Whatever arrangements he may make with the English government I agree to and confirm and no alteration shall be made.'[34]

Initially, it seems, Akbar Khan still felt the need of a Sadozai figurehead to legitimise his rule: despite the taint the dynasty had suffered by allying themselves with the hated Kafirs, such was the charisma of the lineage of Ahmad Shah Durrani that even now Akbar felt it necessary to keep a Sadozai as head of state.[35] By July, however, he had tired of the fiction, and when in the middle of the month he intercepted a letter between Fatteh Jang and Pollock, he immediately had all the Sadozai shahzadas and the old blind Shah Zaman rounded up and imprisoned at the top of the Bala Hisar. 'Akbar considered this letter to contravene all traditions of honour and to violate the Shah's pact with him,' wrote Fayz Mohammad. 'He thereupon took the Shah into custody and expropriated all the jewels and fine things which Fatteh Jang had acquired. Still not satisfied, the Wazir wanted to punish the Shah with a whipping, and confiscate everything he owned.'[36]

It was at the height of his power as wazir, with the Bala Hisar now his personal palace, that Akbar Khan decided to invite to dinner the British officers who had been captured at the fall of Ghazni, and who had recently been brought to Kabul on his orders to join the other hostages. Among their number was a taciturn young Ulsterman who would later go on to change the course of Indian history, Captain John Nicholson. Nicholson was not easily impressed, but wrote afterwards to his mother that he 'never was in the company of more gentleman-like, well-bred men. They are strikingly handsome, as the Afghan sirdars always are, with a great deal of dignity . . . As I looked around the circle I saw both parricides and regicides – the murderer of our envoy was perhaps the

least blood-stained of the party.'[37] Nicholson's colleague Lieutenant Crawford was also taken aback by Akbar Khan's perfect
manners. 'We met with the kindest reception,' he wrote later.

> I could not bring myself to believe that the stout, good-humoured,
> open-hearted looking young man who was making such kind
> enquiries after our health, and how we had borne the fatigues of the
> journey, could be the murderer of Macnaghten and the leader of the
> massacre of our troops ... He ordered dinner, and sent for Troup
> and Pottinger to see us; when they arrived the whole of us all sat
> down to the best dinner I had had for many a month. The Wuzeer
> chatted and joked away on different subjects during the meal ... the
> following morning the arch-fiend sent us an excellent break-
> fast ... and he desired a list of our wants, regarding clothes &c
> might be made out, and that they should be furnished.[38]

One man who received less courteous treatment from the new
Wazir was Burnes's former munshi and intelligence chief Mohan
Lal Kashmiri. Akbar Khan had intercepted some of Mohan Lal's
correspondence with the British and had discovered that the
munshi had been actively gathering arms and ammunition for
Fatteh Jang. In a stark contrast to the treatment extended to the
British prisoners, Mohan Lal was immediately thrown into solitary confinement, beaten and later tortured. 'I was forced to lie
down and a couch placed over me on which the people are jumping
and are beating me with sticks and tormenting me in a very rude
and unmerciful manner,' Mohan Lal reported in a hastily scribbled
and ungrammatical letter that he managed to get smuggled out to
Jalalabad. 'Akbar wants Rs 30,000 from me, says otherwise he will
pull out my eyes; all my body has been severely beaten. I cannot
promise anything without governments order, but see myself
destroyed. All my feet is wounded from bastinadoing.'[39]

A week later, he got word out that his condition had deterior-
ated: 'Sometimes I am pinioned and a heavy stone is placed over
my back, while red pepper is burnt before my nose and eyes. Sometimes I am bastinadoed. I suffer every imaginable agony. He wants

Rs 30,000 out of which he has hitherto to get Rs 12,000 after using me very rudely. The remainder if not paid in the course of ten days, he says he will pull out my eyes and burn my body with hot iron.' He went on to ask that if he was killed the government should look after his wife, his two children and his old father in Delhi.

After a few days more of torture, Mohan Lal had sunk into despair and began writing about himself in the third person, as if already beyond help: 'Mohun Lall is severely beaten three times and most disgracefully and cruelly treated. He has been hitherto forced to pay Rs 18,000 and God knows what may befall him more than this. Kindly do something for his release from such pains.'[40] But, without Burnes to protect him, Mohan Lal had no friends in Pollock's camp and received no letters or reassurances from his employers in Jalalabad. The only man to attempt to raise money to ransom him was his old Delhi College schoolfriend and fellow 'intelligencer', Wade's munshi Shahamat Ali, who from Indore attempted to organise an immediate loan from the Hindu bankers of Kabul to effect his release.[41] He eventually achieved this, aided by a belated letter of protest from Pollock addressed to Akbar Khan; but apparently not before Mohan Lal had been forced to convert to Islam.[42]

In the meantime, Akbar Khan had the defences of the Bala Hisar rebuilt and the ditches redug, laying in stores of food and ammunition, ready to defend himself against the British, should they attempt to retake Kabul.[43] He also sent men to fortify with sangars and breastworks the narrowest points of the Tezin and Khord Kabul passes. He was only just in time.

On 22 July, after three months of waiting, Pollock and Nott finally received the orders they had been waiting for. Using a form of words that put all responsibility on the shoulders of the generals, Lord Ellenborough authorised the two men 'to withdraw via Kabul', if they so chose. He also ordered them 'to leave decisive proofs of the power of the British army'.[44] A race now began between the two generals to be the first to Kabul, though Nott had by far the furthest to go – some 300 miles against Pollock's 100.

'They have untied my hands and mark me, the grass shall not

grow under my feet,' wrote an excited Nott to his daughters that evening. 'I sit writing here in full confidence that my beautiful, my noble regiments will give them a good licking.'[45]

Only one man was more delighted. 'I am so excited,' noted General Sale in a letter as soon as news of the advance had been announced, 'I can scarce write.'

Amid 'bustle and confusion' General Nott finally marched out of Kandahar for the last time, with his 6,000 troops, on 8 August.[46]

Behind him he left the city under the charge of Shah Shuja's youngest son, Prince Safdarjang. The handsome young prince, said to be the son of a Ludhiana dancing girl, had sworn to hold the city for the Sadozais, though Nott doubted whether the Prince would last long after his departure and privately believed 'great confusion and bloodshed will follow our retirement'.[47] The young Prince was nonetheless determined to try to hold out if he could. 'We should know no other feeling than a bold determination to avenge the King's blood,' Safdarjang wrote to Nott, soon after he had left. 'At present my own blood is in such ferment that I can think of nothing else but the best means to obtain this vengeance. I swear to God that while life is in my body I will attend to no other matter than this: I will either share my father's fate, or I will avenge his death.'

Eleven days later, Pollock marched out of Jalalabad with a slightly larger army of 8,000 troops. His was a much more harrowing passage. The further the Army of Retribution went, the more corpses they passed and the more macabre their journey became. First they saw 'the sixty skeletons scattered on the hill' of Gandamak, 'the officers plainly distinguishable by the long hair which still remained attached to their skulls'. By the time the army came to Jagdalak 'the pass was choked with corpses, and they had to be removed before our guns could pass', wrote Thomas Seaton. 'It was a terrible sight, and we felt it the more deeply from the thought that we could not sufficiently avenge such a disaster . . . All along the road, in every ravine and nook, bodies and skeletons of the Kabul fugitives were found lying as they had been cut down, or had sunk from fatigue and had perished in the intense cold.'[48] 'Some were mere skeletons,' noted Lieutenant Greenwood,

> while others were in better preservation. Their features were perfect, although discoloured. Their eyes had evidently been picked out by birds of prey, which wheeling in endless gyrations above my head seemed to consider me an intruder in their domain. On turning the corner of a large rock, where five or six bodies were lying in a heap together, a vulture which had been banqueting on them, hopped carelessly away to a little distance, lazily flapping its huge wings, but too indolent to fly. I turned away from the sickening sight with a sad heart, but with a stern determination to lend my best efforts to paying the Affghans the debt of revenge we owed them.[49]

Worse was to come. At the holly barrier near Jagdalak, they came across hundreds of corpses impaled on the hedge, still slumped where they were shot down as they tried to claw their way over the thorns in the darkness. Just beyond that, within the low mud walls of the Jagdalak mud fort, they saw 'skeletons thrown into heaps of eighty to one hundred' where the column had halted for a day and two nights, exposed to the fire from the Ghilzais' jezails on two sides, waiting in vain for Shelton and Elphinstone to return from their negotiations with Akbar Khan. 'They were killed in ranks,' wrote Seaton, 'and in ranks we found them, the flesh still on their bodies, and every face perfectly recognisable to those by whom they were known.' Near by, at the top of the valley, was a small round watchtower. Here they found the massed bodies of the hundreds of sepoys and camp followers whom the Afghans had captured, stripped of their clothes and driven out into the snow to die.

> The whole of the room was filled with skeletons and decaying bodies, up to the very roof; and there was a mound of them outside, half way up to the door, extending to a distance of twenty-seven feet

from the wall, completely covering the steps. It was a ghastly sight. The poor fugitives appear to have crept in here for shelter, the last comers treading on and suffocating those who had preceded them, and then throwing out their bodies, only to be themselves served in the same way – trampled on, suffocated and thrown out by those that followed.

War carries in its train one pre-eminently dreadful evil – it engenders and nurses the spirit of revenge, stirs up all the malignant passions that lie dormant in man's breast, and urges him to acts that are more suitable to a demon than to a being created in God's image ... Now the sepoys took vengeance wherever they could on the living, and if not on the living then on the dead.[50]

Any place believed to be associated with Akbar Khan came in for especially harsh treatment. One lovely village surrounded by orchards and gardens was thought by the troops to be one of the Wazir's favourite summer residences, and despite surrendering without a fight, 'every house was destroyed, every tree barked or cut down; after which the detatchment having collected a considerable spoil of bullocks, sheep, and goats, marched back to camp'.[51]

Nott's progress was initially more disciplined and less violent than that of Pollock. But after several troops were killed in one village after the Ghilzai elders had formally surrendered, a full-scale massacre ensued: all males over puberty were bayoneted, the women were raped and their goods plundered. 'Tears, supplications, were of no avail,' wrote Neville Chamberlain. 'The musket was deliberately raised, the trigger pulled, and happy was he who fell dead. These horrible murders (for such alone must they be in the eyes of God) were truly wicked ... This is one of the most beautiful valleys in Affghanistan, but we left it a scene of desolation; the Hindustanis being so exasperated against the Affghans, they can never spare anything they can destroy, and all the forts and places within reach were soon on fire.'[52]

Nott's chaplain, the Rev. I. N. Allen, was even more shocked and wrote that rarely had a clergyman had to witness such scenes. 'Every door was forced,' he wrote, 'every man that could be found was slaughtered, they were pursued from yard to yard, from tower to tower, and very few escaped . . . One door, which they refused to open upon summons, was blown in by a six pounder, and every soul bayoneted.'[53] One soldier who visited the village fort the following day described seeing 'about 100 dead bodies lying about, and six or eight children were found roasted to a cinder. They had been concealed beneath heaps of chaff which had burned. One woman was the only live thing in the fort. She was sitting, the picture of despair, with her father, brother, husband and children lying dead around her. She had dragged all their bodies to one spot, and seated herself in the midst.'[54]

On arrival outside Ghazni, Nott fought a brief but fierce battle with 12,000 Durranis under the Barakzai Governor of the Province. After the defenders had retired within the walls, Nott then camped just outside the range of the artillery. The following morning the British found the city entirely deserted: the Ghilzai 'had lost heart', despite having recently received reinforcements from Kabul under Sultan Jan, and had evacuated during the night. At dawn, Nott blew down the city gates and, as he put it tersely in his official report, 'I directed the City of Ghuznee, with its citadel and the whole of its work, to be destroyed.'[55]

Only one last ritual remained. Through his reading of James Mill's *History of India* – a book which Mill famously wrote without ever bothering to visit India, knowing any Indians or learning any Indian languages – Ellenborough had absorbed the entirely false idea that the doors of the tomb of Mahmud of Ghazni (998– 1030) were the legendary sandalwood gates that the Sultan had allegedly stolen while looting the great Hindu temple of Somnath in Gujarat. In reality the gates were of a piece with the tomb itself – Seljuk work of the eleventh century – as Rawlinson could immediately see from the Arabic inscriptions on the woodwork which were contained in notably Islamic-looking six-pointed stars and surrounded by intricate arabesques. It made no difference – Ellenborough had asked for the gates, and the gates he would get.

A proclamation was duly issued by Ellenborough, addressed to the chiefs and princes of northern and western India, in which the Governor General spoke of how an insult of 800 years was finally avenged and centuries of Indian subjugation to Afghans in pre-colonial times had been reversed: thanks to the British, the gates that were once a memorial of Hindu humiliation had become instead a record of Indian superiority in arms over the nations beyond the Indus. The gates were duly paraded around India, accompanied by an imposing escort, where they were ceremoniously displayed to bewildered bystanders in an attempt to impress upon the people of India the undiminished power and benevolence of British rule. There was, however, no reaction from the Indian princes, and still less from the Hindus, neither of whom had been aware that they were missing any gates.[56] As Rawlinson observed while supervising the removal of the beautiful Seljuk woodwork: the gates could hardly be restored because they were not from Somnath; the temple had been in ruins for a thousand years; and the Hindus were anyway totally indifferent to the whole farce.[57]

Nor were the Afghans particularly upset to see the gates go. According to Rawlinson, the custodian of the shrine merely shrugged his shoulders and said: 'Of what use can these old timbers be to you?'[58] Mirza 'Ata was more cutting: 'Ellenborough ordered the gates to be sent to India, where they could be used to publicize the re-conquest of Khorasan and justify the huge expense of operations in a country which produced so little revenue. As the saying goes, real power does not need tawdry propaganda! A more lasting monument until today is the quantity of rotting corpses of the English troops that still block the highways and byways of Khorasan.'[59]

Throughout July there were several attempts at negotiating an exchange of prisoners. First Mackenzie then Lawrence was despatched to Jalalabad to try to make a deal with Pollock; but in the end the talks came to nothing, and both men honourably returned to their captivity having given Akbar Khan their word that they would do so.

Pottinger in particular wrote a letter cautioning Pollock against making a deal which freed all the British officers and their women while leaving large numbers of helpless sepoys stranded in Afghanistan. 'The name and character of the British must suffer in the opinion of our own subjects and soldiers in India if we were to pay for the release of a few Europeans,' he wrote,

> while so many thousands of our native soldiery & camp followers are reduced to the condition of slavery throughout this country. Many other poor wretches who are deprived of their hands and feet or otherwise mutilated or diseased are supporting their precarious existence by begging. If these latter persons be not released many if not all must die in the coming winter, and it appears to me that the Government will lay itself open to the odium and charge of undue partiality if it release us alone by ransom.[60]

There was, moreover, some urgency to the situation of the stranded Indians. A slave trader who visited the fortress where the hostages were being kept told Lady Sale that '400 Hindoostanees have been entrapped at Kabul, under an assurance of safe conduct to Jalalabad . . . Men sell for forty-six rupees; and women for twenty-two, each.' Uzbek slave traders who dominated the Afghan market were especially feared for the merciless brutality they habitually displayed to their captives. When Josiah Harlan had passed through Khulm he described the 'diabolical contrivance' by which the Uzbeks literally sewed their captives to their saddles. 'To oblige the prisoner to keep up, a strand of course horsehair is passed by means of a long crooked needle, under and around the collar bone, a few inches from its junction at the sternum; with the hair a loop is formed to which they attach a rope that may be fastened to the saddle. The captive is constrained to keep near the retreating horseman, and with his hands tied behind his person, is altogether helpless.'[61] When Akbar warned Pollock that, if he attempted to retake Kabul, all the British prisoners of war would immediately be sent north to be sold as slaves in the Bukhara slave markets, the hostages had good reason to be apprehensive.

The British prisoners were staying in relative comfort in a fort just outside Kabul when Akbar Khan heard that the armies of Pollock and Nott had begun advancing on his capital from two different directions. His closest ally, Mohammad Shah Khan Ghilzai, encouraged him to prepare for a final life-or-death struggle with the Kafirs. 'War they want,' he told his son-in-law. 'Let them have it – war to the knife. Let us destroy them all.'[62] That Friday the Wazir rode to the Pul-i-Khishti Masjid and from the pulpit made a passionate appeal for a last and conclusive jihad against the British.

On the night of 25 August, just as the hostages were preparing to retire for the night, they received the ominous order that they were immediately to be moved northwards into the Hindu Kush. By the light of the moon they were made to load their few remaining goods on to the ponies and camels that had been sent for them by Akbar Khan. The women were told for the first time to wear full-length Afghan burkhas. Mackenzie, who had gone down with a severe fever and believed he was dying, was placed in a wicker basket called a *kajawah* slung from the side of a camel.[63] Off they set, past the outskirts of Kabul and the walls of Babur's Tomb, and out on to the Kohistan road. Their initial destination, they learned, was to be Akbar Khan's northernmost fortress which commanded the old Buddhist valley of Bamiyan, famous for its monumental Buddhas.[64]

The head of their escort of 400 irregular horse was a Qizilbash cavalry officer named Saleh Mohammad Khan. He had been in the service of Shah Shuja until he went over to Dost Mohammad on the latter's return from Bukhara in 1840. George Lawrence and Hugh Johnson both knew him a little from this time, while Eldred Pottinger discovered that ten of the guards were his former troopers who had assisted him during the siege of Herat in 1838. There were even two of Mackenzie's jezailchis who had fought by his side during the cantonment siege.[65] Pottinger, Lawrence, Johnson and Mackenzie all quickly realised the opportunity and opened communications to see if any of their guards would be receptive to bribery. At first they all demurred. But as the party headed north on the steep and precipitous caravan route over the wild mountains of Kulu and hence through the high-altitude faultlines of the Hazara country, and as reports began coming in of the crushing victories of Pollock and Nott, the attitude of the guards began to change.

It was Johnson who first made some progress. 'Salih Mahomed is a good humoured, jolly fellow,' he wrote in his journal on 25 August,

> and without any prejudices against us kafirs. He is a soldier of fortune who cares little whom he seizes, has been to Bokhara, and was at the taking of Coucem a few months ago. I rode with him the whole march and was very much amused by his traveller's tales. He is the greatest hero in his own estimation. There is no end to his feats of valour to which I am a ready listener and for two reasons. First that I am amused, secondly that he is flattered by my being a good listener, by which I hope to turn him to good account.

A few days later, Johnson chose a moment when the two were alone together to make his offer. 'As I have become pretty intimate with our commandant,' he wrote, 'I took advantage of no third person being within hearing to whisper in his ear that we would give him a mountain of rupees, if instead of carrying us to Bameean, he would take us in the opposite direction towards General Nott's army, extolling the delights of Hindoostan should he feel inclined to go there after liberating us. At first he seemed rather surprised at the proposition which I mooted half-jokingly half-seriously, not knowing in what way he might view it.'[66] Before long Saleh Mohammad had made it clear that 'he wished to know what we would do for our liberation', and asked the prisoners to make a serious offer.[67]

Negotiations continued after the party arrived in Bamiyan, aided by a series of promissory notes sent by the ever-resourceful Mohan Lal, which he arranged through his Qizilbash friends in Kabul.

When a letter arrived from Akbar Khan ordering Saleh Mohammad Khan to move the hostages still further north, to Khulm, Lawrence raised his bid and offered to make him an immediate down-payment of 20,000 rupees in cash and a monthly payment thereafter for life of Rs 1,000. As 'Ata Mohammad put it: '"Gold is a wonderful substance: the sight of it gladdens the eye; the sound of it drives away melancholy." The offer turned the Khan's head, and he prepared to have the prisoners set free.'[68]

Aided by Saleh Mohammad Khan, at a given signal the prisoners took over the fortress in which they were being held, offering their former guards four months' extra pay if they helped defend it until they were rescued. When Saleh Mohammad handed the prisoners a pile of muskets to help with the defence, the prisoners were so surprised to have control over their own destinies after many passive months in captivity that at first none volunteered to join the guard – until Lady Sale stepped in. 'Thinking the men might be shamed into doing their duty,' she wrote later, 'I said to Lawrence, "You had better give me one, and I will lead the party."'[69]

Before long, under Lady Sale's watchful eye, the hostages had gained sufficient confidence to run up the Union Jack on the flag-pole. Pottinger then resumed his duties as political agent in Kohistan and called upon all the neighbouring chiefs to attend his durbar and receive dresses of honour. 'Our conspiracy continues to prosper,' wrote Johnson in his diary on 14 September.

> Almost all the influential Chiefs for several miles round have come in to pay their respects . . . swearing faith to us & to tender aid in fighting men if required. Although we are still in the dark as to what our troops are doing or where they are we suppose they must be somewhere near Kabul & probably have had a fight with Akbar – in which case we shall not be surprised to see the latter with some 5 or 600 horsemen at any hour in our valley. We have turned our attention to the strengthening of our forts & clearing out the loop holes so as to give them a warm reception in the event of their interference with us.[70]

A week later, with Lady Sale at their head, the former hostages had even begun to tax passing caravans.

Early in the morning on 1 September, a solitary horseman rode up to a picket outside Pollock's camp at Jagdalak. When challenged by the sentry, the rider announced himself to be Shah Fatteh Jang.

It had been rumoured in the Bala Hisar towards the end of August that Akbar Khan had been making plans to kill the young successor to the Sadozai crown, after first having branded him with hot irons. As the rumour spread, the old retainers of the fort took action: they cut a hole in the mud roof of the prison where the Shah was being held and helped him out through a tunnel under the walls, then out to the Qizilbash quarter of Chindawal. There horses were waiting for him, ready saddled. Twenty-four hours later he was breakfasting with General Pollock.[71]

According to the traditions related by Fayz Mohammad, the young Shah then accused the British of failing his father Shuja and demanded that the British honour their commitment to the dynasty. 'The English campaign to seize Afghanistan had no other purpose aside from what the English thought might ultimately benefit themselves,' Fatteh Jang is supposed to have told Pollock.

'They never helped or even gave a thought to my murdered father . . . However I still consider myself bound to the [Tripartite] treaty which was concluded between the English government and my father and I have come to you so that if you still stand by your commitment, you will assist me and march on Kabul. Otherwise, there is no obligation on the part of the English government on my behalf, and your ambitions and your hostility will be revealed to all.' Shah Fatteh Jang's words were embarrassing to General Pollock and he prepared to aid the Shah out of a sense of decency, and so as to banish from people's lips the bad name ascribed to the English.[72]

Whether this conversation ever took place, Pollock certainly welcomed Fatteh Jang and from the first treated him with deference, giving him the same honours that Macnaghten had accorded to Shuja when he travelled through the same valley to retake his throne three years earlier. Privately, however, Pollock wrote dismissively of 'the unhappy prince . . . a slender and rather good-looking young man, but neither gifted with brains, nor entitled to much respect on the score of morality – apparently a reference to the Shah's predilection for "amusing himself with the occasional homosexual rape on members of the garrison" when stationed in Kandahar in 1839–40'.[73] Pollock also wrote that he deliberately withheld from the Shah the fact that the British were planning to withdraw from Kabul after they had achieved the limited objectives Ellenborough had set for them: defeating Akbar Khan, liberating the hostages and prisoners of war, recovering as many sepoys as possible and punishing the Afghan tribes for their perceived treachery.[74]

A week later, on 8 September, Pollock's force marched out of Jagdalak towards the mouth of the Tezin Pass, ready for the final push on Kabul. Sniping from the hilltops increased in intensity as the day progressed and, as darkness fell, fire from unseen jezails peppered the camp, despite Pollock having carefully placed pickets on all the peaks round about. 'The troops were of course turned out and kept on alert,' wrote Lieutenant Greenwood in his diary. 'The enemy continued firing into the camp from every height that was not absolutely in our possession; and their bullets were flying like hail among our tents. The sides of the hill were illuminated in every direction by the constant flashes of their jezails and the muskets of our piquets.'[75] The following morning at daybreak, Pollock's scouts brought in the news that Akbar Khan, supported by Mohammad Shah Khan Ghilzai and Aminullah Khan Logari, had moved forward from the positions they had prepared in the Khord Kabul and were now massing their 16,000 troops just ahead of them on the heights of Tezin.

Pollock split his force into three columns, with columns made up of kilted Highland Scots and long-robed Afghan jezailchis

mounting the slopes on either side of the pass and with the guns
and the cavalry of the advance guard moving cautiously along the
valley floor under the direction of General Sale. 'We moved forward
in column without seeing any indication of any enemy,' recounted
Greenwood. 'We had proceeded about two miles into the defile,
when suddenly a long sheet of flame issued from the heights on
either side, and a thousand balls came whizzing and whistling
about our heads. The hills were lined with the enemy, and they
began a most heavy fire.'[76] Among those who had a narrow escape
at this point was Dr Brydon, who had resumed his duties as a regimental surgeon. 'He was sitting on a pole by which a dooly is
carried, when a six pound shot from one of the enemy's guns struck
and splintered the bamboo, but without injuring him in the least.'[77]

Unlike the last time Brydon had been in the pass, with his
colleagues stumbling snow-blind and unresisting to their slaughter,
this time Pollock's troops were ready. Abbott opened up with his
guns and at the same time 'Sir Robert [Sale] gave the word for the
13th [Regiment] to ascend and storm the heights on the right, and
the 9th and 31st those on the left,' remembered Greenwood.

> Up we went, helter skelter. The hill was very high and precipitous,
> and not easily ascended at any time; the shot of the enemy, however,
> quickened our motions, and in a short time we were up and at
> them. The fire was tremendous; the bullets were hopping and
> whistling among us in every direction. The enemy were very
> numerous, and seemed disposed to fight to the last for possession
> of the heights. No sooner, however, had our men arrived at the top
> than they fixed bayonets, and with a loud hurrah they charged the
> enemy . . . The Afghans were shouting their war cry of 'Allah il
> Ullah' and reproaching us with various elegant names, such as
> dogs, kafirs and the like, and assuring us we would never reach
> Kabul. Captain Broadfoot's sappers in particular gave as good as
> they got, in right good Billingsgate.[78]

Once the Afghans had been dislodged from their position, Sale
kept his men driving them along the heights of the ridge, from peak

to peak. Down below, meanwhile, the cavalry were charging Akbar's cannon, all of which had been captured from Elphinstone's force and were now manned by renegade Company sepoys who had taken their chances with Akbar Khan; as the cavalry closed in, the unfortunate Hindustani deserters were immediately 'put to the sword'.[79] The fighting went on all day, with the Afghans resisting with great bravery and refusing to yield an inch until driven off each successive peak with bayonets. By late afternoon, however, the hilltops had all been captured and Akbar Khan's men had no option but to turn and flee, with their leader and the Ghilzai chiefs doggedly bringing up the rear. So complete was the defeat that the following day the British passed along the even steeper heights of the Khord Kabul without having to fire a shot.

On the evening of 15 September, Pollock's weary force finally marched into Kabul to find that almost the entire population, including Akbar Khan, had fled the city. That night they set up camp on the race course built on Macnaghten's orders three years earlier, and the following day Shah Fatteh Jang was restored to the Bala Hisar, but this time with the Union Jack flying from the flagpole.

Nott and his Kandahar army marched in two days later; and on 21 September news arrived that the 120 prisoners of war were approaching too.* Pollock had sent one of his young officers, Sir Richmond Shakespear, ahead to find them, along with a troop of 700 Qizilbash cavalry. Unaware that they had already liberated themselves, to his surprise Shakespear met them coming confidently down the road towards him, protected by an escort of their former jailers. Amid the cheers and the cries of 'we are saved', there was a single dissenting voice. 'Brigadier Shelton could not forget the honour due to his rank as the senior military man,' wrote Lady Sale, 'and was much offended at Sir Richmond not having called on him first, and reported his arrival in due form.'[80] Mackenzie was now so ill and foggily feverish that he was unable to lift himself off the ground and said only 'Ah!' when told he had just been rescued: 'When he saw Sir Richmond exchange turbans with Saleh Mohammad the only thought which

---

* The Qizilbash had been instrumental in the negotiations to free the hostages and had provided the necessary bribe which secured their release.

passed through his mind was a lazy wonder "if Shakespear would be covered in vermin in the process".'[81]

The day before the hostages made it back to Kabul, the party was met by General Sale, who had headed north to greet them. 'It is impossible to express our feelings on Sale's approach,' wrote Lady Sale, who had not seen her husband for nearly a year. 'To my daughter and myself happiness so long delayed, as to be almost unexpected was actually painful, and accompanied by a choking sensation which could not obtain relief in tears.'[82] When the still feverish Mackenzie stumbled over and said, '"General, I congratulate you!" the gallant old man turned towards him and tried to answer, but his feelings were too strong; he made a hideous series of grimaces, dug his spurs into horse, and galloped off as fast as he could.'[83]

When the prisoners of war finally arrived in Kabul they were greeted with a twenty-one-gun salute, and the infantry lined up to cheer all the captives as they passed into the camp. 'They presented an extraordinary appearance,' wrote Ensign Greville Stapylton, 'being all in Afghan costume with long beards, moustaches. It was with some difficulty that one could recognise one's friends.'[84]

The Army of Retribution stayed in Kabul for only two weeks. For the first few days, the troops amused themselves with eating fresh grapes and apples from the Kabul vineyards and orchards, and by visiting the sights of the town. Many sought out the sites where atrocities had taken place the previous winter. Those who had known Kabul during the occupation were especially shocked. 'Great and terrible changes had taken place in my absence,' wrote the artist James Rattray. 'Razed houses and blackened walls met my view. No one appeared. The city was deserted, its habitations darkened and empty. We rode through the streets without encountering a living soul, or hearing a single sound, save the yelp of a half-wild dog who had lapped up English blood perchance, our own suppressed voices and the echoes of our horses' hoofs sent back through the long grim avenues of the closed bazaars.'[85] Neville Chamberlain had last been to Alexander Burnes's house during his Christmas party in 1839 when Burnes had appeared in full Highland dress and danced reels on a table top in his kilt. Now the house had been burned to the ground and its charred foundations had been dug up by treasure hunters. 'Sir Alexander's house, where I had spent many a happy hour, was a heap of ruins,' wrote Chamberlain in his journal. 'The cantonments were a perfect waste, and where so much money had been spent, not a house or barrack or tree was left.'[86]

Hugh Johnson was even more shocked: 'On passing the corner of the street where I formerly lived I could not forego the desire of looking on the ruins of a house in which I had passed a period of 2 years of happiness,' he wrote in his journal immediately after his return to Kabul. 'Although I had expected to see the whole place unroofed I was not prepared for such a scene of desolation. Not one brick was left standing on another in either my house or that of Sir Alexander Burnes adjoining it. They were nothing but a heap of dirt covering the mouldering remains of our unfortunate people. A spot was pointed out to me in Sir Alexander's garden as that in which his body had been interred. Peace to his ashes!'[87]

More heartbreaking still was the sight of the maimed and crippled sepoys who had somehow managed to survive the winter by begging in the streets of Kabul. The more conscientious officers now threw their energies into trying to reassemble what was left of their regiments: the most successful was Lieutenant John Haughton, who had escaped from Charikar with Eldred Pottinger, and who now succeeded in finding, and in many cases liberating from slavery, no fewer than 165 of his Gurkhas whom he managed to track down in the fields, streets and slave markets of Kabul. In all, some 2,000 sepoys and camp followers were found to have survived. They were collected together with two officers appointed to provide for them and give them access to medical treatment, including, in some cases, amputations.[88]

Parties also began to be sent out to begin digging graves for the thousands of British and Indian cadavers still lying scattered around the city, 'calling out to us to avenge them', as Mohan Lal put it.[89] Soon the troops were pressing Pollock to make some public demonstration to punish the people of Kabul. Pollock needed little encouragement.

On his defeat, Akbar Khan had fled northwards to Khulm and was now well out of reach, but Naib Aminullah Khan Logari and his tribesmen along with the Ghazis of Parwan had decided to fortify themselves in the pleasure resort of Istalif, just thirty-five miles north of Kabul.

Istalif was always renowned as one of the most beautiful places in Afghanistan – the Emperor Babur fell in love with it in the sixteenth century and used to hold wine parties in his summer house and rose garden there; 300 years later Burnes had come here to relax and get away from the diplomatic complexities of Kabul amid the plane and walnut trees, the mountain streams full of fish and 'the richest orchards and vineyards'. It was here that Pollock decided to concentrate his revenge.

As they marched out of Kabul through the vineyards of the Shomali Plain, Pollock's troops were also enchanted by the 'clear streams and green fields' around the hilltown which had charmed so many travellers before them. But it did not stop them laying waste to the place. The town was surrounded, attacked and then systematically pillaged. When 500 enslaved sepoys were found chained in pitiful conditions in the basements, the Afghan wounded were collected in heaps and 'the sepoys set fire to the cotton clothing of their victims', burning them alive. The women of Istalif were then divided among the troops by throws of the dice.[90]

Neville Chamberlain's cavalry were part of the rearguard. By the time he got to Istalif, the scene, he wrote, was 'beyond description . . . Tents, baggage, things of all descriptions lying about the streets, besides the bodies of the unfortunate men who had delayed their departure too long, or were too brave to fly and leave their wives and children to our mercy without first sacrificing their own lives in their defence.' He went on:

> I suppose I need not tell you that no males above fourteen years were spared . . . Several were killed before me. Sometimes they were only wounded and were finished by a second ball . . . Some of the men (brutes except in form) wanted to wreak their revenge on the women . . . The greatest part of the merchandise of Kabul and the harems of the principal chiefs had been removed to Istalif on hearing of our advance on the capital, as it had always been deemed impregnable by the Afghans . . . The scene of plunder was dreadful. Every house filled with soldiers, both European and native, and completely gutted. Furniture, clothes, and merchandise of all sorts flung from windows into the streets . . . Some took arms, some jewels, others books . . . When the soldiers had finished the camp followers were let loose into the place, and they completed the business of spoliation . . . All this day the sappers have been employed in burning the town and the soldiers and camp followers in bringing away anything that had been left worth having.

The plight of the innocent women and children of Istalif made an especially strong impression:

> Whilst we were taking the town we saw a poor chubby-faced boy sitting on the side of the road, crying fit to break his heart; the poor little fellow had been deserted or in the hurry left by his parents . . . At one place my eyes were shocked at the sight of a poor woman lying dead, and a little infant of three or four months by her side, but both its little thighs pierced and mangled by a musket ball. The child was conveyed to camp, but death soon put an end to its sufferings. Further on was another women in torture from a wound and she had been exposed to a night without any covering; she clasped a child in her arms, and her affection seemed to be only increased by the agonies she endured . . . Scattered about the streets lay the bodies of old and young, rich and

poor . . . As I was returning to camp, sad and disheartened, I saw a poor emaciated old woman who had ventured to leave her hiding place thinking we had left; she was endeavouring to drag herself to a small stream to satisfy her thirst . . . I filled her vessel for her, but all she said was, 'Curses on the Feringhees!' I returned home disgusted with myself, the world and above all my cruel profession. In fact we are nothing but licensed assassins.[91]

From Istalif, the Army of Retribution descended the mountain, and pillaged and burned down the provincial centre of Charikar where Pottinger and Haughton and their Gurkhas had been besieged nearly a year before; as Sultan Mohammad Khan Durrani put it in the *Tarikh-i-Sultani*, 'they set the entire district on fire'.[92] Laden with loot, the Army of Retribution then stumbled back to Kabul.

Here they found that their colleagues had also been hard at work in their absence: Broadfoot's sappers had placed charges in the spandrels of the great Char Chatta covered bazaar, originally built during the reign of Shah Jahan and renowned not just as one of the supreme wonders of Mughal architecture but as one of the greatest buildings in all Central Asia. The superb structure with its painted wooden vaulting and intricate tilework, said by some to be the single most beautiful building in Afghanistan, had been chosen for destruction by Pollock, for it was here that Macnaghten's body had been displayed on a butcher's hook for public humiliation. For Mirza 'Ata the destruction was but another sign of British duplicity and weakness: 'After entering Kabul, the English demolished with their cannon all the larger buildings of the city, including the lovely four-roofed market, in revenge for Macnaghten. As the proverb says "When you're not strong enough to punish the camel, then go and beat the basket carried by the donkey!"'[93] It was one of the many ironies of the war that while British interest in promoting commerce between India and Afghanistan had been one of the original motives for sending Burnes on his first trip up the Indus, the final act of the whole catastrophic saga was the vindictive demolition of the main commercial centre of the region.[94] The much vaunted Indus Navigation Scheme had of course come to nothing; and now, before the British retired behind the Sutlej, the largest market in Central Asia was to be reduced to rubble.

The dynamiting of the great bazaar unleashed in Kabul a wave of rape, pillage and murder similar to that which had destroyed Istalif. 'Soldiers and camp-followers from both [Jalalabad and Kandahar] camps are plundering the town,' wrote Chamberlain on his return on 7 October. 'Here and there the smoke rising in black clouds showed that the firebrand had been applied to some chief's house . . . Part of the town also on fire.'[95] There was nothing accidental about the blaze. 'After we had been in Kabul about a fortnight,' Lieutenant Greenwood recorded in his diary,

[we] were ordered one evening to be in readiness to march the following day into the city. The object was not stated, but we could form a pretty good idea of what we were to do, and our expectations were correct. We proceeded the next morning, and blew up all the principal chowks and bazaars, and set fire to the city in many places. The houses were of course gutted in a very short time, and bales of cloth, muslins, fur cloaks, blankets and wearing apparel of every description were turned out and destroyed . . . Some of the men found a number of English cases of hermetically sealed grouse, and other meats, on which, as may be imagined, they had a fine feast . . .

This work of destruction continued until nightfall and exhaustion set in.

Many of our men looked just like chimney-sweeps from the fire and smoke. On succeeding days other parties were sent, and the city of Kabul, with the exception of the Bala Hisar and the Qizilbash quarter, was utterly destroyed and burned to the ground . . . The houses were all built of light dry wood, and when once a fire was kindled it would have been impossible to stay the ravaging element. The conflagration lasted the whole time we were encamped in the vicinity . . . A large mosque which the Affghans had built in honour of

their success over Elphinstone's army, and called the Feringhees'
Mosque, was also blown up and destroyed.[96]

What Greenwood's jaunty narrative does not make clear is that, as
well as destroying the empty shops and houses of their supposed
enemies, the marauding British troops also committed what today
would be classified as war crimes against their Qizilbash and Hindu
allies. Indeed the peaceable Kabul Hindu trading community that
had for centuries survived arbitrary arrests and torture by a whole
variety of Afghan rulers bent on extorting their money was wiped
out in just forty-eight hours by the depredations of the British, as
an official inquiry later acknowledged. 'That much violence was
committed at Kabul is unfortunately true,' Augustus Abbott later
admitted to Ellenborough.

> The Afghans had all deserted the city before we arrived there, and
> only the Hindus and Persians remained. The Hindus, having fed
> and sheltered hundreds of our unfortunate soldiers after the
> destruction of the Kabul Force, naturally expected protection
> from us, and the Hindu quarter, tho' much exposed, remained
> fully occupied by the inhabitants with their families and property.
> The Persians [i.e. the Qizilbash] assisted in recovering our captive
> officers and men and were considered as friends. Their quarter, the
> Chindawol, was however too strong to be in danger for any rabble
> acting in defiance of orders. Then on the 9th October, 1842, the
> Engineers went down to destroy the market place, and a general
> idea seemed to arise in camp that Kabul was to be given up to
> plunder. Sepoys, many European soldiers and thousands of camp
> followers, crowded down and had little difficulty in entering the
> imperfectly walled town. The Troops sent as a covering party to
> protect the Engineers were assembled at one or two gateways and
> near the market place and knew nothing of the violence that was
> committed in the Hindoo quarter, where houses were broken
> open, women violated, property taken by force and the owners
> shot like dogs . . .[97]

Henry Rawlinson, the man whose sighting of Vitkevitch on the Afghan border in 1837 had started the first movements towards war, and who up to this point had just about managed to maintain his belief in the benevolence of British rule, was especially disgusted by the tawdry spectacle of the final days of the British occupation of Kabul. 'Numbers of people had returned to Kabul, relying on our promises of protection,' he wrote in his journal that evening.

> They had, many of them, reopened their shops. These people have now been reduced to utter ruin. Their goods have been plundered, and their houses burnt over their heads. The Hindoos in particular, whose numbers amount to some 500 families, have lost everything they possess, and they will have to beg their way to India in the rear of our columns. The Chindawol has had a narrow escape. I doubt if our parties of plunderers would not have forced an entrance had not the Gholam Khana [the elite Qizilbash household guard] stood to their arms, and showed and expressed determination to defend their property to the last.[98]

Nott was equally disillusioned. 'What we are staying here for I am utterly at a loss to know,' he wrote on 9 October, 'unless it be to be laughed at by the Afghans, and the whole world.'[99]

On the 10th, the British woke to find the first snows of winter dusting the hills around Kabul. Keen to avoid being caught in the sort of blizzards that had helped obliterate Elphinstone's army, and having now burned down almost all of the town, Pollock issued an order that morning that the British were to withdraw two days later.

That the British were about to march out of Afghanistan had been kept a strict secret, and much of the Kabul nobility had come over to the British camp assuming that the occupation was to continue as before. Mohan Lal, who in many cases had been the go-between, was especially appalled by what he saw as an outright betrayal. 'I could hardly show my face to them at the time of our departure,' he wrote later. 'They all came full of tears, saying that "we deceived and punished our friends, causing them to stand against their own countrymen, then leaving them in the mouth of lions".' Mohan Lal realised, as everyone else did too, that Akbar would almost certainly return to Kabul as soon as the British had left and would 'torture, imprison, extort money from and disgrace all those who had taken our side'.[100] Shah Fatteh Jang knew this to be the case too; within a day of Pollock's announcement he had abdicated the throne and announced he would be returning to India with his blind uncle, Shah Zaman. His younger brother Shahpur, Shuja's favourite son, volunteered to stay on in his place, but few believed his rule would last more than a few weeks.

In an effort to give Shahpur's rule a chance of survival, on 11 October Pollock dragooned what was left of the Kabul nobility up to the Bala Hisar to swear an oath of allegiance. A document pledging loyalty was hastily drawn up, to which they all attached their seals, and one by one confirmed this by placing their hands on a Quran: 'At this happy moment when the sultan son of the sultan, Shahpur Shah, is our sovereign, we swear and certify by God and His Prophet and all the prophets . . . that we will not choose as Shah anyone but this illustrious ruler; with heart and soul we will not stint in our service to him; we consider obligatory that his orders be carried out by us, by the country, by the soldiery, and by the populace.'[101] Pollock refused however to supply the assembled nobility with any arms or ammunition, despite their pleas, so making their vows almost impossible to keep.[102] The speed of the army's departure not only doomed the pro-British nobility; it also left many of the Company's own sepoys in captivity. 'We ought to have remained longer to have recovered more of our captive people,' wrote a disgusted Colin Mackenzie. 'Hundreds were left in slavery.'[103] Years later, he met an enslaved sepoy who had managed to escape from captivity and make his way back to India. From this man he learned, as he had suspected, that 'the mountains were then full of our prisoners, many of whom were [later] sent off to Balkh as slaves. There were some English among them. Had our troops only been allowed to stay a few days longer they could all have been brought in.'[104]

At sunrise on 12 October 1842, the British lowered the Union Jack on the Bala Hisar, and, in the words of the Rev. I. N. Allen, 'turned our backs on the scene of former disgrace and present outrage – a melancholy and disgraceful scene'.[105] Behind them, Neville Chamberlain could see 'the whole face of the sky was red with flames' and the last remaining quarters of Kabul still standing – all that was left of the city of gardens which Burnes had once thought the most beautiful in the region – well on their way to becoming a smouldering wreck. 'Ruin and revenge had uprooted families and dwellings,' wrote Munshi Abdul Karim. 'Few distinguished citiziens were left; the bazaars had been pulled down; open spaces were heaped with corpses and filth and stench polluted the air. Once fine gardens were now the haunt of scavengers and owls: wretched beggars were left scrabbling in the dust.'[106]

If many of the troops were pleased to be heading back home to their Indian cantonments, the procession which left the city was nonetheless a sad spectacle, for along with the British trudged a whole variety of groups whose lives had been uprooted and ruined by Auckland's failed adventure: the Afghan nobility who had stood with the British, especially the more Anglophile Qizilbash, who now had little option but hastily to pack up and follow their retreating allies; the long lines of maimed and crippled sepoys who had been left to their fate on the 1842 retreat by Elphinstone's officers, and many of whom were now gangrenous amputees who had to be carried home in swaying dhoolies and camel panniers; the 500 destitute Hindu families who had been left both ruined and homeless by the rape and destruction of their quarter in Kabul; and, bringing up the rear, the surviving members of the Sadozai dynasty and the harems of Shahs Shuja, Zaman and Fatteh Jang, all of whose hopes of recovering their Kingdom had been thwarted by the incompetence and unpopularity of the British occupation, and who now again faced an uncertain future in a foreign land. As Mohammad Husain Herati wrote in conclusion at the end of his postscript to the *Waqi'at-i-Shah Shuja*: 'Thus did the English accomplish the destruction of the Afghan royal house of Sadozai.'[107]

For even as Pollock was marching his weary troops back along the skeleton-strewn Via Dolorosa of the Khord Kabul, past the sad detritus of Elphinstone's army – 'gloves and socks, sepoys' hair combs, broken china all serving to remind us of the misery and humiliation of our troops', and with the wheels of the horse artillery crushing the skulls of the fallen troops – news arrived that Ellenborough had presided over one last betrayal of the dynasty in whose name the British had invaded Afghanistan.[108] Two weeks earlier, on 1 October, the Governor General had issued from Simla a Proclamation which formally distanced the British government from the Sadozais. It did this on the entirely spurious grounds that Shah Shuja's actions had 'brought into question his fidelity to the government by which he was restored'. This was a straightforward lie: whatever his many failings, Shuja remained strikingly faithful to the British, even after they had single-handedly torn up their treaty with him and left him to his fate in December 1841. From now on, continued Ellenborough, 'the Governor General will leave it to the Afghans themselves to create a government amidst the anarchy which is the consequence of their crimes'. The Proclamation ended with a suitably Orwellian flourish: 'To force a sovereign upon a reluctant people would be as inconsistent with the policy as it is with the principles of the British government. The Governor General will willingly recognise any government approved by the Afghans themselves which shall appear desirous and capable of maintaining friendly relations with the neighbouring states.'[109]

In reality, however, Ellenborough believed there was only one man who could restore order in Afghanistan. At the same time as the Simla Proclamation was issued, Amir Dost Mohammad was quietly released from house arrest in Mussoorie. 'The Amir held a feast for all and sundry to celebrate, before leaving for Ferozepur,' wrote Mirza 'Ata.

There he had an audience with the Governor General and took his leave, accompanied by an official escort of 500 cavalry and foot-soldiers, as well as elephants, camels and bullock-carts to carry baggage. Haidar Khan, the Amir's son [who had been captured during the taking of Ghazni] and Haji Khan Kakar [who had delayed Outram's search party and given the Amir time to escape to Bukhara] were all sent to Ludhiana to join the Amir's entourage. After two months the Amir and his party left for Afghanistan; Lord Ellenborough granted him a rich cloak of honour, and sat in private session with him for a whole watch, urging him never to cross or confront the English government, and to maintain peaceful relations with the Sikhs and to refrain from hostilities. He advised that the Amir should restrain his son, Akbar Khan. Then they parted, and the Governor General ordered that the Amir's daily allowance should be paid until he entered the Khyber.[110]

The second retreat from Kabul began peacefully enough.

The long lines of soldiers, refugees and camp followers passed down the Khord Kabul and Tezin passes with barely a shot being fired. It was only when they neared the eastern Ghilzai heartlands just before Jagdalak that the sniping began.

It was Neville Chamberlain's fate to bring up the end of the column:

> I was walking in rear of all with my orderly, rifle in hand, taking shots at the rascals, when my orderly's horse, from which I had been firing, was riddled through the neck. I had not gone many paces when I was struck myself. I spun around and fell to the ground, but soon got up again and staggered on in great pain. I was determined that the Affghans should not even have the satisfaction of thinking they had done for me. On putting my hand on my back I thought it was all over with me, but on getting into camp we found the ball had not penetrated the skin, and it tumbled out on the doctor touching it.[111]

Others were less lucky. Chamberlain recorded how in an echo of the first retreat, the camp followers and refugees were now beginning to fall by the roadside. There they had to be left 'to be murdered by the Ghilzai, we not having any means of conveying them. I have myself given my own charger and made the men dismount to bring on the poor creatures, but after they were so weak as not to be able to ride or hang on a horse, I was obliged to abandon them to the knives of those merciless villains who gloried in cutting the throats of poor emaciated helpless beings. Every march we passed the bodies of those abandoned by the columns ahead of us.'[112]

In Jalalabad, Chamberlain arrived in time to see Broadfoot's engineers mining the walls of the fortress they had twice rebuilt and then defended with such success. A massive charge was placed under each bastion, and smaller ones along each stretch of curtain.[113] On 27 October, immediately after Pollock had marched out, there was a colossal explosion and Jalalabad was left as Kabul had been before it, a smoking mass of ruins.[114]

It was on the next stage of the retreat, the descent of the Khyber, that the British encountered the most determined resistance. The Afridis as usual streamed out of their mountain villages to snipe, gut and pillage the passing columns, and again the British exacted bloody reprisals. 'No quarter was given,' scribbled Chamberlain on the night of the 29th. 'We killed between 150 and 200 men . . . All the stacks and villages plundered and fired.' On 1 November, at the top of the pass, John Nicholson was briefly reunited with his younger brother Alexander, before John was sent to join Chamberlain in the rearguard.

The following day, Chamberlain and John Nicholson corkscrewed down the path just below Ali Masjid, accompanied by the chaplain Allen. Turning a sharp corner the three found the road thickly strewn with the bodies of their colleagues from whom they had parted the previous afternoon. Their entire party had been trapped and overwhelmed by an Afridi ambush. Now their remains were 'lying here and there, stripped and mangled, some already partially devoured by dogs and birds of prey. Among them were two native women, one young and well looking.'[115] Among the dead was Nicholson's younger brother. His body was stark naked, and hacked to pieces. In accordance with Afridi custom, Alexander had had his genitalia cut off and stuffed in his mouth.[116] The incident left Nicholson with a visceral, almost psychopathic loathing of all Muslims, and with an appetite for their destruction that he was able to indulge in periodically over the next few years, and slake fully during the Great Uprising of 1857.[117]

The next morning, his last in Afghanistan, it was Chamberlain's turn to be ambushed. He was again in the rearguard and as he descended the final section of the road towards the fort at Jamrud his party were caught in a hail of bullets from jezail marksmen hidden high in the gullies above them. 'I was riding a few paces in advance of the corps,' he wrote,

> the balls striking rather close. I turned around and said to an officer, 'Those fellows do not fire badly.' And true enough, for the moment afterwards I was struck. The ball hit me so hard that my friend answered, 'You are hit, old fellow,' but I needed not to be told to make me aware of it. The regiment galloped on to get from under the fire. I was obliged to dismount, or rather half fell from my horse, and dragged and supported by my groom and a sepoy, I lay down behind a piece of rock which sheltered me from the fire, until after some time a dhoolie was brought for me and I was carried into camp at Jamrud.[118]

Chamberlain had been hit with the very last shots of the war. Jamrud marked an invisible boundary, after which the murderous violence of Afghanistan abruptly stopped. By evening, the Rev. I. N. Allen had reached the very different world of the outskirts of Peshawar. 'Men were sitting by the roadside selling grain and sweetmeats,' he wrote in amazement. 'These were strange sights to us who had for months been without seeing a human being, except as an enemy.'[119]

There followed a long five-week march through the Punjab to the boundary of the Company territories on the Sutlej, near

Ferozepur. Chamberlain was carried the whole way in a litter, 'too ill to be amused or see the country . . . Hundreds of men died during our march from fatigue or wounds. Comparatively speaking I was one of the lucky ones. But I hope I shall never again go through what I then suffered.'[120]

The first troops reached Ferozepur just before Christmas, on 23 December. As they marched over the bridge of boats spanning the river, Lord Ellenborough was waiting in person to greet the troops, with a regimental band playing 'See the Conquering Hero Comes'. As Colin Mackenzie's sister-in-law, Julia Margaret Cameron, the pioneering photographer, memorably described him, Ellenborough was 'flighty and unmanageable in all matters of business . . . [but] violently enthusiastic on all military matters, and they alone seem to occupy his interests or his attention'.

A great ceremonial arch of bamboo, coloured cotton and bunting had been erected, 'so closely resembling a gigantic gallows', wrote Mackenzie, 'that the soldiers marched under it with peals of laughter'.[121] Beyond stretched a row two miles long of 250 caparisoned elephants, whose trunks the Governor General had personally helped paint.[122] He had also organised a cavalcade of celebrations and parades to mark what he termed the victorious return of the army to the same grounds which they had left three years earlier. There were twenty-one-gun salutes for Sale, Pollock and Nott, and even one for the supposed Somnath Gates which were brought into camp covered in marigold garlands. A succession of banquets were then laid on in vast shamiana marquees, though many had little appetite for such festivities after what they had just gone through. Mackenzie retired to his tent, writing that few 'felt anything like the joy which might have been anticipated . . . All the [former] captives suffered from depression of spirits, some of them, as Eyre, to a terrible degree. Some of the ladies dreamt of the horrors they had witnessed night after night for months after their release.'[123]

Also disenchanted with all the junketing was the Commander-in-Chief, Sir Jasper Nicholls. After watching the troops march in for a while he returned to his desk to begin drawing up his official report on how his army had suffered such an unparalleled disaster.

'I would not have counselled that invasion *for any honour* which could have been conferred on me,' he wrote.[124] After all the waste and destruction of an expensive and unnecessary war of dubious legality, with the honour and reputation of British arms tarnished and British authority undermined; after spending £15 million [well over £50 billion in modern currency], exhausting the Indian treasury, pushing the Indian credit network to the brink of collapse and permanently wrecking the solvency of the East India Company; after losing maybe 40,000 lives, as well as those of around 50,000 camels; and after alienating much of the Bengal army, leaving it ripe for mutiny, the British had left Afghanistan much as they found it, he concluded: in tribal chaos, with Dost Mohammad about to return from exile and on the verge of retrieving his throne. Just ahead of the troops, the news had just come in by express that both Prince Safdarjang in Kandahar and Prince Shahpur in Kabul had been forced out by their Barakzai enemies.

In truth, no one except the bombastic Governor General himself was convinced by Ellenborough's claims of victory, least of all the Afghans. As Mirza 'Ata put it: 'The remaining troops when they were safely out of Afghanistan were welcomed by speeches by the Governor General: for the proverb says Afghanistan is the land of hawks, but India is a land of carrion crows . . .' He continued:

It is said that the English entered Afghanistan a second time merely to free the English prisoners, spending lakhs and lakhs to bribe the Afghans into allowing them passage, leaving thousands more dead behind, and then revealing their true nature by demolishing the markets of Kabul and promptly returning to India. They had hoped to establish themselves in Afghanistan, to block any Russian advance – but for all the treasure they expended and for all the lives they sacrificed, the only result was ruin and disgrace. If the English had been able to conquer and keep Afghanistan, would they ever have left a land where 44 different types of grapes grow, and other fruits as well – apples, pomegranates, pears, rhubarb, mulberries, sweet watermelon and musk-melon, apricots and peaches? And ice-water, that cannot be found in all the plains of India?

'The Anglo-Indian invasion of Afghanistan', which had wasted money, military equipment and soldiers' lives, 'both black and white', had been, he wrote,

> an unequal fight between treacherous Indian crows and brave Afghan hawks: whenever they took one mountain, the next mountain was always still left in open rebellion. In truth the English would never ever, even after years and years, have managed to pacify Khorasan. The English with their crow-like Indian troops stayed with their bones scattered and unburied on the mountain-slopes of Afghanistan, while the brave Afghan fighters looked for martyrdom, and were victorious in this world and the next: blessed they are indeed who taste the cup of martyrdom![125]

Whether or not Mirza 'Ata's ghazis received the blessings they were expecting either in post-war Afghanistan or in paradise, it was certainly true that very few of those who participated in the war, especially those on the Anglo-Sadozai side, saw their lives prosper in any way. Even before the war, many Afghans had warned the British that a curse was attached to the *kumbukht* [that unlucky rascal] Shah Shuja, who always saw his best-laid plans end in disaster.[126] Now, long after Shuja's death, this bad luck seemed to be passed on to any who were involved in his attempt to depose Dost Mohammad.

Ranjit Singh, Burnes, Vitkevitch and Macnaghten were already long dead, while Wade had been sacked from his jealously guarded position on the Frontier at the request of the Khalsa and had been bundled off to the less important Residency at Indore in central India. Burnes's unfortunate Suffolk dray horses that he had escorted up the Indus with such trouble had also passed on: Ranjit Singh soon lost interest in them once it became clear that they were incapable of charging. They were penned up and soon died as no one in Lahore knew what to do with them.

Charles Masson, another survivor from pre-war Kabul, also came to a sad end. After the failure of the 1837–8 Burnes mission, he found himself sidelined by the Company as it prepared for war with Afghanistan, even though he knew the country much more intimately than any other Englishman. Later, while attempting to make his way back to Kabul in 1840, walking along the British line of march through country which he said had been devastated by the passage of the Army of the Indus, he had got as far as Qalat when the British stormed the city. On its capture Masson found himself arrested and imprisoned as a traitor and a spy. It took him over six months to prove his innocence and gain his release. When Henry Rawlinson later ran him to ground in Karachi, he was horrified by what had happened to the man he had long revered as the greatest archaeologist in the region: 'Whilst at Kurrachee Camp I rode into the town to see Masson of whom I have heard and read so much,' he wrote in his diary.

I found him in a wretched hovel talking with some Belochees nearly naked and half drunk. I remained with him several hours and was extremely pained with all I witnessed. His language was at first so insolent that I thought he had become quite foolish. But at last he told me, having sat up writing he had dined of a bottle of wine and had risen at daylight with the fumes still in his head. I almost think however that his mind is really giving way – he gave me several papers to read which were written in the same vague and dreary style as he spoke in and all his information appeared to me to be lost by his method in putting it together. He is most bitter against Burnes and Wade and Lord Auckland . . . He has already written two volumes relating to his travels and his work in Afghanistan and was busy with his third – many parts of this which he showed me are very curious, but they will not stand publication – there is a sort of stilting in his language and vague fanciful fleeting in his ideas that the taste of the age will never tolerate. If Pottinger allows the MSS to be printed as it now is Masson will pass for a presumptuous ignoramus instead of the conscientious, hard working fellow he really is. I trust something will be done to get him to Bombay.[127]

But nothing was done, and Masson was forced to sit and watch as Macnaghten blundered fatally around Afghanistan, unable to do more than write anonymous embittered letters to the press. 'In your paper today,' reads one of his submissions, 'I observe that jackasses are to be employed in Afghanistan. What can be the reason for such a step? Are the camels of the country exhausted? Seeing that jackasses have been for a long time employed in the Political Department, is it the commencement of a system to introduce them to the military one, with a view to establishing uniformity in the services?'[128] He eventually made his way back to England where his publications received the derisory reviews Rawlinson had predicted, and where his reputation as an antiquarian was belittled by his stay-at-home rivals. He died in poverty near Potter's Bar in 1853 'of an uncertain disease of the brain'. He could have no idea that 160 years later he would be revered as the father of Afghan archaeology.

Eldred Pottinger, who received no reward for his work in Afghanistan, resigned from the Company. He went off to stay with his uncle, Sir Henry Pottinger, in Hong Kong, the island which Pottinger senior had just bullied the Chinese into handing over to him, and of which the former Great Game operative had just appointed himself the first governor. There Eldred died in 1843 from 'the combined effects of his wounds, of hardship, and of depression of mind and body'.[129]

Brigadier Shelton was, somewhat surprisingly, exonerated by a court martial from responsibility for the catastrophic handling of the uprising, but remained as unpopular as ever: when he was thrown from his horse and died in Dublin in 1844, his men turned out on the parade ground and gave three cheers to celebrate his demise.

A version of Lady Sale and her husband's Afghan adventures was turned into a popular act at Astley's Circus, 'The Captives at Cabool', but the real 'Fighting Bob' Sale was killed along with George Broadfoot at the Battle of Moodki three years later during the Anglo-Sikh War of 1845, as the Company finally seized its chance to absorb the rich lands of the Punjab. Lady Sale emigrated as a widow to South Africa and died in Cape Town in 1853. Her grave is marked with the epitaph: 'Underneath this stone reposes all that could die of Lady Sale.'[130]

Dr Brydon, the sole European in Company employ to make it through to Jalalabad during the retreat from Kabul, lived on to survive the next great Imperial catastrophe in the region: fifteen years later in 1857, during the Great Uprising, he helped defend the Lucknow Residency under George Lawrence's younger brother Henry. In 1873 he eventually died in his bed, in peaceful retirement at Nigg opposite the Black Isle in the Scottish Highlands.

Auckland lived on in semi-disgrace in Kensington, and died aged only sixty-five in 1849, succeeded three months later by his sister Fanny.[131] Empire-building did not prove to be a family talent: the next Eden to try his hand, Anthony Eden, presided over the debacle of Suez 114 years later.[*]

The heroic and ingenious Mohan Lal, who had taken out large loans in his own name for the benefit of Macnaghten during the siege, partly to raise a bounty for the assassination of the rebel Afghan leaders, and who again in 1842 borrowed more money to secure the release of hostages, was never repaid the 79,496 rupees he calculated he was owed; as a result he was dogged by debt for the rest of his life. In pursuit of justice, he eventually travelled to Britain in the company of his fellow munshi Shahamat Ali, where between attempts to lobby the Company directors he was enter-tained by the newly retired Colonel Wade and his young bride on the Isle of Wight; he also visited Scotland where he delivered Burnes's surviving letters and journals to his family in Montrose. In Edinburgh, Mohan Lal was photographed by the pioneering Scottish photographers David Octavius Hill and Robert Adamson in an exotic confection of Afghan-Kashmiri dress which *The Times* called 'magnificent Hindoo costume'.[132] While in Britain he published in English a memoir of his Central Asian travels with Burnes and an enormous 900-page, two-volume biography of Dost

---

[*] The Edens did however make an enduring name for themselves in New Zealand where the then capital was named after Gèorge, while the present cricket ground is named Eden Park. Lord Melbourne, the Prime Minister at the time, got his name on the map of Australia instead.

Mohammad. He even had an audience with Queen Victoria and Prince Albert. But the Afghan War haunted his life and effectively ended his career.

On his return to Delhi from London he never received the appointments he applied for as Persian secretary to the prestigious residencies of Lucknow and Hyderabad. British officials distrusted him, frequently writing that he was 'presumptuous' and 'had risen above his station'. Not only did he remain unemployed by the government, he also remained outcaste from his own Kashmiri pundit community. After narrowly escaping with his life during the 1857 uprising, when the mutinous sepoys tried to hunt him down as a prominent sympathiser with the British, he died in 1877 in poverty and obscurity, alienated from the society of both colonised and colonisers.[133]

A similar fate awaited the Sadozai princes. By March 1843 they were all stuck in Lahore, able neither to return to Afghanistan nor to enter British India, and living like their father thirty years earlier in daily fear of being plundered of their remaining wealth by their Sikh hosts.[134] When permission was eventually granted for them to cross the border and return to their childhood home of Ludhiana, it was done with the explicit proviso that they should have lower pensions and smaller premises than those once given to Shah Shuja.[135] All the Shahzadas ended up in debt and the National Archives of India contains long reams of correspondence between the government and their creditors who were attempting into the 1860s to sue the princes for unpaid loans. Without exception, they all died in poverty.

Colin Mackenzie, who was posted to Ludhiana to raise the Frontier Brigade, wrote movingly of the plight of the large Afghan refugee community in Ludhiana which he found struggling to survive when he arrived there, newly remarried, in 1847. 'The miseries inflicted by our interference on those whom we professed to support ought not to be forgotten,' he wrote in his memoirs. 'It was sad to see men of rank and property reduced to absolute want. In one case a father and son, nearly connected with Shah Shuja, never paid a visit together because they had only one *choga* [cloak] between them. Another man of rank was obliged to sell even his sword for food. An old retainer of Shah Shuja said sadly: "I live upon fasting, and the day when a little dal is cooked in my house is a feast.""[136]

A request by the old blind Shah Zaman that he should be allowed to retire as a poor dervish to the Sufi shrine of Sirhind was vetoed by the Maharajah of Patiala.[137] The Maharajah did eventually relent on Shah Zaman's death in 1844, and the old Shah was laid to rest there, beside the grave of his sister-in-law, Shuja's chief wife and Dost Mohammad's sister, Wa'fa Begum.[138]

The last glimpse we have of the Sadozai princes is the memoir of Robert Warburton, the son of the happy marriage between a British officer and Shah Jahan Begum, the niece of Dost Moham-mad, who grew up in Ludhiana among the Afghan exile community.

> Whatever may have been their public failings, I was not old enough to judge in those days, but the kindness of some of them to me, carried over a series of years, was always of the same uniform char-acter. I was not debarred from going inside their *harem-sarais*, and my knowledge of Persian permitted me to converse with the wives of all the Shahzadas . . . There were two brothers, Shahzada Shah-pur and Shahzada Nadir, the youngest sons of the unfortunate Shah Shujah-ul-Mulk, who particularly took my fancy. For resignation in the midst of their troubles, for gentleness to all who were brought into contact with them, and for a lofty regard for the feelings and wishes of others, I have seldom seen finer types of the true gentle-man than these two brothers. The elder was in receipt of a pension of Rs 500 and the younger of Rs 100 a month from the Indian government – small sums indeed with which to bring up their fami-lies and support the number of ancient servitors who had been driven out of house and home at Kabul and had followed the fortunes of this royal family into the heat and plains of India.[139]

There were few happy endings either for the Afghan victors of the war. Nawab Zaman Khan Barakzai was quickly marginalised by Dost Mohammad and never again received any major government posts.[140] Aminullah Khan Logari was judged to have become too ambitious and disruptive, and was imprisoned for life shortly after the end of the war, because of his predilection, according to Fayz Mohammad, 'for inciting peaceful people to engage in mischief'.[141] Mackenzie was later told by Aminullah's brother, who ended up a refugee in Ludhiana, that Dost Mohammad, 'having married a daughter of Aminullah, had then murdered him with his own hands, smothering him with a pillow'.[142]

Wazir Akbar Khan enjoyed a year of power after the British left, but on the return of his father in 1843 was sent off to be governor of Jalalabad and Laghman. His durbar soon came to be seen as a centre of opposition to Dost Mohammad. When Akbar Khan was poisoned in 1847 it was widely rumoured that it was on his father's orders.[143] Just before he died, Akbar wrote a last letter to Mackenzie, 'affectionately reproaching him for his neglect of the duties of friendship in not giving him news of his welfare'. Mackenzie was forbidden by the government from answering the letter 'as it was from an enemy'.[144] Mackenzie did however answer a letter from Mohammad Shah Khan Ghilzai, who, having become too powerful for the liking of Dost Mohammad, had fallen from favour and been ruined soon after the death of his son-in-law. Forced to flee into exile among the Kafirstanis of Nuristan, he wrote to Mackenzie in Ludhiana to remind him 'of their former friendship and to ask if it continued'.

> The letter was brought by a Sayad, to whom he had given a token whereby he might judge of Mackenzie's disposition towards him. The Sayad began: 'Mohammad Shah Khan says to you, "when you were in peril of life by the fort of Mahmud Khan [after the murder of Macnaghten] how did I act?"' Mackenzie answered: 'When the sword was raised to strike me, he put his arm round my neck and took the cut on his own shoulder.' Then the Sayad knew he might deliver the letter. Mackenzie replied that he 'would always acknowledge him as a friend'.[145]

The only man who clearly gained from the First Anglo-Afghan War was the very man whom the war was designed to depose. In

April 1843, after staying as the guest of the Sikh Khalsa in Lahore, Dost Mohammad rode to Peshawar and mounted the switchbacks of the Khyber. At Ali Masjid he was greeted by Akbar Khan and escorted by him back to Kabul. 'The residents of that city lined the route,' wrote Fayz Mohammad. 'Old and young alike cheered his arrival and the eyes of his supporters were dazzled and their breasts swelled with pride at the sight of him. With joy increasing, they sang his praises, and together they entered Kabul in a state of complete euphoria. For seven days and nights there were joyous celebrations. The nights were brightened with lights and the days with the sounds of people reciting ghazals [love lyrics] and singing. Joy and festivity rang out and everywhere there was gladness and cheer.'[146]

Intelligence reports collated by the British from their spies and sympathisers in Afghanistan maintained in 1843 that 'the authority of the Ameer and his family is merely nominal and nothing whatever will be collected from the Kohistanis, the Ghilzais, the people of Koonur or the Khyburees. Dost Mohammad spends his time and his money in vainly endeavouring to raise disciplined battalions and in a silly emulation of the state of the princes of India.'[147]

As before, however, British intelligence had underestimated Dost Mohammad. Slowly, the Amir increased his power and expanded his dominions in eastern Afghanistan, so laying the foundations for his subsequent achievement, of conquering first Bamiyan and Badakhshan, then Khulm and the whole of northern Afghanistan. By the early 1850s he had subdued the Ghilzai tribes around Ghazni and in 1855 ousted his half-brothers from control of Kandahar. By the time of his death in 1863, having remained completely true to his treaties with the British, he had increased his tax revenues from 2.5 to 7 million rupees and was ruling over almost all of the modern state of Afghanistan. It was the limits of Dost Mohammad's conquests that came to form the frontiers of modern Afghanistan – containing Herat, but shorn of Peshawar – still a source of disgruntlement to Afghan and especially Pashtun nationalists.

Ironically it was the Amir who was the ultimate beneficiary of the administrative reforms enacted by Macnaghten to strengthen the rule of Shah Shuja, which reduced the power of the Durrani tribal chiefs and created a more professional army and a working tax structure.[148] Indeed this was only one of a number of ways in which British colonialism played a strong formative role in shaping and creating the Afghan state which now came much more clearly into being than it had done before the occupation. Yet the more coherent Afghanistan now ruled by Dost Mohammad was also a more impoverished and isolated country than it had ever been before in its history. No longer was it the rich and cultured cross-roads of the Silk Route, nor were the great days of high Timurid Persianate culture ever to return. For the first time in its history, under the Barakzais Afghanistan would become to some extent a backwater.

The last town to fall to the Amir was Herat, which he had just finished besieging when he died. There Dost Mohammad was laid to rest in the most beautiful Sufi shrine in Afghanistan, the Gazur Gah. In stark contrast to his rival Shah Shuja, whose probable tomb is to be found unmarked in the basement of the mausoleum of his father, Timur Shah, Dost Mohammad lies beneath a large and beautifully carved marble monument in the place of honour beside the region's most revered Sufi saint and poet Khwaja 'Abd Allah Ansari. Dost Mohammad's descendants continued to rule a united Afghanistan until the revolutions of the 1970s.

Today Herat is the most peaceful and prosperous town in Afghanistan, and the Gazur Gah is still a popular place of pilgrimage. Robert Byron wrote in the 1930s that 'everyone goes to the Gazur Gah. Babur went. Humayun went. Shah Abbas improved the water supply. It is still the Heratis' favourite resort.' It remains so eighty years later. The shrine lies on the edge of the hills that surround the city. A tall arched Timurid gateway leads into a cool and peaceful courtyard full of superbly calligraphed tombs and memorial stones. House martins swoop through the pine trees and ilexes. Old men lie asleep in the shade, using their white turbans as pillows. Others gently finger their rosaries as the pigeons coo around them.

Elsewhere in Afghanistan and Pakistan, the return of the Taliban has meant in many places the banning of gentle, heterodox Sufi devotions: the shrines have been closed or blown up, and the instruments of the musicians broken. Yet here at the Gazur Gah, the Sufis survive intact. When I was there in 2009 a group of devotees began to chant the zikr immediately behind Dost Mohammad's tomb, kneeling in a circle, and as a long-haired cantor sang one of Khwaja sahib's poems in a high tenor voice, his followers clapped and chanted: 'Haq! haq!' – 'Truth! Truth!' On they chanted, faster and faster, pitch rising, until finally reaching their mystical climax, and falling backwards on to the carpets and bolsters with long ecstatic sighs. Dost Mohammad could have no more honoured resting place.

In the summer of 1844, soon after Dost Mohammad had returned to reclaim his throne and began the rebuilding and unification of his wrecked and plundered kingdom, on the other side of the world Tsar Nicholas of Russia invited himself to stay with Queen Victoria and Prince Albert at Windsor Castle.

With the Tsar came his Foreign Minister Count Nesselrode, the man who had despatched Vitkevitch on his mission to Dost Mohammad in 1837. If it was Anglo-Russian rivalry and suspicion which had ultimately caused the catastrophe of the Afghan War, here surely was the best possible chance to lay the ghosts of that conflict peacefully to rest.

The Tsar, who had been travelling with his courtiers incognito under the name Count Orlov in order to avoid possible assassination attempts by Polish terrorists, arrived at Woolwich docks unannounced on a Dutch steamer on 1 June. After a night at the Russian Embassy at Ashburnham House in Westminster he made his way to Windsor by train.

Victoria, who was then twenty-five years old and heavily pregnant, had half expected some sort of Tartar savage, and there was much apprehension when, on the Tsar's arrival, their visitor sent to the stable for some straw to stuff the leather sack which served as the mattress for the military campbed on which he always slept. In the end, however, the Queen was most taken by her visitor. 'He is certainly a *very striking* man,' she wrote to her uncle on 4 June,

> still very handsome. His profile is *beautiful*, and his manners *most* dignified and graceful; extremely civil – quite alarmingly so, as he is so full of attentions and *politesses*. But the expression of the *eyes* is *formidable*, and unlike anything I ever saw before. He gives me and Albert the impression of a man who is *not* happy, and on whom the weight of his immense power and position weighs heavily and painfully; he seldom smiles, and when he does the expression is *not* a happy one. He is, however, very easy to get on with.[149]

At the end of the visit, Prince Albert took the Tsar to the villa at Chiswick House – a piece of the Palladian Veneto strangely marooned on the banks of the Thames amid the countryside and market gardens just to the west of London. Here the Duke of Devonshire, the lynchpin of the Whig establishment, was to host a grand ceremonial breakfast in his honour which would be attended by all the country's most powerful politicians and the entire diplomatic corps. The real business of the visit would take place in this unlikely spot, just beyond the fashionable riverside promenade of Chiswick Mall.

On 8 June, a bright summer day, the royal cavalcade entered the gates of Chiswick House at five minutes to two, preceded by outriders in state liveries, while the bands of the Coldstream Guards and Horse Guards played the Russian national anthem. The Imperial Standard was raised over the Summer Parlour and the Royal Standard over the Arcade, while a twenty-one-gun salute was fired from a battery erected within the grounds of the villa. The Tsar was then conducted, past the Duke's four giraffes, to the summer parlour which had been specially decorated in the style of a medieval pavilion. During the levee, the Tsar talked mainly to the Duke of Wellington, but also chatted with Lord

Melbourne and the Prime Minister, Sir Robert Peel. Count Nesselrode made straight for his former opposite number, Lord Palmerston, who in office had been known for his strong line against Russia, and the two remained locked in conversation for much of the afternoon.[150]

The visit was intended to cement relations between the two great powers, and to avoid the sort of misunderstandings and suspicions which had just caused so much unnecessary bloodshed in Central Asia. As the Tsar told Peel, 'Through our friendly intercourse, I hope to annihilate the prejudices between our countries.'[151] As an exercise in public relations, the Tsar's visit was certainly a great success. London society women were especially charmed by his good looks and perfect manners. 'He is still a great devotee to female beauty,' noted Baron Stockmar, 'and to his old English flames he showed the greatest attention.' Yet unwittingly, for all the good intentions, the conversations at the Chiswick Breakfast sowed instead the seeds for future conflict.

The Tsar, who had little understanding of the influence of Parliament and the opposition parties on government, left England believing that the private conversations he had had with the Queen and her senior ministers, especially Sir Robert Peel and his Foreign Secretary Lord Aberdeen, could be interpreted as expressions of government policy. Specifically he believed that Britain would now join him to partition the Ottoman Empire. But the British saw the conversations merely as a private exchange of ideas and not some sort of binding gentlemen's agreement as the Tsar believed.[152]

Symbolically, the breakfast ended in absurdity and chaos: as some of the guests including the King of Saxony crossed the lake in boats punted by the Duke's watermen for the purpose of inspecting the Devonshire giraffes, the giraffes decided to wade across the water in the opposite direction, before running amok on the lawns of Chiswick House and stampeding the Tsar's party who were waiting on the other bank. The giraffes were eventually led away by the groundsmen in their state liveries, but from this point a long chain of accidents, gaffes and diplomatic misunderstandings would lead inexorably to Russia and Britain going to war against each other in the Crimea nine years later in 1853.

This time, Anglo-Russian rivalry would lead to 800,000 deaths.

At the end of *Kim*, Kipling has his eponymous hero say, 'When everyone is dead, the Great Game is finished. Not before.'

In the 1980s it was the Russians' withdrawal from their failed occupation of Afghanistan that triggered the beginning of the end of the Soviet Union. Less than twenty years later, in 2001, British and American troops arrived in Afghanistan where they proceeded to begin losing what was, in Britain's case, its fourth war in that country. As before, in the end, despite all the billions of dollars handed out, the training of an entire army of Afghan troops and the infinitely superior weaponry of the occupiers, the Afghan resistance succeeded again in first surrounding then propelling the hated Kafirs into a humiliating exit. In both cases the occupying troops lost the will to continue fighting at such cost and with so little gain.

For all the differences, there are of course striking parallels between the twenty-first-century occupation of Afghanistan and that of 1839–42. There is a real continuity in the impact of political geography on the evolution of both conflicts. The significance of Kabul's location is one issue – adjacent to both the Tajik population of Kohistan, on one side, and the eastern Ghilzais on the other. Then there is the tribal issue, as another Popalzai ruler lacking a real power base, Hamid Karzai – astonishingly, from the same sub-tribe as Shah Shuja – faces the brunt of concerted guerrilla attacks led by the eastern Ghilzai who today make up the footsoldiers of the Taliban. They are directed by another Ghilzai tribal leader from the Hotak ruling clan, in this case Mullah Omar.*[153]

On my extended visits to Afghanistan to research this book in

* Mullah Omar is a distant relative of the first Afghan ruler of Southern Afghanistan, Mir Waiz Hotaki.

2009 and 2010, I set myself two goals. Firstly I wanted to try to find the elusive Afghan sources telling of the war which I was certain had to exist and which I have in due course used to write this book. Secondly, I was keen to see as many of the places and landscapes associated with the First Afghan War as was possible in a situation where ISAF's* hold on Afghanistan was already visibly shrinking every day. By 2010, the Taliban had a strong presence in over 70 per cent of the country and Karzai's government had firm control of only twenty-nine out of 121 key strategic districts. That 70 per cent included most of the route of the British retreat of January 1842 which I knew I would have to travel if I was to have an idea of the geography I was going to write about. I particularly wanted to try to get to Gandamak and see the site of the British last stand.

The route of the 1842 retreat backs on to the mountain range that leads to Tora Bora and the Pakistan border, the Ghilzai heartlands that have always been – along with Quetta – the Taliban's main recruiting ground. I had been advised not to attempt to visit the area without local protection, so eventually set off in the company of a regional tribal leader who was also a minister in Karzai's government: a mountain of a man named Anwar Khan Jagdalak, a former village wrestling champion and later captain of the Afghan Olympic wrestling team, who had made his name as a Jami'at-Islami Mujehedin commander in the jihad against the Soviets in the 1980s.

It was Jagdalak's Ghilzai ancestors who inflicted some of the worst casualties on the British army of 1842, something he proudly repeated several times as we drove through the same passes. 'They forced us to pick up guns to defend our honour,' he said. 'So we killed every last one of those bastards.' None of this, incidentally, has stopped Jagdalak from sending his family away from Kabul to the greater safety of Northolt in north London.

On the day we were to drive to Gandamak, I had been told to report at seven in the morning to Jagdalak's Ministry in the heart of the administrative district now named Wazir Akbar Khan. Threading my way through a slalom of checkpoints and razor wire surrounding the Ministry, I arrived to find Jagdalak being hustled

---

* The International Security Assistance Force, established by the United Nations in 2001 and taken over by NATO in 2003.

into a convoy of heavily armoured SUVs by his ever-present phalanx of bodyguards, walkie-talkies crackling and assault rifles primed.

Jagdalak drove himself, while pick-ups full of heavily armed Afghan bodyguards followed behind. As we headed through the capital, evidence of the failure of the current occupation lay all around us. Kabul remains one of the poorest and scrappiest capital cities in the world. Despite the US pouring in around $80 billion into Afghanistan, almost all that money has disappeared into defence and security and the roads of Kabul were still more rutted than those in the most negelected provincial towns of Pakistan. There was no street lighting and apparently no rubbish collection. According to Jagdalak, that was only the tip of the iceberg. Despite all the efforts of a dozen countries and a thousand agencies over more than a decade since 2001, the country is still a mess: a quarter of all teachers in Afghanistan are illiterate. In many areas, governance is almost non-existent: half the governors do not have an office, even fewer have electricity. Civil servants lack the most basic education and skills.

We bumped through the potholed roads of Kabul, past the blast walls of the US Embassy and the NATO barracks that has been built on the very site of the British cantonment of 170 years ago, past Butkhak, then headed down the zigzagging road into the line of bleak mountain passes – first the Khord Kabul, then the Tezin – that link Kabul with the Khyber Pass.

It is a suitably dramatic and violent landscape: faultlines of crushed and tortured strata groaned and twisted in the gunpowder-coloured rockwalls rising on either side of us. Above, the jagged mountain tops were veiled in an ominous cloud of mist. As we drove, Jagdalak complained bitterly of the western treatment of his government. 'In the 1980s when we were killing Russians for them, the Americans called us freedom fighters,' he muttered as we descended the first pass. 'Now they just dismiss us as warlords.' At Sarobi, where the mountains debouch into a high-altitude ochre desert dotted with encampments of Ghilzai nomads, we left the main road and headed into Taliban territory; a further five pick-up trucks full of Jagdalak's old Mujehedin fighters, all brandishing rocket-propelled grenades and with faces wrapped in their turbans, appeared from a side road to escort us.

At the village of Jagdalak, on 12 January 1842, the last 200 frost-bitten British soldiers found themselves surrounded by several thousand Ghilzai tribesmen; only a handful made it beyond the holly hedge. Our own welcome that April was, thankfully, somewhat warmer. It was my host's first visit to his home since he became a minister, and the proud villagers took their old commander on a nostalgia trip through hills smelling of wild thyme and wormwood, and up through mountainsides carpeted with hollyhocks and mulberries and shaded by white poplars. Here, at the top of the surrounding peaks, near the watchtower where the naked and freezing sepoys had attempted to find shelter, lay the remains of Jagdalak's old Mujehedin bunkers and entrenchments from which he had defied the Soviet army. Once the tour was completed, the villagers feasted us, Timurid style, in an apricot orchard at the bottom of the valley: we sat on carpets under a trellis of vine and pomegranate blossom, as course after course of kebabs and raisin pullao were laid in front of us.

During lunch, as my hosts casually pointed out the site of the holly barrier and other places in the village where the British had been massacred in 1842, we compared our respective family memories of that war. I talked about my great-great-uncle, Colin Mackenzie, who had been taken hostage nearby, and I asked if they saw any parallels with the current situation. 'It is exactly the same,' said Jagdalak. 'Both times the foreigners have come for their own interests, not for ours. They say, "We are your friends, we want to help." But they are lying.'

'Whoever comes to Afghanistan, even now, they will face the fate of Burnes, Macnaghten and Dr Brydon,' agreed Mohammad Khan, our host in the village and the owner of the orchard where we were sitting. Everyone nodded sagely into their rice: the names of the fallen of 1842, long forgotten in their home country, were still common currency here.

'Since the British went we've had the Russians,' said one old man to my right. 'We saw them off too, but not before they bombed many of the houses in the village.' He pointed at a ridge full of ruined mudbrick houses on the hills behind us.

'We are the roof of the world,' said Khan. 'From here you can control and watch everywhere.'

'Afghanistan is like the crossroads for every nation that comes to power,' agreed Jagdalak. 'But we do not have the strength to control our own destiny. Our fate is determined by our neighbours.'

It was nearly 5 p.m. before the final flaps of naan bread were cleared away, by which time it became clear that it was now too late to head on to Gandamak. Instead we went that evening by the main highway direct to the relative safety of Jalalabad, where we discovered we'd had a narrow escape. It turned out that there had been a battle at Gandamak that very morning between government forces and a group of villagers supported by the Taliban. The sheer size and length of the feast and our own gluttony had saved us from walking straight into an ambush. The battle had taken place on exactly the site of the British last stand of 1842.

The following morning in Jalalabad we went to a jirga, or assembly, of Ghilzai tribal elders, to which the greybeards of Gandamak had come, under a flag of truce, to discuss what had happened the day before. The story was typical of many I heard about Karzai's government, and revealed how a mixture of corruption, incompetence and insensitivity had helped give an opening for the return of the once hated Taliban.

As Predator Drones took off and landed incessantly at the nearby airfield, the Ghilzai elders related how the previous year government troops had turned up to destroy the opium harvest. The troops promised the villagers full compensation and were allowed to plough up the crops; but the money never turned up. Before the planting season, the Gandamak villagers again went to Jalalabad and asked the government if they could be provided with assistance to grow other crops. Promises were made; again nothing was delivered. They planted poppy, informing the local authorities that if they again tried to destroy the crop, the village would have no option but to resist. When the troops turned up, about the same time as we were arriving at nearby Jagdalak, the villagers were waiting for them and had called in the local

Taliban to assist. In the fighting that followed, nine policemen were killed, six vehicles were destroyed and ten police hostages taken.

After the jirga was over, two of the tribal elders of Gandamak came over and we chatted for a while over a pot of green tea.

'Last month,' said one, 'some American officers called us to a hotel in Jalalabad for a meeting. One of them asked me, "Why do you hate us?" I replied, "Because you blow down our doors, enter our houses, pull our women by the hair and kick our children. We cannot accept this. We will fight back, and we will break your teeth, and when your teeth are broken you will leave, just as the British left before you. It is just a matter of time."'

'What did he say to that?'

'He turned to his friend and said, "If the old men are like this, what will the younger ones be like?" In truth, all the Americans here know their game is over. It is just their politicians who deny this.'

'These are the last days of the Americans,' said the other elder. 'Next it will be China.'

Author's Note

In 1843, shortly after his return from the slaughterhouse of the First Anglo-Afghan War, the army chaplain in Jalalabad, the Rev. G. R. Gleig, wrote a memoir about the disastrous expedition of which he was one of the lucky survivors. It was, he wrote, 'a war begun for no wise purpose, carried on with a strange mixture of rashness and timidity, brought to a close after suffering and disaster, without much glory attached either to the government which directed, or the great body of troops which waged it. Not one benefit, political or military, has been acquired with this war. Our eventual evacuation of the country resembled the retreat of an army defeated.'[1]

William Barnes Wollen's celebrated painting of the *Last Stand of the 44th Foot* – a group of ragged but doggedly determined soldiers on the hilltop of Gandamak standing encircled behind a thin line of bayonets, as the Pashtun tribesmen close in – became one of the era's most famous images, along with *Remnants of an Army*, Lady Butler's oil of the alleged last survivor, Dr Brydon, arriving before the walls of Jalalabad on his collapsing nag.

It was just as the latest western invasion of Afghanistan was beginning to turn sour in the winter of 2006, that I had the idea of writing a new history of Britain's first failed attempt at controlling Afghanistan. After an easy conquest and the successful installation of a pro-western puppet ruler, the regime was facing increasingly widespread resistance. History was beginning to repeat itself.

In the course of the initial research I visited many of the places associated with the war. On my first day in Afghanistan I drove through the Shomali Plain to see the remains of Eldred Pottinger's barracks at Charikar, which now lie a short distance from the US Air Force base at Bagram. In Herat I paid my respects at the grave of Dost Mohammad Khan, at the Sufi shrine of Gazur Gah. In Jalalabad I sat by the Kabul River and ate the same delicious *shir maheh* river fish, grilled on charcoal, which 170 years earlier had sustained the British troops besieged there and which had been particularly popular with 'Fighting Bob' Sale. On arrival in Kandahar, the car sent to pick me up from the airport received a sniper shot through its back window as it neared the perimeter; later I stood at one of Henry Rawlinson's favourite spots, the shrine of Baba Wali on the edge of town, and saw an IED blow up a US patrol as it crossed the Arghandab River, then as now the frontier between the occupied zone and the area controlled by the Afghan resistance. In Kabul I managed to get permission to visit the Bala Hisar, once Shah Shuja's citadel, now the headquarters of the Afghan Army's intelligence corps, where reports from the front line are evaluated amid a litter of spiked British cannon from 1842 and upturned Soviet T-72 tanks from the 1980s.

The closer I looked, the more the west's first disastrous entanglement in Afghanistan seemed to contain distinct echoes of the neo-colonial adventures of our own day. For the war of 1839 was waged on the basis of doctored intelligence about a virtually non-existent threat: information about a single Russian envoy to Kabul was exaggerated and manipulated by a group of ambitious and ideologically driven hawks to create a scare – in this case, about a phantom Russian invasion. As John MacNeill, the Russophobe British ambassador, wrote from Teheran in 1838: 'we should declare that he who is not with us is against us . . . We must secure Afghanistan.'[2] Thus was brought about an unnecessary, expensive and entirely avoidable war.

The parallels between the two invasions I came to realise were not just anecdotal, they were substantive. The same tribal rivalries and the same battles were continuing to be fought out in the same places 170 years later under the guise of new flags, new ideologies and new political puppeteers. The same cities were garrisoned by foreign troops speaking the same languages, and were being attacked from the same rings of hills and the same high passes.

In both cases, the invaders thought they could walk in, perform regime change, and be out in a couple of years. In both cases they were unable to prevent themselves getting sucked into a much wider conflict. Just as the British inability to cope with the rising of 1841 was a product not just of the leadership failures within the British camp, but also of the breakdown of the strategic relationship between Macnaghten and Shah Shuja, so the uneasy relationship of the ISAF leadership with President Karzai has been a crucial factor in the failure of the latest imbroglio. Here the US special envoy Richard Holbrooke to some extent played the role of Macnaghten. When I visited Kabul in 2010, the then British Special Representative, Sir Sherard Cowper-Coles, described Holbrooke as 'a bull who brought his own china shop wherever he went' – a description that would have served perfectly to sum up Macnaghten's style 174 years previously. Sherard's analysis of the failure of the current occupation in his memoirs, *Cables from Kabul*, reads astonishingly like an analysis of that of Auckland and Macnaghten: 'Getting in without having any real idea of how to get out; almost wilful misdiagnosis of the nature of the challenges; continually changing objectives, and no coherent or consistent plan; mission creep on a heroic scale; disunity of political and military command, also on a heroic scale; diversion of attention and resources [to Iraq in the current case, to the Opium Wars then] at a critical stage of the adventure; poor choice of local allies; weak political leadership.'[3]

Then as now, the poverty of Afghanistan has meant that it has been impossible to tax the Afghans into financing their own occupation. Instead, the cost of policing such inaccessible territory has exhausted the occupier's resources. Today the US is spending more than $100 billion a year in Afghanistan: it costs more to keep Marine battalions in two districts of Helmand than the US is providing to the entire nation of Egypt in military and development assistance. In both cases the decision to withdraw troops has turned on factors with little relevance to Afghanistan, namely the state of the economy and the vagaries of politics back home.

As I pursued my research, it was fascinating to see how the same moral issues that are chewed over in the editorial columns today were discussed at equal length in the correspondence of the First Afghan War: what are the ethical responsibilities of an occupying power? Should you try to 'promote the interests of humanity', as one British official put it in 1840, and champion social and gender reform, banning traditions like the stoning to death of adulterous women; or should you just concentrate on ruling the country without rocking the boat? Do you intervene if your allies start boiling or roasting their enemies alive? Do you attempt to introduce western political systems? As the spymaster Sir Claude Wade warned on the eve of the 1839 invasion, 'There is nothing more to be dreaded or guarded against, I think, than the overweening confidence with which we are too often accustomed to regard the excellence of our own institutions, and the anxiety that we display to introduce them in new and untried soils. Such interference will always lead to acrimonious disputes, if not to a violent reaction.'[4]

For the westerners in Afghanistan today, the disaster of the First Afghan War provides an uneasy precedent: it is no accident that the favourite watering hole of foreign correspondents in Kabul is called the Gandamak Lodge, or that one of the principal British bases in southern Afghanistan is named Camp Souter after the only survivor of the last stand of the 44th Foot.

For the Afghans themselves, in contrast, the British defeat of 1842 has become a symbol of liberation from foreign invasion, and of the determination of Afghans to refuse to be ruled ever again by any foreign power. The diplomatic quarter of Kabul is after all still named after Wazir Akbar Khan, who in nationalist Barakzai propaganda is now remembered as the leading Afghan freedom fighter of 1841–2.

We in the west may have forgotten the details of this history that did so much to mould the Afghans' hatred of foreign rule, but the Afghans have not. In particular Shah Shuja remains a symbol of quisling treachery in Afghanistan: in 2001, the Taliban asked their young men, 'Do you want to be remembered as a son of Shah Shuja or as a son of Dost Mohammad?' As he rose to power, Mullah Omar deliberately modelled himself on Dost Mohammad, and like him removed the Holy Cloak of the Prophet Mohammad from its shrine in Kandahar and wrapped himself in it, declaring himself like his model Amir al-Muminin, the Leader of the Faithful, a deliberate and direct re-enactment of the events of First Afghan War, whose resonance was immediately understood by all Afghans.

History never repeats itself exactly, and it is true that there are some important differences between what is taking place in Afghanistan today and what took place during the 1840s. There is no unifying figure at the centre of the resistance, recognised by all Afghans as a symbol of legitimacy and justice: Mullah Omar is no Dost Mohammad or Wazir Akbar Khan, and the tribes have not united behind him as they did in 1842. There are big and important distinctions to be made between the conservative and defensive tribal uprising that brought Anglo-Sadozai rule to a close in the colonial period and the armed Ikhwanist revolutionaries of the Taliban who wish to reimpose an imported ultra-Wahhabi ideology on the diverse religious cultures of Afghanistan. Most importantly, Karzai has tried to establish a broad-based, democratically elected government which for all its many flaws and prodigious corruption is still much more representative and popular than the Sadozai regime of Shah Shuja ever was.

Nevertheless due to the continuities of the region's topography, economy, religious aspirations and social fabric, the failures of 170 years ago do still hold important warnings for us today. It is still not too late to learn some lessons from the mistakes of the British in 1842. Otherwise, the west's fourth war in the country looks certain to end with as few political gains as the first three, and like them to terminate in an embarrassing withdrawal after a humiliating defeat, with Afghanistan yet again left in tribal chaos and quite possibly ruled by the same government which the war was originally fought to overthrow.

As George Lawrence wrote to the London *Times* just before Britain blundered into the Second Anglo-Afghan War thirty years later, 'a new generation has arisen which, instead of profiting from the solemn lessons of the past, is willing and eager to embroil us in the affairs of that turbulent and unhappy country ... Although military disasters may be avoided, an advance now, however successful in a military point of view, would not fail to turn out to be as politically useless ... The disaster of the Retreat from Kabul should stand forever as a warning to the Statesmen of the future not to repeat the policies that bore such bitter fruit in 1839–42.'

Despite the central strategic significance of this region, good writing on Afghan history is surprisingly thin on the ground, and what there is invariably uses printed accounts in English or the much mined India Office Archives in London. While the story of the First Anglo-Afghan War has been told many times, in forms ranging from great Victorian three-volume histories to the antics of Flashman, there is still virtually no published material about the war, even in the most specialist academic publications, which utilises contemporary Afghan sources from the early nineteenth century, and which presents Afghan accounts of being invaded and occupied, or makes use of the records of the anti-colonial Afghan resistance.[5]

The First Anglo-Afghan War is a uniquely well-documented conflict and in the writing of it I have made use of a variety of new sources from all sides of the battle lines. Hundreds of tattered letters and blood-stained diaries belonging to the British participants in the war have appeared from trunks in Home Counties attics over the last few years and I have accessed this new material in various family collections, the National Army Museum in Chelsea and the British Library.

Here in Delhi, for the last four years I have been trawling through the voluminous records of the 1839–42 occupation in the Indian National Archives which contains almost all the correspondence, memoranda and hand-written annotations on the subject generated by Lord Auckland's administration in Calcutta as well as that of his army. Among the highlights I found there are some previously unpublished private letters of one of the principal British actors in the story, Alexander Burnes; an inquiry into British army atrocities which reads like a Victorian version of Wikileaks; and some very moving court-martial records of sepoys who had been enslaved, had managed to escape and had then faced charges of desertion when they eventually succeeded in returning to their regiments.

The Indian National Archives also contained the previously unused and untranslated Persian-language account of the war by a returned Persian secretary who was attached to one of the British officials involved in the war, Munshi Abdul Karim's *Muharaba Kabul wa Kandahar*. Munshi Abdul Karim says he embarked on the project of writing the history in the early 1850s 'hoping to drive away the loneliness of old age, and to instruct my children and grandchildren in the many curiosities of the world', but adds, in what could be taken as a coded call for an uprising against the Company in India, that 'the events now seem particularly relevant to Hindustan'.[6] Such an uprising did indeed follow in 1857, and first broke out in regiments where the sepoys had been deserted by their British officers during the 1842 retreat from Kabul.

In the Punjab Archives in Lahore, Pakistan, I mined the almost unused records of Sir Claude Wade, the first Great Game spymaster, under whose care the North West Frontier Agency was created in 1835. Here can be found all the reports of Wade's network of 'intelligencers' scattered around the Punjab, the Himalayas and over the Hindu Kush as far as Bukhara. The Punjab Archives also contained all the correspondence relating to Shah Shuja's exile in Ludhiana and his various attempts to return to the throne of Kabul.

Among the Russian sources, I managed to get access to the printed records of Wade's Tsarist counterpart, Count Perovsky, and his protégé Ivan Vitkevitch. Vitkevitch's papers have always been assumed to have been destroyed in his St Petersburg hotel room just before he blew his brains out, but it turns out that there still survive some of his intelligence reports, including his writings about Burnes and his unravelling of the entire British spy network in Bukhara. These reports appear here in English for the first time.

The real breakthrough, however, was finding the astonishingly rich seam of Afghan sources for the period that turned up in Kabul. In 2009, while staying at Rory Stewart's mud fort near the ruins of the burned-out Curzon-era British Embassy, I began working in the Afghan National Archives. The archives, which are located in a surprisingly undamaged and rather beautiful Ottoman-style nineteenth-century palace in the centre of Kabul, turned out to have disappointingly little material from the era of Shah Shuja and Dost Mohammad. But it was while digging in the stacks there that I befriended Jawan Shir Rasikh, a young Afghan historian and Fulbright scholar. One lunchtime, Jawan Shir took me to a second-hand book dealer who occupied an unpromising-looking stall at Jowy Sheer in the old city. The dealer, it turned out, had bought up many of the private libraries of Afghan noble families as they emigrated during the 1970s and 1980s, and in less than an hour I managed to acquire eight previously unused contemporary Persian-language sources for the First Afghan War, all of them written in Afghanistan during or in the aftermath of the British defeat, but in several cases printed on Persian presses in India for domestic Indian consumption in the run-up to the great uprising of 1857.

The sources consist of two remarkable heroic epic poems – the *Akbarnama*, or The History of Wazir Akbar Khan, of Maulana Hamid Kashmiri, and the *Jangnama*, or History of the War, by Mohammad Ghulam Kohistani Ghulami, both of which read like Afghan versions of *The Song of Roland*, and were written in the 1840s in sonorous Persian modelled on that of the ancient Shahnameh of Ferdowsi to praise the leaders of the Afghan resistance. These epics seem to be the last survivors of what was probably once a very rich seam of poetry dedicated to the Afghan victory, much of it passed orally from singer to singer, bard to bard: after all, to the Afghans their victory over the British was an almost miraculous deliverance, their Trafalgar, Waterloo and Battle of Britain rolled into one.[7]

The single known copy of the *Jangnama* turned up in Parwan in 1951 lacking its front and end pages, and written on East India

Company paper apparently looted from the British headquarters in Charikar. It focuses on the deeds of the Kohistani resistance leader Mir Masjidi, the Naqsbandi Sufi pir who is long known to have been an important figure in the uprising, but who this manuscript maintains was central to the resistance. The *Akbarnama*, which also resurfaced in 1951, this time in Peshawar, by contrast praises Wazir Akbar Khan. 'In this book,' writes Maulana Kashmiri, 'like Rustam the Great, Akbar's name will be remembered for ever. Now this epic has reached completion, it will roam the countries of the world, and adorn the assemblies of the great. From Kabul, it will travel to every gathering, like the spring breeze from garden to garden.'[8]

The *Ayn al-Waqayi* gives a slightly later view of the uprising seen from the perspective of Herat in western Afghanistan, on the border of Persia, while two late-nineteenth-century histories, the *Tarikh-i-Sultani*, or The History of the Sultans, and the *Siraj ul-Tawarikh*, The Lamp of Histories, are official court histories of the kings of Afghanistan and give the perspective from the point of view of Dost Mohammad's successors.[9] The surviving Persian letters of one of the leading resistance leaders, Aminullah Khan Logari, which until the looting of the Taliban survived in the National Museum in Kabul, were recently printed by his descendants as *Paadash-e-Khidmatguzaari-ye-Saadiqaane Ghazi Nayab Aminullah Khan Logari*.[10]

The angry and embittered but perceptive *Naway Ma'arek*, or Song of Battles, of Mirza 'Ata Mohammad tells the story of the war from the point of view of a junior official from Shikarpur (now in Pakistan but then nominally under the sway of Kabul) who starts off in the service of Shah Shuja but later becomes disillusioned with his employer's reliance on infidel support and who writes with increasing sympathy towards the resistance. The style of his Persian is florid provincial Mughal, but he has a more witty and sprightly turn of phrase than any other writer of the period. The book, which holds forth with some venom on the failures of the British, was perhaps surprisingly commissioned by the first English collector of Shikarpur, E. B. Eastwick, and Mirza 'Ata writes rather nervously to his patron in the introduction, begging that 'in accordance with the saying "telling the truth is bitter", even though I have striven to select the most tactful expressions when describing the good and bad in these events, I pray I will avoid giving offence to those enthroned on the peaks of governance. In any case,' he adds, 'the joys and the griefs of this fleeting faithless world do not last: "the world is a dream – however you imagine it, it passes away; until you pass away yourself."'[11]

Perhaps the most revealing source of all is the *Waqi'at-i-Shah Shuja*, Shah Shuja's own colourful and sympathetic memoirs, written in exile in Ludhiana before the war and brought up to date by one of his followers after his assassination in 1842. Shuja explains in his introduction that 'to insightful scholars it is well known that great kings have always recorded the events of their reigns and the victorious military campaigns in which they took part: some writing themselves, with their natural gifts, but most entrusting the writing to skilled historians, so that these pearl-like compositions would remain as a memorial on the pages of passing time. Thus it occurred to this humble petitioner at the court of the Merciful God to record the battles of his reign from the time of his accession at the young age of seventeen, so that the historians of Khurasan should know the true account of these events, and thoughtful readers take heed from these examples.'[12] In these memoirs we have the hopes and fears of the principal player on the Afghan side – a vital addition to the literature.

Yet astonishingly, while most of these sources are well known to Dari-speaking Afghan historians, and were used by them in the nationalist Dari-language histories they wrote between the 1950s and 1970s, not one of these accounts ever seems to have been used in any English-language history of the war, and none is available in English translation, although an abridged translation of a few chapters of the *Waqi'at-i-Shah Shuja* appeared in a Calcutta magazine in the 1840s and a full translation of the *Siraj ul-Tawarikh* is currently under preparation by Robert McChesney at Columbia University, to which I was generously given access.

These rich and detailed Afghan sources tell us much that the European sources neglect to mention or are ignorant of. The British sources, for example, are well informed when talking of the different factions in their own army, but seem largely unaware of the tensions dividing the different groups of insurgents who made up the Afghan side. For the Afghan resistance – it is clear in the Afghan accounts – was in fact deeply fractured: different groups under different commanders camped in different places and often acted with only the bare minimum of co-ordination. Moreover, the rival groups had different aims and formed ever-changing coalitions of self-interest. One particular surprise is how many of the insurgents at the beginning wished to retain Shah Shuja as their king and only wished to drive out his British backers; the loyalties of these same pro-Royalist forces reverted to Shah Shuja as soon as the British army headed off towards its own annihilation in the Khord Kabul Pass. Just as the Soviet puppet Najibullah survived much longer than anyone expected after the departure of the Soviet army in the 1980s, so Shah Shuja might have survived indefinitely as King of Afghanistan had he not been treacherously assassinated by his own godson for reasons of personal pique and jealousy.

The resistance of the Afghan sources has a slightly different dramatis personae to those given in the British accounts: Mir Masjidi and his Kohistanis and Aminullah Khan and his Logaris are both much more prominent than in the British sources, or indeed in those later Afghan accounts written later under Barakzai patronage which emphasise the central role of the victorious dynasty in the uprising – something that was actually only true for the final stages of the revolution.

More importantly, thanks to the Afghan sources the leaders of the Afghan resistance suddenly come into view as rounded figures, human beings with full emotional lives and with individual views and motivations. While the British sources see only an undifferentiated wall of treacherous bearded 'bigots' and 'fanatics', thanks to the new sources it is now possible to understand why it was that individual Afghan leaders, many of them loyal supporters of Shah Shuja, chose to risk their lives and take up arms against the apparently invincible forces of the Company. The venerable Aminullah Khan Logari was insulted by a junior British officer and lost his lands for refusing to pay increased taxes to the Crown. The hot-headed young Abdullah Khan Achakzai had his mistress seduced by Alexander Burnes and was mocked when he tried to retrieve her. Mir Masjidi was about to turn himself in when contrary to all understandings the British attacked his fort and massacred his family; the fort was then seized and turned into the centre of the British provincial government and his lands shared among his enemies. Most fully sketched of all is the sophisticated and complex figure of Akbar Khan, who loved Hellenistic Gandharan sculpture, wanted to import western education and was regarded in Kabul as the most dashing of the resistance leaders. The *Akbarnama* even includes a detailed description of the pleasures of his wedding bed. The caricature 'treacherous Muslim' of the British sources transforms before our eyes into an Afghan matinee idol.

The Afghan sources also present us with a mirror which allows us, in the words of Alexander Burnes's cousin Robbie Burns, 'To see ourselves as others see us'.[13] For according to the Afghan epic poets, Burnes, far from being the romantic adventurer of western accounts, was instead the devilishly charming deceiver, the master of flattery and treachery, who corrupted the nobles of Kabul. 'On the outside he seems a man, but inside he is the very devil,' one nobleman tells Dost Mohammad.[14] Likewise to Afghan eyes the western armies were remarkable for their heartlessness, for their lack of any of the basic values of chivalry and especially for their indifference to civilian casualties. 'From their rancour and spite there will be burning houses and blazing walls,' Dost Mohammad warns Akbar Khan in the *Akbarnama*.

> For such is how they show their strength
> Terrorising those who dare to resist them
>
> As is their custom, they will subjugate the people
> So that no one makes a claim to equality[15]

It is, moreover, a consistent complaint in the Afghan sources that the British had no respect for women, raping and dishonouring wherever they went, and riding 'the steed of their lust unbridled day and night'. The British, in other words, are depicted in the Afghan sources as treacherous and oppressive women-abusing terrorists. This is not the way we expect Afghans to look at us.

At the centre of all the Afghan sources is the enigmatic figure of Shah Shuja himself. Shuja emerges through his own writings and those of his supporters as a sophisticated and highly intelligent man who models himself on the Timurid monarchs of the past. The self-portrait in the *Waqi'at* is backed by that of other writers to reveal a resolute, brave and unbreakable figure, weathering all that fate can throw at him. It is a portrait startlingly different to the corrupt and incompetent figure dismissed by the conceited British administrators who first reinstalled then tried to marginalise the heir to the Durrani Empire. He is also a very different figure to the weak quisling demonised in modern Afghanistan after 170 years of Barakzai propaganda. Shuja created around him a highly cultured Persianate world – there is no indication that the Shah ever knew Pashtu, and he certainly did not write in it. He lived, as the Mughals did before him, a life of mobile kingship and in many ways he emerges as the last Timurid, exercising his rule in a country that was still at the crossroads of Iran, Central Asia, China and Hindustan, not the mountainous periphery it would later become.

In retrospect, Shah Shuja's reign marked the end of one world and the beginning of another. For, despite its many costly failures, the First Anglo-Afghan War had important and long-lasting effects. For the British it created a stable frontier. Within a few years, the British had absorbed the Punjab of the Sikh Khalsa and the lands of the lower Indus previously ruled by the Amirs of Sindh; but they had learned their lesson that Peshawar should be the North West Frontier of their Raj.

For the Afghans the war changed their state for ever: on his return, Dost Mohammad inherited the reforms made by the British and these helped him consolidate an Afghanistan that was much more clearly defined than it was before the war. Indeed Shuja and most of his contemporaries never used the word 'Afghanistan' – for him, there was a Kingdom of Kabul which was the last surviving fragment of the Durrani Empire and which lay on the edge of a geographical space he described as Khurasan. Yet within a generation the phrase Afghanistan existed widely on maps both in and outside the country and the people within that space were beginning to describe themselves as Afghans. The return of Shah Shuja and the failed colonial expedition which was mounted to reinstate him finally destroyed the power of the Sadozai dynasty and ended the last memories of the Durrani Empire that they had founded. In this way the war did much to define the modern boundaries of the Afghan state, and consolidated once and for all the idea of a country called Afghanistan.

If the First Afghan War helped consolidate the Afghan State, the question now is whether the current western intervention will contribute to its demise. At the time of writing, western troops are again poised to leave Afghanistan in the hands of a weak Popalzai-run government. It is impossible to predict the fate of either that regime or the fractured and divided state of Afghanistan. But what Mirza 'Ata wrote after 1842 remains equally true today: 'It is certainly no easy thing to invade or govern the Kingdom of Khurasan.'

Notes

List of Abbreviations

BL (British Library)
OIOC (Oriental and India Office Collections)
NAI (National Archives of India)
PRO (Public Records Office)
NAM (National Army Musuem)

Chapter 1: No Easy Place to Rule

1 Alexander Burnes, *Cabool: A Personal Narrative of a Journey to, and Residence in that City in the Years 1836, 7 and 8*, London, 1843, p. 273, for details of the Kabul spring.
2 Sultan Mohammad Khan ibn Musa Khan Durrani, *Tarikh-i-Sultani*, p. 219.
3 Khurasan also included much of eastern Iran, but was not usually thought to include northern Afghanistan.
4 *Waqi'at-i-Shah Shuja*, The Eighteenth Event.
5 Sultan Mohammad Khan Durrani, *Tarikh-i-Sultani*, p. 226.
6 *Waqi'at-i-Shah Shuja*, The Eighteenth Event.
7 Dominic Lieven, *Russia against Napoleon*, London, 2009, pp. 45–7.
8 Quoted in Sir John Malcolm, *Political History of India*, 2 vols, London, 1826, vol. I, p. 310.
9 Iradj Amini, *Napoleon and Persia*, Washington, DC, 1999, p. 112; Muriel Atkin, *Russia and Iran 1780–1828*, Minneapolis, 1980, p. 125.
10 OIOC, Board's Collections: Sec Desp to India, vol. III, Draft to Governor General-in-Council, 24 September 1807, no. 31; J. B. Kelly, *Britain and the Persian Gulf, 1795–1880*, Oxford, 1968, pp. 82–3. For the Russian nobleman beneath the barge see Peter Hopkirk, *The Great Game*, London, 1990, p. 33.
11 Amini, *Napoleon and Persia*, p.129.
12 Sir John William Kaye, *Lives of Indian Officers*, London, 1867, vol. I, p. 234.
13 There is a wonderful account of the two boys' trip written by Edward's descendant Barbara Strachey in *The Strachey Line: An English Family in America, India and at Home from 1570 to 1902*, London, 1985, pp. 100–5. The diaries of both

boys survive in the India Office Library, though Elphinstone's writing is so scruffy as to be partly illegible. Mountstuart Elphinstone's is in BL, OIOC, Mss Eur F88 Box 13/16[b] and Edward Strachey's at Mss Eur F128/196.

14 Fayz Mohammad, *Siraj ul-Tawarikh*, vol. I, p. 40. The 1761 Battle of Panipat was the fifth at the site.

15 Mirza 'Ata, *Naway Ma'arek*, Introduction, pp. 1–9.

16 Fayz Mohammad, *Siraj ul-Tawarikh*, vol. I, p. 63.

17 Olaf Caroe, *The Pathans*, London, 1958, p. 262; Syad Muhammad Latif, *History of the Punjab*, New Delhi, 1964, p. 299; Robert Nichols, *Settling the Frontier: Land, Law and Society in the Peshawar Valley, 1500–1900*, Oxford, 2001, p. 90.

18 H. T. Prinsep, *History of the Punjab, and of the rise, progress, & present condition of the sect and nation of the Sikhs [Based in part on the 'Origin of the Sikh Power in the Punjab and political life of Muha-Raja Runjeet Singh']*, London, 1846, vol. I, p. 260; Fayz Mohammad, *Siraj ul-Tawarikh*, vol. I, p. 84; Mountstuart Elphinstone, *An Account of the Kingdom of Caubul, and its dependencies in Persia, Tartary, and India; comprising a view of the Afghaun nation, and a history of the Dooraunee monarchy*, London, 1819, vol. I, p. 317.

19 Mirza 'Ata, *Naway Ma'arek*, pp. 57–75.

20 Ibid., *Waqi'at-i-Shah Shuja*, Introduction.

21 Sultan Mohammad Khan Durrani, *Tarikh-i-Sultani*, p. 212.

22 *Waqi'at-i-Shah Shuja*, Introduction.

23 Ibid., The Seventh Event.

24 Fayz Mohammad, *Siraj ul-Tawarikh*, vol. I, p. 95.

25 Sultan Mohammad Khan Durrani, *Tarikh-i-Sultani*, p. 217.

26 Ibid., p. 215.

27 Ibid., pp. 244–69. Afghans still have a tendency to talk about Indians and even Pakistanis in this way. As rice and meat eaters they see themselves as infinitely superior human beings.

28 Robert Johnson, *The Afghan Way of War – Culture and Pragmatism: A Critical History*, London, 2011, p. 48.

29 B. D. Hopkins, *The Making of Modern Afghanistan*, London, 2008, pp. 129, 159; Noelle, *State and Tribe in Nineteenth-Century Afghanistan*, p. 281.

30 Noelle, *State and Tribe in Nineteenth-Century Afghanistan*, p. 288.

31 Elphinstone, *Kingdom of Caubul*, vol. I, pp. 2–7.

32 Ibid., p. 13.

33 Ibid., p. 21.

34 Ibid., pp. 52–4.

35 BL, OIOC, Forster Papers, Mss Eur B 14/Mss Eur K 115, 12 July 1785.

36 Adapted from Caroe, *The Pathans*, p. 244.

37 Though widely attributed to Khushhal, many scholars doubt the authenticity of this celebrated couplet.

38 Elphinstone, *Kingdom of Caubul*, vol. I, pp. 67–8.

39 Private Collection, Fraser Papers, Inverness, vol. 30, p. 171, WF to his father, 6 March 1809.

40 *Waqi'at-i-Shah Shuja*, The Twenty-Sixth Event.

41 Sayed Qassem Reshtia, *Between Two Giants: Political History of Afghanistan in the Nineteenth Century*, Peshawar, 1990, p. 18; Noelle, *State and Tribe in Nineteenth-Century Afghanistan*, p. 8.

42 Fayz Mohammad, *Siraj ul-Tawarikh*, vol. I, p. 86.
43 Elphinstone, *Kingdom of Caubul*, vol. I, pp. 82–3, 282.
44 Ibid., pp. 80–1.
45 Ibid., p. 399.
46 Ibid., vol. II, p. 276.
47 Private Collection, Fraser Papers, Inverness, vol. 30, p. 149, WF to his father, 22 April 1809.
48 Johnson, *The Afghan Way of War*, p. 44.
49 Ibid., p. 42.
50 Elphinstone, *Kingdom of Caubul*, vol. II, p. 276.
51 Hopkins, *The Making of Modern Afghanistan*, p. 1.
52 Noelle, *State and Tribe in Nineteenth-Century Afghanistan*, pp. 164–5.
53 Johnson, *The Afghan Way of War*, p. 43.
54 Private Collection, Fraser Papers, Inverness, vol. 30, p. 177, WF to his father, 7 May 1809.
55 Elphinstone, *Kingdom of Caubul*, vol. I, p. 87.
56 Ibid., p. 89.
57 Sultan Mohammad Khan Durrani, *Tarikh-i-Sultani*, p. 223.
58 Private Collection, Fraser Papers, Inverness, vol. 30, pp. 201–6, WF to his father, 19 June and 6 July 1809.
59 Fayz Mohammad, *Siraj ul-Tawarikh*, vol. I, p. 115.
60 Sultan Mohammad Khan Durrani, *Tarikh-i-Sultani*, p. 229.
61 *Waqi'at-i-Shah Shuja*, The Twenty-Sixth Event.

Chapter 2: An Unsettled Mind

1 Mirza 'Ata, *Naway Ma'arek*, pp. 10–12.
2 Khuswant Singh, *Ranjit Singh: Maharaja of the Punjab*, London, 1962.
3 *Waqi'at-i-Shah Shuja*, The Twenty-Sixth Event.
4 Ibid.; Mirza 'Ata, *Naway Ma'arek*, pp. 13–15. Sikh sources give a rather different account.
5 Prinsep, *History of the Sikhs*, vol. II, pp. 14–15.
6 *Waqi'at-i-Shah Shuja*, The Twenty-Sixth Event.
7 Turk Ali Shah Turk Qalandar, *Tadhkira-i Sukhunwaran-Chashm-Didah*, n.d.
8 *Waqi'at-i-Shah Shuja*, The Twenty-Sixth Event.
9 Fayz Mohammad, *Siraj ul-Tawarikh*, vol. I, p. 135.
10 *Waqi'at-i-Shah Shuja*, The Twenty-Seventh Event.
11 Private Collection, Fraser Papers, Inverness, vol. 30, pp. 171–2, WF to his father, 9 May 1809.
12 Fayz Mohammad, *Siraj ul-Tawarikh*, vol. I, p. 136.
13 *Waqi'at-i-Shah Shuja*, The Twenty-Eighth Event; Fayz Mohammad, *Siraj ul-Tawarikh*, vol. I, pp. 136–7; Prinsep, *History of the Sikhs*, vol. II, p. 22.
14 Arthur Conolly, *Journey to the North of India, 1829–31*, London, 1838, vol. II, pp. 272, 301.
15 *Waqi'at-i-Shah Shuja*, The Twenty-Ninth Event.
16 Eruch Rustom Kapadia, 'The Diplomatic Career of Sir Claude Wade: A Study of British Relations with the Sikhs and Afghans, July 1823–March 1840', unpublished PhD thesis, SOAS, c.1930, p. 18. Wade did his best to stamp out the trade:

Sir C.M. Wade, *A Narrative of the Services, Military and Political, of Lt.-Col. Sir C.M. Wade*, Ryde, 1847, p. 33.

17 Jean-Marie Lafont, *La présence française dans le royaume sikh du Penjab 1822–1849*, Paris, 1992, p. 107.

18 Ibid., p. 110.

19 Punjab Archives, Lahore, from Metcalfe, Resident in Delhi, to Ochterlony in Ludhiana, 6 January 1813, book 8, no. 2, pp. 5–8.

20 Sadly this much repeated and thoroughly delightful story may well be apocryphal: certainly I have been unable to trace it back further than Edward Thompson's *The Life of Charles Lord Metcalfe*, London, 1937, p. 101, where it is described as 'local tradition . . . this sounds like folklore'. It may well have been inspired by the famous miniature of Ochterlony in the India Office Library. In his will, BL, OIOC L/AG/34/29/37, Ochterlony only mentions one bibi [an Indian consort, either a legal wife or a mistress], 'Mahruttun, entitled Moobaruck ul Nissa Begum and often called Begum Ochterlony', who was the mother of his two daughters, although his son Roderick Peregrine Ochterlony was clearly born of a different bibi. Nevertheless it is quite possible that the story could be true: I frequently found Old Delhi traditions about such matters confirmed by research, and several Company servants of the period kept harems of this size. Judging by Bishop Heber's wonderful description of him, Ochterlony was clearly Indianised enough to have done so.

21 Punjab Archives, Lahore, from Ochterlony in Ludhiana to John Adam, Calcutta, 9 July 1815, book 14, no. 226, pp. 5–8.

22 Punjab Archives, Lahore, Captain Birch to Adam, Ludhiana, 2 December 1814, book 15, no. 6.

23 Punjab Archives, Lahore, vol. 18, part II, Letters 117 and 118, p. 535. In Urdu the address reads: Banam-i Farang Akhtar Looni Sahib. Ochterlony's name – or rather its Urduised rendering, Akhtar Looni – translates as Crazy Star.

24 Punjab Archives, Lahore, Fraser, Ramgurh to Ochterlony, Ludhiana, 3 September 1816, vol. 18, part II, Case 118, pp. 538–9.

25 Punjab Archives, Lahore, Captain Murray to Sir D. Ochterlony Bart. K.C.B., vol 18, part II, Case 150, pp. 653–8.

26 Mirza 'Ata, *Naway Ma'arek*, p. 39; *Waqi'at-i-Shah Shuja*, Introduction.

27 Punjab Archives, Lahore, Adam to Ochterlony, 5 October 1816, book 9, no. 98, pp. 637–9.

28 Punjab Archives, Lahore, Ludhiana Agency, Murray to Ochterlony, 20 January 1817, book 92, Case 17.

29 Punjab Archives, Lahore, Adam to Ochterlony, 5 October 1816, book 9, no. 98, pp. 637–9.

30 Mohan Lal Kashmiri, *Life of Amir Dost Mohammad of Kabul*, London, 1846, vol. I, pp. 104–5. This was presumably a euphemism for rape.

31 Mirza 'Ata, *Naway Ma'arek*, pp. 29–39.

32 Patrick Macrory, *Signal Catastrophe: The Retreat from Kabul 1842*, London, 1966, p. 35.

33 Fayz Mohammad, *Siraj ul-Tawarikh*, vol. I, p. 140.

34 Punjab Archives, Lahore, R. Ross, Subhatu to Sir D. Ochterlony, Kurnal, 2 September 1816, book 18, Serial no. 116. Ross reported: 'I am writing to you in Goorkhalee libas [dress/disguise] a most perfect image in which after closing this I shall slip out of my house by a by-path into the beds of the Ganges whence

I shall proceed with a Subadar and a Sipahi (*Nusseeree*), out of uniform and like myself in Goorkhalee dress to look at the royal party'.

35 Charles Masson, *Narrative of Various Journeys in Baluchistan, Afghanistan and the Panjab, 1826 to 1838*, London, 1842, vol. III, p. 51.

36 *Waqi'at-i-Shah Shuja*, The Thirtieth Event.

37 Mirza 'Ata, *Naway Ma'arek*, pp. 39–56.

38 Josiah Harlan, 'Oriental Sketches', insert at p. 42a, mss in Chester Country Archives, Pennsylvania, quoted in Ben Macintyre, *Josiah the Great: The True Story of the Man Who Would be King*, London, 2004, p. 18.

39 Harlan's 'Sketches', p. 37a, quoted in Macintyre, *Josiah the Great*, pp. 22–3.

40 Godfrey Vigne, *A Personal Narrative of a Visit to Ghuzni, Kabul and Afghanistan and a Residence at the Court of Dost Mohamed with Notices of Runjit Singh, Khiva, and the Russian Expedition*, London, 1840, p. 4.

41 Punjab Archives, Lahore, Ludhiana Agency papers, Wade to Macnaghten, Press List VI, Book 142, serial no. 44, 9 July 1836. Shah Mahmood Hanifi, 'Shah Shuja's "Hidden History" and its Implications for the Historiography of Afghanistan', *South Asia Multidisciplinary Academic Journal* [online], Free-Standing Articles, online since 14 May 2012, connection on 21 June 2012, http://samaj.revues.org/3384.

42 See, for example, Punjab Archives, Lahore, Captain C. M. Wade, Pol. Assistant, Loudhianuh to J. E. Colebrooke, Bart., Resident, Delhi, 1 June 1828, Ludhiana Agency Records, book 96, Case 67, pp. 92–4, for one round of the slave-girl saga. See also Kapadia, 'The Diplomatic Career of Sir Claude Wade', p. 6.

43 Victor Jacquemont, *Letters from India (1829–1832)*, London, 1936, p. 162.

44 Jean-Marie Lafont, *Indika: Essays in Indo-French Relations 1630–1976*, New Delhi, 2000, p. 343.

45 Ibid.

46 Public Records Office (now The National Archives, Kew), PRO 30/12, Ellenborough, Political Diary, 3 September 1829.

47 M. E. Yapp, *Strategies of British India: Britain, Iran and Afghanistan, 1798–1850*, Oxford, 1980, pp. 247, 111–12; Mark Bence-Jones, *The Viceroys of India*, London, 1982, p. 15.

48 Macrory, *Signal Catastrophe*, p. 39.

49 Norris, *The First Afghan War 1838–1842*, p. 15.

50 Laurence Kelly, *Diplomacy and Murder in Tehran: Alexander Griboyedov and Imperial Russia's Mission to the Shah of Persia*, London, 2002, ch. XIX, pp. 153–61.

51 Edward Ingram, *The Beginning of the Great Game in Asia, 1828–1834*, Oxford, 1979, p. 49; Wellington to Aberdeen, 11 October 1829, Arthur Wellesley, Duke of Wellington, *Supplementary Despatches and Memoranda of Field Marshall Arthur Duke of Wellington*, ed. by his son, the 2nd Duke of Wellington, London, 1858–72, vol. VI, pp. 212–19.

52 Kelly, *Diplomacy and Murder*, p. 54.

53 Orlando Figes, *Crimea: The Last Crusade*, London, 2010, p. 5.

54 Peter Hopkirk, *The Great Game*, London, 1990, p. 117.

55 Ibid., p. 117; PRO, Ellenborough, Political Diary, II, 122–3, 29 October 1829.

56 BL, OIOC, Secret Committee to Governor General, 12 January 1830, IOR/L/PS/5/543.

57 Hopkirk, *The Great Game*, p. 119.

58 Cobden, quoted by Norris in *First Afghan War*, p. 38.

59 National Archives of India (NAI), Foreign, Political, 5 September 1836, nos 9–19, Minute of Charles Trevelyan.

60 Ingram, *Beginning of the Great Game*, p. 169.

61 James Lunt, *Bokhara Burnes*, London, 1969, p. 39.

62 The two cousins may have spelled their surnames differently, but were in fact closely related.

63 Thanks to Craig Murray for pointing out that Burnes was not educated at the Trades School as Kaye had maintained.

64 Alexander Burnes, *Travels into Bokhara, Being the Account of a Journey from India to Cabool, Tartary and Persia, also a Narrative of a Voyage on the Indus from the Sea to Lahore*, London, 1834, vol. I, p. 127.

65 Hopkins, *The Making of Modern Afghanistan*, p. 51.

66 Jacquemont, *Letters from India*, pp. 171–3.

67 Burnes, *Travels into Bokhara*, vol. I, p. 132.

68 Ibid., p. 143.

69 Ibid., p. 144.

70 Lunt, *Bokhara Burnes*, p. 49. The dray horses were all dead by 1843. According to Norris, they 'died in luxury, far from their Kentish meadows, from over-feeding': *First Afghan War*, p. 47. See also Yapp, *Strategies*, pp. 247, 208.

71 Sir John William Kaye, *Lives of Indian Officers*, vol. II, pp. 231–3.

72 Burnes, *Travels into Bokhara*, vol. II, p. 334.

73 Lafont, *Indika*, p. 343.

74 Burnes, *Travels into Bokhara*, vol. II, pp. 313, 341; vol. III, p. 185.

75 Ibid., vol. II, pp. 330–2.

76 Quoted in Norris, *First Afghan War*, p. 57.

77 BL, OIOC, Enclosures to Secret Letters (ESL) 3: no. 69 of no. 8 of 2 July 1832 (IOR/L/PS/5/122), Wade to Macnaghten, 11 May 1832.

78 Ibid.

79 Ibid., attached letter, 'Translation of a note from Shah Shoojah ool Moolk to Hajee Moolah Mahomed Hussein, the Shah's Agent with Capt. Wade'.

80 BL, OIOC, F/4/1466/5766, Extract Fort William Political Consultations of 12 February 1833: Shah Shuja to the Secretary and Deputy Secretary to Govt, received 18 December 1833, and F/4/1466/57660, Macnaghten to Fraser, 8 December 1832.

81 BL, OIOC, Board's Collections, F/4/1466/57660, no. 52479.

82 BL, OIOC, IOR/P/BRN/SEC/372, Item 34 of Bengal Secret Consultations, 19 March 1833, From the Governor General to Dost Mahomed, written 28 February 1833.

83 *Waqi'at-i-Shah Shuja*, The Thirty-Second Event.

84 Lafont, *Indika*, p. 351.

85 Cited in Kapadia, 'The Diplomatic Career of Sir Claude Wade', pp. 178–9.

86 Mirza 'Ata, *Naway Ma'arek*, p. 146.

87 *Waqi'at-i-Shah Shuja*, The Thirty-Third Event.

88 NAI, Foreign, Secret Consultations, 10 April 1834, no. 20.

89 Ibid.

90 Mirza 'Ata, *Naway Ma'arek*, p. 148.

91 Ibid., pp. 148–62.

92 NAI, Foreign, Political Consultations, 5 September 1836, nos 9–19, Minute of Charles Trevelyan. Trevelyan and Arthur Conolly were the ones who really formed the Indus Policy of Lords Ellenborough and Auckland.

93 Macintyre, *Josiah the Great*, p. 18.

Chapter 3: The Great Game Begins

1   Elizabeth Errington and Vesta Sarkhosh Curtis, *From Persepolis to the Punjab: Exploring Ancient Iran, Afghanistan and Pakistan*, London, 2007, p. 5.

2   George Rawlinson, *A Memoir of Major-General Sir Henry Creswicke Rawlinson*, London, 1898, p. 67.

3   Royal Geographical Society, Rawlinson Papers, HC2, Private Journal Commenced from 14 June 1834, entry for 24 October 1834.

4   Ivan Fedorovitch Blaramberg, *Vospominania*, Moscow, 1978, p. 64.

5   Yapp, *Strategies*, pp. 138–9.

6   I. O. Simonitch, *Précis historique de l'avènement de Mahomed-Schah au trône de Perse par le Comte Simonitch, ex-Ministre Plénipotentiaire de Russie á la Cour de Téhéran*, Moscow, 1967, quoted by Alexander Morrison, *Twin Imperial Disasters: The Invasion of Khiva and Afghanistan in the Russian and British Official Mind, 1839–1842* (forthcoming).

7   Sir John MacNeill, *The Progress and Present Position of Russia in the East*, London, 1836, p. 151.

8   Rawlinson, *Memoir*, p. 67.

9   Ibid., p. 68.

10 NAI, Foreign, Secret Consultations, 17 October 1838, nos 33–4.

11 Rawlinson, *Memoir*, p. 68.

12 NAI, Foreign, Secret Consultations, 17 October 1838, nos 33–4.

13 Errington and Curtis, *From Persepolis to the Punjab*, p. 5.

14 NAI, Foreign, Secret Consultations, 17 October 1838, nos 33–4.

15 Blaramberg, *Vospominania*, p. 60; Melvin Kessler, *Ivan Viktorovitch Vitkevich 1806–39: A Tsarist Agent in Central Asia*, Central Asia Collectanea, no. 4, Washington, DC, 1960, pp. 5–8; V. A. Perovsky, *A Narrative of the Russian Military Expedition to Khiva under General Perofski in 1839*, trans. from the Russian for the Foreign Department of the Government of India, Calcutta, 1867; Mikhail Volodarsky, 'The Russians in Afghanistan in the 1830s', *Central Asian Survey*, vol. 3, no. 1 (1984), p. 72.

16 'Peslyak's Notes', *Istorichesky Vestnik*, no. 9, 1883, p. 584.

17 Letter from V. A. Perovsky, Military Governor of Orenburg, to K. K. Rodofinikin, head of the Asian Department at the Ministry of the Foreign Affairs, 14 June 1836, quoted by N. A. Khalfin, predislovie k sb. *Zapiski o Bukharskom Khanstve* (preface to Notes on the Khanate of Bukhara), Moscow, 1983.

18 Blaramberg, *Vospominania*, p. 60.

19 Perovsky, *A Narrative of the Russian Military Expedition to Khiva*, pp. 73–5. Morrison in *Twin Imperial Disasters* points out that this passage was in fact written by Ivanin, not Perovsky.

20 Khalfin, *Zapiski o Bukharskom Khanstve* (Notes on the Khanate of Bukhara)

21 Blaramberg, *Vospominania*, p. 60.

22 Khalfin, *Zapiski o Bukharskom Khanstve* (Notes on the Khanate of Bukhara).

23 Volodarsky, 'The Russians in Afghanistan in the 1830s', p. 70.
24 Khalfin, *Zapiski o Bukharskom Khanstve* (Notes on the Khanate of Bukhara).
25 Volodarsky, 'The Russians in Afghanistan in the 1830s', pp. 73–4.
26 Ibid., p. 70; Morrison, *Twin Imperial Disasters*, pp. 16–17.
27 Khalfin, *Zapiski o Bukharskom Khanstve* (Notes on the Khanate of Bukhara).
28 Cited by Morrison in *Twin Imperial Disasters*, p. 16.
19 Volodarsky, 'The Russians in Afghanistan in the 1830s', p. 72.
30 N. A. Khalfin, *Vozmezdie ozhidaet v Dzhagda* (Drama in a Boarding House), *Voprosy Istorii*, 1966, No. 10; also Yapp, *Strategies*, p. 234. The original source for this is Duhamel's memoirs.
31 Kessler, *Ivan Viktorovitch Vitkevich*, p. 12.
32 Volodarsky, 'The Russians in Afghanistan in the 1830s', p. 74.
33 Ibid.
34 Blaramberg, *Vospominania*, p. 60.
35 Ibid., p. 64.
36 Burnes, *Cabool*, p. 104.
37 Volodarsky, 'The Russians in Afghanistan in the 1830s', p. 70.
38 See Fayz Mohammad, *Siraj ul-Tawarikh*, vol. I, pp. 184–8; Masson, *Narrative of Various Journeys*, vol. III, pp. 307–9; Hopkins, *The Making of Modern Afghanistan*, pp. 101–7; Noelle, *State and Tribe in Nineteenth-Century Afghanistan*, pp. 15–17; Kapadia, 'The Diplomatic Career of Sir Claude Wade', p. 203.
39 NAI, Foreign, Secret Consultations, 15 May 1837, no. 08, Masson to Wade, 25 February 1837.
40 Ibid.
41 Fayz Mohammad, *Siraj ul-Tawarikh*, vol. I, p. 186. The Amir who commissioned the *Siraj* left a marginal note on the mss: 'I heard from some elderly men that Hari Singh was riding on an elephant and heading into the fray when suddenly a bullet struck him in a fatal spot and he died. It is not known who killed him.' Whatever the truth, Afghan literature has always assumed that it was Akbar Khan who personally despatched Hari Singh, and he is credited with the deed in Kashmiri's *Akbarnama* and several other epics.
42 Norris, *First Afghan War*, p. 114.
43 Burnes, *Cabool*, p. 139, and his letter to Calcutta, 9 October 1837, NAI, Foreign, Political Consultations, letters from Secretary of State, 28 September 1842, no. 21.
44 Masson, *Narrative of Various Journeys*, vol. III, p. 445.
45 Ibid., pp. 447–9.
46 See for example Maulana Hamid Kashmiri, *Akbarnama*.
47 Ibid.
48 Ibid., ch. 9.
49 Masson, *Narrative of Various Journeys*, vol. III, p. 97.
50 Vigne, *Visits to Afghanistan*, pp. 176–7.
51 Burnes, *Cabool*, p. 140.
52 Ibid.
53 Ibid., pp. 142–3.
54 Mirza 'Ata, *Naway Ma'arek*, pp. 162–72.
55 Kashmiri, *Akbarnama*, ch. 10.
56 Fayz Mohammad, *Siraj ul-Tawarikh*, vol. I, p. 192.

57   Kashmiri, *Akbarnama*, ch. 11.

58   Masson, *Narrative of Various Journeys*, vol. III, pp. 452–3.

59   Ibid. A more accurate translation of Garib Nawaz would be 'He Who Cherishes the Poor'.

60   NAI, Foreign, Secret Consultations, 19 August 1825, Burnes to Holland, nos 3–4.

61   Sir Penderel Moon, *The British Conquest and Dominion of India*, London, 1989, p. 492.

62   This was of course the same Macaulay who ignorantly remarked in his Minute on Education that 'a single shelf of a good European library was worth the whole native literature of India and Arabia ... the historical information which has been collected from all the books written in the Sanscrit language is less valuable than what may be found in the most paltry abridgments used at preparatory schools in England'. In the 'anglicist' vs 'Orientalist' debate which followed, Macaulay and Macnaghten were on opposing sides. For the procession see Emily Eden, *Up the Country: Letters written to her Sister from the Upper Provinces of India*, Oxford, 1930, p. 1.

63   Emily Eden, *Miss Eden's Letters*, ed. by her great-niece, Violet Dickinson, London, 1927, p. 293.

64   W. G. Osborne, *The Court and Camp of Runjeet Sing*, London, 1840, pp. 209–10. The Venetians, masters of a previous trading empire, had a similar approach.

65   Eden, *Miss Eden's Letters*, p. 263.

66   Ibid.

67   Eden, *Up the Country*, p. 18.

68   Fanny Eden, *Tigers, Durbars and Kings: Fanny Eden's Indian journals, 1837–1838*, transcribed and ed. by Janet Dunbar, London, 1988, p. 72.

69   Eden, *Miss Eden's Letters*, p. 299; Eden, *Up the Country*, p.3.

70   Eden, *Up the Country*, p. 156.

71   Eden, *Tigers, Durbars and Kings*, pp. 77–80.

72   Eden, *Up the Country*, pp. 4, 46.

73   Eden, *Tigers, Durbars and Kings*, p. 124.

74   Ibid., p. 60.

75   Mohan Lal, *Life of Amir Dost Mohammad*, vol. I, pp. 249–50.

76   Yapp, *Strategies*, p. 245; A. C. Banerjee, *Anglo-Sikh Relations: Chapters from J. D. Cunningham's History of the Sikhs*, Calcutta, 1949, p. 53.

77   Mohan Lal, *Life of Amir Dost Mohammad*, vol. I, pp. 250–2.

78   BL, OIOC, ESL 48: no. 87 of no. 1 of 8 February 1838 (IOR/L/PS/5/129), Extract of a letter from Wade to Macnaghten, 1 January 1838.

79   BL, OIOC, ESL 50: no. 18; Kapadia, 'The Diplomatic Career of Sir Claude Wade', p. 385.

80   BL, OIOC, ESL 48: no. 87 of no. 1 of 8 February 1838 (IOR/L/PS/5/129), Extract of a letter from Wade to Macnaghten, 1 January 1838.

81   NAI, Foreign, Political Consultations, 11 September 1837, no. 4.

82   Volodarsky, 'The Russians in Afghanistan in the 1830s', p. 76.

83   NAI, Foreign, Political Consultations, 6 June 1838, nos 21–2.

84   BL, Broughton Papers, Add Mss 37692, fol. 71, Auckland to Hobhouse, 6 January 1838; Norris, *First Afghan War*, p. 139.

85   Johnson, *The Afghan Way of War*, p. 42.

86   Herawi, '*Ayn al-Waqayi*, p. 29; Fayz Mohammad, *Siraj ul-Tawarikh*, vol. I, pp. 189–90.

87   Norris, *First Afghan War*, pp. 129–30.

88   NAI, Foreign, Secret Consultations, 19 August 1825, nos 3–4, 1, 11–14. Extracts from private letters from the late Sir Alex Burnes to Major Holland between the years 1837 and 1841 relating to affairs in Afghanistan.

89   Burnes, *Cabool*, pp. 261–2.

90   BL, OIOC, L/PS/5/130, Burnes to Macnaghten, 18 February 1838.

91   BL, OIOC, ESL 48: no. 100 of no. 1 of 8 February 1838 (IOR/L/PS/5/129), Burnes to Auckland, 23 December 1837.

92   NAI, Foreign, Secret Consultations, 19 August 1825, nos 3–4, 1, 11–14.

93   Norris, *First Afghan War*, p. 141.

94   Volodarsky, 'The Russians in Afghanistan in the 1830s', p. 76.

95   Masson, *Narrative of Various Journeys*, vol. III, p. 465.

96   Mirza 'Ata, *Naway Ma'arek*, pp. 162–72.

97   Norris, *First Afghan War*, p. 151.

98   NAI, Foreign, Secret Consultations, 22 August to 3 October 1838, no. 60, Pottinger to Burnes.

99   Mohan Lal, *Life of Amir Dost Mohammad*, vol. I, p. 281.

100 Michael H. Fisher, 'An Initial Student of Delhi English College: Mohan Lal Kashmiri (1812–77)', in Margrit Pernau (ed.), *The Delhi College: Traditional Elites, the Colonial State and Education before 1857*, New Delhi, 2006, p. 248.

101 Mohan Lal, *Life of Amir Dost Mohammad*, vol. I, pp. 307–9.

102 Burnes to Macnaghten, 24 March 1838, Parliamentary Papers [PP] 1839, Indian Papers 5. For fuller text see PP 1859.

103 NAI, Foreign, Secret Consultations, 22 August to 3 October 1838, no. 602, Burnes to Macnaghten.

104 Kashmiri, *Akbarnama*, ch. 11.

105 Volodarsky, 'The Russians in Afghanistan in the 1830s', p. 77.

106 Morrison, *Twin Imperial Disasters*, p. 22.

106 NAI, Foreign, Secret Consultations, 19 August 1825, nos 3–4, no. 04, Burnes to Holland, Peshawar, 6 May 1838.

108 BL, OIOC, ESL 49: no. 12 of no. 11 of 22 May 1838 (IOR/L/PS/5/130), Auckland's Minute of 12 May 1838.

109 Eden, *Up the Country*, p. 125.

110 Norris, *First Afghan War*, p. 161.

111 Eden, *Miss Eden's Letters*, p. 293.

112 BL, OIOC, ESL 49: no. 12 of no. 11 of 22 May 1838 (IOR/L/PS/5/130), Auckland's Minute of 12 May 1838.

113 Eden, *Miss Eden's Letters*, pp. 299–300.

114 Eden, *Up the Country*, p. 186.

115 Osborne, *The Court and Camp of Runjeet Sing*, pp. 70–89.

116 Ibid., p. 90.

117 Ibid., p. 190.

118 Major W. Broadfoot, *The Career of Major George Broadfoot, C.B.*, London, 1888, p. 121; also Henry Lawrence, in Yapp, *Strategies*, p. 247.

119 BL, OIOC, Mss Eur E359, Diary of Colvin, entry for 1 June 1838.

120 Norris, *First Afghan War*, p. 182.

121 *Calendar of Persian Correspondence of the Punjab Archives abstracted into English*, Lahore, 1972–2004 vol. 2, p. 158. Mirza Haidar Ali, an attendant to Shah Shuja ul-Mulk, to the Political Agent, Ludhiana, 15 September 1837.

122 Maulana Mohammad-Ghulam Akhund-zada Kohistani, b. Mulla Timur-shah, *mutakhallis ba 'Gulam'* (or Gulami Mohammad Ghulam), *Jangnama. Dar wasfi-i mujahidat-i Mir Masjidi-khan Gazi wa sair-i mudjahidin rashid-i milli-i aliya-i mutajawizin-i ajnabi dar salha-yi 1839–1842 i. Asar: Maulina* [sic] *Muhammad-Gulam Kuhistani mutakhallis ba 'Gulami'*, Kabul 1336 AH/1957 (*Anjuman-i tarikh-i Afghanistan*, No. 48) [preface by Ahmad-Ali Kohzad, without index], pp. 184–6.

123 Osborne, *The Court and Camp of Runjeet Sing*, pp. 207–8.

124 *Waqi'at-i-Shah Shuja*, The Thirty-Fifth Event.

125 Eden, *Miss Eden's Letters*, p. 290.

126 Ibid., p. 311.

127 Moon, *The British Conquest and Dominion of India*, p. 505.

128 NAI, Foreign, Secret Consultations, 21 November 1838, no.104, Mackeson to Macnaghten, 16 August 1838.

129 Masson, *Narrative of Various Journeys*, vol. III, p. 495.

130 Yapp argues convincingly for Macnaghten being the main driving force behind the invasion – see *Strategies*, pp. 246–7.

131 Colonel William H. Dennie, *Personal Narrative of the Campaigns in Afghanistan*, ed. W. E. Steele, Dublin, 1843, p. 30.

132 Sir John William Kaye, *Lives of Indian Officers*, vol. 2, p. 254.

133 Yapp, *Strategies*, p. 253.

134 Sir John William Kaye, *History of the War in Afghanistan: From the unpublished letters and journals of political and military officers employed in Afghanistan*, London, 1851, vol. I, p. 375.

135 Henry Marion Durand, *The First Afghan War and its Causes*, London, 1879, p. 81.

Chapter 4: The Mouth of Hell

1 BL, Broughton Papers, Add Mss 36474, Wade to Auckland, 31 January 1839.

2 Yapp, *Strategies*, p. 263.

3 Dennie, *Personal Narrative of the Campaigns in Afghanistan*, p. 51.

4 Norris, *First Afghan War*, p. 254.

5 Ibid., p. 248.

6 Ibid.

7 *Calendar of Persian Correspondence*, vol. 2, p. 1119, 11 December 1838, Shah Shuja ul Mulk to Political Agent, Ludhiana.

8 Eden, *Miss Eden's Letters*, p. 305.

9 Eden, *Tigers, Durbars and Kings*, p. 162.

10 Ibid., p. 159.

11 J. H. Stocqueler, *The Memoirs and Correspondence of Sir William Nott, GCB*, London, 1854, vol. I, p. 79 .

12 Osborne, *The Court and Camp of Runjeet Singh* pp. 213–14.

13 Eden, *Up the Country*, pp. 205–6.

14 Henry Havelock, *Narrative of the War in Affghanistan in 1838–9*, London, 1840, vol. I, p. 72; Kaye, *History of the War in Afghanistan*, vol. I, p. 392.

15 Eden, *Tigers, Durbars and Kings*, p. 182.

16 Ibid., p. 175.

17 Kaye, *History of the War in Afghanistan*, vol. I, p. 393.

18 Saul David, *Victoria's Wars: The Rise of Empire*, London, 2006, p. 27.

19 Stocqueler, *The Memoirs and Correspondence of Sir William Nott*, vol. I, p. 91.

20 Mirza 'Ata, *Naway Ma'arek*, p. 162, The English in Sindh and the Bolan Pass.

21 Ibid.

22 Kaye, *History of the War in Afghanistan*, vol. I, p. 419.

23 Ibid., p. 415.

24 NAI, Foreign, Secret Consultations, Burnes to Holland (pte), 21 March 1839, 8/43, 28 September 1842.

25 Kashmiri, *Akbarnama*, ch. 11.

26 Major-General Sir Thomas Seaton, *From Cadet to Colonel: The Record of a Life of Active Service*, London 1873, p. 74.

27 Broadfoot, *The Career of Major George Broadfoot*, p. 7.

28 Mirza 'Ata, *Naway Ma'arek*, p. 162, The English in Sindh and the Bolan Pass.

29 Seaton, *From Cadet to Colonel*, p. 85.

30 G. W. Forrest, *Life of Field Marshal Sir Neville Chamberlain GCB*, Edinburgh, 1909, pp. 31–2.

31 *Calendar of Persian Correspondence*, vols. 2 and no. 3, contains many of the letters sent out by Shah Shuja and Wade in an attempt to raise the tribes of Afghanistan for the Sadozai restoration. E.g. vol. 3, no. 206, 19 February 1839, p. 30.

32 Kaye, *Lives of Indian Officers*, vol. I, pp. 262–3.

33 Mohan Lal, *Life of Dost Mohammad*, vol. II, p. 198.

34 Major William Hough, *A Narrative of the March and Operations of the Army of the Indus 1838–1839*, London, 1841, pp. 83–4.

35 Seaton, *From Cadet to Colonel*, p. 89.

36 Stocqueler, *The Memoirs and Correspondence of Sir William Nott*, vol. I, p. 122.

37 Hough, *March and Operations of the Army of the Indus*, p. 68.

38 George Lawrence, *Reminiscences of Forty Three Years in India*, London, 1875, p. 7.

39 Sita Ram Panday, *From Sepoy to Subedar*, trans. Lt. Col. J. T. Norgate, London, 1873, pp. 88–9. This is an irresistible text, but also a somewhat problematic one. The Hindustani original, supposedly written down in Devanagari by Sita Ram in retirement, has never come to light, and the earliest version of it appeared in English in the 1870s. It was then translated *back* into Arabic-script Hindustani (as the *Khwab o Khiyal*) for use as an examination text for the Indian Civil Service (ICS). It is always possible that there is no original, and that the text was actually written by the British officer who first published it. However, having read many other letters allegedly written by sepoys to the Delhi press, and in fact clearly written by their British officers, I am inclined to accept the authenticity of this text.

40 Mirza 'Ata, *Naway Ma'arek*, p. 170, The English in Sindh and the Bolan Pass.

41 *Calendar of Persian Correspondence*, vol. 3, p. 155, no. 1000, 9 June 1839, Shah Shuja to Colonel Wade.

42 Mirza 'Ata, *Naway Ma'arek*, p. 171, The English in Sindh and the Bolan Pass.

43 National Army Museum, NAM 2008–1839, Gaisford Letters, p. 1, Camp Artillery Brigade Near Kabool, 20 August 1839.

44 Stocqueler, *The Memoirs and Correspondence of Sir William Nott*, vol. I, p. 101.

45 National Army Museum, NAM 1983–11–28–1, Gaisford Diary, p. 1.

46 Lawrence, *Reminiscences of Forty Three Years in India*, pp. 12–13.

47 Stocqueler, *The Memoirs and Correspondence of Sir William Nott*, vol. I, p. 115.

48 National Army Museum, NAM 1983–11–28–1, Gaisford Diary, p. 1.

49 Mohan Lal, *Life of Dost Mohammad*, vol. II, p. 206.

50 Haji Khan Kakar had already sent a verbal message to Shah Shuja, but this was the first sign that he was planning to act on his word – see NAI, Foreign, Secret Consultations, 16 October 1839, no. 70, Abstract of letters received by Shah Shooja from different Chiefs West of Indus in reply to communications addressed to them by His Majesty; sent for the perusal of Captain Wade.

51 Kashmiri, *Akbarnama*.

52 Letter of Alexander Burnes quoted by Emily Eden, *Up the Country*, p. 291.

53 National Army Museum, NAM 2008–1839, Gaisford Letter, p. 1, Camp Artillery Brigade Near Kabool, 20 August 1839.

54 BL, Broughton Papers, Add Mss 36474, Macnaghten to Auckland, 6 May 1839.

55 William Taylor, *Scenes and Adventures in Afghanistan*, London, 1842, p. 95.

56 *Waqi'at-i-Shah Shuja*, p. 104, The Thirty-Fifth Event.

57 Ibid.

58 Fayz Mohammad, *Siraj ul-Tawarikh*, vol. I, p. 225.

59 Amini, *Paadash-e-Khidmatguzaari-ye-Saadiqaane Ghazi Nayab Aminullah Khan Logari*, p. 4.

60 Rev. G. R. Gleig, *Sale's Brigade in Afghanistan*, London, 1843, p. 39.

61 Sita Ram, *From Sepoy to Subedar*, London, 1843, pp. 91–2.

62 Forrest, *Life of Field Marshal Sir Neville Chamberlain GCB*, p. 35.

63 BL, Broughton Papers, Add Mss 36474, fols 63–8, Auckland to Hobhouse, 18 June 1839.

64 *Calendar of Persian Correspondence*, vol. 3, p. 111, no. 762, 16 May 1839, Political Agent, Ludhiana to Shah Dad Khan; Noelle, *State and Tribe in Nineteenth-Century Afghanistan*, p. 169.

65 Mohan Lal, *Life of Dost Mohammad*, vol. II, p. 259; Noelle, *State and Tribe in Nineteenth-Century Afghanistan*, p. 43.

66 NAI, Foreign, Secret Consultations, 16 October 1839, no. 70, Abstract of letters received by Shah Shooja from different Chiefs West of Indus in reply to communications addressed to them by His Majesty; sent for the perusal of Captain Wade.

67 William Barr, *Journal of a March from Delhi to Peshawar and thence to Cabul*, London, 1844, pp. 134–5.

68 *Calendar of Persian Correspondence*, vol. 3, p. 50, no. 334, 19 March 1839, Political Agent, Ludhiana to Maharajah Ranjit Singh.

69 Ibid., p. 52, no. 356, 21 March 1839, Political Agent, Ludhiana to Maharajah Ranjit Singh.

70 Ibid., p. 56, no. 382, 27 March 1839; p. 58, no. 399, 1 April 1839; p. 60, no. 410, 3 April 1839; p. 64, nos 443 and 444, 8 April 1839; all Political Agent, Ludhiana to Maharajah Ranjit Singh.

71 Ibid., p. 57, no. 394, 31 March 1839, Khalsa sarkar to General Avitabile.

72 Ibid., p. 87, no. 604, 1 May 1839, Political Agent, Ludhiana to Maharajah Ranjit Singh.

73 Ibid., p. 29, no. 200 and p. 104, no. 716, 13 May (for demands of the Khyber

chiefs) and p. 107, no. 735, 15 and 21 May 1839, Maharajah Ranjit Singh to Political Agent, Ludhiana.

74 Osborne, *The Court and Camp of Runjeet Sing*, pp. 223–4.
75 Eden, *Up the Country*, pp. 292, 310.
76 Yapp, *Strategies*, pp. 363–5.
77 Kaye, *Lives of Indian Officers*, vol. II, p. 264.
78 BL, OIOC, ESL 79: no. 5 of Appendix VI in no. 3 of no. 71 of 20 August 1840 (IOR/L/PS/5/160), Extract from a demi-official letter from Todd to Macnaghten, 15 June 1840.
79 BL, Broughton Papers, Add Mss 36474, Wade to the Governor General, 31 January 1839.
80 NAI, Foreign, Secret Consultations, 12 June 1839, no. 75, Wade to Maddock, 18 July 1839.
81 Taylor, *Scenes and Adventures in Afghanistan*, pp. 101–2.
82 Durand, *The First Afghan War and its Causes*, p. 171.
83 BL, OIOC, Mss Eur D1 118, Nicholls letters, Keane to Nicholls, August 1839.
84 Sita Ram, *From Sepoy to Subedar*, p. 97.
85 Mirza 'Ata, *Naway Ma'arek*, pp. 39–56.
86 Fayz Mohammad, *Siraj ul-Tawarikh*, vol. I, pp. 226–7.
87 Mohan Lal, *Life of Dost Mohammad*, vol. II, pp. 238–42.
88 Durand, *The First Afghan War and its Causes*, p. 174.
89 *Waqi'at-i-Shah Shuja*, The Thirty-Fifth Event.
90 Sita Ram, *From Sepoy to Subedar*, p. 98.
91 Durand, *The First Afghan War and its Causes*, pp. 178–9.
92 *Waqi'at-i-Shah Shuja*, The Thirty-Fifth Event.
93 Mirza 'Ata, *Naway Ma'arek*, pp. 173–6.
94 Lawrence, *Reminiscences of Forty Three Years in India*, p. 17.
95 Forrest, *Life of Field Marshal Sir Neville Chamberlain*, p. 46.
96 National Army Museum, NAM 1983–11–28–1, Gaisford Diary, pp. 71ff.
97 Mirza 'Ata, *Naway Ma'arek*, pp. 173–6.
98 Johnson, *The Afghan Way of War*, p. 53.
99 Durand, *The First Afghan War and its Causes*, pp. 166–7.
100 Mirza 'Ata, *Naway Ma'arek*, pp. 173–6.
101 Ibid.
102 Fayz Mohammad, *Siraj ul-Tawarikh*, vol. I, p. 228.
103 Mohan Lal, *Life of Dost Mohammad*, vol. II, p. 307.
104 Havelock, *Narrative of the War in Affghanistan*, vol. II, p. 97.
105 Mohan Lal, *Life of Dost Mohammad*, vol. II, pp. 236–7.
106 Johnson, *The Afghan Way of War*, p. 53.
107 Kashmiri, *Akbarnama*, ch. 14.
108 Lawrence, *Reminiscences of Forty Three Years in India*, p. 25.
109 Kaye, *History of the War in Afghanistan*, vol. I, p. 461.
110 Hough, *March and Operations of the Army of the Indus*, pp. 251–2.

Chapter 5: The Flag of Holy War

1 Khalfin, *Vozmezdie ozhidaet v Dzhagda* (Drama in a Boarding House).
2 BL, Add Mss 48535, Clanricarde to Palmerston, 25 May 1839.

3 Kaye, *History of the War in Afghanistan*, vol. I, p. 209n.

4 NAI, Foreign, Secret Consultations, 18 December 1839, no. 6, Translation of a letter from Nazir Khan Ullah at Bokhara to the address of the British Envoy and Minister at Kabul dated 15th Rajab / 24 September 1839.

5 Perovsky, *A Narrative of the Russian Military Expedition to Khiva*, pp. 73–5. Also quoted, in a slightly different translation, in Morrison, *Twin Imperial Disasters*, pp. 22–4. Morrison says only four letters from Vitkevitch in Kabul survive in his file in the Russian archives.

6 Khalfin, *Vozmezdie ozhidaet v Dzhagda* (Drama in a Boarding House); also Morrison, *Twin Imperial Disasters*, p. 23.

7 Khalfin, *Vozmezdie ozhidaet v Dzhagda* (Drama in a Boarding House), pp. 194–206.

8 Sungurov's notes were assembled into a memoir by his cousin I. A. Polferov in 'Predatel' (The Traitor), *Istoricheskij vestnik*, St Petersburg, vol. 100 (1905), p. 498 and note. See also Kessler, *Ivan Viktorovitch Vitkevitch*, pp. 16–18.

9 Blaramberg, *Vospominania*, p. 64.

10 Morrison, *Twin Imperial Disasters*, p. 32.

11 George Pottinger and Patrick Macrory, *The Ten-Rupee Jezail: Figures in the First Afghan War 1838–42*, London, 1993, p. 7.

12 Yapp, *Strategies*, p. 268; David, *Victoria's Wars*, p. 35.

13 Eden, *Up the Country*, pp. 205–6.

14 *Waqi'at-i-Shah Shuja*, p. 126, The Thirty-Fifth Event.

15 Gleig, *Sale's Brigade in Afghanistan*, p. 69.

16 Hopkins, *The Making of Modern Afghanistan*, pp. 144–8.

17 James Rattray, *The Costumes of the Various Tribes, Portraits of Ladies of Rank, Celebrated Princes and Chiefs, Views of the Principal Fortresses and Cities, and Interior of the Cities and Temples of Afghaunistan*, London, 1848, p. 16.

18 Mirza 'Ata, *Naway Ma'arek*, pp. 211–24.

19 Gleig, *Sale's Brigade in Afghanistan*, pp. 69–70.

20 Ibid., pp. 71–2.

21 Rattray, *The Costumes of the Various Tribes*, p. 16.

22 Many thanks to Craig Murray for bringing this to my attention. Both Alexander and James Burnes, as well as Mohan Lal Kashmiri, were enthusiastic Masons

23 Lawrence, *Reminiscences of Forty Three Years in India*, p. 27.

24 Eden, *Miss Eden's Letters*, p. 315.

25 Fayz Mohammad, *Siraj ul-Tawarikh*, vol. I, p. 228.

26 Mohammad Ghulam Kohistani, *Jangnama*, p. 70.

27 Lawrence, *Reminiscences of Forty Three Years in India*, p. 20.

28 J. H. Stocqueler, *Memorials of Affghanistan: State Papers, Official Documents, Dispatches, Authentic Narratives etc Illustrative of the British Expedition to, and Occupation of, Affghanistan and Scinde, between the years 1838 and 1842*, Calcutta, 1843, Appendix I, 'The Pursuit of Dost Mohammad Khan by Major Outram of the Bombay Army', p. iv.

29 Ibid., p. ix.

30 Ibid.

31 Mirza 'Ata, *Naway Ma'arek*, pp. 211–24 .

32 Fayz Mohammad, *Siraj ul-Tawarikh*, vol. I, pp. 228–31.

33 BL, OIOC, Elphinstone Papers, Mss Eur F89/3/7; Yapp, *Strategies*, p. 332.

34 Forrest, *Life of Field Marshal Sir Neville Chamberlain*, pp. 54–5.

35 Macintyre, *Josiah the Great*, pp. 264, 308.

36 Gleig, *Sale's Brigade in Afghanistan*, p. 71.

37 Mohan Lal, *Life of Dost Mohammad*, vol. II, pp. 305–12; Noelle, *State and Tribe in Nineteenth-Century Afghanistan*, p. 226; Mirza 'Ata, *Naway Ma'arek*, p. 197.

38 Thomas J. Barfield, 'Problems of Establishing Legitimacy in Afghanistan', *Iranian Studies*, vol. 37, no. 2, June 2004, p. 273.

39 BL, Broughton Papers, Add Mss 36474, fol. 188, Auckland to Hobhouse, 21 December 1839.

40 *Waqi'at-i-Shah Shuja*, p. 127, The Thirty-Fifth Event.

41 Lawrence, *Reminiscences of Forty Three Years in India*, p. 32.

42 Seaton, *From Cadet to Colonel*, p. 109.

43 Sultan Mohammad Khan Durrani, *Tarikh-i-Sultani*, p. 258.

44 NAI, Foreign, Secret Consultations, 18 December 1839, no. 6, Translation of a letter from Nazir Khan Ullah at Bokhara to the address of the British Envoy and Minister at Kabul dated 15th Rajab / 24 September 1839.

45 Ibid.

46 NAI, Foreign, Secret Consultations, 8 September 1842, no. 37–38, Sir A. Burnes Cabool to Captain G. L. Jacob, Rajcote, Private, Cabool, 19 September 1839.

47 Yapp, *Strategies*, p. 339.

48 Eden, *Miss Eden's Letters*, p. 323.

49 Quoted in Yapp, *Strategies*, p. 344.

50 Gleig, *Sale's Brigade in Afghanistan*, pp. 49–50.

51 Ibid., p. 50.

52 National Army Museum, NAM 7101-24-3, Roberts to Sturt, 10 May 1840.

53 Yapp, *Strategies*, pp. 322–3.

54 Mirza 'Ata, *Naway Ma'arek*, pp. 211–24.

55 Kaye, *Lives of Indian Officers*, vol. II, pp. 282–3.

56 Mohan Lal, *Life of Dost Mohammad*, vol. II, p. 399.

57 National Army Museum, NAM 7101-24-3, Roberts to Sturt, 10 May 1840.

58 Jules Stewart, *Crimson Snow: Britain's First Disaster in Afghanistan*, London, 2008, p. 64.

59 *Waqi'at-i-Shah Shuja*, p. 124, The Thirty-Fifth Event.

60 Fayz Mohammad, *Siraj ul-Tawarikh*, vol. I, pp. 235–6.

61 NAI, Foreign, Secret Consultations, 5 October 1840, no. 66, Macnaghten to Auckland.

62 Mohan Lal, *Life of Dost Mohammad*, vol. II, pp. 314–15.

63 BL, Broughton Papers, Add Mss 36474, fol. 188, Auckland to Hobhouse, 21 December 1839.

64 NAI, Foreign, Secret Consultations, 8 June 1840, no. 95–6, Auckland to Shah Shuja.

65 M. E. Yapp, 'The Revolutions of 1841–2 in Afghanistan', *Bulletin of the School of Oriental and African Studies*, vol. 27, no. 2 (1964), p. 342. See also Thomas Barfield, *Afghanistan: A Cultural and Political History*, Princeton, 2010, pp. 118–20.

66 BL, OIOC, ESL, 88, no. 24 of no. 32 of 17 August 1842, Lal, Memorandum, 29 June 1842.

67 Mohan Lal, *Life of Dost Mohammad*, vol. II, pp. 380–1.

68 Noelle, *State and Tribe in Nineteenth-Century Afghanistan*, p. 50.

69 NAI, Foreign, Secret Consultations, 15 January 1840, no. 75–77, Shah Shuja to Auckland.

70 Durand, *The First Afghan War and its Causes*, p. 245.

71 NAI, Foreign, Secret Consultations, 24 August 1840, covering letter of Macnaghten of 22 July 1840.

72 NAI, Foreign, Secret Consultations, 15 January 1840, no. 75–77, Shah Shuja to Auckland.

73 Mohan Lal, *Life of Dost Mohammad*, vol. II, pp. 314–15.

74 *Waqi'at-i-Shah Shuja*, pp. 124–5, The Thirty-Fifth Event.

75 Rattray, *The Costumes of the Various Tribes*, p. 3, and Lockyer Willis Hart, *Character and Costumes of Afghanistan*, London, 1843, p. 1.

76 Shahmat Ali, *The Sikhs and Afghans in Connexion with India and Persia*, London, 1847, p. 479.

77 NAI, Foreign, Secret Consultations, 24 August 1840, Sir A. Burnes' report of an interview with Shah Shooja with some notes of Sir Wm Macnaghten to GG. Capt. Lawrence accompanied Burnes.

78 NAI, Foreign, Secret Consultations, 5 October 1840, no. 66, Macnaghten to Auckland.

79 Fayz Mohammad, *Siraj ul-Tawarikh*, vol. I, p. 245.

80 BL, OIOC, IOR L/PS/5/162.

81 BL, OIOC, ESL 74: no. 5 of no. 24 of no. 13, 19 February 1841.

82 BL, OIOC, ESL 70: no. 35 of no. 99 of 13 September 1840, Burnes Memo of a conversation with Shah Shuja, 12 July 1840.

83 National Army Museum, NAM 7101–24–3, Roberts to Osborne, 18 February 1840.

84 Stocqueler, *The Memoirs and Correspondence of Sir William Nott*, vol. I, pp. 256–7.

85 Kaye, *Lives of Indian Officers*, vol. I, p. 272.

86 Kashmiri, *Akbarnama*, ch. 17.

87 Mohan Lal, *Life of Dost Mohammad*, vol. II, pp. 314–15.

88 Fayz Mohammad, *Siraj ul-Tawarikh*, vol. I, p. 237.

89 Kashmiri, *Akbarnama*, ch. 17.

90 Ibid.

91 Mirza 'Ata, *Naway Ma'arek*, p. 197; BL, OIOC, no. 7 of no. 122 of 16 October 1840 (L/PS/5/152), Macnaghten to Torrens, 22 August 1840.

92 Dennie, *Personal Narrative*, p. 126.

93 Mohammad Ghulam Kohistani, *Jangnama*, pp. 184–6.

94 Ibid, pp. 157–8.

95 Mohan Lal, *Life of Dost Mohammad*, vol. II, pp. 349–50.

96 Mirza 'Ata, *Naway Ma'arek*, pp. 205–10.

97 Mohan Lal, *Life of Dost Mohammad*, vol. II, p. 360.

98 Mohammad Ghulam Kohistani, *Jangnama*, pp. 193–5.

99 Lawrence, *Reminiscences of Forty Three Years in India*, pp. 49–52.

100 *Waqi'at-i-Shah Shuja*, p. 126, The Thirty-Fifth Event. For the tradition of rulers surrendering see the perceptive analysis in Barfield, *Afghanistan: A Cultural and Political History*, pp. 117–18.

101 Mirza 'Ata, *Naway Ma'arek*, p. 209.

102 Kaye, *History of the War in Afghanistan*, vol. II, p. 98.

103 Kaye, *Lives of Indian Officers*, vol. II, pp. 280–1.

104 Mirza 'Ata, *Naway Ma'arek*, p. 210.
105 Fayz Mohammad, *Siraj ul-Tawarikh*, vol. I, p. 240.
106 *Waqi'at-i-Shah Shuja*, pp. 126–7, The Thirty-Fifth Event.
107 Stewart, *Crimson Snow*, p. 71.
108 Mirza 'Ata, *Naway Ma'arek*, p. 211.
109 Lawrence, *Reminiscences of Forty Three Years in India*, p. 53.

Chapter 6: We Fail from Our Ignorance

1 Eden, *Up the Country*, p. 389.
2 Ibid.
3 Eden, *Miss Eden's Letters*, p. 334.
4 Karl Meyer and Shareen Brysac, *Tournament of Shadows: The Great Game and the Race for Empire in Europe*, London, 1999, p. 93.
5 Eden, *Up the Country*, p. 390.
6 BL, Broughton Papers, Add Mss 37703, Auckland to Elphinstone, 18 December 1840.
7 Helen Mackenzie, *Storms and Sunshine of a Soldier's Life: Lt. General Colin Mackenzie CB 1825–1881*, 2 vols, Edinburgh, 1884, vol. I, p. 65.
8 Ibid., p. 75.
9 National Army Museum, NAM 1999–02–116–9–1, Magrath Letters, Letter 9, Cantonment Caubul, 22 June 1841.
10 BL, OIOC, ESL 86: no. 38 of no. 14, 17 May 1842, Elphinstone Memo, December 1841.
11 BL, OIOC, Mss Eur F89/54, Major-General William Elphinstone to James D. Buller Elphinstone, 5 April 1841.
12 Eden, *Miss Eden's Letters*, p. 343.
13 BL, Broughton Papers, Add Mss 37705, Auckland to George Clerk, 23 May 1841. See also Hopkins, *The Making of Modern Afghanistan*, p. 67.
14 Fayz Mohammad, *Siraj ul-Tawarikh*, vol. I, p. 291; Mohan Lal, *Life of Dost Mohammad*, vol. II, p. 382; see also Yapp, *Strategies*, p. 366.
15 See for example the letter from Malik Mohamad Khan and Abdah Sultan in Ghazni to Naib Aminullah Khan Logari, undated but c.1841, reproduced in Amini, *Paadash-e-Khidmatguzaari-ye-Saadiqaane Ghazi Nayab Aminullah Khan Logari*, p. 167. The original was in an album of letters (which now seem to have disappeared) in the Kabul museum.
16 M. E. Yapp, 'Disturbances in Western Afghanistan, 1839–41', *Bulletin of the School of Oriental and African Studies*, vol. 26, no. 2 (1963), p. 310.
17 BL, OIOC, ESL 75: no. 37 of no. 34 of 22 April 1841 (IOR/L/PS/5/156), Aktar Khan's address to Naboo Khan Populzye, and forwarded by that Chief to Ata Mahomed Khan (Sirdar), who transmitted it to Candahar. Translated by H. Rawlinson, February 1841.
18 Stocqueler, *The Memoirs and Correspondence of Sir William Nott*, vol. I, pp. 272–3.
19 Rawlinson, *A Memoir of Major-General Sir Henry Creswicke Rawlinson*, p. 81.
20 BL, OIOC, ESL 81: no. 64a of no. 109 (IOR/L/PS/5/162), Extract from a letter from Macnaghten to Rawlinson dated about 2 August 1841.
21 Colonel (John) Haughton, *Char-ee-Kar and Service There with the 4th Goorkha*

Regiment, Shah Shooja's Force, in 1841, London, 1878, pp. 5–6; George Pottinger, *The Afghan Connection: The Extraordinary Adventures of Eldred Pottinger*, Edinburgh, 1983, p. 117.

22 BL, OIOC, ESL 88: no. 47a of no. 32 of 17 August 1842 (IOR/L/PS/5/169), Pottinger to Maddock, 1 February 1842.

23 Kashmiri, *Akbarnama*, ch. 21.

24 BL, OIOC, Board's Collections of Secret Letters to India, 13, Secret Committee to Governor General in Council, 694/31 December 1840.

25 Burnes to Wood, February 1841, in John Wood, *A Personal Narrative of a Journey to the Source of the River Oxus by the Route of the Indus, Kabul and Badakshan, Performed under the Sanction of the Supreme Government of India, in the Years 1836, 1837 and 1838*, London, 1841, pp. ix–x.

26 NAI, Foreign, Secret Consultations, 28 September 1842, nos 43, Burnes to Holland, 6 September 1840.

27 NAI, Foreign, Secret Consultations, 28 September 1842, no. 37–38, A. Burnes to J. Burnes.

28 Norris, *First Afghan War*, p. 317. For the cost of the Afghan War to the Company economy see also Yapp, *Strategies*, pp. 339–42; Shah Mahmood Hanifi, 'Impoverishing a Colonial Frontier: Cash, Credit, and Debt in Nineteenth-Century Afghanistan', *Iranian Studies*, vol. 37, no. 2 (June 2004); and Shah Mahmood Hanifi, *Connecting Histories in Afghanistan: Market Relations and State Formation on a Colonial Frontier*, Stanford, 2011. See also Hopkins, *The Making of Modern Afghanistan*, pp. 25–30.

29 Yapp, *Strategies*, p. 341.

30 BL, OIOC, IOR/HM/534–45, Papers Connected to Sale's Brigade, vol. 39, Nicholls Papers and Nicholls's Journal, 26 March 1841.

31 National Army Museum, NAM, 1999-02-116-9-1, Magrath Letters, Letter 8 and 9, Cantonment Caubul, 21 May and 22 June 1841.

32 Lady Florentia Sale, *A Journal of the Disasters in Affghanistan 1841–2*, London 1843, p. 29.

33 Broadfoot, *The Career of Major George Broadfoot*, p. 14.

34 Ibid., pp. 15–17.

35 Ibid., p. 8.

36 Ibid., p. 121.

37 Mackenzie, *Storms and Sunshine*, vol. I, p. 99.

38 Broadfoot, *The Career of Major George Broadfoot*, p. 20.

39 Mackenzie, *Storms and Sunshine*, vol. I, p. 99.

40 NAI, Foreign, Secret Consultations, 25 January 1841, nos 80–82, Translation of a letter from His Majesty Shah Shooja ool Moolk to Her Majesty the Queen of England.

41 Lawrence, *Reminiscences of Forty Three Years in India*, p. 54.

42 Yapp, *Strategies*, p. 315.

43 *Waqi'at-i-Shah Shuja*, pp. 124–5, The Thirty-Fifth Event.

44 Fayz Mohammad, *Siraj ul-Tawarikh*, vol. I, pp. 244–5.

45 Mohan Lal, *Life of Dost Mohammad*, vol. II, p. 387.

46 Kaye, *Lives of Indian Officers*, vol. II, p. 286.

47 For the degree to which Afghan debts endangered the financial underpinnings of the East India Company, see Hanifi, *Connecting Histories in Afghanistan*, and Shah Mahmoud Hanifi, 'Inter-regional Trade and Colonial State Formation

in Nineteenth Century Afghanistan', unpublished PhD dissertation, University of Michigan, 2001.

48 David, *Victoria's Wars*, p. 45.

49 Quoted in Macrory, *Signal Catastrophe*, p. 138.

50 BL, OIOC, ESL 81 (IOR/L/PS/5/162), Extract from a letter from Macnaghten to Auckland, dated Cabool, 28 August 1841.

51 Mackenzie, *Storms and Sunshine*, vol. I, p. 96.

52 BL, OIOC, ESL 88: no. 24 of no. 32, dated 17 August 1842 (IOR/L/PS/5/169), Mohan Lal's Memo.

53 Barfield, 'Problems of Establishing Legitimacy in Afghanistan', p. 273; also Barfield, *Afghanistan: A Cultural and Political History*, p. 120; Hanifi, 'Inter-Regional Trade and Colonial State Formation in Nineteenth Century Afghanistan', p. 58.

54 Mohan Lal, *Life of Dost Mohammad*, vol. II, p. 319.

55 Ibid., p. 381.

56 *Waqi'at-i-Shah Shuja*, pp. 131–2, The Thirty-Fifth Event.

57 Kashmiri, *Akbarnama*, ch. 21.

58 BL, OIOC, Mss Eur F89/54, Extract of a letter from Asst. Surgeon Campbell in Medical Charge of the 54th N.I., dated Cabool, 26 July 1841.

59 Pottinger, *The Afghan Connection*, p. 120.

60 BL, OIOC, Mss Eur F89/3/7, Broadfoot to W. Elphinstone.

61 Broadfoot, *The Career of Major George Broadfoot*, pp. 26–8.

62 BL, OIOC, Mss Eur F89/54, Captain Broadfoot's Report.

63 Macrory, *Signal Catastrophe*, pp. 141–2.

64 Seaton, *From Cadet to Colonel*, p. 138.

65 Gleig, *Sale's Brigade in Afghanistan*, p. 80.

66 BL, OIOC, ESL 81: no. 10 of no. 109 of 22 December 1841 (IOR/L/PS/5/162), Macnaghten to Maddock, 26 October 1841.

67 Sale, *A Journal of the Disasters in Afghanistan*, p.11.

68 Quoted in Macrory, *Signal Catastrophe*, p. 149.

69 Seaton, *From Cadet to Colonel*, p. 149.

70 Sale, *A Journal of the Disasters in Afghanistan*, p. 15.

71 Gleig, *Sale's Brigade in Afghanistan*, p. 93.

72 Sale, *A Journal of the Disasters in Afghanistan*, p. 20.

73 Ibid., p. 24.

74 Durand, *The First Afghan War and its Causes*, p. 338.

75 National Army Museum, NAM 1999–02–116–10–4, Magrath Letters, Camp Tezeen 25 October 1841.

76 Sale, *A Journal of the Disasters in Afghanistan*, p. 25.

77 Seaton, *From Cadet to Colonel*, p. 157.

78 Ibid., pp. 156–7.

79 Gleig, *Sale's Brigade in Afghanistan*, p. 118.

80 Seaton, *From Cadet to Colonel*, p. 165.

81 NAI, Foreign, Secret Consultations, 13 December 1841, nos 1–2, Sale to Nicholls, 13 November 1841.

82 Quoted in Hopkirk, *The Great Game*, p. 238.

83 Stocqueler, *The Memoirs and Correspondence of Sir William Nott*, vol. I, pp. 35–9.

84 Ibid., vol. I, pp. 350, 360.

85 Kaye, *History of the War in Afghanistan*, vol. II, p. 161.

86 Sale, *A Journal of the Disasters in Afghanistan*, p. 22.

87 BL, OIOC, ESL 81: no. 64a of no. 109 (IOR/L/PS/5/162), Extract from a letter from Macnaghten to Auckland, dated Cabool, 29 September 1841.

88 Kaye, *Lives of Indian Officers*, vol. II, p. 286.

89 Ibid., p. 287.

90 Kashmiri, *Akbarnama*, ch. 22, The killing of Burnes.

91 Mohan Lal, *Life of Dost Mohammad*, vol. II, pp. 390–1.

92 Mirza 'Ata, *Naway Ma'arek*, pp. 215–20.

93 Kaye, *Lives of Indian Officers*, vol. II, p. 289.

94 BL, OIOC, ESL 88: no. 24 of no. 32, dated 17 August 1842 (IOR/L/PS/5/169), Mohan Lal's Memo.

95 Mirza 'Ata, *Naway Ma'arek*, pp. 215–20.

Chapter 7: All Order Is at an End

1 Private Collection, The Mss Journal of Captain Hugh Johnson, Paymaster to Shah Soojah's Force, p. 1, entry for 2 November 1841.

2 Ibid., pp. 1–2.

3 Pottinger, *The Afghan Connection*, p. 141.

4 Lawrence, *Reminiscences of Forty Three Years in India*, p. 62.

5 Ibid., pp. 63–4.

6 Ibid., p. 65.

7 Mohan Lal, *Life of Dost Mohammad*, vol. II, pp. 401–2.

8 Mackenzie, *Storms and Sunshine*, vol. I, p. 105.

9 Mohan Lal, *Life of Dost Mohammad*, vol. II, p. 407.

10 Mirza 'Ata, *Naway Ma'arek*, pp. 211–24, Events leading to the murder of Burnes and the great revolt.

11 Karim, *Muharaba Kabul wa Kandahar*, pp. 54–7.

12 Kaye, *History of the War in Afghanistan*, vol. II, pp. 163ff.

13 Mohan Lal, *Life of Dost Mohammad*, vol. II, pp. 408–9.

14 Kashmiri, *Akbarnama*, ch. 22, The killing of Burnes.

15 BL, Wellesley Papers, Add Mss 37313, James Burnes to James Carnac, 1 February 1842, Extract of a Persian Letter in exhortation from the Khans of Cabaul to the Chiefs of the Afreedees, a copy of which was received from Captain Mackinnon by Mr. Robertson at Agra on 20 December.

16 Macrory, *Signal Catastrophe*, p. 155.

17 Fayz Mohammad, *Siraj ul-Tawarikh*, vol. I, p. 249.

18 Sale, *A Journal of the Disasters in Afghanistan*, p. 29; Mirza 'Ata, *Naway Ma'arek*, pp. 211–24, Events leading to the murder of Burnes and the great revolt.

19 Quoted by Yapp, 'The Revolutions of 1841–2 in Afghanistan', p. 380.

20 *Waqi'at-i-Shah Shuja*, p. 132, The Thirty-Fifth Event.

21 Ibid., p. 137.

22 Ibid.

23 Mackenzie, *Storms and Sunshine*, vol. I, pp. 106–7.

24 Lawrence, *Reminiscences of Forty Three Years in India*, p. 75.

25 Sale, *A Journal of the Disasters in Afghanistan*, p. 39.

26 Major-General Sir Vincent Eyre, *The Kabul Insurrection of 1841–2*, London, 1879, p. 87.
27 *Waqi'at-i-Shah Shuja*, p. 133, The Thirty-Fifth Event.
28 Sale, *A Journal of the Disasters in Afghanistan*, p. 39.
29 *Waqi'at-i-Shah Shuja*, p. 133, The Thirty-Fifth Event.
30 Stocqueler, *The Memoirs and Correspondence of Sir William Nott*, vol. I, p. 369.
31 *Waqi'at-i-Shah Shuja*, p. 133, The Thirty-Fifth Event.
32 Eyre, *The Kabul Insurrection of 1841–2*, p. 89.
33 Kaye, *History of the War in Afghanistan*, vol. II, p. 187.
34 Sale, *A Journal of the Disasters in Afghanistan*, pp. 29–32.
35 Lawrence, *Reminiscences of Forty Three Years in India*, pp. 67–9.
36 Ibid., p. 69.
37 Sale, *A Journal of the Disasters in Afghanistan*, p. 35.
38 'Personal Narrative of the Havildar Motee Ram of the Shah's 4th or Ghoorkha Regiment of Light Infantry, Destroyed at Char-ee-car', appendix to Haughton, *Char-ee-Kar and Service There with the 4th Goorkha Regiment*, pp. 47–8.
39 BL, OIOC, ESL 88: no. 47a of no. 32 of 17 August 1842 (IOR/L/PS/5/169), Pottinger to Maddock, 1 February 1842.
40 'Personal Narrative of the Havildar Motee Ram of the Shah's 4th or Ghoorkha Regiment of Light Infantry, Destroyed at Char-ee-kar', appendix to Haughton, *Char-ee-Kar and Service There with the 4th Goorkha Regiment*, pp. 47–8, 51.
41 Haughton, *Char-ee-Kar and Service There with the 4th Goorkha Regiment*, p. 15.
42 Ibid., pp. 21–4 .
43 Yapp, *Strategies*, p. 179.
44 BL, OIOC, ESL 88: no. 74 of no. 32 of 17 August 1842 (IOR L/PS/5/169), Court Martial of Himmat Bunneah, 'An European Special Court of Inquiry held at Candahar by order of Major Genl. Nott commanding Lower Afghanistan for the purpose of enquiring into such matter as may be brought before it', Candahar, 15 June 1842.
45 Stocqueler, *The Memoirs and Correspondence of Sir William Nott*, vol. I, pp. 394–5.
46 Sale, *A Journal of the Disasters in Afghanistan*, p. 38.
47 Mohan Lal, *Life of Dost Mohammad*, vol. II, p. 413.
48 Lawrence, *Reminiscences of Forty Three Years in India*, pp. 74–5.
49 Mackenzie, *Storms and Sunshine*, vol. I, pp. 106–7.
50 Ibid., p. 107.
51 Ibid., pp. 108–10.
52 Private Collection, Journal of Captain Hugh Johnson, Paymaster to Shah Soojah's Force, p. 8, entry for 3 November 1841.
53 Karim, *Muharaba Kabul wa Kandahar*, pp. 57–8.
54 Sale, *A Journal of the Disasters in Afghanistan*, p. 46.
55 Mackenzie, *Storms and Sunshine*, vol. I, p. 109.
56 Private Collection, Journal of Captain Hugh Johnson, Paymaster to Shah Soojah's Force, p. 15, entry for 2 December 1841.
57 Ibid., p. 16.
58 Ibid., p. 15.
59 Sale, *A Journal of the Disasters in Afghanistan*, p. 47.
60 Ibid., p. 82.

61 Sita Ram, *From Sepoy to Subedar*, pp. 110–13.

62 Mackenzie, *Storms and Sunshine*, vol. I, pp. 108–10.

63 Eyre, *The Kabul Insurrection of 1841–2*, p. 116.

64 Mackenzie, *Storms and Sunshine*, vol. I, p. 133.

65 Sale, *A Journal of the Disasters in Afghanistan*, p. 66.

66 Ibid., p. 47.

67 *Waqi'at-i-Shah Shuja*, p. 137, The Thirty-Fifth Event.

68 Lawrence, *Reminiscences of Forty Three Years in India*, p. 84.

69 Mirza 'Ata, *Naway Ma'arek*, pp. 211–24, Events leading to the murder of Burnes and the great revolt.

70 Eyre, *The Kabul Insurrection of 1841–2*, p. 124.

71 BL, OIOC, ESL 88: no. 47a of no. 32 of 17 August 1842 (IOR/L/PS/5/169), Pottinger to Maddock, 1 February 1842.

72 Mohan Lal, *Life of Dost Mohammad*, vol. II, p. 416; 'Personal Narrative of the Havildar Motee Ram of the Shah's 4th or Ghoorkha Regiment of Light Infantry, Destroyed at Char-ee-kar', appendix to Haughton, *Char-ee-Kar and Service There with the 4th Goorkha Regiment*, pp. 47–8, 54.

73 'Personal Narrative of the Havildar Motee Ram of the Shah's 4th or Ghoorkha Regiment of Light Infantry, Destroyed at Char-ee-kar', appendix to Haughton, *Char-ee-Kar and Service There with the 4th Goorkha Regiment*, p. 55.

74 Ibid., p. 56.

75 Eyre, *The Kabul Insurrection of 1841–2*, p. 176.

76 Ibid., p. 162; Mackenzie, *Storms and Sunshine*, vol. I, p. 121.

77 Sale, *A Journal of the Disasters in Afghanistan*, p. 85.

78 Sultan Mohammad Khan Durrani, *Tarikh-i-Sultani*, p. 271.

79 Sale, *A Journal of the Disasters in Afghanistan*, p. 86.

80 Sultan Mohammad Khan Durrani, *Tarikh-i-Sultani*, p. 271.

81 Lawrence, *Reminiscences of Forty Three Years in India*, p. 93.

82 Ibid.

83 Fayz Mohammad, *Siraj al-Tawarikh*, vol. I, pp. 251–3.

84 Mackenzie, *Storms and Sunshine*, vol. I, p. 123.

85 Eyre, *The Kabul Insurrection of 1841–2*, p. 182.

86 Kashmiri, *Akbarnama*, ch. 25, Akbar Khan returns to Kabul.

87 Sale, *A Journal of the Disasters in Afghanistan*, p. 120.

88 Yapp, 'The Revolutions of 1841–2 in Afghanistan', p. 347.

89 Mirza 'Ata, *Naway Ma'arek*, pp. 224–9, Sardar Muhammad Akbar Khan arrives back in Kabul after being detained in Bukhara, and kills Macnaghten.

90 Kashmiri, *Akbarnama*, ch. 25, Akbar Khan returns to Kabul.

91 Mirza 'Ata, *Naway Ma'arek*, pp. 224–9, Sardar Muhammad Akbar Khan arrives back in Kabul after being detained in Bukhara, and kills Macnaghten.

92 BL, OIOC, ESL 88: no. 47a of no. 32 of 17 August 1842 (IOR/L/PS/5/169), Enclosure AA: Macnaghten to Maddock, n.d.

93 Macrory, *Signal Catastrophe*, p. 178.

94 BL, OIOC, ESL 88: no. 47a of no. 32 of 17 August 1842 (IOR/L/PS/5/169), Enclosure AA: Macnaghten to Maddock, n.d.

95 Mackenzie, *Storms and Sunshine*, vol. I, p. 123.

96 Macrory, *Signal Catastrophe*, p. 180.

97 Lawrence, *Reminiscences of Forty Three Years in India*, pp. 100–1.

98 BL, OIOC, ESL 88: no. 47a of no. 32 of 17 August 1842 (IOR/L/PS/5/169), Enclosure AA: Macnaghten to Maddock, n.d.

99 Macrory, *Signal Catastrophe*, p. 188.

100 BL, OIOC, ESL 88: no. 47a of no. 32 of 17 August 1842 (IOR/L/PS/5/169), Enclosure AA: Macnaghten to Maddock, n.d.

101 Ibid., Macnaghten to Auckland, Encl with Lawrence to Pottinger, 10 May 1842.

102 *Waqi'at-i-Shah Shuja*, pp. 138, The Thirty-Fifth Event, The death of Macnaghten.

103 Lawrence, *Reminiscences of Forty Three Years in India*, p. 110.

104 Eden, *Miss Eden's Letters*, p. 323.

105 Ibid., p. 329.

106 Ibid.

107 Ibid., p. 355.

108 BL, Broughton Papers, Add Mss 37706, fol. 197, Auckland to Nicholls, 1 December 1841.

109 Mirza 'Ata, *Naway Ma'arek*, pp. 224–9, Sardar Muhammad Akbar Khan arrives back in Kabul after being detained in Bukhara, and kills Macnaghten.

110 Lawrence, *Reminiscences of Forty Three Years in India*, p. 111.

111 Mackenzie, *Storms and Sunshine*, vol. I, p. 124.

112 Lawrence, *Reminiscences of Forty Three Years in India*, p. 111.

113 Ibid., pp. 111–12.

114 Fayz Mohammad, *Siraj ul-Tawarikh*, vol. I, pp. 253–7.

115 Yapp, 'The Revolutions of 1841–2 in Afghanistan', p. 349.

116 NAI, Foreign, Secret Consultations, 28 December 1842, no. 480–82, quoted in Mohan Lal's Memo.

117 Mirza 'Ata, *Naway Ma'arek*, pp. 224–9, Sardar Muhammad Akbar Khan arrives back in Kabul after being detained in Bukhara, and kills Macnaghten.

118 Hari Ram Gupta, *Panjab, Central Asia and the First Afghan War, Based on Mohan Lal's Observations*, Chandigarh, 1940, p. 246. Mohan Lal appears to have doubted the truth of Abdul Aziz's claim.

119 Mohan Lal, *Life of Dost Mohammad*, vol. II, pp. 421–2.

120 BL, OIOC, ESL 88: no. 47a of no. 32 of 17 August 1842 (IOR/L/PS/5/169), Macnaghten to Auckland, Encl. with Lawrence to Pottinger, 10 May 1842.

121 Mirza 'Ata, *Naway Ma'arek*, pp. 224–9, Sardar Muhammad Akbar Khan arrives back in Kabul after being detained in Bukhara, and kills Macnaghten.

122 NAI, Foreign, Secret Consultations, 28 December 1842, no. 480–82, Mohan Lal's Memo.

123 Eyre, *The Kabul Insurrection of 1841–2*, p. 216.

124 Lawrence, *Reminiscences of Forty Three Years in India*, p. 139.

125 Mackenzie, *Storms and Sunshine*, vol. I, p. 127.

126 BL, OIOC, ESL 88: no. 47a of no. 32 of 17 August 1842 (IOR/L/PS/5/169), Macnaghten to Auckland, Encl with Lawrence to Pottinger, 10 May 1842; Mackenzie, *Storms and Sunshine*, vol. II, p.32.

127 Karim, *Muharaba Kabul wa Kandahar*, pp. 66–72.

128 BL, OIOC, ESL 82: Agra Letter, 22 January 1842, (IOR/L/PS/5/163), Pottinger to MacGregor (date unclear).

129 Mirza 'Ata, *Naway Ma'arek*, pp. 224–9, Sardar Muhammad Akbar Khan arrives back in Kabul after being detained in Bukhara, and kills Macnaghten.

Chapter 8: The Wail of Bugles

1   Private Collection, The Mss Journal of Captain Hugh Johnson, Paymaster to Shah Soojah's Force, p. 30, entry for 6 January 1842.
2   Lawrence, *Reminiscences of Forty Three Years in India*, p. 143.
3   Kashmiri, *Akbarnama*, ch. 28.
4   Ibid.
5   Sale, *A Journal of the Disasters in Afghanistan*, pp. 132–4.
6   Ibid., p. 147.
7   Lawrence, *Reminiscences of Forty Three Years in India*, p. 96.
8   Quoted by Peter Hopkirk in *The Great Game*, p. 258.
9   Eyre, *The Kabul Insurrection of 1841–2*, pp. 247–8.
10 Private Collection, Journal of Captain Hugh Johnson, Paymaster to Shah Soojah's Force, p. 30, entry for 29 December 1841.
11 Gupta, *Panjab, Central Asia and the First Afghan War, Based on Mohan Lal's Observations*, pp. 176–8.
12 Sale, *A Journal of the Disasters in Afghanistan*, p. 141.
13 *Waqi'at-i-Shah Shuja*, p. 138, The Thirty-Fifth Event, The death of Macnaghten.
14 Mohan Lal, *Life of Dost Mohammad*, vol. II, pp. 428–9.
15 NAI, Foreign, Secret Consultations, 1 June 1842, no. 19, Shuja's letter to the Governor General on the causes which led to the murder of Sir Wm Macnaghten (free translation).
16 Ibid.
17 Lawrence, *Reminiscences of Forty Three Years in India*, p. 142.
18 Eyre, *The Kabul Insurrection of 1841–2*, p. 249.
19 Sale, *A Journal of the Disasters in Afghanistan*, p. 142.
20 Ibid., p. 143.
21 Private Collection, Journal of Captain Hugh Johnson, Paymaster to Shah Soojah's Force, pp. 30–1, entry for 6 January 1842.
22 Lawrence, *Reminiscences of Forty Three Years in India*, p. 144.
23 Eyre, *The Kabul Insurrection of 1841–2*, p. 258.
24 Mackenzie, *Storms and Sunshine*, vol. I, p. 135.
25 Ibid.
26 Eyre, *The Kabul Insurrection of 1841–2*, p. 259.
27 Lawrence, *Reminiscences of Forty Three Years in India*, pp. 145–6.
28 Ibid., p. 146.
29 Eyre, *The Kabul Insurrection of 1841–2*, p. 261.
30 Ibid.
31 Brydon Diary, quoted in John C. Cunningham, *The Last Man: The Life and Times of Surgeon Major William Brydon CB*, Oxford, 2003, p. 88.
32 Eyre, *The Kabul Insurrection of 1841–2*, pp. 261, 265.
33 Private Collection, Journal of Captain Hugh Johnson, Paymaster to Shah Soojah's Force, p. 31, entry for 7 January 1842.
34 Ibid.
35 Sale, *A Journal of the Disasters in Afghanistan*, p. 149.
36 Eyre, *The Kabul Insurrection of 1841–2*, p. 264.
37 Seaton, *From Cadet to Colonel*, p. 138.
38 Private Collection, Journal of Captain Hugh Johnson, Paymaster to Shah Soojah's Force, p. 33, entry for 8 January 1842.

39 Eyre, *The Kabul Insurrection of 1841–2*, p. 265.

40 Lawrence, *Reminiscences of Forty Three Years in India*, p. 151.

41 Sale, *A Journal of the Disasters in Afghanistan*, p. 155.

42 Private Collection, Journal of Captain Hugh Johnson, Paymaster to Shah Soojah's Force, p. 34, entry for 8 January 1842.

43 Lawrence, *Reminiscences of Forty Three Years in India*, pp. 154–5.

44 Sale, *A Journal of the Disasters in Afghanistan 1841–2*, p. 155.

45 Kashmiri, *Akbarnama*, ch. 28.

46 BL, OIOC, Mss Eur C703, Diary of Captain William Anderson, entry for 9 January 1842.

47 Karim, *Muharaba Kabul wa Kandahar*, pp. 66–72.

48 Sale, *A Journal of the Disasters in Afghanistan 1841–2*, p. 158.

49 Karim, *Muharaba Kabul wa Kandahar*, pp. 66–72.

50 Private Collection, Journal of Captain Hugh Johnson, Paymaster to Shah Soojah's Force, p. 41, entry for 9 January 1842.

51 National Army Museum, Diary of Surgeon-Major William Brydon, NAM 8301/60, entry for 10 January 1842.

52 BL, OIOC, Mss Eur F 89/54, First Elphinstone Memorandum, n.d.

53 Lawrence, *Reminiscences of Forty Three Years in India*, p. 163.

54 Private Collection, Journal of Captain Hugh Johnson, Paymaster to Shah Soojah's Force, p. 36, entry for 10 January 1842.

55 Ibid.

56 Mackenzie, *Storms and Sunshine*, vol. I, p. 142.

57 Sita Ram, *From Sepoy to Subedar*, pp. 114–15.

58 National Army Museum, Diary of Surgeon-Major William Brydon, NAM 8301/60, entry for 13 January 1842.

59 'Personal Narrative of the Havildar Motee Ram of the Shah's 4th or Ghoorkha Regiment of Light Infantry, Destroyed at Char-ee-kar', appendix to Haughton, *Char-ee-Kar and Service There with the 4th Goorkha Regiment*, pp. 57–8.

60 Seaton, *From Cadet to Colonel*, p. 188; Pottinger and Macrory, *The Ten-Rupee Jezail*, p. 197.

61 Sale, *A Journal of the Disasters in Afghanistan*, p. 160.

62 National Army Museum, NAM 6912–6, Souter Letter, Lieutenant Thomas Souter to his Wife.

63 Ibid. The colours were later returned 'though divested of the tassels and most of its tinsel'.

64 National Army Museum, NAM 8301/60, Diary of Surgeon-Major William Brydon, entry for 13 January 1842.

65 Seaton, *From Cadet to Colonel*, p. 186.

66 Mirza 'Ata, *Naway Ma'arek*, pp. 230–2, Pottinger succeeds Macnaghten, leaves Kabul and is plundered.

Chapter 9: The Death of a King

1 *Delhi Gazette*, 2 February 1842.

2 Munshi Abdul Karim's *Muharaba Kabul wa Kandahar* was for example published in Lucknow in 1849 and in Kanpur in 1268/1851; Qasim-Ali-khan 'Qasim' Akbarabadi's *Zafar-nama-i Akbari* (as in Sprenger), or *Akbar-nama* (as in

Peshawar catalogue, completed in 1260/1844), was published in Agra, 1272/1855–6.

3 Charles Allen, *Soldier Sahibs: The Men Who Made the North-West Frontier*, London, 2000, p. 43.

4 BL, Broughton Papers, Add Mss 37707, fols 187–8, Auckland to Hobhouse, 18 February 1842.

5 Hopkirk, *The Great Game*, pp. 270–1.

6 PRO, Ellenborough Papers, 30/12/89, Ellenborough to Peel, 21 February 1842.

7 Pottinger and Macrory, *The Ten-Rupee Jezail*, pp. 162–3.

8 NAI, Foreign, Secret Consultations, 31 January 1842, no. 70a, Clerk to Captain Nicholson, i/c of Dost Mohammad Khan, camp, Saharanpore, 12 January 1842.

9 NAI, Foreign, Secret Consultations, 15 June 1842, no. 34, Captain P. Nicholson with Dost Mohammad Khan, to Clerk, Mussoorie, 2 May 1842.

10 Seaton, *From Cadet to Colonel*, p. 190.

11 BL, Hobhouse Diary, Add Mss 43744, 26 August 1842.

12 BL, Broughton Papers, Add Mss 37707, fols 187–8, Auckland to Hobhouse, 18 February 1842.

13 There is an excellent analysis of this in Yapp, 'The Revolutions of 1841–2 in Afghanistan', pp. 350–1. See also Kaye, *History of the War in Afghanistan*, vol. III, p. 104.

14 *Waqi'at-i-Shah Shuja*, p. 141, The Thirty-Fifth Event, The death of Macnaghten.

15 Kashmiri, *Akbarnama*, ch. 29, Shuja-ul-Mulk sets out for Jalalabad and is killed at the hands of Shuja-ud-Daula.

16 Mirza 'Ata, *Naway Ma'arek*, pp. 236–9, Muhammad Akbar Khan besieges Jalalabad, Shuja al-Mulk is killed in Kabul.

17 Mohan Lal, *Life of Dost Mohammad*, vol. II, pp. 436–8.

18 NAI, Foreign, Secret Consultations, 8 April 1842, no. 32–3, MacGregor to Maddock, Translation of letters received from Captain MacGregor at Jellalabad on 22 March 1842.

19 Ibid., 'From Shah Shoojah to Captain Macgregor dated 8th Feb and written *seemingly* in H.M.'s own hand'.

20 Lawrence, *Reminiscences of Forty Three Years in India*, pp. 173–4, 168.

21 Sale, *A Journal of the Disasters in Afghanistan*, pp. 180–3.

22 Lawrence, *Reminiscences of Forty Three Years in India*, pp. 173–4, 170.

23 Sale, *A Journal of the Disasters in Afghanistan*, pp. 180–3.

24 Karim, *Muharaba Kabul wa Kandahar*, pp. 72–4.

25 BL, OIOC, ESL 88: no. 36 of no. 32 of 17 August 1842 (IOR L/PS/5/169), Eldred Pottinger to Pollock, 10 July 1842.

26 Lawrence, *Reminiscences of Forty Three Years in India*, pp. 173–4, 191.

27 Mackenzie, *Storms and Sunshine*, vol. I, pp. 146–7.

28 Lawrence, *Reminiscences of Forty Three Years in India*, p. 176.

29 Sale, *A Journal of the Disasters in Afghanistan*, p. 237.

30 Mackenzie, *Storms and Sunshine*, vol. I, p. 149.

31 Sale, *A Journal of the Disasters in Afghanistan*, pp. 190–1.

32 Seaton, *From Cadet to Colonel*, pp. 192–4.

33 NAI, Foreign, Secret Consultations, 29 June 1842, no. 8, To: T. A. Maddock Esq, Secr. to the Govt, Political Dept, From: R. Sale, Major General, Dated Jellalabad, 16 April 1842.

34 Seaton, *From Cadet to Colonel*, p. 195.

35 Broadfoot, *The Career of Major George Broadfoot*, p. 82.
36 Seaton, *From Cadet to Colonel*, pp. 195–6.
37 Ibid., pp. 197–8.
38 Pottinger and Macrory, *The Ten-Rupee Jezail*, p. 167.
39 BL, OIOC, ESL 85: no. 20 of no. 3 of 21 April 1842, MacGregor to Pollock, 14 March 1842.
40 See Hopkins, *The Making of Modern Afghanistan*, pp. 75–80, 98–102, 105–7.
41 BL, OIOC, ESL 83: Agra Letter, 19 February 1842 (IOR/L/PS/5/164), Mahomed Akbar Khan to Sayed Ahai-u-din.
42 Ibid., Translation of a letter from Mahomed Akbar Khan to Turabaz Khan Ex Chief of Lalpoora.
43 Mirza 'Ata, *Naway Ma'arek*, pp. 236–9, Sardar Mohammad Akbar Khan besieges Jalalabad.
44 Seaton, *From Cadet to Colonel*, p. 198.
45 Ibid., pp. 207–8.
46 NAI, Foreign, Secret Consultations, 8 April 1842, no. 14–15, n.d., Pollock transmits letter from Captain Mackeson on the wounding of Mohammad Akbar Khan.
47 Mirza 'Ata, *Naway Ma'arek*, pp. 236–9, Sardar Mohammad Akbar Khan besieges Jalalabad.
48 Fayz Mohammad, *Siraj ul-Tawarikh*, vol. I, p. 272.
49 Lawrence, *Reminiscences of Forty Three Years in India*, p. 183.
50 For the complicated politics of Kabul at this period, see Yapp, 'The Revolutions of 1841–2 in Afghanistan', pp. 350–1.
51 Fayz Mohammad, *Siraj ul-Tawarikh*, vol. I, p. 273.
52 BL, OIOC, ESL, 86: no. 30 of no. 14 of 17 May 1842, Lal to Macgregor, 30 January 1842.
53 *Waqi'at-i-Shah Shuja*, p. 141, The Thirty-Fifth Event, The murder of the Shah.
54 Fayz Mohammad, *Siraj ul-Tawarikh*, vol. I, p. 274.
55 BL, OIOC, ESL, 86: no. 30A of no. 14 of 17 May 1842, Lal to Colvin, 29 January 1842; also ESL, 84: no. 27 of no. 25 of 22 March 1842, Conolly to Clerk, 26 January 1842.
56 BL, OIOC, ESL, 85: no. 24 of no. 3 of 21 March 1842, Shuja to MacGregor, recd 7 March 1842.
57 BL, OIOC, ESL, 86: no. 30 of no. 14 of 17 May 1842 (IOR/L/PS/5/167), Lal to MacGregor, 18 March 1842.
58 Kashmiri, *Akbarnama*, ch. 29, Shuja-ul-Mulk sets out for Jalalabad and is killed at the hands of Shuja-ud-Daula.
59 NAI, Foreign, Secret Consultations, December 1842, no. 480–2, Mohan Lal's Memorandum of 29 June enclosed with a letter from General Pollock, Commanding in Afghanistan, to Maddock, Secretary to the Governor General, dated Jelalabad, 10 July 1842.
60 *Waqi'at-i-Shah Shuja*, p. 141, The Thirty-Fifth Event, The murder of the Shah.
61 NAI, Foreign, Secret Consultations, December 1842, no. 480–82, Mohan Lal's Memorandum of 29 June enclosed with a letter from General Pollock, Commanding in Afghanistan, to Maddock, Secretary to the Governor General, dated Jelalabad, 10 July 1842.
62 Kaye, *History of the War in Afghanistan*, vol. III, p. 109n.
63 NAI, Foreign, Secret Consultations, 8 April 1842, no31, Translation of a letter

from His Majesty Shah Soojah ool Moolk to Captain MacGregor written by the Shah himself.

64 Pottinger and Macrory, *The Ten-Rupee Jezail*, p. 165.
65 Ibid., pp. 166–7.
66 Ibid., pp. 169–70.
67 *Waqi'at-i-Shah Shuja*, p. 149, The Thirty-Fifth Event, The murder of the Shah.
68 Mirza 'Ata, *Naway Ma'arek*, pp. 237–9, Shuja' al-Mulk is killed in Kabul.
69 Ibid.
70 *Waqi'at-i-Shah Shuja*, p. 149, The Thirty-Fifth Event, The murder of the Shah.
71 Ibid.
72 Gleig, *Sale's Brigade in Afghanistan*, pp. 303, 309.
73 Kashmiri, *Akbarnama*, ch. 29, Shuja-ul-Mulk sets out for Jalalabad and is killed at the hands of Shuja-ud-Daula.
74 Punjab Archives, Lahore, from Fraser, Ramgurh to Ochterlony, Ludhiana, 3 September 1816, vol. 18, part 2, Case 118, pp. 538–9.
75 NAI, Foreign, Secret Consultations, 10 April 1834, no. 20, Wade to Bentinck, Translation of a letter from Shah Shuja, 12 March 1834.
76 Sultan Mohammad Khan Durrani, *Tarikh-i-Sultani*, p. 212.
77 These were the words of Josiah Harlan on meeting Shuja for the first time in Ludhiana. Josiah Harlan, 'Oriental Sketches', insert at p. 42a, Mss in Chester Country Archives, Pennsylvania, quoted in Macintyre, *Josiah the Great*, p. 24.
78 Masson, *Narrative of Various Journeys*, vol. I, p. ix.
79 *Waqi'at-i-Shah Shuja*, p. 149, The Thirty-Fifth Event, The murder of the Shah.
80 Sale, *A Journal of the Disasters in Afghanistan*, p. 200.

Chapter 10: A War for No Wise Purpose

1 Gleig, *Sale's Brigade in Afghanistan*, pp. 158–9.
2 Seaton, *From Cadet to Colonel*, p. 209.
3 Ibid., p. 210.
4 Quoted in Stewart, *Crimson Snow*, p. 179.
5 Seaton, *From Cadet to Colonel*, pp. 210–11.
6 Gleig, *Sale's Brigade in Afghanistan*, p. 162.
7 Charles Rathbone Low, *The Life and Correspondence of Field Marshal Sir George Pollock*, London, 1873, p. 276.
8 Lieutenant John Greenwood, *Narrative of the Late Victorious Campaign in Afghanistan under General Pollock*, London, 1844, p. 169.
9 Charles Rathbone Low, *The Journal and Correspondence of Augustus Abbott*, London, 1879, p. 315.
10 Ibid., p. 306.
11 BL, OIOC, Mss Eur F89/54, Broadfoot to Lord Elphinstone, 26 April 1842.
12 Stocqueler, *The Memoirs and Correspondence of Sir William Nott*, vol. II, p. 35.
13 Quoted by Hopkirk, *The Great Game*, p. 273.
14 Stocqueler, *The Memoirs and Correspondence of Sir William Nott*, vol. II, p. 57.
15 Low, *The Journal and Correspondence of Augustus Abbott*, p. 320.
16 Ibid., p. 317.
17 Ibid., pp. 318–19.
18 Greenwood, *Narrative of the Late Victorious Campaign*, pp. 173–4.

19 Seaton, *From Cadet to Colonel*, p. 215.

20 Lawrence, *Reminiscences of Forty Three Years in India*, p. 185.

21 Sale, *A Journal of the Disasters in Afghanistan*, p. 203.

22 Lawrence, *Reminiscences of Forty Three Years in India*, p. 187.

23 Ibid., p. 197.

24 Sale, *A Journal of the Disasters in Afghanistan*, p. 211.

25 BL, OIOC, Mss Eur F89/54, Broadfoot to Lord Elphinstone, 26 April 1842.

26 Lawrence, *Reminiscences of Forty Three Years in India*, p. 190.

27 Ibid., p. 194.

28 Gupta, *Panjab, Central Asia and the First Afghan War*, pp. 198–9.

29 BL, OIOC, ESL 86: no. 30 of no. 14 of 17 May 1842 (IOR/L/PS/5/167), Lal to MacGregor, 10 April 1842.

30 Sale, *A Journal of the Disasters in Afghanistan*, pp. 217, 254.

31 Kaye, *History of the War in Afghanistan*, vol. III, pp. 453–5.

32 Noelle, *State and Tribe in Nineteenth-Century Afghanistan*, p. 53.

33 NAI, Foreign, Secret Consultations, December 1842, no. 480–82, Mohan Lal's Memorandum of 29 June enclosed with a letter from General Pollock, Commanding in Afghanistan, to Maddock, Secretary to the Governor General, dated Jelalabad, 10 July 1842.

34 Ibid.

35 Barfield, *Afghanistan: A Cultural and Political History*, pp. 125–6.

36 Fayz Mohammad, *Siraj al-Tawarikh*, vol. I, p. 284.

37 Quoted in Allen, *Soldier Sahibs*, p. 47.

38 Stocqueler, *The Memoirs and Correspondence of Sir William Nott*, vol. II, pp. 316–17.

39 Gupta, *Panjab, Central Asia and the First Afghan War*, p. 186.

40 Ibid., p. 187.

41 Fisher, 'Mohan Lal Kashmiri (1812–77)', p. 249.

42 Gupta, *Panjab, Central Asia and the First Afghan War*, p. 189. Mohan Lal's conversion to Islam is recorded in the *Siraj ul-Tawarikh*, vol. I, p. 282: 'An Indian munshi disobeyed this order by delivering small quantities of powder to the Bala Hisar. When it was discovered, Sardar Muhammad Akbar Khan had the man jailed. After his imprisonment, the Indian converted to Islam and was immediately freed'. Mohan Lal had long used a Shia alias and his conversion may have been part of a much longer game of double identity that he had been playing for several years.

43 BL, OIOC, ESL 88: no. 28 of no. 32 of 17 August 1842 (IOR L/PS/5/169), Pollock to Maddock, 11 July 1842.

44 Stocqueler, *The Memoirs and Correspondence of Sir William Nott*, vol. II, pp. 79–84, 109–10.

45 Ibid., p. 43.

46 The Rev. I. N. Allen, *Diary of a March through Sindhe and Afghanistan*, London, 1843, p. 216.

47 Ibid., p. 217.

48 Seaton, *From Cadet to Colonel*, p. 209.

49 Greenwood, *Narrative of the Late Victorious Campaign in Afghanistan under General Pollock*, pp. 191–2.

50 Seaton, *From Cadet to Colonel*, p. 221.

51 Gleig, *Sale's Brigade in Afghanistan*, p. 169.

52 Forrest, *Life of Field Marshal Sir Neville Chamberlain*, p. 136.

53 Allen, *Diary of a March through Sindhe and Afghanistan*, pp. 241–2.

54 BL, OIOC, Mss Eur 9057.aaa.14, 'Nott's Brigade in Afghanistan', Bombay, 1880, p. 81.

55 Stocqueler, *The Memoirs and Correspondence of Sir William Nott*, vol. II, p. 126.

56 Romila Thapar, *Somanatha: The Many Voices of a History*, New Delhi, 2004, pp. 174–5.

57 Yapp, *Strategies*, p. 443.

58 Rawlinson, *A Memoir of Major-General Sir Henry Creswicke Rawlinson*, p. 132.

59 Mirza 'Ata, *Naway Ma'arek*, pp. 244–69, The second coming of the English to Kabul and Ghazni.

60 BL, OIOC, ESL 88: no. 36 of no. 32 of 17 August 1842 (L/PS/5/169), Pollock to Maddock, 14 July 1842.

61 Josiah Harlan, *Central Asia: Personal Narrative of General Josiah Harlan, 1823–41*, ed. Frank E. Ross, London, 1939, p. 228.

62 Lawrence, *Reminiscences of Forty Three Years in India*, p. 210.

63 Mackenzie, *Storms and Sunshine*, vol. I, p. 187.

64 Sale, *A Journal of the Disasters in Afghanistan*, p. 260.

65 Mackenzie, *Storms and Sunshine*, vol. I, p. 189.

66 Private Collection, The Mss Journal of Captain Hugh Johnson, Paymaster to Shah Soojah's Force, p. 98, entry for 29 August 1842.

67 Lawrence, *Reminiscences of Forty Three Years in India*, p. 220.

68 Mirza 'Ata, *Naway Ma'arek*, pp. 348–54, The march to Bamiyan to release the prisoners.

69 Sale, *A Journal of the Disasters in Afghanistan*, p. 272.

70 Private Collection, The Mss Journal of Captain Hugh Johnson, Paymaster to Shah Soojah's Force, p. 111, entry for 14 September 1842.

71 *Waqi'at-i-Shah Shuja*, p. 141, The Thirty-Fifth Event, p. 147, The fate of Princes Shahpur and Timur.

72 Fayz Mohammad, *Siraj al-Tawarikh*, vol. I, p. 284.

73 Low, *The Journal and Correspondence of Augustus Abbott*, p. 349. For Fatteh Jang's alleged penchant for homosexual rape, see Yapp, *Strategies*, p. 318.

74 BL, OIOC, ESL 90: no. 30 of no. 52 of 19 November 1842 (IOR/L/PS/5/171), Pollock to Maddock, 21 October 1842.

75 Greenwood, *Narrative of the Late Victorious Campaign in Afghanistan under General Pollock*, p. 212.

76 Ibid., p. 213.

77 Ibid., p. 222.

78 Ibid., pp. 213–14.

79 Ibid., p. 223.

80 Sale, *A Journal of the Disasters in Afghanistan*, p. 273.

81 Mackenzie, *Storms and Sunshine*, vol. I, p. 190.

82 Sale, *A Journal of the Disasters in Afghanistan*, pp. 275–6.

83 Mackenzie, *Storms and Sunshine*, vol. I, p. 191.

84 National Army Museum, NAM 9007–77, Ensign Greville G. Chetwynd Stapylton's Journal, entry for 21 September 1842.

85 Rattray, *The Costumes of the Various Tribes*, p. 16.

86 Forrest, *Life of Field Marshal Sir Neville Chamberlain*, pp. 142, 152.

87 Private Collection, Journal of Captain Hugh Johnson, Paymaster to Shah Soojah's Force, p. 116, entry for 21 September 1842.

88 Mackenzie, *Storms and Sunshine*, vol. I, p. 194.

89 Mohan Lal, *Life of Dost Mohammad*, vol. II, p. 88.

90 Joseph Pierre Ferrier, *A History of the Afghans*, London, 1858, p. 376.

91 Forrest, *Life of Field Marshal Sir Neville Chamberlain*, pp. 143–9.

92 Sultan Mohammad Khan Durrani, *Tarikh-i-Sultani*, p. 280.

93 Mirza 'Ata, *Naway Ma'arek*, pp. 244–69, The second coming of the English to Kabul and Ghazni.

94 Hopkins, *The Making of Modern Afghanistan*, p. 69.

95 Forrest, *Life of Field Marshal Sir Neville Chamberlain*, p. 151.

96 Greenwood, *Narrative of the Late Victorious Campaign in Afghanistan under General Pollock*, p. 243.

97 NAI, Foreign, Secret Consultations, 3 May 1843, no. 20, A. Abbott to Ellenborough, 29 March 1843.

98 Low, *The Life and Correspondence of Field Marshal Sir George Pollock*, p. 415.

99 Stocqueler, *The Memoirs and Correspondence of Sir William Nott*, vol. II, p. 163.

100 Mohan Lal, *Life of Dost Mohammad*, vol. II, p. 490.

101 Mirza 'Ata, *Naway Ma'arek*, pp. 254–69, The return of Amir Dost Muhammad Khan to Kabul.

102 Yapp, 'The Revolutions of 1841–2 in Afghanistan', p. 483.

103 Mackenzie, *Storms and Sunshine*, vol. I, p. 194.

104 Ibid., vol. II, p. 30.

105 Allen, *Diary of a March through Sindhe and Afghanistan*, pp. 321, 325.

106 Karim, *Muharaba Kabul wa Kandahar*, pp. 82–4; Forrest, *Life of Field Marshal Sir Neville Chamberlain*, p. 152.

107 *Waqi'at-i-Shah Shuja*, p. 149, The Thirty-Fifth Event, The murder of the Shah.

108 Allen, *Diary of a March through Sindhe and Afghanistan*, p. 326.

109 The text of the Simla Proclamation is given in full in Norris, *First Afghan War*, pp. 451–2.

110 Mirza 'Ata, *Naway Ma'arek*, pp. 254–69, The return of Amir Dost Muhammad Khan to Kabul.

111 Forrest, *Life of Field Marshal Sir Neville Chamberlain*, p. 154.

112 Ibid., p. 155.

113 Allen, *Diary of a March through Sindhe and Afghanistan*, p. 344.

114 BL, OIOC, BSL (1) 27,873, Governor General to Secret Committee 48/, 19 October 1842.

115 Allen, *Diary of a March through Sindhe and Afghanistan*, p. 352.

116 Allen, *Soldier Sahibs*, pp. 53–5.

117 I have written at length about John Nicholson's psychopathic behaviour in 1857 in my *The Last Mughal: The End of a Dynasty, Delhi 1857*, London, 2006.

118 Forrest, *Life of Field Marshal Sir Neville Chamberlain*, p. 158.

119 Allen, *Diary of a March through Sindhe and Afghanistan*, p. 359.

120 Forrest, *Life of Field Marshal Sir Neville Chamberlain*, p. 158.

121 Mackenzie, *Storms and Sunshine*, vol. I, p. 198.

122 Ibid.

123 Ibid., p. 194.

124 BL, OIOC, HM/434, Nicholls Papers, Nicholls's Journal, vol. 40, 7 January 1843. See also Pottinger, *The Afghan Connection*, pp. xi-xii.

125 Mirza 'Ata, *Naway Ma'arek*, pp. 244–69, The second coming of the English to Kabul.

126 Lawrence, *Reminiscences of Forty Three Years in India*, p. 12.

127 Royal Geographical Society, Rawlinson Papers, HC4, Masson Diary, entry for 1 December 1839.

128 BL, OIOC, Mss Eur E162, letter 4.

129 Mackenzie, *Storms and Sunshine*, vol. I, p. 199.

130 Pottinger and Macrory, *The Ten-Rupee Jezail*, p. 167.

131 Eden, *Up the Country*, p. xix.

132 *The Times*, 25 October 1844.

133 See Michael Fisher's excellent essay 'Mohan Lal Kashmiri (1812–77)', in Margrit Pernau (ed.), *The Delhi College*, pp. 231–66. See also Gupta, *Panjab, Central Asia and the First Afghan War*. The book has an admiring introduction by the young Jawaharlal Nehru.

134 NAI, Foreign, Secret Consultations, 29 March 1843, no. 91, From the Envoy to the Court of Lahore, Ambala, 4 March 1843.

135 NAI, Foreign, Secret Consultations, 23 March 1843, no. 539, From Colonel Richmond, Camp Rooper, 18 December 1843.

136 Mackenzie, *Storms and Sunshine*, vol. II, pp. 27, 29.

137 NAI, Foreign, Secret Consultations, 23 March 1843, no. 539, From Colonel Richmond, Camp Rooper, 18 December 1843.

138 Aziz ud-Din Popalzai, *Durrat uz-Zaman*, Kabul, 1959, ch. The Private Life of Zaman Shah from His Dethronement till His Death.

139 Robert Warburton, *Eighteen Years in the Khyber 1879–1898*, London, 1900, p. 8.

140 Noelle, *State and Tribe in Nineteenth-Century Afghanistan*, p. 57.

141 Fayz Mohammad, *Siraj ul-Tawarikh*, vol. I, p. 198. See also NAI, Foreign, Secret Consultations, 23 March 1843, no. 531, From Colonel Richmond, Agent of the Governor General in the North West Frontier, Ludhiana, 27 November 1843.

142 Mackenzie, *Storms and Sunshine*, vol. II, p. 33.

143 BL, OIOC, ESL no. 20 of 3 March 1847 (IOR L/PS/5/190), Lawrence to Curvie, 29 February 1847.

144 Mackenzie, *Storms and Sunshine*, vol. II, p. 23.

145 Ibid., p. 32.

146 Fayz Mohammad, *Siraj ul-Tawarikh*, vol. I, p. 297.

147 NAI, Foreign, Secret Consultations, 23 March 1844, no. 531, From Colonel Richmond, Agent of the Governor General in the North West Frontier, Ludhiana, 27 November 1843.

148 Barfield, *Afghanistan: A Cultural and Political History*, p. 127.

149 *The Letters of Queen Victoria: A Selection from Her Majesty's Correspondence between the Years 1837 and 1861*, ed. Arthur C. Benson and Viscount Esher, vol. II: *1844–1853*, London, 1908.

150 James Howard Harris Malmesbury, *Memoirs of an Ex-Minister: An Autobiography*, London, 2006, vol. I, entry for 6 June 1844, pp. 289–90.

151 Quoted by Figes, *Crimea*, p. 68.

152 Ibid., pp. 61–70.

153 I'd like to thank Michael Semple for pointing this out ot me.

Author's Note

1 Gleig, *Sale's Brigade in Afghanistan*, p. 182.

2 J. A. Norris, *The First Afghan War 1838–1842*, Cambridge, 1967, p. 161.

3 Sherard Cowper-Coles, *Cables from Kabul: The Inside Story of the West's Afghanistan Campaign*, London, 2011, p. 289–90.

4 BL, Broughton Papers, Add Mss 36474, Wade to the Governor General, 31 January 1839.

5 The one striking exception to this is Christine Noelle's remarkable *State and Tribe in Nineteenth-Century Afghanistan: The Reign of Amir Dost Muhammad Khan (1826–1863)*, London, 1997, but its treatment of the First Afghan War is very brief and she has accessed only a small number of the available Dari sources for the period.

6 Munshi Abdul Karim, *Muharaba Kabul wa Kandahar*, Kanpur, 1851, Introduction.

7 In his *Chants Populaires des Afghans*, Paris, 1888–90, p. 201, James Darmesteter mentions a whole body of song and poetry about the war, and adds that Muhammad Hayat sent him a collection from the war, but that it hadn't arrived by the time of publication.

8 Maulana Hamid Kashmiri, *Akbarnama. Asar-i manzum-i Hamid-i Kashmiri*, written c.1844, published Kabul, 1330 AH/1951, preface by Ahmad-Ali Kohzad, ch. 34.

9 Muhammad Asef Fekrat Riyazi Herawi, *'Ayn al-Waqayi: Tarikh-i Afghanistan*, written c.1845, pub. Tehran 1369/1990; Sultan Mohammad Khan ibn Musa Khan Durrani, *Tarikh-i-Sultani*, began writing on 1 Ramzan 1281 AH (Sunday 29 January 1865) and published first on 14 Shawwal 1298 AH (Friday 8 September 1881), Bombay; Fayz Mohammad, *Siraj ul-Tawarikh*, pub. Kabul, 1913, trans. R. D. McChesney (forthcoming).

10 Muhammad Hasan Amini, *Paadash-e-Khidmatguzaari-ye-Saadiqaane Ghazi Nayab Aminullah Khan Logari* (The Letters of Ghazi Aminullah Khan Logari), Kabul, 2010.

11 Mirza 'Ata Mohammad, *Naway Ma'arek* (The Song of Battles), pub. as *Nawa-yi ma'arik. Nuskha-i khatt-i Muza-i Kabul mushtamal bar waqi'at-i 'asr-i Sadoza'i u Barakza'i, ta'lif-i Mirza Mirza 'Ata'-Muhammad*, Kabul, 1331 AH/1952.

12 Shah Shuja ul-Mulk, *Waqi'at-i-Shah Shuja* (Memoirs of Shah Shuja) written in 1836, supplement by Mohammad Husain Herati 1861, published as *Waqi'at-i Shah-Shuja. Daftar-i avval, duvvum: az Shah-Shuja. Daftar-i sivvum: az Muhammad-Husain Harati*, Kabul, 1333 AH/1954 (*Nashrat-i Anjuman-i tarikh-i Afganistan*, No. 29) [pub. after the text of the Kabul manuscript, without notes or index, with a preface by Ahmad-'Ali Kohzad].

13 Robert Burns, 'To a Louse', *The Collected Poems*, London, 1994.

14 Kashmiri, *Akbarnama*, ch. 10.

15 Ibid., ch. 32.

Bibliography

1. Manuscript Sources in European Languages

Oriental and India Office Collections, British Library (Formerly India Office Library), London

Mss Eur A52	Major General Sir Herbert Edwardes Letter
Mss Eur A186	Lady Sale Letter
Mss Eur B14	Forster Papers
and Mss Eur K115	
Mss Eur B191	Auckland Letters
Mss Eur B198	Viscount Howick Letter
Mss Eur B234	William Wilberforce Bird Letter
Mss Eur B330	Outram Journal
Mss Eur B415	Robert Sale Letter
Mss Eur C70	Beresford Journals
Mss Eur C181	Douglas Letters
Mss Eur C260	Captain Henry Fleming Letters
Mss Eur C529	General Sir Arthur Borton Letters
Mss Eur C573	Collister, unpublished book, 'Hostage in Afghanistan'
Mss Eur C634	Herries Letters
Mss Eur C703	Anderson Captivity Diary
Mss Eur C814	Lieutenant George Mein Papers
Mss Eur D160	Webb, 'Reminiscences of a Hostage at Cabul, 1841–42' (of Colonel E. A. H. Webb, compiled by his son Lieutenant Colonel E. A. H. Webb)
Mss Eur D484	Anonymous Diary, 'March from Quettah'
Mss Eur D552	Auckland Letters
Mss Eur D634	Hutchinson Family Papers, including Mss 'Journal of the Campaign in Afghanistan, a manuscript account of the

	First Afghan War compiled from letters of Captain Codrington, Bengal Army, by his widow'
Mss Eur D645	Kabul Relief Fund, Bombay Committee
Mss Eur D649	Besant Letters
Mss Eur D649 and D1118	Jasper Nicholls Letters
Mss Eur D937	Thomas Nicholl Papers
Mss Eur E161–70,	Masson Correspondence
Mss Eur E195	
Mss Eur E262	Carter Journal
Mss Eur E342	Hogg Collection
Mss Eur E359	Colvin Collection, including 'Diaries of John Russell Colvin'
Mss Eur F88–9	Elphinstone Papers, including 'Blue Book on the Disaster in Afghanistan, 1843'
Mss EurF128/196	Edward Strachey papers
Mss Eur F171	Werge Thomas Collection, including Shakespear/Todd letters and 'James Abbott's March from Candahar to Herat'
Mss Eur F213	Broughton Collection, including 'Memorandum regarding the Treaty of Lahore between Ranjit Singh, Shah Shuja, and the British Govt'
Mss Eur F33	Macnaghten Papers
Mss Eur F439	Pollock Papers, including 'Report on the Destruction of the Covered Bazaar, Cabul, 1842, Reports of Atrocities in Jelalabad, Vindication of the Conduct of Captain T. P. Walsh', and Mohan Lal/Shakespear Correspondence
Mss Eur Photo Eur 057	Dennie Letters
Mss Eur Photo Eur 353	Nott Letters
Mss Eur Photo Eur 452	East India Company Letters
IOR, Secret and Political, L/PS/5	Correspondence Relating to Persia and Afghanistan, 1839–42
IOR, Secret and Political, L/PS/20	Correspondence Relating to Persia and Afghanistan, 1834–39
F/4/1466	Extract Fort William Political Consultations
F/4/1466	Boards Collections
IOR/P/BRN/SEC/372, IOR/P/BEN/SEC/380	Bengal Secret Consultations
IOR/HM/534–45 (esp. vol. 39, Nicholls Papers and Nicholls's Journal)	Papers Connected with Sale's Brigade in Afghanistan
IOR/H/546	Letter Book of Major General Sir Willoughby Cotton

British Library, London

Add Mss 36456–83	Auckland Papers
Add Mss 37274–318	Wellesley Papers
Add Mss 37689–37718	Auckland Letter Books
Add Mss 40128	Broadfoot Papers

Add Mss 43144   Aberdeen Papers
Add Mss 43744   Broughton Diaries and Memorandum
Add Mss 46915   Broughton Papers
Add Mss 47662   Rawlinson Notebooks
Add Mss 48535   Palmerston Papers

Royal Geographical Society, London

HC2–7   Rawlinson Papers

The National Archives, Public Record Office, London

PRO 30/12   Ellenborough Papers
PRO FO/705/32   Pottinger Papers
FO 30/12/62   Rawlinson to Hammersley, 3 May 1842
FO 60/58   MacNeill's reports from the Tehran Embassy – MacNeill
                         to Palmerston
FO 65/233   Durham to Palmerston, 28 February 1837
FO 181/130   Palmerston to Durham, 16 January 1837
FO 705/32   Masson Papers

National Army Museum Library, London

NAM 6807–224   Bruce Norton Letters
NAM 8301–60   Brydon Diary
NAM 2002–07–12–2–3   Clunie Letter
NAM 6508–50   Dawes Journal
NAM 2008–1839   Gaisford Letters
NAM 8109–63   Haslock Papers
NAM 1999–02–116–1   Magrath Letters
NAM 1968–07–207–1   Milne Diary
NAM 6308–44–30   Outram Papers
NAM 7604/9   Pennycuik Papers
NAM 7101–24–3   Roberts Letters
NAM 9109–45   Rose Correspondence
NAM 6807–48   Shelton Defence
NAM 6912–6   Souter Letter
NAM 9007–77   Stapylton's 'Journal'
NAM 1968–07–128–1   Trower Journal
NAM 1965–03–65–2–6   Wade Correspondence

National Archives of India, New Delhi

Secret Consultations
Political Consultations
Foreign Consultations
Foreign Miscellaneous
Secret Letters to Court

Secret Letters from Court
Political Letters to Court
Political Letters from Court
Delhi Gazette

Punjab Archives, Lahore

Delhi Residency Papers
Ludhiana Agency Papers

Private Collections

The Fraser Papers, Inverness
Hugh Johnson Journal, Argyll
Walsh Papers, Abergavenny

2. Unpublished Dissertations

Hanifi, Shah Mahmood, 'Inter-regional Trade and Colonial State Formation in Nineteenth Century Afghanistan', unpublished PhD dissertation, University of Michigan, 2001
Kapadia, Eruch Rustom, 'The Diplomatic Career of Sir Claude Wade: A Study of British Relations with the Sikhs and Afghans, July 1823–March 1840', unpublished PhD thesis, SOAS

3. Persian and Urdu Sources

Manuscripts

National Archives of India, New Delhi

Karim, Munshi Abdul, *Muharaba Kabul wa Kandahar, Kanpur, 1851*

Published Texts

Amini, Muhammad Hasan, *Paadash-e-Khidmatguzaari-ye-Saadiqaane Ghazi Nayab Aminullah Khan Logari* (The Letters of Ghazi Aminullah Khan Logari), Kabul, 2010
Azam, Muhammad, *Tarikh-Kashmir Azami*, Lahore, 1303/1885
Busse, Herbert (trans.), *History of Persia under Qajar Rule Translated from the Persian of Hasan-e-Fasai's Farsnama-ye Naseri*, New York, 1972
Durrani, Sultan Mohammad Khan ibn Musa Khan, *Tarikh-i-Sultani*, began writing on 1 Ramzan 1281 AH (Sunday 29 January 1865) and published first on 14 Shawwal 1298 AH (Friday 8 September 1881), Bombay, 1881
Herawi, Muhammad Asef Fekrat Riyazi, *Ayn al-Waqayi: Tarikh-i Afghanistan*, written c. 1845, pub. Tehran 1369/1990
Karim, Munshi Abdul, *Muharaba Kabul wa Kandahar*, Kanpur, 1851
Kashmiri, Maulana Hamid, *Akbarnama. Asar-i manzum-i Hamid-i Kashmiri*, written c. 1844, pub. Kabul, 1330 AH/1951, preface by Ahmad-Ali Kohzad
Kohistani,   Maulana   Muhammad-Ghulam   Akhund-zada   b.   Mulla

Timur-shah, *mutakhallis ba* 'Gulam' (or 'Gulami' Mohammad Ghulam), *Jangnameh, Jang-nama. Dar wasfi-i mujahidat-i Mir Masjidi-khan Gazi wa sa ir-i mudjahidin rashid-i milli-i aliya-i mutajawizin-i ajnabi dar salha-yi 1839–1842 i. Asar: Maulina* [sic] *Muhammad-Gulam Kuhistani mutakhallis ba 'Gulami'*, Kabul 1336 AH/1957 (*Anjuman-i tarikh-i Afganistan*, No. 48) [preface by Ahmad-Ali Kohzad, without index]. Idem: *Aryana*, XXI (1333–4 AH/1955), No. 7, pp. 1–8, No. 8, pp. 1–8, No. 9, pp. 33–40, No. 10, pp. 33–40; XIV (1334–5 AH/1956), No. 1, pp. 29–32, No. 3, pp. 33–40, No. 4, pp. 37–40, No. 5, pp. 41–8, No. 6, pp. 17–24, No. 9, pp. 41–8, No. 10, pp. 41–8; XV (1335–6 AH/1957), No. 1, pp. 41–8, No. 2, pp. 33–40, No. 3, pp. 45–8, No. 5, pp. 49–56, No. 6, pp. 17–24, No. 7, pp. 49–56, No. 8, pp. 41–8, No. 9, pp. 41–8 (see Afshar, *MaQalat*, I, No. 5861)

Mohammad, Fayz, *Siraj ul-Tawarikh* (The Lamp of Histories), trans. R. D. McChesney (forthcoming) (first pub. Kabul, 1913)

Mohammad, Mirza 'Ata, *Naway Ma'arek* (The Song of Battles), pub. as *Nawa-yi ma'arik. Nuskha-i khatti-i Muza-i Kabul mushtamal bar waqi at-i asr-i Sadoza i u Barakza i, ta lif-i Mirza Mirza 'Ata'-Muhammad*, Kabul, 1331 AH/1952 (*Nashrat-i Anjuman-i tarikh*, No. 22) [with a preface by Ahmad-Ali Kohzad, without index]. Idem: *Aryana*, VIII (1328–9 AH/1950), Nos 7–10, pp. 41–8, No. 11, pp. 46–8, No. 12, pp. 49–56; IX (1329–30 AH/1951), Nos 1–12, pp. 41–8; X (1330–1 AH/1952), Nos 1–9, pp. 41–8, No. 10, pp. 49–56

Popalzai, Aziz ud-Din, *Durrat uz-Zaman*, Kabul, 1959

Priestly, Henry (trans.), *Afghanistan and its Inhabitants, Translated from the Hayat-i-Afghani of Muhammad Hayat Khan*, Lahore, 1874

Qalandar, Turk Ali Shah Turk, *Tadhkira-i Sukhunwaran-Chashm-Didah*, n.d.

Shuja, Shah, *Waqiat-i-Shah Shuja* (Memoirs of Shah Shuja), written in 1836, supplement by Mohammad Husain Herati, 1861, pub. as *Waqiat-i Shah-Shuja. Daftar-i avval, duvvum: az Shah-Shuja. Daftar-i sivvum: az Muhammad-Husain Harati*, Kabul, 1333 AH/1954 (*Nashrat-i Anjuman-i tarikh-i Afganistan*, No. 29) [pub. after the text of the Kabul manuscript, without notes or index, with a preface by Aḥmad-Ali Kohzad]. Idem: *Aryana*, X (1330–1 AH/1952), No. 11, pp. 33–40, No. 12, pp. 33–40; XI (1331–2 AH/1953), Nos 1–4, pp. 49–56, No. 5, pp. 49–51, Nos 6–11, pp. 49–56

4. Contemporary Works and Periodical Articles in European Languages

Ali, Shahmat, *The Sikhs and Afghans in Connexion with India and Persia*, London, 1847

Allen, Rev. I. N., *Diary of a March through Sindhe and Afghanistan*, London, 1843

Archer, Major, *Tours in Upper India and in Parts of the Himalaya Mountains*, 2 vols, London, 1833

Argyll, Duke of (George Douglas Campbell), *The Afghan Question from 1841 to 1878*, London, 1879

Atkinson, James, *The Expedition into Afghanistan: Notes and Sketches Descriptive of the Country contained in a personal Narrative During the Campaign of 1839 and 1840 up to the Surrender of Dost Mohamed Khan*, London, 1842

Barr, William, *Journal of a March from Delhi to Peshawar and thence to Cabul*, London, 1844.

Bengal Officer, A, *Recollections of the First Campaign West of the Indus and of the Subsequent Operations of the Candahar Force*, London, 1845

Benson, Arthur C. and Esher, Viscount (eds), *The Letters of Queen Victoria: A Selection from Her Majesty's Correspondence between the Years 1837 and 1861*, 3 vols, vol. II: *1844–1853*, London, 1908

Blaramberg, Ivan Fedorovitch, *Vospominania* (Memoirs), Moscow, 1978

Broadfoot, Major W., *The Career of Major George Broadfoot, CB*, London, 1888

Buckle, Captain E., *Memoirs of the Services of the Bengal Artillery from the Formation of the Corps to the Present Time with Some Account of its Internal Organization*, London, 1852

Buist, George, *Outline of the Operations of the British Troops in Scinde and Affghanistan, betwixt Nov. 1838 and Nov. 1841; with Remarks on the Policy of the War*, Bombay, 1843

Burnes, Alexander, *Travels into Bokhara, Being the Account of a Journey from India to Cabool, Tartary and Persia, also a Narrative of a Voyage on the Indus from the Sea to Lahore*, 3 vols, London, 1834

Burnes, Alexander, *Reports and Papers, Political, Geographical and Commercial, Submitted to Government by Sir Alexander Burnes, Lt Leech, Dr Lord and Lt Wood, Employed on Missions in the Years 1835–36–37 in Scinde, Affghanistan and Adjacent Countries*, Calcutta, 1839

Burnes, Alexander, *Cabool: A Personal Narrative of a Journey to, and Residence in that City in the Years 1836, 7 and 8*, London, 1843

Burnes, James, *Sketch of the History of the Knights Templars*, Edinburgh, 1837

Calendar of Persian Correspondence of the Punjab Archives abstracted into English, 3 vols, Lahore, 1972–2004

Conolly, Arthur, *Journey to the North of India, 1829–31*, 2 vols, London, 1838

Cumming, James Slator, *A Six Year Diary*, London, 1847

Darmesteter, James, *Chants Populaires des Afghans*, Paris, 1888–90

Dennie, Colonel William H., *Personal Narrative of the Campaigns in Afghanistan*, ed. W. E. Steele, Dublin, 1843

Durand, Henry Marion, *The First Afghan War and its Causes*, London, 1879

Eastwick, E. B. (An Ex-Political), *Dry Leaves from Young Egypt, being a Glance at Sindh before the Arrival of Sir Charles Napier*, London, 1851

Eden, The Hon. Emily, *Miss Eden's Letters*, ed. by her great-niece Violet Dickinson, London, 1927

Eden, The Hon. Emily, *Up the Country: Letters written to her Sister from the Upper Provinces of India*, Oxford, 1930

Eden, Fanny, *Tigers, Durbars and Kings: Fanny Eden's Indian Journals, 1837–1838*, transcribed and ed. by Janet Dunbar, London, 1988

Ellenborough, Edward Law, Earl of, *A Political Diary*, ed. Reginald Charles Edward Abbot, London, 1881

Elphinstone, Mountstuart, *An Account of the kingdom of Caubul, and its dependencies in Persia, Tartary, and India; comprising a view of the Afghaun nation, and a history of the Dooraunee monarchy*, London, 1819

Eyre, Captain Vincent, *Journal of Imprisonment in Affghanistan*, London, 1843

Eyre, Major-General Sir Vincent, *The Kabul Insurrection of 1841–2*, London, 1879

Fane, Henry, *Five Years in India, Comprising a Narrative of Travels in the Presidency of Bengal; a visit to the court of Runjeet Sing, etc.*, London, 1842

Fane, Isabella, *Miss Fane in India*, ed. John Pemble, Gloucester, 1985

Forbes, Archibald, *The Afghan Wars – 1839–42 and 1878–80*, London, 1892

Forrest, G. W., *Life of Field Marshal Sir Neville Chamberlain, GCB, GCSI*, Edinburgh, 1909

Forster, George, *A Journey from Bengal to England through the Northern Part of India, Kashmire, Afghanistan, and Persia, and into Russia, by the Caspian Sea*, 2 vols, London, 1798

Fraser, James Baillie, *A Winter's Journey from Constantinople to Tehran with Travels through Various Parts of Persia*, 2 vols, London, 1838

Frontier and Overseas Expeditions from India, Compiled in the Intelligence Branch Division of the Chief of Staff Army Headquarters, India, vol. I: *Tribes North of the Kabul River*, Simla, 1907

Garrett, Lt-Col. H. L. O. and Chopra, G. L., *Events at the Court of Ranjit Singh 1810–1817, Translated from the Papers in the Alienation Office, Poona*, Poona, 1935

Gleig, Rev. G. R., *Sale's Brigade in Afghanistan*, London, 1843

Greenwood, Lieutenant John, *Narrative of the Late Victorious Campaign in Afghanistan under General Pollock*, London, 1844

Griffin, Lepel, *Ranjit Singh and the Sikh Barrier between our Growing Empire and Central Asia*, Oxford, 1892

Harlan, Josiah, *Central Asia: Personal Narrative of General Josiah Harlan, 1823–1841*, ed. Frank E. Ross, London, 1939

Harlan, J., *A Memoir of India and Avghanistaun, with Observations on the Present Exciting and Critical State and Future Prospects of those Countries*, Philadelphia, 1842

Haughton, Colonel (John), *Char-ee-Kar and Service There with the 4th Goorkha Regiment, Shah Shooja's Force, in 1841*, London, 1878

Havelock, Henry, *Narrative of the War in Affghanistan in 1838–9*, 2 vols, London, 1840

Holdsworth, T. W. E., *The Campaign of the Indus: A Series of Letters from an Officer of the Bombay Division*, London, 1841

Honigberger, John Martin, *Thirty Five Years in the East: Adventures, Discoveries, Experiments and Historical Sketches Relating to the Punjab and Cashmere in Connection with Medicine, Botany, Pharmacy, &c*, London, 1852

Hough, Major William, *A Narrative of the March and Operations of the Army of the Indus 1838–1839, in the expedition to Affghanistan, in the years 1838–1839: comprising also the history of the Dooranee Empire*, London, 1841

Jacquemont, Victor, *Letters From India (1829–32)*, trans. Catherine Phillips, 2 vols, London, 1936

Kashmiri, Mohan Lal, *Life of Amir Dost Mohammad of Kabul*, 2 vols, London, 1846

Kashmiri, Mohan Lal, *Travels in the Panjab, Afghanistan and Turkistan to Balk, Bokhara, and Herat and a visit to Great Britain and Germany*, London, 1846

Kaye, Sir John William, *History of the War in Afghanistan: From the unpublished letters and journals of political and military officers employed in Afghanistan, etc*, 3 vols, London, 1851

Kaye, Sir John William, *Lives of Indian Officers*, 3 vols, London, 1867

Kennedy, Richard Hartley, *Narrative of the Campaign of the Army of the Indus in Sind and Kaubool in 1838–9*, 2 vols, London, 1840

Khalfin, N. A., *Vozmezdie ozhidaet v Dzhagda* (Drama in a Boarding House), Moscow, 1973

Khalfin, N. A., predislovie k sb. *Zapiski o Bukharskom Khanstve* (preface to Notes on the Khanate of Bukhara), Moscow, 1983. This volume includes *Zapiska, sostavlennaia po rasskazam Orenburgskogo lineinogo bataliona No 10 praporshchika*

Vitkevicha otnositelno ego puti v Bukharu i obratno (Notes based on the story told by Vitkevich, ensign in the 10th Orenburg manoeuvre battalion, of his journey to Bukhara and back)

Lawrence, Sir George, *Reminiscences of Forty Three Years in India*, London, 1875

Lawrence, H. M. L., *Adventures of an Officer in the Service of Runjeet Singh*, London, 1975

Low, Charles Rathbone, *The Life and Correspondence of Field Marshal Sir George Pollock*, London, 1873

Low, Charles Rathbone, *The Journal and Correspondence of Augustus Abbott*, London, 1879

Lushington, Henry, *A Great Country's Little Wars, or England, Affghanistan and Sinde, being a Sketch, with Reference to their Morality and Policy, of Recent Transactions on the North Western Frontier of India*, London, 1844

Lutfullah, *Autobiography of Lutfullah: An Indian's Perception of the West*, ed. S. A. I. Tirmizi, London, 1857

MacAlister, Florence (Their Grand-daughter), *Sir John MacNeill, GCB and of his Second Wife Elizabeth Wilson*, London, 1910

Mackenzie, D. N. (trans.), *Poems from the Divan of Khushal Khan Khattak*, London, 1965

Mackenzie, Helen, *Storms and Sunshine of a Soldier's Life: Lt. General Colin Mackenzie CB 1825–1881*, 2 vols, Edinburgh, 1884

MacNeill, Sir John, *The Progress and Present Position of Russia in the East*, London, 1836

Malcolm, Sir John, *Political History of India*, 2 vols, London, 1826

Malleson, George Bruce, *History of Afghanistan from the Earliest Period to the Outbreak of War 1878*, London, 1878

Malmesbury, James Howard Harris, *Memoirs of an Ex-Minister: An Autobiography*, 2 vols, London, 2006

Masson, Charles, *Narrative of Various Journeys in Baluchistan, Afghanistan and the Panjab, 1826 to 1838*, 3 vols, London, 1842

Nash, Charles (ed.), *History of the War in Affghanistan from its Commencement to its Close*, London, 1843

Neill, J. Martin Bladen, *Recollections of Four Years' Service in the East with HM Fortieth Regiment under Major General Sir W. Nott GCB*, London, 1845

Osborne, W. G., *The Court and Camp of Runjeet Sing*, London, 1840

Outram, James, *Rough Notes of the Campaign in Sinde and Affghanistan in 1838–9, being extracts from a personal journal kept while serving on the staff of the Army of the Indus*, London, 1840

Panday, Sita Ram, *From Sepoy to Subedar: Being the Life and Adventures of Subedar Sita Ram, a Native Officer of the Bengal Army, Written and Related by Himself*, trans. Lt. Col. J. T. Norgate, London, 1873

Parkes, Fanny, *Wanderings of a Pilgrim in Search of the Picturesque*, London, 1850

Perovsky, Vasily Aleksyeevich, *A Narrative of the Russian Military Expedition to Khiva under General Perofski in 1839*, trans. from the Russian for the Foreign Department of the Government of India, Calcutta, 1867

Polferov, I. A., 'Predatel' (The Traitor), *Istoricheskij Vestnik*, St Petersburg, vol. 100, 1905

Prinsep, H. T., *History of the Punjab, and of the rise, progress, & present condition of the sect and nation of the Sikhs [Based in part on 'The Origin of the Sikh power in the Punjab and political life of Muha-Raja Runjeet Singh']*, London, 1846

Rattray, James, *The Costumes of the Various Tribes, Portraits of Ladies of Rank, Celebrated Princes and Chiefs, Views of the Principal Fortresses and Cities, and*

Interior of the Cities and Temples of Afghaunistan from Original Drawings, London, 1848

Raverty, Major Henry George, *Notes on Afghanistan and Baluchistan*, London, 1862

Rawlinson, George, *A Memoir of Major-General Sir Henry Creswicke Rawlinson*, London, 1898

Rawlinson, H. C., 'Notes on a March from Zohab, at the Foot of Zagros, along the Mountains to Khuzistan (Susiana), and from Thence through the Province of Luristan to Kirmanshah, in the Year 1836', *Journal of the Royal Geographical Society of London*, vol. 9 (1839), pp. 26–116

Rawlinson, H. C., 'Notes on a Journey from Tabriz, through Persian Kurdistan, to the Ruins of Takhti-Soleiman, and from Thence by Zenjan and Tarom, to Gilan, in October and November, 1838; With a Memoir on the Site of the Atropatenian Ecbatana Author', *Journal of the Royal Geographical Society of London*, vol. 10 (1840), pp. 1–64

Records of the Ludhiana Agency, Lahore, 1911

Robinson, Phil, *Cabul – The Ameer, His Country and His People*, London, 1878

Sale, Lady (Florentia), *A Journal of the Disasters in Affghanistan 1841–2*, London, 1843

Seaton, Major-General Sir Thomas, *From Cadet to Colonel: The Record of a Life of Active Service*, London, 1873

Simonitch, I. O., *Précis historique de l'avènement de Mahomed-Schah au trône de Perse par le Comte Simonich, ex-Ministre Plénipotentiaire de Russie à la cour de Téhéran*, Moscow, 1967

Sinha, N. K. and Dasgupta, A. K., *Selections from the Ochterlony Papers*, Calcutta, 1964

Sleeman, Major-General Sir W. H., *Rambles and Recollections of an Indian Official*, Oxford, 1915

Stacy, Colonel Lewis Robert, *Narrative of Services in Beloochistan and Affghanistan in the Years 1840, 1841, & 1842*, London, 1848

Stocqueler, J. H., *Memorials of Affghanistan: State Papers, Official Documents, Dispatches, Authentic Narratives etc Illustrative of the British Expedition to, and Occupation of, Affghanistan and Scinde, between the years 1838 and 1842*, Calcutta, 1843

Stocqueler, J. H., *The Memoirs and Correspondence of Sir William Nott, GCB*, 2 vols, London, 1854

Suri, V. S., *Umdat-ut-Tawarikh: An Original Source of Punjab History: Chronicles of the Reign of Maharaja Ranjit Singh 1831–1839 by Lala Sohan Lal Suri*, Delhi, 1961

Taylor, William, *Scenes and Adventures in Afghanistan*, London, 1842

Teer, Edward, *The Siege of Jellalabad 1841–42*, London, 1904

Trotter, Lionel J., *The Life of John Nicholson, Soldier and Administrator*, London, 1898

Urquhart, David, *Diplomatic Transactions in Central Asia from 1834–1839*, London, 1841

Vigne, Godfrey, *A Personal Narrative of a Visit to Ghuzni, Kabul and Afghanistan and a Residence at the Court of Dost Mohamed with Notices of Runjit Singh, Khiva, and the Russian Expedition*, London, 1840

Wade, Sir C. M., *A Narrative of the Services, Military and Political, of Lt. Col. Sir C. M. Wade*, Ryde, 1847

Warburton, Robert, *Eighteen Years in the Khyber 1879–1898*, London, 1900

Wellesley, Arthur, Duke of Wellington, *Supplementary Despatches and Memoranda of Field Marshal Arthur Duke of Wellington*, ed. by his son, the 2nd Duke of Wellington, 15 vols, London, 1858–72

Wellesley, Richard, Marquess Wellesley, *The Despatches, Minutes and Correspondence of the Marquess Wellesley KG during his Administration of India*, ed. Montgomery Martin, 5 vols, London, 1840

Wellesley, Richard, Marquess Wellesley, *Two Views of British India: The Private Correspondence of Mr Dundas and Lord Wellesley: 1798–1801*, ed. Edward Ingram, London, 1970

Wilbraham, Captain Richard, *Travels in the Transcaucasian Provinces of Russia in the Autumn and Winter of 1837*, London, 1839

Wilson, H. H., *Ariana Antiqua – A Descriptive Account of the Antiquities and Coins of Afghanistan: With a Memoir on the Buildings Called Topes by C. Masson Esq.*, London, 1841

Wolff, Joseph, *Researches and Missionary Labours among the Jews, Mohammedans and Other Sects*, London, 1835

Wood, John, *A Personal Narrative of a Journey to the Source of the River Oxus by the Route of the Indus, Kabul and Badakshan, Performed under the Sanction of the Supreme Government of India, in the Years 1836, 1837, and 1838,* London, 1841

5. Secondary Works and Periodical Articles

Alder, G. J., 'The "Garbled" Blue Books of 1839 – Myth or Reality?', *Historical Journal*, vol. 15, no. 2 (June 1972), pp. 229–59

Alder, G. J., 'The Key to India?: Britain and the Herat Problem 1830–1863 – Part 1', *Middle Eastern Studies*, vol. 10, no. 2 (May 1974), pp. 186–209

Allen, Charles, *Soldier Sahibs: The Men Who Made the North-West Frontier*, London, 2000

Amini, Iradj, *The Koh-i-Noor Diamond*, New Delhi, 1994

Amini, Iradj, *Napoleon and Persia*, Washington, DC, 1999

Anon., 'Sobrannye Kavkazskoi arkheograficheskoi komissiei (AKAK): Instruktsia por. Vitkevichu ot 14 maya 1837, No. 1218' (Acts Collected by the Caucasus Archaeographic Commission: Instruction to Lieutenant Vitkevich of 14 May 1837, No. 1218), *Akty*, vol. 8, pp. 944–5

Anon., 'Poslantsy iz Afganistana v Rossiu' (Envoys from Afghanistan to Russia), Part II, *Russkaya Starina*, no. 8 (1880), p. 789

Archer, Mildred and Falk, Toby, *India Revealed: The Art and Adventures of James and William Fraser 1801–35*, London, 1989

Atkin, Muriel, *Russia and Iran 1780–1828*, Minneapolis, 1980

Avery, Peter, Hambly, Gavin and Melville, Charles, *The Cambridge History of Iran*, vol. VII: *From Nadir Shah to the Islamic Republic*, Cambridge, 1991

Axworthy, Michael, *The Sword of Persia: Nader Shah from Tribal Warrior to Conquering Tyrant*, New York, 2006

Axworthy, Michael, *Iran: Empire of the Mind – A History from Zoroaster to the Present Day*, London, 2007

Baddeley, John F., *The Russian Conquest of the Caucasus*, New York, 1908

Banerjee, A. C., *Anglo-Sikh Relations: Chapters from J. D. Cunningham's History of the Sikhs*, Calcutta, 1949

Banerjee, A. C., *The Khalsa Raj*, New Delhi, 1985

Banerjee, Himadri, *The Sikh Khalsa and the Punjab: Studies in Sikh History, to the Nineteenth Century*, New Delhi, 2002

Bansal, Bobby Singh, *The Lion's Firanghis: Europeans at the Court of Lahore*, London, 2010

Barfield, Thomas J., 'Problems of Establishing Legitimacy in Afghanistan', *Iranian Studies*, vol. 37 (June 2004), no. 2, pp. 263–93

Barfield, Thomas, *Afghanistan: A Cultural and Political History*, Princeton, 2010

Barthorp, Michael, *Afghan Wars and the North West Frontier 1839–1947*, London, 1982

Bayly, C. A., *Imperial Meridian: The British Empire and the World 1780–1830*, London, 1989

Bayly, C. A., *Empire and Information: Intelligence Gathering and Social Communication in India 1780–1870*, Cambridge, 1996

Bell, Herbert C. F., *Lord Palmerston*, Hamden, Conn., 1966

Bence-Jones, Mark, *Palaces of the Raj*, London, 1973

Bence-Jones, Mark, *The Viceroys of India*, London, 1982

Bilgrami, Ashgar H., *Afghanistan and British India, 1793–1907*, New Delhi, 1974

Blanch, Leslie, *The Sabres of Paradise: Conquest and Vengeance in the Caucasus*, London, 2009

Bosworth, Edmund and Hillenbrand, Carole, *Qajar Iran*, Edinburgh, 1983

Bruce, George, *Retreat from Kabul*, London, 1967

Caroe, Olaf, *The Pathans*, London, 1958

Chambers, James, *Palmerston: The People's Darling*, London, 2004

Chopra, Barkat Rai, *Kingdom of the Punjab 1839–45*, Hoshiarpur, 1969

Coates, Tim, *The British War in Afghanistan: The Dreadful Retreat from Kabul in 1842*, London, 2002

Colley, Linda, 'Britain and Islam: Perspectives on Difference 1600–1800', *Yale Review*, vol. LXXXVIII (2000), pp. 1–20

Colley, Linda, 'Going Native, Telling Tales: Captivity, Collaborations and Empire', *Past & Present*, no. 168 (August 2000), pp. 170–93

Collister, Peter, *Hostage in Afghanistan*, Bishop Auckland, 1999

Cowper-Coles, Sherard, *Cables from Kabul: The Inside Story of the West's Afghanistan Campaign*, London, 2011

Cunningham, John C., *The Last Man: The Life and Times of Surgeon Major William Brydon CB*, Oxford, 2003

Dalrymple, William, *City of Djinns: A Year in Delhi*, London, 1992

Dalrymple, William, *White Mughals: Love and Betrayal in Eighteenth-Century India*, London, 2002

Dalrymple, William, *The Last Mughal: The End of a Dynasty, Delhi 1857*, London, 2006

Dalrymple, William and Sharma, Yuthika, *Princes and Poets in Mughal Delhi 1707–1857*, New Haven and London, 2012

David, Saul, *Victoria's Wars: The Rise of Empire*, London, 2006

Davis, Professor H. W. C., *The Great Game in Asia (1800–1844)*, Proceedings of the British Academy, London, 1926

Diba, Layla S. with Maryam Ekhtiar, *Royal Persian Paintings – The Qajar Epoch*, New York, 1998

Diver, Maud, *The Hero of Herat: A Frontier Biography in Romantic Form*, London, 1912

Dunbar, Janet, *Golden Interlude: The Edens in India 1836–1842*, London, 1955

Dupree, Louis, 'The First Anglo-Afghan War and the British Retreat of 1842: the Functions of History and Folklore', East and West, 26(3/4), pp. 503–29

Dupree, Louis, *Afghanistan*, Oxford, 2007

Dupree, Nancy Hatch Wolfe, *Herat: A Pictorial Guide*, Kabul, 1966

Dupree, Nancy Hatch, 'Jalalabad during the First Anglo-Afghan War', *Asian Affairs*, vol. 6, nos 1 and 2 (March and June 1975), pp. 177–89

Dupree, Nancy Hatch with Ahmad Ali Kohzad, *An Historical Guide to Kabul*, Kabul, 1972

Edwards, David B., *Heroes of the Age: Moral Fault Lines on the Afghan Frontier*, Berkeley, 1996

Errington, Elizabeth and Curtis, Vesta Sarkhosh, *From Persepolis to the Punjab: Exploring Ancient Iran, Afghanistan and Pakistan*, London, 2007

Farmanfarmaian, Roxane, *War and Peace in Qajar Persia: Implications Past and Present*, Oxford, 2008

Ferguson, Niall, *Empire: How Britain Made the Modern World*, London, 2003

Ferrier, Joseph Pierre, *A History of the Afghans*, London, 1858

Figes, Orlando, *Crimea: The Last Crusade*, London, 2010

Fisher, Michael, *Counterflows to Colonialism*, New Delhi, 2005

Fisher, Michael H., 'An Initial Student of Delhi English College: Mohan Lal Kashmiri (1812–77)', in Margrit Pernau (ed.), *The Delhi College: Traditional Elites, the Colonial State and Education before 1857*, New Delhi, 2006

Fraser-Tytler, Sir Kerr, *Afghanistan: A Study of Political Developments in Central Asia*, Oxford, 1950

Fremont-Barnes, Gregory, *The Anglo-Afghan Wars 1838–1919*, Oxford, 2009

Gaury, Gerald de and Winstone, H. V. F., *The Road to Kabul: An Anthology*, New York, 1982

Gillard, David, *The Struggle for Asia 1828–1914*, London, 1977

Gleave, Robert (ed.), *Religion and Society in Qajar Iran*, London, 2005

Goldsmid, Sir F. J., *James Outram: A Biography*, 2 vols, London, 1880

Gommans, Jos J. L., *The Rise of the Indo-Afghan Empire c. 1710–1780*, New Delhi, 1999

Goswamy, B. N., *Piety and Splendour: Sikh Heritage in Art*, New Delhi, 2000

Greaves, Rose, 'Themes in British Policy towards Afghanistan in its Relation to Indian Frontier Defence, 1798–1947', *Asian Affairs*, vol. 24, issue 1 (1993), pp. 30–46

Green, Nile, 'Tribe, Diaspora and Sainthood in Afghan History', *Journal of Asian Studies*, vol. 67, no. 1 (February 2008), pp. 171–211

Gregorian, Vartan, *The Emergence of Modern Afghanistan – Politics of Reform and Modernization, 1880–1946*, Stanford, 1969

Grey, C. and Garrett, H. L. O., *European Adventurers of Northern India 1785–1849*, Lahore, 1929

Gulzad, Zalmay A., *External Influences and the Development of the Afghan State in the Nineteenth Century*, New York, 1994

Gupta, Hari Ram, *Panjab, Central Asia and the First Afghan War, Based on Mohan Lal's Observations*, Chandigarh, 1940

Guy, Alan J. and Boyden, Peter B., *Soldiers of the Raj: The Indian Army 1600–1947*, London, 1997

Hanifi, Shah Mahmood, 'Impoverishing a Colonial Frontier: Cash, Credit, and Debt in Nineteenth-Century Afghanistan', *Iranian Studies*, vol. 37, no. 2 (June 2004), pp. 199–218

Hanifi, Shah Mahmood, *Connecting Histories in Afghanistan: Market Relations and State Formation on a Colonial Frontier*, Stanford, 2011

Hanifi, Shah Mahmood, 'Shah Shuja's "Hidden History" and its Implications for the Historiography of Afghanistan', *South Asia Multidisciplinary Academic Journal* [online], Free-Standing Articles, online since 14 May 2012, connection on 21 June 2012, http://samaj.revues.org/3384

Hanifi, Shah Mahmood, 'Quandaries of the Afghan Nation', in Shahzad Bashir (ed.), *Under the Drones*, Cambridge, Mass., 2012

Haroon, Sana, *Frontier of Faith: Islam in the Indo-Afghan Borderland*, London, 2007

Heathcote, T. A., *The Afghan Wars 1839–1919*, Staplehurst, 2003

Hopkins, B. D., *The Making of Modern Afghanistan*, London, 2008

Hopkins, Hugh Evan, *Sublime Vagabond: The Life of Joseph Wolff – Missionary Extraordinary*, Worthing, 1984

Hopkirk, Peter, *The Great Game*, London, 1990

Ingram, Edward, *The Beginning of the Great Game in Asia, 1828–1834*, Oxford, 1979

Ingram, Edward, *In Defence of British India: Great Britain in the Middle East 1775–1842*, London, 1984

Iqbal, Afzal, *Circumstances Leading to the First Afghan War*, Lahore, 1975

Jalal, Ayesha, *Partisans of Allah: Jihad in South Asia*, London, 2008

Johnson, Robert, *Spying for Empire: The Great Game in Central and South Asia, 1757–1947*, London, 2006

Johnson, Robert, *The Afghan Way of War – Culture and Pragmatism: A Critical History*, London, 2011

Keddie, Nikki R., *Qajar Iran and the Rise of Reza Khan 1796–1925*, Costa Mesa, 1999

Kelly, J. B., *Britain and the Persian Gulf, 1795–1880*, Oxford, 1968

Kelly, Laurence, *Diplomacy and Murder in Tehran: Alexander Griboyedov and Imperial Russia's Mission to the Shah of Persia*, London, 2002

Kessler, Melvin M., *Ivan Viktorovich Vitkevich 1806–39: A Tsarist Agent in Central Asia*, Central Asian Collectanea, no. 4, Washington, DC, 1960

Khalfin, N. A., 'Drama v nomerakh "Parizha"' (Drama in a Boarding House), *Voprosy Istorii*, no. 10 (1966), p. 216

Khalfin, N. A., *Predislovie k sb. Zapiski o Bukharskom Khanstve* (Preface to Notes on the Khanate of Bukhara), Moscow, 1983 (this volume includes 'Zapiska, sostavlennaia po rasskazam Orenburgskogo lineinogo bataliona No. 10 praporsh-chika Vitkevicha otnositelno ego puti v Bukharu i obratno' (Notes Based on the Story Told by Vitkevich, Ensign in the 10th Orenburg Manoeuvre Battalion, of his Journey to Bukhara and Back)

Kohzad, Ahmed Ali, *In the Highlight of Modern Afghanistan*, trans. from Persian by Prof. Iqbal Ali Shah, Kabul, 1952

Lafont, Jean-Marie, *La présence française dans le royaume sikh du Penjab 1822–1849*, Paris, 1992

Lafont, Jean-Marie, *Indika: Essays in Indo-French Relations 1630–1976*, New Delhi, 2000

Lafont, Jean-Marie, *Fauj-i-Khas: Maharaja Ranjit Singh and his French Courtiers*, Amritsar, 2002

Lafont, Jean-Marie, *Maharaja Ranjit Singh: Lord of the Five Rivers*, New Delhi, 2002

Latif, Syad Muhammad, *History of the Punjab*, New Delhi, 1964

Lee, Harold, *Brothers in the Raj: The Lives of John and Henry Lawrence*, Oxford, 2002

Lee, J. L., *The 'Ancient Supremacy': Bukhara, Afghanistan and the Battle for Balk 1731–1901*, Leiden, 1996

Lieven, Dominic, *Russia against Napoleon*, London, 2009

Lovell, Julia, *The Opium War: Drugs, Dreams and the Making of China*, London, 2011

Lunt, James, *Bokhara Burnes*, London, 1969

Macintyre, Ben, *Josiah the Great: The True Story of the Man Who Would be King*, London, 2004

Macrory, Patrick, *Signal Catastrophe: The Retreat from Kabul, 1842*, London, 1966; republished as *Retreat from Kabul: The Incredible Story of How a Savage Afghan Force Massacred the World's Most Powerful Army*, Guildford, Conn., 2002

Martin, Vanessa, *Anglo-Iranian Relations since 1800*, Oxford, 2005

Meyer, Karl and Brysac, Shareen, *Tournament of Shadows: The Great Game and the Race for Empire in Europe*, London, 1999

Miller, Charles, *Khyber – The Story of the North-West Frontier*, London, 1977

Moon, Sir Penderel, *The British Conquest and Dominion of India*, London, 1989

Morgan, Gerald, 'Myth and Reality in the Great Game', *Asian Affairs*, vol. 60 (February 1973), pp. 55–65

Morgan, Gerald, *Anglo-Russian Rivalry in Central Asia, 1810–1895*, London, 1981

Morrison, Alexander, *Russian Rule in Samarkand 1868–1910*, Oxford, 2008

Morrison, Alexander, *Twin Imperial Disasters: The Invasion of Khiva and Afghanistan in the Russian and British Official Mind, 1839–1842* (forthcoming)

Mosely, Philip E., 'Russian Policy in Asia (1838–9)', *Slavonic and East European Review*, vol. 14, no. 42 (April 1936), pp. 670–81

Nichols, Robert, *Settling the Frontier: Land, Law and Society in the Peshawar Valley, 1500–1900*, Oxford, 2001

Noelle, Christine, *State and Tribe in Nineteenth Century Afghanistan: The Reign of Amir Dost Muhammad Khan (1826–1863)*, London, 1997

Norris, J. A., *The First Afghan War 1838–1842*, Cambridge, 1967

Omrani, Bijan with Major-General Charles Vyvyan, 'Britain in the First Two Afghan Wars: What Can We Learn?', in Ceri Oeppen and Angela Schlenkhoff (eds), *Beyond the 'Wild Tribes'*, London, 2010

Pottinger, George, *The Afghan Connection: The Extraordinary Adventures of Eldred Pottinger*, Edinburgh, 1983

Pottinger, George and Macrory, Patrick, *The Ten-Rupee Jezail: Figures in the First Afghan War 1838–42*, London, 1993

Preston, Diana, *The Dark Defile: Britain's Catastrophic Invasion of Afghanistan 1838–42*, New York, 2012

Ranayagam, Angelo, *Afghanistan: A Modern History*, London, 2009

Reshtia, Sayed Qassem, *Between Two Giants: Political History of Afghanistan in the Nineteenth Century*, Peshawar, 1990

Richards, D. S., *The Savage Frontier: A History of the Anglo-Afghan Wars*, London, 1990

Roy, Olivier, *Islam and Resistance in Afghanistan*, Cambridge, 1966

Saddozai, Wing Commander Sardar Ahmad Shah Jan, *Saddozai: Saddozai Kings and Viziers of Afghanistan 1747–1842*, Peshawar, 2007

Saksena, Ram Babu, *European and Indo-European Poets of Urdu and Persian*, Lucknow, 1941

Schinasi, May, *Kaboul 1773–1948*, Naples, 2008

Shah, Agha Syed Jalal Uddin, *Khans of Paghman*, Quetta, 1997

Shah, Sirdar Ikbal Ali Shah, *Afghanistan of the Afghans*, London, 1828

Silverberg, Robert, *To the Rock of Darius: The Story of Henry Rawlinson*, New York, 1966

Singer, Andre, *Lords of the Khyber – The Story of the North-West Frontier*, London, 1984

Singh, Khushwant, *Ranjit Singh: Maharaja of the Punjab*, London, 1962

Singh, Patwant, *Empire of the Sikhs: The Life and Times of Maharajah Ranjit Singh*, New Delhi, 2008

Sinha, Narendra Krishna, *Ranjit Singh*, Calcutta, 1933

Stewart, Jules, *Spying for the Raj: The Pundits and the Mapping of the Himalaya*, Stroud, 2006

Stewart, Jules, *Crimson Snow: Britain's First Disaster in Afghanistan*, London, 2008

Stewart, Jules, *On Afghanistan's Plains: The Story of Britain's Afghan Wars*, London, 2011

Stone, Alex G., 'The First Afghan War and its Medals', *Numismatic Circular* (March–June 1967), pp. 1–11

Storey, C. A., *Persidskaya literatura: bio-bibliograficheskyi obzor* (Persian Literature: A Bio-Bibliographical Survey), ed. and trans. Yu. E. Breigel, Moscow 1976

Strachey, Barbara, *The Strachey Line: An English Family in America, India and at Home from 1570 to 1902*, London, 1985

Stronge, Susan, *The Arts of the Sikh Kingdoms*, London, 1999

Sykes, Sir Percy, *A History of Persia*, 2 vols, London, 1963

Tanner, Stephen, *Afghanistan: A Military History from Alexander the Great to the Fall of the Taliban*, Cambridge, Mass., 2002

Thapar, Romila, *Somanatha: The Many Voices of a History*, New Delhi, 2004

Thompson, Edward, *The Life of Charles Lord Metcalfe*, London, 1937

Trotter, Captain L. J., *The Earl of Auckland*, Oxford, 1893

Ure, John, *Shooting Leave: Spying Out Central Asia in the Great Game*, London, 2009

Volodarsky, Mikhail, 'The Russians in Afghanistan in the 1830s', *Central Asian Survey*, vol. 3, no. 1 (1984), pp. 63–86

Varma, Birendra, *English East India Company and the Afghans, 1757–1800*, Calcutta, 1968

Volodarsky, Mikhail, 'Persian Foreign Policy between the Two Herat Crises 1831–56', *Middle Eastern Studies*, vol. 21, no. 2 (April 1985), pp. 111–51

Wade, Stephen, *Spies in the Empire: Victorian Military Intelligence*, London, 2007

Waller, John H., *Beyond the Khyber Pass: The Road to British Disaster in the First Afghan War*, New York, 1990

Wallis Budge, Sir E. A., *The Rise and Progress of Assyriology*, London, 1825

Whitteridge, Gordon, *Charles Masson of Afghanistan: Explorer, Archaeologist, Numismatist and Intelligence Agent*, Bangkok, 1982

Wright, Denis, *The English among the Persians during the Qajar Period 1787–1921*, London, 1977

Yapp, M. E., 'Disturbances in Eastern Afghanistan, 1839–42', *Bulletin of the School of Oriental and African Studies*, vol. 25, no. 1/3 (1962), pp. 499–523

Yapp, M. E., 'Disturbances in Western Afghanistan, 1839–41', *Bulletin of the School of Oriental and African Studies*, vol. 26, no. 2 (1963), pp. 288–313

Yapp, M. E., 'The Revolutions of 1841–2 in Afghanistan', *Bulletin of the School of Oriental and African Studies*, vol. 27, no. 2 (1964), pp. 333–81

Yapp, M. E., *Strategies of British India: Britain, Iran and Afghanistan, 1798–1850*, Oxford, 1980

Yapp, M. E., 'The Legend of the Great Game', *Proceedings of the British Academy*, no. 111 (2001), pp. 197–8

Glossary

akali	A strict and militant follower of Sikhism. In this period the term was used especially of nihangs, an armed Sikh military order who spearheaded attacks on the enemies of the Sikh religion. The word derives from Akal, the Eternal One or Supreme Being of the Sikhs.
alam	A battle standard, also used by Shias as the focus for their Muharram venerations. Usually tear-shaped or fashioned into the shape of a hand, they are highly ornate and beautiful objects, and the best are among the great masterpieces of Islamic metalwork.
amir	Commander, a shortened version of Amir al-Muminin, the Commander of the Faithful.
beg	A chief or ruler.
boosa	Hay or fodder.
chela	A disciple or pupil.
dak	Post, letters (sometimes spelt 'dawke' in the eighteenth and nineteenth centuries).
Dasht	Literally 'meadow'. The area that stretches from Spin Boldak at the foot of the mountains south of Kandahar.
dharamasala	A pilgrims' resthouse.
diwan	Government office.
dhoolie	A covered litter.
durbar	A royal court.
fakir	Literally 'poor'. A Sufi holy man, dervish or wandering Muslim ascetic.

fatwa	A legal ruling.
firangi	A foreigner.
ghazal	Urdu or Persian love lyric.
ghazi	A holy warrior, someone who wages the jihad.
Gholam Khana	The royal bodyguard of the Sadozais.
hamam	A Turkish-style steam bath.
harkara	Literally 'All-doer'. A runner, messenger, newswriter or even spy. In eighteenth- and nineteenth-century sources the word is sometimes spelt 'hircarrah'.
haveli	A courtyard house or traditional mansion.
havildar	A sepoy non-commissioned officer corresponding to a sergeant.
iftar	The evening meal to break the Ramazan fast.
izzat	Honour.
jezail	A long-barrelled matchlock musket, heavy, slow and clumsy to load but deadly accurate at long distances in the hands of a practised handler.
jezailchi	An Afghan infantryman armed with a long-barrelled jezail.
jihad	Holy war.
jihadi	A holy warrior.
jirga	A tribal assembly; the council in which Pashtun elders settle disputes in accordance with the *pashtunwali*, the Pashtun code of laws and ethics.
juwan	A young man.
kafila	A caravan.
kafilabashi	A caravan leader.
kajawah	A wicker basket slung from the side of a camel.
Khalsa	Literally 'the pure' or 'the free'. In this period it was used about Ranjit Singh's Sikh army, but it more properly refers to the whole Sikh nation.
khan	The chief of a Pashtun tribe.
khel	A Pashtun term for lineage.
khutba	The sermon delivered at Friday prayers.
kotwal	A chief of police.
kumbukht	A rascal; a useless, hopeless or unlucky person.
lakh	A hundred thousand.

malang	A wandering fakir, dervish or qalandar.
malik	A village headman or petty chief.
masjid	A mosque.
mooli	A radish.
munshi	An Indian writer, private secretary or language teacher.
naib	A deputy.
namak haram	Literally 'bad to your salt' – someone who is ungrateful or disloyal.
Nauroz	The Persian New Year festival, celebrated on 20 March.
palkee	A palanquin or box litter for travelling in.
Pashtu	The language of the Pashtun people of the North West Frontier of Pakistan and southern Afghanistan.
pir	A Sufi master or holy man.
pirzada	An official at a Sufi shrine, often a descendant of the founding saint.
pishkhidmat	The personal servant of a sardar or king.
pustin	An Afghan sheepskin coat (from 'post', Dari for skin).
qalandar	A Sufi mendicant or holy fool.
Qizilbash	Literally 'redheads', a name given to Safavid soldiers (and later traders), owing to the tall red cap worn under their turbans. These Shia colonists first came to Afghanistan from Persia with the armies of Nadir Shah and later acted as the royal guard of the Durranis. By the 1830s they formed their own distinct community with their own quarters, the Chindawol and Murad Khani, and their own leaders, and their loyalties had to be bought by any potential claimant to the throne.
rahdari	The levy paid to the mountain tribes to keep the road safe and protect the armies and traders travelling along it.
rundi	A dancing girl or prostitute. It has been suggested that this Hindi word could be the root of the English word 'randy'.
sangar	A shallow trench protected by a low mud wall, or breastworks, traditionally built by Afghan fighters to protect jezail snipers.
sardar	A chief, commander or nobleman. Among the Sadozais, it was the military title held by the head of the Durrani clans and the title held by all members of the royal family. Among Sikhs the title was given to all followers of Khalsa, and the word survives in daily use in modern India as a respectful way to address any Sikh.
sawar	A cavalryman. At this period also spelt 'suwar' or 'sowar'.
sepoy	An Indian soldier in the service of the East India Company.

sayyed (f. sayyida)	A lineal descendant of the Prophet Mohammad. Sayyeds often have the title 'Mir'.
shahzada	A prince.
shamiana	An Indian marquee, or the screen formed around the perimeter of a tented area.
Shia	One of the two principal divisions of Islam, dating back to a split that occurred immediately after the death of the Prophet between those who recognised the authority of the Medinian Caliphs and those who followed the Prophet's son-in-law Ali (*Shi'at Ali* means 'the Party of Ali' in Arabic). Though most Shi'ites live in Iran, there have always been a few in Afghanistan and India.
shir maheh	An Afghan freshwater river fish not dissimilar in taste to trout.
sipahee	The original Persian word for soldier, which was turned by British tongues into 'sepoy' and came to mean specifically an Indian soldier in the service of the East India Company.
surwan	A camel driver.
syce	A groom.
talib	A religious student.
takht	A seat or throne.
thannah	A police post or police station presided over by a thanadar.
toman	A Persian unit of currency. At the time of the First Afghan War five tomans were worth around £1.
tykhana	A cool underground room or network of cool rooms.
'ulema	In Arabic, this means 'the ones possessing knowledge', hence 'the community of learned men'. In effect it means the Islamic clergy, the body of men with sufficient knowledge of the Quran, the Sunna and the Sharia to make decisions on matters of religion. The word *ulema* is an Arabic plural; the singular is *alim*, a learned man.
vakil	Representative, headman or ambassador. In modern usage the word usually means lawyer.
waqf	An inalienable religious endowment in Islamic law, usually a religious building or a plot of land reserved for Muslim religious or charitable purposes.
wazir	A councillor of the state, a minister.
Yaghistan	Pashtun notion of their territories as a 'land of freedom and rebellion'.
zenana	A harem, or women's quarters.
zikr	A trance or ecstasy in a Sufi ceremony.

Index

A Note on the Author

William Dalrymple is the bestselling author of *In Xanadu*, *City of Djinns*, *From the Holy Mountain*, *The Age of Kali*, *White Mughals*, *The Last Mughals* and, most recently, *Nine Lives*. He has won the Thomas Cook Travel Book Award, the *Sunday Times* Young British Writer of the Year Award, the French Prix d'Astrolabe, the Wolfson Prize for History, the Scottish Book of the Year Prize, the Duff Cooper Memorial Prize, the Asia House Award for Asian Literature, the Vodafone Crossword Award and has three times been longlisted for the Samuel Johnson Prize. In 2012 he was appointed Whitney J. Oates Visiting Fellow in Humanities at Princeton University. He lives with his wife and three children on a farm outside Delhi.